Mapa Geológico E. 1:200,000: Sintesis De La Cartografia Existente, Issue 39...

Instituto Geológico y Minero de España

WEST VIRGINIA
GEOLOGICAL SURVEY

VOLUME TWO

LEVELS ABOVE TIDE

TRUE MERIDIANS

REPORT ON COAL

By I. C. WHITE, State Geologist.

PRINTED BY THE
MORGANTOWN POST COMPANY,
MORGANTOWN, W. VA.,
1903.

COMMISSION

ALBERT B. WHITE,   *President.*

          GOVERNOR OF WEST VIRGINIA

PETER SILMAN,   *Treasurer.*

          TREASURER OF WEST VIRGINIA

JAMES H. STEWART,   *Secretary and Executive Officer.*

    DIRECTOR STATE AGRICULTURAL EXPERIMENT STATION

D. B. PURINTON,   *President West Virginia University.*

ABRAM McCULLOCH,   *President State Board of Agriculture.*

SCIENTIFIC STAFF

I. C. WHITE,   *State Geologist.*

SUPERINTENDENT OF THE SURVEY

B. H. HITE,   *Chief Chemist.*

E. S. STALNAKER,   *Assistant Chemist.*

RAY V. HENNEN,   *Chief Clerk.*

EMPLOYEES DURING 1901 and 1902

JOHN M. GREGG,   *Chief Clerk.*

MISS R. L. NORRIS,   *Assistant Chemist.*

SAMUEL D. BRADY,   *Chief Coal Collector.*

A. P. BRADY,   *Assistant Coal Collector.*

R. W. EDMONDS,   *Assistant Coal Collector.*

LETTER OF TRANSMITTAL

To His Excellency, Albert B. White, Governor of West Virginia, and President of the Geological Survey Commission:

SIR:—I have the honor to transmit herewith Volume Two of the West Virginia Geological Survey, the same being the long promised Coal Report. Two causes have operated to postpone the publication of this Report so far beyond the time originally promised:—the first and main one, being the failure of the Legislature to appropriate any funds for the Survey during the session of 1899; second, before the funds provided by the Legislature in 1901 became available, the State Geologist, with the approval of the Commission, concluded to broaden the scope of the Report by doing a large amount of chemical and calorimetric work, in order to secure reliable knowledge as to the quality and character of all the West Virginia coals and cokes. The proper sampling, for analysis, of every commercial mine in the State during 1901, consumed a large amount of time, and this work could not be finished with our limited resources until the spring of 1902. Then, the analyses, and the calorimetric determinations, necessarily required many months of arduous labor for the small chemical force available, so that it has been simply impossible to get the volume published earlier.

It is a matter of great regret that no funds were available with which to provide illustrations, cuts, etc., so necessary in describing our coal resources. It is possible that this necessity may be remedied in the future publications of the Survey, since the last Legislature amended the Act establishing the Survey, so as to permit the Commission to use the funds received from the sales of publications in defraying the cost of other publications, etc. There will be published 7,000 copies of this volume, 1,000 of which will be bound in cloth for library use, and the rest in paper. The Commission has fixed the price of the same at $1.50 per copy, delivered to the purchaser either by mail or express, so that a fair publication fund will probably result, if the demand for the volume proves as large as the inquiries therefor would indicate. From the proceeds of such sales it may be possible to undertake the publication of Volume III, on Clays and Ores, and Volume IV, on Limestones, Building Stones, Etc.

The preparation of a new map of the State, on a more accurate base and larger scale, is already under way, by Prof. Walter L. Webb, a skillful engineer and draughtsman, and Mr. Ray V. Hennen of the Survey. This map should be issued by October 1, and will be sold at the same price as the old one, viz: 50 cents.   Its sale is sure to add materially to the resources of the Survey available for publication, since on it will be shown, with a fair degree of accuracy, all the main streams of the State, every railroad, every commercial coal mine, all the oil and gas pools, the principal anticlinal lines, and the different coal series.

The State Geologist approves the plan of selling these publications at the reasonable prices fixed by the Commission, since those who wish them do not object to paying for the same, and it thus preserves the work for those who will appreciate their value.

Very respectfully,

I. C. WHITE,

State Geologist.

MORGANTOWN, June 15, 1903.

CONTENTS

PREFACE

In sending out this volume to the people of the State and the general public, the author knows that they will find much therein to criticise, but hopes they will also find much of permanent value. Aside from the chemical work, and the printing, the volume has not cost the State a penny, since the field notes for the same were collected by the writer during a period of many years at his own expense, and this has made the volume more or less of the patch-work style. No one realizes the imperfections and possibility of error in this volume better than its author, but yet, if one should await publication until every doubtful point is cleared up, the present generation would never get a chance to read any portion of the same. The future rapid development of the coal industry of the State will furnish facts for correcting the most glaring errors into which the writer may have been led by imperfect data and lack of time and means with which to make more detailed investigations. Hence the author not only expects, but invites the kindly criticism of the reader in aiding him to eliminate from future publications any of the errors that may have been committed in this.

It is quite possible that some of the analyses given for the different mines may not represent the same fairly, but this has been fully explained in connection therewith, so that no operator should feel that injustice has been done to his property, since the main object of the analyses was to get a GENERAL AVERAGE for the character and quality of each important coal seam, and the purchaser of fuel will look more to that than the single analysis from any particular mine, no matter how carefully the same may have been sampled.

The Survey is greatly indebted to so many people, who have aided its work in every way, that it is impossible to mention all specifically. The railroads of the State, through their chief officers, have been most generous in granting free transportation, not only for the employees of the Survey, but also for the samples of coal for analysis, thus bringing the same to the chemical laboratory at Morgantown from every portion of the State. For this kindly service the thanks of the Survey are especially due to the officers of the B. & O. Railroad, the C. & O. Railroad, the N. & W. Railroad, the W. Va. C. & Pgh. Railroad, the K. & M. Railroad, and the C. C. & S. Railroad.

To Messrs. Charles Catlett, Frank Haas, and H. M. Wilson, who have kindly prepared, as a "labor of love," their valuable papers printed in this report, the Survey is greatly indebted, as well as to Mr. H. L. Higginson of Boston, President of the Gauley Coal Land Association, for the use of the valuable work of E. V. d'Invilliers, on the Gauley coals. The thanks of the Survey are especially due to Hon. Jas. H. Stewart, the very able and efficient Director of the State Agricultural Experiment Station, for the generous aid given the Survey in the use of the station laboratory and equipments, etc., without which the chemical work of the survey would have been impossible. Also to the Chemist of the Station, Prof. Hite and his assistants, Mr. E. S. Stalnaker, and the late Miss R. L. Norris, who did most of the chemical work on the Pittsburg coal, the Survey is under many obligations for difficult and faithful services.

The same acknowledgement is due to Mr. S. D. Brady, now chief engineer for the Wabash Railroad extensions in West Virinia, who, with his brother A. P. Brady, and R. W. Edmonds, as assistants, collected samples of the coals, and measured the thickness and structure of the different seams at every commercial mine in the State. A very few of these samples were lost in transit, and this will account for the non-appearance of the analyses from some mines that were in operation during 1901, since but few samples have been collected since that time.

The coal operators, one and all, have kindly assisted the Survey, and shown their appreciation of its work in many ways, but acknowledgements are especially due to the Fairmont Coal Company for many courtesies extended through its General Manager, L. L. Malone.

To the several oil and gas companies of the State, notably the South Penn Oil Co., the Carter Oil Co., the Kanawha Oil Co., the Philadelphia Company, the Carnegie Natural Gas Co., and numerous other oil and gas companies, as well as many individual operators whose names appear in the body of this volume, the Survey is under many obligations for valuable well records and data freely given for publication. The valuable work of Dr. John J. Stevenson, David White, M. R. Campbell, E. V. d'Invilliers and many others so liberally drawn upon in the text of this volume, is duly acknowledged under the references and quotations therefrom.

It is the intention of the Survey to begin the preparation and publication of Vol. III on Clays and Ores, and Vol. IV on Limestones, Building Stones, etc., as soon as its resources will permit. The Legislature, at its 1903 session, provided funds for carrying on the topographic map work of the Survey, in cooperation with the U. S. G. Survey for 1903 and 1904. With these appropriations ($15,000 per year) it is hoped that all of the remaining area of the State not yet mapped on any scale, can be completed, and that then the detailed geological work and mapping of the several counties can be undertaken.

ERRATA

Page 1, line 1 from top, for "list" read lists.
" 16, line 13 from bottom, for "Mehldahls," read Meldahls.
" 22, line 12 " , for "Juection," read Junction.
" 26, line 7 from top, for "slations," read stations.
" 27, line 16 " , for "warer," read water.
" 30, line 8 " , for "Eishing," read Fishing.
" 34, line 12 from bottom, for "Burnesville," read Burnsville.
" 35, line 14 from top, for "frrm," read farm.
" 36, line 5 " , for "Bulltowd,' read Bulltown.
" 36, line 1 " , for "Falls Hills," read Falls Mills.
" 36, line 5 from top, for "iu," read in.
" 37, line 12 " , for "he," read he is
" 38, line 13 from bottom, for "abatement," read abutment.
" 41, line 17 from top, for "thts," read this.
" 43, line 3 from bottom, for "Morgantowd," read Morgantown.
" 45, line 4 from top, for "chiee," read chief.
" 46, line 10 " , for "necssary," read necessary.
" 46, line 15 " , for "Adamstown," read Adamston.
" 55, line 4 from bottom, for "Plcsant," read Pleasant.
" 57, line 1 " , ". 219873," read 738.219.
" 59, line 5 " , for "ooposite," read opposite.
" 71, line 8 from top, for "Roanokl," read Roanoke.
" 72, line 2 " , for "Prrkersburg," read Parkersburg.
" 74, line 4 from bottom, for "Ridgo," read Ridge.
" 80, line 3 " , for "througheut," read throughout.
" 83, line 9 from top, for "th," read the.
" 84, line 2 " , for "llke," read like.
" 84, line 5 " , for "beeu," read been.
" 84, line 9 " , for "Mouniain," read Mountain.
" 84, line 17 " , for "tne," read the.
" 86, line 3 from bottom, for "gion" read region.
" 98, line 8 from top, for "measnrements," read measurements.
" 102, line 16 from bottom, for "masstve," read massive.
" 103, line 10 from top, for "foasiliferous," read fossiliferous.
" 103, line 12 from bottom, omit period after near.
" 104, line 21 " , for "sandsfone," read sandstone.
" 106, line 17 from top, for "thickhess," read thickness.
" 108, line 11 from bottom, "she," read the.
" 109, line 4 " , for "ond," read and.
" 110, line 2 from top, for "ot," read of.
" 113, line 21 from bottom, for "Dunkark," read Dunkard.
" 140, line 4 " , for "whos," read whose.
" 171, line 15 " , for "stratigraphical," read stratigraphical.
" 172, line 2 from top, for "Pittsbnrg," read Pittsburg.
" 173, line 12 from bottom, for "beiug," read being.

" 176, line 19 from top, for "Fairmont," read Fairmont.
" 181, line 1   "   , for "openiug," read opening.
" 181, line 18   "   , for "io," read to.
" 183, line 19   "   , for 8th word, read Kanawha.
" 189, line 18   "   , for "Charlesfon," read Charleston.
" 191, line 14 from bottom, for "desceuds," read descends.
" 192, line 17 from top, for "caal," read coal.
" 195, line 17   "   , for "Joscph," read Joseph.
" 197, line 8 from bottom, for "McMinley," read McKinley.
" 207, line 28   "   , for "whtch," read which.
" 217, line 1 from top, for "tne," read the.
" 218, line 11 from bottom, for "eveporated," read evaporated.
" 221, line 11 from top, "Mr. Hass," read Mr. Haas.
" 235, line 4 from bottom, for "ahae," read shale.
" 242, line 12 from top, for "aud," read and.
" 242, line 4 from bottom, for "coai," read coal.
" 243, line 14 from top, for "Slatc," read Slate.
" 252, line 8 from bottom, for "on," read one.
" 258, line 1 from top, for "oj," read of.
" 258, line 5 from top, for "Hemiphronites," read Hemipronites.
" 265, line 18   "   , for "genrally," read generally.
" 273, line 18   "   , for "aud," read and.
" 309, line 1 from bottom, for "Te," read The.
" 344, line 4   "   , for "300," read 310-11.
" 383, line 5 from top, for "Allegany," read Allegheny.
" 423, line 3 from bottom, for "betow," read below.
" 452, line 1   "   , for "folowing," read following.
" 474, line 5 from top, for "mnch," read much.
" 483, for page "433," read 483.
" 503, line 11 from bottom, for "Blaok," read Black.
" 639, line 10   "   , for "Md. Stee," read Md. Steel.

PART I.

LEVELS ABOVE TIDE, TRUE MERIDIANS, ETC.

The lists of elevations above tide level for the stations on all the railroad lines of the State were published in Volume I, Oil and Gas, in 1899. These have proven so useful to both civil and mining engineers that the lists given in Volume I are republished, along with many others obtained since that date, and to these are added the very accurate determinations of the U. S. Geological Survey of many points in the State.

By a comparison of these with the elevations as given on the railroad profiles it is found that many elevations of the latter are often several feet in error. For instance, the elevation given for Burnsville, Braxton county, by the table of elevations for the West Virginia & Pittsburg Railroad by Mr. Fickinger is 748 feet, while the U. S. Geological Survey bench on the bridge pier over the Little Kanawha river there, and at least three feet lower than the station level, is given at 765 feet, a difference of practically 20 feet. These discrepancies will in time be checked off and eliminated, since the Baltimore & Ohio Railroad is now having a new and more accurate level carried over the entire system, and when this work is completed a general correction of elevations can be undertaken, and the whole list brought into harmony with the results of the U. S. Geological Survey's most accurate determinations. It is possible that the large discrepancy revealed at Burnsville may be partly due to some error in reducing the original datum of the West Virginia & Pittsburg Railroad to the Baltimore & Ohio base, since the latter gives the elevation (988') of Grafton only nine feet lower than the U. S. Coast and Geodetic Survey determination (997') of the Grafton bench on the survey from "Ocean to Ocean." This was made with the greatest care, and forms the datum for all the U. S. Geological Survey benches in Northern West Virginia and Western Pennsylvania.

The agreement of the Grafton & Belington Railroad level as given by Mr. Lemley, based upon the U. S. Geological Survey datum, with the West Virginia Central & Pittsburg Railroad levels at Belington—Lemley 1697.9' for base of rail, and West Virginia & Pittsburg 1698.5' for top of rail—is quite remarkable, since the West Virginia Central levels were carried entirely across the Alleghany mountains from Piedmont many years ago by the late James Parsons, Chief Engineer for the West Virginia Central & Pittsburg system. His datum was the orginal profile of the B. & O. R. R. at Piedmont.

In the following lists, when not otherwise stated, the elevation given is the top of the rail in front of the center of the station building.

BALTIMORE & OHIO RAILROAD.

OFFICE OF THE CHIEF ENGINEER,
November 30, 1898.

DR. I. C. WHITE,
        State Geologist,

DEAR SIR:—Replying to your favor of the 22d inst., I beg to attach list giving distances and elevations of various stations along our line in West Virginia.

We have no profiles of short Branches on the Second or G. & B. Division, and, therefore, cannot give the information on these.

Yours very truly,
        W. T. MANNING,
                Chief Engineer.

Main Line.

Distances from Camden Station, Balt.	STATIONS	State	County	Elevation Above Tide
75.6	Brunswick....................	Md	Frederick	......
78,0	Knoxville	......	....	......
78.5	Weverton	......	Washington	......
80.4	Sandy Hook................	...—.	....	......
81.0	Mountain Siding............	......	....	......
81.4	Harper's Ferry...............	W. Va	Jefferson	280
82.4	Island Park	......	....	300
83.2	Peacher's Mill	......	....	335
84.2	Rau Mining & Mfg. Co...	......	....	......
84.8	Engle	......	....	388
87.9	Duffields	......	....	508
88.8	Shenandoah Junction......	......	....	536
89.2	Hobbs.....................	......	....	......
......	Summit	......	....	600
92.1	Stone Crusher Siding	......	....	......
92.3	Kerneysville................	......	Berkeley	550
95.2	Vanclevesville	......	....	477
97.0	Opequon	......	....	400
97.8	Flagg	......	....	......
100.	Martinsburg...............	......	....	445
101.0	Baker's Stone Crusher ...	......	....	475
102.1	Fawver	......	....	......
103.5	Tabb	......	....	535
104.7	Wilson	......	....	533
107.4	North Mountain	......	....	540
107.8	Helper's Switch	......	....	......
112.2	Cherry Run Coal Chute...	......	....	......
113.4	Cherry Run	......	Morgan	410
115.5	Miller.......................	......	....	404
117.3	Sleepy Creek...............	......	....	412
121.8	C. E. Jones................	......	....	......
122.8	Hancock	......	....	......
123.8	Sand Siding	......	....	......
125.8	Round Top............	......	....	433
128.4	Sir John's Run.............	......	....	436
130.5	Henry's Siding.........	......	....	......
132.4	Great Cacapon.............	......	....	437
133.3	Woodmont	......	....	453
135.7	Lineburg	......	....	450
138.7	Orleans Road...............	......	....	501
139.5	Rockwell's Run	......	....	.....
141.9	Doe Gulley.................	......	....	550
143.3	Hansrote	......	....	......
145.6	Baird	......	....	498
148.9	Magnolia	......	....	495
153.8	Paw Paw	......	....	530
156.7	Little Cacapon..............	......	Hampshire	533
158.6	Okonoko	......	....	535
161.4	French	......	....	540
164.1	Green Spring..	......	....	550
168.4	Dan's Run.................	......	Mineral	563
170.9	Patterson's Creek..	......	....	568
172.5	North Branch...............	Md	Allegany	620

LEVELS ABOVE TIDE.

Main Lines—Continued.

177.0	Steel Works	Md.	Allegany	......
177.2	Glass Works	......	......	......
178.0	Cumberland	......	......	639
181.0	Three Mile Water Station	......	......	627
181.3	Robert	......	......	......
183.5	Cedar Cliff	....	......	642
185.0	Brady	......	......	657
187.3	New Potomac Cement Works	......	......	......
187.5	Kenzie	......	......	......
188.1	Potomac	......	......	670
190.0	Lowndes	......	......	......
190.8	Cresap	......	......	692
191.5	Rawlings	......	......	698
195.0	Black Oak	......	......	736
197.0	Dawson	......	......	750
199.2	21st Bridge	......	......	786
201.5	Keyser	W. Va.	Mineral	805
206.5	Piedmont	......	......	910
207.7	W. Va. Central Junction	......	......	......
208.5	Bloomington	Md.	Garrett	1020
209.0	Black Bear	......	......	......
211.8	36 Water Station	......	......	1385
212.2	Crab Tree	......	......	......
214.3	Frankville	......	......	1696
217.9	37 Water Station	......	......	......
219.4	Swanton	......	......	2282
222.3	Wilson	......	......	......
223.3	Altamont	......	......	2620
226.0	Deer Park	......	......	2490
226.3	Deer Park Hotel	......	......	......
228.2	Lake Youghiogheny	......	......	......
229.4	Mountain Lake Park	......	......	2396
231.2	McGowan Switch	......	......	....
231.7	Oakland Water Station	......	......	......
232.0	Oakland	......	......	2374
233.4	Stone Crusher	......	......	......
234.0	Offutt	......	......	2370
235.0	Skipnish Junction	......	......	....
237.6	Hutton	......	......	2486
283.3	Corinth	W. Va.	Preston	2430
239.6	Holmes	......	......	......
240.4	Hazen	......	......	2500
240.6	Rinard	......	......	......
241.6	Riggs	......	......	......
242.1	Terra Alta	......	......	2550
247.3	Rodemer	......	......	......
250.6	Amblersburg, Bradshaw	......	......	1585
253.9	Stoer Mill Siding	......	......	......
254.4	Rowlesburg	......	......	1394
259.0	Anderson	......	......	1855
260.7	Tunnelton	......	......	1823
261.8	West End	......	......	......
263.1	Smoot	......	......	......
263.7	Austen	......	......	1575
267.0	Orr	......	......	......
267.4	Newburg	......	......	1218

268.6	Independence	W. Va	Presto	1155
270.0	Hardman	......	Taylo.	......
271.7	Irontown	......	......	1073
274.7	Thornton	......	......	1040
276.0	Painter Siding	......	......	......
280.2	Grafton	......	......	988
281.8	Fetterman	......	......	986
286.1	Bush	......	......	......
287.9	Valley Falls	......	Marion	971
289.5	Nuzum	......	......	938
292.6	Sand Switch	......	......	....
294.4	Colfax	......	......	885
297.4	Benton Ferry	......	......	885
298.4	King	......	......	......
300.6	Palatine Mines	......	....	......
301.0	Gaston Junction	......	......	885
301.7	New York Siding	......	......	......
302.1	Fairmont	......	......	879
303.0	F. M. & P. Junction	......	......	......
303.5	Central Mines	....	......	......
303.8	Barnesville	......	......	873
304.8	West Fairmont S..aft	......	......	......
307.4	Barrackville	......	......	903
307.7	West Siding	......	......	......
312.8	Farmington	......	......	928
316.3	Downs	......	......	......
320.0	Mannington	......	......	969
324.3	Metz	......	......	....
325.7	Wilfong	......	......	......
327.2	Glover's Gap	......	......	1050
328.0	Well's Siding	......	......	......
331.8	Burton	......	Wetzel	1070
333.5	Hundred	......	......	......
336.2	Quarry Switch	......	......	......
338.0	Littleton	......	......	974
339.0	Jones' Siding	......	......	......
340.0	Floyd Siding	......	Marshall	......
341.2	Board Tree	......	......	1105
344.3	Bellton	......	......	888
346.4	Garrett Siding	......	......	......
348.2	Cogley	......	......	......
351.8	Cameron	......	......	1048
353.8	Loudenville	......	......	......
356.3	Easton	......	......	970
362.0	Roseby Rock	......	......	775
363.6	Gatts	......	......	......
366.4	Gatts No. 2	......	......	......
368.6	Moundsville	......	......	642
369.4	Camp Ground Junction	W. Va	......	......
370.0	Moundsville Coal Shaft	......	......	......
370.0	Moundsville Mining and Manufacturing Comp'y	......	......	......
370.1	Moundsville Glass Works	......	......	....
370.6	Moundsville Brick Works	......	......	......
369.7	Hart	......	......	......

LEVELS ABOVE TIDE.

Main Lines—Continued.

370.9	Glendale	W. Va.	Marshall	......
273.4	Riverview	......	....	......
374.3	McMechen	......	....	......
375.0	Benwood Junction	......	....	......
376.1	Bellaire	Ohio	Belmont	......
375.8	Benwood	W. Va.	Marshall	650
376.5	Nolan	....	....	......
376.5	Riverside Furnace	......	....	......
377.3	Boggs Run	......	....	......
377.3	No. 17 Switch	......	....	......
379.8	Wheeling	......	Ohio	647

Parkersburg Branch—B. & O. R. R.

280.2	Grafton	W. Va.	Taylor	988
282.3	Webster	......	....	1005
286.4	Foster	......	....	1110
287.2	McCartney Switch	......	....	......
287.7	Simpson	......	....	1086
288.2	Giles	......	....	......
288.7	Gramm Switch	......	....	......
290.0	Flemington	......	....	1015
292.3	Tyrconnell	......	Harrison	989
297.6	Bridgeport	......	....	371
300.0	Despard Mines	......	....	......
....	Harrison County Mines	......	....	......
301.9	Pinnickinick Mines	......	....	......
....	Clarksburg, old depot	......	....	1030
302.5	Clarksburg, new depot	.....	....	1014
303.1	W. Va. & Pittsburg, and	......	....	......
....	Monongahela River R.	......	....	......
	R. Junction	......	....	......
304.1	Adamston	....	....	965
306.2	Wilsonburg	......	....	973
309.0	Dolan Mines	......	....	......
309.8	Wolf Summit	......	....	1120
314.1	Cherry Camp	......	....	1016
316.0	Salem	......	....	1034
321.7	Long Run	......	Doddridge	842
324.1	Morgansville	......	....	800
326.1	Middle Island	......	....	......
326.9	Smithton	......	....	784
329.2	Ringer Switch	......	....	......
330.0	West Union	......	....	809
332.1	Ruly Siding	......	....	......
333.0	Central	......	....	802
336.3	Duckworth	......	....	937
337.1	Greenwood	......	....	860
338.7	Toll Gate	......	....	785
342.1	Pennsboro	......	Ritchie	848
347.4	Ellenboro	......	....	771
352.2	Cornwallis	......	....	675
353.0	Reitz Siding	......	....	......
353.9	Fewsmith Switch	......	....	......
354.9	Cairo	......	....	667
357.2	Silver Run	......	....	794
360.3	McTaggart	......	....	......

Parkersburg Branch—B. & O. R. R.- Continued.

361.9	Petroleum	W. Va.	Ritchie	685
364.1	Volcano	......	....	719
364.9	Eaton	......	Wood	763
859.1	Walker............................	......	....	616
370.1	Textor Siding	......	....	......
374.2	Kanawha..........................	......	....	599
375.1	Sherwood Switch	......	....	......
377.2	Davisville	......	....	596
378.1	Ewing	......	....	596
379.2	Jackson	......	....	624
380.1	Stewart	......	....	598
381.2	N. O. C. Co. Tipple	......	....	......
383.5	Parkersburg	......	....	629
384.9	Belpre.............................	Ohio	Washington	......

Wheeling & Pittsburg Branch—B. & O. R. R.

0.	Wheeling..........................	W. Va.	Ohio	647
2.	Mt. DeChantal...............	......	....	672
4.	Carbon	......	....	667
9.	Roney's Point	......	....	829
10.	Point Mills	......	....	896
16.	West Alexander	Penna.	Washington	1043
21.	Claysville	......	....	1143
28.	Chartier	......	....	......
32.	Washington	......	....	1049

Fairmont, Morgantown & Pittsburg Branch—B. & O. R. R.

0.	Fairmont	W. Va.	Marion	879
1.	Junction Bridge...............	......	....	894
3.	Houlttown	......	....	889
4.	Rivesville	......	....	888
7.	Prickett's Creek Bridge...	......	....	882
7.	Catawba	......	....	880
11.	Opekiska	......	Monongalia	......
17.	Little Falls......................	......	....	855
....	Mouth of Tom's Run......	......	....	822
20.	Round Bottom...............	......	....	837
22.	Uffington	......	....	823
26.	Morgantown...................	......	....	816

8

LEVELS ABOVE TIDE.

Monongahela River Branch.

MONONGAH, W. VA.,
December 1, 1898.

DR. I. C. WHITE, State Geologist,
Morgantown, W. Va.

MY DEAR SIR:—In accordance with your recent request I hand you herewith list of stations and elevations on the Monongahela River Railroad, and the West Virginia & Pittsburg Railroad. In the former list we give you the distance to the new B. & O. passenger depot at Clarksburg. In the latter list we begin at the old passenger station. We have no elevation for the new station, neither do I know the exact distance between the old and the new station. This information you will probably get from the data supplied you by the B. & O. R. R. There is a little discrepancy in the elevations between these two roads, owing to the differences in the data furnished by the B. & O., as between Clarksburg and Fairmont. I presume, however, it is sufficiently accurate for the purpose for which you desire it.

Yours truly,   J. A. FICKINGER,
Vice President and General Manager,
Monongahela River Railroad.

Monongahela River Branch.

Distance	STATIONS	State	County	Elevation above tide (Top of rail)
0.0	Fairmont (B & O Depot)	W. Va.	Marion	879.
1.10	Gaston Junction	......	....	883.50
1.95	Watson	......	....	879.30
2.77	Gaston	......	....	876.50
3.50	Thompson	....	....	884.43
5.87	Monongah	......	....	888.70
7.35	Prichard	......	....	892.22
7.80	Bryan	......	....	888.59
8.80	Highland	......	....	890.74
10.00	Chiefton	......	....	893.00
11.14	Worthington	......	....	893.65
11.86	Hutchinson	......	....	901.50
13.24	Enterprise	......	Harrison	900.62
15.91	Shinnston	......		908.80
19.16	Lumberport	......	....	912.23
20.90	Cheswood Park	......	....	916.00
21.60	Maulsby	......	....	921.73
23.31	Clark	......	....	920.50
24.70	Haning	......	....	936.00
25.66	Farnum	......	....	932.21
27.08	Bartlett	......	....	....
28.02	Glen Falls	......	....	928.50
31.25	W. Va. & P. Junction	......	....	991.96
31.43	Monongahela Junction	....	....	....
31.89	Clarksburg (new B & O Depot)	......	....	1014.29

West Virginia & Pittsburg Branch.

0.0	Clarksburg (old B. & O. passenger depot)	W. Va.	Harrison	......
......		......	....	1030
2.0	West Clarksburg	......	....	945
3.2	Monticello	......	....	937
6.3	Lynch's Mines	......	....	947
8.1	Mt. Clare	......	....	1009
11.2	Bond Summit	......	....	1174
13.3	Lost Creek	......	....	1012
18.5	Jane Lew	......	Lewis	1010
21.0	Fisher's Summit	......	....	1222
23.4	Riverside	......	....	1013
23.8	Deanville	......	....	1017
25.4	Weston—pass. station	......	....	1009
26.9	Bendale	......	....	1016
28.8	Brownsville	......	....	1016
32.4	Rohrbough	......	....	1026
36.0	Lias Smith's	......	....	1043
37.6	Roanoke	......	....	1050
39.6	Arnold	......		1092
42.3	Peterson's	......	....	847
46.3	Confluence	......		768
50.7	Burnville	......	Braxton	748
52.7	Coger	......	....	758
57.5	Rollyson	. ...	....	783
59.1	Heater	......	....	851
60.9	Berry	......	....	906
63.0	Flatwoods	......	....	1121
64.6	Hopkins	......	....	1006
65.5	Morrison's	......	....	1074
68.5	Gillespie	......	....	870
70.7	Palmer	......	....	899
73.6	Baker's Run	......	....	917
75.2	Centralia	......	....	933
77.2	Custis	......	....	1056
78.4	Brook's Run	......	....	1132
84.3	Erbacon	......	Webster	1504
85.0	Wainville	......	....	1561
87.6	Weese's	......	....	1706
88.3	Hardwood	......	....	1912
91.3	Halo	......	....	2062
94.7	Cowen	......	....	2229
100.6	Laurel	......	....	2039
103.2	Camden-on-Gauley	......	....	2018

Sutton Branch—W. Va. & P. R. R.

0.0	Flatwoods	W. Va.	Braxton	1121
0.4	Summit	....	....	1165
1.7	McNutt's	......	....	1031
3.5	Karl's Switch	......	....	866
5.6	Sutton	......	....	824

Weston, Buckhannon and Pickens Branch—W. Va. & P. R. R.

0.0	Weston	W. Va.	Lewis	1009
3.9	Smith's	......	....	......
5.3	Nicoles	......	....	......
6.1	Gaston	......	....	1040
7.0	Seymour	......	... .	1035
......	Stone Coal Summit	......	....	1444
12.0	Lorentz	......	Upshur	1435
16.0	Buckhannon.....................	......	....	1405
21.5	Hampton	......	....	1412
23.9	Sago...........................	......	....	1422
28.9	Ten Mile	......	............~	1603
32.5	Bean's Mill	......	....	......
34.2	Alton	......	....	1809
37.8	Alexander	......	....	1817
41.6	Newlon	......	....	1910
43.9	Craddock	......	....	1934
45.9	Avondale Junction..........	......	Randolph	2227
47.5	McCally's	......	....	2324
50.8	Pickens	......	....	2672

GRAFTON & BELINGTON BRANCH—B. & O. R. R.

PHILLIPPI, W. VA.

November 17, 1902.

DR. I. C. WHITE, State Geologist
Morgantown, W. Va.

DEAR SIR:—In reply to your requst of Sept. 24, 1902, I herewith send you tables of distances and elevations of points on the Grafton and Belington Division of the Baltimore & Ohio Railroad; the Hackers Run Branch of the G. & B. Division, B. & O. R. R.; the Point Pleasant, Buckhannon & Tygarts Valley Railroad, and the Burnersville Branch of the same line.

The last column gives the elevation of low water in the streams that are crossed along the line at the points named.

The elevations are based on the U. S. Geological Survey benches at Grafton (1901), and at Philippi, W. Va., (1902).

Yours very truly,   C. McC. LEMLEY,

Assistant Engineer.

Grafton and Belington Branch B. & O. R. R.

Distance	STATIONS	State	County	Base Rail	Low Water
0.	Grafton, center 5th Division track	W. Va	Taylor	1000.2	
0.	Bridge 0A, Three Fork Creek Crossing	....	....		964
2.	Park, Bridge 3A	....	....	1001.4	978
3.5	Yates	....	....		
5.25	Stone House, Bridge 5A..	....	....	1005.9	996
7.	Cecil.........................	....	....	1014.3	990 (river)
	Bridge 6A	....	....	1014.6	1002

Grafton and Belington Branch, B. & O. R. R.—Continued.

		W. Va	Taylor		
	Bridge 8A, Sandy Creek Crossing..................	....	....	1036.5	
9	Sandy Creek..................	....	Barbour	1036.8	1019
	Lusk	....	....	1060.3	
	Bridge 10A	....	....	1068.0	1053
	Bridge 10B	....	....	1088.3	1077
11	Cove Run	....	....	1088.2	1070 (river)
	Bridge 11A, Cove Run Stream ...	....	....	1088.0	1078
	Bridge 12A	....	....	1137.4	1124
	Bridge 13A, Teter's Creek	....	....	1170.0	1149
14	Moatsville	....	....	1169.9	1149.5
	Bridge 16A, Laurel Creek	....	....	1242.8	1232
17	Arden	....	....	1269.5	1260 (river)
	Felton	....	....	1302.0	
20	Fox Hall...	....	......	1295.8	
	Bridge 21A	....	....	1298.3	1280
22	Hacker's Junction	....	....	1301.6	
	Bridge 22A ..	....	....	1299.6	1281
23	Meriden.........	....	....	1300.2	
	Bridge 23A	....	....	1300.9	1284
	Bridge 23B	....	....	1302.9	1291
24	Philippi	....	....	1298.6	
	Bridge 24A ..	....	....	13...	1287
	Bridge 25A	....	....	1312.2	1293
28	Lillian	....	....	1318.5	
30	Tygart's Junction.........	....	....	1333.4	
	Bridge 30A	....	....	1352.1	
	Bridge 31A, Laurel Creek	....	....	1428.5	1406
	Bridge 32A, Laurel Run Crossing	....	....	1450.4	1437
33	Middle Fork.........	....	....	1501.5	
35	O'Brien	....	....	1534.9	
36	Clements	....	....	1580.5	
38	Jones	....	....	1670.3	
19	McLean	....	....	1695.0	
	Bridge 39A	....	....	1693.1	1682
	Bridge 41A	....	....	1696.1	1683
41.2	Belington	....	....	1697.9	1682 (river)

Hacker's Run Branch, B. & O. R. R.

		W. Va	Barbour		
0	Hacker's Junction, Tygart's Valley River Crossing.........	....	....	1301.6	1278
0.5	Trestle, Hacker's Creek Crossing.........	....	....		1283
3	100 Ton Scales....	....	....	1375.4	
3.5	"Fox Grape Summit," water shed, bet. Fox Grape and Simpson's Creek	....	....	1382	
4.3	Berryburg, opp. Southern Coal and Transportation Co's tipple	....	....	1395	

Point Pleasant, Buckhannon and Tygarts Valley Railroad.

o	Tygarts Junction............	W. Va	Brrbour	1333.4	
o	Tygarts Valley River Crossing................	....	....		1317
1	Pitman, Shoals Run Crossing	....	....		1337
4	Lemley Junction.............	....	....	1377.8	

LOCATION,

4	Lemley Junction, base of rail, Burnersville Branch	W. Va	Barbour	1377.8	
6.5	Buckhannon River.........	....	....		1363.2
7.8	Peck's Run	....	....		1384.5
11	Smith's Summit	... .	-	1516	
15.5	Buckhannon River, Post's Mills	....	Upshur		1388.5
15	Leonard Summit..........	....	....	1477.9	
16	Buckhannon River Crossing at Buckhannon......	....	....		1401.4

Burnersville Branch, Pt. P., B. & T. V. R. R.

o	Lemley Junction, Buckhannon River crossing	W. Va	Brrbour	1381.2	1355
0.5	Trestle, Big Run............	....	....	1385.8	
1	Burnersville	....	....	1405.7	
4.7	Century	....	....	1466.2	

WEST VIRGINIA CENTRAL & PITTSBURG RAILWAY.

ELKINS, WEST VA.,
Nov. 26, 1898.

DR. I. C. WHITE, State Geologist,
     Morgantown, West Va.

DEAR SIR:—As per instructions from President Davis of this Railroad, I enclose herewith list of stations with elevations and mileage of same. The elevations are above sea level. This, as I understand, complies with request contained in your letter to President Davis under date of November 21st.

         Yours truly,
            J. W. GALBREATH,
              Chief Engineer.

West Virginia Central & Pittsburg Railway.

Distance.	STATIONS.	State.	County.	Elevations above tide.
0.0	Cumberland	Md.	Alleghany.	625.1
1.2	Ridgely	......	....	622.0
6.1	Seymour	......	....	641.3
9.3	Potomac......................	......	....	664.0
10.4	Frost........................	......	....	....
11.4	Bier........................	......	....	673.4
12.6	Rawlings................	......	....	692.3
16.1	Black Oak...................	......	....	724.8
17.4	Gertstell....................	......	....	738.1
18.1	Dawson......................	......	....	743.7
19.0	Green	......	....	....
20.1	Twenty-first................	......	....	774.8
22.2	Keyser Junction.............	......	....	794.3
27.5	Westernport.................	......	....	904.4
28.8	W. V. C. Junction...........	W. Va.	Mineral.	943.6
31.6	Empire......................	......	....	1078.3
33.4	Warnocks	......	....	1090.0
34.5	Windom	......	....	1129.6
35.1	Barnum	......	....	1151.3
38.3	Shaw........................	......	....	1274.9
42.1	Chaffee..	......	....	1419.4
45.5	Blaine......................	......	....	1560.3
47.2	Harrison....................	......	....	1639.4
52.2	ⁿchell......................	....	....	1943.9
57.8	Stoyer......................	Md.	Garrett.	2245.1
59.9	Gorman	......	....	2267.2
62.3	Bayard	W. Va.	Grant.	2331.1
64.8	Wilson......................	......	....	2508.2
66.3	Dobbin......................	......	....	2596.5
67.7	Henry.......................	......	....	2647.3
69.9	Wilsonia....................	......	....	2744.9
71.5	Beechwood	......	....	2876.6
74.5	Fairfax.....................	......	....	3060.1
76.0	William	......	Tucker.	2967.2
77.7	Thomas	......	....	2883.5
79.0	Coketon.....................	......	....	2844.5
79.9	Douglas.....................	......	....	....
88.0	Hendricks...................	......	....	1702.1
89.0	Hambleton	......	....	1678.6
90.3	Bretz	......	....	1657.6
91.4	Parsons.....................	......	....	1662.4
94.4	Porter......................	......	....	1694.1
95.2	Moore.......................	......	....	....
99.8	Haddix......................	......	....	2178.1
101.5	Montrose	.. ...	Randolph,	1995.1
105.8	Kerens......................	.. ..	....	1937.0
107.9	Whyte.......................	......	....	1825.3
109.4	Gilman	......	....	1920.9
111.0	Read........................	......	....	....
113.2	Elkins......................	......	....	1920.0
114.4	Elkins Junction.............	......	....	1909.7
115.3	Buxton......................	......	....	1914.0
120.8	Roaring Creek Junction......	......	....	1871.3
121.2	Harding.....................	......	....	1846.4

West Virginia Central & Pittsburg Railway—Continued.

124.3	Laurel........................	W. Va.	Randolph.	1753.5
126.9	Junior........................	....	Barbour.	1719.0
128.3	Custer......................	......	....	....
130.8	Belington..................	......	....	1698.5

Davis Branch, W. Va. Central & Pittsburg R. R.

0.	Thomas	W. Va.	Tucker.	2883.5
2.6	Child........................	......	....	3010.5
3.8	Pendleton	......	....	2988.4
6.3	Davis........................	......	....	3001.4

Elk Garden Branch, W. Va. Central & Pitsburg R. R.

0.	Harrison	W. Va.	Mineral.	1639.4
3.3	Switch Back................	......	....	1930.6
7.0	Elk Garden..............	......	....	2268.2

Beverly and Huttonsville Branch W. Va. C. & P. R. R.

0.	Elkins	W. Va.	Randolph.	1920.
1.2	Elkins Junction............	......	....	1909.7
3.1	Yokun.....................	......	....	1926.2
6.7	Beverly....................	......	....	1941.3
8.7	R. R. Bridge over Valley River (top of rail)....	......	... .	.... 2015.6
10.0	Crossing Staunton and Parkersburg pike.....	......	....	.... 2021.6
13.8	Crawford House............	......	....	2046.8
16.3	Mill Creek Bridge.........	......	....	2070.1
17.7	Huttonsville.................	......	....	2077.0

(Preliminary Survey for Gauley River Extension.)

26	Elk Water.................	W. Va.	Randolph	2358
32	Brady's Summit	......	....	2992
34	Riggles	......	....	2714
35	Red Lick Run	......	....	2429
36	Elk River	......	....	2331
38	Whitacres Falls	......	....	2171
39	Big Run................	......	....	2136
46	Burgoo	......	Webster	1904
48	Leatherwood................	......	....	1841
56	Elk River	......	....	1583
59	Addison	....	....	1463
63	Payn's Summit	......	....	2456
71	Gauley River	......	....	2308
78	Williams River	......	....	2215

Elkins and Buckhannon Branch, W. Va. C. & P. R. R.
(Preliminary Survey.)

0	Elkins	W. Va.	Randolph	1920
7	Roaring Creek...............	......	....	1860
11	Roaring Creek Summit...	......	....	2368

Elkins and Buckhannon Survey, W. Va. C. & P. R. R.—Continued.

12	King's Bridge	W. Va.	Randolph	2450
17	Toll Gate	......	Upshur	1851
18	Burnt Bridge	......	.. ..	1840
21	White Oak Summit	......	....	2031
27	Buckhannon River Divide	......	....	1743
32	Buckhannon	....	....	1413

OHIO RIVER RAILROAD.

PARKERSBURG, W. VA.,

December 7, 1898.

DR. I. C. WHITE, State Geologist,

Morgantown, W. Va.

DEAR SIR:—Yours of November 21st, addressed to George A. Burt, Vice President and General Manager, referred to me.

The statement enclosed is as full and correct as we are able at this time to make. The elevations from Wheeling to Raven Rock are correct to the tenth, but south of that point the elevations have been deduced from the original levels, and are liable to the inaccuracies that such levels usually are. Datum is mean tide at Sandy Hook.

Hoping this will be satisfactory, I am,

Yours truly,

L. C. JAMES,

Assistant Engineer.

Ohio River Railroad.

Distance	STATIONS	State	County	Elevations Above Tide
0	Wheeling	W Va.	Ohio	....
3.3	Riverside	......	Marshall	....
4	Benwood	......	....	....
8	Glendale...	......	....	648.4
11.3	Moundsville	......	....	642.2
14.6	Round Bottom...............	......	....	645.5
15.8	Hornbrooks	......	....	645.2
16.4	Chestnut Hill	......	....	644.2
17	Captina Island........	......	....	643.4
19.2	Powhattan.....................	......	... .	646.3
20.2	Cresaps	......	....	642.1
20.5	Underwood	......	....	642
21	Cresap's Grove...............	......	....	640.5
21.5	South Cresap's	......	... .	640.6
22	Foster	......	....	643.2
22.5	Whittaker	......	....	644.1
23.2	Woodland	......	....	640.3
25	Franklin	......	....	641.2
26.8	Clarington.....................	......	....	637.3

Ohio River Railroad.—Continued.

29	Wells' Pit	W. Va.	Marshall	636.6
31.5	Proctor	......	Wetzel	636.4
34	Alexander	......	....	634.6
35	Maud	......	....	634.7
35.9	Baresville	......	....	632
36.5	Bridgeman	......	....	632
37.4	New Martinsville	......	....	633.7
41.1	Sardis	......	....	628.4
42	Paden	......	....	629.9
42.7	Paden's Valley	......	....	630
45.5	Stewart's Crossing	......	Tyler	630.2
47.2	Sistersville	......	....	649.6
48.2	Wells	......	....	637.4
49.2	Cochranville	......	....	629.8
50	Davenport	......	....	627.4
51.5	Hays	......	....	625.5
51.8	Friendly	......	....	624.3
53.7	Blaine Station	......	....	623.9
54	Long Reach	......	....	624.4
56	Selman	......	....	622.3
56.2	Ben's Run	......	....	621.8
57	Engle Run	......	Pleasants	625.6
58	Edmund	......	....	623.8
59	Raven Rock	......	....	623.1
61	Spring Run	......	....	621
62	Grape Island	......	....	622
64.1	St. Mary's	......	....	623
65	Vancluse	......	....	625
67.2	Belmont	......	....	621
69	Eureka	......	....	628
70.6	Salama	......	....	623
71.3	Willow Island	......	....	615
74.6	Waverly	......	Wood	618
75.2	James Lane	......	....	615
80	Jones	......	....	617
81.4	Williamstown	......	....	609
83	Pohick	......	....	610
85.1	Kellar	......	....	613
86.2	Briscoe	......	....	616
88.9	Vienna	......	....	606
93.6	Parkersburg (elevated platform)	......	....	......
....		......	....	624
96.6	Blennerhasset	......	....	......
99.7	Washington	......	....	636
101.6	Walker's Crossing	......	....	......
102.7	Mehldahls	......	....	599
105.1	New England	......	....	......
105.6	Lamps	......	....	......
107.3	Harris Ferry	......	....	595
109.6	Lee Creek	......	....	......
110.1	Humphrey	......	....	......
111.6	Belleville	......	....	590
114.9	Lone Cedar	......	Jackson	......
118.2	Murrayville	......	....	591
120.1	Williams	......	....	......
120.4	Polks	......	....	......
120 6	Muses Bottom	......	....	586
121.1	Coleman	......	....	......

Ohio River Railroad.—Continued.

121.6	Morgan	W. Va.	Jackson	......
123.9	Portland	......	......	......
124.8	Sherman	......	......	586
127.1	Turkey Run	......	......	......
128.2	Ravenswood	......	......	584
128.8	R. S. & G. Junction	......	......	581
132.1	Pleasant View	......	......	578
135.3	Willow Grove	......	......	582
138.6	Ripley Landing	......	......	......
139.2	Millwood	......	......	577
140.6	School House	......	......	......
144.2	Letart	......	Mason	574
148.1	Antiquity	......	......	......
149.9	Graham	......	......	570
153.0	New Haven	......	......	575
154.8	Hartford	......	......	569
157.5	Mason City	......	......	573
154.2	Clifton	......	......	563
161.1	West Columbia	......	......	......
161.9	Spilman	......	......	567
164.3	Brownsville	......	......	563
166.9	Mackers	......	......	575
169.3	Locust Lane	......	......	560
172.5	Point Pleasant	......	......	570
174.2	Henderson	......	......	563
178.1	Gallipolis Ferry	......	......	573
179.1	Beals' Siding	......	......	......
182.1	Elwell	......	......	......
184.0	Ben Lomond	......	......	552
185.1	Hogsett	......	......	......
187.5	Apple Grove	......	......	570
188.6	Mercer's Bottom	......	......	......
189.6	Ashton	......	......	......
192.5	Glenwood	......	......	550
194.1	Lasey's Lane	....	......	......
195.6	McCurdy	......	Cabell	......
198.0	Crown City Ferry	......	......	569
200.1	Green Bottom	......	......	......
201.1	Millersport Ferry	......	......	......
202.7	Lesage	......	......	548
205.4	Coxe's Landing	......	......	548
211.2	Guyandotte	......	......	541
214.6	Huntington	......	......	538
217.3	Central City	......	......	538
221.9	Ceredo	......	......	545
223.0	Kenova	......	......	550

Ripley and Mill Creek Valley Branch, O. R. R.

0	Millwood	W. Va.	Jackson	577
3.0	Cottageville	......	......	583
6.0	Angerona	......	......	586
8.0	Evans	......	......	601
13.0	Ripley	......	......	599

Ravenswood, Spencer and Glenville Branch, O. R. R.

0.0	Ravenswood	W. Va.	Jackson	584
0.6	R. S. and G. Junction	......	....	581
1.0	Bridgeport	......	....	579
3.1	Silverton	......	....	575
6.3	Crow Summit	......	....	637
8.6	Sandyville	......	....	592
12.2	Meadowdale	......	....	611
14.3	Duncan	......	....	626
15.1	Leroy	......	....	635
17.0	Liverpool	......	....	661
19.5	Sandy Summit	......	Roane	889
21.7	Seamans	......	....	695
22.2	Dukes	......	....	684
23.0	Reedy	......	....	669
27.0	Hardman	......	....	695
30.0	Barrs	......	....	899
33.0	Spencer	......	....	710

Little Kanawha River.

0.	Parkersburg (low water)	W. Va.	Wood	563
2.	Lock One	......	....	564
14.	Lock Two	......	....	574
22.	Lock Three	......	Wirt	584
32.	Lock Four	......	....	596
43.	Spring Creek	......	....	612
.....	Buffalo Rock	......	....	625
.....	Lower Leading Creek	......	Calhoun	631
61.	Down's Ripple	......	....	635
63.	Anna Maria Creek	......	....	641
68.	Big Root	......	....	644
76.	Pine Creek	......	....	654
78.	Grantsville	......	....	656
80.	Steer Creek	......	....	666
85.	Acre Island	......	....	671
89.	Mussel Shoals	......	Gilmer	677
92.	Tanner Fork	......	....	682
96.	Cedar Creek	......	....	687
98.	Third Run Shoals	......	....	689
101.	Leading Creek	......	....	690
103.	Glenville	......	....	702
105.	Stewart's Creek	......	....	702
106.	Mud Lick Run	......	....	710
110.	and Fork	......	....	711
115.	Stout's Mill	......	....	723
118.	Hyer's Run	......	Braxton	735
121.	Oil Creek	......	....	741
122.	Burnsville	......	....	741
.....	Bennet's Run	......	....	752
131.	Bulltown	......	....	760

CHESAPEAKE and OHIO RAILROAD.

RICHMOND, VA., November 30, 1898.

DR. I. C. WHITE, State Geologist,
    Morgantown, W. Va.

    DEAR SIR:—In response to attached memorandum I hand you herewith a list of elevations of stations on Main line in West Virginia, above sea level, with distances of same from Ft. Monroe. These elevations were copied from grade profile made in Chief Engineer's Office, 1883.

It is not practicable to give elevations on all branches, for the reason that we have no connected levels, but I have added approximate elevations on Loup Creek Branch.   G. A. LYELL,
                   Chief Draughtsman.

CHESAPEAKE and OHIO RAILROAD.

Distance from Ft. Monroe	STATIONS.	State	County	Elevations above tide
308. 3	Tuckahoe	W. Va.	Greenbrier	2035
311. 9	White Sulphur	......	....	1922
313. 8	Greenbrier	......	....	1865
315. 5	Hart's Run	......	....	1814
316. 4	Howard	......	....	1790
317. 3	Caldwell	......	....	1766
319. 8	Whitcomb	......	....	1698
322. 6	Ronceverte	......	....	1663
326. 6	Rockland	......	....	1650
329. 0	Ft. Spring	......	....	1626
330. 3	Snow Flake	......	....	1607
332. 6	Half Way	......	....	1579
335. 8	Alderson	......	....	1548
337. 9	Mohler	......	Summers	1540
339. 4	Wolf Creek	......	....	1530
340. 5	Riffe	......	....	1524
343. 6	Stockyards	......	....	1530
345. 3	Lowell	......	....	1512
347. 2	Talcott	......	....	1512
349. 5	Hilldale	......	....	1496
352. 6	Don	......	....	1432
357. 0	Hinton	......	....	1372
358. 8	Tug Creek	......	....	1352
362. 0	Brooks	......	....	1338
366. 6	Sandstone	......	... .	1288
369. 6	Meadow Creek	......	....	1265.
374. 3	Glade	......	Fayette	1236
378. 7	Quinnimont	......	....	1196
380. 0	Prince	......	....	1192
383. 1	McKendree	......	....	1141
385. 0	Slater	......	....	1106
386. 0	Buffalo	......	....	1103
387. 0	Alaska	......	....	1090
387. 8	Claremont	......	....	1086
388. 6	Beechwood	......	....	1078
389. 1	Stone Cliff	......	....	1076
390. 8	Thurmond	......	....	1060
392. 2	Dimmock	......	....	1045
393. 2	Beury	......	....	1038
394. 0	Central	......	....	1029
394. 5	Fire Creek	......	....	1029
396. 4	East Sewell	......	....	1009
397. 5	Sewell	......	....	1003

Chesapeake and Ohio Railroad – Continued.

399. 3	Caperton	W. Va.	Fayette	984
400. 4	Keeney's Creek	....	....	965
401. 6	Nuttall	......	....	946
404. 3	Fayette	......	....	900
405. 6	Elmo	......	....	860
406. 8	Sunnyside	....	....	843
407. 5	Gaymont	......	....	832
408. 7	Hawks Nest	......	....	827
409. 0	McDougall	......	....	824
410. 8	Cotton Hill	....	....	792
415. 2	Gauley	....	....	707
417. 9	Kanawha Falls	......	....	669
421. 4	Deep Water	....	....	648
423. 0	Digby	......	....	645
423. 6	Mt. Carbon	......	....	639
424. 3	Powelton	......	....	640
424. 6	Diamond	......	....	641
425. 0	Forest Hill	....	....	642
425. 1	St. Clair	......	....	642
425. 3	Eagle	......	....	641
425. 9	Edge Water	......	....	639
426. 6	Crescent	.....	....	638
427. 5	Montgomery	......	Kanawha	634
428. 1	Union Coal Company	....	....	631
428. 7	Consolidated Mfg. Co	....	....	633
429. 6	Handley	....	....	631
430. 3	Chesapeake	......	....	627
431. 7	Dego	....	....	626
432. 8	Paint Creek	......	....	622
432. 9	Gordon	......	....	621
433. 5	Crown Hill	......	....	623
434. 1	Belmont	......	....	620
435. 0	Black Cat	....	....	620
435. 6	East Bank	......	....	625
437. 5	Coalburg	......	....	625
438. 1	Cabin Creek	......	....	616
440. 7	Winnifrede Junction	......	....	616
444. 5	Brownstown	....	....	608
448. 2	Malden	......	....	606
449. 8	Kanawha	......	....	610
451. 7	South Ruffner	....	....	605
453. 6	Charleston	......	....	603
455. 2	Elk	......	....	601
458. 4	Black Band	......	....	598
459. 2	Spring Hill	......	....	597
462. 9	Huling	......	....	594
465. 5	St. Albans	......	....	592
466. 9	Lewis	......	....	592
456. 6	Scary	......	Putnam	591
473. 2	Scott	......	....	683
475. 1	Cades	......	....	702
476. 4	Henderson	......	....	972
479. 2	Hurricane	......	....	684
480. 5	Kibler	......	....	703
481. 5	Culloden	......	Cabell	703
484. 2	Walton	......	....	619
485. 8	Milton	....	....	586

Chesapeake and Ohio Railroad—Continued.

490.3	Ona	W. Va.	Cabell	622
491.9	Blue Sulphur Springs	....	....	598
494.7	Barboursville	......	....	578
498.2	Wilson	......	....	556
501.0	Guyandotte....................	......	....	560
501.2	D. K. Tower	....	....	563
504.0	Huntington	......	....	566
506.1	Central City	....	....	540
508.5	Kellogg	......	Wayne	544
510.7	Ceredo	....	....	445
511.8	Kenova	....	....	550

Loup Creek Branch—C. and O. R. R.

390.8	Thurmond	W. Va.	Fayette	1060
396.0	Harvey	....	....	1555
397.0	Red Star	....	....	1601
398.0	Glen Jean	......	....	1611
400.0	Dun Loup	......	....	1652
400.5	Turkey Knob	......	....	1677
401.5	MacDonald.....................	....	....	1678

Elk River.

0	Charleston (low water)...	W. Va.	Kanawha	556
21	Big Sandy Creek.............	......	....	591
24	Queen's Shoals	......	....	611
60	Big Otter Creek.............	......	Clay	726
70	Grove's Creek	....	....	751
80	Birch River..................	......	Braxton	770
93	Little Otter Creek...........	....	....	794
.....	Beall's Mills..................	......	....	798
100	Sutton	......	....	806

anley River.

0	Mouth of River (low water)	W. Va.	Fayette	650
...	Twenty Mile Creek (mouth).................	......	....	....
5		......	....	667
..			....	......
10	Little Elk Creek	......	Nicholas	691
15	Peters	......		879
21	Carnifax Ferry...............	....		1208
25	Hughes Ferry	....	....	1546
29	Brock's........................	....		1589
31	Beaver Creek	......	....	1694
40	Cherry River	......	....	1777
43	Cranberry	......		1915
46	Stroud's Ferry	......	....	2009
55	Williams River	......	Webster	2167
75	Laurel Fork	....	Pocohontas	3011
80	Stony Creek	.....	....	3223
85	Marlin's Bottom	......	....	2120

NORFOLK and WESTERN RAILWAY.

ROANOKE, VA., December 13, 1898.

DR. I. C. WHITE, State Geologist,
Morgantown, W. Va.

DEAR SIR :—Your letter of November 21st, addressed to the President of the N. & W. Ry. Company, has been referred to me.

In answer, I attach hereto a list of the stations with elevations of same, in the state of West Virginia; the elevations being uniformly at sub-grade. To get the elevation of base of rail seventeen inches must be added. Probably for publication purposes one foot would be best to use, although this elevation depends on amount of ballast we have under track. Wherever our track is standard ballasted this distance would be one and four-tenths feet above the sub-grade. The elevations given are the heights of sub-grade above mean low water at Norfolk.

Yours truly,
CHARLES J. CHURCHILL,
Eng. M. of Way.

Norfolk and Western Railway.

Distances from Norfolk	STATIONS.	State	County	Elevation above tide
342.41	Wills	W. Va.	Mercer	1614
346.96	Oakvale	......	....	1708
351.08	Hardy	....	....	1865
352.73	Ingleside	......	....	1944
353.89	East River	......	....	1990
356.95	Tulip	......	....	2139
358.73	Ada	....	....	2218
363.08	Bluefield	....	....	2556
371.26	Abbs Valley	....	....	2291
372.92	Dayton	......	....	2287
373.84	Bluestone Junction	......	....	2281
374.94	Wood	......	....	2272
375.29	Cooper	......	....	2266
376.37	Ruth	......	....	2359
376.80	East End Tunnel	......	....	2384
377.42	Coaldale	....	....	2336
379.53	Maybeury	....	McDowell	2147
380.39	Switchback	......	....	2070
381.40	Ennis	....	....	1995
382.94	Elkhorn	......	....	1882
384.86	Powhatan	....	....	1796
385.00	Kyle	......	....	1760
385.99	North Fork Juection	....	....	1700
387.4	Keystone	......	....	1935
388.35	Eckman	....	....	1588
389.30	Landgraff	....	....	1569
390.84	Vivian	......	....	1515
391.54	Vivian Yard	....	....	1494
392.40	Norwood	....	....	1475
396.44	Huger	......	....	1340
390.2	Welch	......	....	1297
400.29	Hemphill	......	....	1285
406.76	Davy	......	....	1183
412.86	Roderfield	....	....	1092

Norfolk and Western Railway, Continued.

417.70	Wilmore	W. Va.	McDowell	1019
421.88	Iaeger	......	....	978
429.29	Panther	......	....	939
432.10	Wyoming	......	....	924
434.00	Alnwick	......	Mingo	897
437.88	Wharncliffe	......	....	826
439.80	Glen Alum	......	....	806
442.78	Gray	......	....	778
446.59	Devon	......	....	754
450.87	Sands	......	....	732
453.73	Delorme	......	....	720
456.21	Thacker	......	....	709
460.70	Matewan	......	....	690
465.80	Rawl	......	....	672
469.59	Williamson	......	....	658
473.42	Barger	......	....	650
477.63	Nolan	......	....	643
484.40	Naugatuck	......	....	630
488.70	Lenore	......	....	635
492.01	Canterbury	......	....	675
496.53	Hale	......	....	880
498.85	Dingess	......	....	1001
501.11	Trace	......	....	915
507.27	Breeden	......	....	811
512.28	Wilsondale	......	Wayne	755
516.59	Doane	......	....	717
519.77	Wells Branch	......	....	701
522.27	Dunlow	......	....	688
527.29	Ferguson	......	....	666
528.89	Radnor	......	....	662
533.40	Genoa	......	....	643
536.48	Coleman	......	....	626
538.86	Echo	......	....	607
543.27	Wayne	......	....	598
549.30	Ardell	......	....	585
552.67	Dickson	......	....	575
555.62	Lavalette	......	....	561
561.38	Buffalo Creek	......	....	556
566.67	Ceredo	......	....	565
567.92	Kenova	......	....	580

Bluestone Branch—N. and W. Railway.

0.00	Bluestone Junction	W. Va.	Mercer	2281
1.47	Pocohontas	......	....	2315

Cooper and Goodwill Branch—N. and W. Railway.

0.00	Cooper	W. Va.	Mercer	2266
1.16	Bramwell	......	....	2247
1.80	Simmons Creek Junction	......	....	2242
5.48	Johnson's	......	....	2216
5.96	Flipping Creek Junction	......	....	2210
6.15	Duhring	......	....	2215
7.91	Goodwill	......	....	2262

Crane Creek Branch—N. and W. Railway.

0.00	Flipping Creek Junction	W. Va.	Mercer	2210
5.17	Mora	......	....	2335

North Fork Branch—N. and W. Railway.

0. 00	North Fork Junction......	W. Va.	McDowell	1699
0. 66	Algoma	....	....	1755
1. 49	Gillian	....	....	1796
2. 75	Rolfe	....	....	1869
3. 98	Arlington	....	....	1939
4. 40	McDowell	....	....	1968
6. 12	Ashland	....	....	2140

Shenandoah Division—N. and W. Railway.

Dist. from Hagerstown	STATIONS	State	County	Elevation above tide
0. 63	Cumb. Valley Junction ...	Md.	Washington	575.
16. 82	Shepherdstown	W. Va.	Jefferson	497.
17. 71	Morgan's Grove	....	....	428.
23. 10	Shenandoah Junction (B. & O.)	....	....	......
....		....	....	509.
24. 47	Aglionsby	....	....	526.
27. 94	Valley Branch (B. & O. Crossing)	....	....	......
....		....	....	492.
28. 32	Charlestown.....................	....	....	512.
32. 56	Wheatland	....	....	501.
33. 70	Rippon.....................	....	....	514.

Ohio Central Railroad—Kanawha and Michigan Division.

Distance	STATIONS.	State	County	Elevation above tide
0	Charleston	W. Va.	Kanawha	600.
4	Lock No. 6	....	....	592.
7	Smith's	....	....	588.
10	Ryans.....................	....	....	588.
12	Sattes	....	....	586.
15	Bowling	....	Putnam	584.
18	Poca	....	....	579.
19	Raymond City.....................	....	....	586.
20	Queen City...	....	....	579.
21	Energetic	....	....	576.
26	Red House	....	....	577.
31	Martins	....	....	572.
35	Buffalo	....	....	570.
38	18-Mile Creek	....	....	564.
40	Grimm's	....	Mason	563.
42	Maupin's	....	....	570.
45	Leon	....	....	567.
48	Beech Hill.....................	....	....	562.
50	Bright's	....	....	564.
51	Rock Castle	....	....	563.
56	River Switch	....	....	557.
57	Ohio River Bridge at Point Pleasant............	....	....	597.

Pittsburg, Cincinnati and St. Louis R. R. —Pittsburg, Wheeling and Kentucky Division.

0.	Steubenville	Ohio	Jefferson	728. ·
1.	Wheeling Junction..........	W. Va.	Brooke	......
3.	Middle Ferry.................	......	....	......
4.	Lower Ferry...................	......	....	......
6.	Cross Creek	......	.. ..	......
9.	Wellburg....................	......	....	......
12.	Beech Bottom	......	....	......
16.	Short Creek	......	Ohio	......
21.	Glenns	·		......
25.	Wheeling	....	....	645.

GUYANDOT VALLEY RAILWAY.

HUNTINGTOWN, W. VA., February 20, 1899.

DR. I. C. WHITE, State Geologist,
  Morgantown, W. Va.

DEAR SIR:—I have your letter of the 15th requesting distances and elevations on the proposed line of the Guyandot Valley Railway Company. I enclose the same from our survey profile, the figures being based upon the elevations at C. & O. R. R. Bridge over Guyandot River in Huntington, W. Va., which is about 550 feet. * We have no survey above Pineville or Rock Castle, except a preliminary survey for about ten miles up the main Guyandot, which shows an elevation of about ten feet to the mile. Trusting the accompanying information will be what you want, I am

Yours truly,   J. L. CALDWELL.

Distance	STATIONS.	State	County	Elevations
....	Huntington (C. & O. R. R. Bridge).................	W. Va.	Cabell	......
0.00	Mouth of Davis Creek ...	......	....	550
8.00	Mouth of Davis Creek ...	......	....	550
14.00	Mouth of Merritt Creek...	......	....	545
20.50	Mouth of Madison Creek	......	·	558
25.75	Mouth of 1-Mile Creek ...	......	Lincoln	570
31.00	Mouth of 6-Mile Creek ...	......	....	585
35.25	Mouth of Laurel Creek...	......	....	390
42.25	Mouth of Big Ugly Creek	......	....	595
....	Mouth of Green Shoals Creek	......	....	620
52.50		......		
60.00	Chapmanville	......	Logan	630
71.00	Logan Court House..... ..	......	....	665
80.50	Mouth of Rich Creek......	......	....	715
....	Mouth of Rock House Creek	......	....	735
85.00		......		
90.00	Mouth of Elk Creek	......	....	760
97.00	Mouth of Gilbert Creek..	......	....	830
101.75	Mouth of Cub Creek	......	Wyoming	870
....	Mouth of Leatherwood Creek	......	....	955
104.00		......		
....	Mouth of Clear Fork Guyandotte	......	....	1110
112.00		......		
123.00	Mouth of Turkey Creek.	......	....	1175
....	Mouth of Rock Castle Creek (Pineville)	......	....	......
130.50		......		1275

*Guyandot station, on the C. & O. R. R. near bridge is 560. (I. C. W.)

CHARLESTON, CLENDENNIN and SUTTON RAIL OAD.

CHARLESTON, W. VA., February 24, 1899.

DR. I. C. WHITE, State Geolog t,
    Morgantown, W. Va.

DEAR SIR:—Complying with your request of November 21st, 1898, which request was referred to our Philadelphia office, I have the pleasure to furnish you the following list of slations on our road between Charleston and Clay Court House, together with the elevation above tide, of the top of the rail in front of each station, show ug also the distance in miles and tenths of miles of each station from Charl ton.

Our railroad is only completed o Clay Court House, but our surveys and location extend to Sutton. Over ...is portion I add the distance from Charleston and the tide elevation of proposed grade of top ot rail at several streams which are crossed by the proposed extension.

The elevation of our grade at   : points mentioned is a little above the ordinary Elk River bottoms.

I trust that this information will reach you in time for your publication.

Yours truly,   CHAS. K. McDERMOTT,
                                Superintendent.

Distance	STATIONS.	State	County	Elevation Top of Rail
0. 0	Charleston......................	......	Kanawha	597. 13
1. 5	Two Mile........................	......	....	597. 33
2. 5	Wilson ....-....	.....	.....:..... ..	600. 83
3. 8	Barlow	....	....	604. 93
6. 0	Mill Creek.....................	......	....	602. 83
7. 3	Masons........ ......-	......	... .	606. 83
8. 5	Indian Creek	......	....	608. 83
10. 0	Pinch	......	....	608. 83
11. 0	Jarrett's Ford................	......	....	615. 83
13. 0	Blue Creek	.....	. ...	613. 83
14. 6	Walnut Grove	......	....	614. 83
15. 8	Rich Creek.....................	......	....	617. 83
17. 0	Falling Rock	......	....	617. 33
18. 6	Reamer	......	....	623. 73
20. 5	Clendennin	......	....	624. 43
22. 7	Morris Creek ....-.....	......	....	633. 23
23. 3	Blyth...........................	....	....	635. 89
24. 4	Queen Shoals..................	......	...........:.	637. 55
27. 6	Porter's	......	Clay	643. 83
28. 9	Rand...........................	......	....	645. 83
30. 3	King	......	....	650. 83
31. 8	Camp	......	....	651. 33
32. 7	Dulis...........................	......	....	652. 83
35. 9	Shelly Junction	......	....	662. 83
38. 4	Birch	......	....	668. 73
39. 5	Little Sycamore	......	....	671. 83
41. 1	Big Sycamore.................	......	....	673. 83
42. 9	Pierson.........	......	....	677. 83
44. 2	Little Beechey................	......	....	582. 33
44. 6	Yankee Dam	......	....	684. 43
46. 4	Big Beechey	......	....	693. 93
47. 2	Middle Creek..................	......	....	698. 43
48. 1	Upper Leatherwood.......	......	....	700. 83

Charleston, Clendennin & Sutton Railroad.—Continued.

50. 8	Clay Court House............	W. Va.	....	706. 03
51. 9	Buffalo Creek.................	......	....	711. 33
70. 7	Grove's Creek	......	....	785. 83
77. 0	Strange Creek	......	Braxton	805. 83
79. 2	Birch River..................	......	....	808. 83
80. 9	Fording Run.................	......	....	813. 88
81. 8	Upper Mill Greek.........	....	....	813. 83
87. 6	Raccoon Creek..............	......	....	827. 13
93. 8	Bear Creek	......	....	840. 23
94. 2	Little Buffalo Creek........	......	....	840. 83
97. 6	Big Buffalo Creek....,......	......	....	840. 83
97. 9	Scidmore Run	......	....	844. 23
98. 1	Opposite Sutton Bridge....	......	....	844. 93
98. 7	Buckeye Creek..............	......	....	846. 33
	High warer, Sutton, 1861	......	....	840. 10
	" " " 1975	......	....	837. 30

DRY FORK RAILROAD.

HENDRICKS, W. Va., January 30, 1899.

DR. I. C. WHITE, State Geologist,
    Morgantown, W. Va.

DEAR SIR :—I herewith enclose table showing distanc ɔ ꞏ ɔ..ɪ Hendricks (which is our junction with W. Va. C. & P. Ry.), elevations, using W. Va. Central and Pittsburg Ry., datum of 1702.1 feet for Hendricks, and elevation of water in Dry Fork River, using same datum. The distances given are correct, the road having been recently measured. I cannot, however, say that the elevations are absolutely accurate, they having been taken from the location notes. I believe, though, that there are no errors greater than a foot or two, at the outside.   Very truly yours,

         F. K. BRETZ, General Manager.

Distance	STATIONS	State	County	Elevations	
				Grade	Low wat.
0. 0	Hendricks	W. Va.	Tucker	1702. 1	1690. 1
3. 06	Red Run	......	....	1804. 1	1795. 1
6. 19	Rich Ford....................	......	....	1864. 1	1843. 1
7. 47	Mill Run.....................	......	....	1890. 1	1880. 1
8. 32	Elk Lick ....---..	......	....	1912. 1	1900. 1
9. 07	Gladwin (old station).....	......	....	1951. 1	1940. 1
12. 06	Flynn's Crossing...........	......	....	2019. 1	2011. 1
13. 50	Mouth of Laurel Fork.....	......	....	2051. 1	2039. 1
14. 59	Carr's	......	....	2072. 1	2066. 1
17. 50	Dry Fork.....................	......	Rand'lph	2177. 1	2170. 1
21. 13	Harman	......	....	2334. 1	2327. 1
24. 78	Lower Dam..	......	....	2497. 1	2492. 1
26. 44	Job...........................	......	....	2578. 1	2572. 1
28. 72	Gandy	......	....	2657. 1	2652. 1
30. 66	Whitmer, C. L. B.&L.Co...	......	....	2757. 1	2750. 1
31. 25	Horton " "	......	....	2805. 1	2799. 1

WEST VIRGINIA SHORT LINE RAILROAD SURVEY.

CLARKSBURG, W. VA., January 20, 1899.

DR. I. C. WHITE, State Geologist,
    Morgantown, W. Va.

DEAR SIR :—In reply to your request I herewith send you a table of distances and elevations of points on the West Virginia Short Line Railroad Survey. In one column is given the elevation of the top of the rail, while in the other column is the elevation of low water in the streams along the lines at the points named. The elevations given are above sea level, based on the Government levels on the Ohio River. The published levels of the B. & O. R. R. in Clarksburg would make these elevations 1.5 feet lower than here shown.   Yours very truly,

             T. M. JACKSON,
                     President.

West Virginia Short Line Railroad Survey.

Distance	STATIONS	State	County	Elevations Top of Rail	Elevations Low Water
0. 0	North end Third Street. Clarksburg	W. Va.	Harrison	......	......
....		....	....	983	......
0 .3	College St., Clarksburg	....	....	975	......
0. 5	West end of Elk Creek bridge..	....	....	968	923
....		....	....	968	923
0. 8	West end of West Fork bridge....................	....	....	966	910
....		....	....	966	910
1. 4	West end of Limestone bridge....................	....	....	967	912
....		....	....	967	912
2. 5	West end Crooked Run bridge....................	....	....	984	922
....		....	....	984	922
5. 5	Hepzibah Summit top of cut,elev'ti'n 1063)	....	....	1031	......
....		....	....	1031	......
7. 2	West end Lambert Run bridge....................	....		986	899
....		....	....	986	899
8. 9	West end of Wolf Pen bridge....................	....	....	961	897
....		....	....	961	897
10. 0	West end of Ten Mile Creek, 1st Crossing (below Fortney's)..	....	....	927	883
....		....	....	......	......
.....		....	....	927	883
10. 2	West end of Ten Mile Creek, 2d Crossing (above McDemott's)	....	....	925	888
....		....	....	......	......
....		....	....	925	888
10. 6	West end of Ten Mile Creek, 3rd Crossing (near school house)	....	....	925	897
....		....	....	......	......
.....		....	....	925	897
11. 6	West end of Ten Mile Creek, 4th Crossing (below Widow Robinson's)	....	....	931	899
....		....	....	......	......
....		....	....	931	899

West Virginia Short Line Railroad Survey—Continued.

11.8	West end of Ten Mile Creek, 5th Crossing (above Widow Robinson's	W. Va.	Harrisan	 932	 901
13.2	West end of Little Ten Mile Creek, 1st crossing (on T. J. Robey)	....	....	 933	 913
14.3	West end of Little Ten Mile Creek, 2d crossing (on A.G. Swiger)	....	....	 947	 926
15.1	West end of Little Ten Mile Creek, 5th crossing (just above Dola)	....	....	 957	 942
15.9	West end of Little Ten Mile Creek, 6th crossing (just above Dola)	....	....	 966	 951
16.9	Wess end of Little Ten Mile Creek, 7th crossing (above Rittenhouse)	....	....	 974	 959
17.3	West end of Little Ten Mile Creek, 9th crossing (near Edgell's ...	....	....	 982	 969
18.0	West end of Little Ten Mile Creek, 10th crossing (belown Brownstown)	....	....	 991	 976
18.6	West end of Little Ten Mile Creek, 11th crossing (below Marsh's)..	....	....	 1000	 985
19.3	West end of Little Ten Mile Creek, 12th crossing (above Marsh's)..	....	....	 1009	 990
20.6	West end of Little Ten Mile Creek, 14th crossing (near Robinson's Mill)	....	....	 1030	 997
21.9	West end of Mud Lick Creek, 1st crossing (at Barnes')	....	....	 1053	 1018
23.1	East end of Tunnel.....	....	....	1075	......
23.7	West end of Tunnel.....	....	Wetzel	1077	......
25.7	West end Fishing Cre'k 1st crossing (on David Talkington.........	....	....	 990	 950
26.3	West end of Talkington Run Crossing...........	....	....	 963	 922
27.6	West end Fishing Cre'k 3rd Crossing (on J. W. Starkey)	....	....	 903	 873
28.3	West end Fishing Cre'k 4th crossing (on Anson Cain)	....	....	 872	 857
29.9	West end Fishing Cre'k 5th crossing (at Smithfield)............	....	....	 883	 820

LEVELS ABOVE TIDE.

West Virginia Short Line Railroad Survey.—Continued.

		W. Va.	Wetzel		
30. 9	West end Falling Timber Creek crossing, (on Edgell's heirs)...	....	....	 823	 811
31. 5	West end Fishing Cr'k 7th crossing at Archie's Fork..........	....	....	 819	 801
33. 0	West end Fishing Cr'k 8th crossing (on Lew-Wyatt)..........	....	....	 802	 782
33. 6	West end Fishing Cr'k 9th crossing (on Alpheus Wyatt	....	....	 792	 772
35. 4	West end Fishing Cr'k 10th crossing (at Morgan Low Gap)	....	....	 770	 749
36. 5	West end Buffalo Creek crossing	....	....	... 749	 731
37. 4	West end Wyatt Run crossing (at Madison Baker's)..........	....	....	 737	 728
39. 2	West end Fishing Cr'k 12th crossing (below Amos Lowe's house)	....	....	 731	 707
39. 7	West end Fishing Cr'k 15th crossing (1 mile above Pine Grove) ...	....	....	 723	 701
40. 6	West end Fishing Cr'k 16th crossing at Pine Grove	....	....	 718	 695
43. 2	West end Piney Fork Creek branch crossing (on Long & Wiley)..	....	....	 698	 680
44. 4	West end Crow Run crossing (on John Lantz..........	....	....	 690	 677
45. 2	West end Brush Run crossing (opposite Reeder	....	....	 689	 676
47. 1	West end Fishing Cr'k 17th crossing (just above Long Point.....	....	....	 687	 660
47. 6	West end Fishing Cr'k 18th crossing (between tunnels)	....	......	 685	 650
47. 8	West end of State Road Run crossing (on Long heirs	....	....	 682	 665
48. 2	West end Fishing Cr'k 19th crossing (above Porter's Falls)........	....	....	 678	 650
49. 2	West end Fishing Cr'k 20th crossing (on Aaron Morgan)......	....	......	 673	 640
51. 7	West end Fluharty Run crossing (opposite Minnie)	....	....	 646	 532

West Virginia Short Line Railroad Survey.—Continued.

59.2	Ohio River R. R. track at Junction, just below New Martinsville	W. Va.	Wetzel	......	......
......		....	....	....	......
......		....	....	629	......
......	Low water, Ohio River, at Bowman. 2 miles below New Martinsville	....	....	......	501

Pittsburg, Washington & Southern Railroad Survey.

(Levels on preliminary survey from Waynesburg, Pa., to Mannington, W. Va.)

0.	Waynesburg (W. &W. R. R	Penn'a	Greene	......
......		......	....	943
0.1	Ten Mile Creek..	......	....	922
2.6	Inghram's School House......	......	....	......
......		......	....	991
4.6	Road at Orndorff's....	......	....	1040
6.3	Road on Bran'ts Summit	......	....	1300
7.2	Private Road at Brick House......	......	....	1127
8.0	Bench Mark, Sugar, Caleb Spragg's Orchard	......	....	... ..
......		......	....	1084
8.5	Road in Spraggtown	......	....	1065
9.2	B. M. 1st Bridge, Roberts Run, below Spraggtown......	......	....	......
......		......	....	1050
10.1	Road upper end John T. Rinehart's land.........	......	......	......
......		......	....	1031
10.5	B. M. Sycamore, between Rinehart's and Thrall's	......	....	......
......		......	....	1023
11.9	M. M., N. E. corner of bridge, at William Mapel's	......	....	......
......		......	....	990
12.1	Johnson's school house ...	......	....	985
12.2	Derrick on the Johnson farm	......	....	(?) 973
13.2	Roberts Run Bridge at Blackville	W. Va.	Monongalia	955
13.6	Washington coal, along road up Dunkard.........	......	....	985
14.3	Wright's Run	......	....	957
14.7	Barber Spring	......	....	968
15.0	B. M., Miracle Run Bridge, on Dunkard Creek	......	....	968
15.0	Dunkard Creek (low water)	......	....	950
15.6	Road above Eliab Tennant's.........	......	....	968

Pittsburg, Washington and Southern Railroad Survey.—Continued.

16.0	Road at J. C. Thomas' scales	W. Va.	Monongalia	
.....				978
16.8	B. M. on Bridge at Bula P. O.			
.....				983
17.6	Road in front of Isaac Strosnider's			
.....				985
18.0	Ground back of Ebenezer Bell's house			
.....				995
18.5	Road in front of Eli Collin's house			
.....				1005
19.1	Road in bend, above Jonathan Fox's			
.....				1010
19.5	Old Road at Josiah Thomas's			
.....				1013
20.0	iracle Run, on Z. S. Wise's farm			
.....				1015
20.3	Road at Lewis Fox's	....		1031
21.3	B. M., N. W. corner of E. Eddy's stable			
.....				1048
21.4	Road (Jollytown coal, 12 feet above)			
.....				1051
21.5	Pike in Cross Roads			1056
22.0	B. M. on School House at Corrother's			
.....				1057
22.9	Miracle Run, E. Tennant's sugar camp			
.....				1071
23.7	Road, lower end of Sol. Shriver's farm			
.....				1097
24.2	Run at Isaac Efaw's stable			
.....				1134
25.7	Road at Fly Blow		Marion	1431
27.4	Coal on Jone's farm (probably Jollytown)			
.....				1175
27.5	B. M. White Oak, Hog Back, Riley Dickens' farm			
.....				1162
28.1	40 feet obove Run at Nancy Thomas's			
.....				1085
29.0	B. M. White Oak, Flat Run Baptist Church			
.....				1016
29.4	Road at Flat Run P. O			1006
30.0	Road, level with derrick, W. B. Sine farm			
.....				993
30.7	Road, bend below Cunningham's (Wash. coal 2 feet above)			
.....				984
31.2	Pyle's Fork (low water)			974
31.9	Pritchard's Run			979
32.8	Mannington, B. & O. depot, top of rail			
.....				978

Coal and Iron Branch, West Va. C. & P. R. R.

O.	Elkins	W. Va.	Randolph	1920
......	Tunnel No. 1, Valley	......	....	......
4.95	Mountain	......	....	2362
9.0	Faulkner.......................	......	....	2174
19.0	Fishing Hawk	......	....	2612
21.0	Cheat River Crossing......	......	....	2770
......	Tunnel No. 2, Shaver's	......	....	......
23.5	Mountain....................	......	....	2934
......	Divide between Glay's	......	....	......
......	Fork of Cheat river and	......	....	......
29.12	Greenbrier river	......	....	3143
47.00	Durbin	......	....	2124

Little Kanawha Railroad.

The following list of elevations on the Little Kanawha Railroad survey of the Wabash system, between Parkersburg and Belington, have been kindly furnished by Mr. S. D. Brady, Chief Engineer. These are all based on the Parkersburg bench of the U. S. Geological Survey, and they check on the Burnsville bench of the same survey within a few hundredths of an inch, and also check accurately at Belington with levels carried there from the Grafton bench mark by Mr. C. McC. Lemley of the B. & O. R. R.

DISTANCE		STATIONS	State	County	Elevation
Via Railroad	Via River				
0.0	0.0	U. S. G. S. bench mark at Parkersburg P. O. (used as datum)	W. Va.	Wood	616.11
......	......		....	....	....
0.0	0.0	Bench mark on bolt, south side of Water street.....	....	....	608.99
......	......		....	....	....
0.0	0.0	Plug, corner Green and Third streets...............	....	....	605.50
......	......		....	....	....
0.0	0.0	Green street crossing, L. K. R. R...................	....	....	605.50
......	......		....	....	....
1.3	......	South Parkersburg, top of ties, L. K. R. R............	....	....	601.10
......	......		....	....	....
1.8	......	Old Hickory, top of ties..	....	....	603.50
2.6	......	Sheffield.....................	....	....	599.80
3.7	......	Johnson's...................	....	....	605.20
4.5	......	Geiger's	....	....	602.90
5.8	......	Nicolette	....	....	608.60
6.8	......	Creels	....	....	605.20
8.6	......	Dewey	....	....	618.23
9.6	......	Kanawha.....................	....	....	608.40
10.4	......	Weekley's..................	....	....	604.80
12.3	......	Cool Springs.................	....	....	605.40
13.9	......	Leachtown Ferry	....	....	617.55
14.5	......	Slate	....	....	608.60
16.7	......	Fishing Camp	....	Wirt	614.70
17.4	......	Hughes River	....	....	617.6

Little Kanawha Railroad.—Continued.

Via New Line	Via River					
18. 7	......	Newark	W. Va.	Wirt	614. 20
20. 9	......	Sandy Bend	....	....	617. 50
22. 5	......	Roberts	....	....	628. 60
23. 2	......	Standing Stone	....	....	622. 10
*24. 5	......	Well's Lock	....	....	619. 30
26. 5	......	Elizabeth...........................	....	....	640. 50
†25. 6	......	Two Ripple Summit...........	....	....	783. 00
29. 7	......	Palestine	....	....	641. 50
30. 1	......	Palestine transfer	....	....	631. 20
Via New Line	Via River		....	....	....
......	31.	Reedy Creek	....	....	599. 00
......	33.	Henderson's Run, Dulon P. O......................	....	....	613. 00
30. 3	39.	Burning Springs Run......	....	....	618. 00
34. 1	......	Opposite Creston.............	....	....	665. 00
......	48.	Creston "O" on water gauge	....	....	621. 37
35. 9	49.	Simpson's Run	....	....	645. 00
......	52.	Katy's Run......................	....	....	660. 00
45. 0	65. 5	Yellow Creek...................	....	Calhoun	647. 00
45. 1	......	Brooksville..	.. ..	....	707. 00
48. 1	69.	Big Root Summit	....	....	940. 80
50. 7	76. 5	Leaf Branch Run.............	....	....	663. 00
51. 4	76. 7	Grantsville	....	....	695. 00
53. 1	79. 5	Bull River..............	....	....	666. 00
60. 5	86. 0	Laurel Run......................	....	....	779. 00
65. 7	91. 5	Tanner Creek...................	....	Gilmer	686. 00
74. 0	100.	Leading Creek.....	....	....	695. 00
......	102.	Sycamore Run	....	....	700. 00
......	102. 3	Turkey Run	....	....	710. 00
76. 8	102. 5	Glennville......................	....	....	735. 00
78. 1	104.	Stewarts Creek..............	....	....	704. 00
81. 2	106. 5	Lynch Run (Trubada P. O.)	....	....	717. 00
83. 1	109.	Sand Fork.......................	....	....	718. 00
84. 9	111.	Dust Camp	....	....	729. 00
85. 3	112. 5	River, ½ mile above Stout's Mill	....	....	733. 00
......	114. 5	Copen Run	....	....	730. 00
88. 0	116.	Long Shoal Run	....	Braxton	740. 00
......	117.	Hyer's Run	....	....	741. 00
92.	120.	Oil Creek........................	....	....	748. 00
92. 5	......	Burnesville, B. M. No. 157 abutment, W. Va. & P. R. R. bridge, over Salt Lick Creek............	....	....	764. 51
97. 3	......	Knawl's Creek.................	....	....	765. 00
101. 5	.....	Knawl's P. O., Knawl's Creek	....	....	825. 00
103. 5	......	Summit bet. Feather Bed Fork of Knawl's Creek and Abram's Run......	....	....	1240. 00
106. 5	......	West Fork river (mouth of Abram's Run)	....	Lewis	1062. 00

*21. 7 New line.   †New line.

Little Kanawha Railroad.—Continued.

108. 5	....	Crane Camp Run............	W. Va.	Lewis	1094. 00
109. 0	....	Laurel Run (Crawford P. O.)	....	....	1101. 00
....	....	Wilson's Summit bet. left fork of Fall Run and French Creek............	....	....	....
113. 5	....		....	....	1513. 00
..... -	....		....	....	....
114. 0	....	French Creek, ½ mile from summit	....	Upshur	1489. 00
115. 5	....	Summit, between French Creek and Slab Camp Creek	....	....	1639. 00
....	....		....	....	....
....	....		....	....	....
116. 5	....	Slab Camp Creek (Hyer's frrm ...	....	....	1456. 00
118. 0	....	Summit bet. Slab Camp Creek and Bull Run (Mt. Pleasand Church)	....	....	1580. 00
....	....		....	....	....
....	....		....	....	....
118. 5	....	Left Fork of Bull kun (Heyner farm).............	....	....	1466. 00
....	....		....	....	....
119. 5	....	Summit between left and right forks of Bull Rnn (Stewarl Hyer farm)	....	....	1557. 00
....	........-		....	....	....
120. 0	....	Right Fork of Bull Run (John Hyer farm).......	....	....	1487. 00
.......-	....		....	....	....
120. 5	....	Summit between Right Fork of Bull Run and Glady Fork of Stone Coal	....	....	1560. 00
....	....		....	....	....
......--	....		....	....	....
....	....		....	....	....
123. 5	....	Glady Fork (John Dowell farm	....	....	1386. 00
....	....		....	....	....
124. 6	....	Summit—Glady Fork—Brushy Fork (J o h n Dowell farm)	....	....	1442. 00
....	....		....	....	....
..... --	....		....	....	....
126. 0	....	Finck Run 1 mile above Buckhannon............	. ...	....	1403. 00
.......-	....		....	....	....
127. 0	....	Clarksburg & Buckhan'n pike, opp. Buckhannon	....	....	1411. 00
....	........-		....	....	....
129. 0	....	Turkey Run	....	....	1390. 00
130. 0	....	Brush Run Summit (Columbus Post farm)	....	......--	1546. 00
....	....		....	......--	......----
....	...... -	B. M. Summit between Sugar Fork of Turkey Run and Pecks Run. Flevation marked by U. S. G. S. —"1558"	....	....	1557. 41
....	....		....	....	....
....	....		....	....	....
....	....		....	....	....
....	....		....	....	........-.-
130. 5	....	Brush Run	....	....	1428. 00
131. 5	....	Summit between Brush and Peck runs............	....	....	1516. 00
....	....		....	....	....
132. 5	....	Peck's Run...........	....	....	1398. 00
134. 0	....	Summit bet. Pecks Run and 2d Big Run..........	....	Barbour	1456. 00
......- .	....		....	....	....
136. 5	....	Second Big Run, 550 feet from Buckhannon River	....	....	1358. 00
....	...--...		....	....	....
....	....		....	....	....
140. 0	....	Buckhannon River (Junction with Tygarts Valley River)	....	....	1314. 00
....	....		....	....	....
....	....		....	.... ..	....
144. 0	....	Middle Fork river (mo'th)	....	....	1479. 00

Little Kanawha Railroad.—Continued.

152.3	....	Tygarts Valley River (1 mile above bridge at Belington)	W. Va.	Barbour	1685.00
....	....		....	....	....
....	....		....	....	....
151.8	....	Hub in center of B. & O. track at Belington station	....	....	1698.70
....	....		....	....	....
....	....		....	....	....
151.3	....	Alston. (Road to Belington	....	....	1741.00
....	....		....	....	....

BRANCH LINE.
Line up Leading Creek to Buckhannon River via Weston and
Hackers Creek.

Distances from mouth of Leading Creek. Via Line.	STATIONS	State	County	Elevation above tide
27.0	Summit bet. Leading and Polk Creeks	W. Va.	Lewis	1200.00
......		......	....	....
33.5	West Fork River (Below dam at Weston High Tide	......	....	999.00
......		......	....	....
......		......	....	....
33.6	Weston B. M. on curb E. cor. Center and Third streets................	......	....	1015.41
......		......	....	....
38.0	Summit bet. Little Stone Coal and Big Hilly Upland Run................	......	....	1246.00
......		......	....	....
......		......	....	....
40.5	Big Hilly Upland Run— 600 feet from mouth, (Hackers)	......	....	1071.00
......		......	....	....
......		......	....	....
50.0	Summit bet. Left Fork of Hackers Creek and and Pecks Run	......	Upshur	1502.00
......		......	....	....
......		......	....	....

LINE UP OIL CREEK.

Dist. from Burnesville	STATIONS	State	County	Elevation
4.5	Oil Creek at Confluence..	W. Va.	Lewis	770.00
12.0	Summit between Clover Fork of Oil and West Fork of Monongahela River	......	....	1282.00
......		......	....	....
......		....	....	....
12.5	West Fork River (one mile above Jacksonville)	......	....	1060.00
......		......	....	....
......		......	....	....

Line Up Little Kanawha River from Knawi's Creek.

100.5	131.0	Bulltowd (Floor County bridge)................	W. Va.	Braxton	787.40
......	....		......	......	....
103.0	133.0	Little Kanawha River, above Falls at Falls Hills................	......	......	799.00
....	....		......	......	....
....	......		......	......	....

MONONGAHELA RIVER.

PITTSBURG, PA., February 1, 1899,
DR. I. C. WHITE, State Geologist,   OFFICE U. S. ENGINEERS.
Morgantown, W. Va.

DEAR SIR:—Referring to your request of the 24th, ultimo, I here enclose list of benches and level points along the Monongahela river from Pittsburg to Dam No. 9, and the same along the West Fork from near its mouth to Clarksburg.

The elevation of the lower sill masonry, lock No. 10, is to be 786.92 and top of lock walls 813.17 feet.

From dam No. 9 to Hoults, the list of benches, etc., is given in the Annual Report of the C. of E., 1897, page 2407, a copy of which is at the Morgantown office, which list Mr. Lucas will copy for you, and furnish, as far as he able, the distances from dam No. 9. From Hoults to Bench No. 12, West Fork river, the list is given on page 2182 of my annual report for 1898, a copy of which is mailed you to-day. Mr. Lucas may be able to furnish the distances of these benches from dam No. 9.

Very respectfully,
CHARLES F. POWELL,
Major Corp of Engineers.

Elevation of Points along the Monongahela River, Referred to Mean Tide Level at Sandy Hook, N. J., per P. R. R. Levels.

*Distance from mouth of river. Miles.	Elevation. Feet.	STATIONS	
0.00	703.0	Pittsburg.—Harbor level, full pool, Davis Island Dam.	
1.95	707.40	Crest of Dam No. 1	B. M., north side 2d Ave. at angle between retaining wall and abutment of B. & O. new bridge over 2d Ave., on first course masonry above ground Elevation 730.46 A. T.
1.95	693.50	Lower sill, lare lock	
11.76	715.10	Crest of Dam No. 2	B. M., N. W. corner bridge seat, south abutment, west side. Elevation, 732.392 A. T.
11.76	701.30	Lower sill, large lock	

*A close aproximation.

Distance from mouth of river. Miles	Eldvation. Feet	STATION
24. 90	723. 10	Crest of Dam No. 3 ⎫ B. M. Stone buried 1 foot between rails north bound track P. R. R. point of curve (glass works) nearly opposite abutment of dam No. 3. Elevation 750. 448
24. 90	709. 46	Lower sill, large lock ⎭ A. T.
41. 33	733. 48	Crest of Dam No. 4 ⎫ B. M. Stone buried 1 foot between rails main track P. R. R., about 100′ below lock No. 4, station building. Elevation 759. 516 A.
41. 33	718. 03	Lower sill, large lock ⎭ T.
59. 45	746. 41	Crest of Dam No. 5.
	730. 28	Fower sill of lock.
69. 25	760. 15	Crest of Dam No. 6. ⎫ Elevations between locks
	742. 84	Lower sill of lock. ⎭ Nos. 4 and 9, not verified.
83. 90	769. 90	Crest of Dam No. 7. ⎱
	754. 19	Lower sill of lock. ⎰
88. 90	780. 80	Crest of Dam No. 8. ⎱
	765. 00	Lower sill of lock. ⎰
94. 20	793. 40	Crest of Dam No. 9. ⎫ Established from R. R. sur-
	775. 55	Lower sill of lock. ⎬ veys brought from Union-
	787. 00	Upper miter sill. ⎭ town, Pa.
*102. 70	820. 601	Eye of ring bolt, north end of Morgantown Suspension bridge abutment, right bank.
	821. 867	North corner, north abutment, railroad bridge, Decker's creek. B. M. cut.
104. 20	822. 130	North corner, north abutment, railroad bridge, Cobun's creek. B. M. cut.
	816. 249	North end of door sill, boiler house of pump station, Eureka Pipe Line Co.
105. 95	828. 852	North corner, north-east abutment, railroad bridge, Booth's creek. B. M. cut.
111. 45	846. 129	North corner, north-east abutment, railroad bridge, Tom's Run. B. M. cut.
112. 20	851. 417	North-east corner, east abatment, railroad bridge, Joe's Run, B. M. cut.
112. 45	857. 352	Point on rock ledge above railroad, right bank, upper end of railroad rock cut, just below dam No. 13. B. M. cut.
117. 20	837. 780	Point on flat rock, left shore, lock No. 14. B. M. cut.
117. 45	863. 515	North corner, north-east abutment, railroad bridge, White Day Creek. B. M. cut.
120. 95	868. 385	North corner, north-east abutment, railroad bridge, Little Creek. B. M. cut.
121. 95	873. 567	East corner, south-east abutment, railroad bridge, Prickett's Creek. B. M. cut.

*Levels from Lock No. 9 to Clarksburg were furnished by J. N. Lucas, Sub-Inspector U. S. Engineer Corps.

Distance from mouth of river. Miles	Elevation Feet.	STATION
123. 20	875. 665	South-west corner of stone foundation of brick warehouse, Montana
127. 20	885. 474	North-east corner center pier, B. & O. R. R. bridge across river below Fairmont.
128. 45	899. 681	South-west corner, bridge seat of abutment, Fairmont Suspension Bridge, Fairmont en l.
129. 95	886. 593	Extreme south-west, or upper corner, north abut-ment, B. & O. railroad bridge, across river above Fairmont
130. 25	882. 516	East corner, north abutment, New England rail-road bridge. B. M. cut
	880. 083	Bottom of New England railroad bridge.
130. 65	887. 728	Highest point on lower wall of abutment, Hon-sacker bridge, left side of river. B. M. cut.
	884. 479	Bottom of Honsacker bridge.
	887. 673	South-east corner, center pier, Monongahela River Railroad bridge. B. M. cut. Bottom of bridge same elevation.
	885. 350	Point on upper wall, railroad culvert, lower end of railroad curve and cut, near below White Rock. B. M. cut.
134. 75	884. 680	South corner, north-east pier, railroad bridge, Booth's creek, Monongah. B. M. cut.
135. 15	873. 386	R. R. spike in Buckeye tree, between railroad and river, lower edge of public road, about 230 feet up stream from Monongah Coal Tipple No. 3.
135. 55	900. 238	Point on rock ledge above railroad; eight feet from center of Main track and about 870 feet up stream from mile post No. 7, and about 750 feet down stream from J. A. Clark Coal Tipple. B. M. cut.
138. 15	894. 853	Point on masonry of railroad culvert, upper side of track, 1200 feet below Clark C. & C. Co. tipple, Chiefton. B. M. cut.
139. 45	874. 499	Seat for rod cut in upper wall of abutment of bridge across river at Worthington, 25 feet back from face of abutment and 2½ feet above surface of ground, left side of river. B. M. cut.
139. 65	893. 323	Point on lower or river end of railroad stone cul-vert, Worthington station. B. M. cut.
140. 93	894. 395	Point on masonry, lower or river end of railroad culvert, 2500 feet up stream from tipple No. 1 of Worthington C. & C. Company.
142. 05	904. 464	Point on north corner east pier Enterprise high-way bridge. B. M. cut.
142. 45	909. 094	Point on rock ledge above railroad, 10 feet from center of the track, lower end of railroad switch, about 645 feet down stream from tipple of Worthington C. & C. Co. No. 2. B. M. cut.

Distance from mouth of river. Miles	Elevation Feet	STATION
142.75	895.071	Point on north corner lower or river end of railroad stone culvert, Harrison's Run. B. M. cut.
143.35	803.030	Point on lower or river end of railroad stone culvert, opposite dairy farm of Wm. Hood.
144.65	911.566	North corner, east abutment, Shinnston highway bridge. B. M. cut.
148.15	917.606	East corner, north pier of Lumberport highway bridge. B. M. cut.
150.55	923.142	South-east corner of upper wing wall, Maulsby highway bridge. B. M. cut.
151.15	907.459	Point on masonry, west corner, lower or river end of railroad culvert, 3000 feet up stream from Maulsby bridge.
152.25	916.647	North corner, east pier, M. R. railroad bridge, across Simpson Creek, Clark station. B. M. cut.
156.45	932.904	River rail, lower end of trestle No. 10, Bartlett station.
157.35	932.325	River rail, Glen Falls coal chute.
157.45	933.005	River rail, trestle No. 11, over Falls Run, lower end.
	933.328	River rail, trestle No. 11, over Falls Run, upper end.
158.95	951.585	River rail, upper end heavy cut, 50 feet down stream from small ravine, 1000 feet down stream from Crooked Run.
159.65	967.638	River rail on trestle No. 12, immediately over stream.
159.75	968.469	River rail, trestle No. 12, upper end.
	966.641	Point on masonry, immediately over tile drain, upper end railroad stone culvert, about 420 feet up stream from trestle No. 12.
160.75	997.135	Point on west corner, north abutment, M. R. railroad bridge over the B. & O. railroad, opposite Adamston.
	970.584	Bolt head, north-west plumb post, B. & O. water tank, left bank, Adamston. B. M. of W. Va. S. L. railroad.
	972.330	Up stream rail, B. & O. railroad bridge, over face of abutment.
	971.674	Up stream rail, B. & O. railroad bridge, over face of abutment on left bank.
160.85	941.782	Top of abutment, left bank, upper inside corner, of Adamston highway bridge. B. M. cut.
161.35	926.005	End of timber of Hart's mill dam.
161.75	941.818	Lower inside corner, left abutment, highway bridge across mouth of Elk Creek, Clarksburg. B. M. cut.
	945.049	Lower inside corner, right abutment, highway bridge across West Fork river, Clarksburg (bridge seat.)
	944.841	Lower inside corner, left abutment, highway bridge across West Fork river, Clarksburg (bridge seat.)

KANAWHA RIVER.

CHARLESTON, W. VA., February 20, 1899.

DR. I. C. WHITE, State Geologist,
Morgantown, W. Va.

DEAR SIR :—In compliance with your request I take pleasure in handing you herewith a blue print profile of the Great Kanawha river from the mouth to Kanawha Falls, giving tide water elevations (Ref. mean tide at Richmond) of miter sills, sill of navigation pass, top of dam, coping of lock, lift of lock, original low water, etc., at each lock and dam on the river, ex-extreme high water elevations, etc., with distances from the mouth of river. All of the lock and dam foundations are built on rock except No. 11 near the mouth of the river. No. 11 is built on hardpan, an indurated clay, from 18 to 24 feet below low water mark. A description of this hardpan is given on page 2452 of the extract from the report of the Chief of Engineers herewith. The bed rock at this site is about 40 feet below low water, or about 470 feet above tide.

Hoping thts will answer your purposes, I am

Yours very truly,

ADDISON M. SCOTT,

U. S. Resident Engineer.

Distance Miles	STATION	ELEVATIONS ABOVE TIDE					
		Extr'e low water	Sill of Lock	Pass of Lock	Pool above Dam	Top of lock wall	Extr'e high water
0.00	Mouth of River............	510.08	....	....	....	....	571.07
1.75	Lock No. 11	509.58	504.0	508.0	521.0	526.0	....
11.50	Thirteen Mile Shoal......	512.15	....				571.64
18.75	Lock No. 10	517.36	514.0	515.0	528.0	533.0	....
21.50	Buffalo............	519.96	....				572.22
25.25	Lock No. 9....................	523.64	520.5	521.25	534.25	539.5	....
36.00	Lock No. 8...................	531.27	526.0	529.25	542.25	547.25	....
44.25	Lock No. 7........	539.63	535.5	537.5	550.50	555.50	....
46.00	St. Albans	....	....				591.28
54.50	Lock No. 6..................	548.01	543.75	546.50	559.00	565.50	....
58.00	Charleston, Elk River...	552.50	....				601.32
67.75	Lock No. 5.................	556.22	552.50	553.50	566.50	572.50	604.88
73.75	Lock No. 4................	564.44	559.75	561.00	573.75	579.75	611.77
80.00	Lock No. 3...............	571.22	566.75		585.75	601.25	622.63
85.00	Lock No. 2...............	581.77	578.75	....	597.75	609.75	....
86.00	Cannelton	586.34	....	....			652.17
95.25	Kanawha Falls, top	637.00	... .	....			....
....	Bed-rock, under Falls...	590.00	....				....
97.00	{ Gauley River } { New River..... }	650.20	....	....		....	665.50

1899.

PRECISE ELEVATIONS.

TAYLOR, MARION AND MONONGALIA COUNTIES, W. VA.

AND FAYETTE COUNTY, PA.

The elevations in the following list are the result of a line of precise levels run during the field season of 1899 from Erie, over the Pennsylvania Railroad, to Leboeuf; thence over the Erie Railroad to Franklin, and from Franklin to Pittsburg over the Allegheny Valley Railway. Also from Grafton, W. Va., over the Baltimore and Ohio Railroad to Leith; thence over the Pennsylvania Railroad to Pittsburg. Between Erie and Pittsburg they are based on an aluminum tablet set in the hospital wing of the Soldiers' Home at Erie, marked "635." The elevation of this is accepted as being 635.640 feet above mean sea level, as derived from the United States Engineer's bench mark at Erie, adjusted in accordance with statements on page 203 of Appendix to Nineteenth Annual Report, and page 298, Appendix to Twentieth Annual Report. Between Grafton and Pittsburg they are based on the United States Coast Survey chisel mark on coping stone at north end of central pier of railroad bridge over Tygarts Valley River. This bench mark was reduced by 0.03 meter, which is applied as a permanent correction from Hagerstown, Maryland, in accordance with the reports of the Coast Survey.

The leveling between Grafton and Pittsburg was done by Mr. E. L. McNair, assisted by Messrs. J. E. Buford and John W. Hodges, rod-men. That between Erie and Pittsburg was done by Mr. C. H. Semper, assisted by Messrs. John W. Hodges and Iddo M. Lewis.

All bench marks set in the course of this work were stamped with word "PITTSBURG," and the date "1899," in addition to the figures of elevations, thus referring them to the central datum tablet accepted for this group of leveling, which is set in the foundation of the Seventh Avenue Hotel in Pittsburg, the adjusted elevation of which is accepted as being 738.527 feet above mean sea level at Sandy Hook. This elevation comes through five precise lines of levels, namely: United States Coast and Geodetic Survey levels from Sandy Hook and from Old Point Comfort to Hagerstown and Grafton; United States Coast and Geodetic Survey and United States Army Engineers to Albany, Oswego, and the lakes, to Erie; United States Geological Survey levels from Albany to Dunkirk; and Pennsylvania Railroad precise levels from Sandy Hook via Harrisburg to Pittsburg.

Grafton, via, Fairmont, to Morgantown, W. Va.

Grafton, W. Va.; B. & O. railroad bridge across Tygarts Valley river; coping stone at north end of central pier, chisel marked (United States Coast Survey bench mark)............................. 996.829

Valley Falls, 2.9 miles east of; bridge seat at north-east corner of girder bridge No. 104, 7 feet east of center of track, 4 feet below top of outer rail of curve; bronze tablet marked "986 Pittsburg 1899"............................. · 985.580

Powell's flag station, ⅔ mile west of; stone arch bridge No. 108, coping stone of wall, 1.1 feet below top of rail, 7 feet north of center of track; aluminum tablet marked "899 Pittsburg 1899" 899.029

Benton Ferry, 160 feet south of sign board at; bridge seat at south-west corner of small girder bridge No. 111, 4½ feet below top of rail and 18½ feet south of center of track; bronze tablet marked "885 Pittsburg 1899"............................. .... 885.090

Fairmont, B. & O. station, 1¼ miles north of the Baltimore & Ohio railroad bridge No. 371, across the Monongahela river; coping stone at north end of east abutment; bronze tablet marked "885 Pittsburg 1899"...................... 885.034

Catawba, o.8 mile south of; B. & O. railroad one-span truss bridge No. 369; coping stone at north end of east abutment, 3 feet below rail and 8 feet north of; bronze tablet marked "873 Pittsburg 1899" 872.611

Little Falls, 1½ miles north-west of; face of rock, bluff, 9½ feet west of west rail and 4 feet above same, ½ mile north of bridge No. 366, bronze tablet marked "859 Pittsburg 1899"...... 858.862

Uffington station, 400 feet north of; coping stone of abutment at north-west corner of one-span truss bridge No. 364, 3 feet below top of rail and 7 feet north of rail; aluminum tablet marked "828 Pittsburg 1899"............................. 827.908

Morgantowd, B. & O. railroad station, 480 feet south of; coping stone of abutment at north-west corner of truss bridge over Decker's Creek; bronze tablet marked "821 Pittsburg 1899".. 820.900

Morgantown. W. Va., to Uniontown, Pa.

Vanvorhis, 1 mile south of; bridge seat at south-east corner of steel
    girder bridge No. 359; bronze tablet marked "815 Pittsburg
    1899" 815.253

Point Marion station, ¼ mile north of; coping stone at east end of
    north pier of six-span truss and girder bridge No. 356 across
    Cheat river; bronze tablet marked "813 Pittsburg 1899".........   812.911

Outcrop flag station, 0. 2 mile south of; northeast of B. & O. tunnel
    east side of track, 3.7 feet above rail; bronze tablet marked
    "1084 Pittsburg 1899"..   1083.891

Fairchance, B. & O. station, 550 feet north of; bridge seat at corner
    of small girder bridge No. 338; aluminum tablet marked "1065
    Pittsburg 1899"..   1065.243

The following letter and list of elevations were received too late for publication in the proper place with the B. & O. levels :

THE BALTIMORE & OHIO RAILROAD COMPANY.

OFFICE OF THE CHIEF ENGINEER,
J. M. GRAHAM.

BALTIMORE, MD., Dec. 16th, 1902.

DR. I. C. WHITE, State Geologist,
Morgantown, W. Va.

DEAR SIR :—Your letter of the 4th inst to Mr. Lemley referred to me, and in answer I send you the enclosed table of distances and elevations, as I was able to obtain. I trust that this will give you the information desired.

Yours truly, P. H. IRWIN,

Asst. Chief Engineer.

Cherry River Extension from Camden-on-Gauley to Richwood.

Station	Distances from Weston Miles	Elevation
Camden-on Gauley		
1. 0	77. 9	2021. 0
Arlington	78. 9	2021. 0
Bonner		2021. 0
Enoch Run Siding		
6. 5 miles		2011. 5
Cranberry		
1. 9 miles	85. 4	1936. 0
Curtin		
4. 0 miles	87. 3	
Lytton		
5. 4 miles	91. 3	2037. 0
Richwood	96. 7	2192. 0

DISAGREEMENT OF LEVELS.

It is not to be expected that the levels of the several railroad lines of the State will be in exact agreement with one another, or with the results given by the river surveys of the U. S. Engineers.

In order to determine the amount of this disagreement at some particular point, Clarksburg was selected, and Prof. T. M. Jackson, President of the West Virginia Short Line Railroad, kindly had the necessary levels carefully made, connecting the Baltimore & Ohio, and the West Virginia Short Line with the levels of the U. S. Engineers, who have carried the Pennsylvania Railroad datum from Uniontown across to the Monongahela river at Lock No. 9, and up the same to Clarksburg. The point chosen for comparison was the Bench Mark of the U. S. Engineers at the "Bolt head, north-west plumb post, B. & O. water tank, left bank, Adamstown, 970.584 feet," according to the river survey above mentioned with the Pennsylvania Railroad datum. The same point (970.584 feet) by the West Virginia Short Lines datum is 969.08 feet, and by the B. & O. datum of 1030 feet for sub-grade of the old passenger station at Clarksburg, is 966.45 feet, thus giving a difference of (970.584—969.08) only 1.504 feet between the Short Line Railroad datum and that of the Government Engineers, and (970.684—966.45) of 4.134 feet between the latter and that of the B. & O., results much nearer in agreement than usually found when different railroad and river levels interlock.

Prof. Jackson also had the elevation of the new passenger station of the B. & O. R. R. at Clarksburg determined, which on the basis of 1033.49 feet for the water table of the old passenger station under west window (a bench accurately established from the B. & O. profile many years ago) gives for the top of the south rail at line of the east wall of tne new passenger station an elevation of 1010.16 feet, and a bench mark on doorstep of the north-east door of the station building 1011 80 feet. Also the top of south rail at west end of the platform, Adamston station, B. & O. R. R., 961.15 feet, and for the B. & O. bridge seat across the

North-Western Turnpike at Adamston, bench mark top of stone wall, south-east corner of abutment, 954.91 feet. The elevation of the new passenger station is given in the table on page 31, vol. I, at 1000 feet, while Adamsion is 952 feet, both of which are too low by 10 feet approximately, even on the B. & O. datum of 1030 feet for sub-grade at the old passenger station. The four points on the B. & O. given above, brought into agreement with the Pennsylvania Railroad datum carried from Uniontown to Clarksburg by the U. S. Engineers, would be for the south rail at Clarksburg new station 1014.294 feet; (for the bench mark on the door sill, same place, 1015.934 feet); for the south rail at Adamston, 965-.284 feet; and for the bench mark on bridge seat over North-Western Turnpike, 959.044 feet, above tide.

PRECISE AND SPIRIT LEVELS.

ESTABLISHED BY THE UNITED STATES GEOLOGICAL SURVEY.
1898-1902.

The following account of the methods pursued by the U. S.
Geological Survey, in its work of establishing accurate elevations
and bench marks in connection with the co-operative topographic
map work of West Virginia, has been kindly prepared for the
Survey by Mr. H. M. Wilson, Geographer in charge of the Atlan-
tic Division of the U. S. Geological Survey.

Mr. Wilson also gives in this connection a list of such elevations accurately determined, together with their locations in the
several regions of the State. It is needless to say that these bench
marks will prove of great value to engineers, railroads, and all
manner of public improvements based upon accurate levels. since
it will enable all work of this kind to be correlated upon the same
accurate and reliable datum   Mining engineers especially should
connect their mine levels in all cases with tide elevations, and for
this reason these elevations find an appropriate and prominent
place in the volume on Coal, so that not only mining engineers,
but all others, may have the data at hand for connecting their
surveys with tidal elevations.

SPIRIT LEVEL ELEVATIONS.

Since 1896 the U. S. Geological Survey has been running very careful spirit levels for the control of its topographic work, and the elevations resulting from the same have been marked by permanent metal tablets, set not farther than six miles apart. These elevations are listed below, the work being executed in accordance with the following instructions issued for the guidance of the field force :

INSTRUCTIONS.
SPIRIT LEVELING.

1. A sufficient amount of accurate spirit leveling will be done to insure the placing of at least two permanent bench marks in each township or equivalent area surveyed, except in forest-clad and mountain areas, and in the region east of the 95th meridian, where at least one shall be established; and these shall be established, whenever practicable, near the township corners of the the public land surveys. In addition to these, other bench marks should be located in prominent places, where they may be of service in the prosecution of future public or private surveys.

2. For each general locality of field work some centrally situated place will be chosen in which an elevation above sea level can be determined with approximate accuracy from railroad or other surveys. In this place is to be established a central datum bench mark, preferably a tablet cemented in some solid masonry structure, to which will be referred all other bench marks in its neighborhood.

3. Permanent bench marks established in the course of the subsequent work should be so located that, like the central datum benches, they will not be liable to injury or disturbance, yet should

be so prominently situated that they will be easy to find. They
should consist of bronze or aluminum tablets, fastened with Port-
land cement into solid rock or masonry structures, as the foundations of buildings or bridge piers; or of the standard bronze-
capped iron posts, which should be so set in the ground as to pro-
ject about one foot. The intersection of the cross lines is the
bench mark.

4. Primary level lines should be run with one or two rodmen and one levelman, and when necessary, a bubble tender.
Wherever practicable such lines should be run in circuits which
will check back upon themselves or other lines. Where long,
unchecked lines are run, two rodmen must be employed.

5. *Single-rodded Lines.* Levelman and rodman must
keep separate notes and compute differences of elevation immediately. As levelman and rodman pass, the former must read the
rod himself, record and compare readings, then compute the H. I.,
and after computations are made compare results with the rodman. No comparisons should be made until the record is complete. If the results differ, each must read the rod before comparing anything but results.

6. Work on primary lines should not be carried on during
high winds or when the air is "boiling" badly. During very hot
weather an effort should be made to get to work early and to
remain out late, rather than to work during midday.

7. Fore and back sights should be of equal length, and no
sight over 300 feet should be taken excepting under unavoidable
circumstances, as in crossing rivers at fords or ferries or in crossing
ravines. In such cases extraordinary precautions must be taken,
as repeated readings at changed positions of rod and level, etc.

8. If it is impracticable to take equal fore and back sights,
as soon as the steep slope is passed take enough unequal sights to
make each set balance. In this case extra care must be taken to
insure correct adjustment of the level.

9. Distances along railroads can be obtained by counting
rails; at other times stadia or pacing may be used, according to
the quality of the work. The distances in feet of both the fore

and back sights must be recorded in both note books in proper columns.

10.   Always level the instrument exactly before setting the target.   After setting it and before giving the signal "all right," examine the level bubble.   If found to be away from center correct it and reset target.

11.   The level must be adjusted daily or oftener, if necessary.   The adjustment of the line of collimation and of the level tube is especially important.

12.   Provide rodmen with conical steel pegs, 6 to 12 inches long, with round heads, to be used as turning points.   Never take turning points on rails, ties, or between them.   Always drive the pegs firmly into the ground.

13.   When the rod is lengthened beyond 6.5 feet, both the rodman and the levelman must examine the setting of the target as well as the reading of the rod vernier.   When the rod is closed see that the rod vernier indicates 6.5 feet, not depending upon the abutting end to bring it back to place.   Keep the lower end of the rod and the top of the turning point free from mud and dirt.

14.   Plumbing levels must always be used and kept in adjustment, and long extensions of the rod avoided.

15.   Leave temporary bench marks at frequent intervals, marked so that they can be easily identified.   These may be on a solid rock well marked, a nail driven in a root of a tree or in a post, or on any place where the mark will not be disturbed for a few weeks. One such bench mark should be left for every mile run, in order to give sufficient points to which to tie future levels. Mark in large figures, in a conspicuous place when possible, the elevation to the nearest foot.   Make notes opposite all elevations at crossings of roads, railroads, streams, bridges, and in front of railway stations and public buildings, and of such other facts as may aid the topographer in his work.

16.   Endeavor to so locate permanent bench marks that the observed elevation shall be within one tenth foot of the marked elevation.   The figures of elevation must be stamped well

into the metal cap before the word "feet," and to the nearest foot only, also name or initial letter of the central datum point after the word "datum."

17. A complete description, accompanied by a large scale-sketch, must be made of each bench mark, giving its exact elevation as computed, from the mean of the two sets of notes. After bench marks are stamped both levelman and rodman must examine them, and record in note books the figures stamped thereon.

18. The limit of error in feet should not exceed .05$\sqrt{\text{distance in miles.}}$

19. Use the regular Survey level books; keep full descriptive notes on title page of every book, giving names, dates, etc. Each man should be responsible for his own note book; and under no circumstances should erasures be made, a single pencil line being drawn through erroneous records.

20. At the end of each day's work columns of fore sights and back sights must be added; the difference between the sums applied with proper signs to original elevations should give the closing elevation.

21. When errors are discovered as the work progresses, they must be reported at once to the topographer in charge.

22. Keep each set of notes separately and independently as taken, paying no attention whatever to other notes except to compare results. If on comparison errors are discovered, correct them only by new observations or computations. All notes must be recorded directly in note book. Separate pieces of paper for figuring, or temporary records must not under any circumstances be used.

23. An index book or list of bench marks must be kept posted in the field, in ink, for all classes of leveling done. In these, location sketches of permanent bench marks may be made, and descriptions should in every case refer, with distance, to some village, section corner, or other place of local importance. All circuit closure errors should be distinctly noted, with cross reference by page to the connecting lines.

24. In long, single rodded lines make two target settings on each turning point, by first signalling "up" or "down" to a set-

ting, which is recorded by the rodman, then unclamping and signalling in an opposite direction to a setting. If the two differ
more tnan .002 of a foot, additional readings must be made. The
rodman should record all readings, using in his computation only
the first of the pair adopted, and the levelman the last.

25. *Double-rodded Lines.*--In running unchecked or single
primary lines with two rodmen, they should set on turning points
10 to 20 feet apart, but each at equal distances for fore and back
sights; otherwise the above instructions are to followed with the
following modifications:

26. The tripod clamping screws should be loosened when the
instrument is set, and tightened only after the legs are firmly
planted; and the instrument must be shaded at all times by the
bubble tender.

27. The laborer should place the steel turning points for
foresights and then return and not remove the back-sight points
until the levelman has set targets on the new fore sight, so that
there shall be in the ground at all times two turning points, the
elevations of which are known.

28. Bench marks left at termination of work at night, or for
rain or other cause, should be practically turning points in a continuous line. They should consist of large wooden pegs driven
below the surface of the ground, with a copper nail firmly imbedded in the top. One of these pegs is to be used as the final turning point for each rodman. They are to be covered with dirt, or
otherwise hidden, their location being marked by sketches in note-
books showing relation to railroad ties, telegraph poles, etc.

GRANT, BERKELEY, HAMPSHIRE AND MINERAL COUNTIES.

The elevations in the following list are based on a bronze tablet set in the Allegany County Court House at Cumberland, Md., and marked "C 688." This bench mark is based on the U. S. Coast and Geodetic Survey transcontinental line of precise levels, and dependent on this its height is accepted as 687.627 feet above mean sea level. These elevations were connected at various places, as shown in the following list, with other bench marks of the Coast Survey transcontinental line besides that at Cumberland. All of these Coast Survey bench marks have been reduced from the elevations published in the Appendix for the report of 1882 by the amount—0.·03 meters, the constant correction found at Hagerstown as published in the Coast Survey Report for 1896.

The leveling was done in 1898 under the general direction of Mr. J. H. Jennings, topographer, by Messrs. Hargraves Wood and C. B. Bailey, levelmen.

All bench marks dependent on this datum are marked with the letter "C" in addition to the figures of elevation :

Pratt Post Office, ¼ mile east of; bronze tablet in ledge of rock south side of road, 150 feet west of Robinette's old house, marked "938 C".. 937. 903

Little Orleans. Chesapeake and Ohio Canal, aqueduct over Fifteen-Mile Creek; north end east coping; bronze tablet marked "459 C".. 459. 288

Hancock, westward along Baltimore Pike to Bench Mark near Harvey's.

Chesapeake and Ohio Canal aqueduct; coping stone middle of north wall, same being about 600 feet east of bridge; U. S. Coast and Geodetic Survey bench mark marked "1878 F" .:................. 420. 813

Hancock Bank, front of; bronze tablet on stone door sill, marked "448 C".. 448. 122

Hancock, 5. 15 miles west of; ¼ mile east of "Harvey's," 100 feet west of road to Woodmont; bronze tablet in solid rock on south side of pike, marked "946 C"................................... 945. 552

Hancock to Sleepy Creek Station, via Berkeley Springs, Rock Gap and Stotler's Corners.

Berkeley Springs, Morgan County Court House; west face of soui h-
west corner stone; aluminum tablet marked "612 C"............... 611. 894

Rock Gap Corners, 700 feet west of Fearnow's house, 10 feet north
of road at summit of gap, in rock; aluminum tablet, marked
"761 C"... .... 760. 755

Stotler's Corners, ½ mile north of, at first ford of Sleepy Creek;
ledge of rock east side of road 25 feet north of north entrance
to ford, in cleft of rock about four feet above roadway, alumi-
num tablet marked "662 C"................................. .... 662. 053

Lock 50, Chesapeake and Ohio Canal, along Chesapeake and Ohio Canal to McCoy's Ferry, thence across and up Back Creek.

Chesapeake and Ohio Canal, Lock 50, northeast wing; aluminum
tablet, marked "402 C" 402. 372

Frankfort, (Alaska), ½ mile northwest of; copper bolt iu west end
of north abutment highway bridge over Patterson's Creek,
marked "589 C"........."............. .... 588. 628

KANAWHA, PUTNAM, LINCOLN, BOONE, LOGAN, MINGO, McDOWELL. WYOMING and MASON COUNTIES.

The elevations in the following list are based on a bench mark determined by trigonometrical leveling by the U. S. Coast and Geodetic Survey at St. Albans west base moṇument. The leveling in connection with this work was done chiefly by Mr. Hargraves Wood, levelman, under the direction of Mr. Hersey Munroe, topographer, during the seasons of 1896 and 1897.

In the spring of 1898 Mr. E. L. McNair, levelman, conected levels brought from Hamden Junction bench mark of the transcontinental line of precise levels of the United States Coast and Geodetic Survey, via Thurman and Gallipolis, Ohio, to Point Pleasant, W. Va. At this place connection was made with bench mark of the United States Engineers on coping of Lock 11, on Great Kanawha River   The result was a difference of 4.780 feet. which is added to the elevations determiued by the United States Engineers on Great Kanawha River, and a permanent bench mark was left in Point Pleasant bearing the accepted elevation as brought from the Coast Survey.

The following elevations are based on a datum tablet placed in the State Capitol building in Charleston in 1897, and marked

"C 602," is now accepted as being 601.597 feet above mean sea level. The bench marks dependent upon this datum have been marked with the letter "C" in addition to the figures of elevation.

Charleston up Two-Mile Creek and along Charleston and Sissonville Road to Wallace's Store on Tupper Creek.

Charleston, State Capitol, in south-west corner of; bronze tablet, marked "602 C" 601. 597

Two-Mile Bridge, 2¼ miles north of; about 200 feet south-west of Methodist church known as Wesley Chapel, copper bolt in boulder, marked "604 C" 604. 751

Wallace's store, ¼ miles east of; copper bolt in boulder on south edge of road and about 600 feet east of James Wallace's house, marked "668 C" 667. 677

Wallace's Store on Tupper Creek, via Martin's Branch and Pocatalico River to Poca.

Martin's Branch Road, south side of and ¼ mile above mouth; 175 feet west first crossing near schoolhouse; copper bolt in rock ledge, one foot above grade, marked "C 592" 591. 942

Poca, along Kanawha and Michigan Railroad to St. Albans.

Poca Station, 300 feet south of; copper bolt on west side south abutment highway bridge over Correly Branch; marked "C 572"... 573. 266

Lock 7, top coping; equals 555. 50 United States Engineer's elevation... 560. 280

Scott railroad station, 75 feet south of; iron post in Pine's orchard, 50 feet south of Chesapeake & Ohio railroad tracks, marked "693 C" 693. 781

St. Albans, west base monument, located in fence line on west side of First street, 60 feet north of the north rail of the C. & O. railway track; center of monument is marked by limestone post projecting one foot above ground in top of which is a copper bolt, the elevation of which is......... .... 595. 616

Lock 6 to Tyler Creek Schoolhouse.

Tyler Creek road, ¼ mile southeast forks of road near Tyler school house; copper bolt in rock 20 feet west of drain across, marked "C 623".. 624. 296

Lock 6 up Middle Fork of Davis Creek to Mouth of Long Branch.

Long Branch, 900 feet north of; between second and third crossings north of school house; copper bolt in large boulder west
side of Middle Fork Davis Creek, marked "C 659 .... 660. 187

Lock 5, up Len's Creek to Racine, and down Coal River to Mouth of Lick Creek.

Lock 5, coping; equals 572. 50 U. S. Engineer's elevation............... 577. 280

Chesapeake & Ohio railway culvert over Rush Creek, ¼ mile northwest of; a copper bolt in middle one of three ledges of rock,
west side of right fork Rush Creek, marked "C 639"............. 639. 868

Hernshaw, about one mile south of; copper bolt in 3x5 foot ledge
of rock south side road, south bank Len's Creek, near A. Hoffman's house, marked "C 722" 723. 110

Peytona, about two miles northwest; copper bolt in ledge of rock,
south side road down Coal river, 100 feet northwest Laurel
branch; one mile below White Oak branch, marked "C 665"... 666. 326

Lick Creek, 200 feet north of mouth of; copper bolt in rack west
side of Coal river road, marked "C 648"................................. 649. 300

Racine, via Comfort and Hopkins, to Mouth Robinson Creek.

Comfort, ¼ mile north of; copper bolt bottom, of rock cliff, ½
mile south mouth of Joe's Creek, east side Coal river road, 4
feet above grade, marked "C 673".. 674. 413

Hopkins Fork, 200 feet southeast mouth of; bronze tablet in face
rock cliff, marked "C 734" 735. 313

Robison Creek and Pond Creek, 500 feet from confluence of; copper bolt sunk in protruding boulder in Ballard Brown's field
on east side of; and 300 feet from road, marked "C 746"......... 747. 772

St. Albans, via Tackett Creek, Young's Store and Tornado, to Starting Point.

St. Albans, west base monument, located in fence line on west side
of First street, 60 feet north of the north rail of the Chesapeake & Ohio railway track; center of monument is marked
by limestone post, projecting one foot above ground, in the
top of which is a copper bolt, the elevation of which is........... 595. 616

Young's store, first house south of; on south side of road, belonging to John Hodges; copper bolt set in east chimney, six feet
from ground, marked "U. S. G. S. 737 feet B. M."................... . 219873

Trace Fork of Mud River, 200 feet below mouth of Two-mile branch, 400 feet northwest of Anderson McAllister's house; copper bolt in huge rock on north side of stream, marked "U. S. G. S. 669 feet B. M." 670. 050

Tornado, 1½ miles southwest of; on road up Fall Creek; iron post on south side of road 150 feet above first crossing of Fall Creek, marked "614" 614. 633

Garrett's Bend to Sand Gap, Sugar Camp Knob, Down Laurel Fork of Horse Creek to Madison.

Garrett's Bend, one mile southeast of, up Trace Fork; nail in root of sycamore tree, east side of road, near foot-log and saw mill   671. 340

Sand Gap, 500 feet west of fork of roads, at; copper bolt in huge rock above John A. Midkiff's house, marked "U. S. G. S. 1079 B. M.".. 1,079. 470

Laurel Fork, 200 feet above confluence with Horse Creek, copper bolt in rock ledge on east bank, opposite James McClure's house, near last crossing of Laurel, marked "U. S. G. S. 673 feet B. M." 673. 547

Trace Branch, one mile above mouth; copper bolt in large boulder on left side of right-hand hollow in Trace Branch of Horse Creek, marked "U. S. G. S. 766 feet B. M." 766. 856

Camp Creek, ¼ mile north of; copper bolt in small ledge of rock on east side of road going up Little Coal river, 300 feet above B. Stolling's, marked "U. S. G. S. 660 feet B. M."................... 661. 095

Lick Creek, 3¼ miles above mouth of and ¼ mile above Chamber's house, on right-hand fork of Lick Creek; copper bolt in boulder above coal bank, 25 feet east of creek, between two walnut trees, one of which is blazed; bolt is marked "U. S. G. S. 820 feet B. M. "........ .... 820. 328

Madison up Spruce Creek to   ng Post Office.

Madison, sheriff's office; bronze tablet in front wall, marked "704"   704. 146

Spruce Fork, ¼ mile above mouth of Beech Creek, on north side of Spruce Fork. 300 feet below splash dam, opposite William Coleman's barn, copper bolt in ledge of rock, marked "U. S. G. S. 846 feet B. M. " 846. 234

From Mouth of Hewett Creek to Peck and up Guyandot River to Logan

Hewett Creek, 300 feet above mouth of; copper bolt in ledge of rock opposite school house and on south side of creek, marked "U. S. G. S. 767 feet B. M. " 767. 954

Peck, ¼ mile south of post office; on the northwest side of Mill creek, 300 feet above mouth; copper bolt in northwest corner of huge bowlder, marked "U. S. G. S. 653 feet B. M."............ 653. 549

Logan, bronze tablet set in wall at northeast corner of court house, marked "678." 678. 822

Logan to Mouth of Big Huff Creek, and up Guyandot River to Gilbert.

Rich Creek, opposite mouth of; copper bolt in rock 20 feet north of Methodist Episcopal Church, marked "U. S. G. S. 725 feet B. M. " 725. 559

Buffalo Creek, ¼ mile above mouth of, opposite Martin Doss' and 60 feet above foot log, on west side of Buffalo; copper bolt in rock. marked "U. S. G. S. 728 feet B. M. ".................. .... 728. 511

Buffalo Creek, west side of valley, 3 miles above mouth of; copper bolt, marked "U. S. G. S. 808 feet B. M. " 808. 539

Rockhouse Creek, west side of and one mile above mouth; copper bolt in rock near south end of cliff, marked "U. S. G. S. 792 feet B. M. ".. .... 792. 749

Big Huff Creek, east side of, and 300 feet above mouth: copper bolt in rock, marked "U. S. G. S. 727 feet B.-M. ".................... 727. 962

Gilbert, via Wharncliffe, to State Corner between Virginia, West Virginia and Kentucky.

Gilbert, opposite Alexander Stafford's store; iron post in field, marked "832" 832. 571

Kentucky, Virginia and West Virginia, corner of state lines, ½ mile south of Wharncliffe; iron post, marked "825"............... 826. 087

Kentucky, Virginia and West Virginia Corner, via Mouth of Long Pole, and up same to near Oak Branch.

Long Pole Creek, 1,200 feet below Oak Branch; iron post on south side of road; marked "1050".. .... 1,051. 209

Up Big Huff Creek, via Cyclone, to Its Head and to Echart.

Cyclone, copper bolt in rock opposite Henchman's house, marked "U. S. G. S. 854 feet B. M. " 854. 917

Toney Fork of Huff Creek, south side of, about two miles above mouth; copper bolt in ledge of rock, marked "U. S. G. S. 1234 feet B. M. " 1,235. 414

Road Gap Branch, 600 feet below; iron post on east side of road
    up Big Huff Creek, 100 feet above D. H. Cook,s store, marked
    "1068"................ .... 1,068. 525

Echart, east bank of Pond Fork of Coal River, opposite mouth of
    Skin Fork; copper bolt in ledge of rock, marked "U. S. G. S.
    1423 feet B. M. "... 1,423. 950

Echart, down Pond Fork of Little Coal River, via Bald
Knob and Crook, to Mouth of West Fork,
and up same to Mouth of
Brown's Branch.

Bald Knob, east side of valley at; copper bolt in boulder opposite
    Eddy Workman's, marked U. S. G. S. 1101 feet B. M. 1,101. 980

Cow Creek, north side of; ¼ mile from mouth and 800 feet from
    Jim Gunnoe's; copper bolt in ledge of rock, marked U. S. G. S.
    1039 feet B. M. "... 1,040. 020

West Fork of Pond, 1000 feet above junction of Pond Fork; copper
    bolt in rock, northeast side, marked "U. S. G. S. 808 feet B.
    M. " 809. 939

West Fork of Pond, 800 feet below Brown's Branch; copper bolt in
    ledge of rock on west side of road, a little above and nearly
    opposite small water mill; bolt is marked "U. S. G. S. 884 feet
    B. M. ".. 885. 250

Junction of West and Pond Forks of Little Coal River
to Madison.

Robinson Creek and Pond Fork, 500 feet from confluence of; cop-
    per bolt sunk in protruding boulder in Ballard Brown's field,
    on east side of and 300 feet from road, marked U. S. G. S. 746
    feet B. M. "..................................... .... 747. 772

MONONGALIA AND PRESTON COUNTIES.
Morgantown Quadrangle.

The elevations published in the following list are based on a bronze tablet 500 feet south of Morgantown station at the northwest corner of coping stone of the Baltimore and Ohio Railroad bridge, marked "821 Pittsburg 1899" set by this bureau, the elevation of which is accepted as 821 058 feet above mean sea level as determined by the U. S. Coast Survey adjustment of 1900, and as published in Appendix No. 8 to the report of the Superintendent of that bureau for 1898-99.

The leveling was done in 1899 under the direction of Mr. Frank Sutton, topographer, by Mr. William Crennell, levelman

All permanent bench marks dependent on this datum are referred, through the precise level net, to an aluminum tablet in the Seventh Avenue Hotel at Pittsburg, the elevation of which is accepted as 738.527 feet above mean sea level, and are marked with the letters "Pittsburg" in addition to the figures of elevation.

Morgantown via Dellslow. Masontown and Cold Spring to Morgantown.

(The error distributed in this circuit slightly exceeds the allowable limit.)

Dellslow, north side of creek; 30 feet east of bridge over; in top of large boulder; aluminum tablet marked "994 Pittsburg 1899"   994. 034

Masontown, Methodist Church; in southeast corner of foundation of; aluminum tablet, marked "1843 Pittsburg".... .... 1842. 609

Cold Spring, o. 5 mile north of; near watering trough west of pike; on large sandstone; aluminum tablet, marked "2113 Pittsburg"... .... 2112. 759

WAYNE COUNTY.
Ceredo Quadrangle.

The elevations published in the following list are based upon bench mark LIII. of the transcontinental line of precise levels of the U. S. Coast and Geodetic Survey, near Hamden Junction, O., the elevation of whicn is accepted as 706.252 feet above mean sea level.

The elevations herein published are based directly upon two bench marks of U.S.G.S., one at Greenup, Ky., a bronze tablet set vertically in a stone at entrance to clerk's office, stamped "538 I," and one at Ironton, O., at the northwest corner Fourth and Railroad streets; a bronze tablet in the southeast corner of Memorial Hall and Public Library, the corrected elevations of which are accepted as 540.692 feet above mean sea level for Greenup, and 546.965 feet for Ironton.

Based upon the above a central datum has been adopted the for the following work, which is a bronze tablet at Kenova, W. Va., in the west side of the door sill at the entrance to the men's waiting room at Union Station. The elevation of this is accepted as 567.606 feet above mean sea level, or about 0.4 foot greater than the elevation derived for this bench mark in the field.

The leveling was executed in 1900 under the general direction of Mr. W. N. Morrill, topographer, by Messers. C. H. Semper and J. E. Buford, levelman.

All bench marks in this list, being referred to Kenova as a local base, are stamped with the letter "K" in addition to their figures of elevation.

Kenova, W. Va., along Ohio & Big Sandy R. R , to Rockville, Ky. (Buchanan).

	Unadjusted Eleva.—Ft.
Kenova, Union Station, west side of door sill of men's entrance to waiting room; aluminum tablet marked " 567 K"...............	567. 606
Savage Branch station, one mile south of; in David Lockwood's house, in foundation on left side of front steps; bronze tablet marked "586 K"	586. 801

Buchanan, 150 feet south of; overhead railroad bridge, (B. S. 189) in top stone east end north pier; bronze tablet marked "554 K 1900" 554. 919

Catlettsburg, Louisa street between Franklin and Clay strets, in courtyard; northwest corner of clerk's office; one foot above water table; aluminum tablet marked "549 K 1900"............... 550. 991

Buchanan, along Big Sandy R. R. to Louisa.

Fullers, 300 feet north of station; 5 feet west of railroad at east edge of highway; 30 feet north of white house; in sandstone ledge; bronze tablet marked "572 K 1900"........ .... 571. 562

Louisa, U. S. Engineers B. M. , No 13 Big Sandy at Lock No. 3, in Engineer's office yard; (by U. S. Engineers, 569. 570) 569. 769

Louisa, county court house; north face west side; in foundation of: aluminum tablet marked "584 K 1900"......... .... 583. 107

Louisa, along Big Sandy R. R. to Gallup.

Gallup, G. C. McClure's house; in stone step to house; bronze tablet marked "591 K 1900"......... .... 590. 059

Gallup, o. 6 mile west of; U. S. Engineer's B. M. , No. 5 Big Sandy, 50 feet south of west end of trestle No. 403; (by U. N. Engineers, elevation 591. 559 feet) ....,................................. · 590. 977

Gallup, via Adam's Store to Hawes' Mill.

Adams, 2 miles south of post office; M. R. Hayes residence; in southwest corner of foundation; bronze tablet marked "667 K 1900" ....·... 667. 279

WETZEL, MONONGALIA, TAYLOR, HARRISON, BARBOUR AND LEWIS COUNTIES.

The elevations in the following list are based upon bench marks of the precise level net at Fairmont, Grafton and Webster, the elevations of which are accepted as corrected by the U. S. coast Survey and published in Appendix No. 8 of their report for 1898 99.

The leveling on the Fairmont and Philippi quadrangles was done in 1901 under the direction of Mr. W. Carvel Hall. topographer, by Mr. G. L. Gordon, levelman, and that on the Clarksburg and Weston sheets under the direction of Mr. W. N. Morrill, topographer, by J. H. Hodges, levelman.

All permanent bench marks are referred through the precise net to an aluminum tablet at the entrance of the Seventh Avenue Hotel at Pittsburg, the elevation of which is accepted as 738.527 feet above mean sea level, and are marked with the letters "PITTSBURG" in addition to their figures of elevation.

Fairmont, via. Farmington, Monongah, Boothsville and Meadville to Bridgeport.

	Unadjusted Eleva.
Fairmont, 1¼ miles north of; B. & O. bridge No. 371, across Monongahela river; north end of east abutment of; bronze tablet in coping stone marked "885 Pittsburg 1889"	885. 175
Farmington, George's Creek Coal and Iron Co's store; northeast corner of front; face of water table; bronze tablet marked "952 Grafton 1901"	951. 843
Monongah, B. & O. R. R. plate girder bridge over Booth's Creek; west face of north pier; two feet from southwest corner in seventh stone from the top; bronze tablet marked "874 Grafton"..	874. 041
Boothsville, covered bridge over Hustead's fork; west face of north abutment; 3. 5 feet from southwest corner and 4. 5 feet from the top; bronze tablet marked "954 Grafton"	954. 241
Meadland, brick house owned by L. J. Stark; front or east face of; foundation, one foot from northeast corner; bronze tablet marked "1319 Grafton"	1318. 640

Bridgeport, railroad bridge No. 6 over Simpson's Creek; west abutment of; south end; third stone from top and second above bridge seat; center of east face of; bronze tablet marked "979 Grafton" 978. 867

Grafton, via. Webster, Simpson, Flemington, Rosemont, Oral and Bridgeport to Clarksburg.

Grafton, B. & O. R. R. bridge, over Tygart's Valley Creek; on top of north side of central pier; chiseled square, marked "United States Coast and Geodetic Survey B. M. 1878"........................ 996. 954

Webster, B. & O. S. W. R. R. bridge No. 2 over Bartlett's Creek; south abutment wall of; 1. 15 feet from east corner; bronze tablet marked "1014 Grafton" 1013. 867

Clarksburg, post office corner Third and Pike streets; northwest corner; two feet above ground; aluminum tablet marked "1006 Grafton" 1007. 791

Monongahela Junction to Monongah.

Shinnston, west branch of Monongahela river; highway bridge over; southwest corner of retaining wall; bronze tablet marked "909 Grafton 1901" 910. 551

Worthington, southwest abutment of highway bridge; south end of; on top of seat; bronze tablet marked "898 Grafton 1901"... 899. 336

Monongah, plate girder R. R. bridge over Booth's Creek; west face of north pier; two feet from southwest corner; in seventh stone from top; bronze tablet marked "874 Grafton 1901"...... .... 874. 041

Bridgeport, via. Berryburg, Switzer and Pleasant Creek to Webster.

Berryburg, Southern Coal and Transportation Company's tipple; retaining wall of; west of tipple and in front of power house; fourth stone from top; bronze tablet marked "1390 Grafton"... 1389. 600

Pleasant Creek, brick residence of A. I. Cole, west corner of south foundation; fifth stone from top and fourth from ground; 1. 45 feet from corner; bronze tablet marked "1170 Grafton"........... 1170. 140

Switzer, via. Philippi, etc., to Peck's Run.

Philippi, brick school house; north side of front entrance; center north face of foundation stone; bronze tablet marked "1311 Grafton" 1310. 781

Philippi, 10. 4 miles south of; (Buckhannon or Tygart's Junction);. Tygart's Valley river; plate girder bridge No. 1 over; west abutment of; north side of first stone above bridge bed; in center of east face; bronze tablet marked "1334 Grafton"........ 1333. 636

Volga, B. & O. R. R. bridge over Wash Run, north abutment of; east face of; iu center of first stone from top; bronze tablet marked "1404 Grafton"..................... .... 1403. 955

Peck's Run, via Peel Tree and Overfield to Pepper.

Peel Tree, residence of Dr. Isaac Smith; retaining wall in front of, at opening for steps; west face of south wall; third stone above third step from sidewalk; in center of; bronze tablet marked "1069 Grafton" 1068. 885

Peck's Run to Buckhannon.

Buckhannon, Upshur county court house; front entrance; west side of; base block of square column; west face; in center of; aluminum tablet marked "1433 Grafton".. 1432. 977

Buckhannon to Ruraldale.

Ruraldale, o. 6 mile west of; near fork of road by old mill; 200 feet east of residence of V. H. Reger; in face of large rock; bronze tablet marked "1121 Grafton 1901'..................................... 1122. 213

Ruraldale, via. Johnstown. Quiet Dell, etc., to West Milford.

Johnstown, o. 1 mile west of; ledge of rock north of road; in face of: bronze tablet marked "1062 Grafton 1901"......... .... 1063. 040

Quiet Dell, o. 5 mile south of: 600 feet from cross roads; large boulder on west of road; aluminum tablet in top, marked "1050 Grafton 1901"... 1050. 872

West Milford, highway bridge over West Fork; southwest corner of; on top of bridge seat; bronze tablet marked "979 Grafton 1901" 979. 459

Clarksburg to West Milford.

West Milford, highway bridge over West Fork; southwest corner of; on top of bridge seat; bronze tablet marked "979 Grafton 1901" 979. 459

Enterprise, up Bingamon Creek West and South, via Wyatt, Margaret (Henpeck) and Brown to Lynchburg.

Margaret, Quaker Fork of Bingamon Creek; covered highway
  bridge over; in northwest corner of; bronze tablet marked
  "1032 Grafton 1901" 1032. 200

Browns, o. 2 mile west of; Short Line Railroad bridge over Little
  Ten Mile Creek trestle 404; southwest abutment of; in top of
  cap stone; bronze tablet marked "999 Grafton 1901"............ 999. 108

Clarksburg. West via. Adamston, Wilsonburg, Wolf Summit and Lynchburg to Bristol.

Wolf Summit; William M. Bolan's store; southeast corner of; in
  end of stone curbing; bronze tablet marked "1133 Grafton
  1901"......................... .... 1134. 422

WETZEL AND MONONGALIA COUNTIES.
Blacksville Quadrangle.

Morgantown, Northwesterly to Blacksville.

Cassville, 20 feet north of road and 20 feet west of road running
  north; stone door step of post office; bronze tablet marked
  "999 Grafton"... .... 999. 386

Core, 2. 2 miles northwest of; 10 feet south of road; bridge over
  east side of Doll's Run, southwest abutment of; bronze tablet
  marked "913 Grafton" .... - 913. 445

Single Spur Line, West to Blacksville.

Blacksville, 3. 9 miles west of Worley and 13 miles west of Cassville; 10 feet east of center of road; bridge over Dunkard
  Creek; 5 feet north of bridge floor; bronze tablet in stone
  abutment, marked "958 Grafton"............ .... 957. 496

Dunkard Creek, South along Highway to Amos, thence Southeast along Highway to Catawba.

Amos or Fairview, 7. o miles south of Ponetown; east side of door
  step to post office; bronze tablet marked "1000 Grafton"......... 1000. 064

OHIO, MARSHALL AND BROOKE COUNTIES.
Wheeling Quadrangle.

The elevations in the following list are based upon bench marks Nos. 90A and 81A of the Army Engineer Corps, near the Ohio River at Wheeling and Short Creek, respectively. The elevations accepted for these are derived by applying corrections to the elevation given by the Army Engineers, by interpolation between Pittsburg and Belpre, at which points connections were made with the precise level net adjusted by the Coast and Geodetic Survey in 1900.

The leveling was done in 1901 under the direction of Mr. W. C. Hall, topographer. by Mr. W. A. Freret, Jr, levelman.

All permanent bench marks dependent on this datum are referred through the precise level net to the U. S. Coast and Geodetic Survey bench mark "M" at Grafton, and are stamped with the letters "Grafton" in addition the figures of elevation.

Wheeling, along National Pike via Elm Grove to Triadelphia.

	Unadjusted Eleva.—Ft.
Wheeling, City building; on north front of; 37 feet east of north-west corner of; a chiseled square, (U. S. Engineer Corps bench mark No. 90A; their elevation 678. 463 feet)	678. 453
Triadelphia, M. E. Church, brick building; southwest corner of; south face, in foundation stone; aluminum tablet marked "745 Grafton" .:... ....……….........	744- 775

Triadelphia, along Middle Wheeling Creek, via Twilight to Valley Grove.

Valley Grove, B. & O. railroad bridge No. 174 (Pittsburg Division) in north face of south pile; bronze tablet marked "953 Grafton"	952. 860

Valley Grove, along National Pike and McGraw's Run to Bethany.

Bethany, 0. 3 mile west of; Bethany College, front face of building; first entrance west of main entrance; north side of en-

trance; east face stone of water table; aluminum tablet marked
"932 Grafton 1901" 931. 988

Bethany, along Pike to Short Creek.

Short Creek, brick store and post office; west face of; 25 feet from
southwest corner and two feet above ground; aluminum tablet
maked "668 Grafton 1901" 668. 178

BRAXTON WEBSTER AND NICHOLAS COUNTIES.
Sutton (Flatwood) Quadrangle.

Heaters, via. Baltimore & Ohio Railroad and County Road
to Sutton.

Shaversville, Dr. M. B. Squires' drug store; o. 8 feet west of and 3. 5
feet south of northwest corner; iron post marked "1071 Graf-
ton" 1071. 013

Heaters, along Baltimore & Ohio Railroad and County
Road via. Sutton to Birch River.

Sutton, suspension bridge over Elk River at; northeast tower; north
face; o. 9 feet above foundation and 2. 4 feet east of corner;
bronze tablet marked "843 Grafton" 842. 953

Sutton, 8.05 miles south of; forks of road, o. 01 mile north of; mouth
of Bear Run, o. 03 mile north of; left side of road; outcrop of
rock; bronze tablet marked "1073 Grafton".................. 1073. 052

Birch River, aluminum tablet at; marked "1108 K N W A"........... 1108. 842

HARRISON, DODDRIDGE, LEWIS AND GILMER COUNTIES.
Vadis Quadrangle.

West Union via. West Union and Milton Pike to New Milton.

Sugar Camp, o. 5 mile southeast of; Middle Island Creek, iron
bridge over; east abutment, southwest corner; bronze tablet
marked "830 Grafton" 830. 0;7

West Union, via. New Milton, Coldwater and Churchville to Weston.

Churchville, 0. 55 mile southeast of; main road to Weston: left side
of road; west side of middle of large rock; aluminum tablet
marked "972 Grafton" 972. 023

Weston, Baltimore and Ohio railroad bridge near round house;
north end of east pier; bronze tablet marked "1017 Grafton".. 1017. 877

West Union, via. New Milton, Coldwater and Churchville to Camden and thence to Alum Bridge.

Camden, P. E. Fetty's front yard at; 1 foot south of fence; 8½ feet
west of porch; iron post marked "1096 Grafton"..................... 1095. 897

Alum Bridge, Alum Fork of Leading Creek at; iron bridge over;
west abutment; southeast corner of; bronze tablet marked
"810 Grafton".. 810. 253

West Union, via. New Milton, Coldwater, Camden, Alum Bridge and Lynn to Vadis.

Lynn, 1. 75 mile northwest of; Fink Creek at; iron bridge over; east
abutment; northwest corner of bridge seat; bronze tablet
marked "766 Grafton" 766. 142

West Union, via. New Milton, Coldwater, Camden, Alum Bridge and Lynn to Hurst and thence to St. Clair.

Hurst, cliff at; facing south; 4½ feet below top of; bronze tablet
marked "815 Grafton" 814. 970

West Union, via. New Milton, Coldwater, Camden, Alum Bridge, St. Clair and New Milton to West Union.

New Milton, 1. 1 mile northwest of; Middle Island Creek; iron
bridge over; east abutment, southwest corner; bronze tablet
marked "830 Grafton" 830. 047

Avon, via. County Road toward Big Isaac.

Avon, 1. 8 mile southeast of; Double Camp Run; forks of road at;
north angle; iron post marked "884 Grafton"........................... 884. 110

LEWIS, BRAXTON AND GILMER COUNTIES.
Burnsville Quadrangle.

Weston, via Baltimore & Ohio Railroad and County Road to Arnold.

Weston, o. 8 mile north of, round house; B. & O. railroad bridge
near; north abutment, southwest corner; bronze tablet marked
"1017 Grafton".. 1017. 877

Weston, via. Roanoke and Arnold to Burnsville.

Roanoke, 1. 8 miles southwest of; Arnold, o. 6 mile northeast of;
B. & O. railroad bridge No. 38, over the Monongahela river;
south pier; southwest corner of; bronze tablet marked "1058
Grafton" 1058. 094

Weston, via. Roanoke, Arnold, Confluence and New Burnsville to Stout's Mills.

Stout's Mills. iron bridge over the Little Kanawha River at; east
abutment, northwest corner; bronze tablet marked "750 Graf-
ton" (marked on bridge truss "B. M. 750")............................. 749. 983

Weston, via. Arnold, Confluence and Burnsville to Bulltown.

Bulltown, Little Kanawha River at; covered bridge over; west abutment, north face; 9. 8 feet below bridge seat and 8. 1 feet west
of corner; bronze tablet marked "777 Grafton"...................... 777. 903

Weston, via. Arnold, Confluence, Burnsville and Bulltown to Rollyson.

Bulltown, 5. 4 miles west of; Cogers, 5. o miles south of; Rollyson,
o. 1 mile north of; B. & O. railroad bridge No. 57D; south abutment, bridge seat; northeast corner; bronze tablet marked
"797 Grafton"........ .... 797. 048

Weston, via. Arnold, Confluence and Burnsville to Cogers.

Confluence, 4. 2 miles southwest of; Burnsville, o. 5 mile north of;
B. & O. railroad bridge over the Little Kanawha river, No. 50A;
northeast pier; top of east corner; bronze tablet marked "765
Grafton" 764. 730

WOOD COUNTY.
Prrkersburg Quadrangle.

Marietta, O., B. M. at Court House to Fleming, M. C. & C. Railway, Ohio.

Marietta, O., bench mark in court house at....... .... 616. 280

Little Hocking, O., foundation of B. &O. railroad bridge over Lit-
tle Hocking Creek 623. 278

Parkersburg, south side of post office near west end at; bronze
tablet placed in water table, marked "616 Grafton 1902" 615. 705

WOOD, RITCHIE AND PLEASANTS COUNTIES.
Waverlv Quadrangle.

Parkersburg, out Northwestern Pike Eastward to Bench Mark 1 1-2 Miles Southeast of Tally Ho Post Office.

Parkersburg, Custom House at; near southwest corner in water
table; bronze tablet marked "616 Grafton 1902" U. S. G. A. 615. 705

Parkersburg, cut on water table; south front, near western corner
of the post office and court house—U. S. G. S 615. 871

Parkersburg, 9. 5 miles east of and 1. 5 mile southeast of Tally Ho
post office, opposite Shiloh United Brethren church; at forks
of road in large boulder; aluminum tablet marked "714 Graf-
ton 1902" 713. 696

Bench Mark 1 1-2 Mile. Southeast of Tally Ho Post Office via Deer Walk Post Office to Borland Post Office.

Borland post office, 100 feet east of, on south side of Bull Creek;
bronze tablet marked "683 Grafton "1902" 682. 963

Briscoe Station, O. R. R. R. and P. O., in face of rock ledge opposite public highway; bronze tablet marked "594 Grafton 1902" 593. 934

Willow Island Station, W. Va., East via. Newport.

Willow Island Station, O. R. R. R.; northeast corner foundation
wall of Joseph Norris' dwelling; aluminum tablet marked
"616 Grafton 1902" 615. 728

PRESTON COUNTY.
Bruceton Mills Quadrangle.

Masontown to Albright.

Masontown, M. E. church at; bronze tablet in foundation............. 1842. 609

Masontown, W. Va., via· Herring, Albrightsville, Lenox and Bruceton Mills to Elliottsville, Pa.

Lenox, M. E. church, about 2½ miles north of; bronze tablet in southwest corner of stone foundation, marked "1851" 1850. 500

Lenox, about 6½ miles north of; residence now occupied by Marshall A. Wolfe on Little Sandy Creek; bronze tablet in the southeast corner of cut stone foundation 1577. 724

Lenox to Bruceton Mills.

Lenox, post office at; aluminum tablet in southwest corner of stone foundation, marked "2123"................................ ....:... 2122. 548

Bruceton Mills, aluminum tablet in northeast corner of stone foundation of Lutheran church at; marked "1549 G".................... 1549. 462

Brandonville, W. Va., to Elliottsville, Pa.

Brandonville, 1½ miles east of; bronze tablet in southwest corner of cut stone foundation of residence of William H. Willett 1832. 000

Masontown to Albright.

Herring post office, church at; bronze tablet in southwest corner of stone foundation of church at Herring post office, marked "2042" 2042. 281

MONONGALIA AND MARION COUNTIES.
Mannington Quadrangle.

From Bench Mark 1 1-4 Miles North of Fairmont on Wheeling and Grafton Branch of B. & O. R. R. to Beilton.

Mannington; bronze tablet placed in pillar on north of door of Exchange Bank, corner of Railroad and Market streets; marked "975 Grafton 1902"... .... 975 15

Mannington, over Wheeling and Grafton Branch of the B. & O. R. R. to Bellton.

Glovers Gap; station B. & O. railroad; bronze tablet placed in south foundation of signal tower, marked "1040 Grafton 1902"........ 1039. 740

Hundred Station, o. 1 mile northwest of; bronze tablet placed in top of bridge seat, northeast abutment of bridge No. 128; marked "1013 Grafton 1902"... 1013. 199

Mannington, 1. 0 Mile Northwest of; up Flat Run via. Gallatin Post Office to Blacksville.

Gallatin postoffice: bronze tablet placed in face of rock on north of road, 300 feet east of Gallatin post office; marked "1452 Grafton 1902" 1452. 168

Cross Roads down Miracle Run to Blacksville.

Cross Roads post office, 2. 9 miles northeast of; in face of large rock on north of road down Miracle Run, 30 feet east of Mrs. Marberley's dwelling, bronze tablet marked "1014 Grafton 1902" 1014. 479

MARSHALL COUNTY.
Cameron Quadrangle.

Moundsville, via. Waynesburg Pike to Limestone.

Moundsville, Marshall county court house; \o1 B: on top of water table of foundation of; bench mark is on front of build-ing, 17. 2 feet east of center of door sill, marked 690. 921

Limestone, brick dwelling of R. S. Peters; front of; on foundation, top stone, 2. 7 feet northwest of center of door; bronze tablet marked "1377 Grafton" 1377. 184

Lone Oak School House, via. a Ridge Road, Hazeldell, i. e., Irish Ridge School House

Pleasant Valley, 5.8 miles northeast of; Hazeldell, or Irish Ridge school house; front of; southwest corner stone, center of; bronze tablet, marked "1322 Grafton" 1321. 942

Moundsville, via. Limestone and Rock Lick to Cameron.

Rock Lick, o. 8 mile south of; school house; south side, southeast
corner; second stone; aluminum tablet marked "1464 Grafton" 1464. 195

Cameron, brick public school building at; west end; water table:
o. 9 feet north of southwest corner; bronze tablet marked "1170
Grafton" 1170. 254

Moundsville, via, Limestone, Rock Lick and Cameron to Bellton.

Woodruff, 1.9 miles south of; o. 1 mile north of Bellton; southeast
corner of northwest abutment of B. & O. railroad bridge No.
136; 2. 7 feet above bridge seat; bronze tablet marked "888
Grafton" 887. 963

Moundsville, via. Limestone Rock, Rock Lick, Cameron, Bellton and Meighen to Roseby Rock.

Meighen, school house No. 5 at; east side; o. 8 foot from southeast
corner, top stone of foundation; bronze tablet marked "691
Grafton" 691. 047

Roseby Rock, Big Grove Creek at; iron bridge over; top of northeast abutment; one foot below bridge seat; 12 feet southeast of
center of bridge; bronze tablet marked "779 Grafton"............ 778. 706

Moundsville, Marshall county courthouse; south front of; 17. 2 feet
east of center of doorway and 1. 2 feet below the above; bronze
tablet marked "690 Grafton" 689. 695

TRUE MERIDIANS.

In 1898, the U. S. G. Survey, in co-operation with the West
Virginina Survey, established true meridians in or near the county
seat of each county in the State. These lines were marked with
stone monuments, properly designated with bronze and aluminum tablets, and the detailed results published in Vol. I., Oil and
Gas, pages 51 to 122, to which the reader is referred for a full de-

scription, since we can publish here only the tabulated results, giving the declination at the date of the determination and also the corrected variation for January 1, 1903.

As known to all surveyors, the variation of the magnetic compass is now increasing uniformly in West Virginia toward the west at the rate of approximately three minutes of arc per annum, so that by adding three minutes for each year from the date of any actual determination of recent years, we shall get for that particular point approximately the variation for any future year during most of the present century. In the early part of last century this secular variation of the compass was to the east in West Virginia, but since that time the line of no variation has passed entirely across West Virginia, and, as stated above, is now uniformly to the west in every county, being greatest in Morgan and least in Wayne, as will be seen from the accompanying table. To obtain the variation for any other date than January 1, 1903, as, say May 1, 1903, instead of adding three minutes, we would add only one-third of that or one minute, or for March 1 one-half minute, the amount to be added to the declination for January 1, 1903, being in direct proportion to the time elapsed. It must also be remembered that the variations given in the table are only for the station or locality where the monuments are placed, and that in our large counties, the variation of the east boundary will be several minutes different from that at the west boundary, and hence, unless the surveyor has determined his local variation by the methods described in Vol. I., he should always state on the plat, of every survey made, the date of the same, and the amount of the variation he had set off, in order that future surveyors may be able to pick up his lines when some of his corners or boundary monuments may have been lost or destroyed.

The table in question is as follows :

Table of True Meridians.

County	LOCATION	Date of Determина'n	Declination West	Declination Jan. 1, 1903	Authority	Resident Referee

PART II.

THE APPALACHIAN COAL FIELD.

CHAPTER I.

GENERAL DESCRIPTION, AREA, STRUCTURE, CLASSIFICATON, ROCK THICKNESS, ETC.

Those who seek gold, silver, copper, tin, lead and other costly metals, should waste no time in West Virginia. Traces she may have of all, but none in commercial quantity. Volcanic disturbances, great faults, quartz veins and extensive metamorphism of sedimentary rocks which always accompany the rare metals are comparatively unknown within her borders. But while precious stones, gems, and metals, have been denied the Little Mountain State, yet generous nature has so richly dowered her with common minerals and with other common things that her natural wealth is unsurpassed by any equal area on the continent. These are some of her riches: A genial climate, midway between the extremes of heat and cold, with an average rain fall of forty-five inches, well distributed throughout the year, giving abundant moisture for crops, as well as ample water supply for the numerous streams and rivers; a fertile soil, yielding abundant returns to agriculture, grazing, horticulture, and unsurpassed for apples, peaches, pears; cherries, and all of the smaller fruits; virgin forests of both hard and soft woods, more extensive than those of any other state in the Union; clays, shales and silica beds, for brick manufacture of every description, and glass of every quality; limestones of purest composition and of exhaustless quantity; building stones of every kind except marble, granite, and other metamorphic rocks; and natural gas fields, far exceeding those of her sister state, Pennsylvania; and last but not least, *coal* in great variety and quantity. These are some of the common possessions of West Virginia which, within the last few years, have attracted to her domain investment capital from many portions of the world.

It is only within the last two years that the richness and value of her coal fields have been realized, first by capitalists outside the State, and finally by her own citizens

To the greatest coal fields in the world, geologists have given the name, Appalachian. Beginning near the northern line of Pennsylvania, latitude 42°, longitude 77°, it extends southwestward through West Virginia, southeastern Ohio, eastern Kentucky, and central Tennessee, ending in Western Alabama, latitude 33°, longitude 88°, nine hundred miles from its northeastern terminus.

The shape of this field is that of a rude canoe, the two prows of which lie in Pennsylvania and Alabama respectively, while the broadest portion of its body is found in West Virginia.

Three great railroads cross this coal field, and a fourth, the Wabash, is building. The B. & O crosses the northern portion of the State, the N. & W. the southern portion, while the C. & O. and the Wabash are intermediate. These railroads all cut the Appalachian field nearly at right angles to its length, and the following distances from the eastern margin of the coal field westward to the Ohio River, as measured along each of them, will give some idea of the coal area of West Virginia:

Baltimore & Ohio R. R., Piedmont to Benwood...................162.1 miles
Chesapeake & Ohio R. R., Hinton to Huntington...............147.0 "
Norfolk & Western R. R., Bluestone Junction to Kenova......194.08 "
W. Va. C. & Little Kanawha R. R., Westernport to Parkers-
    burg ....245.00 "

These are the distances between the southeastern margin of the coal field and the Ohio River boundary of the State. The West Virginia Central, Little Kanawha and the N. & W. lines show greater widths than the others, but this is largely accounted for by the more circuitous routes of these railroads in following the courses of streams, etc., so that the actual distance across the coal field between the eastern edge of the coal field and the Ohio River at all the points named is practically the same, and in straight or air lines would be considerably less than the figures given above —in fact only about one hundred miles.

The length of the West Virginia field is given by the distance table of the Ohio River railroad, which foots up 211.7 miles between Moundsville and Kenova, or about one hundred and fifty miles air line measurement. Hence in a rough way the Coal Measures area of the State may be said to occupy an irregular rectangle, one hundred miles wide by one hundred and fifty in length, and extending from the Alleghany Mountain region northwestward to the Ohio River. This would give 15,000 square miles as the approximate area of the West Virginia field, over and under which the Coal Measure rocks extend. But not all of this 15,000 square miles is underlain by good coal of commercial thickness, since the drill of the petroleum seeker finds many regions in the central portion of the basin where there is apparently very little coal in the entire Coal Measure column of rocks, and hence it is possible that if proper allowance were made for these barren zones, there would remain not more than 10,000 to 12,000 square miles of productive coal territory within the State, reckoned by the standard of thickness and quality as exhibited in the areas now operated by drift mines. This question will be referred to again under the description of the individual coal beds.

As to how far eastward from the Alleghany mountains the Coal Measures may once have extended we can only conjecture, but reasoning from such isolated patches as the Broad Top field of Pennsylvania, preserved in a deep wrinkle of the strata far eastward of the Alleghany escarpment, we can well believe that if the synclines in Morgan and Berkeley counties, near the North Mountain region, which now hold some coal beds of the Pocono, or Lower Carboniferous age, had been two or three thousand feet deeper, we would find, as in the case of Broad Top, several small areas of genuine Coal Measures bound up in their stony embrace, and the coal in all probability, like the Pocono coal there now, converted into a good quality of anthracite by the intense crumpling and consequent slight metamorphism to which all the strata of that region have been subjected. It is even possible, and indeed quite probable, that the Coal Measures may once have extended entirely across the Shenandoah Valley to the ancient shore line of the present Blue Ridge, since the deep trough of Massanutton Mountain, in the center of this valley, is reported still to hold a small area of the Pocono beds in its summit, from which erosion must have removed many thousand feet of sediments in the long aeons since the Carboniferous beds were deposited.

The easily destructible nature of the Greenbrier Limestone, and the soft Mauch Chunk Red Shales, which immediately underlie the Coal Measures, would readily account for the complete removal of the latter over all the steeply folded area between the eastern ridge of the Alleghanies and the Blue Ridge region. Hence, although the deeply buried Coal Measures along the western or Ohio River border of the State have been preserved from erosion, they may in many localities prove comparatively barren of good coal beds, while the same measures which have been destroyed by the ceaseless ages of rain, heat and cold from all the southeastern region of the State, probably once contained richer and thicker coal beds than any of the areas remaining, since the individual coal beds, with rare exceptions, exhibit a tendency to thicken eastward analogous to that of the series themselves.

STRUCTURE.

The central or deepest portion of the Appalachian basin or geo-syncline enters West Virginia from Greene county, Pa., at the southwest corner of the latter state, and crossing Western Monongalia and eastern Wetzel counties continues on through the State in a general southwest course across eastern Tyler, western Doddridge, central Ritchie, Wirt and Jackson, cutting eastern Mason and western Putnam, and central Cabell, to enter Kentucky from northern Wayne, ten miles above the mouth of the Big Sandy river. Where the axis of this great basin enters the State, and on to the southwest as far as Doddridge county at least, the Pittsburg coal is buried to a depth of 1300 to 1500 feet under the highest summits, or say 100 to 150 feet above tide, but from Doddridge county on southwestward, the basin begins to rise, and at the Kentucky line the Pittsburg coal overlooks the Big Sandy waters from an elevation of 800 feet above tide in the deepest portion of the trough.

From this central line of the general basin the strata rise to the northwest at the rate of 30 to 75 feet to the mile, interrupted occasionally by low anticlinal folds, until the last of the Coal Measure rocks pass into the air from southeastern Ohio. To the southeast from the same center, the general basin is traversed by a series of folds which get steeper and higher, (though not deeper) until we come to the eastern boundary of the West Virginia coal fields at the most eastern ridge of the Alleghany mountains.

The most prominent of these anticlinals are shown upon the West Virginia Survey map, where it will be seen that they are rudely parallel to the Alleghany mountains, and have a bearing of 30°–40° S. W. or N. E. as the case may be. One notable exception to this rule is that of the Volcano anticlinal, which runs from the Ohio River in Pleasants county, S. only 11° W. through Wood, Wirt and Ritchie counties into Roane. All of these arches, however, great or small, flatten out and disappear to the southwest, or are replaced by others, which may start up from what was a previous trough or syncline, so that there is not much regularity in the folds.

To the southwest beyond the Great Kanawha river, there appears to be only one prominent anticlinal: viz, the one which enters Kentucky near Warfield. This comparative absence of prominent flexures from the coal area of southern West Virginia has been ascribed by Profs. Fontaine and Stevenson to the great system of faults along the southeastern margin of the coal field in the edge of Virginia, which relieved the tension on the rocks over the southwestern portion of the Appalachian field, and thus prevented their folding as in Pennsylvania and northern West Virginia, being aided in this resistance to flexure by the greatly thickened and massive members of the Pottsville series of the region in question.

CLASSIFICATION.

The Pennsylvania and Virginia geologists, under the lead of the illustrious Rogers brothers, long ago discovered that the Carboniferous system of the Appalachian field could be subdivided into eight series, separated from each other by very distinct and natural features. This generalization was founded upon a very careful study of the rocks over a wide area, and the subsequent work of other geologists has fully established its general truthfulness, as well as its great usefulness in stratigraphic and economic geology.

The more detailed studies of recent years, rendered possible by the vast mining industry, have only modified the Rogers classification, and hence it has become so thoroughly engrafted into geologic nomenclature, and so familiar to practical coal operators, that it would be very unwise to make any radical changes. It is true that in minor details the original nomenclature for some of these series was imperfect, but those slight defects do not materially affect the grand truths expressed in the general frame work of the classification, and hence it has been deemed best to modify and supplement this time-honored work of the nestors in geology, rather than to supplant and throw it away entirely, as some of our iconoclastic geologists have suggested in recent years.

The classification adopted in this report is substantially the same as that proposed by the writer in Bulletin 65 of the U. S. G. Survey, page 19. In this, the attempt is made to preserve whatever of the Rogers nomenclature has been found useful and helpful to geologists, while at the same time such new features are introduced as seem necessary from our wider and more intimate knowledge of these rocks.

The entire Carboniferous system of the northern Appalachian gion splits up naturally into three great divisions founded upon conditions of deposition, and these in turn subdivide into eight series, as shown in the following scheme:

DIVISIONS.	SERIES.		AGE.
Carboniferous System.			
Upper: Fresh, or Brackish Water Deposits.	Dunkard, No. XVI. of Rogers.		Permian, or Permo-Carboniferous.
	Monongahela, No. XV.		Coal Measures.
Middle: Shore Deposits, with Marine Incursions.	Conemaugh, No. XIV.	Upper Half / Lower Half.	
	Allegheny Kanawha } No. XIII.		
	Pottsville, Seral, No. XII.		
Lower: Mostly marine deposits in upper half; earliest coal beds, impure and of irregular thickness in the Pocono.	Mauch Chunk Red Shale. Umbral		
	Umbral	No. XI.	Lower Carboniferous.
	Greenbrier, or Mountain Limestone.		
	Pocono Sandstone, Vespertine } No. X. "Big Injun" Oil Sand.		

In this table, the terms "Upper" and "Lower" Productive Coal Measures, have been discarded as misleading, since at the time they were given by the Rogers brothers to the Monongahela and Allegheny series, it was not known that the Pottsville also held productive coals (New River) in the southern portion of the Appalachian field. The terminology has also been shortened by dropping the term creek, river, etc., as suggested by Dr. William B. Clark, of the Maryland Survey. With the changes thus indicated it is believed that no further simplification of Carboniferous nomenclature is desirable. The term "series" is used instead of "formation" for the larger subdivisions, since there is yet too much variance by different writers in the use of that term, some of the U. S. Survey geologists making it represent a succession of entirely unlike beds, lithologically considered, while others restrict it to a single stratum of the same physical appearance throughout. Of course if the latter usage should prevail, it could not appropriately be used to represent such diverse beds of sandstone, shale, coal, limestone, etc., as those included under the terms Dunkard, Monongahela, Allegheny, etc., and for this reason the name, SERIES, has been retained as more appropriately describing the heterogeneous character of the rocks constituting the beds in question.

As will be seen from the foregoing diagram, the line separating the Middle and Upper carboniferous divisions passes directly through the center of the Conemaugh series. This is due to the fact that marine conditions ceased never to return in the Appalachian field, at least, with the deposition of the Ames, or green crinoidal limestone and its associated beds, midway in the Conemaugh, thus separating it into two divisions, of almost equal thickness, the lower one abounding in marine life, while the upper has nothing but brackish and fresh water forms. The faunal change at this horizon is sufficiently great to warrant the separation of these beds into two series, but owing to the fact that the marine type of the Ames limestone is not persistent over the entire Appalachian field, and that the lithological characteristics are very similar for some distance, both above and below the horizon in question, it is deemed best to maintain the integrity of the Conemaugh formation as modified by the Pennsylvania, Maryland and West Virginia geologists.

THICKNESS OF THE CARBONIFEROUS SYSTEM.

The entire thickness of the rocks in the Carboniferous system varies much in different portions of the State. In a general way the several series composing the system thicken eastward gradually in the northern portion, but very rapidly in the southwestern region. This gives a rapid thickening southwestward along the western flanks of the Alleghany mountain range, as will be shown more fully in a future chapter in connection with a detailed discussion of the series.

There are given here the results of borings which have been drilled to the base of the system, and they are located in several groups, passing from the Ohio river eastward across the State. In these sections, no attempt is made to classify the formations definitely, the main object being to exhibit the general composition of the whole system, and its thickness at the several localities as determined by the oil well drillers.

In order to bring these measurements to the same standard of comparison, there is added to the top of each, in every case, 1100 feet for the thickness of the Dunkard series, which caps the Carboniferous system in the state. This is the greatest thickness yet found for the Dunkard in any of the deep oil well borings, though some isolated peaks in the great trough of the Appalachian basin, along the Wetzel-Marion-Monongalia line, may hold a few feet more, but not over 100 feet in any case, and possibly not so much.

The first line of sections will begin on the Ohio river at Moundsville and pass eastward across the Carboniferous system.

Here we are aided by the carefully kept record of the Gallagher well No. 1, which begins above the Pittsburg coal, and was drilled through the "Big Injun" Oil Sand.

Combining this record with the surface measurements, and adding the Dunkard beds, we get the following:

	Feet
Dunkard	1100
Monongahela	275
Conemaugh	500
Allegheny	280
Pottsville	150
Total	2305

Still farther to the southwest, in Meade district, Marshall county, the well No. 1 on A. S. Leach, bored by the South Penn Oil Company, gives the following:

	Feet
Dunkard	1100
Monongahela	294
Conemaugh & Allegheny	769
Pottsville	157
Total	2320

Farther east, in Church district, Wetzel county, the record of well No. 1, on the Winona Shough farm, gives the following:

	Feet
Dunkard	1100
Monongahela	353
Conemaugh, Allegheny & Pottsville	998
Total	2451

Still east of this, in Battelle district, Monongalia county, the South Penn Oil Company's well No. 1. on Samuel Eakin, gives the following:

	Feet
Dunkard	1100
Monongahela	377
Conemaugh, Allegheny & Pottsville	989
Total	2466

The same Companys' well at Brown's Mill, on Dunkard Creek, and farther east near the Pennsylvania-West Virginia line, gives the following:

	Feet
Dunkard	1100
Monongahela	350
Conemaugh	560
Allegheny	280
Pottsville	180
Total	2470

The thickness at Morgantown, ten miles farther east, as revealed by a boring, is as follows:

	Feet
Dunkard	1100 .
Monongahela................................".........................	370
Conemaugh... ...	585
Allegheny & Pottsville.................................... ...	460
	———
Total	2515

A boring made at Newburg, Preston county, 13 miles south-east of Morgantown, by Hon. J. M. Guffey, reveals the following measurements:

	Feet
Dunkard..	1100
Monongahela.......................................,...........	370
Conemaugh....................................	645
Allegheny......	285
Pottsville..	275
	———
Total	2675

The Potomac basin, near Piedmont, offers the farthest point eastward where it is possible to measure all of these formations except the Dunkard, and estimating it the same as in the others, we get the following:

	Feet
Dunkard...	1100
Monongahela........	360
Conemaugh	600
Allegheny......:	308
Pottsville...	473
	———
Total	2841

These several measurements reveal a gradual and somewhat regular increase in the total thickness of the Upper and Middle Carboniferous system from west to east across the northern line of the State of 536 feet between the Ohio river at Moundsville, and the Potomac river at Piedmont.

In estimating the thickness of the Monongahela in the Piedmont section, the measurement is that found at Frostburg, Md., twenty miles distant, and the top of the Monongahela is there placed, not at the Koontz coal as suggested by Dr. W. B. Clark, State Geologist of Maryland, but at the top of the coal one hundred and twenty feet higher in the measures, the Koontz coal being regarded by the writer as representing the Uniontown coal instead of the Waynesburg.

In the borings at Morgantown and Newburg only the base of the Monongahela is found in the summits of the hills, and the thickness given for it in both cases is the one found nearest on the west.

At the mouth of Ben's Run, on the Ohio river, in Pleasants county, forty-five miles southwest from Moundsville, we get a measurement of the Coal Measure rocks through the record of the James Wells boring No. 1, by adding the usual thickness of the of the absent series:

	Feet
Dunkard	1100
Monongahela	275
Conemaugh, Allegheny & Pottsville	1066
Total	2441

Near Central in Doddridge county, twenty-five miles southeast from Ben's Run, we get another measurement from the records of the Hudson well No. 1, as follows:

	Feet
Dunkard	1100
Monongahela	300
Conemaugh, Allegheny & Pottsville	1135
Total	2535

On east of this, in Lewis county, the South Penn Oil Company's well No. 1, on the Emma Jones land, Freeman's Creek district, gives the following:

	Feet
Dunkard	1100
Monongahela	325
Conemaugh, Allegheny & Pottsville	1169
Total	2594

Near Phillippi, Barbour county, we get another measurement, carefully made by the Elk Creek Oil and Gas Company at its No. 1 well on the Hall farm, which is as follows:

	Feet
Dunkard	1100
Monongahela	350
Conemaugh	720
Allegheny	285
Pottsville	256
Total	2711

On east of this thirty miles, at the head of the Potomac basin near Thomas, on the Black Water, Tucker county, we find the following thickness for these beds:

	Feet
Dunkard	1100
Monongahela	370
Conemaugh	600
Allegheny	315
Pottsville	734
Total	3119

Along this line, which is about forty miles southwest of the former, we find the same progressive thickening eastward, but attaining a greater total by 278 feet, between the Ohio river and the eastern margin of the Coal field.

Passing southwest along the Ohio river seventy odd miles, from Ben's Run to Ravenswood, for another line of measurements southeastward across the system, we get the following on the Ohio river from the record of a well drilled one-half mile below Ravenswood, Jackson county:

	Feet
Dunkard	1100
Monongahela	300
Conemaugh, Allegheny and Pottsville	1086
Total	2486

At Spencer, Roane county, twenty-five miles southeastward from Ravenswood, the measurement of the Asylum well No. 1 gives the following:

	Feet
Dunkard	1100
Monongahela	300
Conemaugh, Allegheny and Pottsville	1468
Total	2868

About forty miles east by south of this, the Haymond well, two miles below Sutton, in Braxton county, gives the following measurement, estimating the Dunkard and Monongahela at the same thickness as in the last:

	Feet
Dunkard	1100
Monongahela	300
Conemaugh, Allegheny and Pottsville	1800
Total	3200

Thirty miles southwestward from Sutton, we get another measurement at Camden-on-Gauley, through the record of a boring made there by the Hon. J. N. Camden. Estimating the Dunkard, Monongahela and Conemaugh at the same thickness as in the last, we get the following:

	Feet
Dunkard	1100
Monongahela	300
Conemaugh	750
Allegheny-Kanawha	650
Pottsville	900
Total	3700

This line of measurements brings out clearly, not only the thickening toward the southeastern rim of the Coal Measures, but also the progressive thickening southwestward, slowly along the Ohio river,—from 2305 feet at Moundsville to 2486 feet at Ravenswood, and rapidly along the southeastern side of the Appalachian coal field,—from 2841 feet at Piedmont to 8700 feet at Camden on-Gauley.

Going fifty miles farther down the Ohio river from Ravenswood, opposite Gallipolis, seven miles below the mouth of the Great Kanawha, we get the following measurements from the record of the C. T. Beale well No. 1, in Mason county:

	Feet
Dunkard	1100
Monongahela	300
Conemaugh, Allegheny and Pottsville	1130
Total	2530

Following up the Great Kanawha river from this southeastward to the margin of the coal field along New River, we get a series of interesting measurements. Twenty five miles southeast from the mouth of the Great Kanawha, and one mile below Winfield, Putnam county, the well No. 1 of the Hurricane Oil Company gives the following, by combining its record with the usual estimates of the Dunkard formation:

	Feet
Dunkard	1100
Monongahela	300
Conemaugh, Allegheny & Pottsville	1500
Total	2900

Twenty miles farther southeast, at Charleston, Kanawha county, we get another measurement by combining the surface exposures with the record of Edwards well No. 3, bored on the banks of Elk river, as follows:

	Feet
Dunkard	1100
Monongahela	300
Conemaugh	800
Allegheny—Kanawha	574
Pottsville	580
Total	3354

About twenty-five miles southeast from Charleston, we get another correct measurement of everything below the Black Flint from the carefully kept record of a well bored by the Powellton Coal Company at its mines on Armstrong Creek, combined with accurate spirit levels from the mouth of the well up to the Kanawha Black Flint. These, added to the other formations as given at Charleston, make the following results at Powellton:

	Feet
Dunkard	1100
Monongahela	300
Conemaugh	800
Allegheny—Kanawha	1050
Pottsville	821
Total	4071

About twenty miles farther to the southeast. and in the vicinity of Fire Creek, Fayette county, we get a complete exposure of the Pottsville series along the gorge of New river, and combining its thickness there with that of the other formations as given above for Powellton, the following total is obtained:

	Feet
Dunkard	1100
Monongahela	300
Conemaugh	800
Allegheny—Kanawha	1050
Pottsville	1400
Total	4650

A result greater by 4650—2530=2120 feet than that found on the Ohio river only ninety miles distant.

One more series of measurements along the Kentucky or southwest border of the state will complete the number.

At Central City, forty-five miles below the mouth of the Great Kanawha, and six miles above the mouth of the Big Sandy River, in Cabell county, the record of a deep boring gives the following thickness, by combining it with the usual measurements above the surface:

	Feet
Dunkard	1100
Monongahela	300
Conemaugh	660
Allegheny and Pottsville	605
Total	2665

About twenty-five miles up the Big Sandy River, and five miles below the mouth of Tug Fork, the Rigdon well No. 2 gives the following results:

	Feet
Dunkard	1100
Monongahela	300
Conemaugh	700
Allegheny—Kanawha and Pottsville	925
Total	3025

At the northern line of Mingo county, and opposite Warfield Kentucky, thirty-five miles southeast of the last locality, we get another measurement for the lower portion of the column through the carefully kept record of a gas well drilled by Guffey & Queen, the upper portion being based on the Charleston measurements as follows:

	Feet
Dunkard	1100
Monongahela	300
Conemaugh	800
Allegheny—Kanawha	700
Pottsville	618
	Total 3518

Ten miles east from this, near Dingess Tunnel, on the head-waters of Twelve Pole Creek, Mingo county, a well was once drilled for gas, which gives another measurement of the system as follows:

	Feet
Dunkard	1100
Monongahela	300
Conemaugh	800
Allegheny—Kanawha	825
Pottsville	1021
	Total 4046

This exhibits a very rapid rate of thickening, especially in the Pottsville beds, which have had 400 feet added in only ten to twelve miles.

About forty-five miles southeast from Dingess is Welch, in McDowell county, and there we get nearly all the Pottsville exposed in the hills, and revealed by borings below the valleys of Elkhorn and Tug river. Combining the surface exposures with the record of a boring on Brown's creek, one-half mile above its mouth, at the Miner's Hospital, and estimating the Allegheny-Kanawha series at only its maximum, 1050 feet, (measured on the Great Kanawha), we get the following for the region of Welch:

	Feet
Dunkard	1100
Monongahela	300
Conemaugh	800
Allegheny—Kanawha	1050
Pottsville	1655
	Total 4905

In this measurement, 300 feet has been added for the portion of the Pottsville estimated to have been removed by erosion from the tops of the hills at Welch, while of course all the other formations above the Pottsville have been so removed, since they come in successively to the north and west. It is possible that the Allegheny-Kanawha formation is really thicker than the 1050 feet given, since no accessible boring records are at hand in the region of Glen Alum and other mining towns, where the top of the formation first appears in the hills along the river, thirty miles northwest from Welch. The indications are that it cannot be less than the 1050 assumed, and it may be 100 to 200 feet more.

We can now compare the measurements shown at the northeastern or Pennsylvania border of the state with those along its southeastern or Kentucky boundary, and also the intermediate stations of the Ohio river on the west, and the eastern margin of the Appalachian coal field on the east, as follows:

	Feet		Feet
Moundsville	2305	Piedmont	2841
Ben's Run	2441	Thomas	3099
Ravenswood	2486	Camden-on-Gauley	3700
Gallipolis	2530	Fire Creek	4650
Huntington	2665	Welch	4905

In other words while the same formations have thickened only 2665' —2305' =360 feet in the 200 miles along the Ohio river, between Moundsville and Huntington, yet they have thickened 4905' —2841' =2064 feet in the 200 miles between Piedmont and Welch, along the eastern border of the coal field. Hence these beds, regarded as a solid, present the form of an irregular wedge, its breadth twice its length, and its northeastern side being thinner than its southwestern, or in other words, the wedge thins away in two directions, northwestward and northeastward, the amount of such thinning being shown in the table above given.

Of course the Dunkard, Monongahela, and most of the Conemaugh formations are absent from the southeastern edge of the Appalachian field in all except the Piedmont and Thomas sections, since owing to the soft and easily disintegrating nature of their beds, they have been eroded, except where preserved in the sheltering embrace of a deep fold like that of the George's Creek basin from Piedmont to Frostburg.

The presence of these highest formations in that far eastern portion of the Appalachian field, however, leads to the conclusion that they were once co-extensive with the Pottsville beds, hence their average thickness at the west has been added to that found found for the Pottsville and Allegheny–Kanawha beds along all the eastern margin of the West Virginia coal field, although as a matter of theory, such thickness should have been increased eastward in proportion to that observed for these latter formations. Should this be done, the result would show a much greater thickening southeastward than that indicated in the measures above tabulated.

CHAPTER II.

THE DUNKARD SERIES, NO. XVI, PERMIAN, OR PERMO-CARBONIFEROUS.

Under the name, Dunkard series, the writer has included all of the beds above the Waynesburg coal of the Monongahela series. The dividing line is drawn where Permian plants have first been observed in the fossil flora. Hence, although there is no observable unconformity between the top of the Monongahela series and the base of the Dunkard as now defined, yet the existence of a thick, coarse, conglomeratic sandstone of wide distribution, just above the Waynesburg coal horizon, denotes a very great change in physical conditions. It is also quite probable that considerable erosion took place in some portions of the Appalachian field during the deposition of this basal conglomerate of the Dunkard series, and hence, although there is no appreciable unconformity in the dip of the beds, there can be no doubt that the currents which brought in the great deposit of coarse sand and gravel just after the epoch of the Waynesburg coal, also transported the elements of a new flora, several species of which are found only in the Permian beds of Europe, while others are even near relatives of Triassic types.

From all of these considerations it is quite possible that the column of rocks included in the Dunkard series should really be split up into two or three divisions each of which would then be comparable in time to any of the other SERIES. The age of these beds will be further considered at the close of this chapter.

Erosion has completely removed these rocks from several thousands of square miles in the State where they once doubtless existed, and also has very probably reduced their total thickness by many thousands of feet, if we can infer that the beds removed above even the highest rocks yet preserved, were of the same soft and easily destructible type as the most of those that remain.

The maximum thickness of the series preserved is somewhere between 1,100 and 1,200 feet. One of the oil wells on the Rush farm, north of Pine Grove, Wetzel county, located on the summit of a high knob near the center of the great Appalachian trough, found 1,100 feet of these Dunkard beds, and it is fairly certain that no other areas can exceed this thickness by more than 100 to 200 feet.

As exhibited in West Virginia, the rocks of this series consist of a succession of brown and gray sandstones, interstratified with much red shale, many beds of limestone, and several thin, impure, and unimportant coal beds, the entire series being slightly gypsiferous throughout, though no accumulations of gypsum have taken place owing probably to the absence of any considerable thickness of limestone beds.

In Ohio and northern Marshall counties, like Greene and Washington of Pennsylvania, this series holds less red shale and a greater proportion of limestone and gray limy shales than farther to the southwest. The coal beds are also more numerous, and the sandstones less massive, the whole resulting in a gently rolling topography, finely adapted to grazing and agriculture, except along the immediate gorges of the streams.

As we pass south-westward, however, the coal beds all disappear except one (the Washington) before we reach the Little Kanawha river, and the Limestones with one or two exceptions thin away into great masses of marly red shales holding only nuggets of lime, while the sandstones thicken up, and, capping the ridges in long lines of cliffs, often make a rugged topography better fitted for grazing and fruit culture than for agriculture. When the massive sandstones disappear from the ridges or uplands, however, there frequently occur limited areas of beautiful, rolling lands which yield abundant crops, the red marly shales being quite fertile from the disseminated limestone nuggets.

The soils formed by the disintegration of the Dunkard beds have the reputation of producing a fine quality of wool in which the fiber is peculiarly firm and strong, so that its area is often known as the "sheep belt" of West Virginia, since probably 90 per cent of the sheep raised in the state are grown upon the outcrops of the Dunkard series.   These rocks occupy a belt about 40–60 miles in width bordering the Ohio river, and extending east from the same over portions or all of the following named counties: Ohio, Marshall, Wetzel, Tyler, Monongalia and Marion (west of the Monongahela river), western Harrison and Lewis, Doddridge, Pleasants, Wood, Wirt, Ritchie, Calhoun, Gilmer, Roane, Jackson, and the uplands of Mason and southern Putnam, but tailing out into a narrow belt, which soon overshoots even the highest hills of Wayne, a short distance east from the Big Sandy river at the Kentucky boundary.

This series was named by the writer from its fine development and exposure along Dunkard creek, a large stream which rises in western Monongalia, and adjoining regions of Greene county, Pennsylvania, and flowing eastward, sometimes in West Virginia, and again in Pennsylvania, empties into the Monongahela five miles north from the West Virginia–Pennsylvania line.

The following sections of the rocks exposed along that stream from the head of its Pennsylvania fork in Gilmore township, Greene county, Pa., to Mount Morris, is taken from Bulletin 65, U. S. Geological Survey, page 22:

DUNKARD CREEK SECTION.

	Ft	In.	Ft	In.
Concealed from top of Shough's knob	165			
Sandstone, massive, Gilmore	40			
Shales, with limestone at base	15			
Sandstone and shales and concealed	100			
Shale, red	2			
Shales, gray	20		480	
Shale, marly	2			
Sandstone and shale	35			
Red shale	3			
Sandstone and Shale	50			
Red Shale	3			
Shales and sandstone, Nineveh	25			
Shales	20			
Coal, Nineveh	1	6		
Shales	28			
Limestone (No. X), Nineveh	7			
Shales, sandstone and concealed	100			

Sandstone, massive, Fish Creek	20				
Shales with fossil plants	10				
Coal, Dunkard { coal ......o′ 5″ / slate .....o 1 / coal......o 6 }	1		223	1	
Limestone	1				
Sandstone	10				
Shales	17				
Limestone, Jollytown	1	6			
Shales and sandstone	25				
Coal, Jollytown	1	1			
Calcerous shale, fossiliferous, fish teeth	0	6			
Limestone, Upper Washington	4				
Shales and sandstone	115				
Limestone, Middle Washington	3				
Shales	40				
Sandstone	35				
Shale	5		276	8	
Coal, Washington "A" { coal, impure 1″ 2″ / fire clay...... 2 6 / coal............ o 6 }	4	2			
Shales and sandstones	60				
Limstone, Lower Washington	5				
Shales	5				
Coal, Washington, slaty	5				
Shales and sandstones, including coal bed near center	110				
Coal, Waynesburg "A"	2	6			
Shales	10				
Sandstone, Waynesburg	50				
Shales, with fossil plants (Cassville)	5				
Waynesburg coal	...				
Total			1162	3	

Shough's knob is wooded, and the rocks in it are not exposed but it probably contains the highest beds of the Dunkard series, existing anywhere in the Appalachian basin.

The following detailed section of these beds made by the writer at Board Tree, Marshall county, combined with the record of an oil well located near. on the Nuce farm, is also taken from Bulletin 65, above cited, page 25:

BOARD TREE SECTION.

	Ft.	In.	Ft.	In.
Sandstone, gray and concealed	55			
Gray limestone, Windy Gap	5			
Red shales and concealed	100			
Coaly slate	1	1		
Concealed to base of a massive sandstone	35		401	
Concealed, sandstone and red shale to Board Tree Tunnel	175			
Sandy shales	15			
Sandstone, Nineveh	15			

Coal, Nineveh..	I	
Gray shales........	15	
Sandstone, massive	12	
Shales	3	
Limestone, Nineveh.. { limestone .... 1′ / black slate .... 3 / limestone and limy beds ....15 }	19	
Variegated shales	9	
Sandstone	5	}261
Shales, limy...	7	
Sandstone to level of track at west portal	5	
Concealed shales and sandstone	100	
Massive sandstone, Fish Creek	30	
Shales	3	
Coal, Dunkard, to level of bore hole....................	2	
Interval, shales, sandstones and limestones, with two thin coal beds	50	
Shales, sandstones and red beds 300		
Coal, Washington....	5	}155
Shales, limestones and sandstone	150	
Coal, Waynesburg		

       Total..1117

• In the vicinity of Bellton, 3 miles west from Board Tree, the exposures are more complete. and there the writer once measured a section which combined with the record of an oil boring gives the following succession, as published in Bulletin 65, U. S. Geological Survey, pages 26 and 27:

BELLTON SECTION.

	Ft.	In.	Ft.	In.
Limestone, Windy Gap..	5			
Shales	30			
Coal, Windy Gap, blossom	0			
Concealed, sandstone and shale.............................	30			
Shales and sandstone	60			
Sandstone, massive, gray............................	20			
Red shales and concealed	75			
Sandstone, massive	40			
Red shales and sandstones	50			
Limestone...	3			
Shales and concealed...................... ──	20			
Coal, Nineveh	I			
Shales and sandstone	35			
Limestone and shales, Nineveh	10			
Shales, sandstone and concealed.................	100			
Sandstone................	5			
Shales...	10			
Limestone......, ...	0	6		
Coal	0	3		
Shales and sandstone	15			
Red shales	5			
Concealed..	20			
Coal	I			
Shales and concealed..	30			

Coal, Dunkard...... { black slate...... 4″ } .... coal .... 11″ }	1	3
Limy shales and fire clay..................................	5	
Shales	13	
Limestone, gray, Jollytown..............................	2	
Shales and sandstones....................................	30	
Coal, Jollytown	0	8
Limestone, gray, Upper Washington, (continued from oil well record	5	
Sandstone	12	
Shale	7	
Sandstone	11	
Shale	12	
Fire clay...	7	
Sandstone..	25	
Shale	12	
Sandstone..	17	
Coaly shales..	9	
Sandstone..	9	
Shale	5	
Sandstone..	4	
Shale	19	
Sandstone	16	
Shale	4	
Sandstone..	30	313
Shale	2	
Sandstone..	35	
Shale	27	
Sandstone..	45	
Coal, Washington...	6	
Sandstone..	20	
Limestone..	8	
Shale	19	
Sandstone	15	
Shale	18	
Sandstone..	25	
Shale	4	148
Limestone..	10	
Fire clay	3	
Limestone..	4	
Sandstone	16	
Place for Waynesburg coal		
Total...1078		8

PRINCIPAL HORIZONS OF THE DUNKARD SERIES.

The Summit of the Dunkard series appears to be crowned by rather massive sandstones separated by red shales and thin limestones with only one coal or COALY horizon.

The Gilmore sandstone of Prof. Stevenson and another massive one 50 to 75 feet higher, have protected these highest members of the Dunkard from complete erosion, although the topmost beds in the great plateau of western Monongalia, Marion, Wetzel, Marshall, Tyler, Doddridge, and western Harrison, remain only in a series of conspicuous knobs, rising 100 to 200 feet above the general level of the surface, and 500 to 700 above the immediate valleys of the draining streams.

The uppermost of these sandstones has not been named, but it caps a high knob one mile south from Windy Gap Church, in Greene county, Pennsylvania. There, an oil well (Barnhardt No. 1) starting on its top, found the Waynesburg coal or base of the Dunkard series at 1075 feet, so that the sandstone in question comes near the very top of the Dunkard beds.

WINDY GAP LIMESTONE.

One of the highest limestones of the Dunkard series, traceable over any considerable area, has been named from a locality in Greene county, Pa., the Windy Gap limestone.

Like all other limestones of this Dunkard series, it is of fresh water origin, and contains only minute fossils, apparently bivalve crustacea, but as these forms have never been studied, nothing definite is known of their specific or even generic type. The rock weathers to a light gray on the surface, but on fresh fracture is dark or bluish in color, and the several layers have a thickness aggregating 8 to 10 feet.

This limestone occurs near the summits of the hills at Board Tree, and Bellton, in Marshall county, and also in most of the high knobs of Marshall, Wetzel, and western Marion and Monongalia.

Oil well No 65 of L. S. Hoyt & Co., situated on a high ridge separating Big and Little Fishing creeks, 5 miles north of Pine Grove, Wetzel county, starts 15 to 20 feet below this limestone, and it reached the Pittsburg coal at 1270 feet and the base of the Dunkard series at 970 feet, thus making the horizon of the Windy Gap limestone practically 1000 feet above the base of the series, or 50 to 75 feet less than that shown in the Board Tree, and Bellton sections. This discrepancy, however, may be accounted for by some westward thinning and also from the fact that the latter were based upon barometric measurements and therefore not so accurate as the oil well result.

At many localities in Wetzel, Marshall, Marion and Monongalia, another limestone several feet thick is found at an interval of 100 to 120 feet below the Windy Gap bed, and this may frequently have been confused with the latter. The L. S. Hoyt oil wells Nos. 30 and 31 of Wetzel county both start at the horizon of this lower limestone and get the Pittsburg coal at 1160 feet. The two limestones in question coming as they do high up on the ridge lands of the counties mentioned, contribute much to the fertility of these upland soils of the Permian area.

THE WINDY GAP COAL.

At 25 to 30 feet below the Windy Gap limestone, there occurs an impure COAL or COALY SHALE which has been observed at a few localities in West Virginia. It is the highest known bed of anything approaching COAL in composition, in the Dunkard series. Where seen in the tops of the knobs near Bellton, Marshall county, or near St. Cloud, Monongalia county, it appears to be little better than a highly bituminous shale, although near Windy Gap, Greene county, Pennsylvania, some actual coal occurs at this horizon, although as far as known it has never been dug for burning, and is of interest only as being the highest known bituminous stratum yet found in the Appalachian basin.

THE GILMORE SANDSTONE.

A massive bed of coarse yellowish brown sandstone, 25 to 30 feet thick comes into the series a short distance below the Windy Gap coal horizon. It was named by Dr. John J. Stevenson, the Gilmore sandstone from its occurrence in the township of that name in Greene county, Pennsylvania, and is there frequently conspicuous in long lines of cliffs near the summits of the hills. It is known under several names at different localities, as the "Fox Rocks," "Pethtle Rocks," etc. In western Monongalia, the same stratum is called "Efaw Rocks" from a locality near Wadestown where it litters up the ground with large boulders.

This sandstone has been, as already stated, one of the principal agencies in preserving the higher portions of the Dunkard series from erosion, and holding up the "ridge lands" into broad arable fields favorably located for agriculture. The stratum is very frequently not exposed in a cliff, but simply makes a well defined bench in the topography.

The interval of 200–250 feet immediately below the Gilmore sandstone is seldom well exposed, but appears to consist of red shales, brown, micaceous sandstones and thin limestones, none of which is sufficiently characteristic to merit a special name.

NINEVEH SANDSTONE.

At a little over 200 feet below the Gilmore sandstone there is quite generally found another great sandstone horizon, and this has been called the Nineveh sandstone from its position a few feet above the coal of the same name.

This, like the Gilmore above, often gives rise to cliffs, especially in Marshall, Wetzel, western Monongalia, Marion, Harrison and Doddridge. · The rock is yellowish gray in color, and has frequently been quarried for building stone, though at times its texture is not firm enough to prevent crumbling when exposed to frost, etc.   An attempt was made to quarry it near the eastern portal of the Short Line [B. & O.] Railroad tunnel in western Harrison, but the sand grains are so loosely cemented that the rock crumbles too easily for building into exposed structures. It appears to be this stratum that crops out in bold cliffs along the B. & O. Railroad between Salem and Long Run in Doddridge county, and also at Littleton in Wetzel county, half way up the hills.   The same sandstone has been quarried on the land of Thomas White, one mile below Maple, Monongalia county.

BELLTON STAGE.

In Bulletin 65, U. S. Geological Survey, the writer has designated the beds beginning with the Jollytown coal and ending with the Nineveh coal as the BELLTON GROUP or STAGE, and the thickness as shown in the Bellton section foots up 284 feet, 8 inches.   These thin coals are rather persistent over the counties of Marshall, Wetzel, and the western portions of Marion, Monongalia and Harrison, but to she southwest they thin away and disappear completely, none of them ever having been seen south of the Parkersburg branch of the B. & O. Railroad.

The coals are five in number at Bellton, but only three of them extend over any considerable area; viz, the Nineveh, Dunkard and Jollytown.   These coals are of no economic importance except locally where other and thicker beds are not available. Occasionally one of them may cover a small area along the valleys of the streams, where only a little stripping will uncover many bushels of fuel.   In such cases these coals can be profitably mined by the farmers for their own use.

THE NINEVEH COAL.

The Nineveh coal, so named by Dr. John J. Stevenson from the village of Nineveh, Greene county, Pa., is the highest member of the Bellton stage. It is frequently seen along the roads and streams in western Monongalia, Marion, Wetzel and Marshall counties and appears to be rather pure, having been used occasionally for smithing purposes. It is seldom more than one foot thick, though occasionally thickening to 25 inches, and also thinning down to 6 inches or less. This coal may be observed cropping out above the arch of Board Tree tunnel on the B. & O. Railroad in Marshall county, and also at the Glover's Gap tunnel on the line between Marion and Wetzel counties.

A coal was once mined in the hill at Burton, Wetzel county, about 130 feet above water level, and it is probably this coal.

THE NINEVEH LIMESTONE.

Below the Nineveh coal at an interval of 25–30 feet, there is found a limestone that appears to have a very wide distribution. It usually occurs in several layers, and these may be separated by marly or sometimes, bituminous shale, the whole often 20 or more feet in thickness. Some of the layers of limestone are of fair quality while others are quite impure. The outcrop of this limestone is finely shown at either portal of Board Tree tunnel, on the Marshall–Wetzel county line; also at the foot of the hill on the road between Maple and St. Cloud, Monongalia county. Its crop may be seen along the public road leading from St. Cloud to Hundred, ¼ mile east of the Winona Shough oil well, and 70 feet above the derrick floor, thus making its position there 960 feet above the Pittsburg coal, since the latter was found at a depth of 890 feet. It appears to be this same Nineveh limestone that crops through Wood, Wirt, and Jackson counties, extending nearly through to the Big Kanawha river, and occurring well up in the summits of the hills. It is known south of the Little Kanawha river as the "Ridge" limestone from its occurrence along the ridges, and it adds much to the fertility of the soil. It gives name to Limestone Hill P. O., on the Parkersburg and Charleston turnpike, near the corner of Wirt, Wood and Jackson counties, where it crops on the summit and appears to be nearly 30 feet thick.

This limestone was called No X in Dr. John J. Stevenson's Report K of the Second Geological Survey of Pennsylvania, while the Windy Gap limestone, 300 feet higher, was called No. XIV.

The rock interval for the next 100 feet below the Nineveh limestone, consists of shales, sandstones and red beds, and occasionally a thin coal may occur 75 to 100 feet down, but it does not appear to be persistent over any considerable area, having been seen only in the region near Burton, Wetzel county.

FISH CREEK SANDSTONE.

At 135 to 150 feet below the Nineveh coal there occurs another sandstone horizon known as the Fish Creek sandstone of Stevenson. It makes great cliffs along the stream of that name in Marshall county, and also along the B. & O. Railroad between Littleton and Burton in Wetzel county, where it has been extensively quarried for building stone, of which it produces a very fair quality.

This stratum, like the Nineveh and Gilmore sandstones above, makes a distinct terrace in the topography, so that its presence can be easily detected, even when it does not stand out as a bold cliff.

THE DUNKARD COAL.

Below the Fish Creek sandstone at an interval of 1 to 20 feet there often occurs another coal which from its outcrop along the bed of Dunkard Creek, for a considerable distance, was named the Dunkard coal by Dr. Stevenson, in his Greene County, Pa. Report. It is seldom more than 12 to 15 inches thick, but is almost always double bedded, having a thin layer of slate near its center. This coal occurs so close to the Jollytown coal below, that it has doubtless often been erroneously identified with the latter. It covers a considerable area in western Marion, Monongalia, and in Wetzel and Marshall counties and has occasionally been mined by stripping along the streams. The roof shales generally contain numerous well preserved fossil plants, and Dr. David White finds among them some well marked Permian types, along with well known Coal Measure forms. This bed crops above the B. & O. Railroad in the vicinity of Bellton, Marshall county, for two or three miles, and may also be seen near Glen Easton in the same county.

In Monongalia county it was once mined by stripping, on the land of Thomas White, one mile below Maple.

JOLLYTOWN COAL.

The lowest coal seam of the Bellton stage is known as the Jollytown bed from its outcrop in the village of that name in Greene county, Pa. It has probably been mined more frequently and used for domestic and other purposes to a greater extent than any other member of the Bellton group, being usually thicker and more persistent, having a wide distribution in western Monongalia, Marion and Harrison counties, and also found quite generally in Wetzel, Marshall, and Tyler. It is a fine "key" rock from which to estimate the depth of the Pittsburg coal below the surface where the latter stratum is so deeply buried in the central portion of the Appalachian basin, since the Jollytown coal is usually found at 750 to 800 feet above the Pittsburg bed, except along the western border of the State where the interval has thinned to 700 feet or even less.

The Jollytown coal has been mined in the vicinity of Wise, Monongalia county, where it is 18 to 24 inches thick and of fairly good quality, on the lands of Mr. Wiley and others. It has also been opened on the land of Zadock Wise, below Cross Roads on Miracle Run.

In Wetzel county it crops along the banks of Fish Creek at Burton, and is frequently seen between there and Littleton, being 30 feet above the bed of the stream at Hundred, 40 to 50 feet above at Littleton, and underlain closely by the Washington limestone.

At Bellton, Marshall county, this coal is only 4 to 6 inches thick and crops near the bed of Fish creek 40 to 50 feet below another [Dunkard] coal bed.

Along the Short Line Railroad this coal crops at railroad grade one-half mile above Wallace, Harrison county, and also comes out on the other side of the divide at Folsom station in Wetzel county, being only 8 to 10 inches thick at either point.

THE WASHINGTON LIMESTONE.

Three limestones were named from Washington, Pennsylvania, by Dr. John J. Stevenson—an Upper, Middle and Lower — and the Upper one comes immediately below the Jollytown coal.

There is frequently a bed of bituminous slate or shale immediately overlying the limestone, which is filled with fish remains.

The Middle Washington limestone while frequently present in Greene and Washington counties of Pennsylvania, does not appear to be persistent in West Virginia.

The Lower one, however, is often seen in the roof shales of the Washington coal, and is one of the factors used to identify that important geological horizon. This Lower Washington limestone is quite generally present in Monongalia, Marion, Harrison, Wetzel, Tyler, Marshall, and Ohio counties, but disappears southwestward in Doddridge, Ritchie and adjoining counties.

THE MARIETTA SANDSTONES.

The interval of rocks 200 feet or more in thickness which separates the Jollytown coal from the Washington coal is often largely occupied by an immense sandstone deposit 100 or more feet in thickness, and in two or three great ledges separated by shales. The writer has termed the sandstone horizon the Marietta sandstones from their occurrence near that city on the Ohio river where they have long been quarried for grindstones, of which they make an excellent quality. The color of the rock is generally of a yellowish brown and they often form immense cliffs as at Raven Rock, on the Ohio river.

In Roane, Jackson, Mason, Calhoun, Gilmer, Wirt, Lewis and Ritchie counties especially, there are many localities where the Marietta sandstones form long lines of cliffs on the summits of the ridges, and often weather into fantastic shapes which from a distance resemble a closely crowded group of immense haystacks. One of these localities in Roane on the lands of Mr. Munson Jackson has given rise to the term "Jackson Rocks" under which name this outcrop is locally known over a considerable region. These sandstones, though frequently coarse in grain, rarely hold pebbles of considerable size, only one such locality (along the Parkersburg and Staunton turnpike near the line between Gilmer and Ritchie counties) being known to the writer. Occasionally the shales which usually separate this sandy horizon into two or three separate strata, thin away as at Rock Lick, Marshall county, and then we get a solid mass of sandstone 100 feet thick,

This horizon has recently been quarried for grindstones to a considerable extent between Parkersburg and Letart along the

Ohio river, and it is quite probable that in many other regions a valuable grindstone grit could be found at this geological level.

THE WASHINGTON STAGE.

Beginning directly beneath the Marietta sandstones and extending down to the top of the Waynesburg sandstone, we find a group of beds which in the northern end of the state contain several quite persistent coals, and which might be called the WASHINGTON STAGE after the name of its principal coal bed.

The coals of this stage which have received distinct names are in descending order the following:

Washington "A."
Washington.
Little Washington.
Waynesburg "B."
Waynesburg "A."

They occupy 180 to 200 feet of measures and are separated by shales, sandstone, and often two or more beds of limestone.

The WASHINGTON "A" coal at the top is of no importance and of very limited extent, occurring principally along Dunkard creek in Western Monongalia where it is often only a mass of bituminous shale and thin slaty layers of coal, the whole being 4 to 5 feet in thickness.

The WASHINGTON COAL is the thickest and most important, and widely extended coal of the Dunkark series. It is generally a multiple seam, having several alternate layers of coal and slate in its upper half, and generally 18 to 20 inches of fairly good coal in its lower portion, the entire seam often attaining a thickness of 10 feet.

The following section from near Farmington, Marion county, will illustrate this latter type of structure:

Coal	0	6"	
Shale	0	3	
Coal and shale	0	8	
Coal	1	0	
Shale	0	4	
Coal	0	5	
Shale	0	3	10' 9"
Coal	1	0	
Shale	0	4	
Coal	1	1	
Shale	0	3	
Coal, fair	2	0	
Slate	0	2	
Coal, good	2	6	

Here the only good coal in the entire 10′ 9″ is the 2¼ feet at the bottom.

This coal was first described by the writer from Brown's Mill, on Dunkard creek near the village of New Brownsville, Monongalia county, where it has the following structure:

```
Bituminous shale..................... 2′   0″ ⎫
Coal, impure.........................1     9 ⎪
Shale .........  .....................0     4 ⎬ 8′ 0″
Coal, slaty..........................1     4 ⎪
Shale ...............................0     3 ⎪
Coal, good...........................2     4 ⎭
```

It is persistent over all of the western half of Monongalia, Marion and Harrison counties, and appears to be universally present in Ohio, Marshall, Wetzel, Tyler, Pleasants, Doddridge, Ritchie, Gilmer, Calhoun, Wirt, Wood, Jackson, and Roane, and hence becomes an important "key" from which to estimate the depths to underlying formations.

The position of this coal at Wheeling, in Ohio county, is only 360 feet above the Pittsburg bed, but this interval increases gradually eastward until in Marion and Harrison counties near Mannington and Brown respectively we find 550 feet of rock thickness intervening.

On the main line of the B. & O. Railroad this coal passes beneath water level about two miles west of Mannington, and does not reappear until we come to near Roseby's rock, Marshall county.

On the Short Line Railroad it goes under water level 2 miles above Brown, Harrison county, on the land of Templeton Smith, and comes out again between Smithfield and Jacksonburg, being frequently seen in the cuts of the railroad for several miles beyond Pine Grove in Wetzel county, and has frequently been mined for domestic supply between there and New Martinsville as well as at the latter town where it is about 160 feet above the Ohio river.

At Sistersville this bed crops near the watering trough on the Middlebourne pike high up in the hills, and looks to be 2¼ to 3 feet thick.

In the region of Marietta, this coal is thin and known as the "Hobson" vein generally by the Ohio geologists.

At Parkersburg it is at low water just below the mouth of the

Little Kanawha, and is slaty and worthless, being only 1½ to 2 feet thick.

On the Parkersburg branch of the B. & O. Railroad, this coal is first observed in the roof of the tunnel just east of Cherry Camp, Harrison county, and it passes below water level at the eastern line of that village to come out again on Middle Island waters two miles east of Long Run station in Doddridge county, and is frequently visible along the railroad to Cairo and beyond, cropping out a few feet above the great cliff sandstone, well up in the hills, but only one to two feet thick and of no economic importance.

In the region of Ritchie Mine, this coal bed is left unchanged by the dike of Grahamite which intersects all the strata from the bottom to the tops of the hills. It is also to be seen near Ritchie Court House where it is only 12 to 18 inches thick. It is mined for local supply at Smithville where it is less than two feet thick and 150 feet above the bed of Hughes river.

On Tanner's Fork in Gilmer county this coal occurs high up in the hills and is from 2 to 3 feet thick. Its occurrence high up on the ridges and hills through Gilmer, Calhoun and Roane counties has led to its being generally known as the "Chestnut Oak" vein, and occasionally as the "Hickory" vein.

This coal has been mined in the vicinity of Spencer, Roane county, where it is 2½ feet thick and crops 75 feet above the level of Spring creek. The coal is slaty and of poor quality except about 12 to 15 inches of the bottom portion.

From Spencer on across to Walton this coal is frequently visible, being mined near Looneyville, and many other points where no other coal is accessible.

One mile and a half below Walton, this vein was once mined on the land of P. H. Lee in the bluff of Poca river, and 50 feet above the same. It is here only 18" thick, rather impure, and comes 40 feet above a great pebbly massive sandstone, the top of which is only 10 feet above water level.

On Rock creek, a tributary of Poca river, emptying from the south near Oakville, Mr. Joseph Moore has mined the same coal to a small extent. It is 12 to 24 inches thick but slaty and sulphurous, and comes only 10 feet above the top of a great pebbly cliff 60 feet high.

This bed may possibly extend farther to the southwest but it has not been reported as mined any farther in that direction.

It is in the roof shales of this coal that the Permian plants, CALLIPTERIS CONFERTA, C. LYRATA, and other Permian types have been found at Price's and Brown's mines below Worley in Monongalia county.

A sample of the Washington coal from the region of Pine Grove, Wetzel county, collected by Mr. Thomas Pettigrew, engineer of the Short Line Railroad was analyzed by Prof. B. H. Hite, Chemist for the Survey, with the following results:

Moisture	8.46 pr. ct.	
Volatile matter	46.75	"
Fixed carbon	31.66	"
Ash	13.13	"
Total	100.00	"
Sulphur	2.64	"

The analysis reveals a coal very high in moisture, volatile matter, and ash, thus keeping up the progressive ratio of increase for these elements in passing upward from the base of the Coal Measures.

WAYNESBURG "A" COAL.

The only other coal in this group which is ever of any economic importance is the Waynesburg "A" bed, 80 to 90 feet below the Washington coal and the same interval above the Waynesburg, or base of the Dunkard series. This bed is quite generally present 10 to 15 feet above the massive Waynesburg sandstone, through Monongalia, Marion, Harrison, Doddridge and Tyler counties, and occasionally attains a thickness of 3½ feet. The coal contains much ash and other impurities, however, and makes only an indifferent fuel. It has been mined to a small extent in western Harrison and eastern Doddridge for local domestic use. Its presence is generally marked by a line of springs which come out of the ground on top of the impermeable clays and shales just below, and which, easily disintegrating, give origin to very bad roads with deep sticky mudholes along their line of outcrop.

These coals, limestones, shales, sandstones, etc., of the Dunkard series, will be described with more minuteness and their floras and faunas carefully studied when the detailed geology of each county is taken up and worked out for publication, since only a small space could be allotted for their consideration in this report, because its main purpose is the description of the important fuel resources of the Commonwealth. These thin and impure beds of the Dunkard will only become important in the far distant future when the thick, pure coals of the other series below have been practically exhausted.

THE WAYNESBURG SANDSTONE.

The Dunkard series began with the setting in of the strong currents which first deposited the Cassville plant shale in immediate contact with the underlying coal (Waynesburg), and also introduced along with many old and well known Coal Measure plants, several new and strange forms which characterize a higher terrane in the fossil flora of Europe.

The grey, sandy, fossiliferous Cassville shales were succeeded abruptly by a coarse, massive, yellowish white conglomerate which the Pennsylvania geologists long ago named the Waynesburg sandstone from its occurrence in great cliffs along Ten Mile creek, just east from Waynesburg, Greene county, Pennsylvania.

The sandstone in question appears to rest conformably upon the underlying Cassville plant shale, so far as dip is concerned, but the latter is frequently absent entirely and then the sandstone rests directly upon the Waynesburg coal. The fact, however, that the Cassville shale has thus frequently been eroded by the rapid currents which transported the coarse sand and quartz pebbles of the Waynesburg sandstone, would lead to the conclusion that a great change in physical conditions had taken place, even although there is no marked unconformity in dip, or any large amount of erosion.

There is some evidence in the south-western portion of the state that there may have been considerable erosion of the underlying Monongahela series in that region during the deposition of the Waynesburg sandstone since the thickness of the Monongahela is about 100 feet less than it is to the northward, and the Waynesburg coal is seldom to be found.

It is a singular coincidence that the dawn of Permian time should have been marked both here and upon the continent of Europe by turbulent currents—in the case of Europe carrying such immense boulders that some geologists see in the deposits, evidence of glacial conditions. The great, coarse, Waynesburg conglomerate so different from any of the beds in the section for several hundred feet below it, and entirely unlike any of the beds above, coming as it does at the beginning of the Dunkard epoch, is certainly good evidence for a marked change in physical conditions and therefore the proper horizon to expect a change in the fauna and flora.

The Waynesburg sandstone has a very wide distribution, extending as a great, coarse deposit entirely across the state. Being seldom less than 50' and often 75' in thickness it makes a line of rugged cliffs along its eastern outcrop from where it enters the state in Monongalla county, across Marion, Harrison, Lewis, Gilmer, Calhoun, Roane, Kanawha, Putnam and Cabell to where it leaves the Appalachian trough in Wayne county near the Big Sandy. It is especially massive and pebbly where it rises from the bed of Poca river just below Walton and for many miles down that stream, as well as in all the country to the southward where the southeastward rise of the strata carries it up into the hill tops before it disappears from the same a few miles west from Elk river.

This same stratum comes out of the Ohio river along the Ohio shore in the vicinity of Blennerhassett Island, and its massive top is frequently visible at low water in the bed of the Ohio at many localities between Parkersburg and Letart. Here the Ohio river veers to the Northwest and the emergence of the Waynesburg sandstone makes "Letart Falls." It appears to be this same stratum that forms the great cliffs along the B. & O. railroad between Ellenboro and Cairo, as well as along Hughes river for long distances above McFarland.

It usually makes a good quarry rock for piers and other large structures, as it splits readily into great blocks of any desired size, dresses easily, and resists weathering action fairly well. It has frequently been used for bridge piers along the line of the B. & O. railroad in Marion, Harrison, Ritchie and other counties.

In its western outcrop in Ohio, Marshall, Wetzel and Tyler counties, this rock, while occasionally massive, is not nearly so thick nor coarse as on the eastern side of the Appalachian basin.

From the fact that this stratum always makes a conspicuous bluff it has been dubbed the "Bluff Sand" by the petroleum drillers in the logs of their well records.

THE CASSVILLE PLANT SHALE.

The first and lowest member of the Dunkard series laid down in immediate contact with the highest bed (Waynesburg coal) of the Monongahela has been named the CASSVILLE PLANT SHALE by Prof. Wm. M. Fontaine and the writer, from the village of Cassville, Monongalia county, seven miles northwest from Morgantown. It varies from 0 to 20 feet in thickness, and its lowest layer is usually interstratified with the Waynesburg coal, since a very rich flora as well as insect fauna occurs in a layer of gray shale 6"-12" thick just below the "roof" member of the Waynesburg coal, and in immediate contact with the main coal stratum.

The first of the new elements discovered in the flora of the Cassville shale was a fragment of TÆNIOPTERIS picked up by the writer in 1875 which the keen eye of Prof. Wm. M. Fontaine at once recognized as a form entirely new to the Coal Measures, and which was later described in Report PP of the Pennsylvania Geological Survey under the name of TÆNIOPTERIS LESCURIANA. Further search by Prof. Fontaine and the writer led to the finding of TÆNIOPTERIS NEWBERRYANA, and the genera BAIERA, and SAPORTEA a nearly allied form, plants unknown in the European flora before the dawn of Permian time.

These facts together with the finding of CALLIPTERIS CONFERTA and other Permian types in the roof shales of the Washington coal higher up in the Dunkard series, led Prof. Fontaine and myself to conclude that this whole series of rocks above the Waynesburg coal should not be included in the Coal Measures, but that they were of Permian age, and this opinion was so published in the Pennsylvania Survey Report PP, 1880, to which the reader is referred for a full discussion of the evidence, Chapter III, 1. c. pages 105 to 120.

While European geologists have almost universally accepted our conclusions, American geologists, for reasons best known to themselves, have not done so. During the present year (1902), however, Mr. David White, the eminent palæobotanist of the U. S. Geological Survey, and of the National Museum, has spent several weeks in the field and in reviewing the collections made from the Cassville shale by Fontaine and the writer. He concludes, in a paper announced for the Washington (December, 1902) meeting of the Geological Society of America, that the Dunkard beds, at least as far down as the roof shales of the Washington coal, are of the same age as the LOWER ROTHLIEGENDE of western Europe, but is not yet fully convinced of the Permian age of the intervening beds down to and including the CASSVILLE SHALE, largely on account of the many Coal Measure types which survive and are found commingled with the Permian forms.

Mr. David White intends to make a more detailed study of these beds later, but as he has accepted our main contention, viz: the Permian age of the larger portion of the Dunkard series, it is to be hoped that American geologists generally will now adopt his opinions, since he has discovered much additional confirmatory evidence.

The following letter from Mr. White will show the nature of the evidence in question:

DEPARTMENT OF THE INTERIOR.

UNITED STATES GEOLOGICAL SURVEY.

WASHINGTON, D. C. DEC. 24, 1902

DR. I. C. WHITE,
    STATE GEOLOGIST;
      MORGANTOWN, W. VA.

DEAR SIR:

    In reply to your inquiry concerning the results of my search for Permian species in the Dunkard series during the past season, I cannot give you a full report, since the collections are not yet completely identified. The following species I regard as characteristic of Permian though some of them may not be confined thereto:

    1. CALLIPTERIS CONFERTA STERNB., small variety in lower Washington limestone, but normal forms in roof shales of Dunkard coal.

    2. CALLIPTERIS LYRATIFOLIA Göpp. var. CORIACEA F. & W. The same as SPHENOPTERIS CORIACEA F. & W., Lower Washington limestone.

    3. CALLIPTERIS CURRETIENSIS Zeill., near Nineveh limestone.

    4. GONIOPTERIS NEWBERRYANA F. & W. =Pecopteris foeminae-formis(Schloth) Zeill., forma DIPLAZIOIDES Zeill., from the Permian of Brieve. Cassville shale.

    5. ALETHOPTERIS GIGAS Gutb., near Dunkard coal.

    6. PECOPTERIS GERMARI (Weiss) F. & W., Cassville shale.

    7. ODONTOPTERIS OBTUSILOBA Naum., near Dunkard coal.

    8. CAULOPTERIS GIGANTEA F. & W. =Ptychopteris gigantea (F. & W.) Zeill., from the Permian of Brieve, Cassville.

9. EQUISETITES RUGOSUS Schimp., Cassville.

10. SPHENOPHYLLUM FONTAINEANUM S. A. Miller, common; probably identical in Europe.

11. SIGILLARIA APPROXIMATA F. & W. In European Permian. To these might be added the species common to the Coal Measures and Permian, such as PECOPTERIS CANDOLLEANA, P. PTEROIDES, P. OREOPTERIDIA, etc.

A new and yet undescribed ODONTOPTERIS from the Cassville shale at Mt. Morris, Pa., seems to suggest TAENIOPTERIS PLAUENSIS Sterzel, but is not that. It, like some of the types of Mesozoic facies, points toward Permian.

ASTEROPHYLLITES EQUISETIFORMIS and SIGILLARIA BRARDII, are among species found this summer. The former goes high up in the Dunkard.

Very truly yours,
DAVID WHITE.

The Permian age of the Dunkard series is also confirmed by the existence of practically the same flora in the Wichita beds of Texas as shown in a paper by the writer published in the Bulletin of the Geological Society of America, Vol. III., pp. 217-218, April 22, 1892. In a small collection from Texas the species of which were identified by Prof. Wm. M. Fontaine, the genus WALCHIA proved to be the only form not yet discovered in the Dunkard beds of West Virginia.

The fossil insects described from the Cassville shale by Prof. Scudder in Bulletin 124, U. S. G. Survey, also furnish additional evidence of Permian age.

A single wing of a fossil insect was found by Fontaine and White in 1876, and described by Scudder under the name of GERABLATTINA BALTEATA in Report PP, of the 2nd Geological Survey of Pennsylvania, 1880. The specimen occurred in a layer of soft gray shale only a few inches thick, on top of the main body of the Waynesburg coal but just under the "roof" member of the latter.

Several years subsequently, the late R. D. Lacoe, of Pittston, Pa., who did such admirable work in collecting fossil plants from the Coal Measures all over the United States, sent one of his keenest-eyed collectors, Mr. C. L. Eakin, of Wadestown, Monongalia Co., W. Va., to make a thorough exploration of the Cassville locality. Mr. Eakin spent several months at the work, and discovered fifty-six (56) species all of which proved new to science, distributed among five (5) genera. This wealth of fossil insects was confined entirely to the few inches of gray shale at the very base of the

Dunkard series between the upper division of the Waynesburg coal, and its thin (6″ to 12″) "roof" member above.

Mr. Lacoe turned over all of the collection made by Mr. Eakin to Prof. Samuel H. Scudder, of Cambridge, Mass., for study and description, the results of which are given in Bulletin No. 124, U. S. G. Survey. The following general statements concerning the Cassville specimens as well as those from near Steubenville, O., given by Prof. Scudder on page 12 of the Bulletin referred to will explain more fully the Permain evidence furnished by the fossil insects in question:

"The West Virginia locality is at Cassville, Monongalia Co., not far from Morgantown, and the specimens were found in rocks lying above the Waynesburg coal, in what is termed by Prof. I. C. White the Dunkard Creek series, and referred very positively by him and Prof. Wm. M. Fontaine to the Permian. The blattarian fauna as thus far determined is unquestionably younger than any known from the Pennsylvania or Illinois rocks, on which we have hitherto depended largely for our knowledge, and consists of a vast assemblage of forms, which will undoubtedly be increased by further search. They number fifty-six species, belonging to five genera, the bulk of them (thirty-six species) to Etoblattina.

The Ohio locality lies at the edge of the township of Richmond, on Wills Creek, in the near neighborhood of Steubenville, Jefferson county, and though far less extensive and less thoroughly worked than Cassville, has already yielded twenty-two species belonging to three genera, of which the larger number (seventeen) belong to Etoblattina and the others to the genera represented at Cassville by more than a single species.

It is a curious fact, to which I called partial attention when first describing some of them, that these species represent for the most part a distinct group of cockroaches of the genera ETOBLATTINA and GERABLATTINA, characterized by great length and slenderness of the internomedian area, by a remarkable openness of the neuration in tha middle of the tegmina, and by their frequently exceptional length and slenderness. They comprise, indeed, nearly 75 per cent. of the species of these two genera at Richmond, and hardly occur elsewhere excepting at Cassville, where they compose about 25 per cent. of the species of these two genera. The only occurrence of a similar form in Europe is ETOBLATTINA ELONGATA from the lower Dyas of Weissig, Saxony. The occurrence of this type of cockroaches is the characteristic feature of Richmond, and must place this fauna high in the series, as the stratigraphical evidence itself warrants. Its horizon, according to Mr. Huston, who alone has explored the location, is in the Barren Coal-measures, a little above the crinoidal limestone.

It is remarkable that, notwithstanding the close relationship in general features of the two rich faunas, of Cassville and Richmond, not a single species has been found common to the two. One species, indeed, I formerly regarded as found in both, but a closer study convinces me that there are in this case two nearly allied forms, and they are accordingly separated in this paper. Further than this, with one or two exceptions, no American species has been found in two different places, and without exception the American species are completely distinct from the European.''

The complete list of these Cassville species as given by Scudder on page 14, Bulletin 124, U. S. G. Survey, is as follows:

Etoblattina lata

sagittaria	Etoblattinna expugnata
mediana	obatra
ovata	imperfecta
debilis	secreta
balteata	invisa
patiens	occulta
mucronata	defossa
detecta	recidiva
exigua	Gerablatina inculta
residua	perita
funeraria	diversinervis
expuncta	cassvici
aperta	abdicata
eakiniana	concinna
accubita	uniformis
expulsata	permanenta
gratiosa	permacra
macerata	eversa
immolata	deducta
mactata	radiata
communis	lata
exsecuta	rotundata
arcta	ovata
praedulcis	Anthracoblattina virginiensis
angusta	Poroblattina gratiosa
macilenta	fossa
rogi	complexinervis
	Petrablattina hastata

CHAPTER III.

MONONGAHELA SERIES, NO. XV. OF ROGERS.

THICKNESS AND GENERAL CHARACTERISTICS.

This series begins at base with the celebrated Pittsburg coal, and extends up to the Cassville shale. The thickness varies from 260 odd feet along the Ohio river boundary to over 400 feet in the central portion of the great Appalachian basin.

Within this interval there belong six distinct coal beds, viz: Waynesburg, Little Waynesburg, Uniontown, Sewickley, Redstone and Pittsburg. These coals have their greatest development along the waters of the Monongahela river, and hence the series was long ago named after that stream by Prof. H. D. Rogers.

In the northern part of the state, nearly one-half of the rock material composing the Monongahela series is limestone, red shales are unknown, while massive sandstones are seldom found except along the eastern side of the Monongahela outcrop. The disintegration of these limestones, limy shales and other soft rocks at the north, gives origin to a gentle topography, and an extremely fertile soil, thus forming in Monongalia, Marion, Harrison, Lewis, Marshall, Ohio and Brooke counties, as well as in portions of Upshur, Barbour and Taylor, the finest agricultural and grazing regions in the state.

In passing southwest from Harrison, Taylor and Lewis counties, however, the limestones practically disappear, along with most all the coal beds, while red shales come in as the limestones go out, apparently replacing the latter, and the sandstones grow more massive than in the northern area, thus giving origin to a rugged topography, and less fertile soils.

These rocks extend over a wide area along the Ohio river and for many miles south of it, as far as the Great Kanawha, and in a narrow belt from that point to the Big Sandy where in the center of the Appalachian trough, the lowest of these beds passes into the air before reaching the Kentucky line.

No marine fossils have ever been discovered in any of the limestones of the Monongahela series, and everything indicates that the deposits are of fresh water origin. The black slates always contain fish remains in the shape of scales and teeth, but nothing is known of their affinities, because they haver never been studied. The water may have been estuarine, and slightly brackish, but the minute Cyprian, and Estherian-like forms whose skeletons—mostly broken and pulverized—make up the principal mass of the Monongahela limestones, testify clearly against their marine origin.

The number and thickness of the several coal beds, and the character of the interstratified rock material as well as the total thickness of the Monongahela series in the different regions of the State will now be shown by several detailed sections. The first one of these is from a few miles north of the State line in Fayette Co., Pennsylvania, where the deep Lambert shaft of the American Coke Co., in the Klondike region just east from the Monongahela river, passes through the entire series. The record of this was kindly furnished by Mr. O. W. Kennedy, General Supt. of the Frick Coke Co., and reads as follows:

	LAMBERT SHAFT SECTION.	FEET.	FEET.
Coal, Waynesb'rg	coal.................................. 3' slate.................................. 2' coal.... .... 3'		8.0
Fireclay...		2.0	
Gilboy sandstone	sandstone. ....12.0' sandy shale..................... 3.0' white sandstone............... 1.0' dark sandy slate........... 17.8'	.. 33.8	71.0
Coal, Little Waynesburg...........		0.2	
Slate............................		7.0	
Limestone, Waynesburg...24.0			
Sandstone 4.0			

COAL, UNIONTOWN..2.0'

Black slate.. .... 2.0

Great limestone of Rogers

limestone........................69.0'		
sandstone.................. .... 3.0'		
limestone.. ....23.0'		
soapstone........................ 1.0'	159.0	186.0
gray slate....................... 5.0'		
limestone......................19.0'		
sandstone.. .... 2.0'		
gray slate....................... 3.0'		
limestone......................34.0'		

Fireclay.. 2.5
Dark sandstone, Sewickley 15.6
Black slate.. .. 6.9

CANNEL SLATE, SEWICKLEY COAL horizon............................. 4.0

Fireclay 3.0
Limestone, Sewickley..18.0   43.5
Fireclay..16.5
Black slate... .... 6.0

COAL, REDSTONE........ .... 1.0

Limestone, Redstone..... ....15.0
Fireclay... .... 6.0   38.0
Sandstone and slate... ....17.0

PITTSBURG "ROOF" COALS

coal........ .... 1.0'	
black slate................... .... 1.0	
coal.................... .... 0.8	
black slate. 0.5	4.9
coal............................. 0.3	
black slate.................... 0.8	
coal............................. 0.5	

Black sandy slate................. ....18.6   20.6
Sandstone....... .... 2.0

COAL, PITTSBURG............ .... 9.0
                                                              ─────
                 Total.. 388.0

Here we find the "roof" coals of the Pittsburg bed separated from the main coal by an interval of slate, etc., of 20 feet, and the Monongahela totaling 388 feet in thickness. Of this mass, 44 feet is included in the several coal beds and black slates of the series, 202 feet is limestone, and the remaining 142 feet is sandy and shaly sediment. But of the 44 feet of bituminous material, only 20 feet or less than half could properly be designated as COAL.

On Scott's Run, Monongalia Co., the writer once measured a section between Cassville and Osage, which gave the following results (Bulletin No. 65, U. S. G. Survey, page 47):

SCOTT'S RUN SECTION.

		Ft. in.	Ft. in.
COAL, WAYNESBURG	coal .... 2' 0'' shale. fossiliferous ... ... 1 0 coal. .... 1 4 shale, gray..... .... 1 6 coal 5 0		10 10
Black slate............		1 0	
Sandy shales, with iron ore...............................		25 0	
Limestone, Waynesburg............................		8 0	99 00
Sandy shales, with limestone layers...........................		30 0	
Sandstone massive........,................................		20 0	
Limestone and shales...............................		15 0	
BLACK SLATE. REPRESENTING UNIONTOWN coal................			2 0
Limestone, interstratified with thin shales, cement beds near base................... ....105 0			145 0
Sandstone, Sewickley...........................		40 0	
COAL, SEWICKLEY			5 0
Shales.........		5 0	
Sandstone		10 0	
Limestone		5 0	
Shales, greenish gray..		8 0	65 0
Concealed.........,...		15 0	
Limestone, steel gray..............		7 0	
Concealed.....		15 0	

		Ft. in.	Ft. in.
COAL, REDSTONE...............			4 00
Limestone, Redstone....................................		18 0	
Shale and fireclay		5 0	28 0
Slate, black...............................		5 0	
COAL, PITTSBURG "ROOF"	coal............... 0' 3'' shale .... 2 0 coal............... 1 0 clay............... 1 0	4 3	
COAL, PITTSBURG, MAIN BENCH	coal............... 3' 6'' slate............ 0 ½ coal............ 0 8 slate............ 0 1 coal .... 1 6 slate .... 0 ½ coal............ 0 6 slate............ 0 ½ coal...... .... 3 3	9 7½	13 10½
Total... ....372 8½			

Near the head of Indian Creek, Monongalia Co., and not far
from Hagans P. O., a test hole was completed during May, 1902,
through the entire Monongahela series by Mr. Joseph E. Barnes,
of Uniontown, Pa. The boring began 126 feet above the Waynesburg coal and as a core was taken out through the whole series,
the record is a very valuable one, since it gives exact measure-

ments between important strata. The boring was made on the land of D. J. Eddy and kindly placed at the disposal of the Survey by Mr. Barnes. It reads as follows:

D. J. EDDY BORING RECORD.

		Ft. in.	Ft. in.
COAL, WAYNESBURG {	coal	0 6	
	shale	1 3	7 7
	coal	5 10	
Shale		1 5	
Shale with streaks of lime		3 0	
Sand shale		23 0	
LIMESTONE, WAYNESBURG		7 0	
Sand shale		7 0	
Sandstone		16 0	
Shale		6 0	
Limestone		1 0	
Sand shale		9 0	
Sandstone		3 0	
Sand shale		9 0	
Limestone		10 6	225 0
Sand shale		13 0	
Limestone		30 6	
Blue shale		2 6	
Limestone		14 6	
Shale		5 0	
Black shale		1 0	
Limestone		9 0	
Blue shale		5 0	
Limestone		10 0	
Limestone		4 0	
Lime shale		6 0	
Sandstone, Sewickley		53 6	
COAL, SEWICKLEY		6 8	6 8
Shale		4 10	6 10
Lime shale		2 0	
Limestone Sewickley {	limestone	3 0	
	lime shale	1 0	
	limestone	8 0	34 0
	soft shale	2 0	
	shale	2 0	
	limestone	18 0	
Lime shale		5 0	8 0
Soft shale		3 0	
COAL, REDSTONE			1 0
Black Slate		14 0	
Sand Shale		1 0	
Limestone, Redstone		1 00	27 6
Blue shale		7 0	
Black shale		4 6	

		Ft.	in.
Coal "roof"..		1	6
COAL, PITTSBURG...		7	7
Total..		355	7

Just east from Farmington, Marion Co., W. Va., a diamond drill boring was made on the land of J. L. Davis by the George's Creek Coal and Iron Co. in 1897, through the Pittsburg coal which there underlies Buffalo creek by about 230 feet. The writer examined the core and connected its record with the surface exposures above the level of the bore hole. The following section of the Monongahela series results:

FARMINGTON SECTION.

		Ft.	in.		Ft.	in.
COAL, WAYNESBURG	coal...	0	6			
	shale..	0	2			
	coal..	1	0		6	0
	fireclay	1	4			
	coal..	3	0			
Concealed		4	0			
SANDSTONE, GILBOY, massive................................		30	0			
Concealed and sandy shales.................................		25	0			
Limestone, yellow magnesian...............................		8	0		104	0
Shales, limy...		7	0			
Sandy shales and massive sandstone......................		30	0			
COAL, UNIONTOWN, impure..................................					2	0
Concealed and sandy shales................................		16	0			
Black slate		1	0			
Limestone..		2	0			
Sandy shale...		10	0			
Sandstone		5	0			
Shales...		5	0			
Limestone, yellow and impure.............................		8	0			
Red shale..		5	0			
Limy shales and concealed to top of bore hole.............		27	0		193	9
Sand and clay (surface)		13	2			
Limestone, yellow and gray...............................		9	6			
Shaly limestone and green shale..........................		30	0			
Limestone, gray...		5	0			
Shale, green...		5	0			
Limestone, gray...		14	0			
Limy shale...		6	0			
Sandstone, Sewickley, micaceous with streaks of sandy shale..........		31	1			
Black slate........		1	0			
COAL, SEWICKLEY	coal.....................3' 0"					
	slate......................0' 2"				6	4
	coal.... ....3' 2"					

Shale, soft and gray..	6	6
Limy shale.....................................	5	6
Sandy shale.........	2	6
Limy shales, gray, and getting sandy at base.............	18	0
Limestone, gray..	20	0
Shales, green..	3	6
Limestone, gray...	3	0
Limy shales and impure limestone	25	8
Sandstone, Pittsburg, micaceous and interstratified with dark sandy shale....	16	5
Shale, sandy..	6	1

107 2

COAL, PITTSBURG	coal, "roof"...........................	1	5
	over clay........	0	7½
	bone coal....................	0	2½
	coal, good...............................	2	8
	coal with thin slates.	0	4
	coal, good.........	3	10

9 1

426 4

This is the thickest measurement known for the Monongahela series, except the one at Berryburg, Barbour Co. The massive, pebbly Waynesburg sandstone crops out in a bold cliff just above the horizon of the Waynesburg coal which is mined in the hills at Farmington, although not visible in the concealed interval at the top of this section.

THE REDSTONE COAL is entirely absent here as also in the vicinity of Fairmont farther east where these rocks are exposed at the surface.

In contrast with this thick section of the Monongahela may be set the one shown in Chapline Hill, Wheeling, Ohio Co., where in the 50 miles of northwestward thinning, between Farmington and the Ohio river, the total section has decreased nearly 160 feet. This measurement was made by the writer and published in Bulletin 65, U. S. G. Survey, page 49, as follows:

CHAPLINE HILL, WHEELING.

	Ft. in.		Ft. in.	
COAL, WAYNESBURG...			2	0
Concealed	5	0		
Flaggy sandstone, filled with plant fragments.............	4	0		
Concealed	4	0		
Limestone, shales and concealed...........	60	0		
Sandstone, massive, gray...................................	5	0		
Limestone and concealed....................................	20	0		
Green shale..	5	0		
Limestone, interstratified with shales........................	55	0		

158 0

		Ft. in.	Ft. in.
COAL, SEWICKLEY	coal................................ 1 0 } sandy shales with plants........ 12 0 } coal................................ 0 8 }		13 8
Shales .... 8 0 }			
Sandstone, rather massive, micaceous, current bedded	20 0 }		29 0
Limestone, impure, flaggy, filled with fossil ferns. 1 0)			
COAL, REDSTONE...............			0 10
Limestone, mostly buffish and impure...... .... 55 0)			55 0
COAL, PITTSBURG	coal "roof"........................ 2 0 } shale.............................. 2 0 } coal, main bench.................. 5 0 }		9 0
Total..........			267 6

Here the Sewickley coal appears to be split into two widely separated -layers, and the REDSTONE representative as well as the WAYNESBURG is thin and unimportant, so that the PITTSBURG bed is the only merchantable coal in the entire series.

Mr. J. E. Barnes, of Uniontown, Pa. has put down several drill holes through the Pittsburg coal in the southwestern portion of Marshall Co., 20 odd miles south from Wheeling and has generously placed these records at the disposal of the State Survey.

One of these drilled on the Anderson farm, Whetstone run, 2 miles south from Fish creek, passes through the Monongahela series and gives the following accurate record of the several strata as kept by the driller:

ANDERSON FARM BORING RECORD.

	Ft. in.	Ft. in.
COAL, WAYNESBURG..		2 0
Sandstone	2 0)	
Shale	6 0	
Sandstone	3 0	
Shale..	0 0	
Sandstone	4 0	
Red shale..	6 0	
Blue shale...	2 0	
Mixed shale...	13 0	
Shale...	5 6	
Red shale...	1 6	
Sandstone	4 0	
Sandshale..	5 6	
Shale..	13 6	
Red shale..	4 0	
Shale and limestone.................................	9 0	
Shale..	1 0	
Limestone	2 0	
Blue shale..	2 0 }	207 0

Red shale........	2	0
Limestone ....….........	1	0
Sandstone ....…............................	4	0
Red shale..	1	0
Blue shale	1	0
Sand shale..	3	6
Red shale...	4	0
Sand shale...	12	0
Limestone	4	0
Sand shale..............................	1	0
Limestone	9	0
Limestone	5	0
Blue shale	2	0
Lime shale..	5	0
Limestone	6	0
Lime shale.....................	22	0
Soft shale......	4	0

COAL, SEWICKLEY ....…............... 3

Sandstone ....…...........	3'	4"
Limestone ....…..................	34	0
Sand shale..	5	0
Blue shale	1	0
Lime shale................................	2	0
Blue shale	1	0
Sandstone	4	0
Blue shale	3	0
Limestone..........	2	0
Dark shale.........	2	0
Limestone	3	0
Green shale..........................	2	6
Lime shale...	5	6
Limestone	9	0
Soft shale.........................	3	0
Sand shale...	1	0
Soft shale	6	7

}...................................87 11

COAL, PITTSBURG.......... .... - 5 5

Total................. ....306 0

This last record gave no trace of either the UNIONTOWN, or REDSTONE COAL, but at another well drilled by Mr. Barnes on the land of David Abersold, one mile north from Proctor, Marshall Co., we find representatives of both these beds as shown in the following:

DAVID ABERSOLD BORING RECORD.

	Ft.	in.		Ft.	in.
Surface	6	0			
Sand and gravel.........	12	0			
Clay...	3	0			
Clay and gravel....................	7	0			
Sandstone	4	0	} 77		0
Sand shale...	17	0			
Red shale	14	0			
Sand shale..	12	0			
Blue shale....................	2	0			

	Ft. in.	Ft. in.
COAL, UNIONTOWN..		0 9
Blue shale.. ..	5 3	
Sand shale......................................	15 0	
Sandstone.......................................	2 0	
Sand shale......................................	3 0	
Red shale.......................................	2 0	
Blue shale	3 0	
Lime shale....	4 0	
Soft shale.......................................	2 0	
Limestone....	4 0	
Red shale............................	1 0	
Limestone	4 0	
Lime shale.	12 0	
Mixed shale	2 0	
Red shale...............	4 0	
Sand shale......................................	3 0	146 3
Mixed shale	2 0	
Limestone	10 0	
Blue shale	4 0	
Red shale.....	1 0	
Blue shale....................................	2 0	
Limestone	10 0	
Lime shale............................:......	5 0	
Limestone	5 0	
Light blue shale.................................	3 0	
Limestone	17 0	
Shale and limestone.............	7 0	
Limestone.	5 0	
Shale and limestone...	6 0	
Blue shale	1 0	
Soft shale.	2 0	
COAL, SEWICKLEY { coal.................	1 8	2 4
{ bone coal.	0 8	
Sandstone	3 8	
Limestone with streaks of shale............	11 6	
Shale..	4 6	
Limestone..................	6 6	
Lime shale.......................................	2 6	59 10
Limestone	3 0	
Lime shale......................	4 0	
Sand shale......................................	18 0	
Sandstone	4 0	
Blue shale....................	2 2	
COAL, REDSTONE...		1 1
Blue shale ... .+............	2 9	
Limestone.............................	14 0	23 7
Blue shale	4 0	
Soft shale.........................	2 10	
COAL, PITTSBURG...		5 11
Total 316 9		

This boring starts where the horizon of the WAYNESBURG COAL
is covered up by the 12 feet of "sand and gravel" near the top,

for in the previous section the interval between the WAYNESBURG COAL and the SEWICKLEY COAL is 207 feet, hence if we subtract this from the interval between the Sewickley coal of the Abersold boring and the surface, we find that it would extend to within about 17 feet of the top of the boring, and there would be the horizon of the WAYNESBURG COAL.

Another hole drilled by Mr. Barnes on the C. Higgs farm near Franklin Station, Marshall Co., in this same region is interesting as showing the "roof" division of the Pittsburg coal as follows:

C. HIGGS BORING RECORD.

	Ft. in.	Ft. in.
Surface...	20 0	
Shale....	3 0	
Limestone and shale............................	9 0	
Limestone	17 0	
Shale...	7 0	
Limestone	1 0	
Shale...	1 0	..............130 0
Limestone..	37 0	
Lime and shale.	3 0	
Limestone..	12 0	
Limestone shale.	8 0	
Limestone	9 0	
Shale.	3 0	
COAL, SEWICKLEY..................................		3 6
Soft Shale..	1 6	
Sandstone..	5 0	
Shale and lime....................................	17 0	
Limestone	6 6	
Sandstone	13 6	
Limestone	6 0	
Lime and sandstone............................	3 0	.............., 83 6
Sand shale.........	11 0	
Shale.	1 0	
Limestone	10 0	
Lime and shale............:	2 0	
Shale.	7 0	
COAL, PITTSBURG. { coal "roof".......	2 0	.... 7 9
{ slate.................	0 6	
{ coal................	5 3	
Total		224 9

This boring begins below the WAYNESBURG COAL, and also below the horizon of the UNIONTOWN as shown in the last record.

Another hole drilled by Mr. Barnes on the Nellie Workman farm, near the mouth of Little Tribble run, on Fish creek in this same region of Marshall Co., gave the following results:

NELLIE WORKMAN BORING RECORD.

	Ft.	in.		Ft.	in.
Surface................	17	0			
Sand, shale and gravel................	9	0			
Red shale................	5	0			
Sand shale................	3	0			
Limestone................	2	0			
Blue shale................	5	0			
Limestone................	9	0			
" with shale partings...	10	0			
" shale.......	5	0			
Soft shale..........	2	0			
Red shale................	1	0			
Sand shale................	2	0			
Limestone shale..	5	0	144	0
Soft shale........	2	0			
Limestone	3	0			
Sandstone................	4	6			
Shale................	3	0			
Lime shale................	11	6			
Limestone...........	10	0			
Green shale................	1	0			
Sand shale................	3	0			
Limestone................	5	0			
Lime and shale mixed........	13	0			
Limestone................	7	0			
Limestone and shale mixed	4	6			
Shale................	1	6			
COAL, SEWICKLEY................				3	6
Sandstone................	8	0			
Limestone................	33	6			
Sand shale........	3	0			
Limestone................	4	0	 60	10
Blue shale................	5	0			
Limestone	3	0			
Hard shale................	1	4			
Blue shale	3	0			
COAL, REDSTONE................				1	2
Shale................	8	3			
Limestone, mixed with shale................	7	0	 27	1
Black shale................	11	10			
COAL, PITTSBURG................				5	7
Total 242	4				

This section shows both the SEWICKLEY and REDSTONE COALS, the latter twenty-seven feet above the PITTSBURG, and the former eighty-nine feet above the same datum.   It started too low, however, to catch the WAYNESBURG BED which should crop in the hills about seventy feet above the top of the boring.   The intervals between the SEWICKLEY and PITTSBURG COALS in these last five sections show remarkable uniformity as follows:

	Ft.	In.
Chapline Hill Wheeling....................................	84	10
Anderson Farm...	87	11
David Abersold...	84	6
C. Higgs..	83	6
Nellie Workman...	89	1

Passing southeast from the region of these Marshall county test borings a distance of twenty odd miles to Pine Grove, Wetzel county, we get an accurate view of the character and thickness of the Monongahela series there, from the record of a bore hole drilled by Hon. J. N. Camden, near the junction of the North and South Forks of Fishing Creek. The writer personally inspected the core and verified the character and thickness of the several strata given in the record as brought up by the core drill. It reads as follows:

PINE GROVE BORING RECORD.

	Ft.	in.		Ft.	in.
COAL, WAYNESBURG....................				0	6
Fireclay..............................	5	3			
Sandstone............................	4	0			
Fireclay..............................	2	0			
Sandstone, Gilboy....................	32	0			
Soft shale, gray......................	7	0			
Sandy shale..........................	3	0		96	0
Soft shale, gray......................	4	0			
Sandy shale..........................	2	0			
Sandstone, blue......................	8	0			
Sandy shale and sandstone..........	23	0			
Soft shale, gray......................	5	9			
COAL, UNIONTOWN, top bony..........				1	6
Fireclay..............................	0	1			
Sandstone............................	7	8			
Soft gray shale......................	2	0			
Sandstone............................	22	0			
Limestone............................	10	0			
Sandy shale..........................	2	0			
Limestone............................	17	0			
Sandy shale..........................	3	0			
Soft gray shale......................	4	0			
Sandy shale..........................	2	0		143	11
Limy shale...........................	5	0			
Limestone............................	20	0			
Gray shale...........................	3	0			
Limestone............................	10	0			
Gray shale...........................	2	0			
Limestone............................	31	0			
Soft gray shale......................	3	0			
COAL, SEWICKLEY.....................				2	2
Sandstone............................	4	0			
Soft gray shale......................	11	10			
Limestone............................	6	0			

	Ft.	In.		Ft.	In.
Limy shale...................................	10	0			
Sandstone	6	0			
Limy shale...................................	4	0	....	79	6
Limestone	5	0			
Sandstone	16	0			
Shales, gray...............	8	0			
Shaly sandstone................................	3	0			
Shale, gray	5	8			
COAL, REDSTONE			....	1	7
Sandy shales...................................	3	9			
Limestone	12	0			
Soft gray shale........................	2	0	....	24	9
Sandstone	2	0			
Shales, gray	5	0			
COAL, PITTSBURG...................................				2	2
				351	9

The WAYNESBURG COAL is only six inches thick here and lies eighty feet below the bed of Fishing creek, while the WASHINGTON COAL of the Dunkard series crops out forty-five feet above the stream, and has been mined to a small extent to supply the village. Curiously enough it contains more fuel than any member of the Monongahela series below, since even the Pittsburg coal has dwindled to only twenty-six inches, the basal three inches of which is slate and bone.

The thickness of the Monongahela rock series has increased to near its normal, and all of its five main coals, though thin and poor, are represented at the proper horizons.

Mr. Camden thought the Pine Grove boring had struck a "roll" or "fault" in the PITTSBURG COAL, and concluded to put down another test boring two miles farther down Fishing Creek, near the mouth of Piney Fork, where an oil well boring had reported six feet of Pittsburg coal. The boring was located only a few feet distant from the oil well, but when the Pittsburg coal was struck the core barrel brought up only twenty-four inches of coal and thirty-six inches of black slate. The records of these two borings constitute the data for drawing the productive outcrop of the Pittsburg coal to the east of Pine Grove.

About twenty-five miles southeast from Pine Grove, Mr. Barnes drilled another test well through the Pittsburg coal, on the land of Mr. J. Hudson, near Sedalia, Doddidge county, three miles west from the Harrison-Doddridge county line, with the following results :

J. HUDSON FARM BORING.

		Ft.	In.		Ft.	In.
Surface		27	0			
Blue sand shale		5	0			
Red shale		12	0			
Sandstone		2	0		61	0
Blue shale		2	0			
Blue shale		2	0			
Sandstone		5	0			
Blue sand shale		6	0			
BLACK AND GRAY SHALE, WAYNESBURG "A" (?)					2	0
Blue shale		4	0			
Sand shale		12	0			
Waynesburg (?)	sandstone	14	0		116	8
	sandstone	69	0			
Blue shale		17	8			
COAL, UNIONTOWN	coal	0	8			
	shale partings	1	3		3	2
	coal	1	3			
Blue shale		15	2			
Lime and shale mixed		7	0			
Lime and shale		31	0			
Red shale		6	0			
Lime and shale		4	0			
Soft blue shale		4	0		184	2
Blue shale		8	0			
Limestone		52	0			
Blue shale		29	0			
Blue shale		28	0			
COAL, SEWICKLEY					0	6
Soft white shale		0	6			
Blue shale		6	0			
Red shale		4	0			
Blue shale		4	0			
Green shale		10	0			
Blue shale		5	0			
Red shale		2	0		83	0
Soft white shale		3	0			
Sandy shale		10	0			
Sand shale		2	0			
Sandstone		26	0			
Black shale		2	0			
Shale		2	6			
COAL, PITTSBURG					6	10
Total					457	4

This boring begins in the base of the Dunkard series and reveals the complete absence of the WAYNESBURG COAL. The UNIONTOWN COAL appears at its proper horizon, 267' 8" above the Pittsburg bed, while a great thickness of sandstone comes into the measures at a short interval above the former coal. It is quite possible that this is the WAYNESBURG SANDSTONE, here having cut into and eroded the upper portion of the Monongahela series including the WAYNESBURG COAL, since this would agree with conditions found nearly everywhere in the southwestern portion of the state, where the interval from the Waynesburg sandstone to the Pittsburg coal appears to be much less than at the northeast.

This last section can be better interpreted by comparison with the carefully kept record of an oil well boring made by the writer and Prof. T. M. Jackson at Brown in Harrison county, only ten miles distant to the northeast. There the WAYNESBURG COAL, the overlying massive pebbly sandstone, Waynesburg coal "A," and the characteristic multiple bedded Washington coal all crop to the surface, so that the identifications are unmistakable. The Monongahela series has there the following structure as revealed by the oil well record in question:

BROWN OIL WELL RECORD.

	Ft.	In.		Ft.	In.
COAL, WAYNESBURG				3	0
Shale	15	0			
Sandstone, GILBOY, hard, white	35	0		130	0
Shale, soft, limy	80	0			
COAL, UNIONTOWN				5	0
Limestone, hard	30	0			
Shale, soft	15	0			
Limestone and shale	112	0			
Shale, soft, some BLACK (Sewickley coal)	60	0		265	0
Limestone, hard	15	0			
Shale	33	0			
COAL, PITTSBURG				10	0
Total				413	0

A comparison of these two records only ten miles distant along a N. E.—S. W. line will be sufficient evidence that the UNIONTOWN COAL is the same in both, since in the Hudson farm boring near Sedalia, the interval from the Uniontown coal to the Pittsburg, as exactly measured there, is 268 feet, while at Brown the interval is 265 feet, or if we allow three feet for "roof" coal at Brown, which is represented by black slate, etc., at Sedalia, they would be exactly the same. Hence, in any event, there can be no possible doubt of the identity of the Uniontown coal in both sections. The conclusion from this is that either the Waynesburg sandstone, a great massive pebbly rock over all the region at Brown, and south-

westward along its crop, has entirely thinned away and its underlying coal has also disappeared from the Sedalia region, or else the
great sandstone mass, struck at seventy-nine feet and eighty-
three feet thick, is the Waynesburg stratum whose depositing current has there eroded at least 100 feet of measures from the top of
the Monongahela series. As already stated, this latter condition
of affairs appears to exist in many other regions, and it seems the
more plausible theory for Sedalia.

At Clarksburg, Harrison county, a hill known as "Pinnickinnick" rises more than 300 feet above the Pittsburg coal, and
probably includes the entire Monongahela series. Mr. J. L. Johnston, C. E., once measured a section from the top of this knob to
the Pittsburg coal which was published in Bulletin 65, U. S. G.
Survey, page 49, as follows :

CLARKSBURG SECTION.

	Ft.	In.	Ft.	In.
COAL, WAYNESBURG, absent or not seen			0	0
Concealed and yellow sandy shales	65	9		
Sandstone	25	0		
Concealed, with some limestone	80	0		
Sandstone	20	0		
Concealed	5	0	251	0
Sandstone	15	0		
Sandy shales	6	0		
Sandstone, SEWICKLEY	25	0		
Shales	10	0		
COAL, SEWICKLEY			1	0
Limestone { shaly 1' 6" / good 7 6 }	9	0		
Concealed	3	0		
Shales, sandy	14	0		
Shale, with iron nodules	1	0	40	0
Shales, sandy	4	0		
Sandstone	1	0		
Concealed	8	0		
COAL, REDSTONE, slaty			3	0
Shale, dark, bituminous	5	0		
Limestone, Redstone	6	0		
Shale, greenish	13	0	25	0
Slate, bituminous	1	0		
COAL, PITTSBURG { coal 3 5 / bone 0 1 / coal 5 0 }			8	6
Total			328	6

Here nothing is seen of the WAYNESBURG COAL, and it has
probably been eroded, if ever present, by the deposition of the

overlying massive rock which appears to correspond to the Waynesburg sandstone.

The SEWICKLEY COAL, which attains a thickness of five to six feet for forty miles along the Monongahela river, between the Fairmont region and the State line, has here dwindled to only one foot, while the REDSTONE BED, which is absent entirely at Fairmont, has reappeared in the section, slaty and worthless it is true, but soon to become a very important member of the series in other portions of Harrison, Barbour and Upshur counties. This condition of affairs is shown by the following section measured in the vicinity of Berryburg, Barbour countyby C. McC. Lemley, Asst. Engineer B. & O. R. R., as follows:

BERRYBURG SECTION, BARBOUR CO.

	Ft. In.		Ft. In.
COAL, WAYNESBURG, not seen (A. T. 1868)			
Concealed to top of bench (sandstone)...128 0			
Concealed (mostly sandstone)............... 98 0			
Concealed (mostly sandstone)............... 62 0	}	413 0	
Concealed, limestone and shales............ 54 0			
Sandstone and concealed 71 0			
COAL, REDSTONE		5 0	
Shales	11 0		
Limestone, yellowish, Redstone............ 11 0	} ....;	32 0	
Shales................................	10 0		
COAL, PITTSBURG (Above T. 1410)..........		8 0	
Total 458 0			

The Waynesburg sandstone is very massive, pebbly, and caps the highest knobs around Berryburg. The white limestone seen about 175 feet above the Pittsburg coal, is only five feet thick, and is the only representative of the Great limestone farther north where it is 150 feet thick.

This location is the farthest east of any point in the state where the total thickness of the Monongahela series has been obtained, and as was to be expected, it exhibits the greatest thickness of rock material.

Nothing was seen of either the Waynesburg or Sewickley coals and they are probably both absent. The measurements from the Redstone coal to the Pittsburg were made west from Berryburg, on Gnatty creek.

The REDSTONE COAL is quite an important bed in this region of the state, having a thickness of four to seven feet, and carrying little or no bony material. It is mined on an extensive scale by the Century Coal Company at Burnersville, and covers an area of several thousand acres in the Berryburg and Burnersville region, where it lies twenty-eight feet above the Pittsburg coal, from which it is separated by shales and yellow limestone.

Southwestward through Lewis, Gilmer, Calhoun, Ritchie, Roane, Mason and Putnam, a great pebbly, massive sandstone corresponding to the Waynesburg stratum is often found, but no corresponding COAL occurs at the proper horizon above the PITTS-BURG to correlate with the WAYNESBURG COAL. True, we often find a thin coal below the sandstone in question just as in the Sedalia well record, but it corresponds to the UNIONTOWN COAL, and not to the WAYNESBURG. As a type of this condition we may take a section from Leading creek near the eastern border of Gilmer county, as given in Bulletin 65, U. S. G. Survey, page 53, as follows:

LEADING CREEK SECTION.

	Ft.	In.	Ft.	In.
COAL, WAYNESBURG (absent)			0	0
Shales	10	0		
Limestone, brecciated	3	0		
Shales and concealed	35	0		
Sandstone, yellow, soft, massive, pebbly	40	0		
Shales	10	0	235	0
Limestone, impure	2	0		
Shales	40	0		
Sandstone, massive	40	0		
Shales	55	0		
COAL, PITTSB'RG { coaly shales	2	0		
clay	0	10		
bony coal	0	6		
coal	2	4	8	0
bony slate	0	4		
coal }	2	0		
Total			243	0

Where the PITTSBURG COAL rises out of the Ohio river, near Hartford, Mason county, we get a great cliff of Waynesburg sandstone high up in the hills, and measuring from its base down, we get the succession published in Bulletin 65, U. S. G. Survey, page 54, as follows:

HARTFORD SECTION, MASON CO.

	Ft.	In.	Ft.	In.
COAL, WAYNESBURG, absent			0	0
Red shale	10	0		
Gray shale	5	0		
Sandstone	6	0		
Shales, brown and sandy	10	0		

	Ft.	In.	Ft.	In.
Shales, red..	2	0		
Concealed	14	0		
Red shale with limestone nodules..........	10	0		
Sandstone	20	0	250	0
Shales, variegated with limestone no- dules near base........................	28	0		
Concealed	20	0		
Red shale.............	5	0		
Concealed	20	0		
Red shale..	15	0		
Sandstone, massive Pittsburg...............	70	0		
Shales, gray, fossil plants.....................	15	0		
COAL, PITTSBURG...			5	6
Total...			255	6

Here the only coal in the series is the PITTSBURG, and all that is left of the great limestone of the northern portion of the State are a few limestone nodules near the center, while much red shale contrasts strangely with its complete absence at the north.

Near Arbuckle, Mason county, on the Great Kanawha and eighteen miles above its mouth, a coal bed comes into the section under a very massive sandstone which appears to be the Waynesburg, and the following section was compiled there by combining the surface exposures with the record of a drilling through the PITTSBURG COAL, as published on page 54, Bulletin 65, U. S. G. Survey:

ARBUCKLE SECTION, MASON CO.

		Ft.	In.	Ft.	In.
COAL, WAYNESBURG	coal, slaty.........	0	10		
	coal, sulpherous	0	8		
	shale, dark.........	0	5	 3	0
	coal, good	0	8		
	coal, slaty.........	0	5		
Shales, sandstone and concealed		150	0		
Sandstone, blue.........		4	0		
Shales, red.		2	0	178	0
Sandstone, blue and hard.....................		14	0		
Shales, variegated...............................		8	0		
COAL, SEWICKLEY...				1	0
Sandstone		6	0		
Shales, red..		4	0	58	0
Shales, variegated................................		48	0		
COAL, REDSTONE HORIZON, impure fireclay.....................				2	0
Sandstone, coarse, white, Pittsburg.......				29	0
COAL, PITTSBURG HORIZON, fireclay and shale with a little slaty coal at bottom...................................				10	0
Total.........				281	0

This coal at the top of the section occupies the same geological horizon as the UNIONTOWN BED in Harrison, Doddridge, Lewis, Gilmer and Calhoun, and is most probably the same stratum instead of the WAYNESBURG as formerly supposed.

About twenty miles farther up the Great Kanawha, at Red House, opposite Winfield, Putnam county, the entire Monongahela series is exposed in the steep hill side and there exhibits the succession given on page 55, Bulletin 65, U. S. G. Survey, as follows:

RED HOUSE SECTION, PUTNAM CO.

	Ft.	In.		Ft.	In.
COAL, WAYNESBURG,				0	0
Red shale with limestone nodules	5	0			
Sandstone, shaly	10	0			
Concealed	10	0			
Red shale	10	0			
Sandstone, flaggy	30	0			
Red shales, with limestone	10	0			
Sandstone, shaly	20	0		250	0
Red shale	25	0			
Sandstone, shaly	10	0			
Red shales	10	0			
Sandstone, flaggy	10	0			
Concealed	10	0			
Red shale with limestone nodules near base	15	0			
Sandstone, red, and gray shales	75	0			
COAL, PITTSBURG HORIZON fireclay				0	0
Total				250	0

This section is peculiar in revealing a complete absence of any coal in the entire Monongahela series. There are doubtless many localities like this in the region southwest from the Parkersburg Branch of the B. & O. R. R.

Farther up the Great Kanawha river the PITTSBURG COAL again comes into the section, and in the vicinity of Raymond City we get the section published in Bulletin 65, page 56, U. S. G. Survey, as follows:

RAYMOND CITY SECTION, PUTNAM CO.

	Ft.	In.		Ft.	In.
COAL, WAYNESBURG, absent				0	0
Concealed, with shale	60	0			
Red shale	30	0			
Sandstone, grey, micaceous	4	0			
Limestone, in red shale	5	0		229	0
Red shale	15	0			
Sandy shale, gray	30	0			

	Ft. In.	Ft. In.
Red shales..	40 0	
Sandy shales, yellowish gray................	45 0	
COAL, REDSTONE HORIZON, black shale....................		2 0
Sandstone, Pittsburg............................	40 0	
Shales...	10 0	50 0

		Ft. In.		
COAL, PITTSBURG, "roof"	coal....................	0 4		
	shale...................	0 4		
	coal....................	0 6	3' 9''	
	shale...................	0 1		
	coal, slaty...........	1 0		
	fireclay...............	1 6		10 7½
COAL, PITTSBURG. main bench	coal, good..	6 0		
	slate....................	0 ¼	6' 10½''	
	coal, slaty	0 10		

Total...291 7½

In the Potomac basin the Monongahela series is no where fully preserved, the Sewickley coal being the highest known member recognized in West Virginia. But in the adjoining region of Maryland, the entire column is found along the George's Creek basin. The summit of the series has there been placed by Dr. G. C. Martin, of the Maryland Survey, at the KOONTZ COAL, which lies only 230 to 240 feet above the PITTBURG BED. This is the proper horizon for the UNIONTOWN COAL of the region west of the Alleghanies, and as there is another coal about 100 feet above the KOONTZ BED in the George's Creek basin, it seems preferable to regard it as the Waynesburg horizon at least tentatively, instead of the Koontz. With this idea in view, the writer has rearranged the nomenclature of the section given by Dr. Martin in page 142 of the Geology of Garrett county, Maryland Geological Survey, as follows:

GEORGE'S CREEK SECTION.

	Ft. In.	Ft. In.
COAL, WAYNESBURG...		4 0
Concealed, with thin coal, (Little Waynesburg) 110 0		110 0
COAL, KOONTZ, (UNIONTOWN)...		1 10
Concealed..................................	20 0	
Limestone..................................	5 7	
Silicious fireclay.........................	3 11	
Sandstone	0 10	
Shale...	4 10	
Sandstone	1 8	115 11
Shale...	20 0	
COAL	0 5	

		Ft.	In.	Ft.	In.
Shale		5	8		
Sandstone, Sewickley		14	2		
Shale		38	0		
COAL, SEWICKLEY (Tyson)	coal	0	10		
	shale	3	0	5	6
	coal	1	8		
Shale		16	0		
Sandstone		4	0		
Shale		25	0	46	0
Sandstone		1	0		
COAL, REDSTONE				2	6
Shale		18	0		
Sandstone		0	10		
Shale		9	6		
Limestone, Redstone		5	6		
Shale		7	8	68	0
Coal and shale, PITTSBURG "ROOF"		7	4		
Shale		18	0		
Sandstone		1	2		
COAL, PITTSBURG.	coal and shale	3	7	13	1
	coal	9	6		
Total				366	9

In this rearrangement of names in Dr. Martin's section, the name "UNIONTOWN" takes the place of what he provisionally termed WAYNESBURG, and the name "REDSTONE" is given to what Dr. Martin called LOWER SEWICKLEY, the REDSTONE of his section being considered more probably a "roof" division of the PITTSBURG similar to that shown in the Lambert shaft section of Fayette county, Pa., page 125 of this volume.

Of course, it may eventually turn out that Dr. Martin's interpretation is the correct one, but as this would necessitate the disappearance of 150 feet of strata between the WAYNESBURG and SEWICKLEY COALS, while the interval from the SEWICKLEY to the PITTSBURG has remained the same as found west of the Alleghenies, the identifications suggested appear to be more in harmony with all the facts, including the general eastward THICKENING of all underlying series.

Having now given a general view of the Monongahela series, the more important individual members will be described in detail.

THE WAYNESBURG COAL.

This highest member of the Monongahela series received its name from Waynesburg, the county seat of Greene county, Pa., just east from which it has long been mined to supply the surrounding region. The seam is always multiple bedded, being generally separated into a "roof," "upper" and "lower" divisions by shale and fire clay partings, the whole often nine to ten feet in thickness. This coal appears to attain its maximum thickness and importance in Marion and Monongalia counties, and the adjoining region of Greene county, Pennsylvania, since it thins down in every direction when traced away from these regions.

The coal is always high in ash and moisture, and hence is a poor steam coal, and is used for that purpose only when nothing better is accessible. Of course there is always some good coal in the bed, but it is generally mixed up with the poorer quality in mining and the resultant fuel is never of first-class grade.

The following section of this coal at David L. Myers' mine on Scotts run, Cass District, Monongalia county, made by Mr. John M. Gregg, will reveal the usual structure of the coal when thick :

	Ft. In.		Ft. In.
Coal	4 5	}	
Impure fireclay	0 8	}	9 2
Coal	4 3	}	

Mr. Gregg collected a sample of this coal entirely across the bed for analysis. It yielded the following results to Prof. B. H. Hite, Chemist for the Survey :

Moisture	1.69
Volatile matter	30.04
Fixed carbon	44.93
Ash	23.34
	100.00
Sulphur	1.98
Phosphorus	0.012

Some of the mines will probably yield a coal lower in ash than this, but none will run much under fifteen per cent. as an average for the whole bed. The lower half of the seam has usually less ash and sulphur than the upper. The "roof" coal is not shown in this section, but it is generally present at one to three feet above the upper bench from which it is separated by a gray shale full of fossil plants and insects in the region of Cassville, Monongalia county.

The following section of this coal near Cassville, will show the triple-bedded structure so common to it in both Monongalia and Marion :

	Ft.	In.		Ft.	In.
Coal "roof"................	1	2	⎫		
Gray fossiliferous shale ..	0	10	⎪		
COAL, upper bench..........	2	6	⎬.............	10	0
Impure fireclay.............	1	6	⎪		
Coal, lower bench...........	4	0	⎭		

This fossiliferous shale on top of the main coal bed contains, as heretofore stated, a rich fossil cock-roach fauna, and many Permian types of plants, so that although apparently a part o the WAYNESBURG COAL, it has been included by the writer as the basal member of the Dunkard series under the term CASSVILLE PLANT SHALE, see page 119 of this volume.

The impure fireclay which separates the two main divisions of the WAYNESBURG COAL, varies much in thickness, often within a few yards swelling from six inches to as many feet. It is usually termed a "horse-back" by the miners, and hence the coal is often locally known as the "horse-back" vein.

The following structure is exhibited by this coal just east of Barracksville, Marion county :

	Ft.	In.		Ft.	In.
Coal, "roof"...............	0	12	⎫		
Shale......................	0	6	⎪		
Coal......................	1	3	⎬.............	6	0
Impure fireclay.............	0	3	⎪		
Coal.......................	3	0	⎭		

This shows a considerable reduction in thickness from the Monongalia county type.

About three miles west of Farmington, Marion county, an opening in the Waynesburg coal, 120 feet above the B. & O. R. R. shows the following:

					Ft.	In.		Ft.	In.
Coal, "roof"..............					0	1	⎫		
Gray shale with fossil......							⎪		
plants.........					3	6	⎪		
COAL, upper bench	coal	0'	12"	⎫	2	8	⎬.............	10	0
	shale	0	6	⎬			⎪		
	coal	1	2	⎭			⎪		
Impure fireclay.............					0	4	⎪		
Coal, lower bench....					3	0	⎭		

Here the upper bench is split into two portions by a layer of shale, but otherwise the coal has the same type as that in Monongalia, except that there is less thickness of actual coal.

Westward from this point the coal dips down and passes under Buffalo creek near the eastern boundary of Mannington, where it thins to less than two feet before going below water level. When this coal comes out to daylight along the Ohio river hills just below Moundsville, it exhibits the following structure :

	Ft. In.	Ft. In.
Coal, bony......................	o 6 ⎫	
Impure fireclay	1 o ⎬ .... 3 o	
Coal, slaty........	1 6 ⎭	

The stratum is here 275 feet above the Pittsburg seam, and although thin and worthless, still retains its double-bedded structure. The coal is of practically no economic importance at any point yet known along the Ohio river.

In the vicinity of St. Marys, Pleasants county, a coal was formerly mined to a small extent under a massive sandstone. It varies from one to two feet in thickness, and was once supposed to represent the WAYNESBURG COAL. It appears, however, to be identical with the Macksburg coal of Ohio, and this correlates with the UNIONTOWN COAL of the Monongahela series.

There is also a coal found at 250 to 275 feet above the Pittsburg seam at many localities in Lewis, Gilmer, Ritchie, Calhoun, Roane, and on through to the Great Kanawha, that has always been considered identical with the WAYNESBURG BED, but it may possibly represent the UNIONTOWN horizon. It has been mined at several places along Tanner's creek, Gilmer county, and is two and one-half to three feet thick, generally single bedded, and makes a fair domestic fuel. It is mined in the hills at Tanner postoffice 140 feet above creek level, and 125 feet vertically above another coal which appears to come at the horizon of the Sewickley coal.

This same coal which is mined in the hills along Tanner creek extends northeastward onto Fink and Leading creeks, and is also found on the tributaries of Sand Fork in Lewis and Gilmer counties. It is seldom more than three feet in thickness and is sometimes called the "Chestnut Oak" vein because it crops high up in the hills where that tree abounds.

Between Long Run and West Union, Doddridge county, a bed of coal two and one-half to three feet thick is frequently seen below a massive, pebbly sandstone, and has been opened in several localities. It furnishes a fairly good fuel for domestic use, and is supposed to represent the WAYNESBURG BED, though it may possibly be the UNIONTOWN.

On account of its high per centage of ash the WAYNESBURG COAL is not of any present economic importance anywhere in the state, except for local domestic use, where no better fuel can be obtained. It is possible that when mined on a commercial scale, and the bone coal discarded, some of the areas in Marion and Monongalia may furnish a marketable grade of steam and domestic coal.

THE LITTLE WAYNESBURG COAL.

Underlying the main WAYNESBURG COAL, at an interval of ten to twenty feet, we frequently find a thin streak of coal from six to twelve inches thick, which Dr. John J. Stevenson has termed the LITTLE WAYNESBURG BED. It never attains minable thickness and hence is of no economic importance.

THE GILBOY SANDSTONE.

Very frequently, and especially along the eastern crop of the WAYNESBURG COAL, a great sandstone mass comes into the section at five to ten feet below that coal, cutting out the LITTLE WAYNESBURG COAL and its underlying limestone completely. This stratum is very prominent in what is known as "Gilboy" cut on the B. & O. R. R., just east from Mannington, and has been designated from that locality. It was formerly termed the BROWNTOWN SANDSTONE from a locality in Harrison county, where it is very massive, but as there is a BROWNSTOWN SANDSTONE in Kanawha county it was concluded best to change the name of this one to GILBOY.

The stratum in question is a very hard, rather fine-grained, grayish white rock, seldom containing any pebbles, and when present forms a bold cliff or bluff below that of the Waynesburg pebbly sandstone above. It is especially prominent in Marion, Lewis and Gilmer counties.

THE UNIONTOWN COAL.

At 90 to 125 feet below the WAYNESBURG COAL, another rather persistent seam is found, which from its occurrence at Uniontown, Pennsylvania, was named by the First Pennsylvania Geological Survey from that locality.

It is seldom more than three feet thick, often only two, and sometimes represented merely ʰ ⸺ ᴋ SLATE, so that from an economic standpoint ⸱ ᵗ value, since in most cases it is rather hⁱ

This stratum crops along the B. & O. R. R. between Farmington and the George's Creek Coal and Iron Company's shaft just east, and may also be seen along Little Ten Mile creek below Brown. Its position above the PITTSBURG COAL is shown in the Brown boring record page 139, and also in the one at Sedalia, from which it appears possible that the coal often found under a massive sandstone through, Lewis, Gilmer, Roane, Jackson and Mason, and usually considered as identical with the WAYNESBURG, may really be the UNIONTOWN BED. The question is left open for future detailed study of the stratigraphy of the region. Should this suggestion of identity prove true, it would show as heretofore intimated a widely spread erosion of at least 100 feet of strata from the top of the Monongahela series, by the rapid currents which deposited the Waynesburg conglomeratic sandstone, bringing with them the new, or Permian flora, which characterizes the Dunkard series.

The MACKSBURG COAL of Ohio is regarded by the Ohio geologists as identical with the UNIONTOWN COAL, and as already stated, this latter is probably the "Koontz" coal of the George's Creek basin.

The interval that separates the WAYNESBURG and UNIONTOWN COALS frequently appears to hold another massive sandstone just above the latter coal, and when present it is called the UNIONTOWN SANDSTONE.

THE GREAT LIMESTONE.

Lying between the UNIONTOWN COAL and the SEWICKLEY COAL horizon, 200 feet lower, we find in northern West Virginia and the adjoining region of Pennsylvania a great mass of limestone and limy shales well shown in the Lambert shaft record, page 125, where they have a thickness of 159 feet. To these limestones the First Pennsylvania Survey gave the name GREAT LIMESTONE. It is a fresh or brackish water deposit, since no marine forms have ever been seen in the entire mass, the only fossils known being minute bivalve crustacea, and other undescribed types, along with fish remains of unknown affinities.

Some of the limestone layers are highly magnesian, and otherwise impure, and these are so interstratified with the purer layers that very little economic use has ever been made of them. Formerly some of these were quarried in the vicinity of Wheeling and used as a flux in the manufacture of pig iron, but such use has now been discontinued entirely. Many of the layers make fine road material, and also burn into a good quality of lime for building and fertilizing purposes, and they are occasionally so used by the farmers.

As already stated, these limestones disappear and are largely replaced by red shale and sandy beds in passing from the northern end of the state southwestward, so that when one reaches the Little Kanawha river only a few thin layers of impure limestone can be found in the entire series, and this condition of affairs continues on southwestward to the Great Kanawha and beyond.

The portion of the Great Limestone immediately below the UNIONTOWN COAL is generally termed the UNIONTOWN LIMESTONE.

SEWICKLEY SANDSTONE.

Along the eastern crop of the Monongahela series, a thick, massive sandstone frequently comes into the section and cuts out a large portion of the Great Limestone. This sandstone overlies the Sewickley coal closely and hence has been termed the Sewickley sandstone. It is especially prominent along the Monongahela river between Morgantown and Fairmont, and may be seen making great cliffs opposite Beechwood, where it is sixty feet thick. Through Harrison, Lewis, Gilmer and other southwestern counties along the line where the Monongahela series crops to the surface, the Sewickley sandstone, together with the underlying Pittsburg sandstone, often forms a bold cliff rising to a height of 125 to 150 feet above the horizon of the PITTSBURG COAL.

Occasionally the Sewickley sandstone is a good building rock, as at the Stokes Tunstill quarry, high up in the hill along Polk creek, two miles south from Weston.

THE SEWICKLEY COAL.

At 100 feet above the basal member of the Monongahela series, there comes a widely persistent coal bed, named the SEWICK-LEY COAL by the First Geological Survey of Pennsylvania. This bed attains its maximum importance along the Monongahela river in Monongalia and Marion counties, so far as its surface outcrop is known, since it is universally present and of workable (five to six feet) thickness entirely across the river front of these two counties from the Harrison-Marion line to the Pennsylvania boundary, a a distance of more than forty miles. The records of oil and gas borings also reveal its presence under all of the great basin between the Monongahela and Ohio rivers, through western Monongalia and Marion as well as under all of Wetzel and Marshall, although when it crops to the surface at the Ohio river it is only three to three and one-half feet thick. It is generally called the "Mapleton" coal (from a village in Greene county, Pa.) by the oil well drillers. This coal also attains considerable importance in Belmont, Harrison, Guernsey, Monroe, Morgan, Muskingum and Noble counties of Ohio, and has there been mined under a variety of names, among which are "Upper Barnesville," "Upper Bellaire," "Cumberland," "Meigs Creek" and several others. The late Dr. Edward Orton while intimating the identity of this Ohio coal with the SEWICKLEY of Pennsylvania, preferred to call it by the name "Meigs Creek" from a stream in Morgan county along which the coal has a good development.

This coal appears to be present everywhere in the George's Creek-Potomac basin, where its horizon has been preserved from erosion, and is always there a coal of good quality, being known as the "Gas" or "Tyson" vein. It also extends over a considerable area in Greene, Fayette and Westmoreland counties, Pennsylvania. Although so constantly present in the northern portion of the Appalachian basin, this bed thins down and disappears entirely southwestward from Marion county, so that little of it is found of workable thickness in Harrison, except for a few miles west of the Marion county line. It appears to thin out entirely as a workable vein before passing the Parkersburg branch of the B. & O. R. R., since it is only six inches thick in the Sedalia bore hole record, and twelve inches in the Clarksburg section.

There is a coal bed which crops along Tanner creek, in Gilmer county, between Tanner postoffice and the mouth of the stream, which may be the Sewickley. It varies from two to three feet in thickness and is of fair quality. If the coal in the hills, 125 feet above it, be the UNIONTOWN SEAM, then there can be no doubt about the lower bed at Tanner representing the SEWICKLEY COAL, but if the "hill" coal be the WAYNESBURG, then the bottom coal would represent the UNIONTOWN instead of the SEWICKLEY. This question will be cleared up in the detailed study of the county geology, to be undertaken in the future. It can be stated as a general fact, however, that there are no areas of the Sewickley coal south from the Grafton-Parkersburg branch of the B. & O. R. R. that will furnish coal of commercial thickness.

The areas in Marion, Monongalia, Wetzel and Marshall, however, together with a portion of northeastern Harrison, may be counted upon as having valuable deposits of this Sewickley bed.

Lying as it does only 100 feet above the great Pittsburg seam below, the two beds can be operated from the same shaft or drift plant as the case may be.

The coal has a fine reputation for domestic use among the farmers of Marion and Monongalia, who generally prefer it to the Pittsburg coal below, on account of its more open burning, and less fusing character in the grate. The coal is usually interlaminated by thin layers of mineral charcoal, and this structure causes it to burn up with a bright flame, leaving only a fine ash with little clinker, although it carries more ash and sulphur than the PITTSBURG COAL below. The coal is rather too hard to coke well without crushing and washing, but it mines in large blocks with no more fine coal than the Pittsburg, and bears transportation equally well.

The coal, when possessing its normal thickness of five to six feet, is generally split into two members by a layer of slate one to three inches thick, near the center, and sometimes one or both members may be again subdivided by one or more thin slates. This coal is now successfully mined on a commercial scale by the George's Creek Coal and Iron Company at its shaft just east from Farmington, Marion county, where its structure is reported as follows by Mr. S. D. Brady, C. E., who collected the sample from it for the analysis reported on a subsequent page :

		Ft. In.	Ft. In.	Ft. In
Upper bench	coal......... 0 9			
	slate........ 0 ¼			
	coal......... 0 6	2 7¼		
	slate .... 0 ½		6 ¼	
	coal......... 1 3			
Slate..			0 1	
Lower bench			3 4	

Butts run S. 78° E.   Face N. 12° E.   Greatest rise, one per cent., elevation 752 feet above tide. The coal is shipped for steam purposes and is reported to give general satisfaction.

Helens run and Tevebaugh run put into the West Fork river, near Worthington, in Marion county, and as the PITTSBURG COAL is there below water level the SEWICKLEY BED has long been mined in the region for local steam and domestic use.

The following sections in that region showing the structure of the SEWICKLEY COAL, as well as the character of the strata immediately above, were measured by Mr. William S. Stevenson, of Fairmont, W. Va., who has kindly placed his results at the disposal of the Survey.

The section at the Charles Jackson Mine, one-fourth mile above the mouth of Tevebaugh Run, is given as follows by Mr. Stevenson :

	Ft.	In.
Limestone, visible..	4	0
Shales and sandstone (Sewickley).....................................	21	0
Shales and soft coaly slate...	2	6

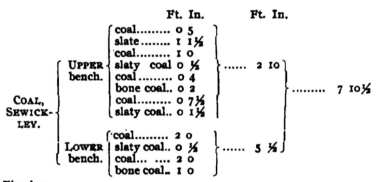

Fireclay ....

Another measurement at the same mine on the working face, 200 feet from the drift opening, gave the following :

	Ft. In.	Ft. In.	Ft. In.
Roof coal, not very good.......... o 7			
Slate, sulphurous..................... o ¼	...... 2 2¼		
Coal........................... I 7		...... 6 6¼	
Coal bony................................. o 1¼			
Coal, lower bench................... .... 4 3			

Thin lenses of slate, from 0″ to ½″ thick and from 0′ to 3′ long, occur irregularly at this mine.

Just below where the Sewickley coal passes under Tevebaugh it exhibits the following structure at the Finley Oakes' heirs opening :

	Ft. In.	Ft. In.
Sandstone		
Slate ....…............	1 0	
Coal, upper bench.	2 3	
Slate ....….	0 ½	
Coal.............................….......	1 11½	6 1½
Slate................................…......	0 1½	
Coal...............................…........	1 9	

At fifty feet in the mine the coal has the following structure :

		Ft. In.	Ft. In.	Ft. In.
Coal, upper bench.	coal......	1 ½		
	slate......	0 1		
	coal......	0 5	2 2	
	slate......	0 1½		
	coal......	0 6		6 2
Slate ....…...........		0 4		
Coal, lower bench, good to bottom..............		3 8		

On Helens run, three-fourths of a mile above its mouth, the SEWICKLEY COAL shows as follows on the land of Mrs. Tetrick:

	Ft. In.	Ft. In.
Hard slate...		1 0
Soft slate...		0 6
Coal, upper bench, thin sulphur bands..........	2 0	
Bone......…...	0 5	5 8
Coal, lower bench	3 3	
Coal, with sulphur balls, bottom not seen.....	.....	

On Mill Fall run which puts into the West Fork river on its north bank just below Monongah, Marion county, this coal shows the following measurement at the Millard Boggess mine, according to Mr. Stevenson :

	Ft. In.	Ft. In.
Coal, upper bench..........................…......	3 5	
Slate..	0 ¼	
Coal...	0 5	5 7¼
Slate...	0 ½	
Coal, lower bench, visible...........................	1 9	

The coal is six feet, three inches thick at the mouth of the entry, and at one point in the mine seven feet, six inches.

Hon. J. W. Paul, State Mine Inspector for West Virginia, made an examination of the SEWICKLEY COAL in this same region of Marion county for Mr. George F. Duck, of Clearfield, Pa., during October, 1900, the results of which have been kindly given the Survey by Mr. Duck, as follows :

Section and analysis of Sewickley coal seam from mine on Tevebaugh creek, about one mile from the West Fork river.

ANALYSES.			SECTION OF COAL.			
	(1)	(2)				
Moisture...............	1.03	0.89	(1) Bone coal roof..........			
Volatile matter........	39 90	41.07	(2) Coal................	o′	6″	
Fixed carbon	47.19	48.18	(3) Bone	o	1	
Ash....................	11.88	9.86	(4) Coal................	o	7	
			(5) Bone	o	1½	
	100.00	100.00	(6) Coal....................	o	9	
			(7) Slate	o	1	
Sulphur	4.80	4.50	(8) Coal................	3	7	
				5	8½	

Analysis No. (1) omits Nos. 3, 5 and 7 of the section.
Analysis No. (2) is of the lower bench No. 8 only.

Section and analysis from mine of D. T. Martin on Little Bingamon creek, near Sturm's Mills :

ANALYSES.			SECTION OF COAL.			
	(1)	(2)				
Moisture................	1.40	1.43	(1) Coal...................	o′	3″	
Volatile matter........	38.15	38.67	(2) Bone and sulphur......	o	1½	
Fixed carbon..........	49.87	51.21	(3) Coal...................	o	11	
Ash	10.58	8.69	(4) Parting	o	0½	
			(5) Coal	o	4½	
	100.00	100.00	(6) Slate...................	o	0¼	
Sulphur...............	3.47	4.42	(7) Coal	3	o	
				4	8¾	

Analysis No. (1) omits Nos. 1 and 2 of the section.
Analysis No. (2) omits Nos. 1, 2 and 6 of the section.
Sulphur balls up to four pounds weight in bottom of No. 7.

On Indian creek, near the Marion-Monongalia line, this Sewickley coal is mined quite generally for local supply, and varies between six and seven feet in thickness, with a thin (one to two inches) slate near the center. It furnishes a very satisfactory steam and domestic fuel. The sample for analysis from that region, given in the table, was collected by Mr. W. F. Hood, of Lowsville, from the mine of Mr. J. A. Cox.

The coal has a good thickness and a fine reputation both for steam and domestic use from Indian creek entirely across Monongalia to the Pennsylvania state line, along all of its eastern crop which borders on and is just west from the Monongahela river.

The following sections, measured by Mr. John M. Gregg, on Scotts and Robinsons Runs, Monongalia county, show its structure there:

WILLIAM DEETS MINE, SCOTTS RUN.

	Ft.	In.		Ft.	In.
Coal, upper bench............	3	0	⎫		
Slate...................................	0	1	⎬	6	1
Coal, lower bench............	3	0	⎭		

On the land of William Baremore, Scotts Run, the Sewickley sandstone comes down and locally cuts out the upper bench of the coal, so that Mr. Gregg found there the following:

	Ft.	In.
Sandstone, Sewickley.........	7	0
Slate..................................	0	7
Coal......	4	0

At the mine of C. C. Lazzell, Robinsons run, this coal shows as follows, as measured by Mr. Gregg:

	Ft.	In.		Ft.	In.
Coal, upper bench...........	2	6	⎫		
Slate..................................	0	½	⎬	5	½
Coal, lower bench............	2	6	⎭		

The chemical character of the SEWICKLEY COAL is approximately shown by the following table of analyses, all of which were made by Prof. B. H. Hite and assistants except Nos. 6 and 7, quoted from Hon. J. W. Paul's Sewickley coal report:

SEWICKLEY COAL ANALYSES.

Analysis No.	Moisture.	Volatile Matter.	Fixed Carbon.	Ash.	Total.	Sulphur.	Phosphorus.	B. T. U.
1......	1.03	35.83	53.93	9.21	100.	2.72	0.011	13355
2...........................	1.64	34.55	51.87	11.94	100.	3.59	0.010	12859
3...........................	1.23	33.23	54.67	10.87	100.	1.45	0.008	13417
4...........................	0.64	34.57	54.22	10.57	100.	2.88	0.005	12983
5...........................	1.25	38.47	51.57	8.71	100.	4.62	0.0057	13231
6...........................	1.13	37.29	49.26	12.32	100.	4.91	0.006	12726
7...........	1.03	39.90	47.19	11.88	100.	4.80	....	....
8...........................	1.40	38.15	49.87	10.58	100.	3.47	....	....
9...........................	0.75	34.17	52.24	12.84	100.	2.82	0.015	12642
Average	1.13	36.24	51.64	10.99	100.	3.47	0.0067	13030
10..................	0.76	19.37	69.38	10.49	100.	1.73	0.025	

LOCATION OF MINES FROM WHICH SAMPLES WERE TAKEN.

1. Wm. Baremore mine, on Scotts run, Monongalia county.
2. Wm. Deets mine, on Scotts run, Monongalia county.
3. C. C. Lazzell mine, on Robinsons run, Monongalia county.
4. J. A. Cox mine, Indian creek, Monongalia county
5. Millard Boggess mine, ¾ mile above mouth of Mill Fall run, Marion Co.
6. Chas. Jackson mine, on Tevebaugh run, Marion county.
7. Mine on Tevebaugh run, 1 mile from West Fork river.
8. D. T. Martin's mine, near Sturm's Mills on Little Bingamon Creek, Marion county.
9. George's Creek Coal & Iron Company's mine, Chetham shaft No. 2, ¼ mile east of Farmington, Marion county.
10. Gas Coal mine, at Windom, Mineral county.

These analyses do not fairly represent the coal, since all except two were collected near the crop, and hence are higher in both ash and sulphur than would be found under normal mining conditions.

Making due allowance for the crop coal character of most of the samples taken from near the surface in country banks, (because the coal has not yet been mined on a commercial scale except at the two localities mentioned, Fairmont and Windom), it is readily observed that the coal will run higher in ASH than the PITTSBURG by three to four per cent., and probably one per cent. higher in SULPHUR, with approximately the same amount of VOLATILE MATTER, but less of FIXED CARBON by two to three per cent., while MOISTURE and PHOSPHORUS are nearly the same.

The open burning character of the coal will largely offset the greater percentage of ash and sulphur, so that for steam and domestic uses this coal, when mined in a commercial way, and properly freed from slate and bone, will not fall much below the Pittsburg coal in general fuel results.

The high percentage of sulphur would appear to forbid its manufacture into coke, unless crushing and washing should greatly reduce this undesirable element.

The sample No. 10, from Windom, belonging as it does in the highly folded, and incipiently metamorphosed region of the semi-bituminous coals, near the most eastern ridge of the Alleghany mountain range, is of course much higher in fixed carbon, and lower in volatile matter, than the unchanged coals west of the Alleghanies, and hence does not properly belong in a table of bituminous coals.

SEWICKLEY LIMESTONE.

At a short interval below the Sewickley coal there nearly always occurs a gray limestone, five to twenty feet in thickness, which bears the same name as the coal. Its position is well shown in the Lambert shaft section, as well as in many of the other sections already given. It is usually fairly pure and makes an excellent building or agricultural lime.

THE REDSTONE COAL.

Lying fifty to seventy feet below the Sewickley coal, and thirty to fifty feet above the Pittsburg bed, there occurs another coal horizon which in two or three districts of the State attains considerable importance. It was first discovered on Redstone creek, Fayette county, Pa., and was designated the REDSTONE COAL by the First Geological Survey of that state, although it does not appear to occur in good thickness at any locality within Pennsylvania.

On Scotts and Robinsons runs, in Monongalia county, five miles northwest from Morgantown, there is a small area where the coal attains a thickness of four to six feet, and is apparently of about the same quality as the Pittsburg bed, forty feet below. It was formerly mined there for domestic purposes to a limited extent, but as the SEWICKLEY coal above and the PITTSBURG below are so convenient, the mines on the REDSTONE have all been abandoned and are now fallen shut, so that no samples for analysis could be secured from that region. It was once analyzed, however, by Dr. John J. Stevenson, who reported it to contain about three per cent. of sulphur. It is a good fuel for either steam or domestic purposes.

In passing both north and south from the Scotts and Robinsons run localities, the coal thins away before reaching the Pennsylvania line on the one hand, or the Marion county line on the other, since in the Fairmont region only a trace of the coal remains in a fireclay horizon at the proper interval above the PITTSBURG COAL.

Still farther south, however, it reappears in the section at Clarksburg, too thin and impure to be valuable, but thickening up farther south into a very important and valuable coal seam, in southern Harrison, and adjoining regions of Barbour, Upshur, Lewis, and possibly some portions of Gilmer.

This coal is mined and shipped to Baltimore and the east on an extensive scale by the Century Coal Company, at Century, Barbour county, near the line between the latter and Upshur county, by a shaft 150 feet in depth. The following sections of the Redstone coal, as measured in the Century mine by Mr. A. P. Brady, exhibit the structure of the coal, and also the analysis, and calorific value of the same as determined in the laboratory of the Survey by Prof. Hite and his assistants.

	Ft. In.	Ft. In.
Slate		
Draw slate............................	1 0	
Coal.............	0 7	
Bone coal	0 ½	} ... 5 5
Coal....................	4 9½	

B. T. U. (British Thermal Units)=13634

ANALYSIS.

Moisture........................	0.67
Volatile matter................	36.89
Fixed carbon..	55.41
Ash............................	7.03
Total............................	100.00
Sulphur........................	2.43
Phosphorus	0.009

"Butts" run S. 78° E., Face S. 12° W., Greatest rise S. 50° E. Sample for analysis taken from southwest side of mine on C. Heading.

Another portion of the Century mine exhibits the following structure for this coal according to Mr. Brady:

	Ft. In.	Ft. In.
Sandrock..............................		
Slate................................		
Bone coal	0 4	
Coal....................	5 0	
Slate....................	0 ⅓	} ... 5 11⅓
Coal..................	0 7	

B. T. U.=13314

ANALYSIS.

Moisture	0.67
Volatile matter	36.21
Fixed carbon..................	54.38
Ash............................	8.74
Total	100.00
Sulphur	2.90
Phosphorus	0.035

Sample for analysis taken from northeast side of mine, A heading, room No. 2.

These analyses reveal a coal of fine quality, which comes out of the mine in handsome cubical blocks, stands shipment well, and has already established a fine reputation for itself as a steam and general fuel coal of the highest excellence. It has an excellent roof, much better than the underlying Pittsburg bed.

This coal covers an area of several thousand acres on the heads of the tributaries of Elk creek, adjoining the Century and Berryburg region, where it overlies the great Pittsburg seam by only twenty-eight to thirty-five feet. The Century company's shaft, 185 feet in depth, goes on through the Pittsburg coal which is found to be eight feet thick and twenty-eight feet under the Redstone.

This coal was not seen at the Berryburg mine which operates the Pittsburg coal exclusively, but Mr. O'Neal, the superintendent, states that the Redstone is present and about four feet thick, thirty to thirty-five feet above the Pittsburg.

On Freeman's creek and Kincheloe creek southward from Jarvisville, Harrison county, there is another large area of this Redstone coal where it is four and one-half to five feet thick, and quite generally mined for domestic use.

In many regions of Lewis county, there are also two coal beds thirty to forty feet apart, and the upper one while generally identified with the Pittsburg seam, may really be the Redstone. The latter always overlies a yellow limestone in the Clarksburg, Berryburg and Century regions, and as a yellow limestone comes a short distance below the upper of the two coals at Weston, Limestone run, Polk creek, and other localities in Lewis where the two are present, it is quite possible that the upper one may represent the Redstone, unless the lower one which is seldom more than three feet thick in Lewis, should be the LITTLE PITTSBURG, since it also occurs under a yellow limestone in Monongalia, Marion and elsewhere.

This stratigraphic question will be cleared up in the later detailed studies for the county reports.

Through Gilmer and Braxton and on across Clay, Roane and Kanawha, only one coal is present, and it has always been identified as the Pittsburg, but should the upper one of the two in Lewis prove to be the Redstone, then the coal in Braxton, Gilmer and on to the Great Kanawha would be the same. The two coal beds lie so close together, that the question is not of serious importance, since both belong in practically the same coal forming epoch.

REDSTONE LIMESTONE.

Lying only a few feet under the Redstone coal, there nearly always occurs, especially when the REDSTONE COAL is of merchantable thickness, a yellowish, impure limestone, named the REDSTONE LIMESTONE by Dr. John J. Stevenson. It has a thickness of five to twenty feet, sometimes extending down nearly to the Pittsburg coal, and giving much trouble in supporting the mine roof of the latter. The limestone is usually too impure for economic use and hence it is seldom quarried except for road material.

THE PITTSBURG SANDSTONE.

In the Fairmont region and especially along the eastern crop of the Pittsburg coal, there is often found a thick, coarse, gray sandstone, usually very soft, and readily disintegrating when exposed to the weather. When this sandstone is present in a massive condition the overlying REDSTONE COAL and LIMESTONE are nearly always absent. For instance on the east side of the Monongahela river at Morgantown, and on eastward to Cheat river, the sandstone is present in a massive condition, only two to five feet above the PITTSBURG COAL, while not a trace of the REDSTONE COAL is to be seen, but on the west side of the Monongahela, only two miles distant, the sandstone is gone entirely, while the REDSTONE COAL and LIMESTONE are both present.

When massive, the sandstone contains much feldspathic material and easily disintegrates into a bed of coarse sand where exposed along the roads, etc. It has been quarried to some extent for building stone in the Fairmont region, but it furnishes a poor quality which stains badly and will not long endure the action of the elements.

Southward through southern Lewis, eastern Gilmer, and southern Braxton a great cliff rock appears to come at this horizon, being very conspicuous for many miles above Glenville, on the Little Kanawha river, as well as southwestward through Braxton, Roane and Kanawha counties. It also forms conspicuous cliffs in the region of Hartford, Pomeroy, Point Pleasant and other localities along the Ohio river between Hartford and Huntington.

It occurs in some high knobs south of Elk river, near the mouth of Strange creek, and possibly in Mt. Pisgah, near Clay Court House, a mile east of the abandoned Chatauqua grounds.

THE PITTSBURG COAL.

Among the rich mineral deposits of the great Appalachian field, the Pittsburg coal bed stands preeminent. Other coal beds may cover a wider area, or extend with greater persistence, but none surpass the Pittsburg seam in economic importance and value. It was well named by Rogers (H. D.) and his able assistants of the First Geological Survey of Pennsylvania in honor of the city to whose industrial growth and supremacy it has contributed so much. Whether or not the prophetic eye of that able geologist ever comprehended fully the part which this coal bed was to play in the future history of the city which gave it a name we do not know; but certain it is that the seven feet of fossil fuel which in Rogers' time circled in a long black band around the hills, and overlooking the site of Pittsburg from an elevation of 400 feet above the waters of the Allegheny and Monongahela, extended up the latter stream in an unbroken sheet for a distance of 200 miles, has been the most potent factor in that wonderful modern growth which has made the Pittsburg district the manufacturing center of the world.

That this claim for the supremacy of the Pittsburg district (including Wheeling and the Monongahela river region) is valid can hardly be doubted, when we see its iron, steel, glass and other products going to every part of the western continent, and even invading the long established manufacturing dynasties of Europe.

AGE.

The Pittsburg coal is the lowest member of the Monongahela series, and so far as one may judge of relative age when comparing the coals of distant countries would correlate closely with the great bed at Commentry in central France.

Just where in the series between the Pittsburg and Waynesburg coals, the Permian flora found in the roof of the latter was first introduced, we do not know, because no systematic collection of fossils has ever been made at any horizon in the Monongahela series, below the top member, in fact, none until marine conditions are found 300 feet under the Pittsburg coal.

The coal making epoch of the Appalachian Carboniferous really culminated and its decline began with the deposition of the Upper Freeport bed at the summit of the Allegheny series of

Rogers (No. XIII), since the few fossil plants found in the 600 feet of the Conemaugh strata, which supervene between the Upper Freeport and Pittsburg coals, are either identical with or closely affiliated to Coal Measure types of plants that survive into the Permian flora of Europe and Texas. This is also mainly true of the last marine faunal types occurring at the horizon of the Ames limestone, about 300 feet below the Pittsburg bed, and therefore in Bulletin 65, U. S. G. Survey, page 19, the dividing line between the Upper and Middle Carboniferous was drawn through the middle of the Conemaugh (No. XIV), at the close of the Ames limestone stage when marine life became practically extinct in the Appalachian sediments. Hence the 600 to 700 feet of strata extending from the Ames limestone to the Waynesburg coal, and enclosing the great Pittsburg bed near the center, may possibly be of Permo-Carboniferous age.

The LESCUROPTERIS MORII SCHIMP. (Lx.) and the large reptilian tracks found by Lyell near Greensburg, Pennsylvania, point to the same conclusion with reference to the age of the Pittsburg bed; namely, that it belongs to the closing stage of the Carboniferous system rather than to the middle of the same.

AREA.

Before the drill of the Petroleum seeker had penetrated every region of the great Appalachian basin, it was supposed that the Pittsburg coal spread in a continuous sheet under every portion of that area where its outcrop was buried from view. This conclusion was based upon the unfailing continuity of the bed southward for 200 miles from Pittsburg to the headwaters of the Monongahela, and also westward into Ohio, and its reappearance on the river of that name at Pomeroy, as also on the Great Kanawha at Raymond City, Pocatallico, and Charleston. But the studies of Prof. Orton and others in Ohio, and my own in West Virginia, aided by the petroleum drilling there, have shown that the coal is absent, or but poorly developed over large areas where it had formerly been considered present. Hence to the list of counties of West Virginia named in Bulletin 65, United States Geological Survey, page 64, viz: Calhoun, Roane, Ritchie, Pleasants and Wood, where this coal is absent or in poor development, must now be added the most of Doddridge, Jackson, Tyler and probably half of Wetzel, since two tests with the diamond drill near the center of the latter county, found only two feet of coal at a depth of 425 feet below the valley of Fishing Creek. This area, together with that previously known to be barren, or to have only a patchy development in West Virginia and Ohio, will aggregate between 4,000 and 5,000 square miles, a rather startling figure when substracted from the supposed area of a coal bed so valuable as the Pittsburg in its developed regions.

There has has been much speculation as to the area which this coal may once have covered. The isolated patches of the bed in the George's creek and North Potomac region; the few knobs of it in Preston, Barbour and Upshur counties of West Virginia, together with its presence in the solitary peak of Round Top in Bedford county, Pennsylvania, forty-five miles from any other outcrop of the bed, and far east of the Alleghany mountains, have led some geologists to believe that it may once have extended northwestward to the Lake region, and eastward possibly to the North mountains, or even to the Blue ridge, having been removed from all this wide expanse by the enormous erosion to which it has been subjected since Carboniferous time. Whether the limits thus assigned were ever attained by the spread of Coal Measure swamps, we shall never know to a certainty, but that there is no inherent improbability in the hypothesis, will appear from the fact that the oldest member of the Carboniferous system, the very hard and erosion-resisting sandstones of the Pocono, with its included coal beds, extends to the North Mountain region at several points along that great ridge. Of course, if the Coal Measures ever covered an area as wide as this lowest member of the Carboniferous, the probabilities are that the area of the Pittsburg bed, which has escaped erosion, is only a fragment of its former extent. But however this may be, its entire area of workable coal remaining in the states of Pennsylvania, Ohio, West Virginia and Maryland, does not probably exceed 6,000 square miles.

STRUCTURE.

Dr. J. J. Stevenson, of the University of New York, was the first geologist to make a detailed study of the Pittsburg coal bed, and to describe the peculiar structure which so distinctly characterizes it, that the coal seam may be thereby identified with considerable certainty over a wide area. In Report K, Second Geological Survey of Pennsylvania, he shows that a series of thin parting slates and clays subdivide the bed into several definite members, which may be grouped as follows :

"Roof" coals.
"Over"-clay.
"Breast" coal.
Parting.
"Bearing-in" coal.
Parting.
"Brick" coal.
Parting.
"Bottom" coal.

"The "roof" coals are a number of thin layers of coal (two to twelve inches each) separated by shales or clays of varying thickness. Some of the layers are good coal, while others contain much dirt and other impurities. Their number ranges from one to eight, or even more, and their combined thickness seldom exceeds three and one-half to four feet, while the separating slates and clays may be only half as much, or they may often exceed the coal in thickness by two or three times. In practical mining operations all this 'roof' coal is wasted, because the coal layers make a good support for the over-lying strata, and are, therefore, left as the roof of the mine. In this way about 2,000 tons per acre of the Pittsburg coal is always lost without any attempt to recover it. This waste is so large that some of the mining companies are considering the question of putting in crushing and washing machinery with a view to taking down these roof coals, and thus preventing the great loss of fuel which their abandonment entails upon any mine. There is no doubt that the time will come, many generations hence, when at great cost, the Pittsburg bed will be remined to secure the coal which is now rejected, both in its roof and bottom members, since all of it would be valuable fuel if freed from the included slates and clays.

The "over-clay" is an impure fire clay, and varies much in thickness, sometimes almost disappearing, and again thickening up to two or even five feet. The clay is usually mottled and much slickensided, so that it becomes a dangerous trap when left as a mine support, since large pieces of it will drop from the roof without any warning sound. Hence it is generally taken down at once, and the miner has, therefore, given it the name of "draw-slate" in many regions. It often contains what appears to be stems and rootlets of plants.

The next succeeding (downward) division of this seam, the "breast coal" of the miners, also often termed the "main bench," is usually the most important and valuable division of the whole bed. Its thickness gradually increases from the Pittsburg region, (where it is usually about three feet), up the Monongahela, attaining a maximum of six feet at Brownsville, while to the eastward in the George's creek and North Potomac basin of Maryland and West Virginia, it increases still more to seven and one-half or even ten feet. The top of this member is nearly always of a bony nature for a thickness of one to four inches, and frequently this must be separated and rejected in mining, but even where this is not required, the top of the "breast" coal is distinctly harder than the rest of it, and inclined to a cannelly structure. Westward to the Ohio river this "breast" division thins, and in the Glendale and Moundsville shafts is only two feet thick, according to A. P. Brady's measurement. It is still perfectly distinct, however, with the twin slates, one-half an inch thick each, and enclosing four to six inches of "bearing-in" coal immediately below.

The "bearing-in" coal is so named by the Monongahela river miner, because in mining operations the under-cutting of the "breast" coal is made in this layer, the latter then being wedged or blown down, and the "brick" division subsequently taken up. The "bearing-in" coal is usually brilliant and pure, varying in thickness from three to six inches, and enclosed by two thin parting slates, so much alike in color and structure as to be almost indistinguishable. Their color is usually a dark, mottled gray, in the Pittsburg to Brownsville region, and they vary in thickness from one-fourth to one inch. In West Virginia, however, especially from Morgantown to Clarksburg, they are generally a dark bone, and will sometimes burn up with the coal. The persistency of these twin slates over all the regions drained by the Monongahela, and east to the George's creek and North Potomac field, while westward to Wheeling, Bellaire and the neighboring regions of Ohio they still appear to be present, is one of the remarkable features of this coal bed. When, however, the areas of this coal south of the Little Kanawha river in West Virginia, and west from the Muskingum in Ohio are examined, these twin slates are not found, or if represented are no longer recognizable as the Monongahela partings, but the "roof" coals and "over-clay" appear to be present.

The "brick" coal comes next under the lower of the twin slates, and was so named by the Monongahela river miners because it comes out in oblong, rectangular blocks, resembling the shape of common bricks. It is usually about one foot thick. The parting which separates the "brick" coal from the next lower member is always present along the Monongahela from Brownsville to Pittsburg, and it is also represented in the George's creek and North Potomac field, but in the Fairmont region it is rarely present, the bed there being generally undivided below the "bearing-in" coal.

The "bottom" member is from twelve to twenty inches thick along the Monongahela in Pennsylvania, and contains so many thin, slaty, sulphurous laminæ, that it is often not taken out in mining, and thus another thousand tons per acre of this bed is wasted, though in the Fairmont and Cumberland (George's creek) regions, it is mined and marketed with the rest of the coal.

The structure here described can be best illustrated by giving an actual section of the coal at its type locality. In the Ormsby mine at Twenty-first street, Pittsburg, where mining operations have been carried on for more than sixty-five years, Mr. J. Sutton Wall took the following measurements (K 4, Second Geological Survey, Pennsylvania, page 177):

		Inches.
	Coal	6
	Clay	2
	Clay	8½
	Parting	0½
	Coal	2
	Clay	9
	Coal	8
"Roof"	Parting	0½
	Coal	9
	Clay	0½
	Coal	5
	Parting	0½
	Coal	2
	Parting	0½
	Coal	2

56″

"Over"-clay		9"
"Breast" coal	33"	61¾"
Parting	0¼	
"Bearing-in" coal	4	
Parting	0¼	
"Brick" coal	10	
Parting	0¼	
"Bottom" coal	14	
Total thickness		10' 6¾"

Substantially this structure may be seen at every mine between Pittsburg and Brownsville, and on beyond for many miles (see Reports K and K 4, Second Geological Survey, Pennsylvania).

East of the Monongahela on the Youghiougheny river, the same structure is well illustrated by a section which Mr. W. S Gresley, F. G. S. A., measured for me with great care at the W. L Scott estate mines, of which Mr. Gresley was formerly superintendent. This section, near Scott Haven, Pennsylvania, reads as follows:

		Inches.	
"Roof"	Coal, several films of dirt	3¼	48¼"
	Shale, black, earthy	2	
	Coal	2¾	
	Shale, gray, streaks of coal near top	11	
	Bone (hard, dull, impure, coaly, layer)	1	
	Coal	2½	
	Shale, black	0¼	
	Coal	1¾	
	Shale, black, coaly	1	
	Coal	3	
	Slale, gray, with irregular coal streaks	4½	
	Coal, compact, free from "binders"	9¼	
	Slate, with coal streaks	1½	
	Coal	2½	
"Over"-clay, impure, fireclay, light gray above, getting browner and then a much darker gray with coal streaks of irregular shapes, especially toward base			10½"
"Breast" coal, (with 1½ inches of bone at top, and next 10" harder than the rest of bench)		41½	72⅜"
Shale, dark grayish brown, mottled		0¼	
"Bearing-in" coal, clear and brilliant		4	
Shale, dark grayish brown, mottled		0½	
"Brick" coal, clear and brilliant.		11	
Shale, parting		0⅛	
"Bottom" coal	Coal with a few thin dirt layers	12½	
	Shale	0¼	
	Coal, bright, clean	2	
Total thickness of bed			10' 5⅜"

How perfectly this great coal-bed preserves the Pittsburg type of structure over wide areas, is shown from the following section sent me by Mr. R. L. Somerville, superintendent of the

George's Creek Coal and Iron Company, Lonaconing, Maryland.
The locality is east of the Alleghany mountains, and 150 miles
from Pittsburg.   It is as follows:

	Inches.
"Roof" coal with slate parting below	20
"Breast" coal, 6" of bone on top	91
"Slate"	1
"Bearing-in" coal	4½
Slate	0¾
"Brick" coal	16
Slate	0¼
"Bottom" coal	15
Total thickness of bed	12' 4½"

This type of structure is practically universal over all of the
Pennsylvania, Maryland and eastern Ohio area of the bed.   The
different members vary considerably in thickness, as for instance
the gradual increase of the "breast" coal from three feet at
Pittsburg to six at Brownsville, 58 miles up the Monongahela
river, or to seven and even ten feet in the Georges creek and North
Potomac regions of Maryland and West Virginia, or a decrease
may take place in the same to thirty and sometimes to twenty
inches, as in the Wheeling and Bellaire regions, but each of the
main sub-divisions can be distinctly recognized, so that whether
at Fairfax Knob, on the summit of the Alleghany mountains,
3,200 feet above the sea, or deep down in the center of the
great Appalachian trough buried under 1,500 feet of sediments,
the explorer can readily identify this great coal-bed, not only
from its associated rocks, but from its stratagraphical elements as
well, and from even the fracture of the coal.   The writer once had
a practical illustration of this latter peculiarity of the Pittsburg
seam.   About the year 1880 a coal-bed was discovered near the
summits of the hills, south from Huntington, West Virginia, and
on one of the excursions to the southern portion of the state,
with the University students of geology, the mayor of Huntington
requested me to determine, if possible, to what horizon the coal
belonged.   It proved an easy problem to identify it since the
Ames and Ewing limestones, with their characteristic fossils, were
readily found in the bed of Four Pole creek, fifty feet above the
Ohio, and above them the ordinary rock succession of the
Conemaugh series.   But, anxious to know what the miner who
was digging the coal thought of the matter, he was interrogated,
and he replied as follows: "I don't know anything about

geology, but I dug coal several years in the Pittsburg seam, along the Monongahela, and this coal reminds me of the Pittsburg in the way it breaks into blocks." Thus had the miner correctly diagnosed the horizon of the bed by his own peculiar methods, though 300 miles distant from where he had learned its structure, with only the tools of his trade and his bright observing mind as his guides, strong testimony to the persistence of even the internal structure of the bed.

The oil-well driller is required to identify this coal correctly in the great petroleum districts of West Virginia and Pennsylvania, between the Ohio and Monongahela rivers, where it is buried from sight by the Permian beds all the way from 500 to 1,500 feet. It is there a key-rock for determining the amount of casing and the depth of the oil sands, and thus many dollars of expense depend upon the correctness of the driller's identification. This he does by observing the character of the drillings as brought to the surface by the sand pump, or in other words he observes the stratigraphic succession in his own peculiar way, and in the hundreds and even thousands of holes drilled in this area, he has only two or three mistakes charged against his accuracy of discrimination.

This coal is always traversed by two systems of joints or cleavage planes approximately at right angles to each other, making in miners' parlance the "butts" and "faces" of the mine. The direction of these planes is fairly constant for the same region, and they give to the coal its characteristic appearance on the cars. Along the Monongahela river in Pennsylvania the butts run from N. 60° W. to N. 70° W., or what is the same thing, S. 60° E. to S. 70° E., and there appears to be a gradual increase in the angle from Pittsburg southward up the river. The "face" bearing is of course at right angles to that of the "butts," and for the Fairmont region generally, the two have the following courses more frequently than any other, viz: "butts" S. 75° E., "faces" S. 15° W., as determined by Mr. S. D. Brady. Further south in the Clarksburg region the angles are S. 78° E., and S. 12° W. respectively. In the Tyrconnell district between Clarksburg and Grafton the angles are 80° to 81½° and 10° to 8½°. Berryburg gives, "butts" S. 79° E., "faces" S. 11° W. In the Wheeling region the angles as reported by Mr. Brady, read S. 73° E. and S. 17° W.

In tne Hartford district, Mason county, Mr. A. P. Brady reports the "butts" running due north and south, while the "faces" run east and west.

The PITTSBURG COAL is also remarkable for the number and size of the "clay veins" which penetrate the bed in every region where it has been mined, whether along the Monongahela or the great Kanawha, 200 miles distant. True, in some districts, they are more frequent than in others, but they occur in all.

Mr. W. E. Gresley, the eminent mining engineer, is inclined to believe them due to earthquakes which opened fissures that have been filled with earthy material from above, but the writer does not concur in this view, preferring to regard them in most cases as due to earth movements which squeezed up the under-clay into and often through the overlying coal.

As already stated they occur in every region where the Pittsburg bed is mined, but are probably more numerous in the Raymond City and other regions along the Great Kanawha river.

In the vicinity of Brownsville, Pa., the "breast" or main upper bench of the Pittsburg coal has a thickness of 5 to 6 feet, while the portion below the "bands", including both the "brick" and "bottom" coals is only about three feet thick.

When this coal is traced into West Virginia, forty miles south from Brownsville, this structure is practically reversed, there being only two to three feet above the "bands", and four to five feet below them, the "brick" and "bottom" divisions having coalesced, the usual separating slate being entirely absent and the whole forming the purest portion of the bed.

Where opened by the Fulmer Coal Co. on the Sturgiss farm, two miles southeast of Morgantown, the following structure is exhibited:

	Ft. In.	Ft. In.
Sandstone, Pittsburg		25 0
Draw slate		0 6
Coal, Pittsburg { breast coal .... 1 8 }		7 6
{ bands .... 0 6 }		
{ bottom coal .... 5 4 }		

Elevation, 1190 feet above tide, by barometer.

Here the dark bands are an inch thick each and enclose four inches of coal, while there is no apparent slate or parting in the sixty-four inches of "brick" and "bottom" coal below, which has here become the main portion of the bed.

One mile east of the Fulmer mine, the coal exhibits this structure at the I. A. Morris bank, near Easton:

		Ft. In.	Ft. In.
Sandstone, visible			10 0
Roof coal	{ coal	0 6 }	
	{ shale	0 4 }	1 4
	{ coal	0 6 }	
Over-clay			0 8
Breast coal		3 2 }	
Bands		0 6 }	7 4
Bottom coal		3 8 }	

Elevation, 1170 feet A. T., by barometer.

In the Beechwood mine of the Fairmont Coal Co., half way between Morgantown and Fairmont, A. P. Brady reports this structure for the Pittsburg coal:

BEECHWOOD MINE

		Ft. In.	Ft. In.	Ft. In.
Sandrock				
Draw slate				
Breast coal	{ coal	1 1 }		
	{ bone	0 2 }	2 5½	
	{ coal	1 2½ }		6 5½
Bands	{ bone	0 ½ }		
	{ coal	0 2½ }	0 4	
	{ bone	0 1 }		
Bottom coal		3 8		

Butts, S. 71° E. Face, S. 19° W. Greatest rise, S. 57° E. Elevation, 907 feet above tide.

Here there is a bony streak near the middle of the "breast" or upper division of the bed. The same structure is also seen in the Opekiska mine of the Fairmont Co. 10 miles below Fairmont as follows:

OPEKISKA MINE.

		Ft. In.	Ft. In.	Ft. In.
Roof coal			0 11 }	
Black slate			0 5 }	1 4
Breast coal	{ coal	1 8 }		
	{ bone	0 ½ }	3 4½	
	{ coal	1 8 }		8 0
Bands	{ bone	0 ¾ }		
	{ coal	0 5 }	0 6½	
	{ bone	0 ¾ }		
Bottom coal		4 1		

Butts, S. 72° E. Face, 18° W. Greatest rise, S. 57° E. Elevation, 1040' A. T.

The following structure is reported by S. D. Brady at the Montana mine, five miles below Fairmont:

MONTANA MINE.

	Ft. In.	Ft. In.	Ft. In.
Sandrock			
Black slate..			
Over-clay			3　0
Breast coal......................................		3　0	
Bands......　{ bone............................ 0　½			
coal .... 0　7		0　8½	7　4½
bone .... 0　1			
Bottom coal..................................		3　8	

Butts, S. 74° E. Face, S, 16° W. Greatest rise, S. 57° E. Elevation, 871' A. T.

Here the third bone or slate has disappeared from the "bands" but it reappears at the Aurora mine, three miles above Montana, as shown in the section measured there by A. P. Brady, as follows:

AURORA MINE.

	Ft. In.	Ft. In.	Ft. In.
Sandrock			
Draw slate...			
Breast coal..2　4			
Bands......　{ slate............................ 0　1			
coal............................ 0　3			
slate............................ 0　¾		0　8¼	6　7¼
coal............................ 0　2½			
slate............................ 0　1			
Bottom coal.....................		3　7	

Butts, S. 74° E. Face, S. 16° W. Greatest rise, S. 57° E. Elevation, 905' A. T.

Here, Mr. Brady calls the partings "slate", but they contain much bituminous matter along with 50 to 60 per cent. of earthy material, and hence, whether called "bone" or "slate", they should always be discarded from the coal, since they rarely hold enough carbonaceous material to permit combustion into ash.

Just west from Fairmont is the Shaft mine of the Fairmont Coal Co., and there the following structure is given by S. D. Brady:

SHAFT MINE.

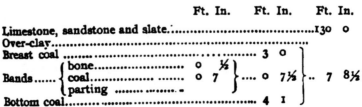

	Ft. In.	Ft. In.	Ft. In.
Limestone, sandstone and slate................................130　0			
Over-clay...			
Breast coal		3　0	
Bands......　{ bone............................ 0　½			
coal............................ 0　7		0　7½	7　8½
parting .... -			
Bottom coal........		4　1	

Butts, S. 76° E. Face, S. 14° W. Greatest rise, S. 54° E. Elevation of pavement (137 feet below surface), 744 feet above tide.

At the George's Creek Coal & Iron Co.'s mine, near Farmington, ten miles west from Fairmont, the following structure was observed for this coal in their Chatham shaft by A. P Brady:

CHATHAM SHAFT NEAR FARMINGTON.

		Ft. In.	Ft. In.	Ft. In.
Breast coal..		3 4		
Bands...... { slate..........................	0 ¼			
coal..............................	0 2			
slate	0 ½		0 7¼	.. 7 11¼
coal..............................	0 3½			
slate..............................	0 1			
Bottom coal..............................		4 0		

Butts, S. 78° E. Face, S. 12° W. Elevation of pavement (230 feet below Buffalo creek), about 685 feet above tide.

The Gaston mine of the Fairmont Coal Co. on the West Fork river, two miles above Fairmont, gave the following succession to A. P. Brady:

GASTON MINE.

		Ft. In.	Ft. In.	Ft. In.
Sandstone.......................................				
Over-clay.............................				
Breast coal...............................		3 11		
Bands...... { bone..........................	0' 1"			
coal..................	0 2			
bone..............................	0 1		0 9	..... 8 5
coal..............................	0 4			
bone..............................	0 1			
Bottom coal.............................		4 9		

Butts, S. 77½° E. Face, S. 12½° W. Greatest rise, S. 54° E. Elevation, 889' A. T.

The New England mine of the same company on the east side of the river just opposite Gaston gives the following as measured by S. D. Brady.

NEW ENGLAND MINE.

		Ft. In.	Ft. In.	Ft. In.
Sandstone..........				
Black slate.................................				
Over-clay.........				
Breast coal...................................		3 0		
Bands...... { bone..........................	0 ½			
coal..........................	0 2½			
bone...	0 1		0 8	...... 8 0
coal..............................	0 3			
bone..............................	0 1			
Bottom coal..............................		4 4		

Butts, S. 78° E. Face, S. 12°W. Greatest rise, 54°E. Elevation, 926' A. T. This mine lies in the junction angle of the Tygarts Valley and West Fork rivers, and a great delta deposit of quicksand, clay, boulders, etc. covers the surface at some points to nearly 100 feet in depth.

There is a good thickness of rock at the mouth of the mine between the coal and the delta deposit, but the eastward rise of the strata brings the coal up to the level of the ancient river bottom (950 to 960 feet above tide) when the Monongahela drained northward into the St. Lawrence system, and hence had cut out the coal entirely over a large area under the thick deposits made during the Glacial Ice Dam epoch, and had also cut away all but a few feet of slate over another considerable area.

In the operation of the New England mine, one of these thin places in the roof rock was encountered a few years ago, and the overlying quicksand broke through and rapidly filled one of the entries where it was more than 100 feet up to the surface of the ground. Since that event, mining under the delta deposit is made with great caution, and frequent tests of the thickness of the rock roof, but in spite of this, many acres of valuable coal will doubtless be lost, owing to the semi-fluid (quicksand) nature of the first Ice Dam deposit which overlies the thin rock roof of the coal, 140 feet above the level of the present rivers.

About 1 mile east from the New England mine, is the plant of the Virginia & Pittsburg Coal & Coke Co., on the west bank of the Valley river, and there A. P. Brady measured the following structure :

	Ft. In.	Ft. In.	Ft. In.
Sandstone..			
Draw slate..			
Breast coal..3	0		
Bands { slate............................. 0 ½		0 7½	8 2½
coal............................. 0 3			
slate....... .... 0 ½			
coal............................. 0 3			
slate............................. 0 ½			
Bottom coal.......................................4	7		

Butts, S. 78° E. Face, S. 12° W. Elevation, 960 feet above tide.

At the Monongah mines of the Fairmont Coal Co., on the West Fork river, 6 miles above Fairmont, the following sections were measured by S. D. Brady :

MONONGAH NUMBER 6 (SLOPE).

		Ft. In.	Ft. In.	Ft. In.
Draw slate...				
Breast coal	bony coal................... 0 10	} 3 4		
	coal 2 7			..... 8 10
Bands	bone 0 1			
	coal 0 7	} 0 9		
	bone...... .... 0 1			
Bottom coal.................................... 4 9				

S. 75° E. Face, S. 15° W. Greatest rise, southeast. Elevation, 820 feet A. T. This mine is 1000 feet north of Monongah station, and the coal is reached by a slope which goes below the level of the West Fork river. The 10 inches of bony coal at the top of the "breast" division is not taken down in this mine, being left for a roof support. This "top" coal contains more ash and sulphur than any portion of the seam, but it is seldom so impure that it will not undergo complete combustion.

The following is the structure at :

MONONGAH NUMBER 2.

		Ft. In.	Ft. In.	Ft. In.
Draw slate.............				
Breast coal...	top coal, bony......... 0 10	} 3 2		
	coal......... .... 2 4			
Bands	bone .... 0 ¾			...8 2¼
	coal...................... 0 3			
	bone..................... 0 ¾	} 0 8¼		
	coal..................... 0 3			
	bone................. .... 0 ¾			
Bottom coal............................... 4 4				

This mine is 600 feet south from the station, and the butts and faces have the same direction as in Number 6 slope. The rise is southeast at the rate of 52 feet to the mile, while the elevation of the coal at the mine mouth is 885 feet above tide.

Monongah No. 3, 1 mile south from the station, shows the following structure for the coal :

MONONGAH NUMBER 3.

		Ft. In.	Ft. In.	Ft. In.
Black slate........ .... 1 8				
Draw slate........................... .... 1 6				
Breast coal......... .... 3 0				
Bands	bone...... .... 0 1			
	coal........................ 0 7	} ..0 9¼		...8 3¼
	bone......................... 0 1¼			
Bottom coal...................................4 6				

Butts, S. 75° E. Face, S. 15° W. Greatest rise, southeast, 70 feet to the mile. Elevation, 892 feet above tide.

The rest of the mine sections between Monongah and Clarksburg as measured by S. D. Brady are so similar to those already given that they can be best exhibited in tabulated form as follows :

Name of Mine.	Breast		Bands		Bottom		Total		Butts	Rise	Elevation.
	Ft.	In.	Ft.	in.	Ft.	in.	Ft.	in.			Ft. A.T.
Marion	3	6	0	9¼	3	10	8	1¼	S.75 °E.	S.8 °E.	885
Pennois	3	3	0	8¼	4	3	8	2¼	S.75¼ E.	S.8 E.	950
Anderson	3	3	0	7½	4	4	8	2½	S.75 E.	S.45 E.	925
Highland	3	2	0	4¼	4	7	8	1¼	S.77¼ E.	S.56 E.	925
Middleton	3	4	0	9	4	4	8	5	S.75 E.	S.45 E.	920
Chiefton	2	8	0	8¼	4	4	7	8¼	S.75 E.	S.45 E.	890
Hutchinson	3	0	0	8	4	7	8	3	S.75 E.	....	860
Enterprise	3	6	0	8½	4	4	8	6½	S.75 E.	S.10 E.	900
Melrose	2	6	0	9½	4	6	7	9½	S.75 E.	S.69 E.	952
Viropa	3	5	0	8	4	0	8	1	S.75 E.	S.69 E.	952
Riverdale	3	0	0	10	4	8½	8	6½	S.75 E.	S.69 E.	908
Harbert	3	0	0	6½	5	0	8	6½	S.74 E.	S.59 E.	912
Gypsy	3	2	0	10½	4	9	8	9½	S.74 E.	....	923
Erie	3	0	0	9	5	1	8	10	S.78 E.	S. E.	1017
Meadow Brook	3	11½	0	6¼	4	3	8	9¼	S.77 E.	S.53 W.	971
Cook C. & C. Co.	3	0	0	6	5	0	8	6	S.78 E.	West	965
Ehlen	3	2	0	8½	4	7	8	5½	S.75 E.	S.15 W.	905
Solon	3	2	0	8½	4	10	8	6½	S.75 E.	N.27 E.	914
Farnum	2	9	0	10¼	4	8	8	3¼	S.79 E.	N.78½ W.	1040
Globe	2	8	0	9½	5	0	8	5½	S.79 E.	N.78½ W.	1033
PinnickinnickNo. 2	3	4	0	½	5	0	8	4½	S.78 E.	West	1050
Briar Hill No. 11	3	6	0	½	5	0	8	6½	S.78 E.	S.65 W.	1045
Glen Falls	2	6	0	9½	4	8	7	11½	S.78 E.	S.50 E.	1027
Perry (Adamston)	2	0	0	10½	4	8	7	6½	S.78 E.	S. E.	1085
Fairmore	2	0	0	6	5	3	7	9	S.78 E.	S. W.	1062
Waldo	2	0	0	10¼	5	1½	7	11¼	S.78 E.	....	1109
Wilsonburg	2	6	0	1	5	0	7	7	S.75 E.	....	1052
O'Neil No. 1	1	1	0	9	4	0	5	10	S.78 E.	East	1123
O'Neil No. 2	1	9	0	10	4	6	7	1	S.78 E.	East	1143
Lydia (Wolf S.)	1	7	0	7	5	0	7	2	S.78 E.	....	976
Pinnick'k No. 1	3	2	0	1	5	2	8	5	S.78 E.	N.60 W.	....
Despard No. 2	3	6	0	7	5	2	9	1	S.76½ E.	N.60 W.	1090
Highland No. 4	3	4	0	1	4	11	8	4	S.78 E.	N.60 W.	1070
Ocean	3	5	0	1	5	0	8	6	S.78 E.	N.60 W.	1150
Reynoldsville	2	7	0	9	4	6	7	10	S.75 E.	East	1098
Dixie	2	6	0	1	5	1	7	8	S.78 E.	S. E.	1100
Lynch	2	3	0	10	4	6	7	7	S.78 E.	N. W.	1097
Two Lick	2	0	0	½	5	2	7	2½	S.78 E.	N.80 W.	1090
West Fork	2	0	0	½	5	0	7	½	S.78 F.	....	1140
Cork near Mt. Clare	2	9	0	1	5	2	8	0	S.78 E.	....	1100
Inter State No. 2	2	6	0	1	5	0	7	7	S.78 E.	S. E,	1209
Inter State No. 1	none		0	8	5	8	6	4	S.78 E.	East	1187
Tyrconn'll (Colon'l)	3	4	0	1½	5	0	8	5½	S.81½ E.	N. W.	1285
Flemington	3	5	0	1½	5	2	8	8½	S.80 E.	N. W.	1200
New York	2	7	0	1½	4	4	7	½	S.78 E.	S. E.	1286
T. B. Davis	2	2½	0	1½	4	9	7	1	S.78 E.	S.45 E.	1205
Sand Lick	3	4	0	1½	4	0	7	5½	S.80 E.	North	1265
Foster	2	10	0	1	3	10	6	9	S.78 E.	East	1250
Rosemont	3	2	0	1½	4	3½	7	7	S.81½ E.	N.80 W.	1325

These several measurements will show the average thickness of the coal throughout the area in Monongalia, Marion, Harrison, and Taylor counties.   They show that after making all due allowance for 6 to 8 inches of bony "top" coal, and some loss in the "bands," as well as occasionally 2 to 3 inches of sulphurous coal at the base of the bed, we shall still have over 7 feet of clean coal as the average of the Pittsburg bed throughout the region in question.   The "roof" coal, 5 inches thick, was noted above the "over-clay" or "draw-slate" at both the Hutchinson and Enterprise mines.

These sections represent what might be called the HEART of the Pittsburg coal region of West Virginia as developed by mining at the present time, and over this area probably ten thousand tons of merchantable coal per acre can be secured by careful mine work.

The Chestnut Ridge anticlinal crosses the Parkersburg branch of the B. & O. R. R., 2 miles east of Bridgeport, and throws the Pittsburg coal into the air along its crest between the Tygarts Valley river near Valley Falls, and the West Fork river at Jackson's Mill, 3 miles below Weston.

The Tyrconnell, Flemington and Simpson field of this great coal bed lies in the trough or syncline east from the Chestnut Ridge uplift, and extends southward into Barbour, Upshur, Lewis and Gilmer counties, in all of which are some valuable areas of Pittsburg coal though no mines on a commercial scale have yet been operated in the last three counties owing to absence of shipping facilities, near where the bed is of good thickness.

In Barbour county, however, a branch of the B. & O. R. R. has recently been built from the Valley river across to the head waters of Elk and Simpson creeks and extensive mines opened at Berryburg, 4 miles west from the river.

The coal has a fine development in the Berryburg region, and sometimes attains a thickness of 10 to 12 feet for short distances. No regular partings or slates have been observed according to A. P. Brady who measured the bed in the two main entries of the Southern Coal & Transportation Co., as follows :

WEST OPENING, BERRYBURG.

Sandstone...
Slate...
Coal ....8 feet.

Butts, S. 79° E. Greatest rise, S. 46° E. Elevation, 1422 feet A. T.

The south opening gave the same succession except that the coal was 8 feet, 2 inches thick, and the elevation 1427 feet A. T.

The Pittsburg coal extends from the Berryburg mines southwestward over a wide area on the head waters of Elk creek and its tributaries, connecting through to the Century mines near Burnersville, where as already stated it exists 8 feet thick and only 28 feet under the Redstone coal which is the only bed mined on that property at present.

This Pittsburg bed is also found over a considerable area in northern Upshur county, and has been mined to some extent in the tops of the hills northwest from Buckhannon for local supply, where its thickness is reduced however to only about 4 feet.

It has also been mined near Lorentz where it rises above the level of the valley and is frequently opened by the farmers between that point and Weston along the line of the B. & O. R. R., but no commercial mining has yet been attempted.

Several local openings in this bed in the vicinity of Weston supply considerable coal io the town, but at none of them does the coal much exceed 4 feet in thickness, the "breast" or upper division appearing to be generally thin, and this is the condition of affairs over a large area in Lewis county.

On Limestone run, south from Weston, two coals are found 35 to 40 feet apart, and separated by several layers of impure yellowish limestone. The upper coal is supposed to represent the Pittsburg, since it is 4 to 5 feet thick, while the lower one is less than 3 and seldom mined, but as previously stated, it is possible that the upper one may represent the Redstone bed, although the probabilities are equal that the lower one is the Little Pittsburg instead of the main Pittsburg bed. The question is not of much economic importance since the two beds lie so close together.

The Pittsburg coal thickens up again and attains much importance along Leading and Fink creeks in the region of Vadis and Alum Bridge in Lewis county.

On the land of James Roony near Vadis, Lewis county, S. D. Brady measured the following section of this coal:

	Ft. In.	Ft. In.
Breast coal	3 10	
Bone	0 2	7 2
Bottom coal	3 2	

The analysis of the coal is given in the table on a subsequent page.

On the Walnut branch of Fink creek, near Vadis, the writer once made the following measurement at the mine of James Davis:

	Ft.	In.	Ft.	In.
Breast coal	3	10		
Bone	0	1	7	11
Bottom coal	4	0		

This rivals the Fairmont coal in thickness, and the quality appears to be quite as good in every way. Just before the coal passes under Fink creek, it exhibits the following structure at the mine of Means and Radcliff:

	Ft.	In.	Ft.	In.
Breast coal	1	9		
Bone	0	1	6	2
Bottom coal	4	4		

At the mouth of Fink creek we are approaching the western edge of the thick Pittsburg coal, and there find the following structure on the land of Homer Farnsworth:

	Ft.	In.	Ft.	In.
Breast coal	0	6		
Bone	0	½	4	5
Bottom coal	3	10½		

This is an illustration of the thinning of the coal all through Lewis and Gilmer counties; i. e., the upper portion is the first to disappear. A short distance west from this and before we reach Troy, the coal disappears entirely.

The Moses Farnsworth bank on Leading creek has thick coal as follows:

	Ft.	In.	Ft.	In.
Breast coal	3	9		
Bone	0	1	7	10
Bottom coal	4	0		

The Eckert bank, one-half mile above this and near the Lewis-Gilmer line, shows the following:

	Ft.	In.	Ft.	In.
Breast coal	3	6		
Bone	0	1	8	0
Bottom coal	4	5		

Near Alum Bridge, Lewis county, the following measurement was made at Mr. A. M. Allman's bank:

	Ft.	In.	Ft.	In.
Breast coal	2	3		
Bone	0	1	6	1
Bottom coal	3	9		

From Linn post office on Leading creek, the coal passes under the divide and comes out on the head of Stewarts creek, which puts into the Little Kanawha, 2 miles above Glenville.

The Peter Messenger mine on Stewarts creek exhibits the following structure :

	Ft.	In.	Ft.	In.
Breast coal	3	0		
Bone	0	2	7	4
Bottom coal	4	2		

Glenville, Gilmer county, is at the western edge of the Pittsburg coal area, since beyond that it appears to thin away entirely in a westward direction, not being known at all on the north bank of the Little Kanawha. On the south bank it occurs however about 250 feet above water level and has long been mined there for local use, being 4 to 5 feet in thickness.

The coal appears to thicken southwestward toward the great trough or syncline that crosses the Little Kanawha at the mouth of Sand Fork creek above Glenville, since it has a good thickness on all of the streams that put into the river above Glenville before the coal dips under water level.

Dry, Duck, and Bear runs put into the Little Kanawha from the south a few miles above Glenville, and the coal has been mined along each, as well as on the north side of the Kanawha, for use in Glenville and the adjoining regions. The structure and thickness shown at several of these mines is as follows :

Name of Mine.	Breast.		Bone.		Bottom.		Total	
	Ft.	In.	Ft.	In.	Ft.	In.	Ft.	In.
Charles Norris	1	9	0	1	4	0	5	10
Hewitt	3	3	0	2	4	2	7	7
John W. Keith	2	4	0	2	3	4	6	7
W. J. Clovis	3	0	0	2	4	1	7	3
Elliott s	2	10	0	2	4	3	6	4
J. P. Coberly	1	1	0	2	4	2	5	5
L. L. D. Peters	3	3			4	3	7	7
Adam Messenger... (Jac's Fork of Ellis)	1				4	0	5	10

The coal comes out in fine large blocks, and being a little
harder than the Fairmont coal, would bear transportation in splendid shape. The SINGLE band, present occasionally in the Fairmont
region, often around Clarksburg, and generally in the Flemington
region, appears to be universal in the Glenville district.

On the South side of Duck run, a local irregularity was observed along the road for some distance, which splits the coal as
follows :

		Ft. In.	Ft. In.	Ft. In.
Breast coal		3 2		
Bone		0 2		7 6
Bottom	coal 0 10		4 2	
	dark shale ... 1 8			
	coal 1 8			

On the north side of the stream, however, the coal resumes its
normal structure as revealed in the Emory Goff bank as follows :

	Ft. In.	Ft. In.
Breast coal	2 0	
Bone	0 2	6 2
Bottom coal	4 0	

Dipping rapidly southeast from the crest of the Chestnut
Ridge anticlinal which crosses the Little Kanawha river at Glenville, the Pittsburg coal passes under water level just above the
Coberly mine, 1 mile below the mouth of Sand Fork creek.   Its
horizon does not get more than 100 feet below the river however
in the broad Sand Fork basin or syncline, since the coal is reported
in oil well borings at about that depth.

To the northeast, in the oil field along Sand Fork, and Indian
creeks, the Pittsburg coal is frequently not found by the drillers,
and is generally quite thin when observed at all.   It is possible
that the coal may be too thin for commercial purposes over a wide
area in Gilmer and Lewis counties, where its horizon is buried from
sight along the Sand Fork trough, since the coal is only 3 to 4 feet
thick where it passes under the West Fork river, near the mouth
of Limestone creek above Weston.

On the east side of the Sand Fork basin along the Little Kanawha, the rocks begin to rise rapidly to the southeast, just below
Stout's Mill, and the coal comes above the water level again about
1 mile above, and ½ mile farther south is 40 feet above water level.
Here it exhibits the following structure on the right bank of the
river at the Charles Whiting mine :

```
                                            Ft. In.        Ft. In.
Breast coal ........................................   1   3  ⎫
Bone .............................................   0   2  ⎬ ......5   3
Bottom coal.......................................   3  10  ⎭
```

Copen run comes into the river from the south nearly opposite the Whiting mine, and ½ mile above it, the coal exhibits the following structure on the left bank of the river at the Isaac Stout mine :

```
                                            Ft. In.        Ft. In.
Breast coal.......................................   2   0  ⎫
Bone .............................................   0   2  ⎬ ......6   0
Bottom coal.......................................   3  10  ⎭
```

The coal is 75 feet above the river and rising rapidly to the southeast. It soon thins down to only 18 to 20 inches as we pass up the river, and at Burnsville, 6 miles above, the coal cannot be found at all, although its horizon is about 300 feet above water level, so that as a merchantable coal the bed disappears completely to the south along the Little Kanawha until its horizon passes into the air 10 miles above Burnsville.

The coal has a fine development along Copen run, as shown by the following sections :

Name of Mine	"Breast" Ft. In.		Bone Ft. In.		"Bottom" Ft. In.		Total Ft. In.	
Hezekiah Stout	3	10	0	2	4	0	8	0
Richard Williams......	3	8	0	2	4	0	7	10
W. T. Brosius.............	3	6	0	2	4	0	7	8
George Nutt..............	1	0	0	2	4	0	5	2
(H d of Copen)								

Hyer run puts into the Little Kanawha above the mouth of Copen, and its upper waters are only a mile south from Copen. There is only one coal mine on it, and at this the upper division is thin like that shown in the George Nutt bank above.

On the waters of Cedar creek, southwest from Copen run, the Pittsburg coal is mined for local use and frequently has a fair thickness. The H. J. Bragg mine on Slab Camp run, has the following structure :

```
                                            Ft. In.        Ft. In.
Breast coal ......................................   3   6  ⎫
Bone ............................................   0   1  ⎬ ......7   7
Bottom coal......................................   4   0  ⎭
```

The coal is here 75 feet above Slab Camp run, and has been opened at several places along that stream and in the vicinity of Cutlipville. At the Meda Cutlip mine near this village we get the following :

	Ft.	In.	Ft.	In.
Breast coal......................................	2	8	} 6	9
Bone ....,...............................	0	1		
Bottom coal...........	4	0		

This is 175 feet above Cedar creek.

Northward from Cutlipville this coal dips rapidly down into the Sand Fork syncline and disappears under Cedar creek, near the mouth of Butchers run, 3 miles above Cedarville, where it is only 4 feet thick. It comes out again one mile and a half above Cedarville however and is there only 2 feet thick, but just south of the village, the coal thickens to 4½ feet, having the "bone" near its top, and at one mine the main "breast" coal comes in so that it shows as follows on Upper Level run at the Jackson Snyder mine :

	Ft.	In.	Ft.	In.
Breast coal	2	8	} 6	9
Bone	0	1		
Bottom coal.......................................	4	0		

The coal is thin on below Cedarville and of little importance. It keeps 20 to 30 feet above the level of Cedar creek, and is seen for the last time ½ mile below the mouth of Lower Bull run, where it was once opened on the land of John Lawson and found to be only 2 feet thick. This is the line of its disappearance west from Glenville, and there are evidently no good areas of the coal, except in a patchy condition, to the northwest of Cedarville.

Southwest from the head of Cedar creek, on the tributaries of Little Otter flowing into Elk river, and the head branches of Steer creek, we find the Pittsburg coal 4 to 5 feet thick over a belt of country several miles wide, extending from the Elk river hills northward to Belfont, Survey, and Sleith, but thinning away almost completely before reaching the Braxton-Gilmer line at Rosedale, and then reappearing in patchy areas around Stumptown, where the coal is only 2 to 3 feet thick.

At the head of Rock Camp run, a branch of O'Brien's Fork of Steer creek, the Pittsburg coal shows as follows on the land of Andrew Skidmore, ½ mile northwest from Belfont post office :

	Ft. In.	Ft. In.
Breast coal	0 4	
Bone	0 1	3 9
Bottom coal	3 4	

On the Mill Fork of Steer creek, 2 miles above Rosedale, the Pittsburg coal has been mined on the land of Martha Cox, and there has the following structure :

			Ft. In.	Ft. In.	Ft. In.
Breast coal			1 4		
Bands	slate.....	0 2			
	coal.....	0 3		6	4 4
	bone....	0 1			
Bottom coal			2 6		

The bed is here 180 feet above creek level and rising rapidly to the southeast.

The coal extends into the high knobs just south from Elk river, opposite Frametown, Braxton county, and has there been mined for a long time on the land of Eli Taylor, where the following structure is exhibited :

	Ft. In.	Ft. In.
Breast coal	3 0	
Slate	0 3	6 10
Bottom coal	3 7	

The coal lies at an elevation of 550 feet above Elk, and a great massive sandstone (Sewickley) caps the knob, 175 feet above the mine.

The coal is mined in the vicinity of Elmira post office by Samuel Gibson, David Hall, Worth Barr, Samuel Morrison and others where it is 3 to $4\frac{1}{2}$ feet thick.

It is probably this coal that is found on the head waters of Sandy creek, north from Newton in Roane county, at Ira Drake's where it is only 30 inches thick.

On the Ashley Camp branch of the Left Hand Fork of Sandy, there is also a coal mined by W. H. Scargent, about 200 feet above water level and $2\frac{1}{2}$ to 3 feet thick, which may represent this same coal.

There are isolated areas of the coal across northern Clay and southern Roane until they connect up with the well known Pittsburg bed in Kanawha and Putnam counties, but the bed is seldom more than $4\frac{1}{2}$ feet thick and often not more than half so much.

The horizon of this coal comes out from under Pocatallico river near the mouth of its West Fork, a mile or two above Sissonville, Kanawha county. The coal however is represented by only a few inches of impuré, slaty coal and some fireclay. The CLAY and COAL HORIZON rises rapidly and opposite the Sissonville mill is 110 feet above water level, but contains no coal until 2 miles below Sissonville when the coal suddenly comes in on the waters of Tupper creek, at John Fishers, Ira Umphries and others. The coal is 3½ to 4 feet thick at the Fisher bank where it has long been mined for local supply, and nas no partings of bone. The coal lies 150 feet above the level of Tupper creek and only ½ mile distant (south) from Poca river. The coal has never been found here on the north side of the latter stream however, and hence is most probably absent.

The Umphries bank, just south from the Parkersburg and Charleston pike, and one mile and a half from Sissonville, is 220 feet above the level of Tupper creek. The coal is 4 feet thick and has 2 inches of bone at top. The quality of the coal is good at both Fisher's and Umphries', and the coal comes out in large blocks characteristic of the Pittsburg bed.

On the Monday branch of Tupper creek the Pittsburg bed is mined for local supply by A. J. Young at whose bank the coal is 44 to 54 inches thick and reported all good. This is only 9 miles north from Charleston.

There are many local mines in this coal on the head waters of Tupper creek, and south from there on the head of Two Mile creek. At one of these mines on the head waters of Two Mile, 8 miles from Charleston, the coal thickens up to a splendid bed and exhivits the following structure at the mine of Beryl Holmes:

	Ft. In.	Ft. In.	Ft. In.
Roof coal	0 6		
Over-clay	1 0		
Breast coal {bony coal... 0 6 / coal .... 3 0}		3 6	....8 7
Bone	0 1		
Bottom coal	3 6		

This is almost the exact type of the coal found along the Monongahela river, and except that the coal is here harder, and more inclined to the "block" condition, one could not convince himself that he is not in a mine on the latter stream. The coal is extensively mined by the farmers along Two Mile among whom are the

Haines Bros., Dr. Davis and many others. The coal is from 5 to 7 feet thick and of most excellent quality. The fuel is wagoned to Charleston and sells at the highest price.

About 2 miles above the mouth of Two Mile creek (which puts into the Great Kanawha river just below Charleston), the crop of the Pittsburg coal occurs in the top of a high knob, 400 feet above the stream, and there the following structure is exhibited at an old abandoned mine :

	Ft. In.	Ft. In.
Sandstone from top of high knob		70 0
Shale		1 0
Roof coal	0 6	
Over-clay	1 6	
Coal	2 0	7 0
Black slate and coal	1 0	
Coal	2 0	

The coal is poor in quality compared to the mines farther up the stream.

The Pittsburg coal has been mined for a long time near Raymond city, Putnam county, on the waters of Pocatallico river which empties into the Great Kanawha from the right bank.

The section of the coal varies much at the different mines of the Marmet-Smith Coal and Mining Co. which carries on the principal operations. The following is given by R. W. Edmonds of Charlesfon, (who collected most of the samples for analysis along the Great Kanawha), as the structure of the Pittsburg coal at one of the Marmet-Smith Co.'s mines 2½ miles northeast from Raymond City :

	Ft. In.	Ft. In.
Sandstone		
Shale		10 0
Sulphurous coal, shaly	2 0	
Draw slate	0 8	
Coal	5 6	8 8¼
Black slate	0 ¼	
Bone coal	0 6	

Elevation, 725 feet above tide. The structure of the "roof" coals as measured here by the writer is given in the general section of the Monongahela series, page 144. The coal is quite hard and interstratified with many laminae of mineral charcoal which gives it the appearance of a "block" coal. The mines are interrupted by many "clay veins," and occasionally a black slate in the roof of the mine will thicken up and supplant the coal entirely, according to Mr. Edmonds. "Rolls" of the overlying sandstone also come down sometimes and cut out the coal completely, this being the condition of affairs in the river hills below the mouth of Poca-tallico, or "Poca" as this stream is popularly called.

Three miles farther down the Great Kanawha, this same coal is operated by the Plymouth Coal & Mining Co., in whose mine Mr. Edmonds measured the following succession :

	Ft. In.	Ft. In.
Sandstone..		
Shale..		8 0
Hard sulphurous coal	2 0	⎫
Draw slate...	1 0	
Coal	5 8	⎬......9 5
Slate..	0 1	
Hard sulphurous coal...............................	0 8	⎭

Butts, S. 58° E.   Elevation, 625 feet A. T.   "Vertical clay veins from 6 inches to 8 feet thick occur frequently in this mine."

The coal at this and the Raymond City mine is shipped by rail and river and used mostly for domestic purposes for which it is admirably adapted.

On the west side of the Kanawha in this region, the Pittsburg coal thins down to an insignificant bed only 2 to 3 feet thick. It was once opened on the land of Hon. Jas. H. Stewart, opposite Raymond City, 220 feet above river level, but was found too thin to warrant mining.

Between Plymouth and Winfield the coal disappears com-pletely, there being nothing but a bed of fireclay to represent the coal horizon at Red House, opposite Winfield.

Three miles below Winfield the coal comes in again on the west bank of the Kanawha and has been mined by the Oak Ridge Coal Co. It is only 20 feet above river level, and the main bench is 4 feet thick, below which is 8 to 10 inches of impure coal.

Near the mouth of Big Hurricane creek, 4 miles below Win-field, the coal is in the bed of the Great Kanawha river on its west shore, and a shaft was once sunk to it there by Mr. J. T. Bowyer, who reports the succession in the shaft as follows :

		Ft. In.	Ft. In.
River clays, sand, etc..............................			40 0
Clays with iron ore.................................			12 0
Sandstone..			18 0
	coal...................0 10	⎫	
	shale 5 0		
[roof	black slate 1 0	⎬...... 10 6	

```
                    (   ( sandstone .........1   8  )
Pittsburg Coal  {   ( black slate .......2   0  )
                    |  over-clay ..............................................   1   3
                    |  coal { coal...............3   3  }......  3  11
                    (        ( slaty coal.........0   8  )
```

To the southeast up Hurricane creek the coal rises and soon comes above water level.   It has been mined by the farmers occasionally along the waters of Big and Little Hurricane creeks between the Kanawha river and Teays valley, but is seldom more than 3 to 4 feet thick and not very pure.

On below the mouth of Big Hurricane creek the coal dips down into the center of the great Appalachian trough and thins away entirely, since a test boring near Arbuckle, Mason county, found only a fireclay and a few inches of slaty coal 90 feet under the Great Kanawha on the land of G. W. Craig, 18 miles from the Ohio river.

In passing down the Kanawha from Arbuckle, the horizon of the coal begins to rise, within a few miles, and at Point Pleasant, along the Ohio river, gets to 20 to 30 feet above the river bottom deposits.   It has been opened here on both sides of the Kanawha, but is only 2 feet thick and rather impure.

From Point Pleasant down the Ohio the horizon of the coal is constantly above water level, and the coal has occasionally been mined for local use, but it is evidently too thin and impure for commercial purposes.

A few miles above Huntington the rocks begin to rise rapidly as one descends the Ohio, and when the hills south from Huntington are reached the Pittsburg coal lies about 400 feet above the river, and covers a few small areas where it exhibits the following structure :

```
                                              Ft. In.     Ft. In.
Coal roof ..........................................   0   6  )
Over-clay ..........................................   0   6  )
Coal................................................   3   6  }......4   8
Slaty coal..........................................   0   1  )
```

The coal is occasionally found along the central line of the syncline across Wayne county, but it never much exceeds 3 feet in thickness.   It is last seen to the southwest, in Wayne county, near the summits of the hills in the center of the syncline, 10 miles above the mouth of the Big Sandy, where it has been mined for local use and is 38 inches thick.   The strata are all rising to the southwest, and none of the hills on the Kentucky side of the river rise high enough to catch the coal, so that probably not a single area of the Pittsburg bed is to be found in that state.

From Point Pleasant northward along ihe Ohio river, the Pittsburg coal remains thin and unimportant and is not mined for commercial use until Spilman is reached, 10 miles above. Here the coal is operated by the Consumers Coal Co., B. D. Spilman, manager, at an elevation of 60 feet above the Ohio River R. R., or 100 feet above the river. The coal has the following structure at the Camden mine No. 1, according to A. P. Brady:

		Ft. In.	Ft. In.	Ft. In.
Sandstone				
Plate				
Coal "roof"		0 4		
Slate		1 6		5 10½
Coal { coal	0 8			
slate	0 ½		4 ½	
caal	3 4			

Butts, north and and south. Face, east and west. Greatest rise, northwest. Elevation, 627 feet above tide.

The "New Castle" mine of this company at West Columbia, and one mile above Spilman, gives the following succession:

		Ft. In.	Ft. In.	Ft. In.
Sandstone				
Slate				
Coal "roof" { coal	0 2			
slate	0 ¼			
coal	0 1½		0 6	
slate	0 ¼			4 2
coal	0 2			
Slate		0 1		
Coal		2 7		

Butts, north and south. Face, east and west. Greatest rise, northwest. Elevation, 607 feet, A. T. The coal is rather high in sulphur, but is a good steam fuel, being used on the Ohio River railroad engines and elsewhere for that purpose. The sandstone above the coal is very massive in this region, and crops in a great cliff forty to fifty feet high.

On above West Columbia, and one-half mile south from Mason City, the coal is mined by the Beech Grove Coal Company in whose entry A. P. Brady reports the following succession:

BEECH GROVE MINE.

	Ft.	In.	Ft.	In.
Draw slate			0	2
Coal	0	2		
Slate	0	½		
Coal	0	3		
Slate	0	½		
Coal	0	3	4	8
Slate	0	½		
Coal	0	3		
"Horn" coal	0	3		
Coal	3	5		

Butts, north and south. Face, east and west. Greatest rise, northwest. Elevation, 600 feet A. T. The layer of bony coal on top of the main bench is locally called "horn" coal by the miners of this region.

The Hope Salt Company's mine, one-fourth mile farther up the river, shows practically the same succession as at Beech Grove. and the coal has an elevation of 588 feet A. T.

The following structure was measured by Mr. Brady at the Klondike Coal Company's mine, one mile and a-quarter above Mason City.

KLONDIKE MINE.

	Ft.	In.	Ft.	In.
Sandstone				
Slate	0	to	20	0
Draw slate			0	½
Coal { coal	0	10		
"horn" coal	0	2	4	10
coal	3	10		

Butts, north and south. Face, east and west. Greatest rise, northwest. Elevation, 590 feet above tide.

One-fourth mile farther up the river the coal shows practically the same structure at the Mason City Mining Company's plant, where the elevation of the coal is 585 feet A. T.

One-half mile below Hartford the coal is mined by the Liverpool Salt and Coal Company for its use in the manufacture of salt, and the following section was measured there by A. P. Brady:

	Ft.	In.	Ft.	In.
Sandstone				
Slate	0	to	20	0
Draw slate			0	1
Coal { top coal	0	7		
"horn" coal	0	2	4	6
coal	3	9		

Butts, north and south.   Face, east and west.   Greatest rise, northwest.   Elevation, 560 feet A. T.

The Hartford City Salt Company has a mine farther up the river where the coal sinks to 520 feet above tide, or only a few feet above low water in the Ohio river, and it shows almost exactly the same structure as that last given.

The coal continues to dip rapidly to the southeast and soon disappears below water level, as one passes up the river, and at Antiquity, five and one-half miles above Hartford City, it has attained a depth of 100 feet below low water, where the coal has long been mined by shafting.   It exhibits the following structure at the bottom of the shaft, 170 feet below the surface:

	Ft.	In.		Ft.	In.
Coal, with a bony band...	2	6	⎫		
Slate	0	2	⎬	5	8
Coal	3	0	⎭		

The coal continues to dip up (southeast) the river and when Letart is reached, four miles above Antiquity, the coal, if present, would be more than 300 feet below the Ohio.   From near Letart the river turns to a northeast-southwest course and the horizon of the coal continues at between 300 and 400 feet below water level on up to Parkersburg and beyond.

Just how far up the Ohio from Antiquity the coal extends in commercial thickness, or how far southward from the river the productive area may he found, are questions that only the core drill can answer satisfactorily.   Some of the well borings report it of fair thickness, while others do not find it at all, but of course the oil well record cannot be depended upon to determine fhe thickness or quality of any coal bed with accuracy.

A well bored just south from Ravenswood, Jackson county, and probably forty-five feet above ow water in the Ohio river. reports finding five feet of coal at 346 feet, which would be near the Pittsburg horizon, but whether the coal is that thick, or whether it is of good quality, is only conjecture.

In the vicinity of Parkersburg, and elsewhere in Wood county, the Pittsburg coal has not been reported in the hundreds of oil wells that have there been drilled, though iust northwest from Parkersburg it is found by the drill in Washington county, Ohio, although thin and patchy.

It is also absent in Pleasants county so far as the oil well records can determine, and when its horizon is brought up to daylight by the great Volcano-Burning Springs anticlinal arch at Eureka, Belmont, etc., no coal whatever is visible at the Pittsburg horizon.

Practically the same conditions are found along the Ohio river through Tyler county, since of the many hundreds of oil wells drilled in Tyler along the Ohio valley, only a very few report finding any coal at the Pittsburg horizon, there being probably a half-dozen that show about three feet of coal 200 feet below river level at Sisterville.

As one proceeds up the river however into Wetzel county, the coal comes in as a regular stratum before New Martinsville is reached, though it is there only three feet thick and possibly not of commercial value. It soon grows thicker, however, since at the David Abersold boring on Beaver run, just north from the Wetzel-Marshall line, seven miles above New Martinsville, a good thickness (5' 11") occurs as reported from the diamond drill record there, (see page 133), by Joseph E. Barnes of Uniontown, Pa., as well as at Franklin and other points in the surrounding region. Hence, there can be little doubt that from, say the mouth of Proctor creek on up the Ohio river to where the Pittsburg coal rises to the surface near Benwood, it is of good development and thick enough to prove of great value commercially.

In the northwest bend of the Ohio river, three miles below Moundsville, the Pittsburg coal comes up to the bed of the stream on the Ohio shore, but is probably fifty to sixty feet below the surface of the river bottoms on the West Virginia side. It dips down toward Moundsville to the southeast from Round Bottom, and in the shaft of the Moundsville Coal Company, as reported by A. P. Brady, lies at an elevation of 494 feet above tide, or 100 feet below the Ohio. The coal has the following structure in the Moundsville Coal Company's shaft according to Mr. Brady:

MOUNDSVILLE SHAFT MINE.

		Ft. In.	Ft. In.	Ft. In.
"Roof" coal		2 0		
"Over-clay"		0 10		
"Breast" coal		2 0		
"Bands"	slate	0 ¼		
	coal	0 6	0 7	8 5½
	slate	0 ¾		
"Bottom" coal	coal	1 0		
	"copper band"	0 ½	3 ½	
	coal	1 6		

Butts, S. 75° E.   Face, S. 17° W.

The "copper band" of this section is a pyritiferous slate which occupies the same relative position as the parting slate on the Monongahela river that separates the "brick" from the "bottom" division of the Pittsburg bed.   This parting is seldom present in the Fairmont and Clarksburg areas of the Pittsburg coal, but is occasionally found in other regions of West Virginia, and appears to be generally present in the Ohio river area of this bed, between Moundsville and Wellsburg.

The Glendale Coal Company also operates this coal by a shaft at its mine on the B. & O. R. R. near Glendale, Marshall county, two miles north from Moundsville, and there A. P. Brady reports the following structure :

GLENDALE SHAFT MINE.

			Ft. In.	Ft. In.	Ft. in.
"Roof" coal, mixed with slate					
"Breast" coal				2 ½	
"Bands" { slate	0	½			
coal	0	4		0 5	
slate	0	½			4 8¾
"Brick" coal				1 5	
Parting slate				0 ¼	
"Bottom" coal				0 10	

Butts, S. 73° E.   Face, S. 17° W.   Elevation, 75 feet below the B. & O. R. R.

The several divisions of the coal here given are not known by those names among the miners of the regions, but they have been so arranged by the writer to show how accurately and completely the detailed frame work of the bed agrees with the type structure of the same coal along the Monongahela river, between Pittsburg and Brownsville, sixty miles distant.   See page 166.

At Benwood, five miles north of Glendale, the coal rises to the level of the B. & O. R. R., and has there been extensively mined by the Wheeling Steel & Iron Company, in whose mines A. P. Brady measured the following structure :

BENWOOD MINE.

		Ft. In.	Ft. In.	Ft. In.
Limestone				
Shales, soft				5 0
Roof coal		1 6		
Draw slate		0 1		1 7
Breast coal		2 6		
{ slate	0	1		

```
Bands { coal ..................  0   4 } ......... 0   6 |
       { slate ..................  0   1 }                |
Brick coal .................................................  1   7  } ......6   7
Trace slate.................... .................                    |
Bottom coal................................................  1   6  |
```

Butts, S. 73°. E.   Face, S. 17° W.   Elevation, 645 feet A. T. Here the main body of the coal foots up six and one-half feet, and including the "roof" division, eight feet.

This section also reveals the complete absence of the Pittsburg sandstone, which is such a conspicuous member of the series at Fairmont and Morgantown along the eastern crop of the coal, as well as at Hartford, Mason, Point Pleasant, Raymond City and Huntington on the southwest. Its horizon is occupied by limestones in the Moundsville-Wheeling region, which extend up to the Redstone coal horizon fifty feet above the Pittsburg seam.

This coal is also mined by the Boggs Run Mining and Manufacturing Company, at Benwood, near the level of the B. & O. R. R., but the section of the coal measured in its mine is so nearly like the one just given that it is simply a duplicate of the latter.

At the mouth of Wheeling creek, in the center of the city of Wheeling, four miles above Benwood, the northward rise of the strata elevates the Pittsburg coal to 100 feet above water level, and this gives fine exposures of this bed for mining purposes along the latter stream until the eastward dip carries it below the same just east of Elm Grove, on the Pittsburg Division of the B. & O. railroad.

There are several mines located near Wheeling and along Wheeling creek, and the structure of the coal at these may be tabulated as follows:

Name of Mine	Roof		Over-Clay		Breast		Bands		Brick		Bot m		Total		Elevation Ft above R.R.
	Ft	In	Ft	In	Ft	In	Ft	In	Ft	In	Ft	In	Ft	In	
Whittaker ...	1	3	1	0	1	11½	0	3½	1	3	1	1	6	10	45
McMinley ...	1	0	1	4	1	11	0	4½	no part'g		2	9	7	4½	65
Jocklum.......	1	0	1	0	1	10½	0	3	1	5	1	3	6	6½	50
Manchester..	1	8	1	6	1	11½	0	5	no part'g		2	8	8	2½	40
Elm Grove (shaft)	2	0	1	6	2	3	0	4	1	8	0	9½	8	6½	600' A. T.

In all of these mines, the butts run S. 73° E., and faces S. 17° W., according to A. P. Brady. In all of the sections there are two bands of slate, each one-half to one inch thick, enclosing two to four inches of bright coal, and corresponding exactly to the "bands" in this bed along the Monongahela river. There is also a parting slate or pyritiferous layer ("copper band") separating the "brick" and "bottom" divisions at all of the mines except the McKinley and Manchester, where Mr. Brady did not note any partings.

Traced north from Wheeling along the Ohio river, the Pittsburg coal continues to rise, and at the Richland mine of Mr. J. P. Gilchist, three miles from the mouth of Wheeling creek, is 145 feet above low water. The following structure is reported from the Richland mine by A. P. Brady:

RICHLAND MINE.

	Ft. In.	Ft. In.	Ft. In.
Roof coal		0 8	
Draw slate		0 6	} 1 8
Breast coal		1 11	
Bands ... { slate	0 ½		
coal	0 3	} ... 0 4½	
slate	0 1		} 4 10½
Brick coal		1 4	
Sulphur streak			
Bottom coal		1 3	

Butts, S. 73° E. Face, S. 17° W.

Two miles south from Wellsburg, and fourteen miles north from Wheeling, the Pittsburg coal has attained an elevation of 340 feet above the Ohio river, and exhibits the following structure at the Brown Coal Company's

BIG FOUR MINE.

	Ft. In.	Ft. In.	Ft. In.
Roof coal		0 5	
Draw slate		1 2	} 1 7
Breast coal		1 11	
Bands ... { slate	0 ½		
coal	0 2½	} ... 0 4	
slate	0 1		} 4 3
Brick coal		1 0	
Slate, trace			
Bottom coal		1 0	

Mr. J. M. Gilchrist operates the Pittsburg bed one-half mile south from Wellsburg at an elevation of 355 feet above the river on the Waltz land, and there A. P. Brady measured the following structure :

	Ft. In.	Ft. In.	Ft. In.
Roof coal	0 5	}	1 7
Draw slate	1 2		
Breast coal	2 8½		
Bands — bone slate	0 1		
coal	0 3	0 5	
slate	0 1		5 1½
Brick coal	1 0		
Slate, trace			
Bottom coal	1 0		

The last mine to the north along the Ohio river operating on this coal at the time of A. P. Brady's sample collecting tour, in December, 1901, is one mile north of Lazearville, and owned by the Gilchrist Coal Company. The structure there is as follows:

	Ft. In.	Ft. In.	Ft. In.
Roof coal	0 5	}	1 7
Draw slate	1 2		
Breast coal	2 1½		
Bands — slate	0 1		
coal	0 2	0 4	4 8
slate	0 1		
Bottom coal	2 2½		

There is a "sulphur" band one inch thick near the middle of the "breast" division, but no parting slate is noted in the "bottom" member.

The detailed analyses showing the chemical composition of the Pittsburg coal in the region along the Ohio from Moundsville to Wheeling and Wellsburg; are given in a subsequent table to which the reader is referred, where all the analyses of this coal from every region of the State are grouped together. The average of the thirteen samples collected from the region in question reveal a coal of the following composition:

Moisture	0.93
Volatile matter	39.46
Fixed carbon	51.35
Ash	8.26
Total	100.00
Sulphur	3.86
Phosphorus	0.0067

This result discloses a coal high in sulphur, but low in phosphorus and moisture. The volatile matter is also high, and were it not for the excessive sulphur, the coal would be of ideal composition for gas making purposes. It is too hard for coking, and the sulphur forbids that, unless crushing and washing would remove considerably more than half of the latter.

It is possible that this could be done, at least the great demand for coke in the Wheeling district would warrant extensive experiments in such attempts, and even if the sulphur could not be reduced low enough for the general manufacture of iron and steel, there is no reason why a fair grade of "foundry" coke might not be secured by the proper treatment of the coal. So far as the writer knows, no tests of the character indicated have been made in the Wheeling district, but the coal is used entirely for steam and domestic purposes.

The thickness of the bed in the Wheeling district will average about five feet exclusive of the "roof" coal, and making due allowance for loss in the removal of slate and sulphur ("copper") bands, will yield approximately four and one-half feet of clean coal, or about two and one-half feet less than the same bed in the Fairmont and Clarksburg districts. With modern mining methods the yield per acre should not be less than 6000 tons of fuel.

A small area of this coal is caught in the deep syncline in the tops of the hills at Newburg, Preston county, but the most of it has already been mined, and that remaining is in isolated knobs.

The writer once measured the coal there and found the following structure in the summit of Scotch Hill:

SCOTCH HILL SECTION.

	Ft. In.	Ft. In.	Ft. In.
Sandstone, Pittsburg			
Roof ..... { coal, slaty	0 8		
{ coal....................	0 9	... 2 3	
{ coal....................	0 10		4 3
Over-clay.........	2 0		
Breast and brick coal...........................	9 0		
Shale	0 3		10 9
Bottom coal, slaty.............................	1 6		

The "bands" probably exist in the main body of the coal here, but they were not noted when the measurement was made.

The next, or Kingwood basin, still east from Newburg, also catches a few small isolated areas of this celebrated coal. One of these is Copeman's knob, near Albrightsville, three miles from Kingwood, Preston county, while several others are found in the same basin just northeast from Belington, Barbour county. None of these areas exceed ten acres in size, and are of interest only in showing the great extent of country from which this bed has been removed by erosion.

This coal has evidently once existed over all the region between the Kingwood-Belington basin and the Elk Garden or North Potomac region, across the entire extent of the Alleghanies, since we find two small areas of it near Fairfax, at the head of the Potomac, and several hundred acres at Elk Garden, Mineral county, as well as several thousand farther to the northeast in the Maryland area of the same Potomac basin.

When this Fairfax knob area was first opened in 1885, it was carefully measured by the late James Parsons, then Chief Engineer of the W. Va. Central R. R., who reported to the writer the following results :

	Ft.	In.	Ft.	In.
Roof coal	2	0	8	0
Shales	6	0		
Coal	8	2	9	6
Slate	0	2		
Coal	1	2		
Shales	5	0	16	0
Limestone	4	0		
Shales	7	0		
Coal, good			4	6
Fireclay and shales			18	0
Coal, slaty			7	0
Total			63	0

It has been considered possible that this sixty-three feet might represent simply the Pittsburg bed with greatly expanded partings separating the "breast" ($9\frac{1}{2}'$), "brick" ($4\frac{1}{2}'$), and "bottom" (7') members, but this interpretation is probably erroneous. The two lower divisions of the coal, four and one-half feet thick and seven feet thick, respectively, very probably represent the LITTLE PITTSBURG COALS, of which there are sometimes two.

The following structure is reported from the Elk Garden mine, in Mineral county, by S. D. Brady :

	Ft.	In.	Ft.	In.
Slate				
Coal	8	0	10	8
Slate	0	4		
Coal	2	4		

Elevation, 2268 feet above tide.

At some localities in the mine the coal thickens to twelve feet. If more than one slate "band" is present here Mr. Brady did not note the fact.

The analysis of a sample of the coal collected from the Elk Garden mine No. 6, by S. D. Brady, is reported as follows by Prof. Hite :

Moisture	0.31
Volatile matter	17.17
Fixed carbon	76.91
Ash	5.61
Total	100.00
Sulphur	0.81
Phosphorus	0.017

B. T. U.
- Parr calorimeter 14285
- Williams calorimeter............................. 14788

This, like the Sewickley coal in the same highly folded region, is of course low in volatile matter, and high in fixed carbon, thus placing it among the semi-bituminous coals, midway between the ordinary type of this coal and anthracite.

Two parting slates are found in the Piedmont region, as shown by the following section of the bed which the writer once measured at the old Franklin mine in the summit of Westernport hill, opposite Piedmont :

FRANKLIN MINE, WESTERNPORT, MD.

		Ft. In.	Ft. In.	Ft. In.
Roof coal	coal	0 8		
	shale	4 0	5 8	
	coal	1 0		
Over-clay			1 0	
Breast coal, no partings			10 0	19 7½
Bands	slate	0 2		
	coal	0 9	0 11½	
	slate	0 ½		
Coal			2 0	

It is possible that only one of the usual "bands" is present, and that the nine inches of coal included within the "bands" of of this section is really the "brick" portion of the bed, instead of the "bearing-in" division of the same, as indicated.

The areas of the Pittsburg coal in the West Virginia portion of the Potomac basin have been largely mined out, since only about 600 acres of it was preserved from erosion, and most of that in one body near Elk Garden.

Hence, although the bed is a splendid type of the ideal steam and general fuel coal, yet on account of its near approach to complete exhaustion, it has little besides a scientific interest for West Virginia, although a few thousand acres of it yet remain unmined in the Maryland area of the George's creek-Potomac basin, so close to the boundary lines of the two states, that the coal will necessarily be used for a long time in the adjoining regions of West Virginia.

CHEMICAL COMPOSITION,
CALORIFIC VALUE, AND ECONOMIC USES OF THE
PITTSBURG COAL.

In this discussion, the bituminous type of the coal west from the Alleghany mountain region, is for reasons just given, the only one considered.

The lack of financial resources has prevented the Survey from undertaking the more detailed and elaborate investigations required in ultimate analyses, so that the work done by Prof. B. H. Hite and his assistants has been confined to that of determining the usual four constituents of the ordinary proximate analysis : viz, moisture, volatile matter, fixed carbon and ash, with separate and usually duplicate determinations of sulphur and phosphorus.

The samples of coal for these analyses were all taken with great care under the immediate supervision of Mr. S. D. Brady, now Chief Engineer of the Little Kanawha Railroad, Parkersburg, W. Va. In all cases, a complete strip of the coal was dug from the working face of the mine, including all partings or slates not separated in mining operations. These samples, averaging about twenty-five pounds in weight, were all shipped in properly labeled bags to the laboratory af the West Virginia Agricultural Experiment Station, Morgantown, where they were resampled, ground and analyzed by Prof. B. H. Hite, Chief Chemist of the Survey, and his assistants, the late R. L. Norris, C. D. Howard, and E. S. Stalnaker.

The calorific determinations of Prof. Hite and his assistants on the Redstone and Sewickley coals, were all made with Parr Standard Calorimeter, a new instrument recently devised by Prof. S. W. Parr, Professor of Applied Chemistry in the University of Illinois, for which accuracy as well as rapidity is claimed by Prof. Parr, after many comparisons of its results with those obtained by the use of the more expensive Bomb calorimeter.   The determinations of Prof. Hite, made with the Parr instrument, check fairly well with Mr. Haas' results obtained by using the Mahler Bomb calorimeter, except that they appear to be systematically 400 to 500 units lower.

The laboratory of the Experiment station has just acquired one of the new and improved Bomb calorimeters, recently devised by Mr. Henry J. Williams, the eminent chemical engineer of Boston, Mass., and the calorific values of the Allegheny and Pottsville coals will be checked and controlled by it.   In accuracy of results it is conceded by all experts to be superior to the best calorimeter in use previous to the improvements made by Williams.

The few checks on the Parr instrument with the Williams that were possible before "going to press," confirm the too low results obtained by the use of the Parr calorimeter.   The average increment seems to be about 500 B. T. U., and this sum should be added to all those given for the Redstone and Sewickley coals which were determined with the Parr instrument.

To those not familiar with the technical term "B. T. U."= British Thermal Units, it may be explained that one British Thermal Unit is a quantity of heat sufficient to raise one pound of water one degree Fahrenheit, and hence when a coal is said to possess say 14,000 B. T. U.s, it means that one pound of the coal will develop in complete combustion sufficient heat to raise 14,-000 pounds of water one degree Fahrenheit, provided all the heat generated could be made effective.   Of course this theoretical heat in the combustion of coal is never attained in actual practice, since combustion is never perfect, and much heat is lost through radiation, and imperfect conduction of boiler plates, tubes etc., and a still larger quantity goes out of the furnace chimney into the air without accomplishing any result, so that but little over half of the heat values locked up in coal are utilized in the heating of water or generation of steam by the ordinary methods.

In order to bring all these analyses made under the supervision of Prof. Hite into a single view for ready comparison, they have been arranged in geographical order, and here presented in tabular form, to be followed by corresponding numbers under which the locations of the several mines are given.

ANALYSES OF THE PITTSBURG COAL.

Analyses Nos.	Moisture.	Volatile Matter.	Fixed C'rb'n	Ash	Total.	Sulphur.	Phosphorus.	B. T. U.
	Pr. Ct.	Pr. Ct.	Pr. Ct.	Pr. Ct.	Pr. Ct.	Pr. Ct.	Pr. Ct.	
1	0.95	37.45	51.59	10.01	100	4.25	0.012	
2	0.63	39.42	50.63	9.32	100	4.43	0.012	
3	0.78	35.18	53.53	10.51	100	4.47	0.007	
4	1.44	37.32	51.36	9.88	100	3.41	0.0105	
5	0.58	40.19	50.66	8.57	100	3.98	0.005	
6	0.58	40.65	50.86	7.91	100	3.32	0.0095	
7	0.90	40.69	53.65	4.76	100	3.02	0.0065	
8	1.07	39.40	52.03	7.50	100	2.97	0.0045	
9	0.97	41.15	50.88	7.00	100	3.67	0.0025	
10	0.69	39.40	50.35	9.56	100	4.29	0.0045	
11	1.34	40.98	50.04	7.64	100	4.66	0.0045	
12	1.07	41.11	49.73	8.09	100	4.16	0.004	
13	1.08	40.05	52.22	6.65	100	3.51	0.005	13949
14	1.40	34.16	56.99	7.45	100	2.88	0.013	
15	0.87	37.10	54.04	7.99	100	3.13	0.007	
16	0.46	34.69	58.89	5.96	100	1.46	0.0045	14143
17	0.55	34.26	58.91	6.28	100	1.97	0.005	
18	0.80	36.21	57.93	5.06	100	1.71	0.040	
19	0.51	36.68	56.26	6.55	100	1.54	0.007	
20	0.44	35.98	57.58	6.00	100	2.02	0.0195	
21	0.39	35.38	56.42	7.81	100	0.71	0.0215	
22	0.47	37.54	54.91	7.08	100	1.72	0.010	
23	0.46	35.89	55.87	7.78	100	1.73	0.028	
24	0.33	37.47	56.31	5.89	100	1.30	0.005	
25	0.70	36.75	55.80	6.75	100	1.62	0.012	
26	0.89	36.58	55.56	6.97	100	1.48	0.007	
27	1.18	37.13	56.67	5.02	100	0.73	0.003	
28	0.74	36.87	54.47	7.92	100	0.62	0.004	
29	0.99	36.53	57.81	4.67	100	0.70	0.012	
30	0.55	35.39	58.45	5.61	100	0.86	0.008	
31	0.76	36.50	58.17	4.57	100	1.06	0.029	
32	0.81	36.87	56.69	5.63	100	0.76	0.015	
33	0.69	37.03	56.21	6.07	100	1.65	0.008	
34	0.79	37.01	55.85	6.35	100	1.10	0.037	
35	0.81	36.42	58.29	4.48	100	0.70	0.0029	
36	0.93	35.78	58.02	5.27	100	0.82	0.0097	
37	0.88	37.34	54.94	6.84	100	1.22	0.008	
38	0.58	38.24	55.76	5.42	100	1.71	0.0019	14332
39	0.74	38.97	54.23	6.06	100	1.76	0.01	
40	1.01	38.65	54.03	6.31	100	2.61	0.004	
41	0.83	38.64	55.04	5.49	100	2.13	0.017	14213
42	0.85	38.84	54.39	5.92	100	1.67	0.010	
43	0.87	38.58	54.66	5.89	100	2.02	0.006	
44	0.83	39.78	52.56	6.83	100	3.43	0.026	
45	0.64	38.71	54.18	6.47	100	2.88	0.021	
46	0.81	38.90	54.70	5.59	100	2.61	0.021	
47	1.07	38.03	53.71	7.19	100	2.96	0.027	13758
48	0.99	39.33	54.06	5.62	100	2.48	0.016	
49	1.03	39.24	52.53	7.20	100	3.21	0.023	
50	0.54	38.40	54.75	6.31	100	1.96	0.009	
51	0.65	38.36	55.25	5.74	100	1.92	0.010	
52	0.44	39.27	54.71	5.58	100	3.27	0.002	

53	0. 85	38. 68	54. 22	6. 25	100	3. 02	0. 007	....
54	0. 93	40. 42	52. 20	6. 45	100	3. 34	0. 0125	....
55	0. 80	39. 57	52. 71	6. 92	100	3. 23	0. 007	....
56	0. 99	39. 28	52. 45	7. 28	100	3. 24	0. 004	....
57	0. 73	38. 41	53. 08	7. 78	100	3. 45	0. 032	....
58	0. 65	38. 39	52. 20	8. 76	100	4. 50	0. 020	....
59	0. 78	40. 12	50. 15	8. 95	100	3. 87	0. 020	....
60	0. 97	37. 81	55. 78	5. 44	100	2. 33	0. 016	....
61	1. 01	39. 72	52. 81	6. 46	100	3. 13	0. 004	....
62	0. 85	41. 39	51. 87	5. 89	100	3. 05	0. 003	....
63	0. 88	40. 66	51. 93	6. 53	100	3. 36	0. 002	....
64	0. 54	39. 70	52. 63	7. 13	100	3. 49	0. 003	....
65	0. 77	41. 37	51. 93	5. 93	100	2. 25	0. 004	14249
66	0. 54	41. 01	52. 88	5. 57	100	2. 52	0. 003	....
67	0. 76	40. 65	52. 01	6. 58	100	3. 31	0. 003	....
68	0. 71	39. 14	53. 96	6. 19	100	3. 13	0. 006	14072
69	0. 28	40. 11	52. 77	6. 84	100	3. 16	0. 004	....
70	0. 50	40. 36	53. 94	5. 20	100	2. 98	0. 006	....
71	0. 58	40. 03	53. 08	6. 31	100	3. 11	0. 008	....
72	1. 51	38. 09	54. 87	5. 53	100	2. 02	0. 013	....
73	0. 37	36. 96	54. 19	8. 48	100	3. 24	0. 004	....
74	0. 31	38. 00	53. 64	8. 05	100	2. 98	0. 021	....
75	0. 35	37. 99	55. 71	5. 93	100	1. 98	0. 008	....
76	0. 51	36. 71	56. 30	6. 48	100	3. 31	0. 005	....
77	0. 66	35. 29	58. 90	5. 15	100	1. 74	0. 022	14062
78	0. 47	37. 60	56. 82	5. 11	100	2. 16	0. 008	....
79	0. 58	37. 95	55. 71	5. 76	100	2. 25	0. 009	14471
80	0. 71	37. 64	56. 25	5. 40	100	2. 78	0. 009	14402
81	0. 74	37. 01	53. 41	8. 84	100	3. 54	0. 006	....
82	1. 01	40. 99	48. 34	9. 66	100	3. 39	0. 0306	....
83	1. 16	40. 74	50. 60	7. 50	100	1. 79	0. 0096	....
84	1. 00	40. 51	50. 40	8. 09	100	2. 17	0. 0061	....
85	1. 30	41. 41	50. 39	6. 90	100	1. 80	0. 0045	....
86	1. 87	39. 25	45. 93	12. 95	100	1. 95	0. 013	....
87	1. 96	41. 29	46. 58	10. 17	100	3. 33	0. 010	....
88	1. 77	39. 50	50. 58	8. 15	100	1. 75	0. 013	....
89	1. 83	42. 47	44. 03	11. 67	100	3. 52	0. 028	....
90	0. 71	43. 63	46. 49	9. 17	100	2. 73	0. 020	....
91	1. 31	38. 78	50. 10	9. 81	100	1. 23	0. 015	....
92	2. 82	36. 94	48. 64	11. 60	100	1. 10	0. 026	....
93	2. 80	39. 79	49. 91	7. 50	100	2. 02	0. 017	....
94	1. 59	39. 44	52. 62	6. 35	100	1. 63	0. 028	....
95	2. 07	38. 08	51. 10	8. 75	100	1. 80	0. 061	....
Average ...	0. 89	38. 52	53. 55	7. 04	100	2. 48	0. 0121	

LOCATIONS OF MINES FROM WHICH SAMPLES OF PITTSBURG COAL WERE TAKEN FOR ANALYSIS.

Sample
No.

1 Gilchrist mine, one mile north of Lazearville, Brooke county.
2 Wellsburg mine, one-half mile south of Wellsburg, Brooke county.
3 Big Four mine, two and one-quarter miles south of Wellsburg, Brooke county.
4 Richland mine, three miles north of Wheeling, Ohio county.
5 Whittaker mine, East Wheeling, Ohio county.
6 McKinley mine, East Wheeling, Ohio county.

7   Jochlum mine, East Wheeling, Ohio county.
8   Manchester mine, East Wheeling, Ohio county.
9   Elm Grove mine, near Elm Grove, Ohio county.
10 Boggs Run mine, near Benwood, Marshall county.
11 Benwood mine, near Benwood, Marshall county.
12 Glendale mine, near Glendale, Marshall county.
13 Moundsville mine, near Moundsville, Marshall county.
14 Garlow mine, on Robinson Run, Monongalia county.
15 Jasper Stone mine, on Robinson Run, Monongalia county.
16 Beechwood mine, about half way between Morgantown and Fairmont,
        and in Monongalia county.
17 Opekiska mine, eleven miles northeast of Fairmont, Marion county.
18 Murray mine, ten miles north of Fairmont, on the F. M. & P.
        R. R.
19 Montana mine, six miles north of Fairmont, on the F. M. & P.
        R. R.
20 Aurora mine, two miles west of Fairmont, Marion county.
21 Chatham shaft No. 1 one-fourth mile east of Farmington, Marion
        county.
22 Shaft mine, near Fairmont, on Wheeling Division of B. & O. R. R.
23 New England mine, at Watson, two miles south of Fairmont, on B.
        & O. R. R.
24 Gaston mine, at Watson, Marion county.
25 Monongah No. 6 mine, at Monongah, six miles south of Fairmont, on
        B. & O. R. R.
26 Monongah No. 2 mine, on east side of railroad, 600 feet south of Mon-
        ongah.
27 Monongah No. 3 mine, on east side of railroad, one mile south of
        Monongah.
28 Marion mine, one-fourth mile south of Everson, which is eight miles
        south of Fairmont, and in Marion county.
29 Pennois mine, one-fourth mile north of Everson.
30 King mine, at Kingmont, about three miles south of Fairmont.
31 Anderson mine, at Anderson, about nine miles south of Fairmont.
32 Highland mine, on east side of railroad, 500 feet south of station.
33 Middleton mine, at Middleton, one-fourth mile south of Highland.
34 Chiefton mine, at Chiefton, ten miles south of Fairmont.
35 Same name and place, (bottom coal of vein).
36 Chiefton mine, on east side of railroad.
37 Hutchinson mine, at Hutchinson, twelve miles south of Fairmont.
38 Enterprise mine, at Enterprise, thirteen miles south of Fairmont.
39 Riverdale mine, one-fourth mile north of Shinnston, which is fifteen
        miles south of Fairmont.
40 Briar Hill mines, Nos. 5 and 7, one-fourth mile below Gypsy, which is
        twenty-one miles south of Fairmont.
41 Briar Hill No. 6 Maulsby mine, about three-fourth mile above Gypsy.
42 Ehlen mine, at mouth of Shinn's run, near Shinnston.
43 Solon mine, one-half mile south of Shinnston, on M. R. branch B. & O.
44 Farnum mine, at Farnum, six miles north of Clarksburg, on the M.
        R. branch of the B. & O. R. R.
45 Globe mine, at Farnum, on south side of railroad.
46 Pinnickinnick mine, No. 2, at Glenn Falls, Harrison county.
47 Briar Hill mine, No. 11, about two miles north of Clarksburg, Harri-
        son county.
48 Glenn Falls mine, about two miles north of Clarksburg.
49 Erie mine, six miles north of Clarksburg on Short Line R. R.
50 Columbia or Highland mine, No. 4, two and one-half miles east of
        Clarksburg.
51 Ocean or Highland mine, No. 5, three and one-half miles east of
        Clarksburg.

52 Perry No. 1 mine, near Adamston, one mile north of Clarksburg.
53 Fairmore mine, near Adamston.
54 Waldo mine, one-half mile east of Wilsonburg, which is four miles
      west of Clarksburg, on the Parkersburg branch of the B. & O.
      R. R.
55 Wilsonburg mine, at Wilsonburg, opened in 1872.
56 Lydia mine, at Wolf Summit, about seven miles west of Clarksburg.
57 Pinnickinnick No. 1 mine, one mile east of Clarksburg on the B. & O.
      R. R.
58 Despard No. 2 mine, about two miles east of Clarksburg.
59 Meadow Brook mine, at Meadow Brook, nine miles north of Clarks-
      burg.
60 Cooke Coal and Coke Company No. 1 mine, on Simpsons creek in
      Harrison county, about one mile south of MeadowBrook.
61 Reynoldsville mine, at Reynoldsville, Harrison county.
62 O'Neil No. 1 mine, at O Neil, Harrison county, on the B. & O. R. R.
63 O'Neil No. 2 mine,   "   "   "   "   "   "
64 Melrose mine, one-half mile north of Viropa, Harrison county.
65 Viropa mine, on east side of railroad at Viropa.
66 Dixie mine, one mile from Clarksburg, on east side of railroad, near
      Monticello.
67 Lynch mine, six miles south of Clarksburg, on the W. Va. & P. R. R.
68 Two-Lick mine, six miles south   "   "   "   "
69 West Fork mine, at Mt. Clare, Harrison county, on the W. V. & P.
      R. R..
70 Cork mine, at Mt. Clare, eight miles south of Clarksburg.
71 Interstate No. 2 mine, near Mt. Clare, eight miles south of Clarksburg.
72 Interstate No. 1 mine, one-half mile south of Mt. Clare.
73 Foster mine, six miles west of Grafton. Taylor county, on the B. &
      O. R. R.
74 New York mine, at Simpson, Taylor county, seven miles west of
      Grafton.
75 T. B. Davis mine, at Simpson, on south side of railroad.
76 Flemington No. 2 and 4 mines, at Flemington, Taylor county, north
      of B. & O. R. R.
77 Sand Lick mine, at Sand Lick, Taylor county.
78 Tyrconnell mine, at Rosemont, Taylor county.
79 Rosemont mine, at Rosemont, Taylor county.
80 West Opening mine, at Berryburg, Barbour county.
81 South Opening mine, at Berryburg, Barbour county.
82 James Rooney mine, at Vadis, Lewis county.
83 W. J. Clovis mine, on Bear run, Gilmer county.
84 Ellis mine, on Coal run, tributary to Big Ellis, Gilmer county.
85 George Nutt mine, on left prong of Middle Fork of Copen Run, Gil-
      mer county.
86 Hope mine, one-half mile south of Mason City, Mason county.
87 Beech Grove mine, one half mile south of Mason City, Mason Co.
88 Klondike mine, one and one-fourth miles above Mason City.
89 New Castle mine, at West Columbia, Mason county.
90 Camden No. 1 mine, at Spilman, Mason county.
91 Mason City mine, one and one-half miles above Mason City, Mason
      county.
92 Jackson Furnace mine, at Hartford, Mason county.
93 Hartford mine, at Hartford, Mason county.
94 Plymouth mine, one mile northeast of Plymouth, Putnam county.
95 Raymond City mine, two and one-half miles northeast of Raymond
      City, Putnam county.

The average results of all these analyses give in round
numbers, moisture, 1 per cent., volatile matter 38½, fixed carbon
53½, ash 7, sulphur 2½, and phosphorus one-hundredth part of
1 per cent.. These figures give the average for the coal over the
entire state, but as some districts are higher in sulphur, ash and
volatile matter than others, the average has also been computed
by districts. In this computation the mines on the Monongahela
and Little Kanawha waters have all been included in one district;
the mines on the Ohio river in Mason county make a second
group; those on the Great Kanawha in Putnam county, a third
and those along the upper Ohio in Marshall, Ohio and Brooke
counties, a fourth. As thus arranged by districts the results are
as follows:

	Moisture	Vol. Mat.	Fix. Car.	Ash	Sulphur	Phosphor.
Fairmont and Clarksburg	0.75	38.16	54.63	6.45	2.30	0.0117
Brooke, Marshall and Ohio	0.93	39.46	51.35	8.26	3.86	0.0067
Mason county	1.88	40.21	47.78	10.13	2.20	0.0160
Raymond and Plymouth	1.83	38.76	51.86	7.55	1.72	0.0450

An inspection of this table of averages will show that the coal
from the Fairmont-Clarksburg district stands first in the order of
excellence, Putnam county, second, Wheeling, third, and Mason
county, fourth, or last, on account of its high percentage of ash
and moisture.

Of course some of these analyses given will prove too high in
sulphur, and some too low for the average of the respective mines
from which the samples were taken, but this could not be avoided
without undertaking the analysis of a greater number of samples
from each mine than the resources of the Survey would permit,
but as the coal has been carefully sampled, and accurately analyzed from a large number of mines in the same region, it is concluded that the general average of all will fairly represent the composition of the coal.

The chemical work of the Survey has very fortunately been
supplemented and checked by the vastly more extensive and elab-
orate analytical work of the chemical department of the Fairmont
Coal Company. Through the courtesy of Mr. L. L. Malone, the
General Manager of that corporation, and the kindness of Mr.
Frank Haas, its Chief Chemist, the Survey is enabled to present

these highly instructive and useful results in the following very interesting article, prepared expressly for these pages.

The letter and report of Mr. Haas follow herewith:

FAIRMONT COAL COMPANY.

GENERAL OFFICES.

FAIRMONT, W. VA.,
December 20, 1902.

DR. I. C. WHITE,
State Geologist,
Morgantown, W. Va.

DEAR SIR :—

I send you under separate cover the paper on the Fuel Value of Fairmont (Pittsburg) coal.

As I have explained to you verbally, the article has been revised by cutting out the coke part. This was done because our coke product will be entirely changed from what it is now and such results as I might have used would not represent the facts as they will exist in the future.

Yours truly,
FRANK HAAS.

ANALYSES AND FUEL VALUE OF THE PITTSBURG COAL IN THE FAIRMONT REGION.

A full discussion of the chemical properties and fuel value of the Pittsburg coal in West Virginia is, perhaps, premature at this time, from the fact that it has only been a year since the coal companies have started a systematic examination of this subject. Furthermore, there is but a very small area of the Pittsburg seam exposed, and this on the extreme eastern border; far too small a portion to draw conclusions for the vast territory still undeveloped. The discussions and conclusions drawn should be taken as apparent tendencies or theories when the whole field is considered, to be substantiated or revised as the work progresses and more territory is exposed.

It would have been desirable from a scientific as well as a practical standpoint to attack the problem with the ultimate analysis of the coal, but the practical demands were so pressing, and the ultimate analysis so laborious, expensive and difficult, that as a preliminary, the universally used and much abused proximate analysis was employed, supplemented by the Mahler Bomb Calorimeter for fuel values.

There is a growing opinion that the proximate analysis, so far as the Volatile and Fixed Carbon determinations are concerned, is worthless and misleading except for the identification of a coal. The Volatile Matter has been used as an index of the coking quality of a coal, and the quantity of gas that it will produce. The first has too often failed and the second is only a very rough approximation as to quantity, and of no information as to quality. The Fixed Carbon as an index to the quantity of coke is only an approximation and fails completely in coking coals of very high Fixed Carbon. As a measure of the heating value of a coal, the Fixed Carbon determination has been extensively used, but the results calculated by this method are so at variance with those actually determined, that with the coal in this region it cannot be relied upon to give even approximate results.

With coals from the same seams and the same region the Volatile matter should, if uniformly determined in all samples, show if any great change has taken place from one mine to another. The indications were, after a few preliminary samples were taken, that there was no great change in the actual coal, but that the sulphur was practically the only disturbing influence and the work resolved itself almost entirely into locating this troublesome element.

It was found that if samples were taken every tenth room on all butt entries, or an equivalent distance, (500 feet), that the average so determined could be relied upon to represent the mine to within two-tenths of one per cent. in sulphur, and one-fourth of one per cent. in ash, even in the extremely high sulphur coals. In taking samples a piece of canvas was spread on the floor of the mine and a groove cut into the face of the coal about two inches wide and two inches deep from top to bottom, bringing down twenty to thirty pounds of coal. This was halved down to about five pounds, which, after taking to the laboratory, was crushed and pulverized to a laboratory sample of two ounces. Following this general rule some 1500 samples were taken.

The extreme limits of this investigation extended from Beechwood, Grays Flat and Chatam mines on the north and west, to Berryburg, Interstate and Wolf Summit mines on the south and west, with the bulk of samples along the West Fork river between Fairmont and Clarksburg. The territory enclosed by the extreme limits is approximately 500 square miles.

The Pittsburg seam in this region has two persistent bands; the lower half consists of one-half to one inch of bone coal four and one-half to five feet from the bottom of the seam. The second band is six to eight inches above the lower bone .A third parting is occasionally present between the two mentioned. The coal immediately below the slate, and known as the top coal, is of an inferior quality and on average about one foot thick. If the height of the seam is diminished below its normal thickness of eight and one-half feet, it is invariably at the expense of the top coal. A general section of the Pittsburg seam of this region may be represented by the accompanying sketch :

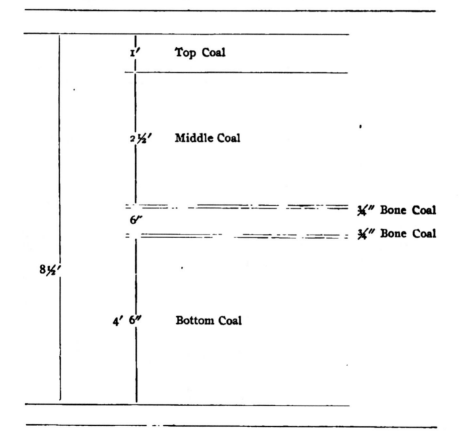

The bottom coal includes most of the bed and is almost invariably better than the rest of the seam. A test made in various parts of the field to determine this, resulted as follows:

MINE.	BOTTOM.		MIDDLE.		TOP.	
	Ash.	Sulphur.	Ash.	Sulphur.	Ash.	Sulphur.
Shaft..............	5.94	2.48	9.12	2.55	17.04	5.19
Anderson.........	6.50	1.38	4.05	1.14	15.15	2.19
Enterprise........	6.42	1.26	6.40	1.70	14.74	3.20
Mon'ng'h, No. 3	6.40	2.48	7.45	3.25	12.65	4.07
Chiefton	6.05	1.03	9.85	1.55	11.50	3.88
Harbert	6.80	3.07	8.60	3.54	14.25	5.32
Ocean	4.68	1.89	7.68	3.43	17.18	3.07

The dividing line between the middle coal and the top coal is not clearly marked and it is probable that, if the facts had been suspected and more care taken in making the separation, the middle coal would have been found more uniform and lower in ash and sulphur, while the top coal would have been more uniformly bad.

In the table of average analyses given below, all mines are arranged in order from Beechwood, the mine farthest down the river, up to the headwaters of the West Fork:

MINE.	Moisture.	Volatile.	Fixed Carbon.	Ash.	Sulphur.	B. T. U.
Beechwood	1.56	35.39	55.18	6.87	1.86	14138
Murray...........	1.44	35.82	56.82	5.92	2.07	14281
Luther	1.40	35.61	56.37	6.42	2.01	14216
Montana.........	1.20	35.49	56.30	7.00	2.05	14151
Aurora	1.58	35.57	55.79	7.06	1.99	14090
Stafford	1.14	35.04	55.94	7.88	1.52	14085
Federal......... ..	1.35	35.65	55.09	7.91	1.74	14021
Chatam...........	1.63	35.74	55.99	6.64	0.92	14256
Shaft.............	1.39	36.63	54.31	7.67	2.46	13969
O'Donnel........	1.61	35.41	56.13	6.85	2.77	14028
Gaston	1.25	37.61	53.77	7.37	2.49	14044
New England...	1.37	36.29	55.36	6.98	2.02	14132
Monong'h No. 6	1.34	35.48	55.70	7.48	2.01	14059
" " 5	1.73	35.88	56.42	5.97	0.97	14356
" " 2	1.45	36.29	55.48	6.78	1.85	14171
" " 3	1.56	37.34	53.29	7.81	2.71	13892
Anderson	1.78	36.01	56.34	5.87	1.34	14321
Highland...	1.39	35.17	57.13	6.31	1.23	14326
Middleton........	1.62	36.21	55.82	6.35	1.35	14270
Chiefton..........	1.64	35.75	54.30	8.31	1.74	13914
Hutchinson......	1.82	36.66	54.23	7.29	1.46	14078
Enterprise........	1.62	36.79	54.44	7.15	1.94	14076
Melrose...........	1.37	37.41	51.85	9.37	3.72	13559
Viropa............	1.09	39.22	52.62	7.07	2.91	14058
Riverdale........	1.27	37.42	52.72	8.59	2.91	13791
Ehlen.............	1.60	38.62	51.34	8.44	3.26	13720
Solon...	1.45	37.93	52.23	8.39	2.97	13788
Harbert...........	1.60	38.74	51.93	7.73	3.35	13823

Gypsy	1.31	39.36	50.95	8.38	3.71	1 725
Maulsby	1.07	38.74	52.87	7.32	2.63	14065
Meadow Brook	1.18	39.99	51.83	7.00	3.18	14024
Globe	1.45	38.97	53.30	6.28	2.65	14156
Farnum	1.54	38.68	52.87	6.91	3.24	13974
Glen Falls	1.46	37.94	53.25	7.35	3.19	13924
Dunham	1.61	36.66	53.77	7.96	2.81	13849
Pinnickinnick	1.53	38.01	53.53	6.93	2.59	14048
Columbia	1.35	37.76	53.23	7.66	2.57	13964
Ocean	1.43	36.26	54.74	7.57	2.96	13921
Colonial	1.34	36.85	55.74	6.07	2.42	14233
Rosemont	1.11	36.90	55.88	6.11	2.47	14257
Flemington	1.20	36.90	54.11	7.79	3.08	13908
Wilsonburg	1.89	38.46	50.23	9.42	4.52	13377
O Neil, No. 1	1.35	40.65	49.47	8.53	3.52	13717
" " 2	1.36	40.98	51.15	6.51	3.29	14060
Wolf Summit	1.48	40.20	51.04	7.28	3.92	13846
Dixie	1.35	40.48	51.23	6.94	3.92	13920
Lynch	1.23	40.54	50.79	7.44	3.72	13884
Two Lick	1.70	38.60	53.25	6.45	2.67	14089
West Fork	1.55	39.20	53.19	6.06	2.87	14149
Interstate	1.27	39.39	51.92	7.42	3.51	13905
Berryburg	0.68	38.60	53.09	7.63	3.06	14017
Average	1.43	37.47	53.83	7.27	2.59	14014

The Moisture column, while it shows a considerable variation, does not follow any regular change from the northern end to
the south. High and low averages are of only local occurrence
and the normal percentage is regained in the following mine.
The Volatile Matter gradually increases from thirty-six per cent.
at the northern end to nearly forty per cent. at the southern. The
increase is due partly to a greater percentage of Volatile Sulphur
in coal around the Clarksburg end than in the northern end of the
field.

Just what relative quantity of Volatile or organic sulphur
exists in the total, has not been determined. The Fixed Carbon
follows inversely the change suffered by the Volatile Matter. The
Ash is fairly constant and such variations as exist are in nearly
every case caused or accompanied by variations in the sulphur.
The sulphur is very erratic, varying from three-fourths of one per
cent. to nearly four per cent.

Efforts to indicate the cause or indications of high sulphur
coals met with failure. All the theories of the practical miner, such as
heavy cover, local basins or depressions in the seam and even the
effect of water courses, failed to throw any light on the subject.
There are areas which can be well defined as development continues that are practically uniform and low in sulphur.

Of the three kinds of sulphur in coal the inorganic, or that combined as sulphide of iron, furnishes the greater quantity. This is indicated by the comparatively high iron content in the ash. The sulphates furnish but a small quantity and this is mostly from the sulphate salts, which are deposited between the joints of the coal by the water percolating through the stratifications above, charging itself with lime and magnesia carbonate, which in part changes to sulphate when in contact with the sulphides in the coal. There is, however, but a small amount that suffers from this change. It has been found that by far the most of the white scaly material, so common in this coal, is either carbonate of lime or magnesia.

The segregated masses of sulphide of iron, known as sulphur balls, are found in nearly all of the mines of this coal. Their frequency occurs in proportion to the sulphur in the coal proper. In such of the mines as run less than one per cent. sulphur, they are comparatively rare, while in coals of three or four per cent. sulphur, they are most abundant. It appears that four per cent. is the point of saturation of this coal, if such a term can be applied to a solid body, and all over this amount is segregated in these masses. An analysis of a sulphur ball shows that the sulphur and iron are in such combination as is equivalent to the bisulphide or pyrite form. These masses go to pieces very rapidly when exposed to atmospheric agencies. The pyrite changes to sulphate or iron and disappears as a soluble compound, leaving a soft, pasty and sooty material behind. This action was shown in the coking of some slack which had been exposed on a dump for several years. The resulting coke had an ash content of seven to eight per cent. and sulphur one per cent., while the coal as taken out of the mine would show eleven per cent. ash and two per cent. sulphur.

In coking, about one-half the sulphur is volatilized; this factor is variable to some extent, depending on the total sulphur present; for all coals containing over one and one-half per cent. sulphur the factor will hold. Roughly, if the sulphur in coal is multiplied by eight-tenths, it will give the sulphur in the resulting coke.

The Heating Value of the average coals of each mine was determined by the method described in the Transactions of the A. I. M. E., Volume XXVII., page 259. Briefly, the method consists in determining a quantity "H" which represents the heating value of the average coal, free from Moisture, Ash and Sulphur, and then deducting the losses due to each of these impurities in any one analysis. This method was successfully employed in the various Ohio coals, and the results so far obtained in this field are as uniform as on any coal yet tried. The general formula as used is :

B. T. U. = "H" (100-Ash-Sul.-Mois.) + (Sul. × 4050). It follows that knowing "H," Ash, Sulphur, and Moisture, the calorific value can be determined. Since the method has not been applied to West Virginia coal, the manner in which the constant "H" was found, will be given, also to show that so far as the work has progressed the Formula can be relied upon to give results within one per cent. of the actual determination of the Calorimeter. The Mahler calorimeter need not be described here, nor the manner of operating it; for such information, reference is made to the paper previously mentioned. It is conceded that the instrument is the best, and perhaps the only reliable one for the practical determination of the calorific values of fuel.

Twenty samples taken at different points in the field were tested with the calorimeter and the B. T. U. actually determined; the results are given in the following table :

Moisture.	Volatile.	Fixed Carbon.	Ash.	Sul.	Calorimeter B. T. U.	Calculated B. T. U.	Diff. Per Ct.
1.40	37.00	55.48	6.12	2.59	14147	14196	— 0.3
1.50	36.84	53.45	8.21	3.13	13819	13790	— 0.2
1.45	35.05	53.20	10.30	2.56	13505	13536	—|-0.2
1.55	35.85	55.05	7.55	1.58	13975	14066	—|-0.6
1.65	39.80	53.45	5.10	2.48	14243	14329	—|-0.6
0.92	37.60	52.56	8.92	3.23	13861	13758	— 0.7
1.85	36.95	55.80	5.40	1.60	14279	14353	—|-0.5
1.07	37.40	55.44	6.09	2.48	14405	14265	— 0.97
1.50	40.15	50.72	7.63	3.48	13818	13840	—|-0.2
2.28	36.12	57.40	4.20	0.76	14660	14571	— 0.6
1.49	36.18	54.79	7.54	2.34	13947	13988	—|-0.3
1.24	36.66	55.95	6.15	1.51	14338	14342	—|-0.0
1.25	37.15	55.38	6.22	1.67	14305	14310	—|-0.0
1.58	35.72	55.56	7.14	2.32	14066	14039	— 0.2
1.38	37.80	54.21	6.61	2.71	14193	14108	— 0.6
1.95	35.85	56.95	5.25	0.83	14453	14451	— 0.0
1.50	35.63	56.86	6.01	1.93	14212	14274	—|-0.4
1.17	35.64	55.59	7.60	2.70	13867	13987	—|-0.9
1.90	35.78	55.78	6.54	1.38	14274	14192	— 0.6
1.25	40.10	51.70	6.95	3.33	14033	14003	— 0.2
1.49	36.96	54.77	6.78	2.23	14120	....	....

The average Moisture, Ash, and Sulphur from the analyses, and the average B. T. U., were substituted in the following formula :

$$\frac{\text{Average B. T. U.}-(\text{Average Sul.}\times 4050)}{100-(\text{Average Ash}+\text{Sul.}+\text{Mois.})}=\text{"H"}$$

"H," the only unknown quantity in the equation, is determined and may be represented by 15675. Now this quantity (15675) is substituted for "H" in the Formula,—B. T. U. = "H" (100 Ash—Sul.—Mois.)+(Sul. × 4050), and applying it to each separate analysis, the seventh column in the table is produced. An eighth has been added to show the difference between the actual and calculated determinations. The largest difference so far found is 0.97 per cent. Considering the fact that duplicates with the Calorimeter sometimes vary one-half to one per cent., the formula gives close results and well within the limits of practical demands. When tests on steam boilers are made that can account for the last one per cent. in the heat balance, it may become necessary to furnish results less in error, but of this there is no immediate danger.

The calorific value of coal in this country, where fuel is abundant and cheap, has not been considered important until within recent years. At the present time, as the practical man is taking this into account, the tendency is to overestimate and exaggerate the relative value of the various coals.

The following table gives a comparison between average Fairmont coal and average samples of Pocahontas, New River, and Kanawha coals:

COALS.	Mois.	Volatile.	Fix. Car.	Ash.	Sul.	B. T. U.	Relative Value.
New River......	1.61	27.16	67.54	3.69	0.68	14976	100
Pocahontas......	0.73	18.10	74.52	6.65	0.59	14588	97
Kanawha........	0.89	32.61	60.10	6.40	1.03	14349	96
Fairmont........	1.50	36.70	54.80	7.00	2.10	14100	94

An average elementary analysis of the coal of this region cannot be given at this time for lack of sufficient data. From some boiler tests, in which elementary analyses were reported, made on Fairmont coal in 1900 by Professors Lord and Hitchcock, of Columbus, Ohio, an average elementary analysis has been calculated.

The tests referred to were on five coals from different parts of the field and samples taken from car lots.

The Carbon-Available Hydrogen ratio was practically constant, showing no great change in the ultimate composition of the coal. The elementary analysis, which may be considered as fairly representative of the field, is as follows :

Carbon	Hydrogen	Oxygen	Nitrogen	Sulphur	Ash
77.00	5.52	6.82	1.56	2.10	7.00

The question is frequently asked: "How much water will Fairmont coal evaporate per pound of coal?" An answer cannot be given unless curtailed with suppositions or conditions. The B. T. U., as given, shows the heat that the coal will deliver if the coal is completely burned, independent of how the coal is fired, or the kind, make or condition of the boiler. With a theoretical boiler, a coal with 14100 B. T. U. will evaporate 14.6 pounds of water from and at 212 degrees Fahrenheit. Since neither the methods of firing are perfect, nor the absorption of boilers complete, the above theoretical figure is never reached and seldom ever approached. Some few plants with modern appliances for automatic firing and boilers of special design and construction have been able to extract eighty per cent. of the heat in the coal and deliver it in available steam. In other words, they have attained an efficiency of eighty per cent. Such performances are very rare and seventy-five per cent. might be called the best practice, while seventy per cent. would be very good, sixty-five per cent. the average and sixty per cent. the common practice in smaller plants.

Assuming now the various efficiences, the following table will give the water eveporated:

With 80 per cent, efficiency Fairmont coal will evaporate 11.68 pounds water from and at 212 degrees F.

With 75 per cent. efficiency Fairmont coal will evaporate 10.95 pounds water from and at 212 degrees F.

With 70 per cent. efficiency Fairmont coal will evaporate 10.22 pounds water from and at 212 degrees F.

With 65 per cent. efficiency Fairmont coal will evaporate 9.49 pounds water from and at 212 degrees F.

With 60 per cent. efficiency Fairmont coal will evaporate 8.76 pounds water from and at 212 degrees F.

Now comparing New River, Pocahontas, and Kanawha with Fairmont, we have the following table :

COALS.	80 per ct.	75 per ct.	70 per ct.	65 per ct.	60 per ct.
New River................	12. 40	11. 63	10. 85	10. 08	9. 30
Pocahontas......................	12. 08	11. 33	10. 57	9. 82	9. 06
Kanawha.,......................	11. 89	11. 14	10. 40	9. 66	8. 91
Fairmont.....................	11. 68	10. 95	10. 22	9. 45	8. 76

Under the ordinary method of firing, Fairmont coal is known as a smoking coal. While smoking qualities are to a considerable extent inherent to the coal, yet it can, to a very great extent, be controlled, and in some cases entirely overcome. The modern contrivances, known as smoke consumers, are very effective in their action on this coal and in smaller plants, where extensive contrivances for this purpose are unwarranted, a care in the manner of firing will in part suppress the dense black smoke. Firing often and not much at one time will remedy the evil to a great extent, and keep the conduct of the stack within the requirements of the law. It has been erroneously supposed that the black smoke was an indication of considerable loss of carbon, but this has been carefully tested and determined by various authorities, and it has been found that the loss in smoke is trifling, less than one per cent., even in extreme cases.

Sulphur has little or no effect on coal as a fuel. It is true that it replaces a certain amount of carbon, but the replacement is not entirely lost, as sulphur is combustible, having a heating value of about three-eighths of that of carbon. Moisture, on the other hand, not only replaces combustible matter, but requires additional combustible for its evaporation.

Clinkering, or running on grate bars, is made possible by the composition of the ash, but it is due more to the manner in which the coal is fired. Sulphur has nothing to do with it, and only indirectly affects the composition of the ash by being a carrier for the iron.

Following is a table of analyses of the ash of some of the coals of this region :

AVERAGE ANALYSES OF ASH FROM COKE.

MINE.	SiO_2	Al_2O_3	Fe_2O_3	CaO	MgO	P_2O_5	SO_3	Na_2O	K_2O	Totals.
Montana	42.08	24.33	28.07	1.70	0.39	0.48	0.15	0.72	0.87	98.79
Mon ng'h No.2	39.34	22.21	28.07	4.60	0.88	0.52	2.24	0.89	1.30	100.05
Mon'ng h No.3	36.44	21.44	29.71	5.70	0.76	0.49	2.62	0.89	1.45	99.50
Beechwood	44.96	25.94	23.57	1.60	0.97	0.47	0.27	1.07	1.33	100.18
New England..	34.15	18.24	29.36	8.20	0.97	0.56	5.25	0.94	1.36	99.03
Gaston	35.39	21.10	30.86	6.04	0.93	0.59	2.41	1.21	1.22	99.75
Enterprise......	36.57	19.67	28.57	6.90	1.14	0.78	4.50	1.03	1.35	100.51

The analyses represent the average of over one hundred separate samples and eliminate, to a considerable extent, the accidental variations of single samples. It appears from this that the real basis of the Ash is Silica and Alumina in the proportion of 1.7 of Silica to 1 of alumina. The iron varies with the sulphur in the coal. The most of the lime appears to be a foreign element to the coal, and an intrusion after the coal was formed in the manner previously suggested. The Alkalies, on which so much stress is laid by some as the cause of clinkering, are here shown to be present in a very small and uniform quantity.

Speculating as to the fusibility of the Ash, from the above analyses, it would appear from the relatively high ratio of Alumina to the Silica, that it would require a very high temperature to convert this compound to cinder. The relative fusibility would be marked by the sum of the Fe_2O_3 and CaO, the higher this quantity the more fusible the compound.

Taking now the physical conditions into account, we find that the Ash is not a simple chemical compound but a mechanical mixture of several. For instance, it has been shown that a considerable portion of the Fe_2O_3 can be removed by mechanical separation. Furthermore, anyone familiar with coal under steam boilers, has noticed that considerable of the Ash is carried over the bridge wall. The Ash so carried over by the draft is practically free from iron and nearly pure Silica and Alumina. This action taking place would soon leave on the grate bars a compound considerable higher in iron and lower in silica, which would tend to a more fusible mixture. This probably explains why, under excessive draft and extreme temperature in the fire box, the coal from this region sometimes clinkers. A sample of clinker taken from a locomotive boiler showed :

Silica (SiO₂) - - - - - 32.40
Alumina (Al₂ O₃) - - - - - 23.38
Sesqui-Oxide of Iron (Fe₂ O₃) - - 38.28

showing a tendency in this direction.

FRANK HAAS, C. E., M. E.

FAIRMONT, WEST VA.,
December, 1902.

It is instructive to place the average chemical results for the Fairmont-Clarksburg region obtained by Professor Hite and his assistants in a comparative column with those for the same district by Mr. Haas, as shown in the following table:

CHEMIST.	Moisture.	Volatile Matter.	Fixed Carbon.	Ash.	Sulphur.	B. T. U.
HAAS............	1. 47	39. 46	51. 36	7. 27	2. 59	....
HITE............	0. 75	38. 16	54. 63	6. 45	2. 30	....

These results agree as closely as one could expect in view of the different methods of sampling, and also in view of the wider area of the coal field covered by Professor Hite's work, viz.: from Monongalia to Gilmer counties, while Mr. Haas' analyses extend only over the Fairmont-Clarksburg district.

The greatest ratio of difference is in the moisture, and this is probably due to the fact that Professor Hite's samples were stored in a rather dry room for some considerable time before analysis.

GAS AND COKE.

The great value of the Pittsburg coal consists in the variety of uses for which it is adapted. Yielding fine results as a general steam and domestic fuel, it is also unexcelled as a gas producer, and with proper care to exclude the sulphurous portion, makes a good quality of coke.

The coal from the Fairmont region has long been used in the principal cities for the manufacture of illuminating gas, the yield per ton being quite as large and the quality as good as that from the same coal obtained at the famous gas coal mines of Westmoreland county, Pennsylvania.

This three-fold use is not a common one to the thick coals of any region, and it is this that adds additional value to the Monongahela river area of the Pittsburg coal, since the excessive amount of sulphur in this coal along the Ohio river would forbid its manufacture into either gas or coke in the Wheeling district, unless some practical method could be devised for largely reducing its quantity of sulphur.

It appears to be a general law that the proportion of sulphur in any of the coals increases westward across the Appalachian field, the purer ones lying along its southeastern side. For instance, if we take the Pittsburg coal as an example, the analyses show its sulphur contents increasing, in round numbers, westward, from its most eastern area as follows:

	Sulphur.
Potomac Basin (Elk Garden)..	0.80
Connellsville Basin..	1.00
Monongahela River (Fairmont)...	2.50
Ohio River (Wheeling)...	3.50
Western Crop in Ohio...4.50–5.00

This law will also hold true, in a general way, for any of the other coal beds of wide geographical extent, and there must consequently be some general cause which has operated to produce such results. It is sufficient here to note the fact as an explanation why the same bed of coal may be of quite different quality in one region from that in another, and hence not well adapted for the same purposes in both.

It has been the custom of the coal operators in the Fairmont and Clarksburg regions to coke only the fine coal, or screenings, the "lump" coal being shipped for steam and fuel purposes, and hence the manufacture of coke has been more in the nature of a by-product, than of the production of coke per se. For this reason the coke product of the region has always held a deservedly poor rating among the iron and steel working fraternity, since the lack of care in excluding impurities, left the resulting coke high in both ash and sulphur. This haphazard method, however, as stated by Mr. Haas in the letter accompanying his article on the Fairmont coal, is not to continue, since his chemical investigations have located the portion of the coal in which the chief quantity of the sulphur occurs, as well as large areas of the same where there is but little more sulphur in the general body of the coal (excluding its top) than there is in the average of the Connellsville basin. With the inauguration of the new methods contemplated by the Fairmont Coal Company for the manufacture of coke, there can be little doubt that a great improvement in quality can be achieved, and that the resultant coke will compare favorably with the present average of the Connellsville product, including Klondike and other new areas recently opened in Pennsylvania. Hence the following analyses of the coke from the Pittsburg coal in the Fairmont-Clarksburg region are to be considered only as the type of the old and careless methods, and not what can and will be done in this line for the future.

FAIRMONT–CLARKSBURG COKE (FROM PITTSBURG COAL.)

Anal. No.	Mois-ture.	Volatile Matter.	Fixed Carbon.	Ash.	Total	Sul.	Phos.	Coking Time.
1	0.18	1.24	83.45	15.13	100	2.17	0.0265	48 hours,
2	0.02	1.02	87.51	11.45	100	1.12	0.0200	72 "
3	0.04	1.20	85.35	13.41	100	1.79	0.0300	72 "
4	0.15	1.29	85.79	12.77	100	1.81	0.0300	72 "
5	0.04	2.00	86.71	11.25	100	1.10	0.0060	48 "
6	0.48	2.67	84.56	12.29	100	1.86	....	72 "
7	0.50	3.58	78.75	17.17	100	2.09	0.0190	48 "
8	0.69	0.76	92.77	5.78	100	2.43	0.0320	48 "
Average..	0.26	1.72	85.61	12.41	100	1.79	0.0243	....

LOCATION OF MINES FROM WHICH SAMPLES FOR COKE WERE TAKEN.

Sample
No,

1 From Beechwood mine, about half way between Morgantown and Fairmont.
2 From Montana mine, six miles north of Fairmont, Marion county.
3 From Gaston mine, at Watson, Marion county.
4 From New England mine, near Watson, Marion county, two miles south of Fairmont, on the B. & O. R. R.
5 From Kingmont ovens, Kingmont, Marion county.
6 From Monongah, No. 3, 1 mile south of Monongah, Marion county.
7 From Hutchinson mine, at Hutchinson, Marion county, twelve miles south of Fairmont.
8 From Briar Hill, No. 1, about twenty miles south of Fairmont.

The Montana and Monongah mines are the only ones that make any attempt to reduce the impurities by washing the fine coal.

There can be little doubt that if a foot or more of the highly sulphurous and bony "top" coal were discarded, and all the rest of the bed properly crushed and washed, a most excellent coke would result.

It is highly proper, before closing this chapter on the Pittsburg coal, to call attention to its exceeding richness in volatile combustile matter, and of the great and unpardonable waste of heat and most valuable by-products when it is coked in the ordinary bee-hive oven. The coal is one which would yield very rich results if coked in some form of the by-product oven, and now that one very strong and wealthy corporation controls practically all of the Fairmont-Clarksburg coal mines, it is hoped that it will not repeat the wasteful folly of the Connellsville producers in its future coke operations.

CHAPTER IV.

THE CONEMAUGH SERIES, NO. XIV.

This is the rock series which was formerly called the Lower Barren Measures, Elk River series, etc.

Dr. William B. Clark, State Geologist of Maryland, has recently called attention to the fact that the name Conemaugh, given to these beds by Franklin Platt in 1878, antedates all other geographical terms, and should, therefore, have precedence. The name is also quite appropriate, since the series in question has a fine development along the stream of that name.

As now limited, it includes all of the strata from the floor of the Pittsburg coal down to the top of the Upper Freeport bed, the whole having an average thickness of 600 feet, though it varies from 400 on the western margin of the Appalachian field in Ohio, to 800 feet near Charleston, W. Va.

The series as thus limited above and below, consists of two widely different members, lithologically considered, the upper composed largely of soft, red, and marly shale, the lower of mas-

sive, pebbly sandstones.   The difference in the rock type is so
marked, and especially in the character of the topography made
by each, that the First Geological Survey of Pennsylvania and
Virginia placed them in two different series, the massive sandstones, at the base of the Conemaugh, being classed with the underlying Allegheny.   That assignment, based primarily upon difference of rock type, was more philosophical than the present
limitations, but the fact that no definite boundary (a sandstone always being subject to sudden and rapid changes in both thickness
and character) could be assigned to either the lower limits of the upper one, or the upper limits of the lower one, led Profs. Stevenson,
Lesley, and other Pennsylvania geologists to extend the limits of
the "Lower Barren Measures" of Rogers down to the horizon of
the Upper Freeport coal, a well marked and widely persistent
stratum.   This arrangement gives definiteness to classification, a
great desideratum, but it has the fault of bringing together rocks
of very different type, and hence, while apparently preferable to
the old and indefinite dividing line between the two series, is yet
not altogether satisfactory.   Hence, it is possible that a future and
more detailed study of the series in West Virginia, may reveal
some more desirable dividing plane between the Conemaugh series
and the underlying Allegheny than the present one, (U. F. coal),
which will retain all of the desirable features of the Rogers classification and at the same time relieve it of indefiniteness.

The sudden appearance or disappearance of RED sediments
Viewed from the standpoint of change in physical conditions
the proper place for such a dividing plane between the Conemaugh and Allegheny beds, would be the first general appearance
of RED ROCKS, near the horizon of the Bakerstown coal about 100
feet under the Ames or Crinoidal limestone horizon.   That a
great physical change took place soon after the deposition of the
Mahoning sandstone rocks, the present basal members of the
Conemaugh series, must be conceded, since no RED BEDS whatever
are found from the base of the Pottsville up to the top of the
Allegheny, and none worth considering until after the epoch of
the Upper Mahoning sandstone.

The sudden appearance or disappearance of RED sediments
after their absence from a great thickness of strata is always
accompanied by a great change in life forms, and the present one
is no exception.   In fact, the invasion of RED SEDIMENTS succeeding the Mahoning sandstone epoch of the Conemaugh may well

be considered as the "beginning of the end" of the true Coal
Measures, both from a lithological as well as a biological standpoint, and hence it is possible that the best classification aside
from the conveniences of the geologist, would leave the Mahoning
sandstone in the Coal Measures, and place the rest of the Conemaugh, as well as the Monongahela series above, in the Permo-
Carboniferous.   This reference is also confirmed by the character of the fauna and flora, both of which contain many forms that
characterize the Permo-Carboniferous beds of Kansas and the west
as may be seen in the lists published on a subsequent page under
the detailed description of the principal Conemaugh strata.

As already stated, the two types of rock (hard and soft) included in this series, give rise to two widely distinct varieties of
both soil and topography. The uppermost 400 feet of soft beds
with their included thin limestones, and limy, red, yellow, and
greenish shales, interstratified with two to three rather massive
sandstones, give origin to a beautiful, rolling topography often
finely adapted to grazing and agriculture, especially where these
beds cover the uplands not deeply trenched by draining streams.
When the hills are high and steep, however, the red marly shales
exhibit a great tendency to landslides, and hence where such
topography abounds, grazing rather than agriculture should be
the chief occupation for these Conemaugh soils.

A wide band of RED marks the crop of this soft portion of the
Conemaugh entirely across the State from the Pennsylvania line
on the north to the Big Sandy river at the Kentucky boundary,
250 miles distant to the southwest.

The line of this RED BAND so distinctly marked by the great
Pittsburg coal at top, and the massive, pebbly sandstones below
that no one could fail to recognize it, passes across eastern Monongalia and Marion, western Taylor, Barbour and Upshur, across the
Pan-handle of Lewis into Braxton, and following the west side of
Elk river, rudely parallel to the same, crosses western Clay, eastern Roane, and central Kanawha counties to the Great Kanawha
at Charleston; then crossing the latter stream, extends in a broad
belt into Putnam, through central Cabell and Wayne to the Big
Sandy river at the Kentucky line.

South from Taylor and Barbour counties, the RED BEDS of the
Conemaugh are reinforced by the REDS which there begin to replace

the limestones of the Monongahela series, so that the belt of RED
SOIL broadens out westward to the Ohio river after crossing the
Little Kanawha, and includes not only the Conemaugh and Monongahela series, but also the Dunkard.   The CONEMAUGH REDS,
however, are sharply delimited from the overlying ones by the
gray, pebbly sandstones at their base, which, together with the
complete absence of RED BEDS from the underlying Allegheny-Kanawha, and Pottsville series, causes the entire disappearance of RED
SOILS at a few miles east from Elk river, until the MAUCH CHUNK
REDS of the Lower Carboniferous are brought to the surface many
miles to the southeast in Webster, Pocahontas, Greenbrier, Summers and other counties along the southeastern border of the state.

The lowest 150 feet of these reds is known among oil well
drillers as the "Big red cave," since it gives much trouble to them
in drilling for gas and oil.   The wall of the well through this portion of the column of rocks must be quickly lined with casing, or
it will "cave" and crumble into the hole from the pressure of the
overlying strata, thus often imprisoning the drilling tools and leading to the abandonment of the boring.   The nuggets of hard limestone scattered through these red shales constitute the chief agent
in this imprisonment, since they readily tumble out from the
walls of the hole, and impinging against the drilling tools, principally at the "jars," prevent their withdrawal.

For these reasons, every oil well driller becomes an expert
stratigrapher in tracing these RED BEDS underground, and they
have been so traced in hundreds of borings entirely across the
state, when deeply covered by the overlying Monongahela and
Dunkard series, so that whether at the surface and visible in broad
bands of RED SOIL around the hills, or buried under 2000 feet of
higher sediments, the same deep purple and red shales exist in this
portion of the geologic column along the belt of country west from
the mountain region of the state.   Hence the *color* is not the result of recent oxidation, but is evidently due to the deposit of RED
SEDIMENTS derived from the erosion of old land areas of pre-carbon-
iferous time.

When these red beds of the upper Conemaugh are traced
eastward into the Allegheny mountain area, however, the colors
often fade out into green, yellow and gray, so that frequently the
geologist might be led to infer their complete absence, if his obser-

vations were confined entirely to the rocks exposed at the surface. The fact that the diamond drills bring up these reds when buried below the level of the present drainage systems in mountain areas, leads to the conclusion that the absence of the red beds, so universal over the area west from the Alleghanies, is only apparent and due to the action of carbonated waters, which have largely leached the iron from the superficial beds in mountain regions, thus decolorizing the strata and almost completely depriving them of the purple and red colors which make the outcrop of this series so conspicuous throughout their entire area in West Virginia, Pennsylvania and Ohio, west from the Alleghanies. The writer has personally observed the RED MATERIALS brought up from these borings in the Alleghany mountain region, and hence can testify that its absence from the surface outcrops in those regions is due to the secondary causes mentioned, and that although there may be an increase of sandstone and gray sandy sediments eastward, yet in the unleached portions of the Conemaugh there are always some RED BEDS to be found.

These RED BEDS cause great expense and trouble, not alone to the oil well drillers, but also to the railroads, highways, trolley lines and other public improvements, which are compelled to be cut through their outcrops. As these reds are reconverted into muddy sediments and "cave" into the oil wells soon after water penetrates them, so they return to mud at the surface, when exposed to the weather in cuttings, and thus give rise to slides which obstruct railroads and highways, and in addition give origin to a deep, sticky mud along the latter, through which wagons pass with the greatest difficulty. The railroad or highway engineer should avoid cutting into the slopes of these red beds wherever possible, since when the angle of repose is once disturbed, they will slide into the excavation continually thereafter, until the condition of equilibrium is again attained. It is these soft red beds which have given the Pennsylvania railroad so much trouble in landslides at Pittsburg, where immense retaining walls have finally been built to hold back the movement of the steep slopes, in the vicinity of the Union depot, and also along the Pan Handle railroad on the south side of the Monongahela river. Where long steep slopes must be traversed with deep cuttings through these rocks, it would be less expensive to construct tunnels, or heavy retaining walls, in the beginning.

In strong contrast with these soft, yielding, unstable beds, which make the upper two-thirds of the Conemaugh series, may be placed the massive, gray, pebbly sandstones, which form its basal members. These rocks are quite hard, and the sand grains being cemented with peroxide of iron, or silica, resist erosion and form a protecting roof to the underlying Allegheny-Kanawha coal series, long after the soft red beds above have disappeared. Along all the larger streams, they crop in bold, precipitous cliffs, and on the smaller tributaries form narrow gorges, water falls and rugged scenery generally. As a topographic element in the landscape, they can be followed with the greatest ease from knob to knob, and hill to hill.

In the northern portion of the state these massive sandstones occupy 150 to 200 feet of the basal portion of the Conemaugh, but in passing southwestward they thicken up and occupy 250 to 300 feet of the series on the Elk and Kanawha rivers, and the same condition of affairs continues to the Big Sandy river, and beyond into Kentucky.

Having given a general description of the Conemaugh series, some sections will now be presented which exhibit the measurements and detailed character of these strata in several widely distant regions of the state.

At Morgantown, the Pittsburg coal is in the summit of the hills and the Upper Freeport comes up to the bed of the Monongahela river, on the crest of a low anticlinal wave, near the Eureka Pump Station, thus giving an almost complete exposure of the Conemaugh series, as published in Bulletin 65, U. S. G. Survey, page 79.

MORGANTOWN, MONONGALIA COUNTY.

	Ft.	In.	Ft.	In.
Pittsburg Coal..........................				
Fire Clay..........................	2	0		
Sandy shales and sandstone............	32	0		
Coal, Little Pittsburg....................	1	6		
Sandy shales	17	0		
Limestone.................................	1	0		
Yellowish shales with iron ore..........	10	0		
Sandy shales, and concealed............	17	0	227	6
Sandstone, rather massive..............	25	0		
Sandy shales, and concealed............	15	0		
Massive sandstone, Connellsville......	20	0		
Bluish green sandy beds.................	20	0		
Black slate, fossiliferous................	1	0		
Limestone, Clarksburg....................	1	0		

Shales and sandy beds.....................45   0 }
Sandstone, Morgantown..........................20   0 }
Elk Lick Coal...   3   0
Shales, and concealed...........................   55   0
Limestone Crinoidal, Ames.............................   1   6
Variegated shales...   85   6
Limestone, Upper Cambridge............................   1   0
Shales....................................... 14   0 }
Sandstone, Buffalo.......................... 3   6 }
Shales and Shaly sandstone.............. 30   0 } 187   6
Massive sandstone, Upper and Lower
    Mahoning 100   0 }
Shales....................................... 40   0 }

       Total... 561   0

In the vicinity of Little Falls, nine miles above Morgantown, the basal members of the Conemaugh can be seen more in detail than in the Morgantown section, and the following gives the structure there. Bulletin 65, U. S. G. Survey, page 80:

LITTLE FALLS, MONONGALIA CO.

	Ft. In.	Ft. In.	Ft. In.
Pittsburg coal...			
Shales, sandstone and concealed.......100 0			
Sandstone, in knob 5 0			
Shales...................................... 15 1			
Massive, coarse yellow sandstone, Connellsville 21 7			
Coaly shale, Little Clarksburg 0 6			
Limestone. fossiliferous Clarksburg .. 1 0		205 9	
Concealed, shales and sandstone 47 0			
Limestone, nodular 3 0			
Gray and yellow shales..................... 9 0			
Black slate 3 7			

Coal, Elk Lick { Coal { coal...12 / slate.. 1 / coal... 4 }... 1 5 }
    Concealed with red
       shale .... 15 0 } 16 11
    Coal, good............ 0 6 }

Shales......... .... 8 6		
Limestone, gray and buff in several layers, Elk Lick 6 0		
Flaggy sandstones and shales......... 22 10	83 4	
Sandstones, massive, pebbly at base for four feet 15 0		
Concealed, probably shales 31 0		
Fossiliferous shale, crinoidal (Ames L. 8) 10 0		
Concealed, red shales and impure limestone 65 6		
Limestone, light gray, Upper Cambridge........... 1 0		
Shales and flaggy sandstones 24 6		
Sandstone, rather massive............. 10 10	105 1	
Concealed and shales 16 3		
Sandstone, Upper Mahoning, massive 53 6		
Coal, Mahoning 1 0		

	Ft.	In.		Ft.	In.
Shales and concealed......................	29	0			
Shale, greenish, sandy	11	0			
Sandy shale and flaggy sandstone...	5	2			
Shale, greenish yellow	12	0	}	98	8
Concealed, probably shale	17	0			
Lower Mahoning sandstone	26	6			
Coal, Upper Freeport.....................					

Total..................................587   3

Near Webster, Taylor Co., in the syncline east of the Chestnut Ridge anticlinal, the Pittsburg coal is caught in the summits of the hills. A diamond drill boring was recently sunk near the B. & O. R. R. at Webster to test the Allegheny coals underlying the valley. Mr. Charles H. Washburn kept a careful record of the strata penetrated by the drill, and combining those results with measurements up to the Pittsburg coal in the summits of the hills one mile south, he obtained the following section :

WEBSTER, TAYLOR COUNTY.

	Ft.	In.		Ft.	In.
Pittsburg coal					
Concealed 104	0	to	104	0	
Connellsville sandstone	20	0	"	124	0
Concealed, flaggy sandstones and shales..	53	0	"	177	0
Limestone, massive, visible............	3	0	"	180	0
Concealed, variegated shales and sandstone...............101	0	"	281	0	
Sandstone, flaggy......................	24	0	"	305	0
Shale, sandy............................	3	0	"	308	0
Limestone, Crinoidal, Ames	1	0	"	309	0
Shales, dark........................	3	0	"	312	0
Coal, Crinoidal, Ames.................	2	0	"	314	0
Shales, variegated....................	30	0	"	344	0
Limestone.............................	10	0	"	354	0
Shales, variegated, and flaggy sandstone..	23	0	"	377	0
Shales, yellow.......................	5	0	"	382	0
Coal, Bakerstown, Barton, etc	2	0	"	384	0
Red shales, sandstone, and concealed......	77	0	"	461	0
TOP OF DIAMOND BORING.					
Yellow clay, gravel, etc	10	6	"	471	6
Fire clay and shale....................	6	4	"	477	10
Shale	14	10	"	492	8
Shale, limy, probably horizon Lower Cambridge Limestone	8	0	"	500	8
Fire clay and black shale.............	2	10	"	503	6
Coal, Mason	0	9	"	504	3
Limestone, impure, Irondale...........	12	11	"	517	2
Fire clay	11	6	"	528	8
Shale, light green....................	7	0	"	535	8
Fire clay	17	6	"	553	2
Sandy shale and massive sandstone, Upper Mahoning	32	3	"	585	5
Sandy shale	15	7	"	601	0
Fire clay and shale	7	3	"	608	3
Shale, sandy	5	0	"	613	3

Shale, streaked with coal seams.............	11	0	" 624	3
Coal, Mahoning	2	0	" 626	3
Fire clay and sandy shale	19	11	" 646	2
Limestone, dark greenish gray, Mahoning.......................	7	0	" 653	2
Shale and fire clay, with lime nodules.....	14	0	" 667	2
Sandy shale and micaceous sandstone, Lower Mahoning	12	1	" 679	3
Coal, Upper Freeport......				

It is possible that the measurement was made a few feet thicker than it should be in connecting the surface outcrops with the mouth of the bore hole, but the error is probably not greater than 25 to 30 feet, since a few miles east of this at Newburg, Preston Co., where the Pittsburg coal has been mined in the summits of the hills, and the upper Freeport is mined by a shaft below the level of the valley, the following section was once measured by the writer :

NEWBURG, PRESTON COUNTY.

	Ft.	Ft.
Pittsburg coal		
Fire clay...................................	5	
Concealed...................................	14	
Sandy shales	30	259
Concealed	210	
Coal, Elk Lick, slaty...................................		4
Concealed	16	
Sandstone, pebbly...................................	30	
Concealed	15	
Sandstone, flaggy	10	94
Shales, sandy	10	
Shales, dark, fossiliferous, (Ames Limestone horizon)...................................	13	
Coal, Crinoidal, Friendsville.........		2
Concealed	20	
Red, marly shale	5	
Concealed	40	
Sandstone, yellow...................................	10	95
Concealed	15	
Fire clay and shales................................	5	
Sandstone, massive...................................	20	
Sandy shale	10	
Sandstone, massive	10	49
Surface in shaft...................................	9	
Coal, Mason...................................		1
Sandstone, Upper Mahoning................................	35	60
Shales...................................	25	
Coal, Mahoning		1
Lower Mahoning { Sandstone	40	
Shale...................................	2	
Sandstone	34	80
Shale...................................	1	
Sandstone	3	
Coal, Upper Freeport		
Total...................................		645

On east from this in the central portion of the Alleghany mountains, and not far from the northern line of Preston county, Dr. G. C. Martin, Geologist of the Maryland Geological Survey, measured the following section near Friendsville, Md., Geology of Garrett county, pages 130-131 :

FRIENDSVILLE, GARRETT COUNTY, MD.

	Ft.	In.	Ft.	In.
Probable position of Pittsburg coal				
Strata removed by erosion			10	0
Concealed			62	0
Coal, Little Pittsburg { coal	0	6		
shale	0	2		
coal	1	5	3	8
shale	0	1		
coal	1	6		
Limestone			1	0
Concealed			6	0
Flaggy sandstone			26	0
Concealed, and massive conglomeritic sandstone			50	0
Fine grained sandstone			8	0
Shale			2	0
Limestone, Clarksburg { limestone	2	6		
shale	1	0	7	0
limestone	3	6		
Shale			1	0
Concealed			15	0
Shale			5	0
Concealed			18	0
Sandstone and shale			15	0
Fine-bedded sandstone			21	0
Massive conglomerate			9	0
Shaly, cross-bedded sandstone			18	0
Coal, Elk Lick			0	6
Gray, calcareous shale			3	0
Massive sandstone			20	
Shaly limestone and fossiliferous shale, Ames L. S.			10	0
Coal, Friendsville			1	3
Yellow shale			5	0
Fine-grained, cross-bedded sandstone			30	0
Gray shale			1	0
Concealed			31	0
Sandy, fossiliferous shales			4	0
Yellow shales and concealed			15	0
Black shale			2	0
Coal, Bakerstown			1	6
Shale and sandstone			36	0
Red shale			2	0
Limestone			2	0
Red and green shales			7	0
Sandy shales			10	0
Limestone			1	0
Sandy shales			27	0

		Ft.	In.
Black fossiliferous shales		5	o
Limestone, Lower Cambridge		o	6
Black shale		5	o
Coal, Mason		I	9
Concealed		80	o
Black shale, with coal smut on top		6	o
Coal, Mahoning { bone o 7 / shale o 6 / coal o 9 }		I	10
Black shale		10	o
Sandstone		o	4
Shale		4	o
Concealed		25	o
Approximate position of Upper Freeport coal			
Total		**635**	**4**

At Fairfax Knob, Tucker county, the following measurement results by combining the exposures there with the record of a well drilled to test the Upper Freeport coal below the bed of the North Potomac near its headwaters :

		Ft.	In.	Ft.	In.
Shales				5	o
Limestone				4	o.
Shales				7	o
Little Pittsburg { coal 4 6 / fire clay and shales 18 0 / coal, slaty 7 0 }				29	6
Shales, and concealed				85	o
Coal, Little Clarksburg { coal 2 9 / slate o 6 / coal o 6 }				3	9
Shales				40	o
Coal .. { coal, slaty o 10 / coal I 5 / slate I o / coal I o }				4	3
Fireclay and shales				10	o
Blue shales with iron ore				15	o
Black slate				2	o
Coal, Elk Lick { coal o 8 / slate o 4 / coal I o }				2	o
Concealed with sandstone and shales				200	o
Coal and black slate, (Mason)				3	o
Shales				50	o
Sandstone, massive				25	o
Concealed				9	o
Sandstone, soft				I	o
Clay, yellow				6	o
Sandstone				20	o
Limestone, Mahoning				20	o
Soft shale				I	o
Hard shale				9	o
Soft shale				I	o
Slate, light blue				10	o
Slate, dark				19	o

	Ft.	In.
Sandstone	2	0
Upper Freeport coal....................................		
Total..583		6

This section is the same as the one published in Bulletin 65, U. S. G. Survey, page 82, except that a different interpretation is put upon the two layers of Little Pittsburg coal which with the 16 feet of strata above them was referred to the main Pittsburg bed in Bulletin 65, but is now considered to belong to the Conemaugh series. Since these strata are now removed from the Monongahela series, the next underlying coal bed will be the Little Clarksburg instead of the Little Pittsburg as correlated in Bulletin 65.

The 3 feet of coal and black slate 200 feet under the Elk Lick coal has been correlated with the Mason coal horizon, but it may be a little too high above the Upper Freeport coal for that bed, since in the Henry shaft, as well as in the Elk Garden section, the Mason coal lies only one hundred and twenty feet above the base of the Conemaugh.

At Elk Garden, Mineral county, the Pittsburg coal is mined in the summits of the hills, and in descending from it to the North Potomac river at Blaine, Dr. G. C. Martin obtained the following section, Geology of Garrett county, page 128 :

BLAINE, MINERAL COUNTY.

		Ft.	In.	Ft.	In.
Coal, Pittsburg					
Concealed		180	0		
Sandstone		3	0		
Concealed		108	0		
Sandstone		2	0		
Concealed		60	0		
Sandy shales...		4	0		
Coal, Bakerstown..	coal............... 1 2			2	0
	shale............... 0 1				
	coal............... 0 5				
	bone 0 4				
Concealed		26	0		
Shale		6	0		
Coal...	coal............... 0 4			2	1
	shale............... 1 6				
	coal............... 0 3				
Concealed		36	0		
Black shales..		10	0		
Fossiliferous, disintegrated limestone. Lower Cambridge		0	8		
Black shales..		8	0		
Coal, Mason	coal 1 2			1	9
	bone 0 1				
	coal 0 6				

Concealed 110   o
Flaggy sandstone..   7   o
Sandy shales   5   o
Coal, Upper Freeport........ ....
                                                     ————
     Total........ 571   6

Barton, Allegany county, Md., in the George's Creek-Potomac coal basin is a type locality for the Barton coal (Bakerstown), and the following section of the Conemaugh series constructed there by Dr. Martin is given in the Geology of Garrett county, page 127, as follows :

BARTON, ALLEGANY COUNTY, MD.

		Ft. In.	Ft. In.
Coal, Pittsburg			
Concealed, shale toward the base...........................		41	o
Gray shales...............		8	o
Concealed.........		18	6
Black bituminous shale.....................................		2	o
Yellowish shales, with iron-band markings...........		26	9
Concealed, with sandstone near base		29	o
Arenaceous shales and thin-bedded sandstones........		8	o
Concealed		10	6

Coal, Franklin...
- coal........................... o 9
- shale.......................... o 2
- coal............................ o 3
- Bituminous shales ... 1 o
- coal............................ o 8
- shale.......................... 2 o
- coal........................... 2 o

  } 6   10

Ferruginous shales		4	3
Concealed		26	9
Dark gray shales...		20	9
Coarse, sandy shales		10	6
Massive gray cross-bedded sandstone.....................		9	9
Concealed		94	9
Brownish gray massive sandstone		7	9
Concealed		84	6

Coal, Bakerstown..
- bone.................. o 4
- coal.................... 2 4
- coal and shale...... o 4

  } 3   o

Concealed		77	o
Sandy shales		15	o
Coal, Mason		1	7
Sandy shale		3	5
Shale		12	o
Sandstone		28	o
Shale .... -		8	o
Sandstone		33	6
Shale		3	6
Coal, Upper Freeport			

                                                     ————
     Total.... 594   7

About five miles northwest from Philippi, on the head waters of Elk creek, the Pittsburg coal crops high up in the hills, and an oil well record on the Hall farm, beginning at the horizon of the Crinoidal Limestone, gives the lower portion of the Conemaugh. Mr. C. McC. Lemley, Assistant Engineer of the B. & O. R. R., Philippi, W. Va., is authority for the following measurements made on the Hall farm and connected by him with the record of the Hall well No. 1 of the Elk Creek Oil and Gas Company.

HALL FARM SECTION.

	Ft.	Ft.
Pittsburg coal, base 1365 A. T.		
Interval, shales, sandstones and concealed.........259		
Sandstone, massive, Morguntown 20		
Shales... 3		
Coal, Elk Lick.. 2		
Limestone, Elk Lick.... 5		331
Shales, and concealed...... 16		
Red shales, containing two layers of fossiliferous (marine) limestone, Ames 15		
Bore hole record begins here..........................		
Surface sand and wash..................................... 14		
Black slate and coal, Friendsville...........................		6
Black lime 15		
Lime shell...... 20		
Red and black lime 20		
Red rock and slate...................................... 15		
Light slate and lime..................................... 10		
Sand... 25		270
Red rock and sand shell 13		
Black slate 62		
Blue lime.. 75		
Sand, white 5		
Sand, black 10		
Coal, Mason		5
Black sand 15		
White sand.. 10		
Black lime... 15		110
Black sandy lime.. 55		
Sand 15		
Coal, Upper Freeport...		
Total...		722

The oil well driller makes use of the word "lime" to indicate any rock whose drillings come up fine and limy-looking. The rock may be a sandy shale, or even a shaly sandstone, with scarcely a trace of lime in it, so that terms given in a welldriller's log often fail to convey an adequate idea of the rock in question.

This section near Philippi shows a thick measurement of the Conemaugh, but that it is correctly made is confirmed by the next one, several miles to the southwest, also the result of accurate leveling by a civil engineer.

In the Pan Handle of Lewis county, near Ireland, both the
Elk Lick coal and the Bakerstown, or Barton beds have been
mined, and as the Pittsburg caps some of the highest summits in
the vicinity, a vertical section from it to the Upper Freeport coal
has been accurately measured by Mr. J. Perry Thompson, of Fairmont, by combining the surface outcrops with the record of a boring, as follows :

IRELAND SECTION.

	Ft.	In.	Ft.	In.
Pittsburg coal				
Interval			240	6
Coal, Elk Lick { coal............	1	3		
slate	0	2		
coal............................	1	4	4	6
slate	0	1		
coal............	1	8		
Interval			127	8
Coal, good, bright, Bakerstown			2	4
Concealed			40	0
Shaly sandstone................... ..			15	0
Coal, thin................................ .				
Interval			182	7
Coal, Mahoning { coal........................	1	6		
black slate	0	3	3	5
coal........................	1	8		
Sandstone, Lower Mahoning, massive...............			84	0
Coal streak				
Interval			21	0
Upper Freeport coal...................................				
Total...			721	0

This measurement exhibits the same tendency to thicken eastward and southwestward shown by the previous one near Philippi.
In the region of Charleston on the Great Kanawha the Conemaugh
appears to attain its greatest development, as shown by the following section compiled by the writer along Two Mile creek, and
southward to the junction of the Elk and Kanawha rivers, as
follows :

TWO MILE-KANAWHA SECTION.

	Ft.	Ft.
Pittsburg coal..		
Concealed, sandstone and red shales...................	150	
Sandstone, massive, Connellsville....................	30	
Red shales, sandstone and concealed	80	320
Sandstone, massive, Morgantown	20	
Concealed and sandy shales............................	40	
Coal, impure, Elk Lick...................................		1
Dark limestone	2	
Concealed and massive sandstone	27	
Deep red shales, with Two Mile limestones and iron ore	50	

Flaggy sandstone	20	} 162
Coal, impure, Bakerstown (Barton)	3	
Sandstone, massive	15	
Shales, with gray limestone, two feet thick	20	
Sandstone, massive..	25	
Fireclay		8
Sandstone and concealed..................................	85	} 160
Sandstone, massive, pebbly, Buffalo..................	75	
Coal, Mason....................		2
Shales................................	10	
Sandstone, with streaks of coal near center, (Mahoning)...................	120	} 147
Shales, sandy...	10	
Black flint...	5	
Shales...	2	
Upper Freeport coal...		
		———
Total...		800

The 50 feet of deep red shales with two gray fresh-water limestones 20 feet apart appears to represent the horizon of the Ames or Crinoidal limestone of the northern portion of the state, though here the limestones hold only a spirorbis like form of fossil. About 50 miles west from Charleston, however, the marine type of the Ames limestone appears in the vicinity of Huntington between which town and Kenova Prof. A. G. Selby once measured the following section of the Conemaugh, see page 84, Bulletin U. S. G. Survey :

HUNTINGTON-KENOVA SECTION.

	Ft.	Ft.
Pittsburg coal...		
Red shale, containing limestone nodules............	28	
Sandstone, shaly..	16	
Red shales and sandstones.................................	101	} 197
Coal, Little Clarksburg.....	2	
Sandstone, massive, Morgantown	50	
Elk Lick coal..		2
Fireclay	3	} 106
Shales, deep red	103	
Limestone, crinoidal, Ames................		2
Coal, Crinoidal, Friendsville...............................		2
Red shales....	4	
Limestone	4	} 183
Shales and sandstones......................................	175	
Limestone, Lower Cambridge...............................		2
Shales		10
Coal, Mason		1
Shales..	30	} 155
Sandstone, Mahoning....	125	
Upper Freeport coal..		
		———
Total...		660

This Huntington-Kenova section reveals all of the main features shown at the northern line of the state, 250 miles distant. The Mahoning sandstone is double bedded at Kenova, where it crops along Twelve Pole river, and the Mahoning coal is occasionally present about midway between the Mason and Upper Freeport seams.

The Ames and Lower Cambridge limestones are still filled with their characteristic marine fossils, although only fifty miles distant from Charleston, where only fresh water or estuarine types are to be found at these horizons.

To show the wide spread uniformity of this Conemaugh series, there will now be introduced a section from the region of King's creek, Brooke county, the most northern outcrop in West Virginia of the Pittsburg coal, where it is possible to measure a section between it and the Upper Freeport, as follows:

OSBURN'S MILL, BROOKE COUNTY.

	Ft.
Pittsburg coal, about 1195 feet A. T	
Concealed, red shales and sandy beds 175	
Sandstone, massive, Morgantown..............................	25
Shales. with thin coal (Elk Lick)	10
Concealed and shales.............................	40
Limestone, Crinoidal (Ames) very fossiliferous.............	10
Red and marly shales and concealed	60
Massive sandstone..................	40
Coal, Bakerstown, Barton...2—4	
Shales and concealed............................	25
Limestone, fossiliferous, Upper Cambridge	2
Red shales.. ...	10
Shales, sandstone and concealed	60
Dark, fossiliferous shales, Lower Cambridge L. S.........	5
Coal, Mason, blossom	1
Limy shales	5
Concealed and massive sandstone.............................	45
Coal, Mahoning (No. 7) ....3—5	
Concealed and sandstone..................	60
Coal, Upper Freeport................................	
	———
Total...580	

In the deeply buried region between the Ohio and Monongahela rivers, where even the top of the Conemaugh series is occasionally 1500 feet below the summits, the continuity of the beds remains unbroken, as revealed by numerous oil well borings.

The Brice Wallace well No. 1, just east from Fairview, Marion county, drilled by the South Penn Oil Company, is one of the few in which the Upper Freeport coal has been observed, as well as the

Pittsburg above.   The record of this well reads as follows through the Conemaugh series :

BRICE WALLACE WELL NO. 1, MARION COUNTY.

	Ft.
Pittsburg coal	
White slate :	31
Limestone	40
Slate, light	15
Red rock	25
Shale and white sandstone	50
Red rock and sandstone	165
Limestone	15
Red rock aud slate	40
Sandstone	25
Coal and slate (Mason)	30
Sand, hard, (Upper Mahoning)	35
Slate, dark	45
Sandstone, (Lower Mahoning)	40
Coal, Upper Freeport	
Total	556

Here the Mahoning sandstone is clearly differentiated into two members, and the coal above apparently belongs at the horizon of the Mason bed.

In Grant district, Doddridge county, near the Tyler county line, this series has the following thickness according to the record of the William Sandy well No. 1, drilled by the South Penn Oil Company :

WILLIAM SANDY WELL NO. 1, GRANT DISTRICT, DODDRIDGE COUNTY.

	Ft.
Pit'sburg coal	
Slate	10
Limestone	30
Slate	35
Red rock	15
Sand	30
Limestone	10
Red rock	10
Slate	5
Red rock	75
Sand	100
Slate	10
Limestone	35
Red rock	10
Limestone	25
Coal	8
Slate	15
Limestone	20
Sand	25

Slate 15
Limestone 20
Slate and shells.. 25
                                                          ——
      Total..528

The records of borings to the southwest across the state reveal a thickening in that direction, thus confirming the observations from the surface outcrops.

The Hudnall well No. 1, near Stouts Mill, Gilmer county, reveals the following structure for the Conemaugh series on the Little Kanawha river, as recorded by the Guffey & Galey Oil Company :

HUDNALL WELL NO. 1, STOUTS MILL, GILMER COUNTY.

	Ft.
Pittsburg coal..	
Limestone	29
Slate	2
Sand....................	68
Red rock	7
Slate	5
Limestone	33
Red rock	10
Slate	5
Red rock	30
Morgantown { sand	65
slate, break..	?
sand, hard	18
Slate..	5
Limestone	5
Sand, hard	31
Slate..	10
Coal, Friendsville.....................................	3
Limestone	17
Red rock..	4
Slate	5
Red rock	40
Limestone	15
Slate..	10
Pink rock	35
Limestone	15
Sand..	20
Slate..	30
Pink rock..	20
Slate..	10
Sand, Upper Mahoning...................................	65
Limestone. Mahoning...................................	15
Sand, Lower Mahoning	65
	——
Total...	694

Having now given a general view of the Conemaugh series,

we shall give a more particular description of the important members of the same.

The chief coals of the series are quite variable both in thickness and quality, and they are generally high in ash and other impurities. Locally, however, some of the beds thicken up into quite important coals of commercial quality and thickness, over limited areas. Considered as a whole, the series was very appropriately named by the First Geological Surveys of Pennsylvania and Virginia, the "Lower Barren" Measures, on account of the uncertain, impure and variable nature of the coal beds in the same.

The following beds represent the more important and widely distributed members of the Conemaugh series, and have received Geographical names:

Lower Pittsburg sandstone.
Little Pittsburg coals.
Pittsburg limestones.
Connellsville sandstone.
Little Clarksburg coal.
Clarksburg limestone.
Morgantown sandstone.
Elk Lick coal.
Birmingham shale.
Ames limestone.
Friendsville coal.
Pittsburg red shale.
Saltzburg sandstone.
Bakerstown coal.
Upper Cambridge limestone.
Buffalo sandstone.
Lower Cambridge limestone.
Mason coal.
Upper Mahoning sandstone.
Mahoning coal.
Lower Mahoning sandstone.

Other beds, like the Kanawha black flint, Upper and Middle Cannelton coals, etc., have received distinct names, but as they are of limited distribution, they are not enumerated in the general table of the nomenclature.

The interval immediately below the top of the Conemaugh, for about 100 feet, is probably the most variable portion of the series in its rock constitution. Sometimes there will occur shales, limestones, thin coals, with some red beds, down to the horizon of the Connellsville sandstone, and again a very massive sandstone may appear only three to ten feet below the Pittsburg coal.

At only one locality in the state (eastern Monongalia) do the Olyphant iron ore beds, so conspicuously developed in Fayette county, Pa., make any show of their presence in the column of rocks.

The first stratum under the Pittsburg coal would naturally be a fire clay deposit, but such is seldom found ; in fact, the coal often rests on sandy shales, without any apparent intervening clay, or old fossil soil, except a very thin veneer, which makes no show whatever at the surface. This absence of underclays from the coal beds is quite general in all of the upper two-thirds of the Conemaugh series, and it also is universal in the Monongahela series above, since at no locality in the Appalachian field has any fireclay deposit been noted in the latter series of rocks. The highest known fireclay deposit of any economic value is one at the horizon of the Mahoning coal, near the base of the Conemaugh.

THE PITTSBURG LIMESTONES.

Two well marked limestone horizons belong in this variable 100 feet of measures at the top of the Conemaugh—one five to six feet thick, and usually found twenty-five to thirty-five feet below the Pittsburg coal, the other eight to ten feet thick and fifty to sixty feet below the latter. They are usually known as the Upper and Lower Pittsburg Limestones, and are excellent landmarks for determining the horizon of the Pittsburg coal above. They are often rather earthy and impure, and hence of little economic importance, except for farm use.

The lower of these two beds may be seen in fine exposure along the B. & O. R. R., just west from the station at Fairmont, Marion county.

THE LITTLE PITTSBURG COALS.

Two coal beds of little economic value are also often seen in this variable interval at the top of the Conemaugh—one immedi-

ately UNDER the Upper Pittsburg Limestone thirty to forty feet
from the Pittsburg coal, and the other immediately OVER the next
underlying Pittsburg limestone.   Both coals are seldom present in
the same section, and hence it is frequently difficult to distinguish
the one from the other on account of the extreme variation in the
character of the enclosing rocks, so that both horizons have been
designated Little Pittsburg coal.

In the section at Fairfax Knob, Tucker county, given on page
235 of this volume, the two beds appear to be only eighteen feet
apart.   The upper one is there four and one-half feet thick, and
has been mined commercially.   It is known as the "Coking seam"
locally, from its columnar structure resembling a typical coking
coal.   Formerly the writer was inclined to believe that this bed
represented the "Brick" division of the Pittsburg coal, the main
body of which lies only sixteen feet above, but further studies of
the structure of the Pittsburg coal in the Potomac basin has convinced him that this conclusion was erroneous.

On Limestone run, and other regions of Lewis county, near
Weston, a coal bed two and one-half to three and one-half feet
thick occurs over a considerable area at forty feet below what has
always been considered the Pittsburg coal.   A yellow limestone,
eight to ten feet thick, overlies the coal in question, and the latter
would appear to represent the Little Pittsburg bed, unless the coal
forty feet above should be the Redstone (which hardly seems possible), and in that event the lower bed would be the Pittsburg
proper.   The detailed studies soon to be undertaken in Lewis
county will settle this question finally, but with the ·present
knowledge the coal under the yellow limestones on Limestone run,
and other localities in Lewis county, where it has occasionally
been mined, must be regarded as the first coal below the true
Pittsburg bed, and therefore one of the Little Pittsburg seams.
Where mined for local use, it is reported as of good quality, fully
equal to that of the main Pittsburg bed above.

The lower one of the two Little Pittsburg coals is seldom of
·any economic value in West Virginia, so far as known, and is
often absent entirely, or represented by only a few inches of BLACK
SLATE or impure coal, just above the Lower Pittsburg limestone.

Dr. G. C. Martin, of the Maryland Geological Survey, identifies with this coal a bed which has some economic importance in
Garrett county, Md., where it overlies immediately the lower of

the Pittsburg limestones, the quarrying of which by the farmers has frequently exposed the coal.

In a section near Friendsville, Garrett county, (page 130 Geology of Garrett county) Dr. Martin places this coal at seventy-two feet under the horizon of the main Pittsburg bed, and finds it exhibiting the following structure :

	Ft.	In.	Ft.	In.
Coal	o	6		
Shale	o	2		
Coal	1	5	3	8
Shale	o	1		
Coal	1	6		

The writer was at first inclined to believe this a thin representative of the main Pittsburg coal, but as Dr. Martin appears to be quite confident his conclusions are correct, and as he has studied the region in great detail, his decisions should be conclusive.

THE CONNELLSVILLE SANDSTONE.

Only a few feet below the Lower Pittsburg limestone there is often found a massive sandstone of great economic importance. The stratum in question rises from the bed of the Youghiogheny river at Connellsville, Pa., and was named by Dr. John J. Stevenson from that locality.

When massive, this rock is one of the finest building stones in the entire Coal Measures. The sand grains being cemented by silica and peroxide of iron, are almost weather proof, so that for all structures like bridge piers, outside walls, etc., it has no superior. The iron in the rock often permeates the entire mass so thoroughly as to give it a uniform reddish tint, and again it may have a speckled type, much resembling gray granite.

The Asylum for the Insane at Weston, as also the B. & O. station building there, were constructed largely from this rock, obtained at Mt. Clare, Harrison county, while the suspension bridge piers at Morgantown, as well as the postoffice building there, are built of the same stratum. The suspension bridge piers have stood for more than fifty years, and exhibit no tendency to disintegration.

The rock splits readily into any desired size and, although quite hard to carve into delicate shapes, yet it "masons" very readily into beautiful forms for natural or uncut "rock face" work.

Being one of the chief rocks in the Conemaugh series, it has played a very important part in shaping their topography. It is especially hard, massive, and often pebbly in the Potomac and George's Creek basin, and the rounded hills that hold the "Big" (Pittsburg) "vein" rest upon a platform of this Connellsville sandstone which, owing to its resistance to erosion, makes a bold terrace far up the mountain sides, after the Pittsburg coal and all other soft beds above its horizon have disappeared. It is this hard bed of pebbly sandstone that caps the summits in the center of the Potomac basin southwest from Elk Garden, forming almost level plateaus over thousands of acres where the great Pittsburg coal is missed by only a short interval.

This stratum varies in thickness from twenty to fifty feet, and may be seen making huge cliffs at many places along the Monongahela river between Morgantown and Fairmont. It is also conspicuous near the base of the hills at Berryburg, Barbour county, and at many localities along Elk creek in Barbour and Harrison. It forms the principal quarry rock in the vicinity of Clarksburg, and is now extensively used at Morgantown for all building work, street curb, etc.

The interval between the Connellsville sandstone and the Pittsburg coal is seldom less than sixty feet, and often ninety or more. When the sandstone is not present as a massive rock, its place is filled with sandy shales or flaggy sandstone.

THE LITTLE CLARKSBURG COAL.

Just under the Connellsville sandstone there comes a widely persistent COAL bed, which the writer named from the city of Clarksburg where it crops along the valley of Elk creek and the West Fork river. The coal is often double, with two to three feet of slate or shale separating as many feet of impure, bony coal, so that in the Allegany and Garrett county, Maryland, area, the bed is frequently termed the "Dirty Nine-Foot" coal. This double character of the coal is exhibited along Elk creek, below Quiet Dell, in Harrison county, and also in the vicinity of Berryburg, Barbour county, as well as on Gnatty Creek and other tributaries of Elk in

Harrison county.   The same feature has been noted in Lewis and Upshur.

Economically considered, the coal is of little importance, since it is coarse and bony, and makes a very indifferent fuel, even at its best.   The bed has been termed the Franklin coal at many localities in Maryland, and Dr. Martin gives it the following structure at Barton, Allegany county, Md.:

	Ft.	In.	Ft.	In.
Coal	0	9		
Shale	0	2		
Coal	0	3		
Bituminous shales	1	0	6	10
Coal	0	8		
Shale	2	0		
Coal	2	0		

Its position is 130 to 150 feet below the top of the Conemaugh series, and as the coal overlies directly a widely distributed lime-stone, it is easily identified.

Very frequently a few inches of BLACK SLATE is the only representative of the Little Clarksburg coal, and it is generally filled with the teeth, scales and bones of fossil fishes.   In fact, when the coal is present, it is often underlain by this fossiliferous stratum, which then rests directly upon the Clarksburg limestone. This stratum was named the Little Clarksburg coal by the writer because in the vicinity of Clarksburg, where the bed was first studied and described, the main Pittsburg coal, which is there extensively mined, is locally known as the "Clarksburg" coal.

THE CLARKSBURG LIMESTONE.

Directly below the last described coal and its underlying fossiliferous black slate, there often occurs a limestone which is finely exposed in the vicinity of Clarksburg along Elk creek, at its junction with the West Fork river, and was named by the writer from that locality, the Clarksburg limestone.   Its upper portion is generally rather slaty and filled with fossil ostracoids and fish remains, but the lower layers are compact and massive.   The whole stratum is often twenty to thirty feet thick, and some of the layers are quite ferruginous, so much so that they were once mined as ore and used in the manufacture of iron at an old charcoal furnace on Elk, near Clarksburg.   Some iron ore was also obtained for this furnace from the ferruginous shales just above the Little Clarksburg coal.

The Clarksburg limestone has a wide distribution in the northern end of the state, and has frequently been quarried and burned into lime for fertilizing purposes. It also makes excellent road material and has been extensively used for that purpose on the streets and roadways in the vicinity of Clarksburg.

THE MORGANTOWN SANDSTONE.

At a few feet below the Clarksburg limestone, and separated from it by soft shales, there occurs another of the great sandstone horizons of the Conemaugh series. This stratum was named by Dr. John J. Stevenson from its fine exposures in the vicinity of Morgantown, Monongalia county, where it was once extensively quarried and used in the construction of the State University buildings and other structures. At this typical locality the top of the sandstone lies a little more than 200 feet below the Pittsburg coal, and the stratum has a thickness of twenty-five feet. It is usually of a yellowish gray cast, and splits readily into building blocks of any desired size. The rock contains much feldspathic material, and occasionally some lime, and in weathering the rock changes from a bluish gray cast to a dirty brown, and frequently decomposes readily, so that as a building stone for exposed surfaces, it is not a success, some of the stone work at the State University in Morgantown having disintegrated badly within a period of only twenty-five years.

Several of the locks along the Monongahela river, between Morgantown and Pittsburg, have been constructed of this stone, and the disintegration of the lock walls is a constant source of expense.

This sandstone is one of the most persistent members of the Conemaugh series, and usually forms a line of cliffs or steep bluffs wherever its outcrop extends. Although the stratum is usually only twenty-five to thirty feet thick, yet occasionally, as on Crooked run in Monongalia county, near the West Virginia-Pennsylvania line, it thickens up to one hundred feet in a solid and massive wall.

Through Monongalia, Marion, Tyler, Preston, Barbour, Upshur, Lewis, Braxton, Clay, Kanawha, Putnam, Mason, Cabell and Wayne, this stratum can be traced from the Pennsylvania line on the north to the Kentucky boundary on the southwest. ¶ It is well exposed along the Ohio river in the region of Huntington, where it makes cliffs fifty to sixty feet high along the hills back from the river valley.   It is also conspicuous in cliffs along the Guyandotte, Mud, and Coal rivers, as well as along the Great Kanawha, where it has been frequently quarried and used in building the locks below Charleston.

This stratum produces oil in the "Shallow sand" districts of Washington, Noble and Monroe counties of Ohio, as well as at some localities in Wirt and Ritchie of West Virginia, where it has occasionally been confused by the oil well drillers with the Dunkard or "First Cow Run" sand of Ohio.   It also produced oil in one well on Dunkard creek, Greene county, Pennsylvania, at about 200 feet below the Pittsburg coal.

THE ELK LICK COAL.

Immediately under the Morgantown sandstone, or separated from it by only a few feet of shale, there comes a coal of very wide distribution which often obtains workable dimensions.   The name, Elk Lick, was given the coal in question by the First Geological Survey of Pennsylvania, but the exact place of the bed in the Conemaugh series remained uncertain till the Messrs. Platt, of the Second Pennsylvania Survey, determined the matter finally by identifying the massive sandstone above it at the type locality in Somerset county, Pennsylvania, as the Morgantown.   The coal attains a thickness of four feet on Elk Lick creek (which puts into the Castleman river from the southwest near Meyersdale, Somerset county, Pennsylvania), where it was once mined for local use.

This coal is quite generally present in eastern Monongalia and has been mined along Deckers creek in Morgantown, and farther up the stream, where it is three to four feet thick, but contains much ash and bony material.   It burns well, however, if broken into small lumps.

It has been mined for local use at a few localities in Preston county, north from Cheat river, where it is known as the "top vein," and is close to four feet thick.

In Scotch Hill, at Newburg, Preston county, it was once opened along the old incline leading up to the Pittsburg coal, where it is 260 feet below the latter bed and called the "Four-Foot" seam. The coal is slaty, however, and could not be mined for commercial purposes.

In Taylor and Barbour counties this bed has occasionally been opened high up in the hills along the Tygart's Valley river, and mined by the farmers for domestic use.

In the deep syncline, east from Philippi, this coal has been mined locally by the farmers, and it is also caught in the summit of Friedly Knob, near the crest of the Laurel Hill anticline, where it has been mined on the lands of Hessel, Upton and others, and is three feet thick. The crop of the coal is visible here along the Nestorville road, near the school house. It also makes a broad band of black crop in the fields north of the road, and has there been mistaken for the Pittsburg bed, which belongs two hundred and fifty feet higher.

In the vicinity of Buckhannon, a coal has been mined quite extensively for local use by Maj. Heavner, Mr. Reger and others, and exhibits the following structure at the Reger bank :

	Ft.	In.	Ft.	In.
Sandstone, massive				
Slate	1	6		
Slaty coal	0	5		
Coal	0	8		
Slate parting	0	½	3	10
Coal	1	1		
Slate	0	1½		
Coal	1	6		

The coal makes a fair domestic and steam fuel, and appears to be identical with the Elk Lick, although its interval (300') below the Pittsburg bed appears large.

This coal is the source of domestic supply for a large area in the vicinity of Vandalia, Lewis county, where it is mined by many of the farmers and is called the "Four-Foot" vein.

It first emerges from the bed of Big Skin creek at the upper end of the Gould farm, one mile below Vandalia, and is well exposed in a cutting along the road, where it has the following structure :

	Ft.	In.	Ft.	In.
Coal...	0	10		
Bone..	0	3		
Coal	0	9½	4	11½
Slate and bony coal	0	5		
Coal, good................................	2	8		

The bed lies 250 to 275 feet below the Pittsburg coal, and will furnish fuel of commercial value over a considerable area in this portion of Lewis.

The coal thins down to two feet or less a few miles above Vandalia, however, and is no longer mined to the eastward:

This coal has also some importance southeast from Arnolds, in the vicinity of Ireland, along the West Fork river, where Mr. J. P. Thompson reports it as exhibiting the following structure:

	Ft. In.	Ft. In.
Coal	1 3	
Slate..	0 2	
Coal	1 4	4 6
Slate..	0 1	
Coal	1 8	

At Glenville, Gilmer county, there is a small bed of coal reported eighteen to twenty inches thick near the level of the Little Kanawha river, and as its horizon is about 250 feet below the Pittsburg bed, it is probably this Elk Lick coal.

Southeast from the Little Kanawha, through Braxton, Clay, Roane and Kanawha counties, the Elk Lick coal is usually quite thin, and of little importance so far as surface outcrops would indicate.

In the section on Two Mile creek, near Charleston, it is represented by one foot of black, coaly slate, at 320 feet under the Pittsburg coal.

The same coal thickens up to two and one-half to three feet just south of Huntington, where it has been mined to a small extent under the massive Morgantown sandstone along the waters of Four Pole Run.

In the section from Huntington to Kenova, page 240, Prof. Selby reports this coal as only two feet thick.

In the northern Pan Handle of Brooke and Hancock, this coal is thin (12″) and slaty, and never of any economic importance, so far as developed at present. Its crop may be seen along the road leading up from Colliers station, at an interval of two hundred feet below the Pittsburg coal, and forty feet above the Ames, or Crinoidal Limestone.

The Elk Lick coal is not reported as having been mined in the Potomac basin of Garrett and Allegany counties by Dr. Martin, since the sections given for the Conemaugh show it only a few inches thick.

In the Fairfax Knob section, given on page 235 of this volume, the Elk Lick bed has been identified as the one a little over 200 feet below the top of the Conemaugh, but it is there only two feet thick and parted with four inches of slate.

THE ELK LICK LIMESTONE.

Lying only a short distance below the coal just described, and 210 to 225 feet below the Pittsburg coal, the Messrs. Platt found in Somerset county, Pennsylvania, a widely persistent limestone to which they gave the name Elk Lick in Report HHH, of the Second Geological Survey of Pennsylvania.

This limestone is of common occurrence in Monongalia, Marion, Taylor, Barbour and Lewis counties, at a few feet below the Elk Lick coal, and a thin representative of it may be seen as far to the southwest as Two Mile creek, near Charleston.

The stratum is frequently ten to fifteen feet thick in several layers, separated by shales. The limestone is of fresh or brackish water origin like all of those in the series above it, but some of the layers are fairly pure, and burn into a good quality of lime for building or fertilizing purposes.

The place of this limestone in the series is shown in the Morgantown section on page 230, and the Hall farm section on page 238 of this volume. It is usually gray in color and resembles the Clarksburg limestone, sixty to eighty feet higher, so closely in physical aspect, that it has probably been frequently confused with the latter.

THE BIRMINGHAM SHALE.

The interval between the Elk Lick limestone and the Ames, or Crinoidal, limestone, forty to fifty feet lower, is quite variable, often being occupied by a sandy shale, and again a massive, pebbly sandstone makes its appearance therein. Dr. Stevenson named the shales from their fine exposure at Birmingham, on the south side of the Monongahela river, Pittsburg, where they have a jointed appearance, and give much trouble to the Pan Handle R. R. by sliding down onto its tracks from the almost vertical face of the hill.

In the region of Grafton, Taylor county, a massive, pebbly sandstone appears to crop out at the same horizon, only twenty to thirty feet above the Ames or Crinoidal limestone. It has been quarried in that vicinity and yields a fair building stone of a yellowish gray color. The same massive stratum is visible at many localities along Three Fork creek, and also in the vicinity of Newburg, where it clearly underlies the Elk Lick coal opened in the hills above. But for this evidence, the rock in question would be considered as representing the Morgantown sandstone, with the interval between it and the Ames limestone greatly reduced.

RICHMOND, OHIO, INSECT FAUNA.

In the shales a short distance above the Ames limestone, at the edge of the township of Richmond, on Wills creek, near Steubenville, Ohio, Mr. Samuel Huston, of the latter city, has discovered a rich fauna of fossil cockroaches. These have been described by Prof. S. H. Scudder in Bulletin No. 124 of the U. S. G. Survey, and of the twenty-two species enumerated, all except five belong to the Etoblattina which is so largely represented in the fauna of the Cassville plant shale. The following is the list of species and genera given by Prof. Scudder from the Steubenville or Richmond locality.

Etoblattina fossa.
      strigosa.
      jeffersoniana.
      fasciata.
      remosa.
      willsiana.
      maledicta.
      benedicta.
      funesta.
      exsensa.
      tenuis.
      hustoni.
      hastata.
      marginata.

Etoblattina gracilenta.
    stipata.
    variegata.
Gerablattina apicalis.
    richmondiana.
    minima
Poroblattina longinqua.
    ohioensis.

These fossil insects are described by Professor Scudder in connection with those given on page 123 of this volume, from the base of the Dunkard creek series at Cassville W. Va., 600 feet higher in the stratigraphic column. The Richmond insects, while entirely different specifically from those at Cassville, nevertheless agree with them in their resemblance to the Permian types found in Europe, only in the lower Dyas of Weissig, Saxony. The comments by Prof. Scudder on the geological relations of both the Cassville and Richmond fossil insect faunas are quoted at length on pages 122-123 of this volume, and are of special interest as confirmatory of the Permo-Carboniferous age of the main portion of the Conemaugh series suggested by the writer as a possibility.

THE AMES, OR CRINOIDAL, LIMESTONE.

We come now to one of the most interesting deposits, from a geological standpoint, in the entire Appalachian field, the "Green Fossiliferous" limestone of the First Geological Survey of Pennsylvania, the "Crinoidal" limestone of Stevenson, and the "Ames" limestone of Andrews and Orton in the Ohio Geological Survey Reports.

This stratum, and its overlying limy shales, are the first beds found in descending the column of rocks through the Carboniferous beds, that contain clearly marked marine fossils. True, there occurs occasionally a "Black Fossiliferous" limestone, in the vicinity of Pittsburg and elsewhere in Pennsylvania, twenty-five to thirty feet above the Ames limestone, which is sometimes fossiliferous, but this is only the upper limit of this same marine fossiliferous zone, which then disappeared never again to reappear in the Appalachian field.

During the time (1868-1871) that Dr. John J. Stevenson was

Professor of Geology in the State University at Morgantown, he made a large collection of the fossils found in the Ames limestone and its associated limy shales above, which was carefully studied and its fossils identified by the late F. B. Meek. The list of fossils thus obtained, together with the letter of Mr. Meek making interesting comments on the same, was published in the Third Annual Report of the Board of Regents of the West Virginia University, 1870, pp. 67-71. Since this publication is out of print, and only a few copies of the same are extant, the letter of Mr. Meek to Dr. Stevenson, under date of November 8th, 1870, and its accompanying list of fossils, are herewith republished as follows :

"The specimens sent from the lower Coal Measures are nearly all forms common in the coal series of Indiana, Illinois, Missouri, Kansas, Nebraska, etc. , though few of them have before been found so far eastward. In some of the states mentioned, nearly all of these species range through the whole of the Coal Measures. Some of them, however, are locally more restricted. This great range of the species of invertebrate remains in the Coal Measures of the western states has long since satisfied me that these fossils cannot generally be relied upon as a means of identifying particular beds or horizons in our Coal Measures throughout wide areas; though particular grouping of species may sometimes serve as guides in this respect, within limited areas. The Coal Measure forms, however, enable us at once to distinguish beds of that age from any of the lower Carboniferous or older rocks.

The great length of time through which most of these fossils must have continued to live, will be better understood when it is stated that nearly *all* of the species enumerated in this list from the lower Coal Measures of West Virginia, also occur even in the upper Coal Measure beds in Nebraska, referred by Profs. Marcou and Geinitz to the *Permian* or so-called *Dyas*. Indeed, the collections from these two widely separated localities and horizons, contain so many of the same species, that if shown to almost any geologist unacquainted with the range of species in our Coal Measures, he would scarcely hesitate to adopt the conclusion that they came from *exactly* the same horizon in the series. Yet from what is known of the geology of your region, and that of the states farther west, it is probable that the beds from which your collections were obtained, hold a position from 1,000 to 1,500 feet or more below those alluded to in Nebraska.

From such facts as this, it would seem that although there were many elevations and depressions, as well as other consequent changes, the climatic and other physical conditions affecting animal life, must have remained remarkably uniform throughout the whole of the long continued coal period.

Very truly yours,

F. B. MEEK. "

List of Fossils identified by F. B. Meek from horizon of the Crinoidal or Ames Limestone, near Morgantown, West Virginia:

*Crinoidal fragments—Some pentagonal, star-shaped discs of columns. Crinoidal columns.

Hemiphronites crassus *Meek* and *Hayden.*

Chonetes smithii *Norwood* and *Pratten.*

Chonetes. Seem to differ from *C. granulifera* Owen, only in being smaller.

*Productus nebrascensis *Owen.*

*Productus prattenanus *Norwood.*

*Productus semireticulatus *Martin* sp. Seems to be rare in our beds.

*Discina nitida? (?)

*Pseudomonotis. (Monotis of some authors but not of Brown.) A fragment, but showing exactly the irregular regulating costæ and striæ, with vaulted scales seen on the ribs in that genus.

*Aviculopecten carbonarius *Stevenson* sp. —Pecten broadheadi *Swallow,* and Pecten hawni *Geinitz.*

*Myalina subquadrata *Shumard,* var. *ampla.*

Myalina. Undetermined species. Very small. Probably a young shell.

Allorisma. Undetermined species.

*Nucula ventricosa *Hall.*

*Nucula parva *McChesney.*

†Nucula anodontoidea *Meek.*

*Nuculana bellistriata *Stevenson,* sp. A very small attenuated variety. Common in the so-called upper Dyas, Nebraska City, Nebraska.

Astartella. Undetermined species.

†Macrodon obsoletus *Meek.*

Macrocheilus primigenius *Conrad.*

*Macrocheilus ventricosus *Hall.*

Macrocheilus. Undetermined species.

*Bellerophon montfortianus *Norwood* and *Pratten.*

*Bellerophon percarinatus *Conrad.*

*Bellerophon carbonarius *Cox.*

Bellerophon meekianus *Swallow.*

*Pleurotomaria grayvilliensis *Norwood* and *Pratten.*

Pleurotomaria. Undetermined species. A very small depressed species.

*Orthoceras cribrosum *Geinitz.*

*Nautilus occidentalis *Swallow.*

Nautilus. Undetermined species.

Productus. Undetermined species. Very small, concentrically wrinkled.

*Athyris subtilita *Hall.* Very abundaut and presenting all the usual varieties.

*Spirifer (Martinia) planoconvexus *Shumard.*

*Spirifer cameratus *Morton.*

*Species known to range through the whole of the Coal Measures in the West, even into the upper beds at Nebraska City, Neb., referred by Profs. Marcou and Geinitz to the Permian or so-called Dyas.

†New species.

Aviculopecten.   Undetermed species.   Probably *A.* occidentalis *Shumard.*

Dr. John J. Stevenson was the first geologist who adequately described and recognized, the value of this limestone as a geological horizon or "key" rock for Coal Measure geology.   Coming almost exactly midway in the Conemaugh series, it forms a splendid datum plane, easily recognizable, from which the observer can measure either up, or down, to determine the identity of important strata.   When once thoroughly known, it cannot be confused with any other stratum in the series, since in addition to being the highest limestone to contain marine fossils, it has a peculiar lithology over a wide area that is distinctly different from any other rock in the series.   Dr. Stevenson thus aptly describes its main characteristics : "Dark bluish or greenish gray, tough, and breaks with a granular surface, much resembling that of a coarse sandstone. * * * In all cases it is fossilliferous, and contains immense numbers of crinoidal stems and spines or plates."

The marine type of the bed can be traced from central West Virginia in Lewis county northward into Pennsylvania, and continuously through Greene, Fayette, Westmoreland, Allegheny and Beaver counties into Ohio, whence it can be followed without a break across that state to where it reenters West Virginia near Huntington in Cabell county, to disappear finally under water level at the Kentucky line in Wayne county, eight miles above the mouth of the Big Sandy river.

The same type of fossiliferous bed is also exhibited all along the great Volcano anticlinal from the Ohio river at Eureka across Pleasants, Wood and Wirt counties to Burning Springs on the Little Kanawha river.   Dr. Martin has also recognized this important fossiliferous horizon away up on the Alleghany mountain plateau of Garrett county, and there can be little doubt that the fossiliferous Mill creek limestone near the summit of the Pennsylvania anthracite coal series in the Wilkesbarre basin, represents the same geological plane, since nearly every species described from it by Prof. Angelo Heilprin (see Geological Survey of Pennsylvania, Annual Report, 1885, pp 451–458) is found in this list published above from the Crinoidal or Ames limestone in the vicinity of Morgantown.

The only commentary necessary to make on Mr. Meek's letter

is to state the fact that the Ames horizon does not belong so low in the Coal Measures as he supposed, so that instead of coming 1000 to 1500 feet below the Nebraska horizon holding the same fossils, it probably comes at about the same geological level, and hence as previously stated in the beginning of this chapter, it is possible that the Ames limestone and all the rest of the Conemaugh series down to near the top of the Mahoning sandstone, should, with the overlying Monongahela series, be classed among the Permo-Carboniferous beds. The great series of RED SEDIMENTS which underlie the Ames limestone fossiliferous beds give credence to this idea of their relationship to Permian time.

The Ames limestone is seldom more than 1 to 2 feet thick, and often is represented simply by a row of limestone nuggets imbedded in fossiliferous shale. In the Northern Pan Handle, however, opposite Steubenville, Colliers, and other localities, the limestone has a thickness of 10 feet. This stratum and its accompanying fossiliferous beds are finely exposed in the vicinity of Morgantown, in Falling run, Purinton's hollow, the "Peninsula," and other localities. It can also be seen in the hills at many points between Morgantown and Fairmont whenever the Pittsburg coal is 350 feet or more above the Monongahela river. It may also be observed cropping in a bold layer 1½ to 2 feet thick along the B. & O. R. R. for three or four miles in the vicinity of Colfax, and is constantly present in the hills from that point to Grafton, where it may be seen in the roadside at Mr. Poe's residence, near the Northwestern Turnpike, 280 feet above the station level.

In the section at Newburg, this horizon is marked by fossiliferous shales only, though the limestone is present high up in the hills near Austen, three miles above.

At Bridgeport, Quiet Dell, Haymond's Mill, and many other points along Elk creek in Harrison county, this limestone is conspicuous, as also on the headwaters of the same stream in Barbour, near Philippi, and in the summits of the hills around that town.

The Chestnut Ridge anticlinal brings this bed up to daylight along the West Fork river in Lewis county where it is well exposed between the old Jackson Mill and Woodford's Crossing below Weston, and also for a considerable distance below the Jackson mill.

At Burning Springs, California House, Petroleum, Volcano,

Eureka and at hundreds of other localities along the great anticlinal passing through these points, this limestone and its characteristic fossils may be seen, sometimes down near the valley floors, and again high up in the summits, along the crest of the arch.

Southwest from Eureka, the Ames limestone dips rapidly under the Ohio, and its horizon remains below the same until we come to the vicinity of Huntington, 150 miles below, where it again emerges from its rocky covering, and is finely exposed in the banks of Four Pole creek, south from the C. & O. Station, where both it and the overlying shales are still filled with the marine fossils that characterize them in the northern portion of the state.

When this geological horizon rises from the bed of the Great Kanawha, however, below Charleston, in the region of thickening sediments, the limestone horizon and its accompanying red beds below, are present, but the marine fossils are gone, and only Spirorbis, and other fresh or brackish water types are found. The same thing is also true at Burnsville in Braxton county, where this horizon comes out from under the Little Kanawha river, and at all localities between there and Charleston where this horizon is exposed in the hills along Elk river, and its tributary streams coming in from the north.

The inference from these facts is that in passing southeastward from the parallel of Charleston, Burnsville, etc, we are approaching the mouths of those ancient rivers that transported the thick delta deposits which filled up the Appalachian gulf, and hence the estuarine waters would be too fresh to permit the existence of marine life.

THE CRINOIDAL OR FRIENDSVILLE COAL.

The sudden transition from peat bogs to marine limestone making conditions which recur several times in the history of the Appalachian field, is finely illustrated by the thin coal which frequently underlies the Ames limestone without any intervening shale or other rock whatever. In fact large unbroken shells of ALLORISMA, MYALINA and other forms, are frequently found partly imbedded in the upper part of the coal itself, although still in contact with the overlying limestone. This is especially noticeable in the vicinity of Burning Springs, Wirt county, where the coal has been mined for use in drilling for oil, although only eighteen to twenty inches thick.

This bed has usually been termed the CRINOIDAL COAL, on account of its relationship to the overlying limestone. Recently, however, Dr. G. C. Martin, of the Maryland Geological Survey, has proposed the name Friendsville as a geographical term, from its occurrence near the village of that name in Garrett county, Maryland, and since this is the first clear geographical designation the coal has received, it has been adopted into the West Virginia nomenclature. Dr. Martin finds the coal of some economic importance in the Castleman river valley, where it is locally known as the "Fossil" coal, and is frequently mined by the farmers for domestic use, being fifteen to eighteen inches thick. He has also identified this bed one mile west from Mt. Savage, Allegany county, Md., where it has been mined with a thickness of twenty-eight inches. He adds that Charles Lyell visited a mine in the same coal bed, nearby, in 1842, and listed the fossils observed in its limestone (Ames) roof.

Splendid exposures of this coal, and its accompanying limestone, may be seen in the great cuttings along the Pan Handle R. R. in the vicinity of Saw Mill run, and westward at Pittsburg, Pa., where the Ames limestone is in direct contact with the coal.

So far as known, there are only two or three regions in West Virginia at which this coal has been mined by drifting. One of these is at Burning Springs, Wirt county, previously referred to, where the coal was mined for fuel in the petroleum developments of the early '60's. Another locality is in the vicinity of Haymond's Mill, on Elk Creek, five miles above Clarksburg, Harrison county. At this latter locality the bed is known as the "Shell" coal, from the fossil shells in its roof, and it has been mined by several farmers for domestic use. It is twenty-one inches thick, without any perceptible partings, and is a bright, pitchy-looking coal of fair quality.

This coal has also been dug into in the ravine at Newburg, Preston county, where it crops 135 feet above the shaft to the Upper Freeport and Lower Kittanning beds, and appears to be twenty to twenty-four inches thick.

About two miles south-east from Newburg, the same coal has been mined for domestic use by the farmers high up on the hillside.

This coal crops along the hills at Grafton, Taylor county, about 320 feet above the river, and also at many points along the

B. & O. R. R. between Grafton and Clarksburg, in the vicinity of Webster, Tyrconnell, and Bridgeport, but it is there never more than two feet thick, and frequently only one.

In Lewis county this coal is seen above Woodford's Crossing, below Weston, where it is only four to eight inches thick, and quite impure.

In Monongalia county the coal is frequently absent from the measures, and when present it is only six to twelve inches thick, so that generally it is not of much economic importance.

The writer has not seen this bed in the southwestern end of the state, but Prof. Selby reports it as two feet thick in his Huntington-Kenova section, page 240.

It is possible that at some of the localities in the Potomac basin, and other regions of the state where the Ames limestone is absent, this coal may have been confused with the one (Bakerstown) which comes fifty to one hundred feet lower in the series.

PITTSBURG RED SHALE.

As a rule the Friendsville coal, or in its absence the Ames limestone, rests directly upon a soft red, or purple shale which, from its fine exposure along the grade lines of many railroads at Pittsburg, has been named from that locality. Occasionally there is some limy, gray, or red shale under the overlying coal or limestone, as the case may be, and then comes another limestone bed quite different in color and texture, and only slightly fossiliferous. This limestone is found occasionally in Ohio, and has there been named the EWING LIMESTONE, by the Ohio geologists.   It has been seen at Huntington and a few other localities in West Virginia, but does not appear to be very persistent. As a rule, the measures below the Ames limestone and Friendsville coal, consist of deep red and variegated shales, often marly and containing nuggets of impure limestone and iron ore.   The red beds extend from the Ames limestone downward from fifty to one hundred feet. Although RED SEDIMENTS may occur at any horizon in the Conemaugh series, between the Mahoning sandstone and the Pittsburg coal, yet these near the middle of the series are the thickest, most persistent, and striking of all. It is this band of PITTSBURG RED SHALE, thirty to 100 feet thick, which makes such a conspicuous belt of red soil entirely across the state, from the Pennsylvania line at the north to the Kentucky border on the Big Sandy river.

All of the red shales in the Carboniferous system are soft, yielding, and easily reduced to mud, but this one is particularly so, giving rise to bad roads, slips, landslides and other troubles at the surface, and great annoyance and anxiety to those who attempt to drill through it, even when buried from sight hundreds of feet below ground. Its peculiar character of returning to mud when wet, and "caving" or running into the holes drilled by the oil and gas well contractors, adds from $1,000 to $1,500 to the cost of every deep well bored through it in the state, and frequently by imprisoning the drilling tools, leads to the loss of both well and tools, so that the derrick must be moved to a new location. Occasionally this disaster happens not only once, but even twice and thrice before the oil or gas well contractor succeeds in completing an open, steel-lined hole to the coveted oil or gas sand, 1,000 to 2,000 feet below this red horizon. On account of this tendency to "cave," this particular stratum has been dubbed the "Big Red Cave" by the oil well drillers of West Virginia and Pennsylvania. It is the belief of the drillers that it is not the RED SHALE itself which imprisons the drilling tools, but the nuggets of hard limestone imbedded in these soft shales which, falling out from the wall of the well with the "caving" muddy sediments, impinge against the drilling tools, principally at the "jars," and thus prevent their withdrawal. It is on account of this tendency of these beds to "cave" and give trouble in drilling through them, until a lining of steel or iron casing is firmly anchored on the top of the Mahoning or Dunkard sand below, that these beds have been so readily traced underground across the state, with much certainty from the Pennsylvania line to the Great Kanawha, and on beyond to the Big Sandy river, even when buried from sight by huudreds of feet of superincumbent strata.

Very little economic use has as yet been made of these red shales of the Conemaugh in West Virginia. They would make a fine grade of red brick, and some of the layers would doubtless make a good quality of ornamental tiling for hearths, mantels, etc., as they do in the vicinity of Pittsburg.

At Huntington, Cabell county, a good grade of red roofing tile is manufactured from these red shales of the Conemaugh, the State University Library, at Morgantown, having recently been roofed with the Huntington tile. They are quite hard and great durability is claimed for them by the manufacturers.

THE SALTZBURG SANDSTONE.

Sometimes a very massive sandstone comes into the series and displaces, or has eroded, a large quantity of the red beds described above. In the vicinity of Saltzburg, on the Kiskiminitas river, Westmoreland county, Pennsylvania, such a stratum occurs with a thickness of 100 feet, and its top extends to 260 odd feet above the horizon of the Upper Freeport coal. To this sandstone Dr. John J. Stevenson gave the name, Saltzburg sandstone. This stratum is quite prominent in Preston county, in the vicinity of Reedsville, Masontown, Kingwood and other points, where it overlies the Bakerstown (Barton) coal at a short interval, and is often quite pebbly and massive.

This stratum is seldom seen in Monongalia county, or if represented, it is not very massive; but in the tier of counties extending from Braxton along Elk to the Great Kanawha and beyond, it appears to be genrally present and quite massive. It is possible that this stratum may represent what has often been termed the "First Cow Run Sand" of the oil drillers, since its position in the series would correspond very closely to the horizon of this petroliferous rock at Moundsville and elsewhere in West Virginia.

This stratum has a great development along the Pan Handle R. R. near Colliers, in Brooke county, where it immediately overlies the Bakerstown coal, and extends half way up to the Ames limestone.

It also appears to be this rock which crops in great cliffs along Buffalo creek, near its mouth, at Wellsburg, in the same county.

THE BAKERSTOWN (BARTON) COAL.

At an interval of sixty to one hundred feet below the Ames limestone, and three hundred and fifty to four hundred feet below the Pittsburg coal, there occurs a coal bed of wide persistency and of considerable economic value, which the writer once described under the name BAKERSTOWN COAL, from its occurrence near a village of that name in Richland township, Allegheny county, Pennsylvania. (See Report Q, Second Geological Survey of Pennsylvania, pp. 162-3).

The following section from page 163, l. c., will show its structure and relationship to other well-known horizons:

		Ft. In.	Ft. In.
Ames (Crinoidal) limestone		2	
Concealed		90	
Coal, Bakerstown. { coal	1 6		
	slate	0 ¼	
	coal	0 4	
	slate	0 ½	2 8
	coal	0 3	
	slate	0 ½	
	cannel	0 6	
Interval to Upper Freeport coal, about		200	

The coal is seldom more than four feet thick and is sometimes called the "Three-Foot" seam, and again the "Four-Foot," being locally designated by both terms in the George's creek-Potomac basin, according to Dr. Martin, of the Maryland Survey, who correlates with it the Barton coal of Allegany county, as shown in his section from that region reproduced on page 237 of this volume, where the bed in question is three feet thick, with impure top and bottom.

The Barton coal was so named by Prof. Philip T. Tyson in his description of the "Frostburg Coal Formation of Allegany county, Maryland," published in the Trans. of the Maryland Academy of Science and Literature, 1837, and hence it has priority over the name Bakerstown, which was not given until 1876, and first published in 1878. This Barton coal lies 183 feet above the Upper Freeport bed in the Barton section of Dr. Martin referred to above, and 408 feet below the Pittsburg coal. Should this suggested identity be confirmed by further detailed studies, then the name, Bakerstown, will become a synonym, and be replaced by "Barton" in agreement with the law of priority.

The Bakerstown or Barton coal has been mined extensively for several years near Collier's station, Brooke county, on the line of the Pan Handle R. R., at what is known as the Blanche mine of the Pan Handle Coal Company. The principal output is used in coaling the engines of the railroad company. There has been much local discussion as to the horizon of the coal at the Blanche mine, some even regarding it as identical with the Pittsburg bed. The writer, however, finds it 370 feet below the Pittsburg coal, which

crops in the high knobs south from Colliers. It is about 100 feet
under the Crinoidal or Ames limestone which, filled with its characteristic fossils and ten feet thick, crops in the hills above, while
twenty-five to thirty feet under the coal in question lies the Upper
Cambridge limestone, also fossiliferous and unmistakable, so that
there can be no doubt that the Blanche mine bed comes at the
horizon of the Bakerstown coal of Allegheny county, Pennsylvania.

Mr. A. P. Brady, who collected the sample of coal from the
Blanche mine for analysis, reports the following section there.

	Ft. In.	Ft. In.
Sandstone (Saltzburg)		
Slate		12 0
Coal...{ coal, softer	1 11	} 4 2
{ coal, hard	2 3	

Butts run N. 68° W. Face N. 22° E. Elevation above R.
R., 20 feet.

Prof. Hite's analysis of the coal sample gives the following
results :

Moisture	0. 78
Volatile matter	41. 25
Fixed carbon	52. 36
Ash	5. 61
Total	100 00
Sulphur	3. 15
Phosphorus	0. 0055

The coal is rather high in sulphur, but as it is low in ash,
it gives excellent results as a steam producer. The deposit near
Colliers appears to be quite patchy, since in passing eastward the
overlying Saltzburg sandstone comes down and cuts out the
coal entirely within a short distance from the mine entry. The
bed is also thin or poorly represented on the south side of the
Pan Handle R. R. tracks.

In the vicinity of Morgantown this coal appears to be absent
entirely, there being only some impure fireclay and limy deposits
at its horizon, but the coal comes into the section six miles east,
along the Ice's Ferry road, near its junction with the Tunnelton
pike. It has there been mined by Mr. Bayles for domestic use,
and has a thickness of three feet, but thins to less than two feet
where last seen along the Morgantown road a few hundred yards

west. It lies 100 feet below the Ames limestone and its underlying Friendsville coal, visible at the roadside farther up the hill
to the west, and appears to be of fair quality.

.The coal is also seen above the road just west of the Cheat
Canyon Club House, where it is 200 feet above the level of Cheat
river at the point where the Upper Freeport coal rises out of the
same.

On the east side of Cheat at Ice's Ferry, this coal was once
mined by stripping and used at the old Green Spring iron furnace
operated there half a century ago. It is reported as three and
one-half to four feet thick, and of very fair quality for general
fuel purposes.

This coal thickens and obtains its best development eastward
from Monongalia and Marion counties, since it is unknown at the
numerous localities along the Monongahela river between Morgantown and Fairmont, where its horizon is exposed, and it also
appears to be absent, or but feebly represented, between Fairmont
and Grafton.

East from the Chestnut ridge anticlinal, however, in the vicinity of Masontown, Reedsville and other points in the Preston
county basin, this coal has frequently been mined and has a thickness of three to four feet, being known as the "Four-Foot" bed.
It is highly valued as a domestic fuel, and generally preferred to
that of the Upper Freeport coal below.

The writer described this coal in the vicinity of Masontown
in Bulletin 65 of the U. S. G. Survey, as the one which underlies
the Lower Cambridge limestone, and named it the Masontown
coal. This was an error due to an unexpected and unperceived
rapid dip in the strata, which greatly increased the
supposed interval between this coal, which crops at Masontown, and the Upper Freeport mined along Decker's creek,
just west of the village.

The interval was supposed to be only 125 to 140 feet, but recently a bore hole starting eleven feet below the level of the coal
in question, passed though 180 feet, $8\frac{1}{2}$ inches of rock material
before encountering the Upper Freeport coal. It also passed
through the Lower Cambridge limestone, and its accompanying
dark, fossiliferous shales, at a depth of sixty-seven feet, or one
hundred and thirteen feet above the Upper Freeport coal, so

that the conclusion is unavoidable that the coal hitherto known as the Masontown at its type locality, is in reality the Bakerstown, and hence the name Masontown must be dropped from the nomenclature, since the coal it was intended to designate belongs just under the Lower Cambridge fossiliferous limestone and dark shales. The rock cores brought up by the diamond drill from the boring referred to on the land of Amos Ashburn, along Dillon creek, two miles southwest from Masontown, were presented to the State University Museum by the Hon. S. B. Elkins, under whose direction the drilling was done. The writer has carefully examined these cores and they reveal the following succession between the Upper or "Four-Foot" coal bed, mined in the hills at Masontown, (cropping near the bore hole) and the Upper Freeport coal at the base of the Conemaugh below:

	Ft.	In.	Ft.	In.
Coal, Bakerstown, Barton....................................			4	0
Concealed and shales	11	0		
Surface clays from top of drill hole.........	12	0		
Green shale and clay　..	17	10	77	9
Gray sandstone & conglomerate, Buffalo	23	11		
Dark shales, fossil plants and shells	13	0		
Limestone, Lower Cambridge, fossiliferous.............			1	3
Shales, dark, sandy, fossiliferous...........	7	0		
Fireclay ....　.........................	10	9		
Gray and green shales........　.......　......	8	0	112	8½
Gray, massive sandstone, Mahoning	86	4		
Black slate, pyritous	0	7½		
Upper Freeport coal......................................				
Total...			195	8½

This section reveals the two members of the Mahoning sandstone united into one solid mass eighty-six feet thick, with only a few coaly streaks to indicate the Mahoning coal horizon, sixty to seventy feet above the Upper Freeport seam.

There is also a massive sandstone which makes a steep bluff at a short interval above the Bakerstown coal, and this would represent the Saltzburg sandstone horizon.

This coal has been mined on the land of Samuel Kirk by stripping, a short distance west from the Presbyterian church and cemetery at Masontown, where it lies fifty feet above a massive, pebbly sandstone, and the same distance below the top of another gray, massive sandstone, which caps the knob above it. The coal has the following structure:

	Ft. In.	Ft. In.
Gray and yellow shales..	5	0
Bituminous shale	0	6
Coal, bony	1 4 }	4 0
Coal, good, hard..	2 ·8 }	

The coal has been mined on many of the farms in the central portion of the syncline east from Chestnut ridge in Preston county. An opening just north from Reedsville gives the following measurement:

	Ft. In.
Dark shale	1 0
Bony cannel..	1 3
Coal, good...	3 0

It is possibly this coal that has been mined in the summit of the hill, 350 feet above Sandy creek, and one-half mile west of Bruceton, instead of the Elk Lick bed as supposed.

This coal has been mined by stripping along the road near Albright's bridge across Cheat river, three miles east of Kingwood, and there the following succession may be seen:

	Ft. In.
Sandstone, rather massive, Morgantown....................	30
Concealed..	55
Shale, drab..	15
Sandstone..	2
Shale and fireclay..	8
Shale, green, sandy..	10
Sandstone, massive, Saltzburg..............................	30
Shale, drab..	15
Shale, dark blue..	8
Coal, Bakerstown (Barton)......................................	2 6
Concealed	5
Limestone, nodular..	2
Concealed	23
Sandy shale..	7
Sandstone, greenish..	13
Shale	5
Concealed to Cheat river at the Albright bridge.....	25

This is the same section published by the writer in the Proceedings of the American Philosophical Society, 1882, page 493, in a paper read before the Society October 20th of that year. At that time, however, this coal shown in the section was supposed to belong lower down in the measures, but as the Mahoning sandstone rises out of the Cheat nearby, and the well-known Upper Freeport coal has recently been opened up under it, there can remain scarcely any doubt that the coal in the section above is the

Bakerstown bed, since it comes about 200 feet above the Upper Freeport, and 400 feet below the Pittsburg bed, of which latter coal a few acres are caught in the summit of Copeman's Knob, one-half mile distant.

It is probably this Bakerstown coal that has been mined along the Morgantown and Kingwood turnpike, one mile west from Kingwood, and also along the W. Va. Northern R. R., a mile or so southwest from the town, at each of which localities the coal is three feet thick, and a very good domestic and steam fuel.

It is probably this bed which caps the summits near Mr. A. G. Harshbarger's house, at Anderson, Preston county, two miles east from Tunnelton.

There are also frequent openings in this coal high up in the hills along the Valley river, between Grafton and Philippi, where it has been mined by the farmers for domestic supply.

In the deep syncline between Philippi and Big Laurel mountain, this coal has been opened on many of the farms lying along that great trough from Fellowsville, past Valley Furnace, Nestorville, Meadowville, and Belington. It is usually called the "Three-Foot" bed in this region, but occasionally the name "Four-Foot" is heard. Its reputation is good as a domestic fuel.

Southwestward through Upshur, at Centreville, or Rock Cave, and vicinity, this coal is frequently mined, although only two and one-half feet thick, or less in many cases.

In the Pan Handle of Lewis county, near Crawfordsville, Walkersville, Ireland, Duffy and other points, this coal appears to furnish the main local supply, together with the Elk Lick bed, which, in the region of Ireland, overlies the Bakerstown coal by an interval of 127 feet, according to J. Perry Thompson, C. E., who has accurately determined the same. Through all this region it varies from two and one-half to three feet in thickness, and appears to be a satisfactory fuel.

This coal was once opened near the eastern end of the tunnel, at Morrisons, Braxton county, but is there rather poor in quality.

It is probably this same bed that has been reported as present, eighteen to twenty-four inches thick, in some of the cellars excavated at the town of Sutton, since its horizon would come at about that level.

It appears to be this coal which has been mined in the vicinity of Newton, at the Three Forks of Sandy creek, in the southern portion of Roane county, where it is twenty-eight to thirty inches thick, with a slate parting near the middle.

Along Two Mile creek in Kanawha county, a coal has been mined occasionally, one mile above the mouth of the stream, at sixty to eighty feet under the Ames limestone horizon. This appears to be identical with the Bakerstown horizon. It is reported as three feet thick and rather impure.

In the Castleman basin of Garrett county, Maryland, the Bakerstown coal has considerable value, according to Dr. Martin, of the Maryland Survey, and is locally known as the ''Honeycomb'' seam.

At some localities in the George's Creek-Potomac basin, this coal is mined and shipped on a commercial scale, and appears to give satisfactory results as a fuel. It is probably this bed which has been opened thirty feet above the mouth of the shaft at Henry, on the line of the W. Va. C. & P. R. R., where it is two feet thick, and about 240 feet above the Upper Freeport coal in the shaft.

In Somerset county, Pennsylvania, the ''Price'' and possibly the ''Rose'' coals are found at this geological horizon.

IRONDALE LIMESTONE AND IRON ORE.

Near Albright's Bridge, Anderson, and other points in Preston county, a bed of ferruginous limestone immediately underlies the Bakerstown coal. At Gladeville and Irondale in the same county, a limestone 4 to 5 feet thick overlies ½ to 2 feet of silicious, limy iron ore, and although no coal is to be seen immediately above the limestone, it is quite probable that it represents the limestone frequently found just under the Bakerstown coal, since its geological horizon appears to be not far from that level. The limestone is of fair quality but not of marine origin, and was used as a flux in the Irondale furnace. The iron ore is a carbonate but rather lean, having only 35 per cent of metallic iron, and 12 to 15 per cent of silicious matter. It was mined by stripping at Gladeville, and at Irondale by both stripping and drifting, the limestone above being taken out for flux, and thus making room to get the ore. The latter was roasted before mixing with ''Lake'' ores for use in the furnace. The ore is too lean for successful iron manufacture, and the furnace has been out of blast for twenty years.

UPPER CAMBRIDGE LIMESTONE.

At an interval varying from ninety to one hundred and twenty feet below the Ames or Crinoidal limestone, there often occurs another fossiliferous limestone which sometimes has a slight resemblance to the Ames, and may have been occasionally confused with it. This resemblance is notably marked along Harmans creek, between Colliers and Hollidays Cove, Brooke county, where the Lower Cambridge limestone, one to two feet thick, and filled with marine fossils, immediately overlies a bed of dark red shale. The presence of the Ames limestone in the hills 120 feet above, and also the presence of the Pittsburg coal bed on above the latter limestone at the proper interval, forbid any error of identification here.

This same Upper Cambridge limestone has a wide distribution in Brooke and Hancock counties, being seen on King's creek and also just below the summits of the hills at New Cumberland, where it overlies the Mahoning coal (No. 7 of the Ohio series), by an interval of 140 feet, and is 210 feet above the Upper Freeport coal horizon, while the Ames bed, much thicker, caps the summits farther east, 100 to 120 feet higher.

This bed was termed the 'Pine creek' limestone by the writer in Report Q of the Second Geological Survey of Pennsylvania, from a locality in Allegheny county where it comes 120 feet below the Ames bed, and 60 feet above the underlying Lower Cambridge ("Brush creek") limestone.

But as the names Upper and Lower Cambridge had been used by Dr. Orton to designate the same horizons in Ohio, the "Pine creek" and "Brush creek" terms have been replaced by the former in the nomenclature of the Conemaugh series.

The Upper Cambridge limestone is present in the section at Morgantown, and generally along the Monongahela and Tygarts Valley rivers between Morgantown and Grafton. It is usually dark colored on fresh fracture, but weathers to an ashen hue on exposed surfaces, and while not so full of marine fossils as the Ames above, yet it contains an abundance of them. No systematic collection has been made from it in West Virginia, but the forms are apparently much the same as those in the Ames above, except that Crinoidal fragments are not so abundant. The rock is generally quite silicious, and has seldom been burned for lime.

It is possible that this marine type of the Upper Cambridge limestone may belong at the same geological horizon as the fresh or
brackish water Irondale limestone, since both have never been
observed in the same section.

THE BUFFALO SANDSTONE.

The last described limestone immediately overlies a massive
sandstone in northern Allegheny and southern Butler counties,
Pennsylvania, which from its great development along the waters
of Buffalo creek in Eastern Butler county, was named by the
writer the Buffalo sandstone, in Report Q of the Pennsylvania
Reports.

At its type locality the stratum is very massive and quite
conglomeritic, its top being 175 feet above the base of the Conemaugh, and its bottom 125 above the same datum.

The rock is exposed in a massive stratum along Decker's
creek at Morgantown, in the rear of the High School building,
where its deposition has eroded the underlying shales in a very
striking manner, well illustrated in the cuttings of the Morgantown and Kingwood railroad, so that at this horizon there is much
local unconformity. The sandstone itself is seen to vary from five
to twenty feet in thickness within 200 feet.

The sandstone has a fine development in the vicinity of Grafton, Taylor county, where it makes great cliffs along the bluffs, fifty to one hundred feet above the B. & O. railroad grade, and has
been extensively quarried for building purposes. From Grafton
southward, along the Valley river to Philippi, in Barbour county,
it is almost constantly in sight above water level, and frequently
high up in the hills. It is apparently this stratum which covers
the surface for several acres, three miles above Grafton, and has
recently been quarried for use in rebuilding the bridge piers along
the Grafton and Belington branch of the B. & O. railroad. It is
usually a grayish-white rock with a tinge of pink, and splits readily into blocks of any desired size.

It makes high cliffs half way up the hills around the town of
Philippi, and immense blocks of the sandstone lie scattered over
the surface along the little stream which enters the Valley river from the south. These blocks have been quarried for building stone at Philippi, of which they make an excellent quality.

This sandstone is most probably the one which underlies, by twenty to thirty feet, the town of Buckhannon, in Upshur county, and rises to the surface two miles south along the Buckhannon river, where it has been quarried for building stone on the lands of Mont. Reger and Minter Jackson.

Farther up the Buckhannon it makes prominent cliffs in the hills, especially between the mouth of Cutright's run and Sago. It is a grayish-white rock, slightly reddened with iron, and makes excellent building material.

This stratum is generally below the horizon of all the soft red shales of the Conemaugh series. When any red shales are found under this stratum and still in the Conemaugh, the color is seldom original, but is superinduced by weathering of exposed ferriferous shales.

Southwestward from Upshur, through the Pan Handle of Lewis, to Sutton in Braxton county, this stratum appears to be always present at the proper horizon, and is generally conspicuous as a bold cliff around the hills. It caps the summits at Gillespie, and Palmer, and may be seen at many points along Holly river n Webster county where it crowns the highest points with its massive layers.

It rises from the bed of Elk river, one mile above Sutton, and makes great cliffs along that stream southward to the mouth of Holly and beyond.

A few miles below Sutton this stratum comes above the level of Elk river again, and is constantly in sight from there to Charleston, sometimes down near the water, and again high up in the summits of the hills as at Clay, and other points where the dip of the strata elevate or depress its horizon as the case may be. It is probably this stratum that makes such a massive cliff near the mill at the Three Forks of Sandy or Newton in the southern end of Roane county.

At Clendennin, Mason, and on down Elk through Kanawha county to Charleston, this stratum is constantly in sight, and it forms the top of the bold bluffs at the junction of the Elk and Great Kanawha rivers.

It extends southwestward from the Great Kanawha across Lincoln, Boone, Cabell and Wayne counties to the Kentucky line, making great cliffs along the Big and Little Coal, Mud, Guyandot, Twelve Pole, and the Big Sandy rivers.

The stratum is frequently very pebbly, and occasionally the disintegrated matrix leaves a thick bed of rounded quartz gravel, some an inch or more in diameter, on the summits of many ridges, between the Great Kanawha and Big Sandy rivers.

Should the dividing plane (Upper Freeport coal) now used to separate the Conemaugh series from the underlying Allegheny, ever be changed, it would naturally be moved up to either the base, or top of this Buffalo sandstone, since immediately above it RED SEDIMENTS begin to appear, denoting a great change in physical conditions. The frequent evidences of erosion at the base of this rock render it probable that this stratum is more closely allied with the overlying beds than with the underlying ones, and hence if any portion of the Conemaugh series belongs in the Permo-Carboniferous rather than in the Coal Measures, the most natural place at which to draw the division plane would be at the base of this Buffalo sandstone, or the limestone just below.

THE LOWER CAMBRIDGE LIMESTONE.

In Allegheny, Butler and Beaver counties of Pennsylvania, there frequently occurs a dark, very fossiliferous limestone over some black shales in the roof of a rather persistent coal bed. Its geological horizon varies between sixty and ninety-five feet under the Upper Cambridge limestone, and 180 to 200 feet below the Ames or Crinoidal bed. The limestone in question was first designated from Brush creek, a stream in Cranberry township, Butler county, where it is frequently seen above the dark roof shales of a coal bed, and it was described as the ''Brush creek'' limestone in Report Q of the Pennsylvania Geological Survey.

The following section quoted from page 176 of the above named Report, measured in the steep bluffs of Killbuck run, one mile above its mouth in Ohio township, Allegheny county, will show the relationship of this Brush creek (Lower Cambridge) limestone to the well-known and important strata above, as follows:

KILLBUCK RUN, ALLEGHENY COUNTY, PENNSYLVANIA.

	Ft.
Massive sandstone (Morgantown)	20
Concealed	65
Limestone, Crinoidal (Ames)	2
Red clay (Pittsburg)	30
Concealed	85
Pine creek (Upper Cambridge) limestone	2
Massive sandstone, Buffalo	75

```
Shales..................................................................................    3
Brush creek (Lower Cambridge) limestone ..................    1
Concealed to level of run ..........................................    3
                                                                    ———
    Total...............................................................286
```

Another section from the same Volume (Q) page 181, measured in the steep bluffs of the Ohio river, opposite Economy, Beaver county, will further illustrate the stratigraphic horizon of this bed :

SECTION OPPOSITE ECONOMY, BEAVER COUNTY, PENNA.

```
                                                          Ft.      Ft.
Limestone, Crinoidal(Ames)...........................    4
Red shales (Pittsburg)..................................   25 ⎫
Concealed ...................................................  100 ⎬ ...195
Finely laminated sandstone, Buffalo...............   70 ⎭
Brush creek (Lower Cambridge) limestone......    4
Dark shales.................................................   12
Coal, Brush creek (Mason)...........................   1⅓
Sandstone, Mahoning, visible............. ..........   35
Concealed to horizon of Upper Freeport coal....   50
                                                         ————
    Total............. .........................................  301⅓
```

One more section from Allegheny county, giving all three of these fossiliferous limestones and their relation to each other, as well as to the base of the Conemaugh below, obtained from the record of a diamond drill boring at Sewickley, Pennsylvania, will be useful here in illustrating the varying interval between the Lower Cambridge limestone and the base of the Conemaugh. It is taken from Bulletin 65, U. S. G. Survey, page 73, and only the portion of the section from the Ames limestone down is given as material to the point in question. It reads as follows :

SEWICKLEY, ALLEGHENY COUNTY, PENNSYLVANIA.

```
                                          Ft. In.      Ft. In.
Limestone, Crinoidal(Ames).............................     2   0
Coal, Crinoidal (Friendsville)...........    1   0 ⎫
Red shales and sandy beds.................  110   0 ⎪
Limestone, gray, Upper Cambridge......    2   0 ⎪
Shales and concealed .......................   40   0 ⎬ 196   0
Sandy shale (Buffalo S. S.) ................   32   0 ⎪
Dark slate ...................................   11   0 ⎭
Limestone, dark, Lower Cambridge......... ..........     1   0
Dark shales.............................................. .........    11   0
Coal, Masontown (Mason)..................................    0   5
                         ⎧ sandstone, mica- 
                         ⎪   ceous, gray.........   13   8 ⎫
Sandstone,               ⎨ fire clay, sandy......    0   6 ⎬ 36   2
Upper Mahoning           ⎪ sandstone, lt. gray   22   0 ⎭
```

Shale, dark gray.........	8	4
Sandstone, gray	0	8
Shale, sandy..	6	8
Shale, blue	6	5
Sandstone	0	8
Slate, gray	3	4
Fire clay, variegated at base, impure	25	11

	sandstone, gray, micaceous	38	5		
Sandstone, Lower Mahoning	shales, sandy, blue..	8	6	55	5
	sandstone, lt. gray..	8	6		

Upper Freeport coal		
	———	
Total	354	0

The base of the Conemaugh is correctly identified in this bore hole record, since the boring was continued on below the Lower Kittanning coal. It reveals an interval of 147 feet between the Lower Cambridge limestone and the Upper Freeport coal, or practically double the minimum rock thickness between these two important horizons, when the Mahoning sandstones are poorly developed, or mere sandy shales.

This Lower Cambridge limestone is seldom exposed at the surface in West Virginia, since its horizon is so often concealed by the debris from the massive Buffalo sandstone above.

In the bore hole near Masontown, Preston county, the record of which is given on page 269 of this volume, this limestone is very fossiliferous, as also the dark shales immediately above and below, and its interval above the Freeport coal is 112 feet, 8½ inches.

It has also been observed by the writer a short distance below the mouth of Cutright's run, four miles above Buckhannon, Upshur county, where the underlying coal and the fossiliferous shales are both well exposed in a cutting along the Weston and Pickens branch of the B. & O. R. R., one-tenth mile below the forty-fourth Clarksburg mile post. Here the dark shales just below the irregular lens-like layer of fossiliferous Lower Cambridge limestone, is a mere mass of fossils, only twelve to eighteen inches above the underlying thin coal, which there emerges above the railroad grade, while the massive Buffalo sandstone forms a great cliff along the hills a few feet higher. At this locality the following section was measured :

BELOW MOUTH OF CUTRIGHT'S RUN, UPSHUR COUNTY.

	Ft.
Massive sandstone, Buffalo and concealed.....................	65
Blue shales, with lenses of fossiliferous limestone (Lower Cambridge)	10
Dark fossiliferous shales	5
Coal, { coal......... 0' 8'' / slate........ 0 4 / coal......... 0 6 }	1½
Concealed to Buckhannon river...............................	25

The horizon of the limestone and its fossiliferous shales is about 160 feet above the Upper Freeport coal, which rises out of the Buckhannon river two miles above this locality. In the fossiliferous shales were noted Chonetes mesolobus, Productus Nebracensis, a species of Bellerophon, and many crinoidal fragments.

In the Huntington-Kenova section of Prof. Selby, page 240 of this volume, the Lower Cambridge limestone is placed 166 feet above the Upper Freeport coal, and 185 feet below the Ames, or Crinoidal limestone.

On Twelve Pole river, Wayne county, three miles above Ceredo station, on the N. & W. R. R., this limestone horizon is exposed in a railroad cutting where the Wayne turnpike leaves the river, as follows :

	Ft.
Massive sandstone...	10
Sandy shales	6
Sandy limestone, fossiliferous	4
Shales	10
Limestone, dark, fossiliferous, Lower Cambridge	½
Dark blue shales..	10
Coal, Mason........	1
Concealed and shales................................	14
Sandstone, Upper Mahoning, massive, visible in bed of Twelve Pole	10

Here the sandy limestone is filled with crinoidal stems as well as other marine forms, and on its weathered surface exactly resembles the ''fossil sandstone'' found by Dr. G. C. Martin in Garrett county, Maryland, at this same horizon.

The dark, Lower Cambridge limestone, ten feet below the ''fossil sandstone,'' is also quite fossiliferous, though thin and impure.

This same section is also exposed three miles farther up Twelve Pole, near the mouth of Buffalo creek, in a cutting along the N. & W. R. R.

Along the Big Sandy river, in Wayne county, this fossiliferous limestone is frequently seen in the roof shales of the Mason coal, opposite Louisa, Kentucky, and on northward to the mouth of Blaine creek and beyond. It is also to be seen in the Ohio river hills near Catlettsburg, at the mouth of the Big Sandy.

These limy, fossiliferous shales are present high up in the hills at New Cumberland, Hancock county, at 120 feet above the Upper Freeport coal horizon, and eighty feet below the Upper Cambridge limestone. They are also present in the section at Osburn's Mill, on King creek, in the same county, though no distinct stratum of limestone was observed either there or at New Cumberland.

In Garrett county, Maryland, Dr. G. C. Martin, of the Maryland Geological Survey, finds this Lower Cambridge limestone and its accompanying dark fossiliferous shales, the most persistent and characteristic members of the Conemaugh series, so that they have proven most valuable stratigraphic guides in tracing and identify-the coals of the Allegheny mountain plateau, where the dips are frequently steep and the exposures few.

Dr. Martin's section on the North Potomac at Blaine, near Elk Garden, Mineral county, quoted in this volume, page 236, reveals the presence of the Lower Cambridge limestone there, imbedded, as usual, in black, fossiliferous shales. Its horizon in the Blaine section is 132 feet above the Upper Freeport coal, and 439 feet below the Pittsburg bed.

Dr. Martin has kindly sent the Survey a list of fossils, which he has identified from the Lower Cambridge limestone. He states that the list is preliminary and incomplete, since he has only partially studied the collections from this horizon. He also states that the Mason shales, below, contain a marine fauna somewhat different from the overlying limestone, and that it has not yet been carefully studied. The locality from which these fossils were collected is in Garrett county, Maryland, one mile north from Selbysport. This list as determined by Dr. Martin is as follows :

LOWER CAMBRIDGE LIMESTONE FOSSILS.

Phillipsia sangamonensis Meek and Worthen.
Orthoceras sp.
Temnocheilus sp.
Pleurotomaria tabulata Hall.

Pleurotomaria sp.
Macrocheilus sp.
Bulimorpha sp.
Straparollus catilloides Conrad.
Bellerophon percarinatus Conrad.
Bellerophon carbonarius Cox.
Allorisma subcuneatum Meek and Hayden.
Astartella vera Hall.
Nucula ventricosa Hall.
Yoldia carbonaria Meek.
Productus nebracensis Meek.
Chonetes mesolobus Norwood and Pratten.
Derbya crassa Meek and Hayden.
Seminula sp.
Eupachycrinus mooresi Whitfield.
Zaphrentis sp.

This list reveals about one-half of the species common to the Ames limestone above, as given by the determinations of Mr. Meek on page 258. Possibly when larger collections are made, and thoroughly studied, a larger proportion of species may be found common to the two horizons.

THE MASON SHALES.

The dark or black shales immediately under the Lower Cambridge limestone, frequently contain marine fossils, in their upper half especially, in Pennsylvania, Maryland and northern West Virginia, while in the basal portion of the same, many fossil plant remains occur. They are especially rich in fossil plants at Mason, on Elk river, seven miles above Charleston, Kanawha county, and this shale has been designated from that locality. The same horizon is rich in fossil plants in many other regions, viz: in Wayne, Clay, Braxton, Upshur, Preston and other counties.

Mr. David White, the eminent paleobotanist of the U. S. G. Survey, has studied the collections of fossil plants made by himself, Mr. M. R. Campbell, and others, from these shales at Mason, Clendennin, Pleasant Retreat, and other localities in Clay and Kanawha counties, and from apparently the same horizon at Furnace Hollow and Lavalette, Wayne county. The lists of plants identified from this horizon are given in a paper published by Mr. White March, 1900, in the Bulletin of the Geological Society of America, pages 170-172, inclusive, from which the following quotations are made :

FLORAS SUCCEEDING THE KANAWHA FORMATION

PLANTS LESS THAN 200 FEET ABOVE THE "BLACK FLINT."

"As bearing upon the question of the position of the Stockton flora in the Pennsylvania region, while further showing the occurrence of the typical Pennsylvania floras, it is of interest to glance at the floras succeeding the Stockton in the southern West Virginia section. I therefore append three lists of plants from higher horizons in the same section."

"The first of these floras, from localities * which Mr. Campbell informs me lie 200 feet above the Black Flint, is as follows:"

Name.	Locality.
Pseudopecopteris obtusiloba (Sternb.) Lx.	Wayne.
" *squamosa* (Lx.),† large	Clen., Wayne.
Mariopteris sillimanni (Lx.)‡	Gr., Wayne.
" *nervosa* (Brongn.) Zeill.	Wayne, Liz.
" *newberryi* (Lx.)†	Clen.
Sphenopteris solida Lx.†	Wayne.
" *chærophylloides* (Brongn.) Presl †	Clen.
" *mixta* Schimp.†	Wayne, Liz.
" *ophioglossoides* (Lx.) †	Clen., Cob., Wayne, Liz.
Pecopteris emarginata (Goepp.) Presl. †	Cob., P. R.
" *unita* Brongn†	Clen., Wayne, Liz.
" *solida* Lx. †	Clen.
" *villosa* Brongn. ? †	Gr., Clen., Cob., Wayne, Liz.
" *vestita* Lx. †	Clen.
" *oreopteridia* (Schloth.) Sternb. †	Gr. ?
" cf. *jenneyi* D. W. †	Wayne
" *miltoni* (Artis) ? †	P. R., Wayne
Alethopteris serlii (Brongn.) Goepp.	Wayne.
Neuropteris rarinervis Bunby †	P. R., Liz.
" *vermicularis* Lx. †	G. H.
Neuropteris fimbriata Lx. †	Clen., Wayne.
" *ovata* Hoffm. †	Clen., P. R., Wayne.
" *scheuchzeri* Hoffm. †	Gr., Clen., P. R., Wayne.
Odontopteris subcuneata Bunby†	Gr.
" *æqualis* Lx. †	Liz.
Calamites cistii Brongn.	Clen.
Annularia ramosa Weiss	Wayne

---

* The collections here roughly listed are Graham mine, Mason (Gr.); along the Elk river, one mile above Clendennin (Clen.); Cob mine, near Clendennin (Cob.); from an horizon about 200 feet above the Black Flint, one-half mile east of Pleasant Retreat (P. R.); Left Fork of Mill creek, Wayne county (Wayne); south of summit on Belva and Lizemore road (Liz.); Gunter hollow, near Mason (G. H.).

† Forms apparently identical with those in the Allegheny series.

Name.	Locality.
Annularia stellata (Schloth.) Wood *............Gr., Cob., P. R. Wayne.	
" *sphenophylloides* (Zenk.) Gutb. *...Gr., Wayne.	
Sphenophyllum emarginatum Brongn. *.........Clen., Cob., Wayne, Liz.	
" *majus* Bronn*.....................Clen., Wayne.	
Lycopodites pendulus Lx...........................Wayne.	
Lepidophyllum brevifolium Lx ....Clen.	
" *oblongifolium* Lx* ....Clen., Liz	
Lepidocystis vesicularis Lx ....Wayne, Liz.	
Sigillaria camptotænia Wood* ....Clen.	
" *fissa* Lx* ....Wayne.	
Cordaicarpon gutbieri Gein*..................Wayne.	
Carpolithes ellipticus Sternb* ....Cob.	

PLANTS 200-300 FEET ABOVE THE "BLACK FLINT."

"A small collection of plants from the road north of Clay Court House is reported by Mr. Campbell as probably between 200 and 300 feet above the Black Flint, although his stratigraphic field notes are not yet compiled so as to more precisely fix the position of the horizon. Another lot of fossils, from an horizon possibly no higher, is from Granny branch of Indian creek, near Mason. These small lots contain:"

Name.	Locality.	
Pseudopecopteris squamosa (Lx.)†..............Gran.		
Mariopteris sphenopteroides (Lx.) Zeill†...........Gran.		
" *sillimanni* (Lx.)† ....Gran.		
Sphenopteris pinnatifida Lx?†.....Clay.		
" cf. *stipulata* Gutb ....Gran.		
" *sagittatus* (Lx.)†.......Clay.		
Pecopteris dentata Brongn†...........Clay.		
" *villosa* Brongn†..........Gran., Clay.		
" *miltoni* Artis†...........Clay.		
Neuropteris rarinervis Bunby†...........Clay.		
" *ovata* Hoffm† ....Gran., Clay.		
" *fimbriata* Lx.† ....Clay.		
" *scheuchzeri* Hoffm†....Gran., Clay.		
Linopteris obliqua (Bunby) Pot* ....Clay.		
Odontopteris wortheni Lx* ....Gran.		
Annularia stellata (Schloth) Wood*.............Gran., Clay.		
Sphenophyllum emarginatum Brongn* ....Gran., Clay.		
Lepidodendron modulatum Lx*.........Gran.		
Lepidophyllum jenneyi D. W.* ....Gran.		
" *hastatum* Lx*...........Clay.		
Sigillaria camptotænia Wood* ....Clay.		
Carpolithes ellipticus Sternb*...........Gran.		

*Forms apparently identical with those in the Allegheny series.
†Identical species in the Allegheny series.

SPECIES 300-400 FEET ABOVE THE "BLACK FLINT."

"Two other small collections from horizons said by Mr. Campbell to be between 300 and 400 feet above the Black Flint were obtained near Lavalette (Lav.), on the Huntington pike and Furnace Hollow† (Fur.), Wayne county. They include :"

Name.	Locality.
Mariopteris nervosa (Brongn.) Zeill	Fur.
Pecopteris dentata Brongn	Fur.
" *villosa* Brongn.?	Fur.
" *oreopteridia* (Schloth.) Sternb	Fur., Lav.
" *polymorpha* Brongn	Lav.
" n. sp?	Lav.
Alethopteris pennsylvanica Lx.?	Fur.
Callipteridium inæquale Lx	Fur.
Neuropteris rarinervis Bunb.?	Fur.
" *scheuchzeri* Hoffm	Fur.
" *agassizi* Lx.?	Fur.
Annularia sphenophylloides (Zenk.) Gutb. var. *intermedia* Lx	Fur., Lav.
Sphenophyllum emarginatum Brongn	Fur.
" *majus* Bronn	Fur.
" *thoni* Mahr. ?	Av.
Lepidodendron modulatum Lx	Fur.
Lepidophloios sp	Fur.
Lepidophyllum oblongifolium Lx.	Fur.

ALLEGHENY FLORAS ABOVE THE "BLACK FLINT."

"It needs but a glance at the first two of the three preceding lists to recognize the typical constitution of the Allegheny floras. While it is not my present purpose to attempt by analysis to arrive at an estimation of the approximate positions of these plant associations, I may here express the opinion that the collective flora enumerated in the first list shows so high a degree of identity and so similar a composition to the floras of the Kittanning group of Pennsylvania, as to strongly argue for a reference of some portions at least of the beds within 200 feet above the Black Flint to the latter group. Likewise, for reasons which cannot here be discussed, I am inclined to believe that the small flora from beds between 200 and 300 feet above the Black Flint may be from terranes not later than the Freeport group. The species in the third list, though few in number, do not appear to indicate a stage very far above the horizon of the Upper Freeport coal, the upper limit of the Allegheny series. The evidence on this point is, however, at present too insufficient to justify further consideration."

---

*Identical species in the Allegheny series.
†Near the mouth of Labor creek.

The resemblance of this flora to that in the Allegheny series below is so great and well marked that it misled Mr. David White into placing these shales in the Allegheny series, 150 to 200 feet lower, based not upon any stratigraphic evidence, but solely upon the presence of many fossil plants which had survived into this horizon from the older beds below. This fact is another argument showing the close relationship of these basal members of the Conemaugh series, and especially of those which precede the appearance of RED SEDIMENTS, with the Allegheny series beneath, and confirms the correctness of the old Rogers classification which included them in the same series with the Allegheny.

As already suggested by the writer, on pages 226-7, 260, and elsewhere in this volume, in discussing the age of the Conemaugh series from entirely different lines of evidence, it would be more philosophical to return substantially to the old classification, except that the dividing plane might be drawn at the base of the Buffalo sandstone just above the Lower Cambridge limestone, instead of at the top of the Mahoning sandstone, as was done by the Rogers classification. This is a question which the detailed study of the beds carried from county to county, may be expected to settle definitely when it is taken up systematically hereafter.

THE MASON COAL.

It has already been related on pages 268 and 269 how the writer was once led into error in defining the place in the Conemaugh series of a coal which crops in the vicinity of Masontown, Preston county, and that consequently it becomes necessary to drop the name Masontown entirely, since at its type locality the bed designated as the Masontown turns out to be the Bakerstown, or Barton coal, at an horizon sixty to seventy-five feet above the coal bed which it was intended to describe. So far as known, the region around Masontown is the only locality where this error was made, and as one of the most widely persistent coals of the Conemaugh series belongs at the horizon for which the name was intended, it becomes necessary to adopt another. Fortunately this can be done by simply dropping the final syllable of the old name, since the coal it was the intention to name has long been mined at the village of Mason, on Elk river, seven miles above Charleston, Kanawha county, so that in this volume the coal which belongs next under the Lower Cambridge limestone horizon, has been designated as the Mason coal.

In the Graham mines, operated by Mr. J. G. Vaughan, at Mason, Kanawna county, Mr. R. W. Edmonds measured the following structure for this coal at its type locality:

		Ft. In.	Ft. In.
Sandstone			
Shale, Mason			3 0
Coal, Mason	coal	2 10½	
	slate	0 2½	
	coal	0 6	
	bone coal	0 ¾	4 7¾
	coal	0 1½	
	slate	0 4	
	coal	0 6½	

Butts run N. 45° E.   Face S. 45° E.   Elevation 630 feet A. T.

Prof. Hite reports the following analysis of the sample collected by Mr. Edmonds:

Moisture	0. 72
Volatile matter	36. 58
Fixed carbon	52. 25
Ash	10. 45
Total	100. 00
Sulphur	2. 69
Phosphorus	0. 006

The coal is hard, bright, and makes an excellent fuel for both steam and domestic purposes.

The dark gray shale (Mason) in the roof of the coal is filled with fossil plants, and from the mines in this vicinity the fossils in one of the lists of species previously given were obtained by Mr. David White.

The dip of the rocks carries this coal below the water level of Elk on above Mason, and it is not mined to any considerable extent until Clendennin is reached, at the mouth of Sandy creek, twenty-five miles above Charleston, where the coal again comes above water level, and has been mined at several local banks for the village supply.   One of these mines, on the north bank of Elk river, a mile above the mouth of Sandy creek, operated by Jackson and Osburn, exhibits the following structure:

	Ft. In.	Ft. In.
Shale................................		
Fire clay, impure..	1 6	
Coal { coal..	0 10	} 3 0
{ bone	0 2	
{ coal......................................	2 0	

Farther back under the hill, the portion of the coal above the bone increases to twenty inches, and the entire bed is then four feet thick. The bottom portion is the best coal, clean, bright, and highly valued for domestic use. The coal has an elevation of thirty to forty feet above Elk, but on the south side of the stream is considerably higher, and it has been opened and mined there in several places.

The strata continue rising up Elk from Clendennin, and the Mason coal gets higher and higher above water level until the underlying KANAWHA BLACK FLINT comes up to the bed of Elk, and makes Queen Shoals in the same, five miles above Clendennin.

The Mason coal is mined near Queen Shoals by the Elk Run Collieries Company, and shipped to market over the C. C. & S. R. R.

Mr. S. D. Brady, who collected the sample for analysis from the mine, reports the following section there:

	Ft. In.	Ft. In.
Sandstone		
Slate, gray..	1 6	
Coal..	1 0	
Sandstone	1 6	
Shale, dark, Mason, filled with fossil plants............	3 0	
Coal, Mason...... { coal	0 5	} 4 4½
{ bone	0 ½	
{ coal..............................	1 0	
{ slate, gray..................	0 1	
{ coal	2 10	
Mostly sandstone to level of the Elk river.............	200 0	

Butts run S. 55° E.   Face S. 35° W.   Greatest rise, S. E.

The analysis of the sample from this mine yielded the following results to Prof. Hite:

Moisture.....	1.09
Volatile matter....................................	38.14
Fixed carbon	54.88
Ash..	5.89
Total..	100.00
Sulphur	0.93
Phosphorus	0.005

This analysis illustrates a coal of the highest excellence, and the demand for it in the coal markets exceeds the capacity of the mines. It is shipped west and north, principally for gas and steam purposes. The coal is very hard, but very bright and pure looking, and if crushed would make a most excellent coke.

The stratigraphical position of the coal is here about 175 feet above the KANAWHA BLACK FLINT, the horizon of which is above water level along Elk, immediately below the mine. The following section of the rocks between the MASON COAL and the KANAWHA FLINT is exposed immediately below the mine:

SECTION NEAR QUEEN SHOALS.

	Ft.
Mason coal...	
Fireclay and shales..........	2
Sandstone, massive..	20
Shales. sandy, gray, containing nodules of iron ore.......	40
Sandstone and concealed	20
COAL blossom, Mahoning...	
Concealed and massive sandstone to level of C. C. & S. R. R.	80
Concealed...	15
KANAWHA BLACK FLINT horizon, here concealed by debris..	

This is in the region of thick sediments, where the Conemaugh series is 800 feet or more in thickness, and where the lowest RED SEDIMENTS of that series lie 410 feet above the horizon of the Kanawha black flint, or more than 200 feet above the Mason coal, the most of which latter interval is made up of the greatly thickened Buffalo and Saltzburg sandstones, which make great pebbly cliffs along Elk above the Mason coal horizon.

The KANAWHA BLACK FLINT comes out from under its covering of rock debris at the mouth of Spread Shoals creek, a mile or more above the Elk Run Company's mine, where it is five to seven feet thick and quite massive, presenting the typical appearance of this peculiar stratum along the Great Kanawha, so that there can be no doubt of its identity with the latter rock. Then, too, at the mouth of Porter creek, a mile above Spread Shoals, the thick coal, which so frequently underlies the Kanawha flint, makes its appearance seven feet below the latter. Hence, here on Elk, the horizon of this important MASON COAL may be said to be about equally distant (200 feet) between the LOWEST RED BEDS above, and the KANAWHA BLACK FLINT below.

This Mason coal extends along the Elk river hills from Queen

Shoals to Clay, with a thickness of three to three and one-half feet, and has been exploited on the lands of the Thompson estate, one mile above Yankee Dam, and five miles below Clay, where it has been opened at 450 feet above the C. C. & S. railroad grade, and 310 feet above the Splint, or Coalburg, seam. The Mason coal exhibits the following structure on the Wilson survey of the Thompson estate:

	Ft.	In.	Ft.	In.
Coal	0	9		
Slate, gray	0	½	3	4½
Coal	2	7		

The coal is very bright, pure, and Mr. Thompson reports that it cokes well. It lies 150 feet below the top of a great pebbly sandstone, above which come reddish shales, with deep red beds 100 to 150 feet higher.

This coal has been opened near the pike on the north side of Elk, at Clay Court House, by Mr. Reed. It is high in the hills —350 feet above Elk River—and reported to be three feet thick, with a thin slate or bone near the top.

Its crop is also visible on the new road which ascends to Mt. Pisgah, or Asbury Heights, on the south side of Elk, twenty feet above the massive pebbly sandstone (Upper Mahoning), which forms the top of the great cliffs that surround Clay, 300-400 feet above the valley of Elk. Since this coal is an important link in connecting the Kanawha coals with those in the typical Allegheny series at the northern line of the state, a section measured from the summit of Asbury Heights to the bed of Elk river below, will now be given to illustrate the associated rocks, as follows :

SECTION AT CLAY COURT HOUSE, CLAY COUNTY.

	Ft.
Concealed, and much deep red shale	90
Coarse, gray, pebbly sandstone	60
Concealed and shales, some pale red	100
Sandstone, very massive large quartz pebbles	60
Concealed and sandy shales	130
Coal, blossom, Mason	2-3
Fireclay and shales	10
Sandstone, Upper Mahoning, very massive, pebbly	90
Concealed and massive sandstone (Lower Mahoning)	160
Black slate and thin coal (Upper Freeport)	3
Massive sandstone, and concealed	100
Coal, Coalburg (Lower Freeport?)	6
Sandstone and concealed to Elk river	15

It is from the horizon of this MASON COAL at Clay that the collection of fossil plants, listed on page 283, was obtained by Mr. David White.

The KANAWHA BLACK FLINT thins away as we pass up Elk beyond Porter's Creek, twenty miles below Clay, where it is last observed in a massive condition, but as its geological horizon is constantly above Elk, and since the MASON COAL can be readily traced, the horizon where it belongs is well known, viz: just above the three feet of black slate and coal, 121 feet from the bottom of the section.   In fact, a thin layer of the flint is reported as present at this horizon, in the rear of the Court House, on the north side of Elk.

The coal at the base of this section is the same one that has been mined at several points in the vicinity of Clay, and also near Yankee Dam, six miles below, where it lies 310 feet vertically below the Mason coal, which has been exploited in the hills above by M. Thompson, Jr.   The interval of 363 feet in the Clay section, between the same coal beds, is probably thirty to forty feet too great, since the rocks are rising southward, and the section traverses the rocks northward with no allowance for dip.

This is in the region of greatly thickened deposits, and where the Conemaugh series is probably thicker than at Charleston (800') since 700 feet of these beds may be seen in this section, and the Pittsburg coal horizon must over-shoot the deep red shales at the top by an interval of not less than 200-300 feet.   There are some PALE RED SHALES in the mostly concealed interval, 190 feet above the Mason coal, but nothing that resembles the great PITTSBURG RED SHALE until we come to ninety feet below the summit of Asbury Heights, when the dark purple shales, so characteristic of that horizon, make their appearance in the section.

About two miles south of Clay the Mason coal has been mined by Hedge Triplett, near the Nicholas county road, where it is reported as three feet thick, with only one thin bony streak.

This coal has been mined occasionally high up in the Elk river hills, between Clay and the mouth of Big Otter creek, and it is probably this same coal which is reported to be two feet thick on the latter stream, three miles above its mouth.

A coal is reported as four feet thick near the junction of Birch river with the Elk, one-half mile up the former stream, and it is possibly this bed. It overlies a heavy sandstone bluff, which extends along Elk to Frametown, four miles above.

A coal was once mined there, forty feet above the Elk river, just above a massive ledge of sandstone, on the land of David Evans. It is reported as two and one-half feet thick and very probably represents the Mason coal, since it is 140 feet above it up to the lowest red bed of the Conemaugh, and 550 feet up to the Pittsburg bed, which crops in the summits of the hills on the land of Mr. Evans, one-half mile north from Frametown. Here very deep red shales with gray limestone (Two Mile) crop about 300 feet below the Pittsburg coal, and 250-300 feet above the one (Mason) near the Elk river. The dip to the northwest is more than 100 feet to the mile, so that at least 700 feet of the Conemaugh series would be above water level at Frametown.

A few miles above Frametown the horizon of the Mason coal dips under the Elk, and does not reappear until the course of the river veers to the southeast above Sutton, when it comes up with a rapid rise in that direction, one mile above the town, and has long been mined on both sides of the river for local supply. At the Josiah Hawkins mine the coal is twenty to twenty-four inches thick, having two inches of soft coal on the bottom, and the rest rather hard, but very pure and bright, except a streak of bone near the top.

About two miles above Sutton, Mr. Henry Evans has a mine in this coal, eighty feet above Elk river, one-fourth mile below the mouth of Bee run, where it is twenty-two to twenty-four inches thick, bright and clean, and overlain by three feet of dark gray shales (Mason), filled with fossil plants, above which is a layer of coal four inches thick.

Near Palmer, at the mouth of Holly river, this coal has been mined to a small extent by Mr. O. W. Gum, high up in the hill, one-half mile northwest from the town, where it is about 150 feet above the Upper Freeport coal, and 160 feet below the first red beds above. The coal is twenty-eight inches thick at Mr. Gum's bank, with four inches of bony coal at the top.

On the stream which puts into Elk river below Gillespie, this coal has been mined by both Mr. Hoover and Mr. P. G. Gillespie, along the B. & O. railroad track one mile south of Morrison's tunnel, and 140 feet below the Bakerstown coal. The Mason plant

shales are very fossiliferous here and are exposed in the following
section at the old Hoover mine :

		Ft.	In.	Ft.	In.
Dark gray plant shales (Mason) visible..............		3	o		
Coal, Mason... { coal		o	4		
shale, gray		o	5	2	5
coal, good.........		1	8		

The same coal, apparently, was once mined by the Hardwood
Lumber Company in the summit of the mountain south from Elk
river, five and one-half miles below Addison, where the coal lies
1250 feet above the level of Elk river, and exhibits the following
structure:

		Ft.	In.	Ft.	In.
Gray slate with fossil plants (Mason).........		2	o		
Coal, Mason { coal		o	9		
dark bony slate		o	5	2	11
coal, good		1	9		

The coal gave excellent results as a steam producer on the
heavy grades of the Hardwood Lumber Company's railroad.

This coal has also been opened in a few places by the farmers
along the high ridges west from Holly river, in Webster county,
as also in the Pan Handle of Lewis, where it is 150 feet above the
Upper Freeport coal, and two and one-half to four feet thick, frequently being mined by the farmers for domestic use.

One mile below Abbott's store, on the waters of French creek,
Upshur county, this Mason coal has long been mined on the old
Burr farm, now owned by Taylor Heavner, Guy Colerider and
others, where it exhibits the following structure :

	Ft.	In.	Ft.	In.
Slate, dark..				
Coal, hard...................................	o	9		
Black slate...............................	o	1		
Bone coal....................................	o	6		
Coal, good........................	2	10	5	4
Black slate...................	o	3		
Coal, hard, good................................	o	11		

The two feet and ten inches of coal is softer and purer than
the rest, and known as "shop coal," since it is used for smithing
purposes. A very massive, pebbly sandstone (Upper Mahoning)
crops only ten to fifteen feet under this coal, along French creek,
and makes bold cliffs around the hills.

This same coal is also mined on the land of A. A. Morgan, near the Burr farm on French creek. where it has the following structure :

	Ft.	In.	Ft.	In.
Coal and bone	o	8		
Coal, good..	4	0		
Shale, gray...	o	2	6	2
Coal	I	4		

The best coal is the lower two-thirds of the four-foot bench, the top of it being more or less bony.

This coal was once mined on French creek by Dr. Newlon and others, of Buckhannon, who built a branch railroad to it from the Pickens line of the B. & O. R. R., about three miles up French creek from its mouth. The slate and bone in the coal at that locality proved quite thick, however, and the mine has been abandoned.

At Sago, on the Buckhannon river, this coal has been mined by stripping, on the land of W. L. Burner, where the following section is visible:

	Ft.	In.	Ft.	In.
Shales, gray, visible...	3	0		
Dark shale	I	0		
Coal	o	8		
Coaly slate...	o	3		
Coal, good...	2	6	4	2
Shale, gray	o	3		
Coal, hard...	o	6		

The coal has a good reputation as a domestic fuel. It lies at an elevation of 150 feet above the Upper Freeport coal, which was once mined along the base of the hills just above the grade of the B. & O. (Pickens branch) R. R. at Sago.

At the mouth of French creek, near Hampton, the Mason coal has been mined on the lands of Messrs. Westfall, Cutright, and others, where it is sixty to seventy-five feet above the B. & O. R. R. grade, and three and one-half feet thick.

A short distance below Hampton, this coal is exposed at a quarry in the underlying massive Upper Mahoning sandstone, where there is only five to seven feet of fire clay and shales between the two strata.

A short distance above the mouth of Cutright's run, the Mason coal has been mined by M. A. Cutright, and there the following section is exposed in the steep bluffs of the Buckhannon river :

CUTRIGHT SECTION.

	Ft.
Silicious limestone, top of knob	5
Deep red shales and concealed	70
Massive sandstone, Saltzburg	30
Coal, blossom, Bakerstown	
Marly shales and concealed	35
Massive sandstone	25
Concealed	50
Coal, Mason	3
Fire clay and shales	6
Sandstone, massive, Upper Mahoning to B, & O. R. R. grade	30
Concealed to Buckhannon river	25

Here a thin coal is reported in a well boring just under the bed of the Buckhannon. It would represent the Mahoning coal, since the Upper Freeport would lie at least eighty feet below the river at this point.

The silicious limestone which caps the summit here, is very probably a representative of the Crinoidal or Ames limestone, but it appears to be non-fossiliferous.

The massive sandstone, which has been identified with the Saltzburg, is the same one which underlies the town of Buckhannon, five miles north, and whose top comes about 120 feet under the coal, which has there been identified as the Elk Lick, at the mines of Major Heavner, Mr. Reger, and others. Its horizon would come about fifty feet above the top of the Cutright section. This section is an important one in stratigraphy, since only one mile north of this the Lower Cambridge limestone, with its underlying fossiliferous (Mason) shales, is seen at the B. & O. R. R. grade.

In this connection the structure of the Elk Lick coal in Maj. Heavner's mine, near Buckhannon, has an important bearing on the stratigraphic succession, and is as follows :

	Ft.	In.	Ft.	In.
Slate				
Coal	0	8		
Bone	0	1½		
Coal	1	1	3	8½
Slate	0	1		
Coal	1	10		

That this coal holds the above structure over a wide area in
Upshur and Lewis counties, may be seen by reference to pages 252
and 253 of this volume, and also by the following additional section of it, three miles southeast of Roanoke, Lewis county, measured by Mr. W. T. Blackiston, of Piedmont, W. Va.

	Ft. In.	Ft. In.
Coal	0 7	
Slate	0 3	
Coal	1 3	4 3
Dark slate	0 2	
Coal	2 0	

This digression is pertinent here because there is no doubt
that the Buckhannon coal belongs about fifty feet above the
top of the limestone in the Cutright section, and the above structures prove it to be the Elk Lick bed, because at Vandalia and
elsewhere in Lewis and Upshur a coal with this same structure
lies 250 to 275 feet below the Pittsburg bed. This would put the
Elk Lick coal 265 feet above the MASON COAL of the Cutright section, and as the latter is 150 feet above the Upper Freeport coal at
Sago, only two miles above, it would be about 415 feet above the
base of the Conemaugh series, another line of evidence that the coal
mined 120 feet above the river at Buckhannon is the Elk Lick bed.

At the mouth of Cutright's run, a short distance north of the
last locality, the Mason coal has been mined twenty feet above the
B. & O. R. R. grade, and reported to be three feet thick. It overlies the Upper Mahoning sandstone by an interval of only ten feet,
and the latter crops out in a bold ledge along the run and river.

On Cutright's run, one mile above its mouth, Mr. Jacob Cutright mines the Mason coal for local use, and it is there three and
one-half feet thick, though farther up the run, near the Beverly
pike, it contains only two feet of good coal where stripped out of
the bed of the stream on the land of J. W. Strader.

One mile below the locality of the Cutright section, the Lower
Cambridge limestone, and Mason shales filled with marine fossils,
come down to the B. & O. R. R. grade, as shown in the section on
page 278. It is possible that the coal shown there may belong
twenty to twenty-five feet above the regular Mason vein, and is
simply a "roof" member of the latter, since such a coal is occasionally present a few feet above the Mason bed. The Mason coal is
mined on the land of Mr. Shaw, opposite the mouth of Cutright's
run, and in the region between Sand run and the Buckhannon

river, there are several mines operated on this coal for domestic use by the farmers, blacksmiths, and others.   It varies
from two to four feet in thickness and appears to give very satisfactory service as a general fuel, as well as smithing coal.

In the vicinity of Philippi, Barbour county, the Mason coal
crops in the hills eighty to one hundred feet above the Valley river,
and ten to thirty feet below the massive Buffalo sandstone, which
makes such a great cliff around the hills at that point. It is known
as the "Three-Foot" bed, and has been dug at several localities,
but not mined to any extent.

It is well exposed along the Nestorville road, two miles southeast from Philippi, where the road descends to Ford's run, in the
following section :

FORD'S RUN SECTION.

	Ft. In.	Ft. In.
Sandstone, massive Buffalo	30 0	
Concealed	10 0	
Black shales (Mason) containing fossil plants	10 0	
Mason coal { coal ... 0 10 / bone ... 0 6 / coal ... 2 1 }		3 5
Concealed and sandstone (Upper Mahoning).	75 0	
COAL, Mahoning		3 6

Farther down Ford's run the Freeport coal comes out and is
mined at Meriden, forty feet under the Mahoning coal, thus making the Mason coal about 118 feet above the base of the Conemaugh
series in the Philippi region.

This coal has been mined on the land of Samuel Moats, one
mile up Teter's creek from its mouth, and high up in the hills to
the south, where it is about four feet thick, and has a thin slate or
bony coal ten inches above the bottom, and another near the top.
It lies ninety-nine feet below another coal bed eighteen inches
thick, and 150 feet below a deep red shale with marly shales, and
a coaly streak, above which, thirty-two feet, comes another coal
bed, possibly the Bakerstown, four feet thick, on the land of Jasper England.

Just below the mouth of Teter's creek, at Moatsville, and 250
odd feet above the Valley river, the Mason coal appears as a bed
of cannel in the following section on the land of Daniel Moore :

		Ft. In.	Ft. In.
Coaly slate			2 6

Fireclay shales		2	0
Coal, Mason {coal, bituminous...... 11 2} {coal, cannel............ 3 0}		3	2
Massive sandstone (Upper Mahoning) and concealed		84	0
Coal, Mahoning		3	0
Fireclay and shales		5	0
Sandstone, very massive, Lower Mahoning		31	0
Concealed		22	0
Coal, Upper Freeport, visible		3	0
Concealed		10	0
Massive sandstone, Upper Freeport and concealed to bed of Valley river		90	0
Total		255	2

Here the Mason coal turns to a fairly good bed of cannel, which has been mined and burned to a small extent by Mr. Moore. By the thickening up of the Mahoning sandstone members at this locality, the Mason coal is thrown 146 feet above the base of the Conemaugh.

A bed of cannel coal is frequently found along the waters of Sandy creek, in Preston county, and it very probably belongs at the horizon of the Mason coal.

The Daniel Moore section just given is an important one, since the massive pebbly rocks below the Upper Freeport coal here were formerly (Bulletin 65, U. S. G. Survey, page 128) considered by the writer as belonging in the Pottsville series, instead of the Allegheny, while both the Mason coal at the top of the section, and the Mahoning coal below it, were included in the Allegheny series. The section given for Moatsville in Bulletin 65, referred to above, was made about one-half mile above the mouth of Teter's creek, where the exposures are not so good as at the Daniel Moore locality, below the mouth of the same stream. The occurrence of RED BEDS, however, only 150 feet above the Mason coal, and the Bakerstown coal on above in the hills back from Moatsville, render it certain that the former interpretation of the Moatsville section was in error, and that the great, pebbly, massive sandstones in the bluffs and bed of the Valley river there, are the Upper and Lower Freeport sandstones respectively, since the entire series can be traced from Moatsville to Philippi, where the measures extend up to the Pittsburg coal in the hills, two miles west from the river.

The Masontown coal is occasionally mined between Moatsville and Grafton, Taylor county, but in approaching the latter place, it appears to grow thin and slaty, since in a cut one-fourth

mile below the B. & O. railroad station in Grafton, it exhibits
the following structure in the section measured there from the summit of the hill :

GRAFTON, TAYLOR COUNTY.

	Ft.
Massive, yellowish gray, pebbly sandstone..............	20
Shales and concealed..	25
Limestone, fossiliferous, Ames..	2
Coal, Friendsville.........	1
Shales, marly, gray and red..	30
Shales, sandstone and concealed....................................	160
Sandstone, massive, Buffalo	55
Dark shales (Mason) fossil plants........................	5
Coal, Mason	½
Fireclay and sandy shales...	15
Sandstone, top of Upper Mahoning............................	10
Concealed to Valley river................................	35

The base of the Conemaugh would probably underlie the
river here at about sixty to seventy feet, since the Upper Freeport
coal comes out of Three Forks creek, one mile east from this locality, at about 125 feet below the Mason coal.   Here the Ames limestone and its underlying coal are finely exposed at a cutting on the
road at Mr. Poe's residence, near the summit of the hill, and as
the limestone (although earthy and shaly) is a mass of fossils,
there can be no doubt about the place of the Mason coal and other
rocks in this section.

The massive sandstone above the Ames limestone, which has
been much quarried around the Grafton hills, appears to be a new
member of the Conemaugh which comes into the series along
Three Forks, at a short interval below the Elk Lick coal, and it
might be appropriately named the Grafton sandstone.   It makes
cliffs along the hills at many points between Grafton and Newburg.

In the coal shaft at Newburg, the Mason bed is reported as one
foot thick, and it is apparently this seam which crops under a
heavy sandstone along the B. & O. railroad tracks a few hundred
feet west.

Three miles east from Newburg, the Upper Freeport coal rises
to the level of the B. & O. railroad at Murray tunnel, near Austen,
and the basal members of the Conemaugh are there well exposed
in the following section descending from the hills above :

MURRAY TUNNEL SECTION.

	Ft.
Massive, pebbly sandstone, Buffalo	25
Concealed	20
Coal, Mason	2
Concealed	20
Massive sandstone (Upper Mahoning)	40
Concealed, with fireclay at base (Mahoning coal)	40
Massive sandstone (Lower Mahoning)	50
Upper Freeport coal	

The MASON COAL was once opened here by a farmer, who reports it as two feet thick, and fairly good. The drift was closed when the locality was visited, so that the coal could not be seen.

In the Belington region of Barbour county, this coal has been mined within the limits of the town, and just east of it for local supply. It is two and one-half to three feet thick, cropping twenty to thirty feet above the top of the Upper Mahoning sandstone, and about 140 feet above the Upper Freeport coal.

It has been mined by many farmers along the western edge of Randolph and eastern Upshur, between the Tygart's Valley and Little Kanawha rivers, and is seldom less than two and one-half feet thick.

Through Webster and Nicholas counties, this coal increases in importance, and has frequently been opened by the farmers high up in the summits of the hills. In Powell mountain, Nicholas county, it makes a large outcrop along the Sutton pike, 150 feet above the Upper Freeport bed, which was once mined at that locality.

About one mile southwest from there, the Mason coal has long been mined for domestic supply on the land of James McCarron, 450 feet above the level of "Muddlety" (Mumble-the-peg) creek, where it exhibits the following structure:

	Ft.	In.	Ft.	In.
Coal	1	0		
Bone	0	4	3	10
Coal	2	6		

The coal is very bright and rich looking. It is used by the smiths and appears to be a very pure coal. Through this district it is known as the "McCarron" vein.

In the region of North Coalburg (Shrewsberry) and Cedar Grove, Kanawha county, this MASON COAL thickens up to a large size, and is locally known as the "Big" bed. It lies 160 to 175 feet above the Kanawha black flint, and exhibits the structure shown in the following section measured by the writer in 1884:

NORTH COALBURG, KANAWHA COUNTY.

	Ft. In.	Ft. In.
Shales, with iron ore..		10 0
Massive sandstone, Buffalo		50 0
Shale, blue (Mason plant shale)		3 0
Coal, Mason ... { coal .... 1 6 / black slate................... 0 6 / coal, good.................. 4 2 / shale............................ 2 6 / coal .... 0 6 / shale.......................... 5 0 / coal, slaty .... 3 6 }		17 8
Massive sandstone (Upper Mahoning) and concealed..		90 0
Coal "No. 5," Mahoning { coal............... 0 8 / shale............. 0 2 / coal.............. 1 0 / bone............. 0 4 / coal............. 1 8 }		3 10
Concealed and sandstone, Lower Mahoning		65 0
Kanawha black flint		7 0
Concealed, with Stockton coal near top		65 0
Sandstone, massive.		25 0
Coalburg coal.. { coal, splint................... 0 5 / bone or "niggerhead".. 0 6 / coal, splint .... 3 0 / fire clay, shale .... 2 6 / coal, soft .... 1 6 }		7 11
Concealed		300 0
Sandstone, visible...		10 0
Coal, Cedar Grove { coal .... 0 3 / shale................ 0 8 / coal .... 2 8 }		3 7
Concealed, containing "Peerless" coal bed, thirty above base..		100 0
Coal, Blacksburg...		4 0
Concealed to level of the Great Kanawha		20 0

This section, measured between North Coalburg and Cedar Grove, is introduced to show the relation of this MASON COAL to the KANAWHA BLACK FLINT bed, as well as to the underlying KANAWHA COAL SERIES, which is here exposed nearly to its base, since the Blacksburg bed is the lowest member of the Campbell's creek coal, the "Peerless" being the upper member of the same.

The Cedar Grove Colliery Company has a mine in the Mason coal near Cedar Grove, where Mr. S. D. Brady measured the following structure :

	Ft. In.	Ft. In.	Ft. In.
Slate (Mason)			
Black slate..			0　3
Coal, left up...........................	0　3	⎫	
Coal	1　3			
Bone or "niggerhead".............	0　1			
Coal	0　6	⎬ 5　8	⎫
Bone or "niggerhead"..........	0　1			⎬ 14　8
Coal	0　9			
Slate	0　2			
Coal	2　7	⎭	
Sandy shale		5　6	
Coal, reported		3　6	⎭

Butts, E.　Face, N.　Elevation, 1300 feet A. T.　Greatest rise, S. E.

The three and one-half feet of coal at the bottom of the bed is not mined, and it represents the impure coal of the same thickness shown in the North Coalburg section.

The analysis of the sample collected here by Mr. Brady gave the following results:

Moisture	1.03
Volatile matter.................................	33.73
Fixed carbon	53.07
Ash..	12.17
Total	100.00
Sulphur	0.73
Phosphorus	0.009

The Kanawha and Hocking Coal and Coke Company's mine, in the same coal, one-half mile below Cedar Grove, Kanawha county, is given by Mr. Brady as follows:

	Ft. In.	Ft. In.
Sandstone		
Shales (Mason),..................................		3　0
Coal	1　4	⎫
Slate	0　6		
Coal	4　10	⎬ 12　9
Hard slate..	3　7		
Coal	2　6	⎭

Butts S. 60° W.　Faces S. 30° E.　Elevation 1350 feet A. T.
Analysis of sample:

Moisture	0.60
Volatile matter	36.24
Fixed Carbon	55.14
Ash..	8.02
Total	100.00

Sulphur .... I. 21
Phosphorus 0. 002

What Mr. Brady identifies as the same coal is operated by the
K. & H. C. & C. Company, on Kelly's creek, one mile above
Mammoth, Kanawha county, where he measured the following
succession :

		Ft. In.	Ft. In.
Sandstone	....		
Slate	....		
Coal	....	I o	
"Niggerhead"	....	o 4	6 4
Coal	....	5 o	
Slate	....	? ?	
Coal	....	? ?	

Elevation 1325 feet A. T.   Greatest rise S. E.
Analysis of sample :

Moisture 0. 91
Volatile matter 36. 35
Fixed carbon 55. 02
Ash 7. 72
                                                         _____
     Total 100. 00
Sulphur 0. 70
Phosphorus.. .... 0. 003

The coal is highly valued as a steam and domestic fuel, and
is shipped both east and west by rail, and south by river.
These analyses show more ash and a little less volatile matter than
the same coal at Queen Shoals, the analysis of which is given on
page 287.

The general section at North Coalburg also demonstrates that
the "Big bed" there is the same as the one at Queen Shoals, since
both have practically the same interval above the Kanawha black
flint.

In the region of Cedar Grove and North Coalburg (or Shrewsberry) this Mason bed has been confused with the Mahoning coal
below it, and termed "No. 5" in the local mining parlance,
whereas No. 5 is ninety feet under the Mason bed, as shown by
the general section at Cedar Grove and North Coalburg on page 300
above.

In passing north down the Great Kanawha from Coalburg,
the Mason coal gets thinner, and is not mined to any extent except
for country use.

On Lick, Porter, and Ferry runs, which put into the Kanawha

river from the south, a mile or more above the Charleston C. & O. R. R. station, this coal was formerly mined to a small extent for domestic use. It is known there as the "Joel Ruffner" bed, from a mine on Lick Run, where the coal is forty inches thick, with some bone at the top and much black slate in its roof.

Captain Swan and others have exploited it on Porter's run, where it appears to be split into two beds by a layer of sandstone, as exhibited in the following section:

PORTER'S RUN SECTION, NEAR CHARLESTON.

	Ft. In.	Ft. In.
Sandstone, massive, Buffalo		80 0
Coal		0 4
Fireclay, impure		4 0
Concealed		20 0
Iron ore, sandy		0 6
Blue shale		3 0
Coal, Mason... { coal 0 2 / shale 1 6 / coal 0 6 }		2 2
Black slate		1 6
Massive sandstone		15 0
Coal, good, "Joel Ruffner" (Mason)		1 6
Sandstone, Upper Mahoning, massive		60 0
Coal, slaty, Mahoning		1 6
Sandstone, Lower Mahoning		50 0
Shales and concealed		30 0
Kanawha black flint		5 0

The lower bench of the Mason coal is the only one mined, and it varies from eighteen to thirty inches in thickness.

It is probably this coal which comes down to the level of the C. & O. R. R. grade one-half mile below the C. & O. R. R. Charleston station, where it has the structure exhibited in this section:

	Ft. In.	Ft. In.
Sandstone, massive, Buffalo		75 0
Coal...... { coal 0 6 / black slate 2 6 / coal 1 6 }		4 6
Concealed to Kanawha river		50 0

It is also possibly this same coal that is mined on the land of Col. Robert Carr, three miles southwest from Charleston, along a branch of Davis creek, and waggoned extensively to the city for domestic use. It is about three feet thick, and Col. Carr reports it as having one or more bony streaks. It makes an excellent domestic fuel when properly freed from bony material.

This bed occurs at many localities along Twelve Pole river, between Ceredo and Wayne, ten to fifteen feet under the fossiliferous Lower Cambridge Limestone, and has been mined three miles above Ceredo where it is reported as two feet thick.

It is possibly the same coal that crops above the N. & W. R. R. at Wayne, and has been mined at a few localities in that region, and southward, but is only two to two and one-half feet thick.

No particular study of this bed has been possible between the Kanawha and Big Sandy rivers in Lincoln. Boone, Logan and Mingo counties, but it doubtless exists in workable conditions at many localities across the counties mentioned.

It is possibly this bed which has been opened high up in the hills along Big Sandy, one mile above Nolan, Mingo county, by the Hatfield Colliery Company, where it lies 480 feet above the coal (Winifrede?) mined by that company, and 650 feet above river level. The coal in question comes sixty feet above three and one-half feet of splint coal (Mahoning) and 170 feet below the the top of a great, pebbly sandstone, above which are red beds. The coal exhibits this structure at the opening :

		Ft. In.	Ft. In.
Massive sandstone, pebbly		90 0	
Sandy shale		0 6	
Coal... { coal		0 5 }	2 1
{ gray shale		0 4 }	
{ coal, good		1 4 }	

The coal now described under the term "MASON" was formerly given the name "Brush Creek" by the writer from a locality in Cranberry township, Butler county, Pennsylvania, (see Report Q, Second Geological Survey, pages 34 and 35), where it was supposed to be only seventy-five feet above the base of the Conemaugh, and to be identical with the coal which is now termed the Mahoning. But subsequent investigation revealed the fact that the coal along Brush Creek lies more than 100 feet above the base of the Conemaugh, and is the SECOND coal above the Upper Freeport seam, instead of the FIRST, so that the name "Brush creek," having been given under a misapprehension, had to be dropped.

The coal which was thus described has the following structure
at the type locality, Mr. Hains' bank, on Brush Creek, Butler
county. See page 35, Report Q, referred to above:

		Ft. In.	Ft. In.
Limestone, Lower Cambridge (Brush creek)............		1 0	
Dark shales			10 0
Coal { coal 1 0			} 2 5
slate.. 0 1			
coal 1 4			

In the Potomac basin of Mineral and Garrett counties, this
Mason coal is almost universally present at 110 to 140 feet above
the base of the Conemaugh. In the deep shaft at Henry, it was
struck at 138 feet above the Upper Freeport coal and is sixteen
inches thick.

It is also present in every region of Garrett county, where its
horizon is exposed, according to Dr. G. C. Martin.

This coal does not appear to be present in Monongalia county,
unless the one at ninety-eight feet above the Upper Freeport bed,
in the Little Falls section, page 231 of this volume, should be
the Mason instead of the Mahoning, which is not at all improbable.
Of course, in that event, the overlying massive, pebbly sandstone
would be the Buffalo sandstone instead of the Mahoning, as given
in the section indicated.

In Hancock county this coal is only about one foot thick, and
crops high in the hills at New Cumberland, 50 to 60 feet above
the Mahoning coal.

THE MAHONING SANDSTONE STAGE.

Separated from the Mason coal by five to thirty feet of fireclay and shales, there comes in below, almost universally, a very
massive sandstone group, sometimes in one massive solid ledge
eighty to one hundred feet thick, but more frequently separated
into two sandstones by an intervening coal, and an underlying
limestone—fireclay, or both; so that when all of the members are
present the Mahoning stage is made up of the following succession: Upper Mahoning sandstone.
Mahoning coal.
Thornton fireclay.
Mahoning limestone.
Lower Mahoning sandstone.

The sandstone members of this stage have played a very conspicuous part in shaping the topography along their lines of outcrop, since, together with the massive Buffalo and Saltzburg sand-

stones above, they form a friendly cover which has often protected the underlying Allegheny series from complete erosion. Being hard, freqently pebbly, and the sand grains cemented largely by peroxide of iron and silica, these sandstone beds often cap the high ridges and peaks with an almost indestructible roof, and thus preserve the underlying softer rocks from destruction. This is especially true in the southwestern portion of the state, from Upshur, Webster and Randolph counties, across Nicholas, Clay, Kanawha, Fayette, Boone, Lincoln, Logan, Wayne, Mingo, and western Wyoming and Raleigh, while the same massive beds make the steep bluffs along the Ohio river through Hancock county in the northern Pan Handle of the state. The elevated peaks of "Turkey Bone," in Randolph, and Cottle Knob, in Nicholas, rising more than 1200 feet above the nearest valleys, are each crowned by the hard rocks of this stage, while in western Fayette, Raleigh, and Wyoming, and on through Logan and Mingo to the Kentucky line, the summits formed by these massive, pebbly sandstones often attain an elevation of 1500 feet above the valley floors.

Wherever they emerge, whether along the lower slopes of the hills, midway up the same, or capping the summits, long lines of cliffs and rough, broken topography result.

The massive sandstone beds are generally traversed by two systems of jointing planes, and hence large blocks of these sandstones frequently descend into the valleys or litter up the slopes wherever they can find a lodgment.

These sandstones split readily into blocks of desirable size, and have been frequently quarried for building and bridge masonry. The stone in the Capitol at Charleston, the Court House at Buckhannon, and many other structures throughout the state, come from the rocks of this stage. Occasionally, either from the presence of pyrites, or other easily destroyed constituents, these sandstones break down and weather into all kinds of shapes, a fine example of which may be seen in Monongalia county, one-half mile east of the Monongahela river, along the banks of Booth's creek, at the locality known as "Raven Rocks." There the Upper and Lower Mahoning beds, having united into one mass, make a cliff nearly one hundred feet high, the face of which is weathered into many fantastic shapes and pitted with holes and cavities of every description.

The Upper Mahoning is generally the more massive member, and the better quarry rock of the two. Occasionally its basal beds take on a greenish tinge, as at Philippi, Barbour county, where they have recently been quarried for building purposes by Mr. Hall, along the west bank of the Valley river.

The name Charleston sandstone was given to these beds, and the overlying Buffalo sandstone, by the U. S. G. Survey in its Charleston Folio, but as the name Mahoning, given by the First Geological Survey of Pennsylvania from the Mahoning river in that state, has priority, the new one cannot be adopted without violating one of the fundamental laws of nomenclature.

The oil well drillers usually term these beds either the "Dunkard" or "Cow Run" sand, and the Upper Mahoning especially is often quite rich in petroleum, some of the wells in Wood and Pleasants counties having produced as much as fifty to one hundred barrels an hour for many days when first completed.

THE MAHONING COAL.

Lying between the two Mahoning sandstones just described, there frequently occurs a coal bed which is of considerable economic importance in some regions of the state. The bed in question was once (Report Q, Second Geological Survey of Pennsylvania) termed the "BRUSH CREEK" coal by the writer under an erroneous view of the geological horizon of the type locality on Brush creek, Butler county, Pa., which turns out to be the same as the Mason coal, or the next higher bed of this report, and hence in Bulletin 65 of the U. S. G. Survey the term "Brush creek" was abandoned and that of "Mahoning" substituted for this important coal horizon.

In Ohio this bed is known as No. 7, and is occasionally an important coal, especially in Columbiana county, where it is often termed the "Groff vein" along the Ohio river.

In the adjoining county of Hancock, this Mahoning bed has long been mined, high up in the hills at New Cumberland, and recently a standard gauge railroad has been built up Hardins run to reach the new mines of the Marquette Coal Company, which operates this seam two and one-half miles east from the town, and 350 feet above the Ohio river. The coal at the Marquette mine has been assigned to most every horizon from the Pittsburg bed down to the Upper Freeport, but it is the same one that has been mined in the river hills at New Cumberland fifty to sixty feet below the Mason coal, and its overlying fossiliferous limy shales, and eighty to ninety feet above the "Roger" vein of that region, which, by the Ohio geologists, has always been considered identical with the Lower Freeport bed of the Allegheny series.

The coal at the Marquette mine is single bedded, aside from a streak of "sulphur," which is not regular in its position. The following section was measured there by A. P. Brady, who also collected the sample for analysis:

		Ft. In.	Ft. In.
Sandstone, Upper Mahoning			
Slate		10 0	
Coal, Mahoning { coal .... 3 0 } { sulphur .... 0 ¼ } { coal .... 2 2 }			5 2¼
Fireclay			

Butts run N. 68° W. Faces N. 22° E. Greatest rise, northeast.

Prof. Hite reports the following analysis of the sample collected here:

Moisture	1. 15
Volatile matter.	36. 38
Fixed carbon	56. 55
Ash	5. 92
Total..	100. 00
Sulphur	1. 45
Phosphorus...	0. 005

The coal is shipped east and west by the Pan Handle railroad for steam and domestic purposes, and is in very high favor for either.

This coal is also extensively mined by Mr. Porter, adjoining the Marquette mine, and waggoned to New Cumberland for use in the brick factories. It is from three and one-half to five feet thick in the Porter mine, with no visible partings.

The bed was also once extensively mined in the hills northeast from the New Cumberland cemetery, at the old Chatam mines, and taken to the valley below over a long incline, but these mines have now been abandoned.

The coal has a coarse, massive sandstone (Upper Mahoning) at a short interval above.

The thick deposit of this coal covers only a limited area and appears to thin down to only two or three feet when traced away from the region of Hardins run and one or two farms adjacent.

The coal is mined for local purposes on the land of Thomas Doak, just above the "Falls," on Hardins run, and 200 feet vertically over the bottom of the same, and 330 feet above the Ohio river. The coal shows five and one-half feet at the entrance to the mine without any visible partings, but within less than one-half mile to the south it is only three feet thick, and is mined no more in that direction on the West Virginia side of the Ohio river.

The horizon of this coal dips below water level on the Ohio river just above Steubenville, and remains below it along that stream until the rise of the strata brings it up to daylight again near Ceredo, in Wayne county, nearly 250 miles below. Here there is some CLAY and LIMESTONE (Mahoning) between the two massive members of the Mahoning sandstone. but no COAL is visible.

When we pass eastward to the waters of the Monongahela, however, the coal is generally present, though thin in many regions. In the diamond drill boring to the Upper Freeport coal, made on the Gamble lot, Deckers creek, by Hon. S. B. Elkins, a coal was encountered at a depth of 104 feet, as shown by the following record :

DECKERS CREEK BORING, MONONGALIA COUNTY.

	Ft.	In.
Surface	8	10½
Shale, green	7	4
Shale, red	13	5
Sandy shale, gray	3	4½
Sandstone, gray, Buffalo?	12	0
Fireclay	2	0
Sandstone, Upper Mahoning?	47	3½
Black slate	8	8½
Dark limestone, very fossiliferous	1	0
COAL, MAHONING?	1	3
Fireclay, soft, Mahoning	19	0½
Sandstone, shaly, Lower Mahoning	30	3½
Slate	1	3½
Bone coal	0	6
Slate	0	2½
Bone coal	0	5
Fireclay shales	6	3
Upper Freeport coal		
	———	
Total	163	3

Te coal is quite bright and pure looking, and comes at an

interval of fifty-eight feet above the base of the Conemaugh series, immediately below which is the typical Upper Freeport
coal.

The black slate and dark fossiliferous limestone in the roof of
this little coal bed are exactly like that seen in the roof of the coal
found in the Ashburn boring, Preston county, page 269, above, at
an interval of 112 feet above the Upper Freeport coal, and also in
the Watson farm boring, page 310, below, at only 86 feet above
the same coal.   The marine fossils are quite numerous, and the
limestone rests in direct contact with the underlying coal; and,
although the interval is only 58 feet here, or but a few feet more
than half what it is in the Watson boring, the conclusion is unavoidable that it is the same limestone and coal in each of the three
borings; and hence, if the fossiliferous limestone in the Watson
farm boring is the Lower Cambridge, then that in the Ashburn
and Gamble borings is also, and the overlying sandstone would be
the Upper Mahoning. It is possible that the Mahoning and Mason
coals may have been frequently confused on account of such rapid
changes in the character and thickness of the intervening rocks.
These problems can only be solved by careful, detailed studies in
the future county work contemplated.

The steep southeast rise of all the strata toward the Chestnut
ridge anticlinal from Rock Forge, or the locality of the last section, soon brings this little coal to the surface, and it is exposed along the Decker's creek road, where it descends the steep
hill to the valley of the stream, between Rock Forge and Dellslow.

The bore hole on the Sanford Watson farm, Dillon creek,
Preston county, less than a mile distant from the Ashburn
boring, found a thin coal at a depth of ninety feet, and eighty-five
feet above the Upper Freeport coal, but it was only nine inches
thick and must be the same as the Mason bed of the Watson boring,
since a fossiliferous limestone is in the roof of each. The record of the
Watson diamond drill boring, as given by Mr. Davis Elkins, president of the M. & K. R. R., reads as follows from the surface
down to the base of the Conemaugh :

SANFORD WATSON FARM BORING, PRESTON COUNTY.

	Ft.	In.
Interval from crop of Bakerstown (Barton) coal (no allowance for dip) to top of boring	45	5
Surface.......	2	0
Sandstone, fine grained, gray, Buffalo...................	8	6

Fireclay	4	0
Shale, green, sandy	15	2
Sandstone, gray, large pebbles for 20 feet near the middle	54	7
Black slate..	4	1
Limestone, fossiliferous	1	8
COAL	0	9
Fireclay, soft, limy.................................	10	6
Green shale and sandstone, mixed	20	1
Fireclay, soft...	11	10
Sandstone, gray, some green, shale in lower half, Lower Mahoning	35	4
Slate	0	6
Bone coal and slate	0	11
Slate and shale	5	11
Upper Freeport coal		
Total...	221	3

This section is a good illustration of the rapid changes which take place in the Mahoning sandstone stage, since in the Ashburn boring, less than one mile distant, a solid mass of sandstone, eighty-six feet thick, occurs, while in the Watson boring thick fire-clays and shales replace the Lower Mahoning sandstone, thus largely decreasing the interval between the little coal and the Upper Freeport coal bed, so that instead of the 112 feet as shown in the Ashburn boring, on Dillon creek, page 269, it is here eighty-five feet, or twenty-seven feet less.

The limestone in the roof of the little nine-inch coal bed is full of marine fossils, corals, gastropods, brachiopods, etc., and lenses of it are interstratified with the top layers of the coal. The writer was inclined to regard this thin coal bed of the Watson boring as a different coal from the one found in the Ashburn boring at 112 feet above the Upper Freeport coal, but when he saw the core, showing the same dark shales and fossiliferous limestone in its roof as found in the latter, the conclusion is inevitable that they are one and the same. It is even possible that both may represent the Mahoning coal, instead of the one that has been termed the Mason bed in this report.

In many regions of southern Preston, eastern Barbour, western Randolph, eastern Upshur and the Pan Handle of Lewis counties, a bed of coal identified with the Mahoning thickens up to three and one-half and four feet, and becomes an important bed of fuel. When the Lower Mahoning sandstone is thin and shaly, this coal is found within forty feet of the Upper Freeport bed, as at Philippi, Nestorville, and other localities, but when the sandstone in question thickens, and grows massive, the interval increases to seventy-five feet or more in Randolph, Upshur, Lewis, Braxton, Webster, Nicholas, Kanawha and southwestward.

Opposite the western end of the mill-dam at Philippi, the Mahoning coal is mined on the land of Mr. Hall and there the following section is exposed :

PHILIPPI SECTION.

	Ft.	In.	Ft.	In.
Sandstone, massive, Buffalo			40	0
Shales and concealed			30	0
Coal, Mason, slaty			3	0
Concealed			25	0
Sandstone, Upper Mahoning, massive, flaggy at base			50	0
Mahoning coal { coal	3	0		
{ bone	0	2	4	3
{ coal	1	1		
Concealed to Upper Freeport coal just under the bed of Valley river			40	0

The coal is bright, hard, and makes a fairly good domestic and steam fuel.

The coal has long been mined at the Tolbert bank, just below the west end of the wooden bridge across the Valley river at Philippi, and there, in the mines of the M. E. Tolbert Coal Company, Mr. A. P. Brady measured the following section:

	Ft.	In.	Ft.	In.
Blue sandstone, Upper Mahoning				
"Draw" slate			0	6
Coal { coal	2	5		
{ slate	0	1	3	11
{ coal	1	5		

Elevation, 1295 feet, A. T.

The analysis of the sample collected at the Tolbert mine is reported as follows by Prof. Hite :

Moisture	0. 74
Volatile matter	31. 17
Fixed carbon	57. 37
Ash	10. 72
Total	100. 00
Sulphur	2. 69
Phosphorus	0. 018

At the W. T. Ice mine, on the west side of the Valley river, above Philippi, Mr. A. P. Brady reports the following section :

	Ft.	In.	Ft.	In.
Blue sandstone, Upper Mahoning				
"Draw" slate			0	6
Coal { bone coal	0	2		
{ coal	2	6½		
{ slate	0	½	4	2
{ coal	1	5		

The analysis of a sample collected from this mine gave the following results as reported by Prof. Hite :

Moisture	0. 81
Volatile matter	30. 71
Fixed carbon	56. 14
Ash	12. 34
Total	100. 00
Sulphur	2.37
Phosphorus	0. 015

These analyses reveal a coal rather high in ash and sulphur. It is used for both steam and domestic purposes at Philippi, and appears to give general satisfaction.

The coal is mined on the land of Mrs. Morrill, one mile below Philippi, near the mouth of Morrill's run, on the east bank of the Valley river, and there the following section is revealed :

		Ft. In.	Ft. In.
Sandy shales			3 0
Black slate			0 3
Coal, Mahoning	coal .... 2 4 shale, gray .... 0 3 coal 1 4		3 11
Concealed			5 0
Sandstone, flaggy, Lower Mahoning		35 0	
Upper Freeport coal			

Here the Upper Freeport coal has been stripped out of the bed of Morrill's run, directly under the Mahoning coal.

At the Lillian mines, two miles above Philippi, and the Meridan mine, two miles below the town, this coal has been pierced by the air shaft from the Upper Freeport bed below, and the exact interval is reported to be forty feet in each case.

This coal was once mined on Laurel creek, seven miles from Philippi, by J. W. Miller, where it has a massive sandstone (Upper Mahoning) above, is forty-five feet above the Upper Freeport coal, and is reported as three and one-half to four feet thick. Mr. Miller has abandoned this bed and mines the Upper Freeport below.

About one mile beyond Laurel creek, the Mahoning coal is mined along the Nestorville, or Valley Furnace pike by A. O. Bennett, at whose bank the following structure is exposed:

	Ft. In.	Ft. In.
Sandy shales		

		Ft.	In.		
Coal, slaty		1	0		
Coal, good		3	0		5 3
Shale, dark gray		0	3		
Coal		1	0		

A very massive sandstone (Upper Mahoning) crops only a few feet above the coal. This bed is also mined by J. D. Stemple on the opposite side of the road, where the following structure is visible :

		Ft.	In.	Ft.	In.
Sandstone, massive, Upper Mahoning		30	0		
Shales, sandy		3	0		
Coal { coal		2	9		
slate		0	1		3½ 0
coal		0	8		

There are several openings in this coal at Nestorville, and it is the principal source of domestic supply from there over a wide region.

It is mined below Nestorville at the junction of Brushy Fork of Teter's creek with the main stream, just above the Valley Furnace road, where it is four feet thick and lies forty-five to fifty feet above the Upper Freeport coal which was once mined at this locality by stripping along the bed of Brushy Fork.

In the section at Nestorville, page 297, this coal is reported as only three feet thick by Daniel Moore, who opened it fifty-eight feet above the Upper Freeport bed.

In the Roaring creek basin of Randolph county, and extending southwestward into eastern Barbour, Upshur and Lewis counties, there is quite a large area of the Mahoning coal, where the bed is three and one half to four feet thick, and will prove of much economic importance in the general fuel resources of the region. The coal lies seventy-five to eighty feet above the large Upper Freeport seam, and is usually called the "Four-Foot" vein.

About one mile southwest from Roaring Creek Junction this coal has been opened on the land of Patrick O'Connor, where it lies seventy-five feet above the Upper Freeport bed, opened along Grassy run below, and is four and one-half feet thick. It mines in large blocks, which exhibit the "peacock" hue throughout, thus indicating the presence of sulphur in considerable quantity.

This coal has also been mined for local supply on the land of Peter Kain, where it is four and one-half feet thick and has six inches of bony coal and slate near the center.

This coal was once opened high up in the hills near Ford's Hotel, on the Beverly and Buckhannon pike, 70 feet above the Upper Freeport bed.

Several openings in this coal have been operated by the farmers for domestic use between Kingsville and Talbot, and on beyond to Hall's mill, on the Middle Fork river, where the Mahoning coal has been mined along the pike and dug into at several localities. It lies here eighty feet above the Upper Freeport seam, and above it two other thin coals crop at 65 and 115 feet respectively.

Just over the divide, between Laurel run (which empties into the Buckhannon river) and the Middle Fork of Valley river, one mile from D. O. Hall's mill, the Mahoning coal has been mined quite extensively for local supply on the land on Peach Campbell, where it exhibits the following structure :

	Ft.	In.	Ft.	In.
Shale roof				
Coal	2	0		
Slate	0	1		
Coal	0	4	4	3½
Slate	0	½		
Coal	1	10		

This is called the "Four-Foot" bed, and near Mr. Campbell's house the "Three-Foot," or Mason coal, was once opened 80 feet above the Mahoning.

Several openings in the Mahoning coal have been made along Laurel run between P. Campbell's and the Buckhannon river, three to four miles distant.

On Sand creek, Upshur county, which empties into the Buckhannon river ten miles below Buckhannon, this Mahoning coal has been mined by nearly every farmer between its mouth and several miles above. In this region the coal is from three to four feet thick, and has the usual slaty partings near the middle. It is mined by "Poke" Foster, M. H. Kiesley, Luther Shreeves, B. F. Hamilton and many others. The interval appears to be thinner between it and the underlying Upper Freeport coal along Sand creek than elsewhere, since at some localities it is only thirty to thirty-five feet above the latter coal, as illustrated in the following section measured just below the mouth of Big Laurel Fork of Sand creek :

		Ft.	In.	Ft.	In.
Black slate					
Coal, Mahoning........... { coal................	0	2			
slate	0	1½			
coal................	1	3		3	10
slaty coal........	0	9½			
coal	1	6			
Flaggy sandstone and sandy shale				18	0
Coal, local.................. { coal...............	0	1			
shale..............	0	3			
coal........	0	2½		2	10½
shale.............	0	10			
slaty coal	1	6			
Gray, sandy shales... ..				10	0
Black slate........ ....·..........				0	3
Gray, sandy shales............				2	6
Upper Freeport coal········................					
Total..				37	5½

Here a sporadic, slaty coal makes its appearance (as frequently happens) a few feet above the main Upper Freeport bed. .

At Mr. Kiestling's mine on Sand creek, one mile below the mouth of Big Laurel branch, the Mahoning coal is sixty feet above the stream, and has the following structure :

	Ft.	Iu.	Ft.	In.
Coal	0	3		
Slate...........	0	½		
Coal	1	7	4	2½
Slate and coal ....…	0	8		
Coal	1	8		

The Upper Freeport coal crops along the bed of the stream here, and a BLACK SLATE and COALY STREAK shows in the hills 70 feet above the Mahoning coal, while 115 feet higher a massive sandstone makes a terrace around the hills, capping which, at 235 feet above the Mahoning coal, is a bold cliff of massive, pebbly sandstone.

The Mahoning coal has been mined along the Buckhannon river just below the mouth of Sand creek, and at the mouth of Handy Camp branch, where it is thirty-five feet above the water level.

Just below this the coal has been gouged out of the hills along the left bank of the Buckhannon, only twenty feet above the water, while above it occurs a rather massive sandstone cliff (Upper Mahoning) at fifty feet, and a very bold one near the top of the hill 250 to 300 feet higher.

One mile below the mouth of Handy Camp the Buckhannon

river veers east, and the Mahoning coal rises rapidly to seventy-five feet above the same, where it exhibits the following structure at the mine of J. H. Wentz:

		Ft. In.	Ft. In.
Soft, gray sandy shales...		10 0	
Coal	coal	1 0	
	slate..	0 3	3 3
	bone...	0 2	
	coal..	1 10	

The heavy sandstone, just under the Upper Freeport coal, comes up to the bed of the Buckhannon here, and makes rapids along the same.

In the southwestern portion of Upshur, and the adjoining region of Lewis and Braxton counties, the Mahoning coal has frequently been mined for domestic use. It comes about eighty feet above the thick (10′–15′) and impure Upper Freeport bed of that region, and is two and one-half to four feet thick.

About one mile above the mouth of Cherry Fork of the Little Kanawha, the Mahoning coal has been mined on the land of George Davis, where it is four feet thick, with a slaty streak of three to four inches, near the center. The same coal is mined on Glady creek by Lee Cochran, where the section is as follows:

		Ft. In.	Ft. In.
Massive sandstone, Upper Mahoning			
Shale		2	
Coal, Mahoning	coal	1 6	
	slate	0 2	4 2
	coal	2 6	

On Cherry Fork, two and one-half miles above its mouth, both the Mahoning and Upper Freeport coals have been mined on the land of Harrison Clayplole, where the following section is exposed near the Lewis-Upshur county line:

		Ft. In.	Ft. In.
Shale			
Coal, Mahoning	coal	0 9	
	bony coal.........	0 8	4 2
	shale, gray	0 3	
	coal	2 6	
Concealed and sandstone		80 0	
Upper Freeport coal			

The same coal has been mined in the hills above the Upper Freeport bed at the head of Fallen Timber run, Lewis county by Lorenz Farnash. It has also been opened along the pike high up in the hills above Little Wild Cat Creek, west from the Little Kanawha river.

Below Bulltown, Braxton county, a coal eighteen to twenty inches thick, has been mined at an elevation of thirty to forty feet above the Little Kanawha, which is either this coal or the Mason bed above.

On the Great Kanawha river, in southern Kanawha county, as well as northern Fayette and the adjoining region of Nicholas county, a bed of coal has been mined to a considerabe extent high up in the hills under the name of "No. 5," or "Block" coal." It lies from sixty to seventy feet above the KANAWHA BLACK FLINT, and was formerly supposed to be identical with the "Big" bed at North Coalburg, but the section given on page 300 shows that view to be erroneous, since the "Big," or Mason coal, is there found ninety feet above coal "No. 5." The Mason bed has thus been confused with the true No. 5, which was named long ago in the region of Montgomery, where it is only sixty to seventy feet above the Kanawha black flint, because it was regarded as the fifth workable bed above the valley floor.

The Mason coal over-shoots the hills in the Montgomery region, however, or is not mined, at least, and hence further south, near Cedar Grove, North Coalburg, etc., where the Mason coal becomes workable, it, too, has been dubbed "No. 5" by the operaators, simply because its horizon lies above the Kanawha black flint.

The general section referred to, however, on page 300, sets the matter at rest, and shows that the "No. 5" of the Montgomery, Eagle, and Powelton regions, is not the "Big" or Mason coal bed, but one nearly between it and the Kanawha black flint, and that it answers to the horizon of the Mahoning coal of the northern end of the state.

The coal is a genuine "block" in its structure and aspect, and was formerly used in the "raw" state to some extent in the Ashland, Kentucky, furnaces. In these "block" coals, the thin, bright, pitchy layers of coal are interstratified with layers of "mineral charcoal," which cause the fuel to burn freely without fusing to any considerable extent.

The bed in question is operated in the summit of the mountain at Mt. Carbon, by the Great Kanawha Colliery Company, and there A. P. Brady measured the following section.

	Ft. In.	Ft. In.
Sandstone, Upper Mahoning..................................		
Coal	1 4	
Fireclay.......	0 4	
"Block" coal..	0 8	8 4
Slate, trace...		
"Block" coal...	6 0	

Elevation, 2060 feet A. T.

The analysis of the sample is reported by Prof. Hite as follows :

Moisture	1. 20
Volatile matter.................	33. 36
Fixed carbon	60. 46
Ash	4. 98
Total..............	100. 00
Sulphur....................	0. 76
Phosphorus..	0. 004

The coal is shipped north and west by the C. & O. R. R. for steam purposes.

The Carver Bros. have a mine in this coal one-half mile west of Eagle, Fayette county, nine miles below Mt. Carbon, where A. P. Brady reports the following :

	Ft. In.	Ft. In.
Sandstone		
Coal.. ...	0 3	
Slate...	10-20 0	
"No. 5"... { "gas" coal.................... 1 7 / slate .... 0 1½ / "block' coal................. 5 10 }		7 6½

Elevation, 1639 feet, A. T., or 1000 feet above the C. & O. R. R. grade.

The analysis of the sample is reported by Prof. Hite as follows:

Moisture..	0. 84
Volatile matter..	37. 78
Fixed carbon...............................	57. 08
Ash	4. 30
Total	100. 00
Sulphur..	0. 84
Phosphorus..	0. 004

Mr. W. R. Johnson mines the coal at Crescent, a mile below the last locality, and there A. P. Brady reports the following structure :

		Ft.	In.	Ft.	In.
Sandstone					
"Draw" slate				1	6
"No. 5"...	top coal, left up	1	0		
	slate	0	3		
	coal	0	11	7	5
	slate	0	1		
	block coal	5	2		

Elevation, 1593 feet A. T.

Analysis of sample, reported by Prof. Hite as follows :

Moisture	1. 11
Volatile matter	34. 63
Fixed carbon	59. 07
Ash	5. 19
Total	100. 00
Sulphur	0. 74
Phosphorus	0. 01

Here the thick overlying slate of the previous section has thinned to only a few inches.

The Davis Gordon Company mines this coal in the same region between Eagle and Montgomery, and there A. P. Brady measured the following succession:

		Ft.	In.	Ft.	In.
Sandstone					
Draw slate				0	6
"No. 5"	hard ("block") coal	0	8½		
	slate	0	1		
	hard ("block") coal	4	0	5	7½
	"gas" coal	0	10		

Elevation, 1584 feet A. T.

Analysis of sample reported by Prof. Hite as follows:

Moisture	1. 07
Volatile matter	34. 46
Fixed carbon	59. 31
Ash	5. 16
Total	100. 00
Sulphur	0. 77
Phosphorus	0. 004

These analyses all reveal a coal of great excellence, being

very low in both ash and sulphur and high in fixed carbon. It is greatly prized as a steam coal, and bears transportation extremely well. The coal from all of these mines is sent to market both east and west over the C. & O. R. R., being carried down to its grade over long, steep inclines, 1000 feet in vertical elevation.

The analysis of this coal, so different in the amount of ash from that of the "Big" bed (Mason) in the Cedar Grove region, is almost sufficient in itself to prove the two beds are separate and distinct coal horizons, as the section on page 300 conclusively demonstrates.

Traced northward along the Kanawha river from the region of Montgomery, this "No. 5," or Mahoning coal, appears to dwindle in size, so that no extensive mining operations have been undertaken upon it below Montgomery, so far as known to the writer. At the old Peabody mines above Watson's Hollow, on the north bank of the Kanawha, near Cedar Grove, ten miles north from Montgomery, the main body of the coal is only three feet thick, and that is split with a bone or "niggerhead." The coal still retains its "blocky" character and lies ninety feet below the "Big" or Mason bed, which is mined in the hill above, and sixty-five feet above the Kanawha black flint, which crops around the slopes below.

In the region of Charleston, where this coal horizon dips under water level, the bed is only a few inches thick, and occasionally disappears entirely in the great sandstone (Upper and Lower Mahoning) mass, which surrounds that city.

In the region between the Great Kanawha and Big Sandy rivers, through Boone, Lincoln, Logan, and Mingo counties, this coal has not been studied, but it doubtless exists in good development at many localities, since in northern Wyoming county the writer has observed a bed of coal cropping at this horizon under the great cliffs of sandstones which cap the mountains north from Huff creek.

One mile above Nolan, Mingo county, the Hatfield Colliery Company has exploited a coal bed at 420 feet above the one (Winifrede) now mined, and 600 feet above the Tug Fork of Big Sandy river, which is most probably this same coal, since it possesses the "block" or splinty type, so characteristic on the Kanawha, and appears to come at the proper geological horizon in a great sand-

stone (Mahoning) mass, that crowns the river hills. It has the
following structure at the locality near Nolan :

		Ft. In.	Ft. In.
Massive, coarse sandstone, Upper Mahoning, visible		10 0	
Coal	soft, slaty coal	0 5	
	splint, or "block" coal	1 3	3 11
	bone	0 2	
	splint or "block" coal	2 1	

A coal which would correlate with the Mason bed has been
opened in the hill, sixty feet above this, and then at 230 feet, over
immense cliffs of sandstones (Upper Mahoning, Buffalo, etc.),
reddish shales make their appearance near the summits, so that as
this is practically the same succession as that found on the Great
Kanawha above the "No. 5," or Mahoning coal, there can be but
very little doubt about the correctness of the suggested identity.

The Hatfield Colliery Company is extending its "incline" up
the hill to this bed, and will mine it on a commercial scale.

Where opened in the opposite side of the mountain, on the
land of Virginia Hatfield, the following structure is reported by
the Hatfield Co.'s mine superintendent :

	Ft. In.	Ft. In.
Soft coal	1 1	
Slate	0 2	5 5
Coal, splint	4 2	

The same softer coal in the roof of the bed appears to characterize this coal on Tug river as on the Great Kanawha.

In the section at Irondale, Preston county, the Mahoning
coal is three feet thick and seventy feet above the Upper Freeport
bed. The same coal is also exposed in the cuts along the B. & O.
R. R., between Grafton and Fairmont, on either side of the Chestnut ridge anticlinal, but the bed is only two to two and one-half
feet thick, and about sixty feet above the base of the Conemaugh
series.

THORNTON FIRECLAY.

Just under the Mahoning coal, and occasionally replacing it,
there occurs a fairly good bed of fireclay in a few regions of the
state. It appears to have more importance in the vicinity of
Thornton, Taylor county, than elsewhere, and the stratum has

been designated from that locality, where it is mined and shipped to the brick factory at Hammond and other points.

It crops along the B. & O. R. R. for several miles between Grafton and Tunnelton, and should prove of considerable value, since it contains both the hard and plastic varieties of clay. The bed appears to have a thickness of five to six feet where exploited. It has not been mined in any other portion of the state so far as known to the writer, but a fireclay is frequently present at this horizon.

MAHONING LIMESTONE.

A bed of gray, impure limestone is occasionally found in the shale interval which separates the two members of the Mahoning sandstone. The stratum occurs in the vicinity of Irondale furnace, and is there four to six feet thick and of a buff or yellowish hue. No marine fossils have been seen in the rock, and it is evidently a fresh or brackish water deposit.

It is also present about twenty feet above the Upper Freeport coal at the Meriden mines, below Philippi, where it is exposed in a cutting along the B. & O. R. R. It crops in the hill at Moatsville, ten miles below Philippi, twenty feet above the Upper Freeport coal, and was there erroneously referred by the writer to a much lower horizon (just above the Lower Kittaning coal) in Bulletin No. 65, U. S. G. Survey, page 128.

It is possibly this limestone which has been mined for agricultural purposes in the hills, sixty to seventy feet above the level of Sandy creek, near Bruceton, Preston county.

In the southwestern portion of the state, limestone is very rare at this horizon, but near Ceredo, Wayne county, some nuggets of limstone may be seen just under the Upper Mahoning sandstone in the cuts of the N. & W. R. R.

The Johnstown Iron ore of Cambria county, Pennsylvania, belongs at this horizon, but aside from scattered nuggets of ore, and ferruginous shales occasionally present, no iron accumulations have been noted at this geological level in West Virginia.

THE UFFINGTON SHALE.

The interval which separates the Lower Mahoning sandstone from the Upper Freeport coal varies greatly both in thickness and

character.   Frequently a massive, and usually bluish-gray,
sandstone, rests directly upon the underlying coal without any intervening shales whatever.   At other times a dark, sandy, fossiliferous shale, twenty to forty feet thick, will intervene for short
distances, to be entirely displaced by massive sandstones within a
few hundred feet, mostly by erosion, which took place during the
deposition of the sandstone.

These shales are well developed at the village of Uffington,
near the mouth of Booth's creek, three miles south from Morgantown, Monongalia county, and they have been designated from
that locality.

They contain marine fossils as well as many plant remains,
and it is from this horizon, and mostly from the Uffington locality,
that Dr. John J. Stevenson collected the specimens identified by
Mr. Meek, and published in the Third Annual Report of the
Board of Regents of the West Virginia University for the year
1870.

Since this publication is now unobtainable, the list of fossils
is herewith republished.   The letter of Mr. Meek transmitting
this list to Dr. Stevenson, along with that from the Crinoidal, or
Ames limestone, has already been given on page 257.

As this is the only systematic collection of marine fossils
made at this horizon in West Virginia, and identified by one so
eminent in paleontology, the list which follows possesses especial
interest for all geologists:

*List of Fossils in Roof Shales of the Upper Freeport Coal, Near Morgan-
town, Monongalia County, West Virginia.*

*Crinoidal columns.
Erisocrinus.   Undetermined species.
*Aviculopecten carbonarius *Stevenson sp.* —Pecten broadheadi *Swal-
low,* and Pecten hawni *Geinitz.*
Allorisma.   Undetermined species.
*Nucula ventricosa *Hall.*
†Nucula anodontoides *Meek.*
*Nuculana bellistriata *Stevensou sp.*—A very small attenuated variety.
Common in so-called upper Dyas, Nebraska City, Nebraska
†Yoldia carbonaria *Meek.*
†Yolda stevensoni *Meek.*
*Schizodus.   Undetermined species.
*Edmondia aspenwalensis *Meek.*
Astartella.   Undetermined species.

Macrocheilus primigenius *Conrad.*
*Macrocheilus ventricosus *Hall.*
Macrocheilus. Undetermined species.
Polyphemopsis peracutus *Meek* and *Worthen.*
*Euomphalus rugosus *Hall.*
*Bellerophon montfortianus *Norwood* and *Pratten.*
*Bellerophon percarinatus *Conrad.*
*Bellerophon carbonarius *Cox.*
Bellerophon meekiana *Swallow.*
*Pleurotomaria grayvilliensis *Norwood* and *Pratten.*
*Orthoceras cribrosum *Geinitz.*
*Nautilus occidentalis *Swallow.*
*Phillipsia sangamonensis *Meek* and *Worthen.*
*Productus nebrascensis *Owen.*
*Productus prattenanus *Norwood.*
*Athyris subtilita *Hall.* Very abundant and presenting all the usual varieties.

Productus. Species undetermined. Very small, concentrically wrinkled.

*Spirifer (Martinia) planoconvexus *Shumard.*
*Spirifer cameratus *Morton.*
Aviculopecten. Undetermined species. Probably *A. occidentalis Shumard.*
*Hemipronites crassus *Meek* and *Hayden.*

A considerable number of these species will be found common to the Lower Cambridge limestone fauna, as given by Dr. G. C. Martin, page 280-1 of this volume, while several also pass on up into the Ames limestone fauna, 200 feet higher. (See list given on page 258.)

No large collections of fossil plants have been made from the Uffington shale in the northern end of the state, but in the Great Kanawha valley Mr. David White has made large collections from the roof shales of the Stockton coal, which the writer considers as identical with the Upper Freeport bed at the north. A list of the fossil plants identified by Mr. White from the shales above the Stockton coal has been published in the Bulletin of the Geological Society of America, Vol. II., pp. 168-9, from which the following quotations are made :

---

*Species known to range through the whole of the Coal Measures in the West, even into the upper beds at Nebraska City, Nebraska, referred by Profs. Marcou and Geinitz to the Permian or so-called Dyas.

†New species.

Plants in the roof of the Stockton coal.—"The Stockton coal, which has been identified with the Upper Freeport coal of the Allegheny valley by Dr. I. C. White, and has accordingly been made by him the topmost stratum of the Allegheny series in his correlations of the terranes along the Kanawha river, lies from 30 to 50 feet below the Black flint, beneath which the upper boundary of the Kanawha formation is drawn by Messrs. Campbell and Mendenhall.

The plant collections from the roof of the Stockton coal at a number of localities † include the following species:"

Name.	Locality.
Pseudopecopteris cf. *nummularia* (Gutb.) * Lx.......	Bel. , Buff. . Sp.
Mariopteris muricata (Schloth.) Brongn..............	Hur.
" *nervosa* (Brongn.)Zeill. ‡...................	Bel.
Sphenopteris karwinensis Stur........................	Buff., P. G.
" cf. *trichomanoides* Brongn. *	Buff.
" cf. *broadheadi* D. W. *	P. G.
" *tenella* Brongn. [Lesq.]...................	Buff. , P. G.
" *mixta* Schimp. *	Bel. , P. G.
" cf. *crepini.* Boul.......	Buff., St.
" *ophioglossoides* (Lx.)?*	Buff.
" *hymenophylloides* Lx. *	Hur., St , P. G.
Pecopteris villosa Brongn. ?* [Lesq.]...............	P. G.
Alethopteris serlii (Brongn.) Goepp....................	Buff. , Sp.
Neuropteris cf. *gigantea* Sternb...................	St.
" *rarinervis* Bunby *	Bel.,Huff.,Hur.,St.,P.G.
" *ovata* Hoffm. *...........................	P. G.
" sp. cf. *carrii* Lx. *.....................	Sp.
" *scheuchzeri* Hoffm. *...................	Bel., Hur., St. , Sp.
Calamites ramosus Artis........................	St.
Asterophyllites equisetiformis (Schloth.) Brongn. *..	Bel.
Annularia ramosa Weiss..........................	Bel., St.
" *stellata* (Schloth.) Wood *	Bel. , St. , P. G.
" *sphenophylloides* (Zenk.) Gutb..............	Buff., St., P. G.
Sphenophyllum cuneifolium (Sternb.) Zeill............	Buff., St. , Sp., P. G.
" *lescurianum* D. W.*...................	Buff. , P. G.
" *emarginatum* Brongn. *.................	Sp.
Lycopodites meekii Lx. *........................	Hur., St.
Lepidodendron cf. *brittsii* Lx. *........	Bel.
" *lanceolatnm* Lx. *........	Hur., St.
" *modulatum* Lx. *.......	P. G.
Bothrodendron cf. *minutifolium* Boul	St.
Lepidostrobus cf. *variabilis* L. and H..............	Bel. , St.
Lepidophyllum lanceolatum L. and H. ?	St.
Lepidocystis vesicularis Lx.....................	Buff. , St.
Sigillaria cf. *fissa* Lx. *.....................	Hur.
Poacordaites sp..............................	P. G.

Cordaicarpon cinctum * ....P. G.
       "   *circularis* Lx. ?* ....St.
Palæoxyris appendiculata Lx. * ....St.

THE STOCKTON COAL FLORA AN ALLEGHENY FLORA.

"It needs but a brief comparison of the foregoing lists with the lists of Allegheny plants to show the large proportion of forms (marked with the asterisk) identical with those found in the Allegheny valley. Moreover, the forms so designated are in general typical of the Allegheny series, and, so far as I recollect, have not been found elsewhere than in that or the higher terranes. The Stockton flora is almost completely composed of species found in the Allegheny valley in Pennsylvania, at Mazon creek, Illinois, or in Henry county, Missouri. In short, we have here a normal association of the identical and characteristic forms of the Allegheny series—a typical Allegheny flora.

It is not within the scope of this paper to more precisely discuss the equivalence in the Pennsylvanian section of the several Kanawha terranes. It is, however, proper to add that the absence of the higher Pecopterids, the presence of certain phases of the species, certain older elements, as well as the proportion and range of the identical forms, bespeak for the Stockton flora a place not higher than the Clarion group in the Allegheny series. It seems very improbable that it can in any event be so high as the Upper Kittanning."

From these observations of Mr. David White, it will be seen that his preliminary conclusions, based solely upon his fossil plant studies, differ vitally from those of the writer, based largely upon the stratigrapic order, since the Stockton fossiliferous shale, which the writer would correlate with the Uffington shale of the northern region of the state, is, from the standpoint of its included fossil plants, regarded by David White quite as low down in the Allegheny series as the roof shales of the Clarion coal. In other words, while the writer places the Stockton coal of the Great Kanawha valley at the TOP of the Allegheny series upon stratigraphic and other grounds, Mr. David White, on paleobotannic evidence, would place it at the BOTTOM of that series. The question as to which is in error has very important economic consequences, and

---

† Belmont mine, near Crown Hill (Bel.); Buffalo Lick fork, five miles above Cannelton (Buff.); near the mouth of Hurricane creek (Hur.); Stanton mine on Kellys creek (St.); Spanglers fork of Blue creek (Sp.), and from the drift back of the schoolhouse north of Pond gap (P. G).

‡ Form characteristic of the Allegheny series.

* Identical with species in the Allegheny series.

hence is of more than purely theoretic interest. The evidence pro and con will be more fully discussed in the next chapter, and reference is made to the question here merely to call the reader's attention to the fact of the difference in conclusions as to the geological horizon of the shales in the roof of the Stockton coal of the Great Kanawha valley.

THE KANAWHA BLACK FLINT.

In the midst of the shales (Uffington) which separate the Stockton coal from the massive sandstone (Lower Mahoning) above, in the Great Kanawha valley, there rises from the bed of the river at Charleston, a very peculiar and characteristic deposit, known as the KANAWHA BLACK FLINT. The stratum soon rises to the level of the C. & O. R. R. grade, and is well exposed in the cuts of the same a short distance south from its Charleston station.

It is a popular but a mistaken belief, first voiced by the late Prof. William B. Rogers, in his Fifth Annual Geological Report of Virginia, that this stratum passes under the bed of the Kanawha river at the mouth of Elk, and thus gives origin to the "shoals" which formerly existed there before the Kanawha was slack-watered, but this view is erroneous, since the BLACK FLINT is only ten feet from water level just under the highway bridge across the Kanawha, and its rapid northwest dip would carry it beneath water level at the old ferry, near the C. & O. R. R. station, and since this rapid dip continues on northward to the mouth of the Elk, one-half mile distant, the horizon of this rock must be many feet (40-60) below the beds of both rivers at their junction.

Hence if any rocks other than loose boulders are ever exposed in either river at Elk "shoals," it would be one of the massive Mahoning sandstones which crop above the BLACK FLINT.

The character of this KANAWHA BLACK FLINT can be very well seen along the C. & O. R. R. at the point referred to between the C. & O. Charleston station and a few hundred yards south. Every gradation between a compact, structureless flint and a dark, stratified, sandy, fossiliferous stratum may there be observed. In it the writer has recognized Productus, Spirifera, Discina, and fragments of other marine forms which appear to be of the same type as those collected by Dr. Stevenson from the Uffington shale at the northern end of the state.

This fact has an important bearing upon the origin of the flint deposit, whether it is an original accumulation of silicious matter like the flint in chalk, from the silicious skeletons of diatoms and other minute forms of life, or whether the silica is derived by solution from the overlying sandstones, and has invaded this horizon from above by a kind of chemical replacement. The latter theory appears the more plausible from the facts already at hand, although it is possible that both agencies may have operated to produce the flint in question.

In weathering this rock breaks up into rudely rectangular forms two to three inches thick and eight to ten inches long which, being practically insoluble, line the streams and cover the ground with their bluish-black fragments up to the line of outcrop.

The weathered surface of this bed presents a peculiar wavy or undulating structure which appears to be characteristic of the deposit over a wide area. The distribution of this KANAWHA BLACK FLINT was formerly supposed to be confined entirely to Kanawha and Fayette counties, but the writer has recently found it in Clay and northern Nicholas.

From Charleston southward this rock rises rapidly, and soon attains an elevation of several hundred feet above the Kanawha, its hard and resisting nature having contributed much to the preservation of the precipitous slopes of the Kanawha valley, as well as the underlying coal series. Its crop gets higher and higher above the valley floor until it escapes from the summits at Ansted, in Fayette county, where it overlooks the junction of the Gauley and New rivers from an elevation of more than 1500 feet above the valleys.

On the Elk river the horizon of this FLINT is below water level, from Charleston to twenty-five miles above, where the emergance of the hard massive flint stratum from the bed of the river makes the rapids known as Queen "shoals." A mile farther up Elk the stratum crops along Spread "shoals" run and at Porter creek, another mile beyond it rises to the level of the C. C. & S. R. R. grade in a massive ledge 7 feet thick.

Between this point and Clay, it disappears as a conspicuous

bed, but traces of it are reported to occur near the Court House in
the town of Clay.

Buffalo creek puts into the Elk from the south at Clay, and
although the horizon of the flint is constantly above water level,
it has not been observed until near the head of its Lily fork at the
northern edge of Nicholas county.   Mr. W. Thompson, Jr. first
reported its presence in that region, on the line between Clay and
Nicholas counties, and the writer subsequently found its outcrop
three miles eastward where the Clay-Nicholas road crosses the
Lily branch.   It there juts out of the bank, 10 feet above the water, in a ledge 5 feet thick.

No one has reported its presence definitely in Boone county,
and the writer has not made the necessary examinations to determine its presence or absence there.

Being so conspicuous in appearance, when once carefully observed, it can never be confused with any other stratum in the
Kanawha series, and hence it was long ago designated by Prof.
Wm. B. Rogers as the dividing line between the two coal series.
His description of this bed is so apt that it may well be quoted
from his Fifth Annual Geological Report to the State of Virginia
in 1839, as follows :

"The landmark to which I here allude, and which was first recognized,
and afterwards diligently traced by my brother Prof J. B. Rogers, consists
of a band of black or bluish black silicious rock, approaching the character
of a flint or hornstone, which is found in the hills at the height of several
hundred feet above the river near the falls (Kanawha), and which, accompanying the subjacent strata in their various undulations, and their ultimate
steady western dip as they extend down the river, is seen to disappear below
the water level at the Elk river shoals.

This stratum from its striking peculiarity of character, and its constancy of geological position, furnishes a standard line with which to compare
the rocks and coal seams both above and beneath, and may be regarded in
this region as clearly defining the boundary between the upper and lower
series. As will be seen hereafter, throughout the tract extending from the
falls (Kanawha) to the point at which the flint comes down to the river level, no seams of coal, but such as are local and of insignificant extent, occur
in the hills above this stratum, but as we proceed toward the west, and thus
in virtue of the westerly dip of the rock, pass successively into strata higher
in the geological order, we meet with one or more coal seams (Pittsburg)
associated with the shaly rocks already noticed as predominating in the upper series."

And again on a subsequent page, l. c., he says :

"BLACK SILICEOUS ROCK, FLINT OR HORNSTONE."

"This remarkable deposit which here appears of the thickness of seven feet, and at an elevation in the hills above the road at Ryder's creek of 466 feet, may be traced by its debris from near the falls (Kanawha), and seen capping the hills in broken masses at the head waters of Scrabble creek. It is found up the northwest side, forming the tops of the hills, but cannot be traced in this direction above Twenty Mile creek. Thence it proceeds with a general gentle dip to the northwest, and is found up all creeks flowing into the Kanawha river. At Smither's, Ryder's and Hughes's creeks it occupies a considerable elevation in the hills, being overlaid by a coarse sandstone, which as low down as Keller's (Kelley's) creek, is found to be a conglomerate. It is readily distinguished from all the associated strata by the resistance which it furnishes to disintegrating agency; and by its always presenting a regular bedding and an angular sharp structure. No fossils can be detected in it, but at Ryder's creek the blue shales upon which it reposes are observed to contain a few impressions of shells.

Although throughout, the structure of this rock is remarkably uniform, sometimes it assumes the character of a black siliceous shale, particularly in its lower portion. And above, it is so dense and vitreous as to be readily mistaken for true flint, and properly entitled to the name of hornstone. "

This bed has been used as a "key" rock in the correlation of the Kanawha coals by everyone who has attempted their classification since Rogers (W. B.) first described and named it the BLACK FLINT, sixty-five years ago. It was one of the sources of arrow material made use of by the Indians, and arrows manufactured from it are scattered through many adjoining counties.

A light gray flint occurs in this same geological zone at the crest of the Volcano-Burning Springs anticlinal, on Hughes' river, near the California House, Wirt county, and a silicious shale, having the same peculiar physical aspect, crops near the western end of Cut No. 80 at Anderson, Preston county, ten to fifteen feet above the Upper Freeport coal.

A few feet above the BLACK FLINT in Fayette county, West Virginia, there occurs an impure, slaty bed of coal which in Bulletin No. 65. U. S. G. Survey, was termed the "Middle Cannelton" coal, the "No. 5 Block" coal above being named the "Upper Cannelton," and the Stockton coal below the FLINT, the "Lower Cannelton." It is now believed that the "No. 5 Block" coal represents the Mahoning bed, and that the thin, impure Middle

Cannelton layer is simply the "rider" so often observed in the roof of the Upper Freeport bed, a few feet above the main body of the latter coal, and since the name Stockton coal, or Stockton cannel bed, is much in vogue for the name of the first coal under the BLACK FLINT, the entire list of "Cannelton" names is dropped from the terminology in this volume.

CHAPTER V.

THE ALEGHENY SERIES, NO. XIII.

Below the last described (Conemaugh) rock series, and bound up between two great sandstone deposits, the Mahoning above and the Homewood, or Tionesta, below, the First Geological Survey of Pennsylvania discovered a group of strata holding valuable coal beds, not sporadic and irregular as those in the Barren or Conemaugh series above, but extending in valuable thickness and quality over wide areas. Since these beds were first developed and explored along the Allegheny river, this coal series was designated from that stream, and also termed the Lower Productive Measures, as well as No. XIII in the Rogers scheme of Formation Numbers.

As already related, the original nomenclature of Rogers included the Mahoning sandstone in this series, thus extending 100 to 150 feet above the present top of the Allegheny beds as limited by later geologists. That these sediments thus formerly included in the Allegheny measures are more nearly related to the main portions of the Allegheny beds below than to those which overlie the Mahoning sandstones with great masses of red shale, and holding faunas and floras closely related in many respects to the Permo-Carboniferous rocks of the west, has already been stated. Whether convenience and reasonable certainty in classification should outweigh real affinity, is the only question involved as to whether the classification should remain as now constituted, and used in this volume, or whether it should be revised by a a substantial return to the less convenient but more philosophical usage of the earlier geologists of Pennsylvania. This question can hardly be decided until after the entire Coal Measure sediments have been carefully studied in detail, with the aid of the new and more accurate maps, and vaster mining enterprises, shafts borings, etc., to which the younger school of geologists will have access, but which were denied to their predecessors.

The Allegheny series, as here limited, is capped at the top with the widely distributed, easily recognized, and valuable Upper Freeport coal bed, and extends down through several beds of fire-clay, limestone, coal, shale, and sandstone, until a marked change in lithology takes place, the sandstones becoming harder, more massive, often very pebbly, and of a lithologic type quite different from the ordinary sandstones of the Allegheny series, accompanied, of course, with a change in the character of the imbedded fossil plants. The physical change at the base of the series is generally very striking, so that the observer, once familiar with the lithologic type of the Allegheny sediments, finds but slight difficulty in differentiating the basal beds of the latter from the underlying Pottsville. True, sometimes the members of the Freeport sandstone grow very massive and conglomeratic and assume a type that is so like the Pottsville as to readily lead the stratigrapher into error, especially where the full series is not exposed, but this is only a local and temporary phase, and can always be avoided by a careful study of the overlying Conemaugh beds.

The thickness of this Allegheny series varies greatly in different portions of the field. Entering the state from Pennsylvania in Monongalia and Preston counties, the series has in Monongalia a minimum thickness of about 225 feet, which soon expands eastward to 275 to 300 in Preston, and slightly more in Mineral and Grant.

Traced southwestward, the series rapidly expands along its eastern crop through Barbour and Upshur, so that at the head of the Buckhannon, in Randolph, and on the Little Kanawha, in Webster and Lewis, the series has a thickness of 500 to 600 feet, which thickens up still more through Nicholas, Clay, and Fayette, so that when the Great Kanawha is reached, 1000 feet of sediments occur between the UPPER FREEPORT COAL, or the closely overlying KANAWHA BLACK FLINT, and the top of the undoubted Pottsville beds below.   This thickness holds through southern Kanawha, Boone, northern Wyoming, southern Logan and Mingo, to the southern line of the state, and may even be greater there.

Just how this great thickening of the sediments takes place is not exactly clear, whether by the gradual introduction of new and older beds entirely unrepresented at the northeast, or by the thickening of the sandstones, shales, etc., which separate the several coal beds.

From the fact that the same number of commercially valuable coals exist on the Great Kanawha river as on the Allegheny, together with the known fact that the interval between the KANAWHA BLACK FLINT and the CAMPBELLS CREEK COAL thickens from 410 feet at Campbell's creek to 650 feet at Montgomery, twenty miles south, in which distance both beds are constantly above water level, and can be traced without probability of error—these facts led the writer to believe that as the Upper Freeport coal, at the top of the series, appeared to extend through to the Kanawha river continuously from the northern line of the state, so too, the other coal horizons, persistent over all of western Pennsylvania, very probably extended on southwestward like the Upper Freeport, and that the sediments separating them at the north simply expanded three to four fold in passing southward to the Great Kanawha region, where observations had shown that not only the Allegheny series had greatly expanded, but also the Conemaugh beds above, as well as the Pottsville, Mauch Chunk, and Greenbrier series below.

Mr. David White, the eminent authority on Carboniferous fossil plants, however, has reached conclusions opposed to those outlined above.   He concludes on the evidence of the flora alone, not that the main mass of the Kanawha series belongs in the Pottsville (for his views coincide with the writer's as to the top of the Pottsville beds on the Kanawha), but that the bulk of the sediments represent new elements unknown at the north, and intermediate between the Allegheny and Pottsville sediments, and representing the Lower Coal Measures of Europe, the flora of which had not previously been found in America until Mr. White took up the study of the Kanawha series.   Whether the one or the other of these views is correct, or whether the truth will finally be found in a combination of causes which partially supports both theories, must be left for future and more detailed studies, since it has been impossible as yet (owing to lack of time and the undeveloped condition of large intervening areas) to trace the Allegheny series as a whole continuously from Barbour county, where the thickening begins, across to the Great Kanawha, although it has been possible to follow the Upper Freeport coal at its top with a high degree of certainty until it merges into the Stockton cannel seam, the first coal below the KANAWHA BLACK FLINT, thus confirming the conclusions of Rogers and his assistants in placing the BLACK FLINT at the base of the Conemaugh series instead of at the base of the Allegheny, where Mr. David White's conclusions would correlate the KANAWHA FLINT with the FERRIFEROUS, or VANPORT LIMESTONE of Western Pennsylvania.   This conflict of evidence, in which the fossil plants must yield to the stratigraphic results at the top of the Kanawha series, of course, weakens the argument derived from them as to the other coal beds of that region, 300 to 600 feet below the BLACK FLINT, being older and lower in the geologic time scale than any of the coals of the Allegheny series.

This question will be further considered when the UPPER FREEPORT COAL is discussed, and traced from the northern line of the state southwestward to the Great Kanawha river, in subsequent pages of this volume.

TOPOGRAPHY.

The topography made by the Allegheny series is generally very much the same, except where the thickness is greatly increased. The outcrop of the beds makes a fairly rich soil, covering slopes often quite broken and rugged, and frequently too steep for convenient tillage, but usually bearing a fine growth of timber, and forming excellent grazing lands.   The hills are usually terraced with a series of benches, rudely parallel to each other, which, as Prof. Lesley long ago showed in his classic work, "Coal and Its Topography," mark the outcrops of the several coal beds, since the soft rocks (shales and clays), usually found in connection with every coal bed, are more readily eroded than the hard beds (sandstones) either above or below. The coal bench terraces are not confined to the topography of the Allegheny series, since they are due to a general law of erosion, and occur in the Conemaugh and Monongahela series above, as well as in the Pottsville below. The terraces are more strikingly illustrated in the Allegheny, however, because the coals are closer together and more numerous in these measures than in the others.

Through the southwestern portion of the state, where the Allegheny-Kanawha series attains great thickness, say from Webster county on through to the Big Sandy river at the Kentucky boundary, the crop of these rocks is marked by such steep and cliff-like slopes, that much of the surface is not arable, while a considerable portion is even too steep for grazing, except along the narrow valleys, from which the slopes rise at angles of 25°–40° up to the long narrow ridges capped by the Mahoning sandstones, 1000 to 1500 feet above.

When these beds dip beneath the surface of the ground, westward from the eastern margin of the Appalachian field, the only knowledge of them obtainable is from the records of oil and gas well borings, since, except in Hancock county, along the northern Pan Handle of the state, they do not come to the surface again until the northwestern side of the Appalachian field is exposed in Ohio.

The records of many hundreds of gas and oil wells, drilled in nearly every portion of this deeply buried area, do not bear out the promise of valuable coal beds in the Allegheny series over a considerable portion of the state, since very many records reveal no coal whatever, and others find only thin streaks at the horizon where valuable beds occur at the surface. Except for the general thinning westward, the series holds its thickness all right, but the coal beds are simply not present in valuable quantity if we can believe the evidence of the oil well drillers. True, they do not drill for coal, and the latter is only noted incidentally, as a rule, and hence there is a slight chance that in some of the areas at least, where no coal has been reported by the oil and gas well drilling, the diamond or core drill may yet be able to discover one or two workable beds.   Still, it is merely a chance, and hardly probable in view of the many wells giving the same negative results over such wide areas.

In the early operations for oil and gas, which were confined largely to the northern region of the state, especially the vicinity of Mannington, Marion county, a thick bed of coal was generally reported about 200 feet below the top of the Allegheny series. The same reports came also from Wheeling and Parkersburg, and hence in discussing this subject of the existence of valuable fuel in the Allegheny series, under the central portion of the Appalachian field, in Bulletin 65 of the U. S. G. Survey, the evidence appeared to be in favor of the presence of at least one or more coals of merchantable thickness under the entire area where these beds are deeply buried.   Since then, however, so many more oil and gas wells have been drilled in the other counties of the state, where no coal of any importance was found in the Allegheny series, that the writer is prepared to believe that but little or no coal of commercial value will be found in the Allegheny series under the counties of western Monongalia, Marion, Wetzel, Tyler, Pleasants, Wood, Ritchie, Doddridge, Harrison, Lewis, Gilmer, Calhoun, Wirt, Roane, Jackson, Mason, and large areas of central Cabell and Wayne, and hence that the original idea of Dr. John J. Stevenson may finally prove the correct one, viz: that most of our principal coal beds were deposited in a fringe or zone, many miles in width around the edges of the Appalachian field, while the main inner area was barren ground so far as coal deposition is concerned.

We know this is true for the Pottsville coal series of Pennsylvania, Ohio and West Virginia, and except over the northern end of the Appalachian trough, appears to be true for the great Pittsburg bed of the Mongahela series.   Of course, this fringe of productive coal beds is twenty to thirty miles in width, but even that is a narrow belt compared with the great barren areas lying between the two borders of the trough.

The main beds of the Allegheny series, which have received distinct names in western Pennsylvania, are the following:

Upper Freeport coal.
Upper Freeport limestone.

Upper Freeport sandstone.
Lower Freeport coal.
Lower Freeport limestone.
Lower Freeport sandstone.
Upper Kittanning coal.
Johnstown (cement) limestone.
Middle Kittanning coal.
Lower Kittanning coal.
Lower Kittanning fireclay.
Lower Kittanning sandstone.
Buhr stone, iron ore.
Ferriferous (Vanport) limestone.
Clarion coal.
Brookville coal.

Other beds in this series have been named whose distribution is only local, but those given above are the principal ones which can be traced and identified over wide areas.

The late Dr. Edward Orton, Sr., State Geologist of Ohio, has shown that all of the main strata in the Allegheny series of western Pennsylvania, can be traced bodily across that state from where they enter it in Columbiana county to where they leave it to enter Kentucky from Lawrence county, 250 miles from the Ohio-Pennsylvania boundary.

In this intervening distance, some of the coal beds may change in thickness, or disappear entirely over areas of considerable size, but they ultimately come into the section again, so that the integrity of the persistent beds of the Allegheny series in Pennsylvania, is maintained entirely across the state, and this is true, not only of the COAL BEDS, but also of the LIMESTONES, SANDSTONES, FIRECLAYS and even the IRON ORES, so that a section in Lawrence county is practically a duplicate of one in Columbiana.

This simplicity and regularity of the stratigraphic column in Ohio along the northwestern crop of the Appalachian coal field, does not hold good when we cross to the southwestern border and attempt to follow it southwestward across West Virginia, since in the intervening region between the Pennsylvania-West Virginia boundary, and the Kentucky-West Virginia border, there occurs that enormous thickening of the entire Coal Measure column of rocks, which interrupts the continuity of individual beds, so beautifully illustrated in Ohio, where the measures maintain practically the same thickness, and hence a section through the Allegheny series in Monongalia and Preston counties, at the northern line of the state, bears very little physical resemblance to one in Mingo county at the Kentucky border, through what appears to be the equivalent of the Allegheny series at the northern line of the state.

It is known with a high degree of certainty that the great coal bed (Upper Freeport) at the top of the Allegheny series, extends across this southeastern border of the Appalachian field in an almost continuous sheet, but whether or not the five other main coal beds below, viz: Lower Freeport, Upper Kittanning, Middle Kittanning, Lower Kittanning, and Clarion, maintain their continuity through the mass of thickening sediments and emerge on the Great Kanawha as the five coal beds found there in the Kanawha series, below the Stockton cannel (Upper Freeport) viz: the Coalburg, Winifrede, Cedar Grove, Campbells creek, and Eagle beds respectively, cannot yet be demonstrated. The evidence drawn by inference from the continuity of the coals on the northwestern side of the Appalachian field tends to induce the belief that as we find the same number of more or less persistent coal beds between the Conemaugh series and the Pottsville beds in the southwestern portion of the state that we do at the northeastern border, it may be possible that they represent the same coal horizons with greatly thickened intervening sandstones and shales.

Of course, the other view of the matter is that held by Mr. David White, the paleobotanist, in his paper on the "Relative Ages of the Kanawha and Allegheny Series as Indicated by the Fossil Plants," published in the Bulletin of the G. S. A., Vol. XI., pp. 145-178, March, 1900, in which he maintains from the evidence of fossil plants, that the Kanawha coals, except possibly the two highest beds, (Stockton and Coalburg), are entirely below the Allegheny series; that they represent a series hitherto unknown in the Appalachian field, viz: the Lower Coal Measures of Europe, between the Allegheny series and the Lower Pottsville.

While the writer is convinced that Mr. White is in error concerning the Upper limits of the Allegheny series on the Kanawha river, he cannot say that there may not be coal beds in the lower half of the Kanawha series which are unrepresented in the typical Allegheny series of Pennsylvania, and, as heretofore stated, the question remains open for future investigation. In this volume wherever the thick sediments are found, we shall term them the Allegheny-Kanawha series, thus leaving the question of identity an open one.

There will now be given a number of detailed measurements of the Allegheny series in the different regions of West Virginia, adding two or three from Pennsylvania, Maryland and Ohio for ready comparison.

The following section from Miller's Eddy, near the mouth of the Clarion river, Report VV, Second Geological Survey of Pennsylvania, page 123, represents the Allegheny series in that region of the Allegheny river:

MILLER'S EDDY SECTION, CLARION COUNTY, PA.

	Ft.	In.
Coal, Upper Freeport	3	0
Interval	28	3
Iron ore	2	0
Concealed and slate	103	0
Coal, Upper Kittanning, (Middle)	1	6
Interval	20	0
Sandstone	30	0
Interval	16	6
Coal, Lower Kittanning	3	6
Interval	10	0
Sandstone	19	10
Limestone, Ferriferous, (Vanport)	9	0
Shales	6	0
Sandstone	28	6
Coal, Clarion	2	4
Blue shales	29	0
Sandstone, massive, (Pottsville)		
Total	312	5

The words in parenthesis have been added by the writer:

Another typical section from the banks of the Allegheny river at Kittanning, Armstrong county, Pennsylvania, will be of service here to show the continuity of the series along that stream. This section was made by the writer and is quoted from Bulletin 65, U. S. G. Survey, page 109, as follows:

KITTANNING SECTION, ARMSTRONG COUNTY, PA.

	Ft.	In.	Ft.	In.
Coal, Upper Freeport			4	0
Shales and concealed			35	0
Coal, Lower Freeport			2	0

Concealed and massive sandsone............	35	0	}	75	0
Shales and sandstone	40	0			
Coal, slate in center, *Middle Kittanning*................				1	6
Fireclay	4	0			
Sandy shales	6	0			
Fireclay	3	0	}	70	0
Flaggy sandstone	17	0			
Shales, dark, sandy, with iron ore............	40	0			
Coal, Lower Kittanning { coal	1	10			
slate	0	2			
coal	0	8	}	3	3
bone.............	0	1			
coal ......,......	0	6			
Fireclay	5	0			
Sandstone and sandy shales	40	0	}	50	0
Shales, with iron ore.............................	5	0			
Iron ore, Buhrstone	0	6			
Limestone, Ferriferous, Vanport............	11	6	}	27	0
Sandy shales	15	0			
Coal				0	3
Sandy shales and sandstone				21	0
Coal, Clarion..				1	0
Concealed to top of No. XII. sandstone................				25	0
Total..				315	0

The interval between the Upper and Lower Freeport coals, in the above section, is probably too small by twenty to thirty feet, since a subsequent visit reveals a greater interval than that given in the section, due to the discovery of a new exposure where the crops of both coals may be seen in a nearly vertical section.

The exposures at the classic locality of Freeport, on the Allegheny river, twenty miles below Kittanning, have also much interest in a study of the coals in the Allegheny series, and the following from a detailed section by the writer, made at Freeport and published in Bulletin 65, l. c., page 111, will prove convenient for reference:

FREEPORT, PENNSYLVANIA.

	Ft.	In.		Ft.	In.
Coal, Upper Freeport { coal................... ...	2	8			
slate, gray......	0	1½			
coal........	0	6½	}	3	9½
slate, dark gray.....	0	0½			
coal sulphurous.....	0	5			
Fireclay..	1	6			
Limestone, Upper Freeport.........	3	6			
Sandy shales	20	0	}	66	0
Coal, Middle Freeport............................	2	0			
Sandy shales and sandstone	39	0			

			Ft. In.
Coal, Lower Freeport	cannel slate .... 5 o		14 o
	slaty coal.............. 4 o		
	fireclay with lime-		
	stone 2 6		
	slaty coal............ 2 6		
Fireclay and shales.................................... 2 o			
Freeport sandstone	sandstone, massive... 45 o		64 o
	coaly slate, U. Kittan 0-4 o		
	sandstone, gray,mas. 15 o		
Coal, Middle Kittanning..........................			1 6
Fireclay, with limestone nodules in upper half.........			6 o

Total...155 3½

It will be observed that the Upper Freeport coal is multiple bedded at its type locality, a characteristic which it maintains everywhere in West Virginia. Also, that there is a local coal twenty-five feet beneath it before reaching the Lower Freeport bed 66 feet below, and that the horizon of the Upper Kittanning coal is in the middle of the Lower Freeport sandstone.

Coming still closer to West Virginia, we find the following section of the Allegheny series reported from the Ligonier Basin of Fayette county, Pennsylvania, by Dr. John J. Stevenson, in Report KKK, Second Geological Survey of Pennsylvania, page 89:

FAYETTE COUNTY, PA., SECTION.

		Ft.	Ft. In.
Coal, Upper Freeport...........................			3 o
Clay		3	
Limestone, Freeport.............................		5	44 o
Fireclay, Bolivar, and shale		16	
Shale, sandy, (Upper Freeport sandstone).....		20	
Coal, Lower Freeport			o 8
Shale, sandy			30 o
Coal, Upper Kittanning	coal....2' 3"		5 11
	clay......o 4		
	coal......3 4		
Clay		3	83 o
Sandstone, Lower Freeport, in part............		40	
Concealed, mostly sandstone		40	
Coal, Middle Kittanning........................			blossom
Sandstone........................		10	35 o
Concealed		25	
Coal, Lower Kittanning			blossom
Concealed			60 o
Coal, Clarion or Brookville			2 3
Shale and clay..................................			10 o
Sandstone, massive, top of No. XII......................			

Total 273 10

In the adjoining county of Preston, West Virginia, and in the same (Ligonier) basin, Hon. S. B. Elkins has recently completed a diamond drill boring through the entire Allegheny series, the core of which the writer has inspected. The boring is located on the land of Sanford Watson, Dillon creek, near Masontown, and the record reads as follows:

SANFORD WATSON FARM, DILLON CREEK,
PRESTON COUNTY.

		Ft.	In.	Ft.	In.
	coal	0	4¼		
	bone	0	3¾		
	coal	0	2		
	bone	0	1½		
	coal	0	7¼		
	coal, bony streaks	0	10		
Upper Freeport coal.....	coal	2	11¼	10	2½
	slate	0	2½		
	coal	1	1½		
	slate	1	0		
	coal	1	5½		
	slate	0	1½		
	coal, slightly sulphurous	0	11½		
Fireclay, limestone, (Upper Freeport) and sandstone		21	1½	64	11½
Green shale and sandstone		14	2		
Gray sandstone, Upper Freeport..............		29	8		
Coal, Lower Freeport...	bony coal	0	2	1	1
	coal...................	0	11		
Fireclay, very soft		4	2	83	10
Green shales and sandstone.........		3	4		
Gray sandstone, hard, pebbly, Lower Freeport..		76	4		
Black slate, upper half very bituminous, *Middle Kittanning coal horizon*				8	5
Slate, streaked with sandy layers		37	11	44	8
Shale		6	9		
Fireclay, top of this, horizon of *Lower Kittanning coal*		17	0	42	5
Shale		10	10		
Gray sandstone, very hard.......................		6	1		
Slate................................		0	11		
Coal streak		0	1		
Shale		7	6		
Coal, Clarion	coal and slate.................	1	5	9	1
	Fireclay....................	6	5		
	coal, slaty and bony	1	3		
Fireclay				12	10
Gray sandstone, very hard, top Pottsville series........					
Total				277	6

This boring is the continuation of the section given on page 300, where the lower portion of the Conemaugh series above was penetrated. It also passed through the underlying Homewood or Tionesta sandstone, the great top member of the Pottsville conglomerate series, so that the section is a very important one, since it gives an exact measurement of the thickness and character of the Allegheny sediments near the northern line of the state, where there can be no controversy as to the identity of the several elements of the series, since nearly all of the principal members of the same are present or represented in such manner as to be unmistakable. The Freeport stage, as the upper portion of the Allegheny series might be termed, is in typical development, all of its members being represented except the Upper Kittanning coal, the horizon of which belongs near the middle of the Lower Freeport sandstone, which is here seventy-six feet thick in one solid mass of coarse, gray sandstone, very pebbly toward the base.

Although the middle and Lower Kittanning coal beds are completely absent as COAL, yet their horizons are distinctly marked—in the case of the first by a cannel-like stratum of very bituminous slate, four and one-half feet thick, and the latter by its underlying Kittanning fireclay, indicating that its accompanying coal is only locally absent, and may appear at any other locality not far removed, as it actually does at Newburg, in the same basin, a few miles distant to the southwest.

The great multiple-bedded coal, (Upper Freeport), at the top of the series, reveals here the same characteristics, only on a larger scale, that we find at its type locality in the section given on page 343. The pure and valuable portion of this coal is the five and one-half feet near the center of the bed, which is separated into three benches by two layers of slate, one twelve, the other two and one-half inches in thickness, known respectfully as the "Big" and "Little" slates of the miners. Including these, the workable coal bed measures six feet, eight and three-quarter inches.

The coal at the base of the series, split by the large bed of fireclay into two members, has been identified as the Clarion coal, since, as Mr. Chance has well shown, the Clarion bed is nearly always double in Pennsylvania, and it reveals the same characteristics where exposed at the surface in Preston county. It is possible that the "Brookville" coal of Pennsylvania is only the lower member of the Clarion bed.

The boring on the Gamble lot, near Rock Forge, Monongalia county, a portion (the Conemaugh) of which record is given on page 309 preceding, was also continued by Mr. Elkins down nearly to the base of the Allegheny series. This locality is about seven miles northwest from the Watson farm boring, near the bottom of the steep dip of the rocks along the western slope of the Chestnut ridge anticlinal, and one mile southeast from the center of the Connellsville syncline. It is of interest as showing the changes which take place in the character of the fragmental or clastic sediments that constitute the main mass of the Allegheny series. The writer has also examined this core, (which, together with that obtained at the Watson farm, is now in the museum of the West Virginia University) and it gives the following record:

GAMBLE BORING, ON DECKER'S CREEK, NEAR ROCK FORGE, MONONGALIA COUNTY.

		Ft. In.	Ft. In.
Upper Freeport coal	bone coal.............. 0 2½		
	coal 3 4½		
	slate 0 2½	5 7	
	coal 1 0		
	slate 0 3		
	coal 0 6½		
Fireclay, Bolivar...		7 7	
Upper Freeport sandstone	gray sandstone 15 8		
	fireclay and sandstone... 8 8	53 2	
	gray sandstone 28 10		
Fireclay, with streak of coal (*Lower Freeport*) at top..		22 8	
Lower Freeport sandstone	sandstone and fireclay... 7 7		
	black slate with streaks	22 11	
	of gray sandstone......15 4		
Upper Kittanning coal	coal 2 6½		
	slate 0 0¾	2 10½	
	coal 0 3¼		
Slate		1 10½	
Fireclay, greenish cast, sandy streaks		29 2	
Black slate		1 6	
Middle and Lower Kittanning coals	coal, slaty.............. 0 11		
	bone coal 0 3¼		
	black slate, streaks	8 0½	
	of gray sandstone 6 9		
	coal 0 1		
Fireclay, streaks of sandstone...............		14 11½	
Sandstone, streaks of slate		19 2	
Gray sandstone, Clarion...............		35 0	
Shale		2 4	
Coal, Clarion...		1 6½	
Fireclay to bottom of boring		11 6½	
Total..239 11			

It cannot be more than ten feet additional in this boring down to the base of the Allegheny series, thus giving these beds a total of 250 feet in thickness, or a thinning of thirty feet in the seven miles between the Watson and Gamble borings.

At the horizon where the great Lower Freeport sandstone occurs in the Watson boring, seventy-six feet thick in one solid mass, we find in the Gamble boring mostly clays and sandy shales, with the Upper Kittanning coal near the center of the mass.

At the head of Booths creek, two miles or more above Clinton Furnace, Monongalia county, and about seven miles southwest from the location of the Gamble boring, the following section of these members is exposed on the lands of Samuel Dalton and E. J. Jeffry:

BOOTHS CREEK SECTION.

		Ft. In.	Ft In.
Coal, Upper Freeport	coal, bony	2 0	
	coal, good	2 6	
	slate	0 2	
	coal, good	0 10	6 0
	slaty coal	0 2	
	coal, good	0 4	
Concealed			60 0
Coal, Lower Freeport, reported			4 0
Concealed, with a thin coal above middle			120 0
Coal, Lower Kittanning, good			2 3
Concealed to top of Pottsville series			50 0
Total			242 3

The Lower Freeport bed was once mined at this locality, but the mine is now abandoned and has fallen shut.

At Newburg, Preston county, on the main line of the B. & O. R. R., and near the center of a deep syncline which holds small areas of the Pittsburg coal in the summits of the hills, both the Upper Freeport and Lower Kittanning coal beds have been penetrated by a deep shaft, and the section continued on below by a diamond drill boring. The Lower Kittanning bed was formerly mined there, but a disastrous mine explosion, and the great expense of sinking an additional shaft for ventilating purposes, caused the abandonment of the lower coal bed, so that now operations are confined to the Upper Freeport seam. The combination of shaft and drill hole records gives the following as the structure of the Allegheny series under Newburg:

SHAFT AT NEWBURG, PRESTON COUNTY.

		Ft. In.	Ft. In.
Coal, Upper Freeport	coal	3 0	5 4
	coal and slate	2 4	
Shales		8 0	

Sandstone 18	0			
Limestone, Upper Freeport................... 8	0		45	0
Shales 6	0			
Iron ore 1	0			
Shales 4	0			
Fireclay, (horizon of Lower Freeport coal)			2	0
Shales, gray 14	0			
Shales, dark..11	0		108	0
Shales, gray 9	0			
Sandstone, Freeport.......... 74	0			
	coal 1	0		
	slate............... 0	3		
Coal, Middle Kittanning	coal, slaty 2	0	7	3
	fireclay.......... 2	0		
	coal, good 2	0		
Fireclay and shales, with iron ore nodules			15	0
	coal 0	10		
	shale, gray...... 0	10		
	coal 0	6		
Coal, Lower Kittanning	coal, bony 0	3	9	5
	coal, main bch. 4	6		
	black slate..... . 0	6		
	coal 2	0		
Sandstone and shale			38	0
Pebbly sandstone, top of Pottsville series				
Total......................... 230				0

This locality is in the same basin as the Watson farm boring, given on page 344, above, and not more than ten miles distant therefrom in a southwest direction, and yet the Lower Kittanning coal bed, of which only a trace exists in the Watson boring, comes into the Newburg section with a fine development, although a few miles east, at Tunnelton, it is again thin and unimportant where struck in a boring.

The Middle Kittanning coal also comes into the section here according to the record given by the Superintendent of the Aurora Coal Company.

The top member of the Pottsville was eighty-eight feet thick in one solid mass of hard, pebbly sandstone in the boring, which passed on below the bottom of the shaft.

A deep well was drilled for oil at this last locality, and as it began near the mouth of the shaft, it will prove interesting to give its record of the strata passed through in the Allegheny series. The well was drilled by Hon. J. M. Guffey, of Pittsburg, Pennsylvania, and according to the contractor the following strata were penetrated:

OIL WELL BORING RECORD AT NEWBURG.

	Ft.
Slate in place of coal (Upper Freeport) at 170 feet below surface...	20
Slate, white, and shale............ ....…...............	120
Sandstone, hard, firm (Lower Freeport)................…...	30
Slate, white . ...…….....	20
Coal (Lower Kittanning)...…...................................	10
Slate, white ...…...............…..... ....…... .	15
Sandstone, gray, very hard, top of Pottsville.............	
Total...	215

The drill probably encountered a locality where the Upper Freeport coal had been mined out, and hence none was found, although its proper horizon is noted at 170 feet below the surface. This would add at least five feet to the total thickness of the Allegheny series, thus making it 220 feet as against 230 in the diamond drill and shaft record, an agreement quite as close as one could expect.

All of these measures come to the surface along the B. & O. R. R. in descending the Cheat river grade from Cut 80, near Anderson, seven miles east from Newburg, and there the following succession may be seen:

CUT 80, B. & O. R. R., PRESTON COUNTY.

		Ft. In.	Ft. In.
Coal, Upper Freeport	coal, slaty 2 0		8 6
	shale 0 3		
	coal 2 8		
	fireclay shale...... 0 8		
	hard, dark slate, bony 1 5		
	coal, slaty 0 6		
	shale 0 2		
	coal 0 10		
Fireclay and sandy shale............... .... 8 0			55 8
Sandstone 8 0			
Shales, with ferruginous nuggets 5 0			
Limestone, Upper Freeport	limestone, gray pure 1 8	12 8	
	fireclay shales..5 0		
	limestone, gray shaly 6 0		
Shales, with much iron ore in nuggets......17 0			
Sandy shales and hard sandstone 5 0			
Dark, coaly slate, Lower Freeport coal horizon.........			0 2
Fireclay, with ferruginous nuggets 10 0			85 0
Concealed, estimated on dip.....................60 0			
Massive sandstone, Lower Freeport, visible 15 0			
Coal, Middle Kittanning, slaty, visible................…...			2 0
Concealed and shales, estimated 60 0			90 0
Fireclay and sandy shales, some coaly appearance, iron ore nuggets.................30 0			

		Ft.	In.
Coal, slaty..		I	o
Fireclay and sandy shales.....................................		18	o

| Coal, Clarion | { coal, slaty....................... 2 3 }
{ fireclay............................ 5 0 }
{ coal .... I 0 } | 8 | 3 |

| Black slate .... | I | o |
| Very massive white sandstone, top of Pottsville series .... | | |

| Total....................................271   9 |

Here we find, resting almost in immediate contact with the uppermost member of the Pottsville conglomerate, the same coal, split with a thick bed of fireclay, as that observed in the basal portion of both the Watson and Gamble drill holes. I have called this the Clarion coal, but of course it may represent the Brookville bed, and the coal next above it may be the Clarion.

The iron ore nuggets in the thirty feet of shales have an oolitic appearance and remind one of the Ferriferous or Buhrstone ore of Pennsylvania. This is the same geological horizon as the latter, but no limestone is visible here.

These sections across Preston and eastern Monongalia reveal the normal thickness of the Allegheny series as found in the adjoining regions of Pennsylvania. This condition of affairs continues on eastward, as shown by the following section published by Dr. G. C. Martin in "The Geology of Garrett county, Maryland," page 116, from the locality of Jennings Mill, Garrett county. It is the result of a diamond drill boring, and the record is as follows:

SECTION OF ALLEGHENY SERIES IN BORE HOLE AT JENNINGS MILL, GARRETT COUNTY.

		Ft.	In.	Ft.	In.
Coal, Upper Freeport	{ coal .... 0 2 } { bone.................. 0 3 } { black shale.........10 10 } { coal .... 2 2 }			13	5
Shale				4	o
Shaly sandstone				9	o
Gray shale...........				35	5
Brecciated fireclay				o	8
Gray shale...				12	o
Coal				o	2
Gray shale...............				II	7
Black shale...				o	9
Coal, Lower Freeport				I	2
Black shale.............				I	o
Gray shale..............................				18	9
Sandy shale				15	o

Coarse sandstone....		12	0
Gray shale.		1	0
Coarse sandstone.		3	0
Black shale		8	10

Coal, Middle and Lower Kittanning	coal	1	4	
	black shale	3	0	
	gray shale	2	4	14 1
	coal	0	10	
	gray shale	5	3	
	coal	1	10	

Gray shale.		8	6
Coarse sandstone....		10	0
Coarse cross-bedded sandstone		20	0
Coarse sandstone.		11	0
Shaly sandstone		10	0
Gray shale.		6	6
Sandy shale		7	0
Dark gray and black shale		7	0
Coal, Clarion		0	8
Gray shale.		4	0
Gray sandy shale		5	0
Black shale		5	0
Coal, Brookville(?)		1	0
Total		257	6

In Mineral county, on the North Potomac, the Allegheny series is well exposed from Piedmont up to Gorman. Dr. Martin measured a section of these beds on the east, or West Virginia, side of the Potomac, opposite Harrison, which is published on page 115, l. c., as follows:

SECTION OF ALLEGHENY SERIES AT HARRISON.

		Ft.	In.	Ft.	In.
Coal, Upper Freeport...	coal	1	3		
	shale	0	1		
	coal	0	6	5	4
	shale	0	6		
	coal	3	0		
Concealed				134	0
Black shale.				3	0
Coal, Upper Kittanning				3	7
Concealed				37	0
Sandstone				5	0
Coal, Middle and Lower Kittanning	coal	2	0		
	shale	0	9–12		
	coal	0	6	6	4
	shale	0	6		
	coal	2	4		
Concealed				20	0
Massive sandstone				45	0
Concealed				15	0
Coal, Clarion.				2	4
Concealed				35	0
Total				311	7

About one mile and a-half above Harrison, the writer once measured the following section in the steep bluffs of the North Potomac, opposite the Maple Swamp Water Tank.   (See page 127, Bulletin 65, U. S. G. Survey:

MAPLE SWAMP WATER TANK SECTION.

		Ft.	In.	Ft.	In.
Coal, Upper Freeport...	{ coal	0	5		
	bone and slate.....	1	4	4	3
	coal	2	6		
Concealed				60	0
Coal, Lower Freeport..				1	2
Concealed				55	0
Coal, Upper Kittanning				1	0
Concealed and slate........				45	0
Coal, Lower Kittanning	{ coal	3	0		
	slate	2	0	6	5
	coal	1	5		
Concealed and sandstone...............................				85	0
Coal, Clarion				2	6
Shales and concealed.............................				45	0
Massive sandstone, top of Pottsville.......................					
Total				305	4

Above Gorman and Bayard, on the North Potomac, the Allegheny series sinks entirely below water level, and for several miles its structure is known only through borings and shafts.   A boring was sunk by the Davis Coal & Coke Company at Hambleton, near Henry, Grant county, West Virginia, the record of which is published by Dr. G. C. Martin on pages 112-113 of "The Geology of Garrett County, Maryland."   It shows a slight thickening in the measures, and reads as follows:

SECTION OF ALLEGHENY SERIES.   BORE HOLE NO. 1,
HENRY, GRANT COUNTY.

		Ft.	In.	Ft.	In.
Mahoning sandstone, etc					
Coal, Upper Freeport...	{ bony coal............	1	10		
	coal	3	4	5	2
Shale				2	2½
Limestone..				0	11½
Shale				7	6½
Sandstone with streaks of shale............................				10	3
Sandstone				13	3
Conglomerate				1	7½
Conglomeritic sandstone..................................				5	6
Light gray sandy shale............				13	3
Sandstone..				17	5
Shale				2	0
Shaly sandstone				21	3
Shale				15	1

Shaly sandstone	24	10
Bone	0	2
Shale	3	0
Sandstone......	1	10
Shale	1	1
Limestone....................	1	0
Shale	16	3
Black shale with streaks of bone	1	1
Shale	11	6½
Sandstone and shale	14	5½
Black shale	3	1½
Sandy shale	3	8
Sandstone	2	3½
Black shale	2	4

Coal, Middle and Lower Kittanning	coal .... 0 2 shale .... 0 1 coal .... 2 9½ shale .... 0 4½ bone .... 0 7½ coal .... 2 0 shale .... 0 1½ coal .... 2 0 shale .... 0 1 bone 0 2½		8	5½

Shale	19	2½
Rough coal and shale ("split six")	2	1½
Sandstone and black shale..................................	4	4
Black shale.....:..	4	5
Shale and bone	0	7½
Shale	6	5
Limestone	2	8
Shale	12	8½
Hard flinty sandstone	13	0
Conglomerate	7	4½
Sandstone...	5	11
Shale and sandstone	22	11½
Sandstone	8	4½
Shale	1	2

Coal, Clarion	coal with sulphur .... 0 11 shale .... 0 0½ coal .... 0 6 sulphur 0 1	1	6½

Shale	10	2

Coal, Brookville	coal .... 1 5 shale .... 0 8½ bone............................ 0 2½ shale and bone............ 0 5½ coal 0 8	3	5½

Shale	4	7½
Homewood sandstone, etc		
Total..	341	8½

Dr. Martin identifies the coal at the bottom of the section with the Brookville, but it probably represents simply the Lower Clarion, or the "split" division of the latter, just as the "split-six" division higher up in the section represents the lowest layer of the Lower Kittanning or "Six-Foot" vein.

At the head of the North Potomac, and just over the divide on the Cheat river drainage, the shafts of the Davis Coal & Coke Company, at Thomas, together with the surface outcrops along the Cheat river grade of the W. Va. C. & P. R. R., reveal the following section of the Allegheny series:

		Ft. In.	Ft. In.
Coal, Upper Freeport...	coal .... 2 6 bony coal............ 2 6 coal 3 0		8 0
Sandy shales..			50 0
Coal, Lower Freeport ..	coal .... 0 2 shale .... 0 4 coal 1 0		1 6
Shales			20 0
Sandstone, massive, Lower Freeport, pebbly at base			75 0
Fireclay and shales...			40 0
Coal, Middle and Lower Kittanning	coal .... 1 5 slate.................... 0 4 coal .... 1 0 slate.................... 0 3 coal .... 3 6 shale, gray............ 1 6 coal, slaty .... 3 ●		11 0
Fireclay and shales.....................................			5 0
Sandstone, massive			20 0
Shales...			2 0
Iron ore (Buhrstone?)			1 0
Limestone, gray, horizon of Ferriferous or Vanport ..			2 0
Shales and sandstone.................................			35 0
Coal, Clarion, slaty			3 0
Shales and concealed to top of Pottsville series........			40 0
Total..			313 6

Here, at the proper horizon below the Lower Kittanning coal, we find a gray limestone supporting a layer of silicious iron ore, in the same manner as the Vanport or Ferriferous limestone of Pennsylvania. It does not contain marine fossils, however, and hence, while its geological horizon is the same as that of the Pennsylvania stratum, it evidently originated in fresh or brackish water.

Passing westward to Valley Falls, Taylor county, where the Chestnut ridge anticlinal elevates the strata to daylight, we get the following section in the steep bluffs on the south side of the Tygarts Valley river:

VALLEY FALLS, TAYLOR COUNTY, SECTION.

	Ft. In.	Ft. In.
Coal, Upper Freeport........................		3 0

		Ft.	In.		Ft.	In.
Concealed and shales.		60	0	}		
Sandstone		15	0	}	79	0
Blue shales		4	0	}		
Coal, Lower Freeport...	coal	0	3	}		
	slate, gray	0	6			
	coal	1	3			
	shale	2	11		7	8
	coal, bony, cannel	0	6			
	coal	0	8			
	gray shale	0	4			
	coal	1	3	}		
Dark shales		37	0	}		
Sandstone, Freeport		15	0	}	55	0
Shales, blue		3	0	}		
Coal, Upper Kittanning	coal	3	1	}		
	shale, gray	0	1		3	9
	coal, bony	0	7	}		
Shales, dark grayish		16	0			
Coal, Middle Kittanning		1	0			
Shales and flaggy sandstone		8	0	}		
Limestone, silicious		1	0			
Sandstone, flaggy		2	0	}	37	0
Shales, containing iron ore nodules		5	0			
Limestone, dark blue		1	0			
Shales		20	0	}		
Coal, Lower Kittanning	cannel slate	0	5	}		
	coal	1	9		5	0
	bone	0	1			
	coal	2	9	}		
Fireclay		5	0	}		
Sandstone, flaggy		5	0	}	45	0
Sandy shales and concealed		20	0			
Sandstone, hard, micaceous		15	0	}		
Coal, Clarion ..	coal	0	2	}		
	shale	0	10		1	2
	coal	0	2	}		
Shales and concealed		25	0			
Sandstone, massive		15	0			
Coal, Brookville ...	coal	1	7	}		
	slate	0	5		3	6
	coal	1	6	}		
Fireclay and gray shales		11	0			
Massive sandstone, top of Pottsville						
Total					308	1

It is barely possible that the coal identified in this section as the Lower Freeport bed, may prove to be the Upper Freeport, with the interval between it and the Lower Kittanning much reduced at this locality.

The writer formerly regarded the massive sandstone above the lowest coal in the Valley Falls section as the Homewood or Tionesta, and that may yet be the correct reference, but the coal under it would then be in the Mercer group. If, however, there be a Brookville coal in the Allegheny series, distinct from the Clarion, the coal under the massive sandstone, at the base of the section above, would represent that bed. It has some importance in the vicinity of Valley Falls, but its crop is near water level above the Falls, and the coal soon goes under the river on a rapid southeast dip.

Near Webster, Taylor county, on the Parkersburg branch of the B. & O. R. R., a diamond drill hole was recently put down to test the Allegheny series by Messrs. Wilgus and Grant, of Morgantown. The record of the strata passed through was carefully kept by Mr. Charles H. Washburn, of Webster, and is given herewith :

UNDER WEBSTER, TAYLOR COUNTY:

		Ft.	In.	Ft.	In.
Coal, Upper Freeport..	coal	0	1		
	black slate	0	2		
	coal	0	4	4	9
	gray shale	1	2		
	black slate	1	6		
	coal	1	6		
Dark slate and sandy shales		13	4		
Limestone, Upper Freeport		9	6		
Shale		10	0		
Black slate, thin seams of coal		2	0	44	0
Fireclay		2	4		
Shales, sandy		6	10		
Coal, Lower Freeport...	coal	0	2		
	black slate	1	2		
	bony coal	0	2	5	10
	coal	2	4		
	bony coal	0	4		
	coal	1	8		
Fireclay, hard				6	0
Shale, sandy, some limestone				4	0
Sandstone, hard, massive, light gray	27	4			
Sandstone or sandy shale, dark	12	0			
Sandstone, hard, base pebbly, coal streaks in center, base of Lower Freeport sandstone	39	0		78	4
Sandstone and sandy shale				31	10
Sandstone, hard, white, pebbly				60	0
Dark sandstone, with coal seams				3	0
Very hard conglomerate, Pottsville					
Total				237	9

This is a very curious section, as it reveals the complete absence of the entire Kittanning series of coals, unless thin streaks of coal in sandstones and conglomerates may be said to represent coal beds. This is a continuation of the boring, the Conemaugh part of which is given on page 232 of this volume. The drill passed on into the hard Pottsville conglomerate, at the base of the Allegheny for forty-seven feet, and was still in it when the hole was abandoned.

We are here approaching a region where the Kittanning group appears to be cut out occasionally by massive conglomeratic sandstones, which are difficult to distinguish from the Pottsville beds, even at the surface. They are very massive and pebbly, between Grafton and Philippi, especially in the region of Moatsville, where they make the falls and rapids in the bed of the Valley river, and crop along its bluffs, in great vertical cliffs so bold and pebbly, that the writer was once deceived into correlating them with the Pottsville series, instead of with the Upper and Lower Freeport sandstones of the Allegheny, to which they really belong, unless, indeed, it could be possible that the Allegheny beds could thin away and be crowded into an interval of less than 100 feet upon a great mass of Pottsville conglomerates. As already explained on page 297, the section given by the writer in Bulletin 65, U. S. G. survey, page 128, from Moatsville, Barbour county, is erroneous, if the Allegheny beds maintain their customary thickness along the Valley river.

In the region of Philippi, Barbour county, several holes have been bored for oil, and they all passed through the Allegheny series. Well No. 2 of the Tygarts Valley Mineral and Oil Company begins on top of the great Buffalo sandstone, which surrounds the town with its bold cliffs, 150 feet above water level, and the contractor reported for it the following record:

OIL WELL RECORD AT PHILIPPI.

	Ft.	Ft.
Surface	5	
Iron ore and hard limestone	5	
Very hard sandstone, Buffalo	30	100
Shale, blue, tough	60	
Coal, Mason		2
Fine grained sandstone	19	
Shale	59	
Coal, Mahoning	3	106
Shale	10	
Fine, hard sand	15	

Coal, Upper Freeport	4
Shale	20
Sandstone, hard, close...	45
Coal, Lower Freeport	7
Very hard sandstone	30
Shales	40
Hard sandstone...........	60
Slate..	5
Dark limestone?........	15
Shale	10

236

Hard sandstone, water, top of the *Pottsville*	
series...	25
Slate	5
Limestone (?) very hard	8
Slate rock 100	
Hard sandstone..	50
Slate and ''shells''	40
Hard sandstone.:..	20
Hard ''limestone''	18
Slate rock...	10
Hard, close sandstone, base of Pottsville	
series... 14	

290

Bright red shale, Mauch Chunk series.......................

The POTTSVILLE SERIES, below the ALLEGHENY, is given here to show the thickness of the same down to the undoubted MAUCH CHUNK beds.   The Bakerstown coal comes into the hills about forty feet above where the record begins, and then at 130 feet higher, in the midst of red shales, another coal bed, probably the FRIENDSVILLE, has been opened.

The MASON, MAHONING, and UPPER FREEPORT coal beds have all been mined along the Valley river, near Philippi, and the interval from the MASON to the UPPER FREEPORT found to be 115 feet by accurate measurements, hence the driller's record of 106 feet is not more in error than might have been expected.   The principal error of the record appears to be in the measurement of the interval between the MAHONING COAL and the UPPER FREEPORT.   This is given as only twenty-five feet, whereas, two or three accurate measurements at Philippi give it as forty feet.

The section is of interest as revealing a complete absence of the Kittanning group of coals, just as was shown in the diamond drill record at Webster, Taylor county, their horizons being occupied by massive sandstones.   The ''limestone'' of the driller's record may be only a hard, sandy stratum, or fine grained sandstone, and hence the base of the Pottsville series is supposed to extend down to where the ''bright red'' Mauch Chunk shale was struck.

About four miles northwest from Philippi another well was

drilled for oil on the Hall farm, and its record was kept with much care by Mr. C. McC. Lemley, Assistant Engineer of the B. & O. R. R. Company. The top or Conemaugh portion of this record is given on page 238 down to the Upper Freeport coal. The mouth of the well is near the crop of the Ames limestone, filled with its marine fossils, while the great Pittsburg coal is mined in the hills 300 feet higher, and hence the record of the boring, combined with the surface outcrops, gives a measurement of the entire Coal Measure column of the region. In the Hall well record the Pottsville series will also be included as in the previous section, as follows:

ELK CREEK OIL AND GAS COMPANY'S HALL WELL, FOUR MILES NORTHWEST OF PHILIPPI.

	Ft.	Ft.
Upper Freeport coal	3	
Limestone and sandstone.	15	
White slate...	30	
Black slate (Lower Freeport coal horizon)........	5	
White slate..	5	
White sandstone.........	52	
White slate..	25	
Limestone..	10	
Coal, Middle Kittanning?	5	285
Sandstone, dark	15	
Coal, Lower Kittanning?............................	5	
Sandstone, pebbly at base............................	56	
Brown shale	24	
Coal, Upper Clarion?	2	
White slate..	18	
Coal, Lower Clarion?	2	
White slate..	13	
Sandstone, dark, top of *Pottsville series*............	40	
Black Slate.....	35	
Coal (one of the Mercer group)......................	3	
Shale, brown	23	
Black "lime"..	20	
White sandstone..	25	256
Black slate	10	
White sandstone..	55	
Black slate	30	
White "lime"..	5	
Black slate, base of *Pottsville series*...............	10	
Red rock and lime, Mauch Chunk series.....................		

The total thickness of the Allegheny and Pottsville series in the Hall well foots up 541 feet, as against 506 feet for the same measures in the Philippi well, or a difference of only thirty-five feet.

It will also be noted that the Kittanning group of coals, as well as the Clarion, was noted in the record. An interrogation point has been placed after these members, since the identity in each case is uncertain.

Southeastward from Philippi there appears to be a great development of sandstone and conglomerate in the Allegheny series, as well as a thickening up of the same, and a decrease in the quantity of the coal usually found in the Kittanning group, as we learn from the records of borings made with the diamond drill in the Roaring creek basin of Randolph county.

The Upper Freeport coal bed is extensively mined in the western edge of Randolph county by the Junior Coal Company and others, between the mouth of Roaring creek and Belington, and especially along Beaver creek, where it crops 200 to 250 feet above the level of Valley river. The W. Va. C. & P. R. R. Company put down a diamond drill hole one mile north from the mouth of Beaver creek, in 1892, to test for coal below the Upper Freeport bed. The exposure between the mouth of the drill hole and the latter coal is complete, so that the following record, furnished by Mr. F. S. Landstreet, Vice President of the W. Va. C. R. R. Company, gives the structure of the rocks to a depth of 417 feet under the Upper Freeport, or "Roaring creek" seam, as it is locally termed:

DIAMOND DRILL HOLE ON COBERLY FARM, ONE MILE NORTH OF BEAVER CREEK, RANDOLPH COUNTY.

	Ft.	In.	Ft.	In
Upper Freeport coal. coal, slaty	1	6		
shales dark	2	0		
coal	2	8		
bony coal and slate	1	3		
coal	3	1	14	0
slate, gray	0	6		
coal	1	8		
slate	0	4		
coal, slaty	1	0		
Fireclay and sandy shales	10	0		
Gray sandstone	60	0		
Hard, dark sand rock	23	6		
Soft, brown sand rock	19	8		
Hard, coarse sand rock, with streaks of conglomerate	78	7		
Coarse, dark sand rock	5	2		
Soft fireclay	2	5		
Hard sandrock, light	6	8	292	4
Dark sandy slate	7	2		
Small pebbled conglomerate rock	15	3		
Soft, smooth blue clay	1	2		
Small pebbled conglomerate rock	26	3		
Light, soft fireclay	1	10		

Small pebbled conglomerate rock............	10	8		
Fine grain sand rock..............................	13	10		
Black slate................................	2	0		
Hard gray sand rock...........................	0	6		
Black slate...........................	1	8		
Dark sandy slate................................	6	0		
Coal, Lower Kittanning..			0	4
Black slate	1	0		
Dark gray shale	12	0		
Hard, dark sandstone, fine grain..............	1	2		
Hard gray sand rock...........................	37	5		
Dark sandy slate	1	10		
Dark sand rock............ ...	5	0		
Dark sandy slate ....·.·..	2	6	103	10
Gray sand rock	0	6		
Dark smooth slate.........................	4	4		
Black slate	2	0		
Dark, sandy slate..............................	22	11		
Fine gray sand rock	5	9		
Dark sandy slate	7	5		
Coal, Upper Clarion?....................................	1	2		
Dark sandy slate ....;........	11	11	15	1
Coal, Lower Clarion?............................	2	0		
Light smooth fireclay ....·............................·			3	3
Dark sand rock to bottom of boring			2	5
Total...			431	3

Here we get, immediately under the Upper Freeport coal, a great sandstone and conglomerate mass 282 feet thick, 187 feet of which is without any partings of shale or fireclay. It is this coarse conglomerate which makes the "falls" in Roaring creek and gives origin to the name of the stream. The entire mass represents the Upper and Lower Freeport sandstones of the Allegheny series.

A thin (4") streak of coal at 292 feet below the Upper Freeport bed, may represent either the Middle or Lower Kittanning, while the double bed at $396\frac{1}{2}$-$411\frac{1}{2}$ may represent the Upper and Lower Clarion beds. The section reveals the fact that unless the coal at $409\frac{1}{2}$ feet should thicken up into a merchantable one, there are no workable beds in the Allegheny series below the Upper Freeport.

The Junior Coal Company also bored a test hole for these lower coals opposite the mouth of Laurel run, and its results have been given the Survey through the courtesy of its president, Mr. John T. Davis, of Elkins. The Upper Freeport coal crops about 200 feet above the top of the boring, and connecting the surface rocks with the record of the well the following section results :

SECTION AND BORING OPPOSITE MOUTH OF LAUREL RUN, NEAR
THE RANDOLPH-BARBOUR COUNTY LINE.

	Ft. In.	Ft. In.
Upper Freeport coal, three partings........................		10 0
Concealed and massive sandstone to top of diamond drill hole 200 0		
Boulders and gravel................................. 12 2		
Gray sandstone...................................... 8 10		293 10
Sand, slate, fireclay, streaks, sandstone ... 24 8		
Gray sandstone 25 5		
Sandstone and sand slate, mixed.............. 22 9		
Coal, Lower Kittanning............................		1 2
Sand slate, fireclay and sandstone streaks 29 1		
Sandstone and sand slate, mixed.............. 18 0		
Gray sandstone.................................... 7 4		
Black slate 8 9		94 11
Sand slate.. 5 3		
Gray sandstone 11 5		
Sand slate and sandstone, mixed.............. 15 1		
		399 11
Gray sandstone; top of Pottsville series 141 11		
Coal 0 6		
Gray sandstone, pea conglomerate, mixed 2 10		10 9
Sand slate, little streaks of sandstone...... 5 1		
Coal, little sulphur mixed...................... 2 4		
Fireclay and sandstone........................... 9 4		
Gray sandstone..................................... 24 5		62 9
Gray sandstone, little streaks of slate and conglomerate, mixed........................ 29 0		
Total...		615 4

The coal struck at 294 feet below the Upper Freeport bed in
this bore hole, appears to be the same as the one at 292 feet in the
previous section, but the double bed, 103 feet below, has no representation whatever in the Laurel run section, which foots up 398
feet as the thickness of the Allegheny series down to the top of
the great (142 feet) sandstone mass beginning at that depth.

This is the region where both the Allegheny and Pottsville series begin that wonderful expansion toward the southwest, which
quadruples both at the Kanawha and New rivers over their average
thickness near the northern line of the state.

This thickening is first clearly visible in the surface outcrops
at the head of the Buckhannon river between Newlon and Pickens,
where we first recognize the Allegheny-Kanawha series and find
nearly 600 feet of measures between the unmistakable UPPER
FREEPORT COAL BED at the top and the undoubted POTTSVILLE at the
base.

No complete exposures between the Upper Freeport coal and

the top of the massive Pottsville beds below, has been obtained at the head of the Buckhannon, since where the Pottsville comes above river level below Pickens, the crop of the Upper Freeport bed is thrown out of the tops of the hills, and the dip being 200 to 300 feet to the mile, renders an accurate vertical section impossible. The Upper Freeport bed is caught in the summit of Turkey Bone mountain, south from Pickens, and in other high points west from the Buckhannon river, so that the following is an approximate section of the region around Pickens:

		Ft. In.	Ft. In.
Upper Freeport coal, blossom large.......................			
Concealed, with very massive sandstone...................			150 0
Coal... { coal, good..............................	1 0		
{ shale.................................	0 6	}	1 9
{ coal, bony..............................	0 3		
Shales and sandstones, with several thin coals			300 0
Coal			2 0
Shales................................			25 0
{ coal	1 9		
Coal, Pickens.. { slate	0 1	}	3 0
{ coal	1 2		
Concealed, sandstone and shales with another coal bed ("Gimmel") near base, to top of the Pottsville series...			100 0
Total......			581 9

The Pickens coal of this section has been mined for local use around the village of that name by James Pickens, James Thomas and others. It correlates with the Campbell's creek bed of the Kanawha series, which, on the theory of the latter being the expanded Allegheny, would represent the Lower Kittanning coal of the latter.

The "Gimmel" coal has been mined in the bed of the Buckhannon river, three miles below Pickens, and is three and one-half feet thick with a streak of bone near the center. It is a coarse-grained, blocky coal, and lies only about ten feet above the top of the Pottsville series.

The Upper Freeport coal bed has a great development from Roaring creek, on the Valley river, across to the Buckhannon, and from there to the head of the Little Kanawha. Being several feet in thickness, including its parting slates and other impurities, it is readily traced and identified from one point to another.

On the left bank of the Little Kanawha river, above the

mouth of Glady creek, the following section was observed in descending from the W. T. Wilson coal bank :

MOUTH OF GLADY CREEK, LEWIS COUNTY.

		Ft.	In.	Ft.	In.
	coal, soft, some bone	5	o		
	shale	1	o		
	coal	o	7		
	bone	o	4		
Upper Freeport coal	slate	o	9	12	9
	coal	2	6		
	slate	o	7		
	coal, hard	1	6		
	coal, soft	o	6		
Sandstone and concealed..........................				125	o
Coal, blossom					
Concealed				80	o
Coal, blossom					
Concealed and sandstone..........................				175	o
Coal, blossom...............................					
Sandstone				20	o
Shales to level of Little Kanawha river....				25	o
Interval to top of Pottsville in borings for oil with a thick (7-10 feet) coal bed reported 20 feet above base...				65	o
Total..502				502	9

In the region of Little Wild Cat, and the mouth of Glady creek, along the Left Fork of the Little Kanawha, several wells have been sunk for oil, and most of them are reported to pass through a thick bed of coal a few feet below water level, and its horizon is indicated near the base of the section given above. It is possibly the same as the "Gimmel" bed of the Pickens section.

The Upper Freeport bed is easily traced from the Little Kanawha across the divide to the head of Holly river, where it keeps well up in the summits along that stream to its mouth at Palmer.

In descending the left bank of Holly at Allen Anderson's mill, two miles below Hacker's Valley P. O., Webster county, the following section is visible:

SECTION OF ALLEGHENY-KANAWHA SERIES AT ALLEN ANDERSON'S MILL, HOLLY RIVER, WEBSTER COUNTY.

		Ft.	In.	Ft.	In.
	coal, splinty............	3	2		
	slate, dark	o	4		
Upper Freeport coal	coal, soft...............	1	4	6	10
	bony coal	o	4		
	coal, soft................	1	8		

Concealed and sandstone 120 0
Coal, visible ....: 0 6
Concealed 110 0
Coal, blossom..............................,...................................
Concealed 150 0
Massive sandstone 25 0
Concealed 10 0
Coal, blossom............................. ....
Concealed 85 0
Massive, grayish white sandstone 20 0
Black slate 0 6

Coal .. { coal, hard, coarse...... .... 2 0 }
         { slate and bony coal .... 0 6 } 4 0
         { coal .... 1 6 }

Interval below Hollow river to top of Pottsville se-
    series, about..30 0

    Total...561 10

    The coal near the base of the section is mined at many points along Holly river between its head waters and the Forks of Holly above Palmer. It appears to be the first bed of merchantable coal above the top of the Pottsville series, and is possibly identical with the Eagle coal of the Kanawha valley.

    The thick coal at the top of this section can be followed down to the mouth of Holly river, at Palmer, where it is 300 feet above water level and ten feet thick, with two to three feet of sandy shale and rock in its middle. It and the coal near the base of the Allegheny-Kanawha series, appear to be the only ones of workable thickness along the Left Fork of Holly river.

    The same Upper Freeport coal can be followed up Elk river from Palmer until it over-shoots the tops of the mountains, five miles below Webster Springs, where nearly all of the Pottsville has risen above the surface.

    The following measurement of the Allegheny-Kanawha series and Pottsville beds was made from the summit of the mountain at the head of Cold Spring hollow, which puts into the left bank of Elk river one-fourth mile above the mouth of Big run, six miles below Webster Springs, Webster county:

COLD SPRING HOLLOW SECTION, SIX MILES BELOW
WEBSTER SPRINGS.

                             Ft. In.   Ft. In.

Upper Freeport coal { cannel, impure ...... 2 0 }
                     { coal .... 1 2 } 5 11
                     { slate, gray.............. 0 3 }
                     { coal .... 2 6 }

```
Concealed ................................................................ 30   0
Sandstone, massive and concealed............................150   0
Concealed ............................................................170   0
Sandstone, massive.................. ......................... 25   0
Dark shales and concealed............. .................. ...... 85   0
Coal, blossom ...... ...........................
Shales and concealed........................................ 100   0
         ( coal ...................................... 0  11  )
Coal ..{ bone ...................... .................... 0   2½ }  1   9½
         ( coal ...................................... 0   8   )
Shales and concealed to top of Pottsville series......... 40   0
                                                        ─────────
         Total............................... ................607   8½
Pottsville conglomerates, with several thin coal beds
   to Mauch Chunk red shale.....................................700   0
```

The coal near the base of the Allegheny-Kanawha series is most probably the one seen along Holly river near the water level for several miles.

The MAUCH CHUNK RED BEDS come out of Elk river a few hundred yards above the line of section, thus bringing the entire Pottsville series above water level in the same section with the Allegheny-Kanawha series.   There are four or five coal beds in the Pottsville here, none of which appear to be more than two and one half feet thick, but they are of the soft, coking, or New River type, and at Webster Springs, six miles southeast, one of them attains a thickness of five feet.

It is interesting to observe that as we pass southwest from the northern portion of the state, both the Allegheny and Pottsville series thicken at nearly the same rate.

Passing southwest over to the waters of Laurel creek, we find the Upper Freeport coal ranging along under the summits of the highest peaks, protected by the great overlying Mahoning sand-stone series.   Here, in the vicinity of Weese station, twelve miles above the mouth of Laurel creek, the following section is exposed:

```
                                                        Ft.   Ft.
Coal, Upper Freeport, large blossom ........................... 5
Concealed ........................................... 10  }
Massive sandstone......................... .................. 90  } 100
Coal, blossom.....................................................
Sandstone .............................................110  }
Dark slate................... ............... ................. 5  } 285
Concealed ........................................170  }
Black slate, with coal blossom ............................ .........
Concealed ...................................... 10  }
Massive sandstone, visible........................... ......... 30  } 70
Concealed ...................................... ................ 30  }
```

Coal 2
Blue shales.. 15 } 25
Concealed 10

Campbells creek coal { coal ...... 2′ 5′
slate...... 0 1
coal ...... 0 6 } ....

Concealed 100

Eagle coal { coal ...... 1′ 2″
slate...... 0 1
coal ..... 0 9 } 2

Shales and concealed to top of Pottsville......... 25

Total................... 617

This is practically a vertical measurement, and as the Pottsville conglomerate series forms bold cliffs at the base for 75 to 100 feet above the bed of Laurel creek, there can be no doubt about either the top or bottom of the Allegheny-Kanawha series in this section.

We are here approaching the region in which the coal bed termed the Campbells creek can . be traced continually across to Gauley river, and down the tributaries of the same through Webster, Nicholas, and Fayette counties to the Great Kanawha river, where it merges into the "No. 2 Gas," or lower bench of the Campbells creek bed.

Likewise the Upper Freeport coal, at the top of the section, can be followed across to the Gauley river waters, and down to the Kanawha, keeping high in the summits of the ridges, crowned and preserved by the Mahoning sandstone series above, until it passes into the STOCKTON CANNEL BED, just under the famous KANAWHA BLACK FLINT.

Where this coal emerges to daylight on the Gauley river side, at the head of Stroud creek, five miles north from Camden-on-Gauley, it exhibits the following structure on the land of William Hayhurst:

	Ft. In.	Ft. In.
Cannel, impure, slaty	2 0	
Coal, soft..	2 3	8 2
Shale, gray......	0 5	
Coal, splint..	3 6	
Dark slate, floor		

There is probably another division of the coal not exposed under the dark slate at the bottom.

The same impure layer of cannel shown here was also observed in the sections on Laurel and Elk.

Cottle Knob is a conspicuous point five miles below Camden-on-Gauley, which rises almost sheer from the broad plain along its base to a height of 1100 feet above the level of Gauley river, or about 900 feet above the terrace of the Pottsville beds at its base. The summit is capped by great cliffs of the Mahoning sandstone, and the entire Allegheny-Kanawha series is found in its steep slopes facing Gauley river. The Upper Freeport coal bed is not exposed, but its place is closely defined by the great Mahoning cliffs above, and a prominent bluff just below its "bench" or line of crop. The following measurements were made here in descending Cottle Knob to the southeast:

SECTION IN COTTLE KNOB, WEBSTER COUNTY.

	Ft. In.	Ft. In.
Massive Mahoning sandstone in three ledges, for 200 feet from summit of Cottle Knob to horizon of *Upper Freeport coal* bench......		
Concealed and massive sandstones 255		0
Coal .. { coal .... 0 8 / slaty coal .... 0 3 / coal .... 0 8 / bone................. .... 0 2 / coal .... 1 3 }		3 0
Concealed and sandstone with two or three thin coals	300	0
Sandstone, massive and concealed	30	0
Coal, Campbells creek, 4 to 6 inches of slate near the middle..............................	3	6
Concealed	20	0
Coal	1	0
Concealed (estimated) to top of Pottsville	50	0
Total... 662		6

The concealed interval at the base of the section is an estimate only, since a wide plain, a mile or more in width, extends from the crop of the lowest coal bed at the foot of the steep slopes southeastward to the Gauley river. This plain is underlain by the Pottsville series, the bold crop of which makes great cliffs along the immediate banks of Gauley, but the massive beds at its top dip northwest under the plain toward the base of Cottle Knob and are concealed by a thick covering of debris, so that the interval between the Pottsville and the small coal, where the steep slopes of the mountain begin, could not be measured. This interval, however, cannot be less than the fifty feet given, and may possibly be fifty feet more. The section reveals the gradual expansion of the Allegheny-Kanawha series southwestward toward the Kanawha river, since at the mouth of Gauley, forty miles distant, the series is 1000 feet thick.

The three and one-half feet of coal seventy-one feet above the base of the series is identical with the Campbells creek bed of the Kanawha series, since from this point it can be traced continuously southwestward to Summersville in Nicholas county, and thence in a constant line of workings down Peter's creek, Bell creek, and Gauley to the Kanawha river. Both it and the coal 330 feet above have been mined in Cottle Knob by Mr. John Woods, though the lower one is not now operated. The upper one comes near the horizon of the Winifrede coal, and may be identical with that bed.

The Upper Freeport coal just misses the top of the high knob called Summersville mountain, at Summersville, or Nicholas Court House, while the Campbells creek coal is mined at many localities around the base of the mountain, and about 600 feet below the summit.

At Gilboa, on Peter's creek, six and one-half miles below Summersville, the following section is seen in descending the high mountain, along the new road, which crosses to Twenty-Mile creek:

GILBOA, NICHOLAS COUNTY.

	Ft. In.	Ft. In.
Upper Freeport coal, large blossom under 150 feet of massive Mahoning sandstone		
Concealed and massive sandstone	70 0	
Coal, blossom		
Concealed	60 0	
Coal, blossom		
Concealed	30 0	
Coal, blossom		
Concealed and massive sandstone	90 0	
Coal, blossom		
Concealed	90 0	
Cannel coal and black slate...................................	3 0	
Concealed and massive sandstone	100 0	
Concealed	75 0	
Shales, gray	15 0	
Sandstone, flaggy..	10 0	
Shale, blue	2 0	
Coal, Campbells creek.. { coal ....)......... 1 0 / slate .... 0 4 / coal .... 2 0 / splint .... 0 2 }		3 6
Concealed to top of Pottsville series..........................	120 0	
Total...		668 6

The great pebbly cliffs of both the Upper and Lower Mahoning sandstones, with the Mahoning coal showing between them, here crown the summit of the mountain. Just under the lower one and at the roadside, an uprooted tree exposes a very thick, rotten outcrop of coal, which is the Upper Freeport bed. The other outcrops of coal are exposed in cuttings along the road, and their thickness can only be surmised.

The Campbells creek coal, at the bottom, is mined for local supply on the land of Curtis Stevenson, where it exhibits the structure indicated.

This is a very important section, since it reveals the Allegheny Kanawha series with nearly its typical thickness between its top and the important Campbells creek coal, so that the main expansion from here to the Kanawha river takes place between the Campbells creek bed and the top of the Pottsville. Then, too, only two miles west from this, the KANAWHA BLACK FLINT comes into the section, high up in the mountain, just over the great coal bed at the top, which, with its overlying sandstone mass, has been followed from Sago, on the Buckhannon river, in a practically continuous outcrop of thick coal, to this point, where it crowns the summit of the Kanawha series, below which is at least 1000 feet of Pottsville sediments.

Mr. James Livesay, of Zela, Nicholas county, reports the KANAWHA BLACK FLINT, and its underlying coal, high up in the hills on the waters of Twenty Mile creek, only two miles west from where this section begins, and showing the following succession:

				Ft. In.	Ft. In.
Kanawha black flint				8 0	
Shales				10 0	
Coal, Upper Freeport	coal, slaty	5 0			15 4
	shale	4 0			
	coal, "splint"	2 4			
	slate	2 0			
	coal, "splint"	2 0			

This same thick coal, with much slate and other impurities, can be followed into the summits of the hills along Peter's creek and Twenty Mile, down to the mouth of the latter and on to the Great Kanawha, where, at the mouth of Armstrong creek, the following succession was once measured by the writer:

MOUTH OF ARMSTRONG CREEK, FAYETTE COUNTY.

		Ft. In.	Ft. In.
Sandstone, massive, Upper Mahoning.....................		80 0	
Shales..		10 0	
Coal, Mahoning, ("No. 5, Block").. { coal .... 1 8 / bone.................... 0 2 / "block"................ 3 6 }			5 4
Concealed.............			5 0
Sandstone, massive, Lower Mahoning..			65 0
Concealed............			5 0
Kanawha black flint			10 0
Shales and concealed to base of Conemaugh series.....			12 0
Coal, Upper Freeport..............			3 0
Sandstone and concealed 170 0			
Sandstone, massive....................... 60 0			
Concealed and sandstone....... ....115 0			372 0
Limestone, silicious.................... 2 0			
Sandstone, massive, gray................... 25 0			
Coal, Cedar Grove { coal .... 0 6 / shale .... 0 8 / coal ...,......... 0 5 / shale .... 0 6 / coal .... 0 4 }			2 5
Fireclay and concealed........................... 5 0			
Sandstone, massive............. .... 20 0			
Shales, concealed, and sandstone 20 0			
Concealed 20 0			
Sandstone and shales.......................... 20 0			165 0
Sandstone, massive.. .... 25 0			
Shales and concealed...................... 20 0			
Sandstone................................ 25 0			
Sandy shales..................................... 10 0			
Coal, local { coal............................... 1 1 / shale .... 0 1 / coal .... 0 6 }			1 8
Shales, sandy			12 0
Coal, Campbells creek { coal, "Peerless" .... 2 0 / shales, bluish.............. 15 0 / coal, sulphurous .. 0 5 / slate .... 0 0½ / coal .... 0 6 / coal, splint .... 0 11 / parting....................... 0 0¼ / coal .... 0 7 / slate .... 0 0¼ / coal .... 2 10 }			22 4
Fireclay......			5 0
Shales and sandstone...			35 0
Coal .. { coal......... .... 1 0 / shale .... 2 6 / coal.................. .. .. 0 10 }			4 4
Shales and sandstone............................			15 0
Coal			1 2
Concealed and sandy shales 40 0			
Limestone, silicious 1 0			51 0
Shales........ .... 10 0			
Coal, local { coal......... .... 0 8 / shales .... 1 4 / coal, slaty .... 0 6 }			2 6

Sandy shales................................			20	0
Coal, Eagle { coal	0	2		
shales	0	8	3	8
coal	2	10		
Shales and sandy beds			20	0
Coal, Little Eagle............................			1	6
Fireclay and shales............................	5	0		
Sandstone, massive	10	0	55	0
Shales, sandy	40	0		
Limestone, fossiliferous, Eagle...............			1	0
Dark shales, fossiliferous	5	0	80	0
Shales, sandstone and concealed............	75	0		
Bituminous shale			2	0
Shales	30	0		
Limestone, silicious..............	1	0	131	0
Shales, sandstone and concealed............	100	0		
Mussive sandstone, top of Pottsville series............				

Total of Allegheny-Kanawha series........ 1006   7

Here the Allegheny-Kanawha series has thickened up to more than 1000 feet, and contains an immense amount of massive sandstone, just under the Upper Freeport coal.

Cannelton, on the north bank of the Great Kanawha river, is a classic locality for the study of the Kanawha coals, and a section which the writer once measured there, reads as follows, beginning in the Conemaugh series :

CANNELTON SECTION.

	Ft.	In.	Ft.	In.
Massive, pebbly sandstone, and concealed 200				0
Coal, "No. 5 Block" (Mahoning) in several divisions 6				6
Concealed and massive sandstone ....· 75				0
Kanawha black flint ....···· 7				0
Shales........ 15				0
Coal, Stockton Cannel, { coal	0	5		
Upper Freeport slate	0	2	5	0
coal	1	8		
cannel	2	9		
Shales........			15	0
Coal, several partings			6	0
Sandstone and concealed............ 500				0
Coal, Campbell's creek			5	0
Concealed and shale			75	0
Silicious limestone, cement rock			2	6
Shales and concealed............................			35	0
Coal, Eagle			2	6
Concealed to level of Great Kanawha......			10	0
Interval to top of Pottsville, estimated 250				0

Thickness of Allegheny-Kanawha series............906   0

The portion of this section, below water level, is only an estimate, based upon the known thickness of the rocks between the

Eagle coal and the top of the Pottsville a few miles farther to the south.

One more section of the Allegheny-Kanawha series on the Great Kanawha river will be given from the Wyoming Coal Company's mines, near Handley, Fayette county, in order to show the relation of the several beds, in the upper portion of the series, to each other, and to the KANAWHA BLACK FLINT, as follows:

ALLEGHENY-KANAWHA SERIES NEAR HANDLEY.

		Ft. In.	Ft. In.
Kanawha black flint...			5 0
Shales and concealed..			25 0
Coal, Stockton, Upper Freeport	coal, "splint" 2 0		
	coal, soft........... 0 4		
	coal, slaty 1 0		
	coal, "splint" 1 4		
	coal and slate...... 4 2½	12 1	
	slate................. 0 9		
	coal, "splint" 0 9½		
	slaty coal............ 0 1		
	coal, soft.............. 1 7		
Concealed			30 0
Coal, Coalburg	coal, "splint"................. 0 10		
	"niggerhead"................. 0 3	4 0	
	coal, "splint"................. 3 9.		
Concealed and massive sandstone			53 6
Coal, local	coal 0 6		
	rock 0 6	1 6	
	coal 0 6		
Shale and sandstone			20 0
Coal, Winifrede	coal, "splinty" 3 6		
	slate 0 2		
	coal 0 6	5 3	
	dark rock.................. 0 4		
	coal 0 9		
Concealed			370 0
Coal, Peerless..			2 0
Concealed			25 0
Coal, Campbells creek, "*No. 2 Gas*"....................			4 0
Concealed to Kanawha river.....................................			85 0
Interval to *Eagle seam*..			25 0
Interval to Pottsville, estimated			250 0
Total..			917 4

Only one other important coal bed of the Kanawha region is not shown in this section, and that is the CEDAR GROVE BED, which belongs about 120 feet above the PEERLESS BED in the concealed interval of 370 feet.

The Peerless seam is simply the upper bench of the Campbell's creek bed, which separates from the lower, or Blacksburg member, the "No. 2 Gas," in coming southward up the Kanawha river.

The KANAWHA BLACK FLINT and the twenty-five feet of shales below it, at the top of this section, belong in the Conemaugh series and, of course, should be deducted from the Allegheny-Kanawha series in estimating the thickness of these measures.

Guyandot mountain is a high, broad ridge, extending around the heads of Big and Little Coal rivers, through Raleigh and Wyoming counties. Several years ago Captain M. A. Miller, Chief Engineer for the Trans-Flat Top Land Association, made a section from the top of Guyandot mountain eastward, along the Oceana pike to the Marsh Fork of Big Coal river, which exhibits the following succession:

GUYANDOT MOUNTAIN, RALEIGH COUNTY.

		Ft.	In.	Ft.	In.
Coal, Upper Freeport, not seen					
Sandstone, massive,				83	0
Shales				15	0
Coal, Coalburg	coal	3	10		
	slate	0	1	4	8
	coal	0	9		
Shales				43	0
Coal				2	5
Shales				12	2
Coal, Winifrede	coal	1	3		
	slate	0	2		
	coal	2	3	3	10
	slate	0	1		
	coal	0	1		
Sandstone, hard, gray		28	0		
Shale		81	0		
Sandstone		8	0		
Shale		14	0	247	0
Sandstone, hard, gray		53	0		
Shale		32	0		
Sandstone		24	0		
Shale, yellowish		7	0		
Coal, Cedar Grove ?	coal	0	7		
	slate	0	1		
	coal	0	9		
	slate	0	0½	4	0
	coal	1	1		
	slate	0	4		
	coal	1	1½		
Sandstone, soft, yellow		19	0		
Coal		0	1	56	3
Fireclay		1	2		
Shales, yellowish		36	0		
Coal	coal	0	1		
	fireclay	2	0	3	2
	coal	1	1		

Fireclay	o	6	}	
Sandstone, soft, yellow......................15		o		
Sandstone, hard, gray.............. 22		o	} 125	
Sandstone, soft, yellow, micaceous...........21		o		
Shales, yellowish 67		o	)	
Coal.......			o	2
Fireclay	1	4	}	
Slate, black.......................................16		o		
Sandstone, soft, yellow......................35		o	} 91 4	
Shales, yellow 39		o	)	

	coal	1	3	⌐	
	slate	4	o		
	fireclay	2	o		
	coal	o	1		
Coal, Eagle..	clay	o	3	} 9 8	
	coal	o	9		
	clay	o	2		
	coal	o	1		
	clay	1	o		
	coal	o	1	⌐	

Sandstone, hard, gray......................13		o	} 46 o	
Sandstone, soft, yellow......................33		o		
Coal, Little Eagle			o	3
Fireclay	1	o	}	
Shales, sandy, yellow....................	46	o		
Sandstone, soft, yellow.....................	70	o	} 208 o	
Shales, sandy, yellowish...........................	58	o		
Sandstone, flaggy	7	o		
Shales, yellow, to top of Pottsville series ..	26	o	)	

Total		955	5

The two highest coals appear to be the COALBURG AND WINI-
FREDE, respectively, but the identity of the ones between the WIN-
IFREDE and EAGLE beds is a matter of conjecture.

Practically, this same thickness of Allegheny-Kanawha deposits extends across Wyoming and McDowell counties to the Tug
Fork of Big Sandy at the Kentucky line.

No mining operations have been undertaken, however, on the
Upper coals of the series until we come to the Norfolk & Western
railroad along Tug river.

In recent years a valuable coal bed, known as the THACKER
VEIN has been extensively mined in southern Mingo county, re-
ceiving its local name from the town of Thacker, near which it
was first opened.

The Grapevine Coal Company has mines in this bed, high up
in the hills between Thacker and Delorme, and in descending
from the mines to Tug river, we get the following section :

SECTION BETWEEN THACKER AND DELORME, MINGO COUNTY.

			Ft. In.	Ft. In.
Sandstone, massive				
Slate				4 0
Coal, Thacker	coal, soft	3 0		
	"splint" coal...................	2 6		
	coal, softer.....................	1 8		
	fireclay	0 4		
	coal	0 7		
	fireclay	0 11		12 2
	coal	0 2		
	bone................................	0 2		
	coal, soft......	1 4		
	slate, gray	0 2		
	coal, soft........................	1 4		
Concealed				5 0
Sandstone, massive...				65 0
Coal, reported				5 0
Concealed				25 0
Sandstone, massive...				200 0
Concealed and sandstone, with some thin coals, to level of Tug river...				385 0
Total...				701 2

There has been much speculation as to the geological horizon of this Thacker coal bed. There must be at least 300 feet of measures below water level here, down to the top of the Pottsville, which would put it near the summit of the Kanawha series, so that it would be either the Stockton or Coalburg seam, most probably the former, since its great thickness and multiple character resembles the structure of the Stockton or Upper Freeport coal in the Handley section on the Great Kanawha river, page 373, above.

This same coal has been mined high up in the hills near Naugatuck by Dr. Waldron, where we get the following section in descending from the summits to Pigeon creek:

SECTION NEAR MOUTH OF PIGEON CREEK,
MINGO COUNTY.

	Ft. In.	Ft. In.
Mostly sandstone, coarse, massive............................		120 0
Concealed and massive sandstone		40 0
Shales		10 0
Coal, No. 5 Block (Mahoning)		4 0
Concealed and massive sandstone		100 0
Slate		0 2

		Ft.	In.	Ft.	In.
Thacker coal *Stockton* *Upper Freeport*	coal, "splint"	2	0		
	slate	0	0½		
	coal	0	4		
	gray slate.........	0	2½	8	6
	coal	I	0		
	"splint," bony at top.	2	0		
	dark slate..................	I	8		
	coal, softer..............	I	3		

Concealed and sandstones ....230　0

Coal, Winifrede ..	coal	0	8		
	slate	0	I		
	coal	I	2	3	6
	bone........................	0	I		
	coal	I	6		

Concealed .... 70　0
Sandstone, massive .... 65　0
Coal, "splint," one inch of bone below center........... 1　9
Sandy shales................ .... 20　0
Coal.. 0　6
Shale .... 5　0
Sandstone and concealed to bed of Pigeon creek...... 40　0

Total of Allegheny-Kanawha series................444　3

It cannot be less than 300 feet under Tug river down to the top of the Pottsville, thus making the Allegheny-Kanawha series about 750 feet thick at this locality.

About eight miles south of Naugatuck, a long section, which takes in the lower half of the Conemaugh series, was obtained in descending from the summit of a high knob, about one mile above Nolan, Mingo county, where the Hatfield Colliery Company has its mines. The section there, between the summit of the mountain and Tug river, is as follows:

ONE MILE ABOVE NOLAN, MINGO COUNTY.

		Ft.	In.	Ft.	In.
Sandstone, massive, very little shale				90	0
Reddish, limy shales				30	0
Sandstone, very massive, pebbly				45	0
Concealed and shales......................................				35	0
Sandstone, massive, pebbly..................................				90	0
Sandy shales..				0	6
Coal, Mason	coal	0	5		
	shale gray....................	0	4	2	1
	coal, good	I	4		
Concealed and massive coarse sandstone..................				60	0
Coal, *"No. 5 Block"*	soft, slaty coal	0	5		
	"splint" coal................	I	3	3	11
	bone	0	2		
	"splint" coal	2	I		
Fireclay, ...				5	0
Mostly very massive coarse sandstone, with a "bench" and concealed near middle..............................150 0					

		Ft.	In.	Ft.	In.
Coal, Stockton	coal, "splint"..............	1	0	2	0
	slate, dark.....................	0	4		
	coal, "splint"..	0	8		
Concealed				100	0
Coal blossom,...					
Concealed..				150	0
Coal, Winifrede	coal, "splint"	0	8	4	0
	gray slate	0	3		
	coal, "splint"	1	8		
	coal, softer...............	0	8		
	slate, dark	0	1		
	coal, "splint"	0	6		
	clay	0	1		
	coal, soft..................	0	1		
Concealed				160	0
Coal				2	6
Concealed to Tug river.........				50	0
Total..				980	0

This looks like the same succession as that observed in the previous section near Naugatuck, at the mouth of Pigeon creek, seven miles below, except that the STOCKTON COAL is not fully exposed, and may have thinned very much also. If we regard this bed as the STOCKTON SEAM there will be 466½ feet of the Allegheny-Kanawha series above water level here, and 511½ of the Conemaugh beds, while at least 300 feet more of the Kanawha series would extend below water level down to the top of the Pottsville beds.

In the region of Dingess, near the northern line of Wayne county, we get a complete measurement of the Allegheny-Kanawha series by combining the surface measurements with the record of a gas well, bored there by Guffey and Queen, which gives the following succession:

DINGESS, MINGO COUNTY.

		Ft.	In.	Ft.	In.
Massive sandstone					
Coal, Stockton Upper Freeport	coal	1	6	8	1
	fireclay	1	10		
	black slate................	0	2		
	fireclay	0	5		
	coal	1	6		
	bone..................	0	5		
	coal	2	3		
Concealed and sandstone				140	0
Coal, visible, *Winifrede?*..				1	0
Concealed and sandstone				195	0

		Ft.	In.	Ft.	In.
Coal, Cedar Grove?	coal	I	2		
	gray shale	o	4		
	coal	o	5		I
	dark slate	o	2		
	coal	I	o		
Sandstone, massive				40	o
Coal				o	10
Shales, dark		10	o		
Sandstone, massive		25	o		
Shales, dark		30	o	100	o
Sandstone, massive		25	o		
Shales, gray		10	o		
Dingess coal	coal	I	3		
Campbells creek	dark slate	o	I		
	coal	2	o	4	8
	bone	o	I		
	coal	I	3		
White sand (gas well record)		15	o		
Slate, black		10	o	71	o
Sand, white		46	o		
Coal				I	o
Slate, sandy		78	o		
Slate, black		80	o	233	o
Sand, white		10	o		
Slate, white, to top of Pottsville		65	o		
Total				797	8

There can be little doubt that the big bed at the top is the STOCKTON or UPPER FREEPORT, while the DINGESS COAL is the CAMPBELLS CREEK bed, and the same as the one mined at Warfield, Kentucky, along Tug river, a few miles distant.

In the gas well record at Dingess, we get 1021 feet of POTTS-VILLE SEDIMENTS before reaching the MAUCH CHUNK RED SHALE at its base.

In passing northwest from the region of Dingess, the Allegheny-Kanawha series dips under the waters of Twelve Pole river, within a few miles, and at the same time thins rapidly down to its normal thickness at the northern end of the state, since, when the series comes up again near Ironton, Ohio, just below the southwestern corner of West Virginia, and fifty miles distant from Dingess, the following section of typical Allegheny beds is exposed. See Bulletin 65, U. S. G. Survey, page 135:

SECTION, NEAR IRONTON, OHIO.

	Ft.	In.	Ft.	In.
Coal, Upper Freeport			2	o
Shale and sandy beds			50	o
Lower Freeport coal			3	o
Massive sandstone	40	o	45	o
Shale	5	o		

		Ft. In.	Ft. In.

Middle Kittanning coal
{
coal 1 0
fireclay.............. 1 0
coal .... 1 0 } 7 0
fireclay.............. 2 0
coal 2 0
}

Fireclay.. 5 0 } 45 0
Sandstone, massive 40 0
Lower Kittanning coal... .... 2 6
Shales and fireclay 25 0
Limestone, Ferriferous, (Vanport) ....•......... 5 0
Fireclay and shales.. 10 0
Coal, Clarion.. 1 0
Shales and concealed........................... .... 40 0
Massive sandstone, top of Pottsville.....................

Total 235 6

Above these beds come the typical Conemaugh series, and below them 250 feet of Pottsville carries the section down to the Mauch chunk shale, or Greenbrier limestone, so that the 1728 feet of Coal Measures (including the Pottsville) at Dingess, dwindle to less than 500 feet near Ironton, only 50 miles distant.

Passing now to the extreme northern point of West Virginia, at the mouth of Little Beaver river, we find the Allegheny series exhibiting the following structure near the corner of West Virginia, Pennsylvania, and Ohio:

MOUTH OF LITTLE BEAVER RIVER AT NORTHERN LINE OF HANCOCK COUNTY.

	Ft. In.	Ft. In.

Upper Freeport coal 3 0
Sandy shales.. 50 0
Lower Freeport coal.................... .... 2 0
Sandy shales 20 0)
Sandstone, massive ....50 0 } 105 0
Sandy shales 35 0)
Middle Kittanning coal..................................... 2 0
Fireclay .... 5 0 } 20 0
Shales, containing nodules of iron ore 15 0
Lower Kittanning coal.. 2 6
Fireclay, Lower Kittanning ....10 0 } 60 0
Sandy shales and shaly sandstone............50 0
Limestone, Ferriferous, Vanport............................. 1 0
Sandy shales.. 8 0
Bituminous shale, Clarion coal 5 0
Shale, sandy.. .. 15 0
Massive sandstone, top of Pottsville.....................

Total..273 6

As will be observed, except for a slight expansion in thickness, this section is nearly an exact duplicate of the previous one near Ironton, 250 miles distant, and is in remarkable contrast with the change that takes place in the structure of the series in the fifty miles, only, between Ironton and Dingess, when passing in a southeastern direction across the southern portion of the Appalachian coal field.

Practically the same structure as that found at the mouth of the Little Beaver occurs at New Cumberland, Hancock county, where the Allegheny series is all exposed in the Ohio river hills except its basal portion, which is largely concealed under the covering of gravel and debris along the valley floor. The following measurements at New Cumberland give an idea of the structure of the series there:

NEW CUMBERLAND, HANCOCK COUNTY.

	Ft. In.	Ft. In.
Upper Freeport coal, not present......................................		
Fireclay and limestone, Upper Freeport	5 0	
Concealed and sandstone, massive...............................	40 0	
Flaggy sandstone and sandy shales...............................	20 0	
Coal, "Roger" vein, { coal 2 0		3 4
Lower Freeport { slate 0 2		
{ coal 1 2		
Shales and concealed..	30 0	
Sandstone, massive, Lower Freeport...........................	70 0	
Middle Kittanning coal { coal 1 0		2 11
{ shale 0. 1		
{ coal 1 10		
Fireclay and sandy shales..	30 0	
Lower Kittanning coal, bony at top........................	3 0	
Fireclay, Lower Kittanning...	8 0	
Sandy shales and concealed to low water in Ohio river	50 0	
Interval, estimated, to top of Pottsville	25 0	
Total...287 3		

The Ohio geologists have always regarded the "Roger" bed along the Ohio valley as identical with the LOWER FREEPORT COAL of the Allegheny series, the UPPER FREEPORT being thin or wanting altogether as in the New Cumberland section. The late Dr. Orton regarded the "STEUBENVILLE SHAFT" COAL, as also the one in the deep shaft at Wellsburg, in Brooke county, as the same LOWER FREEPORT COAL.

When the Allegheny series passes under the overlying Conemaugh, Monongahela and Dunkard series, deep down into the Appalachian basin of the state, we know its constitution only through the records, more or less imperfect, of the oil and gas wells drilled over a wide region. As already stated, while the rock series can be universally recognized in these records, many of them exhibit no coal whatever, and hence it is possible that over large areas, where these beds underlie the surface, they may not contain any coal of commercial thickness and value. True, the oil and gas well contractors do not drill for COAL, and the presence of the latter is noted only incidentally, and hence there is some slight chance that in many wells where no coal has been reported, it has either been overlooked or passed through at night, when it might have been classed as BLACK SLATE or missed entirely. We shall now present some of these records selected at random from different portions of the area where the Allegheny series lies deeply buried, and let them speak for themselves.

As a rule the record of the first well drilled in any region is kept with more detail and with greater care than any of those subsequently bored, so that in making selections from hundreds of records throughout the state, we shall, wherever possible, give those that were first drilled in their respective localities.

The South Penn Oil Company drilled a gas well on the Brown Heirs land, Dunkard creek, in western Monongalia, near the Pennsylvania-West Virginia state line, where the Upper Freeport coal was struck at a depth of 1090 feet, and the following record made of the Allegheny series there:

BROWN HEIRS WELL NO. 1, NEAR ANDY, MONONGALIA COUNTY.

	Ft.
Upper Freeport coal	2
Slate and shells	53
Sand, white, "*Big Dunkard*," (2d Cow Run)	15
Slate and shells	30
Upper Kittanning coal	3
Slate and shells	72
Sand, gray	40
Slate and shells	35
Sand, gray	20
Clarion or Brookville coal	2
Slate	8
White sand, top of *Pottsville*	
Total	280

The same Oil Company drilled a well on the Lee R. Shriver farm, only one mile east from the Brown Heirs well, where the UPPER FREEPORT COAL was also noted, and it will be interesting to compare the two records, since both were kept with more than usual detail.   The top of the Allegany was struck at 1110 feet in this well, and the record reads as follows:

LEE R. SHRIVER WELL NO. 1, ONE MILE EAST OF

ANDY, MONONGALIA COUNTY.

	Ft.
Upper Freeport coal	2
Slate	93
Upper Kittanning coal	2
Slate and shells	73
"*Gas sand*," *Freeport*	40
Slate	7
Sand	43
Slate	6
White sand, top of *Pottsville*	
Total	266

These records are especially valuable in giving the exact thickness of the Allegheny series, since the UPPER FREEPORT COAL BED was noted in each, at the proper interval (565 feet) below the thick PITTSBURG COAL above, and then the base of the Allegheny was sharply defined by a great thickness of white POTTSVILLE ("Salt Sand" of the drillers) sandstone below.

While three of the Allegheny coals are reported in the Brown well, and two in the Shriver, none of them appear to be thick enough to be considered commercially valuable at present, although in the distant future any good coal of three feet in thickness, or only two, for that matter, will be mined even at great depths, just as such beds are now in Britain, France, Belgium, Germany, and other older countries, where the easily won coal has long been exhausted.

Just south from Monongalia county, in the northern edge of western Marion county, the Allegheny series is well defined in a well drilled by the South Penn Oil Company on the land of Brice Wallace, just east from Fairview, or Amos.   The record is as follows:

BRICE WALLACE WELL NO. 1, ONE MILE EAST FROM AMOS, MARION COUNTY.

	Ft.
Coal and slate, Upper Freeport	20
Dark slate and sandstone	160
Sand	30
Slate and sandy shells	60
White sand, top of Pottsville	
Total	270

Here the Upper Freeport coal was noted at a depth of 1090 feet, but its thickness was not separated from that of the accompanying slate. Its interval below the Pittsburg coal is here 556 feet.

West from this in Wetzel county, the D. H. Cox well No. 1, three miles east from Pine Grove, gave the following record through the Allegheny series, the top of which was struck at 1176 feet, and 568 feet below the Pittsburg coal:

NEAR PINE GROVE WETZEL CO.

	Ft.
Slate and shells	38
Slate	17
Sand	44
"Cave" (fireclay, possibly)	5
Slate	10
Sand	50
Slate and shells	15
Slate to top of Pottsville series	22
Total	201

Here no coal whatever is reported, and this is only a sample of hundreds of borings in Wetzel county, so that if the Allegheny series does hold valuable coal there, no oil well records known to the writer have yet disclosed the same.

In the adjoining county of Marshall, the Carter Oil Company drilled a well five miles north from Loudensville, (near Cameron) and this record reveals one coal bed in the Allegheny series, as follows :

COX FARM, FIVE MILES NORTH FROM LOUDENS-VILLE, MARSHALL COUNTY.

	Ft.
Upper Freeport coal, absent	
Slate	20
Sand	20
Slate	35

Lower Freeport coal... 5
Slate 10
"Gas sand," Lower Freeport................................ 70
Slate to *Pottsville series* 70
———
Total 230

The coal given above was struck at a depth of 1195 feet, 615 feet below the PITTSBURG COAL, and hence is most probably the "STEUBENVILLE SHAFT" or "ROGER" VEIN, of the Ohio valley, which appears to correlate with the LOWER FREEPORT BED of the Allegheny series.

In Ohio county, next north from Marshall, where the Pittsburg coal rises to the surface, and is 100 feet above water level at Wheeling, two coals have been reported in a boring made for gas at the Central Glass Works, within the city limits, as follows:

CENTRAL GLASS WORKS, WHEELING, OHIO COUNTY.

Ft.

Upper Freeport coal, absent ....
Shale, blue 50
Lower Freeport coal... 7
Sandstone and shales... 96
Upper Kittanning coal 5
Shales and sandstone to *Pottsville*....................... 112
———
Total... 270

The coal at the top of the series was struck at 556 feet below the Pittsburg coal, and 450 feet under the bed of the Ohio river, and hence has been correlated with the LOWER FREEPORT COAL, or ROGER VEIN of the Ohio valley, rather than with the UPPER FREEPORT BED, although it may possibly be the same.

At Wellsburg, Brooke county, next north from Ohio county, the record of Barclay well No. 1, drilled at the mouth of Buffalo creek, gives the following for the Allegheny series there:

BARCLAY WELL NO. 1, WELLSBURG, BROOKE COUNTY.

Ft.

Upper Freeport coal, absent ....
Fireclay 40
Slate 12
Coal, Roger vein, Lower Freeport 5
Fireclay 10
Slate 20
Slate and shale 40
Sand, white 40
Slate and shale to top of *Pottsville*........................ 74
———
Total... 241

The coal given above was once mined at Wellsburg, by a shaft 235 feet in depth. It has always been regarded as identical with the "STEUBENVILLE SHAFT" COAL, only a few miles above, which, as already stated, the Ohio geologists are quite certain represents the LOWER FREEPORT COAL of the Allegheny series. In this report the writer has accepted that determination, although not entirely satisfied as to its correctness, since he had always inclined to the view of Dr. Newberry: viz, that it was the UPPER FREEPORT COAL. It is certainly one or the other, and as the two horizons are only fifty to sixty feet apart along the Ohio valley, it does not make much difference in the economic results.

The coal in question lies 324 feet below the Ames limestone at Wellsburg, and 554 feet below the Pittsburg coal, both of which crop in the Ohio river hills.

The Allegheny series does not apparently hold coal of much value under Harrison county, if we may judge from the oil well records.

About four miles southeast from Clarksburg, a well was bored on the Carr farm by the Harrison County Oil Company, and a very careful record of the strata penetrated was kept by Prof. T. M. Jackson, of Clarksburg, one of its officers, which exhibits the Allegheny series as follows:

CARR WELL NO. 1, NEAR QUIET DELL, HARRISON COUNTY.

	Ft.
Upper Freeport coal. absent	
Slate, black	33
White slate and shells	25
Limestone and sand	8
Soapstone	7
Sandstone, gray	33
Shales, sandy	35
Sand, black	4
Slate, white	21
Black, hard sand	4
Sand, white	6
Lower Kittanning coal	1
Shale, black	31
Slate, black	15
Slate, white, to top of white sandstone, (*Pottsville*)	27
Total	250

Here the only coal in the entire series is a thin streak near the horizon of the Lower Kittanning bed.

In a boring made within the city limits of Clarksburg, a

slightly different result was obtained from that given above. This boring is known as the Despard gas well, and it was located near the junction of Elk creek and West Fork river. Prof. T. M. Jackson furnishes the following record of this well in its passage through the Allegheny series.

UNDER CLARKSBURG, HARRISON COUNTY.

	Ft.	Ft.
Upper Freeport coal, absent.............................		
Shales, sandy	29	
Sandstone, white........	7	
Shales..	6	124
Sandstone, white, Lower Freeport	72	
Sandstone, dark	10	
Middle Kittanning coal		1
Shales, black	21	
Sandstone, gray	12	49
Sandstone, white...................................	16	
Lower Kittanning coal, with slate		4
Sandstone, hard, gray	4	
Sandstone, hard, white.....	36	54
Shale	14	
Top of *Pottsville* white sandstone		
Total......................................		232

Here another thin streak of coal was found above the LOWER KITTANNING, but the Lower one has thickened up to four feet, though half of this may be black slate, from the fact that the driller noted slate in connection with the coal.

In Taylor county, near the Harrison line, the South Penn Oil Company drilled a well on the land of R. L. Reed, in the Booth's Creek District, where the following record was made through the Allegheny series:

R. L. REED WELL NO. 1, BOOTH'S CREEK DISTRICT, TAYLOR COUNTY.

	Ft.
Upper Freeport coal..........	5
Slate and shells...................................	110
Sand, Lower Freeport..............................	60
Slate	20
Sand	20
Slate	25
Total..	240

In Doddridge county very few of the wells report coal in the Allegheny series, the top of which is there buried from 800 to 1500 feet below the surface.

The following record, from Well No. 1, on Ruley Brothers land, in Central District, is a fair sample of the records the drillers report from Doddridge county for the Allegheny series:

RULEY BROTHERS WELL NO. 1, CENTRAL DISTRICT, DODDRIDGE COUNTY.

	Ft.
Upper Freeport coal, absent	
Slate..................................	50
Limestone	40
Slate	15
Limestone	25
Sand	20
Slate and limestone..	10
Sand, white..	55
Slate, black...	7
Limestone	21
Siate..	15
Limestone	15
Total.................................	273

The word "limestone," or "lime," as used by the average oil well driller, can usually be translated into "light gray shale," so that the excessive quantity of LIMESTONE reported in many oil well records, is thus accounted for. The top of the Allegheny series was struck at a depth of 1025 feet in the Ruley Brothers well.

About two miles from Long Run station, on the B. & O. R. R., the South Penn Oil Company driled a well on the land of J. D. Crabtree, where a coal was found in the Allegheny series of Doddridge county, as follows :

J. D. CRABTREE WELL NO. 1, NEAR LONG RUN STATION, DODDRIDGE COUNTY.

	Ft.
Upper Freeport coal, absent	
Slate..................	63
Lower Freeport coal.....	5
Slate	31
Sand	45
Slate	10
Sand	59
Slate, to top of *Pottsville*......................................	19
Total..232	

The coal was struck at a depth of 1088 feet, 652 feet below the Pittsburg bed, and hence has been identified with the LOWER FREEPORT COAL, rather than with the UPPER one.

In the adjoining county of Ritchie, many hundreds of wells have been drilled, and the contractors report a general absence of coal in the Allegheny series. Sometimes thin traces of it are encountered, but no thick or valuable beds, according to their records.

The Keystone Oil and Gas Company drilled a well near Harrisville of which a fairly good record was kept, and, although some coal was found, both in the Monongahela series and the Conemaugh, above, only a trace appeared in the underlying Allegheny series, which was recorded as follows:

KEYSTONE OIL AND GAS COMPANY'S WELL NO. 1, HARRISVILLE, RITCHIE COUNTY.

	Ft.
Upper Freeport coal, absent......................................	
Slate, blue..	23
Sand, hard	15
Slate, white..........	6
Limestone	31
Sand, sharp..	36
Slate, dark (show of coal at 1320 feet)	38
Sand..	6
Slate, white..	4
Sand, white..	57
Slate and shells, dark, to top of *Pottsville*..............	52
Total..	268

In the Whiskey run oil pool of Ritchie county, the record of well No. 1, on the Baumgardner farm, was very carefully kept by Mr. John F. Carll, the geologist of Venango county, Pennsylvania, who reports the following succession through the Allegheny series:

BAUMGARDNER WELL NO. 1, WHISKEY RUN OIL POOL, RITCHIE COUNTY.

	Ft.
Upper Freeport coal, absent..............................	
Slate, light gray	145
Slate, dark, limy.......................................	80
Coal, Lower Kittanning..................................	2
Slate and shells to top of *Pottsville*	68
Total..	295

The coal was struck at a depth of 1355 feet, 850 feet below where the Pittsburg bed had been noted, and 402 feet above the Mountain, or Greenbrier limestone.

Near Cairo, Ritchie county, the record of a well on the Lee farm was kept for the Survey with much care by Mr. William A. Clark, of the Clark Oil Company, who reports the following succession through the Allegheny series:

LEE FARM WELL NO. 6, NEAR CAIRO, RITCHIE COUNTY.

	Ft.
Upper Freeport coal, absent..	--
White slate and "shell"	50
Sandstone	25
Black slate and "lime shells"	47
Sand..	15
Slate, black	33
Sand	35
Dark *coaly* shales ("cave"), cased at 1310, 6¼ inch	45
"*Casing sand*"	40
Slate, black, to top of *Pottsville*	15
Total..............	305

Here the only coal in the entire series is a thin bed found in connection with the "black cave," as the shales which cave so badly are named by the drillers. This "black cave" comes at about the horizon of the LOWER KITTANNING FIRECLAY and its overlying dark shales.

In the neighboring county of Tyler an oil well has recently been drilled by the Carter Oil Company, two miles south of Wick Post Office, the record of which was kept with great care by the drilling crew, and a set of the samples was kindly presented to the Survey by Mr. W. H. Aspinwall, of the Carter Oil Company. The well begins in the Permian, and found petroleum in the Pocono or "Big Injun" sand of the Lower Carboniferous, so that it penetrated nearly all of the Carboniferous system. The record is a very interesting and important one, and is here given in full as follows:

Samp.	Strata.	Top.	Bot.	Thick.
1	Soil and clay.....................	0	5	5
2	Red rock...........................	5	55	50
3	Brown shale........................	55	67	12
4	Red rock...........................	67	90	23
5	Sandstone	90	150	60
6	Green slate........................	150	160	10
7	Sandstone, hard	160	180	20
8	Dark gray slate....................	180	192	12
9	Sandstone	192	230	38
10	Sandstone	....	....	...
11	Green slate........................	230	234	4
12	Red rock...........................	234	280	46

13	Sandstone, hard......	280	295	15	
14	Slate	295	305	10	
15	Slate, *trace of coal at 315*........	305	325	20	
16	Sandstone, micaceous	325	410	85	
17	Red rock..........................	410	425	15	⎫
18	Limestone .... {	425	......	...	
19	Limestone .... {	440	450	25	
20	Slate	450	452	2	
21	Red rock	452	472	20	
22	Sandstone, gray coarse...........	472	502	30	
23	Black slate, *trace of coal at 506* (*Uniontown?*)	502	510	8	
24	White slate......................	510	530	20	
25	Sandstone	530	540	10	
26	White slate..................	540	542	2	⎬ Monongahela
27	Red rock..........................	542	557	15	series 349 feet.
28	Slate, 10-inch casing 557 feet ..	557	597	40	
29	Limestone......	597	629	32	
30	Slate	629	635	6	
31	Lime and sand shells	635	690	55	
32	Sandstone ....•••	690	700	10	
33	Slate	700	710	10	
34	Limestone	710	730	20	
35	Limestone	730	742	12	
36	Sandstone	742	759	17	⎭
37	*Pittsburg coal?*	759	760	1	⎫
38	Sandstone	760	800	40	
39	Sandstone	800	806	6	
40	Lime and sand shells	806	856	50	
41	Limestone, sandy....................	856	881	25	
42	Sandstone	881	893	12	
43	Black slate, *trace of coal*.........	893	908	15	
44	Red rock, "Big Red"	908	960	52	
45	Limestone, sandy..................	960	990	30	
46	Coarse sand, *steel line*..........	990	1030	40	
47	Black slate	1030	1046	16	
48	Limestone, sandy..................	1046	1052	6	
49	Red rock.........................	1052	1058	6	
50	Limestone and limy shales... {	1058			⎬ Conemaugh
51	" " .. {	1080		103	series 493 feet.
52	" " ... {	1120			
53	Limestone .... {	1140	1161		
54	Slate .... {	1161			
55	" .... {	1175	1200	39	
56	Sandstone, hard.....................	1200	1212	12	
57	Shale	1212	1237	25	
58	Sandstone	1237	1247	10	
59	"	1247	1253	6	⎭
60	Limestone, hard	1253	1288	35	
61	"Break," soft.................	1288	1293	5	
62	Limestone, hard....................	1293	1299	6	
63	Freeport sandstone........... .. {	1299			⎫
64	*Steel line*........................ {	1319			⎬ Allegheny series
65	" 8-inch casing 1310' {	1339			211 feet.
66	" .... {	1429	1434	135	
67	"Break" of black slate, *trace coal at 1464*	1434	1464	30	⎭
68	⎧	1464			⎫
69	⎨ Salt sand, Pottsville, water {	1479			⎬ Pottsville series.
70	⎩ at 1550. {	1549			⎭

71		1652			
72					
73		1658	1666	202	
74	Black slate 1666		1752	86	
75	Sandstone 1752		1764	12	
76	Black slate, 6⅝ casing 1776'...1764		1776	12	
77	Black grit, very hard and wore bits 1776		1826	50	Mauch Chunk
78	Shells........ 1826		1836	10	series 225 feet.
79	Maxton sand 1836				
80	"				
81	"		1891	55	
82	Black lime rock....................1891		1910	19	
83	Limestone, "big lime" .... { 1910				
84	" .... {		1976	66	
85	"Keener" sand 1976		2008	32	
86	Top of Big Injun 2008				Steel line, little gas.
87	Big Injun sand......................				
88	" " 2018				Gas.
89	" " oil. Steel line ..2029				
90	" " 2095				
	Total depth, steel line...........		2101		

Commenced November 29, 1902; completed January 11, 1903.
Drilled by the Wilson Drilling Company. Drillers, John Sayres and Chas Swab. Tool dressers, Earl Martin, Ross Monroe and Edward Williams.

It is possible that the suggested identification of the Pittsburg coal in this record is not correct, and that its horizon would belong higher up in the well. The identification is based upon the position of the lowest RED BED which is seldom more than 400 feet below the Pittsburg coal. Then, too. this identification gives the interval between the Pittsburg coal and the top of the "Keener" division of the "Big Injun" oil sand as 1216 feet, which is about right. The important thing of the section is that it reveals no merchantable coal in the whole Carboniferous system. The large quantity of limestone found by the drillers is significant in this connection, pointing as it does to conditions of sedimentation unfavorable to the accumulation of coal.

The trace of coaly material first noted at 1464 feet was skimmed from the water which rose in the well and was brought up in the bailer.

Pleasants county adjoining Tyler has the same reports of the absence of thick coal veins as the latter, and Wood county is but little better, as the following record of the Judge John J. Jackson well No. 1, drilled by the South Penn Oil Company, will illustrate. It begins in the Permian red beds, and goes through the entire column of Carboniferous beds below, down to the Berea Grit of Ohio in the top of the Devonian, and reads as follows:

JUDGE JOHN J. JACKSON WELL NO. 1, FIVE MILES N. E. OF PARKERSBURG.

		Feet.
Conductor	25 to	25
Red rock	25 "	50
Sand, gray	50 "	100
Slate, white	25 "	125
Sand, gray	25 "	150
Red rock	15 "	165
Limestone	10 "	175
Slate, white	25 "	200
Red rock	15 "	215
Sand, gray	15 "	230
Slate, white	10 "	240
Red rock	25 "	265
Sand, white	25 "	290
Red rock	100 "	390
Slate, white	10 "	400
Sand, white	5 "	405
Slate, white	15 "	420
Limestone	10 "	430
Sand, white	15 "	445
Red rock	20 "	465
Limestone	10 "	475
Slate, black	25 "	500
Red rock	30 "	530
Slate, black	20 "	550
Sand, white	25 "	575
Slate, white	25 "	600
Red rock	105 "	705
Slate, white	50 "	755
Sand, white	20 "	775
Slate, white	10 "	785
Sand, white	15 "	800
Red rock	30 "	830
Slate, white	20 "	850
Sand, white	15 "	865
Slate, black	25 "	890
Cow Run" sand (*Mahoning*) water at 915 feet	110 "	1000
Slate, white	50 "	1050
Sand, gray	30 "	1080
Slate, white	37 "	1117
Slate, black	30 "	1147
Sand, white	120 "	1267
Slate, white	30 "	1297
Slate, black	60 "	1357
"*Salt Sand*" (water at 1390) Pottsville	100 "	1457
Limestone	15 "	1472
Slate, white	15 "	1487
"*Big Lime*"	18 "	1505
"*Big Injun*" sand { sand, white, water at 1525 ...140; sand, black ...10; sand, white ...40; sand, black ...15 }	205 "	1710
Slate and shells	283 "	1993
Slate, black	30 "	2023
Shells, (*Berea*), dark and poor, no oil or gas	52 "	2075

The top of the Allegheny series would come at about 1000 feet in this well, and extend down about 250 feet. No coal whatever is reported from any of the wells drilled in the oil fields of Wood county, but in a well bored at Parkersburg by the Camden Oil Refinery a bed of coal, seven feet thick is recorded at a depth of 1095 feet. This would probably be a representative of either the Middle or Lower Kittanning seam. It is possible that some portion of the seven feet was bituminous shale, since the oil well drillers do not, as a rule, distinguish between the two.

In Wirt county some of the wells report four feet of coal in the Allegheny series. In Casto well No. 1 the record gives four feet of coal at 1156 feet, and 555 feet above the top of the Big Injun oil sand. This is most probably one of the Kittanning beds, and the same as that reported in the Camden boring at Parkersburg.

The Roberts well No. 1, near Burning Springs, Wirt county, does not report any coal in the Allegheny series, and gives the following record through it :

ROBERTS WELL NO. 1, NEAR BURNING SPRINGS, WIRT COUNTY.

	Ft.
Upper Freeport coal, absent	
Gray and blue shales..	57
Sand	31
Shale..	33
Sand, gray, shelly, "Gas" sand, Lower Freeport...........	55
Shale, gray, to *Pottsville*...	79
Total...	255

The base of the Allegheny beds comes here, 475 feet above the top of the "Big Injun" oil sand, and hence the coal reported in the Casto well would come just under the Lower Freeport or "Gas" sand of the drillers, and be one of the Kittanning beds.

A coal is also reported in the Allegheny series under Calhoun county at about 600 feet above the Big Injun oil sand and it is probably the same as the one found in Wirt county.

The Cornell well, drilled by Messrs. Courtney and McDermott in Calhoun county had eight feet of coal reported at a depth of 1300 feet and 590 feet above the Big Injun oil sand. In order to show the character of the strata in the Allegheny series of Calhoun as well as the geological horizon of the deep coal found there we shall give the complete record of a well in the Yellow creek oil field drilled on the Jackson farm by Hon. J. M. Guffey, of Pittsburg, as follows :

JACKSON WELL NO. 1, ON YELLOW CREEK, CALHOUN COUNTY, ONE-HALF MILE N. E. OF METZ WELLS.

Feet.

Unrecorded	0 to	45
Sand	15 "	60
Red rock	15 "	75
Lime	15 "	90
Slate	15 "	105
Lime	10 "	115
Red rock	20 "	135
Slate	85 "	220
Red rock	111 "	331
Shell	5 "	336
Red rock	20 "	356
Slate	10 "	366
Sand, white	15 "	381
Red rock	71 "	452
Sand, white	23 "	475
Slate	10 "	485
Lime	20 "	505
Red rock	10 "	515
Sand, white	45 "	560
Lime	10 "	570
Red rock	122 "	692
Slate	53 "	745
Sand	40 "	785
Slate	30 "	815
Sand	15 "	830
Slate	10 "	840
Sand	20 "	860
Broken lime	35 "	895
Sand	200 "	1095
Black shale	40 "	1135
Sand	30 "	1165
White lime	10 "	1175
Black shale	34 "	1209
White sand	26 "	1235
Slate and shell	50 "	1285
Lime	20 "	1305
Sand	25 "	1330
Slate	30 "	1360
Lime	15 "	1375
Slate and shale	90 "	1465
Sand	25 "	1490
Slate	10 "	1500
Sand	30 "	1530
Lime	10 "	1540
Red rock	20 "	1560
Slate	10 "	1570
Lime	20 "	1590
Sand	30 "	1620
Little lime	25 "	1645
Slate	10 "	1655
"Big Lime"	70 "	1725

Allegheny series 314 feet.

Pottsville series 321 feet.

Mauch Chunk series 125 feet.

"Big Injun".............................. 45 " 1770
White slate...... .... 40 " 1810
Slate and shell ....270 " 2080
Black shale................................... 26 " 2106
Berea sand .... 12 " 2118
Slate, black .... 5 " 2123
Slate and shell ....246 " 2369
Slate and shell to bottom................... 2442

As will be perceived, no coal whatever is recorded from this well, but it is possible that the BLACK SHALE struck at 1095 feet may hold the coal reported in the Cornell well by Courtney and McDermott, since the bottom of this stratum (1135) comes 590 feet above the top of the Big Injun Oil sand, or exactly the same as the top of the eight foot coal in the Cornell farm well, so that there may be unnoted by the drillers, a coal bed of good thickness masked in the forty feet of BLACK SHALE in question.

In the W. L. Camden well No. 1, drilled by the South Penn Oil Company in Sherman District, Calhoun county, the following succession is reported for the Allegheny and Pottsville series:

W. L. CAMDEN WELL NO. I, SHERMAN DISTRICT, CALHOUN COUNTY.

	Ft.
Sandstone	172
Slate	20
Sand	95
Black shale...	164
Sand	40
Black slate	20
Sand, hard	26
Slate and shell.....................................	155
Sand, white, base of *Pottsville*..............	51
Black slate	10
Red shale...	8
Shale	2
"Big Lime"..	118
Big Injun oil sand ....:................................	
Total...........	881

The heavy sandstone at the top of this section was struck at a depth of 927 feet, and is evidently the same one as that at the top of the Allegheny series in the Jackson well, since the top of the latter lies 830 feet above the "Big Injun" Oil sand, and the top of the sandstone of the Camden well comes 881 feet above the same datum. It is possible that the upper half of this immense thickness of sandstone may belong in the Conemaugh series, the driller not observing any slate division between.

In the region of Stumptown, Gilmer county, the Stumptown Oil and Gas Company has drilled several wells for gas, and found a coal bed of fair thickness in the Allegheny series at a depth of over 1100 feet below the level of Steer creek. This is in the region where the great eastward expansion of the Allegheny-Kanawha series has begun, and the following record of the Gas Company's well No. 4, received from Mr. John T. Harris, of Parkersburg, Secretary of the Stumptown Company, shows this succession:

NEAR STUMPTOWN, GILMER COUNTY.

	Ft.	Ft.
Unrecorded..	140	
Red rock, lime and shells	185	
Coal, Bakerstown...................................	4	615
Red rock, lime and shells	166	
First Cow Run sand (Mahoning) base of Cone-		
maugh series	120	
Upper Freeport coal, absent		
Limestone, shells and slate	95	
Sand..	18	
Limestone and slate.......................................	67	
Sand, Lower Freeport	113	615
Limestone, shells and slate	287	
Coal	9	
Limestone, to top of *Pottsville* (gas)	26	

This well starts about 100 feet below the horizon of the Pittsburg coal and hence the thick sand struck at 495 feet is the basal member of the Conemaugh series, and the coal in question comes 580 feet lower. It is barely possible that this coal is in the Pottsville series, since in a deep well drilled near Stumptown the top of the Big Injun sand was reported at a depth of only 400 feet below five feet of coal struck at a depth of 1145 feet, which must be the same as the one showing nine feet in the record just given.

About two miles southwest of Stumptown, Gilmer county, the Rush well No. 1 got two beds of coal ninety feet apart, the upper one seven feet at 953 feet below the surface, and the lower one six feet at 1050 feet, the top of the "Big Injun" Oil sand being reported at 1550 feet. These beds would both belong in the Allegheny-Kanawha series, since the LOWEST RED BED of the Conemaugh series is only 370 feet above the top of the upper one.

Near Spencer, Roane county, the record of No. 1 well on the Asylum farm was kept with much care. It begins near the base of the Dunkard series, and was drilled through the entire Carboniferous system. The only coal reported by the drillers was some coal and slate ten feet thick at 1224 feet, and 227 feet below the base of the Conemaugh series. Hence it would be in the Allegheny beds and probably at the horizon of the Lower Kittanning coal.

In the southern edge of Roane county, Geary district, Mr. Grosscup, of Charleston, drilled a gas well on the W. A. Geary farm, in which five feet of coal is reported at a depth of 347 feet, and 1132 feet above the top of the Big Injun Oil sand. This is in the region of the thickened Allegheny-Kanawha series, and would probably be about the horizon of the Upper Freeport coal, since the lowest red beds crop only 100 feet above the level of the boring.

The Elk River Oil and Gas Company drilled a well on the P. A. Tallman farm near the line between Clay and Roane counties, and the President of the Company, Mr. E. M. Hukill, of Pittsburg, reports the finding of two coal beds, one ten feet thick at 440 feet, and the other six feet thick at 525 feet, while the "Big Injun" Oil sand was struck at 1670. These two coals belong at the top of the Allegheny-Kanawha series, and probably represent the Upper and Lower Freeport beds, or what is the same, the Stockton and Coalburg coals of the Kanawha valley. The bottom of the Pottsville series was struck at 1400 feet, 870 feet below the lower of the two coal beds.

The Carter Oil Company drilled a deep well near the line between Roane and Calhoun counties, four miles southeast of Triplett Post Office, the record of which was kept with much detail and kindly given the Survey by Mr. W. H. Aspinwall, of the Carter Oil Company. The well begins in the base of the Dunkard series and passes through the Carboniferous system into the Devonian. Its record reads as follows:

WELL NO. 1, ON S. CONLEY FARM, NEAR ROANE-CALHOUN LINE, FOUR MILES SOUTHEAST OF TRIPLETT.

Feet

Unrecorded	55 to	55
Sand	15 "	70
Red rock	10 "	80
Sandstone	20 "	100
Slate	50 "	150
Lime	25 "	175
Slate	25 "	200
Sand	25 "	225
Red rock	15 "	240
Lime	20 "	260

Sandstone .... 10 " 270
Slate .... 30 " 300
Lime.. 35 " 335
Lime.. 15 " 350
Slate .... 30 " 380
Shell.. 4 " 384
Coal .... 4 " 388
Lime.. 12 " 400
Slate .... 55 " 455
Lime.. 15 " 470
Slate .... 10 " 480
Red rock.. 15 " 495
Lime.. 5 " 500
"Big Red" cave................................. 80 " 580
Lime.. 20 " 600
Slate ....100 " 700
Red rock.. 10 " 710
Slate .... 40 " 750
Lime .... 25 " 775
Sand .... 8 " 783
Lime.. 7 " 790
Slate .... 60 " 850
Lime.. 29 " 879
First Cow Run sand (Mahoning)... 59 " 938

Upper Freeport coal............ .... 2 " 940 ⎫
Sand .... 20 " 960 ⎪
Slate and lime................................. 52 " 1012 ⎪
Sand .... 10 " 1022 ⎪
Lime.. 18 " 1040 ⎬ Allegheny–Kanaw-
Slate .... 20 " 1060 ⎪ ha series 402 feet.
Lower { "Gas sand".................... 75 " 1135 ⎪
Freepo't { Slate, "break"............... 5 " 1140 ⎪
{ Sand .... 60 " 1200 ⎪
Slate .... 55 " 1255 ⎪
Sand .... 45 " 1300 ⎪
Black slate (cave)........................... 40 " 1340 ⎭
Sand .... 50 " 1390 ⎫
Slate .... 80 " 1470 ⎪
Lime .... 30 " 1500 ⎪ Pottsville series
Slate .... 45 " 1545 ⎬ 375 feet.
Lime.. 35 " 1580 ⎪
Slate .... 10 " 1590 ⎪
Salt sand, water (1620 feet).... ......135 " 1725 ⎭
Unrecorded....................................... 53 " 1778
Maxton sand.................................... 9 " 1787
Slate.. 13 " 1800
Little Lime....................................... 15 " 1815
Slate.. 5 " 1820
Sandstone, hard................................ 10 " 1830
"Pencil cave"................................... 5 " 1835
"Big Lime"....................................... 61 " 1896
Big Injun sand ....104 " 2000
Small gas at 1936 feet..
Slate.. 30 " 2030
Lime...... .... 24 " 2054
Slate.. 71 " 2125
Sand.. 10 " 2135
Slate.. 50 " 2185

```
Lime.................................................. 15 "  2200
Slate................................................ 160 "  2360
Limy sand (Berea) ...................... 10 "  2370
Slate.................................................. 50 "  2420
Shells................................................ 50-55 "  2475
Slate.................................................. 53 "  2528
Sand, limy, "stray", gas show..... 7 "  2535
Slate.................................................. 15 "  2550
Gordon sand (shell)...................... 3 "  2353
Slate to bottom ............................ 51 "  2604
```

The coal at 384 feet may possibly be the Pittsburg bed, although its interval (550') above the base of the Conemaugh series is hardly large enough for that seam.

A deep well was drilled for oil in the Great Kanawha valley about five miles below Charleston, which begins about 300 feet under the Pittsburg coal. Its record as given by J. W. Penhale is as follows :

NEAR LOCK NO. 6.

	Ft.
Conductor	45
Sandstone to base of Conemaugh series......	405

Coal, Stockton, Upper Freeport..................	5	
Sandstone	35	
Slate and shale	220	
Sandstone..	220	
Slate and shale	10	
Sandstone..	40	
Shale...	50	Allegheny-Kanawha series 495 feet.
Lime..	10	
Sandstone..	35	
Coal..	45	
Sandstone..	3	
Shale to top of Pottsville.......................	7	
Sandstone, Pottsville, to top of Greenbrier limestone	35	
	480	

The coal at the top of the Allegheny-Kanawha series is near the horizon of the Upper Freeport coal, since the Pittsburg bed crops at about 300 feet above where the boring begins, and this would give an interval of 750 feet between it and the Stockton coal as against 800 feet between the Pittsburg coal and the Stockton bed at Charleston.

The coal near the base of the Allegheny-Kanawha series in the record may be either the Eagle or Campbells creek bed, most probably the former.

About one mile below Winfield, Putnam county, a boring was once made for oil on the left bank of the Great Kanawha river, twenty miles north from the locality of the last boring. It begins near the horizon of the PITTSBURG COAL, and the record reads as follows, according to Mr. M. R. Campbell, in the Huntington Folio, U. S. G. Survey, page 3:

BORING NEAR WINFIELD, PUTNAM COUNTY.

	Feet.	
Shale	20	⎫
Sandstone	7	
Limestone	5	
Slate	87	
Sandstone	25	
Shale	5	
Red shale	10	
Shale	5	
Red rock	25	
Sandstone	15	
Red rock	15	
Sandstone	10	Conemaugh series
Slate	85	609 feet.
Sandstone	10	
Slate	37	
Sandstone	40	
Slate	43	
Sandstone	35	
Slate	25	
Sandstone	10	
Slate	25	⎭
Sandstone, Lower Mahoning	70	⎫
Coal (Upper Freeport) and slate	20	
Sandstone	108	
Slate	52	
Sandstone	20	
Slate	37	
Sandstone	21	
Slate	15	Allegheny–Kanaw-
Sandstone	19	ha series 420 feet.
"Shells"	13	
Sandstone	45	
Slate	10	
Sandstone	20	
Slate	15	
Coal (Eagle?) and slate	25	⎭
Sandstone	45	⎫
Slate	45	
Sandstone	15	Pottsville series
Slate	20	400 feet.
Sandstone	255	
Dark sandstone	20	⎭
Limestone, *Mauch Chunk*	15	
Sandstone	5	
Limestone, Greenbrier	175	
Slate	25	
Sandstone, "Big Injun" oil sand	25	

This record shows the gradual thinning of the Allegheny-Kanawha and Pottsville series northward from Charleston after the members of the same have all passed below water level.   The coal beds at the top, and near the base of the series were not separated by the driller from the enclosing shales, and hence the coal reported may not be of commercial thickness.   These two beds are evidently the same as the two in the boring five miles below Charleston, given above.   It will be observed that in the Lock No. 6 well the Allegheny-Kanawha series has a thickness of 495 feet as against 420 in the Winfield boring, while the POTTSVILLE thins from 480 feet at Lock 6, to 400 at Winfield, and thus each series decreases northward at about the same rate, and maintaining practically equal thicknesses, just as the Allegheny and Pottsville do everywhere in western Pennsylvania and in the northern portion of West Virginia.

In a boring at Charleston, five miles south from the Lock No. 6 well, the Allegheny-Kanawha series has thickened to 516 feet, and the Pottsville to 580 feet.

Passing northward to the Ohio valley and five miles below the mouth of the Great Kanawha, the C. T. Beale well in Mason county, opposite Gallipolis, gives the following intervals between the Pittsburg coal and the base of the Pottsville series.

C. T. BEALE WELL NO. 1, MASON COUNTY, OPPOSITE, GALLIPOLIS, OHIO.

	Feet.	
Pittsburg coal		
Interval to derrick floor	150	
Quick sand and gravel	58	
Red rock	72	
Sand, white	7	
Slate and red rock	113	
Sand and slate	10	
Limestone	5	
Slate	7	
Coal	2	
Slate	18	
Sand	10	Conemaugh series
Slate and very soft red rock	50	597 feet.
Sand, gray	5	
Slate	25	
Sand, white (Mahoning) base of Conemaugh series	67	
Slate	63	
Coal	7	Allegheny series
Sand, white, salt water	213	
Slate	30	528 feet.
Sand, salt water, Pottsville	170	
Slate to top of the *Greenbrier limestone*	45	Pottsville series

Here the Allegheny and Pottsville series thin from 820 feet at Winfield to only 528 feet in the Ohio valley, thirty miles distant, and again attain their normal proportions, while the Conemaugh series above, retains its average thickness of nearly 600 feet. The coal bed at sixty-three feet below the top of the Allegheny series is probably a representative of the Lower Freeport bed.

At Huntington, Cabell county, one boring reports three good beds of coal within an interval of ninety three feet, beginning at a depth of 475 feet at the C. & O. R. R. round-house, while a few miles below, the Central City deep well passed entirely through the Allegheny and Pottsville series without recording any coal whatever, except about two feet somewhere in the Pottsville series. The Allegheny and Pottsville beds have a combined thickness of 605 feet in the Central City well, probably about equally divided between the two series. The record of the well at the C. & O. R. R. round-house is probably not reliable.

No one should take it for granted that the Allegheny series holds valuable coals anywhere within the large area where its beds lie deeply buried from view, without first making thorough tests with the core or diamond drill, since the records of oil and gas wells, so far as thickness and quality of the coal are concerned, cannot be depended upon.

Having now reviewed the general structure of the Allegheny series in the several regions of the state, we shall take up the individual coal beds and consider them in detail, beginning with the highest one.

THE UPPER FREEPORT COAL.

At the top of the Allegheny series, and marking it off from the Conemaugh rocks above, there occurs a very important coal bed. The First Geological Survey of Pennsylvania long ago named it from the town of Freeport on the Allegheny river, where the coal in question crops half way up the hills, and has the structure shown by the section given on pages 342-3. As may be noted in the section at its type locality, the Upper Freeport coal is a composite or multiple bed, and this peculiarity characterizes it everywhere in the state.

Next to the great Pittsburg bed, at the other limit of the Conemaugh series, the Upper Freeport coal is probably of more importance than any other single bed of coal in the entire Appalachian basin.   Unlike the Pittsburg, it does not thin down and vanish to the southwest, but appears to extend entirely across the state, at least along the belt of its eastern crop, and is quite as important in southern Mingo county at the Kentucky line as in eastern Monongalia and Preston at the Pennsylvania border.

Like the Pittsburg bed, however, it thins away when followed westward from the belt of its thick development, and disappears or becomes unimportant under a large area of the state where its horizon underlies the surface.   Along many of the principal streams, like the Buckhannon, Little Kanawha, Elk, Great Kanawha, Guyandot, Twelve Pole, and Tug rivers this westward thinning may be observed, just like that of the underlying New River beds, before the coal bed in question dips under the grade of the streams, thus confirming the results of oil and gas well drilling as to its general absence over such a wide area of the state deep down in the central sweep of the Appalachian basin.

When this coal horizon comes up to daylight again on the western side of the Appalachian trough near Kenova on the southwest, and New Cumberland on the northeast, it is either missing entirely as at New Cumberland, (unless, indeed, the "Roger" vein of the Ohio valley may prove to be this bed) or is thin, slaty and worthless as at the Big Sandy river near Kenova.   Hence, it follows, that aside from the limited area of this coal in the Potomac basin of Mineral, Grant, and Tucker counties, its principal area in valuable thickness and quality will be found in a belt ten to thirty miles in width, extending across the state through Monongalia, Preston, Taylor, Barbour, Randolph, Upshur, Webster, Braxton, Clay, Nicholas, Fayette, Kanawha, Boone, Lincoln, Wyoming, Logan, and Mingo counties.

Westward from this belt of thick coal, the presence of this bed is so uncertain that nothing but extensive exploration with the diamond or other form of core drill can be relied upon to locate any areas of the coal where it may possess valuable thickness and quality.

The character of this coal changes gradually in its passage across the state from a soft, typical, coking coal with columnar structure in Monongalia, Preston, Taylor, Barbour and Randolph, to a harder or "splinty" type, which beginning in southern Upshur and Webster, continues a feature of the coal on southwestward to the Kentucky line, although usually a portion of the bed will contain some layers of soft coal.

Another peculiarity of this coal worthy of note, is its tendency to cannel, especially in the southwestern end of the state, since nearly all of the cannel deposits of Fayette, Kanawha, and Wayne counties appear to come at this horizon. An impure, slaty cannel is also often present, in the roof of this coal, in the northern end of the state.

This coal bed enters Monongalia county from Fayette county, Pennsylvania, along the steep northwest slope of the great Chestnut Ridge anticlinal, and has been mined at several localities for domestic use near the foot of the mountain, between the Pennsylvania line and Cheat river. It rises above this latter stream on a steep northwestern dip just above Ice's Ferry, and was long ago mined there for use at the old Green Spring Furnace. This was probably the first coal to be made into coke for the manufacture of iron anywhere within the state, it having been burned for that purpose fifty to sixty years ago in heaps covered with earth, after the manner of charcoal manufacture, and used along with charcoal in the old Green Spring Furnace, which stood on the right bank of Cheat river, near Ice's Ferry.

The coal rises rapidly to the southeast from Ice's Ferry, and comes up to the level of the Bruceton pike just opposite Mt. Chateau Hotel, where it has been mined for local use and exhibits the following section:

		Ft. In.	Ft. In.
Sandstone, massive			
Shales, sandy, gray		10 0	
Coal ..	coal, bony	1 8	
	coal................	2 8	5 8
	"little" slate, gray...........	0 2	
	coal	1 2	

Under the bottom portion here, there should be another ply of coal, just below what is termed the "big slate," the thin one, shown above, being termed the "little" slate in mining parlance, but its horizon is concealed at this level, and it is not known whether the lower division of the coal is present or otherwise.

This bed soon passes into the air southeastward over the great Chestnut Ridge anticlinal, and does not come down again in that direction till we come to Pisgah, Preston county, where it catches the highest knobs, just east from the village, dipping rapidly down into what corresponds to the Ligonier basin of Pennsylvania, and which has its main axis along the waters of Sandy creek, in Preston county.

About one-half mile east from Pisgah, the Upper Freeport coal is mined on the land of Mr. D. A. Ryan, where it exhibits the following structure:

	Ft. In.	Ft. In.
Gray shale...	......	
Cannel, impure	0 2	
Coal, fair...	1 6	
Coal, bony	1 0	
Coal	2 11	6 9
"Little" slate.. ...	0 2	
Coal, good...	1 0	
"Big" slate...		

Another ply of coal belongs under the "big" slate, but it was not seen at this opening.

The coal shows practically the same section at J. T. Gribble's bank, two miles south from Pisgah, and at P. J. Rogers' opening, one mile southeast of Gribble's, it has the following section:

		Ft. In.	Ft. In.
Sandstone, massive, Lower Mahoning...................		40 0	
Gray, sandy shales..		8 0	
Coal...	bony coal...................................	0 4	
	coal	1 6	
	bony coal..........	1 0	
	coal	3 0	6 11
	slate, "little"...............................	0 1	
	coal	1 0	

The upper portion of the coal, above the three-foot bench, is seldom taken down, since it is bony and slaty. The bed will average about four feet of clean, soft coal, excellent for both coke and steam purposes. The same coal is mined by O. Walls and Brother, and also by Lockard Birtcher in the bluff of Sandy creek, near the center of the syncline, 600 feet above water level, and 550 feet above the base of the Pottsville series, since the bright RED SHALES of the Mauch Chunk crop fifty feet above Sandy creek and almost vertically below the Birtcher mine, where the Upper Freeport bed exhibits the following structure:

	Ft. In.	Ft. In.
Sandy shales		8 0
Bony coal	0 4	
Coal	1 3	
Bony coal	1 0	
Coal	2 11	6 8
"Little" slate	0 2	
Coal	1 0	

Many farmers have openings on the coal in this basin, north from Cheat river, and there is not much variation from the type given above. The two and one-half to three feet of coal in the roof of the mine contains some good coal, but if it is all rejected there will remain about four feet of pure fuel. If the roof coal could be crushed and washed, not less than two feet of good fuel could be obtained from it.

At Bruceton, this coal has long been mined for village use, and appears to be thinner than elsewhere in the basin, since it gives the following section in Mr. William Miller's bank:

	Ft. In.	Ft. In.
Slaty coal	1 0	
Coal	1 10	
Slate, gray	0 2	4 3
Coal	1 3	

This is just east from the center of the trough, since the coal dips to the northwest.

The coal continues rising to the southeast and arches into the air again over the crest of Laurel Hill anticlinal, the eastern boundary of the Ligonier basin of Pennsylvania. This coal comes down again, however, and has a good development in the Muddy creek basin of Preston county, or the Wilmore basin of Pennsylvania, which lies along the eastern slope of Laurel Hill, and crosses Cheat river just below Albright, where it carries the Upper Freeport coal below the level of Cheat river, and is deep enough to catch a small area of the Pittsburg coal in Copemans Knob, between Albright and Kingwood.

In this Muddy creek basin the Upper Freeport coal bed has practically the same structure as in the Pisgah region, so that the portion of Preston county north from Cheat river, holds two valuable basins of this coking coal, while Monongalia county holds another just west from the Chestnut ridge arch. This last area lies between Chestnut ridge and the Monongahela river, being practically the southwestward extension of the Connellsville syncline.

These three troughs or synclines, viz: the Connellsville, Ligonier, and Muddy creek, extend completely across both Preston and Monongalia counties, and appear to hold good coal throughout their entire extent, although in the westernmost one (Connellsville) the Upper Freeport coal gets thinner in southern Monongalia than it is farther north.

The next eastern one, (Muddy creek), which corresponds to the Wilmore basin of Pennsylvania, as already stated, crosses Cheat river just below Albright, and its central line, cutting across Copemans knob, passes east of Kingwood, half way between that town and Cheat river, and, crossing the B. & O. R. R. near Anderson, goes on southwestward through Preston into Barbour and Randolph.

The Upper Freeport coal has not been mined for shipment in a commercial way from the northern end of this basin, except at Tunnelton, and between Tunnelton and Kingwood. There it has the same structure (see section page 349) as in the Ligonier or Sandy creek basin, north from Cheat river, except that the lowest ply of coal is present or exposed under the "big" slate, the latter being only eighteen to thirty inches thick.

Near Howesville, Preston county, the Kingwood Coal Company operates a mine on the West Virginia and Northern railroad, the output being shipped east for general steam and fuel purposes. A. P. Brady reports the following section at this mine:

HOWESVILLE MINE.

	Ft.	In.	Ft.	In.
Bone coal..	0	4		
Coal	2	3		
"Little" slate	0	2		
Coal	0	6		
Sulphur streak	0	0½	6	9½
Coal	1	2		
"Big" slate	0	10		
Coal, not mined	1	6		

Butts run S. 73° E. Face S. 17° W.

The coal below the "big" slate is not taken out, and was not included in the sample taken for analysis, for which Prof. Hite reports the following composition:

Moisture	0. 57
Volatile matter	30. 52
Fixed carbon	54. 91

Ash 14.00

Total..100. 00

Sulphur... 3. 45
Phosphorus .... .008
B. T. U. Wil. Cal. 13,031

The Irona Coal Company also mines this bed along the West Virginia & Northern railroad, between Tunnelton and Kingwood, and Mr. Brady reports the following structure at the

IRONA MINE.

	Ft. In.	Ft. In.
Slate	10 0	
Bone coal..	1 3	
Coal	2 8	
"Little" slate...	0 1	7 11
Coal	1 5	
"Big" slate...	1 0	
Coal	1 6	

ANALYSIS.

Moisture. 0. 65
Volatile matter 28. 46
Fixed carbon 62. 54
Ash 8. 35

Total...100. 00

Sulphur 1. 47
Phosphorus.. 0. 026

Butts run S. 62° E.   Face, S. 28° W.   Greatest rise, N. 70° W.

The Merchants Coal Company, of Baltimore, has extensive mines on this coal at the eastern end of Kingwood tunnel, Tunnelton, Preston county, just east from the crest of the Laurel Hill anticlinal, and there A. P. Brady made the following measurements:

MERCHANTS COAL COMPANY'S TUNNELTON MINES.

	North Side Mine.		South Side Mine.	
	Ft.	In.	Ft.	In.
Bone coal...................................	0	10	0	11
Coal	2	7	2	4
Slate, "little"	0	2	0	2
Coal	1	9	1	6
Slate, "big"	1	3	not measured	
Coal	1	6	"	
Totals	8	1	4	11

Butts run S. 73° E.   Face S. 17° W.   Elevation A. T.,
1872.

ANALYSES

	North Side Mine.	South Side Mine.
Moisture	0. 62	0. 72
Volatile matter	31. 00	28. 75
Fixed carbon...................	57. 66	63. 84
Ash	10. 72	6. 69
Totals...........................100. 00	100. 00	
Sulphur........	3. 41	1. 31
Phosphorus...	0. 009	0. 025
B. T. U. (Wil. Cal.)	13,846	14,807

These mines supply the B. & O. R. R. locomotives with fuel.
The above analyses probably show too much sulphur for the average coal at the North Side mine, and too little at the South Side
mine.

The coal, as may be seen from the calorific determinations,
gives very efficient results as a steam fuel, although, owing to the
large sulphur contents, there is a tendency to "clinker," which
the firemen do not like. The "bottom" division of the coal is not
mined, and was not sampled for analysis.

Just west from Kingwood Tunnel, the Gorman Coal and Coke
Company operates two mines on the Upper Freeport coal, where
A. P. Brady made the following measurements:

GORMAN COAL AND COKE COMPANY'S MINES.

	No. 1 Mine.		No. 2 Mine.	
	Ft.	In.	Ft.	In.
Bone coal...	0	8	0	8
Coal...	2	8	2	11
Slate, "little"...................	0	2	0	2
Coal...	1	7	1	9
Slate, "big"	1	6	not measured.	
Coal........	1	6		
Totals	8	1	5	6

Butts run S. 73° E.   Face S. 17° W.   Altitude No. 2, 1662
A. T. Greatest rise, N. 65° E.

ANALYSES.

	No. 1 Mine.	No. 2 Mine.
Moisture	0. 83	0. 91
Volatile matter.................................	28. 26	29. 15

Fixed carbon.......	62.42	58.76
Ash	8.49	11.18
Totals..	100.00	100.00
Sulphur	1.11	2.81
Phosphorus	0.032	0.003
B. T. U. Wil Cal.................................	13,515	

Just west from these last mines, we come to those of the Austen Coal & Coke Company, where this coal has been mined and coked for probably forty years, and there A. P. Brady made the following measurement:

AUSTEN COAL & COKE COMPANY'S MINES.

	Ft. In.	Ft. In.
Bone coal..	0 8	
Coal	2 8	
Slate, "little"..	0 2	8 1
Coal	1 7	
Slate, "big"	1 6	
Coal	1 6	

Butts run S. 73° E.   Face S. 17° W.   Elevation 1535 A. T. Greatest rise S. E.

ANALYSES.	Coal.	Coke.
Moisture	0.72	0.18
Volatile matter	28.67	1.30
Fixed carbon	63.78	86.33
Ash	6.83	12.19
Totals...	100.00	100.00
Sulphur	0.94	0.86
Phosphorus	0.048	0.067
B. T. U. Wil. Cal	14,403	

The bottom ply of coal is not mined, and was not sampled for analysis.

This same coal is mined west from Austen by the Orr Coal & Coke Company, and also by the Hite Coal & Coke Company, at their "Vulcan" and "Dixie" mines respectively, but the measurements of the coal, reported by Mr. Brady, are practically the same as those given for Austen.   Prof. Hite reports the analyses of the coal in each as follows:

ANALYSES,	Dixie Mine.	Vulcan Mine.
Moisture	0.69	0.73
Volatile matter	30.01	30.02
Fixed carbon ....:............................	57.72	61.23
Ash	11.58	8.02
Totals	100.00	100.00
Sulphur........	3.04	2.41
Phosphorus	0.069	0.03

At the Newburg shaft, two miles west from the Vulcan and Dixie mines, the Upper Freeport coal has dipped 150 feet below water level, or from 1360 feet above tide at the Vulcan mine to 1038 feet above the same datum in the bottom of the deep syncline, where even the Pittsburg coal is caught in the summits of the hills. The Newburg shaft was sunk through the Upper Freeport bed down to the Lower Kittanning coal, and the latter was the only one mined until a disastrous explosion of mine gas partially wrecked the mine, and led to the abandonment of operations on the Kittanning coal.

In recent years, the Upper Freeport bed, which lies 170 feet down in the shaft, has been mined by the Newburg Coal & Coke Company, and A. P. Brady reports the following measurement for the same:

NEWBURG SHAFT MINE.

	Ft. In.	Ft. In.
"Draw" slate	0 3	
Coal	2 4	
Slate, "little"	0 1½	
Coal	1 5	6 2½
Slate, "big"	1 6	
Coal	0 10	

Butts run S. 76° E.   Face S. 14° W.   Greatest rise, southwest.   Elevation 1038 A. T.

Prof. Hite reports the following analysis for sample collected from the shaft:

Moisture	0. 64
Volatile matter	30. 42
Fixed carbon	56. 72
Ash	12. 22
Total	100. 00
Sulphur	2. 33
Phosphorus	0. 007
B. T. U. Wil. Cal	13,516

This is near the center of the deep syncline west from the Laurel Ridge anticlinal, and the rocks rise to the northwest, and also to the northeast, so that the coal comes to the surface on Three-Fork creek, and has long been mined in the region of the old Hardman Furnace. It was also manufactured into coke until that furnace went out of blast several years since. Recently the mines have been reopened by the Monarch Coal and Mining Company, one mile and a-quarter north from Hardman, and there A. P. Brady reports the following succession :

VICTORIA MINE, NEAR HARDMAN, TAYLOR COUNTY.

	Ft.	In.	Ft.	In.
Coal	I	6		
Draw slate	I	6		
Bone coal....................	0	3		
Coal	I	7		
Bone coal	0	2	7	9¼
Coal	2	5		
Slate, "little"...................................	0	0¼		
Coal	0	4		

Prof. Hite gives the following analysis for the coal below the upper bone:

Moisture	o. 81
Volatile matter...	28. 78
Fixed carbon	61. 46
Ash	8. 95
Total...	100. 00
Sulphur	1. 99
Phosphorus	0. 097

There has been some discussion among the local mining fraternity as to the horizon of the coal at the Victoria mine, some even claiming it to be identical with the Lower Kittanning, but while, the structure of the bed has changed slightly, there is no difficulty in recognizing the main features of the Upper Freeport seam. The "little" slate is thinner than usual, as well as the ply of coal immediately under it, but the main body of the coal above the slate has the same thickness and quality as in the other mines farther east. True, a new layer of coal makes its appearance in the roof of the mine, but this is a common feature with the Upper Freeport bed. Then, too, there is only a slight rise of the strata from the Newburg shaft northwestward, and for the Lower Kittanning to get up to the surface on Three Fork, it must rise over 300 feet in less than three miles, an impossible proposition from the known rate of dip.

In the region of Masontown, Preston county, near the center of this same coal basin, (Ligonier), Hon. S. B. Elkins has recently put down two test borings for coal. One of these, on the Sanford Watson farm, published on page 344 of this volume, and summarized, shows the Upper Freeport coal with the following structure:

	Ft. In.	Ft. In.
Coal and bone mixed	2 4¾	
Coal	2 11¼	
Slate, "little"	0 2½	
Coal, "mining ply"......	1 1½	10 2½
Slate, "big"	1 0	
Coal, bottom { coal...... .... 1 5½ / slate .... 0 1½ / coal..................... 0 11½ }	2 6½	

Here the "bottom" division of the coal has nearly doubled
its usual thickness, but otherwise the coal has its typical structure
for Preston county. The coal was struck in this boring at 176 feet
below the surface.

In another test boring made by Senator Elkins, on the Amos
Ashburn farm, about three-fourths of a mile distant from the Watson, this coal was struck at a depth of 181 feet, and exhibits the
following structure:

	Ft. In.	Ft. In.	Ft. In.
Coal, "top".......... { coal, sulph. 0 2½ / bone.......... 0 8 / black slate.. 0 11½ / coal, sulph.. 0 8½ / bone.......... 0 3 / coal .... 0 2½ / bone.......... 0 ½ }		3 0½	
Coal, "main bench"....`..............................	2 3		
Slate, "little".......................................	0 2½		10 5½
Coal, "mining ply" { coal .... 1 2½ / slate.......... 0 ½ / coal .... 0 4 }		1 7	
Slate, "big"	0 11		
Coal, "bottom"....... { coal, sulph.. 1 4½ / slate........... 0 2 / coal .... 0 11 }		2 5½	
Fireclay..			5 0
Limestone, in several layers, separated by fireclay shales...			20 0

Here, although the bed shows a thickness of nearly eleven
feet, it holds only four feet of available coal, unless the "big"
slate should be taken up and the "bottom" coal mined. It would
be a great loss of fuel to leave so much coal in the ground as a
waste product, but under present mining conditions no other result may be feasible. It is possible that in the far off future both
the "top" and "bottom" members of the coal may be crushed
and washed, and thus three to four feet more of valuable fuel recovered from this bed.

The Upper Freeport coal rises above water level on Deckers creek, one-half mile northwest from Masontown, and has been mined for village supply at the Scott bank, where it exhibits the following structure:

	Ft. In.	Ft. In.
Gray shales...		5 0
Slaty and bony coal	2 2	
Coal, good, main bench	2 9	
Slate, "little"...	0 2	
Coal, "mining ply"	1 4	9 4
Slate, "big"	0 9	
Coal, "bottom," visible...........................	2 2	

The bottom division of the coal is not fully exposed, and it holds two inches of bony slate near the center. The "big" slate, which is really an impure fireclay, varies from six to twelve inches in thickness, and is occasionally taken up in this mine to secure the underlying coal, which the farmers "report" as the best in the mine. Its appearance, however, would not confirm the "report," since it looks coarse in grain and rather high in ash. The "mining" ply and the "main bench" above, however, are both very pure, bright, and clean-looking, of the typical coking facies.

At the "Falls" tract opening, near this, the coal has practically the same structure as at the Scott mine, and the Lower Mahoning sandstone makes a massive cliff only five feet above the coal.

This coal has been mined at many localities on either side of the basin, just north from Masontown, and also near the center of the same where Bull run cuts down to it on its course to Cheat river. The central line of the basin appears to pass between Nicholas Posten's opening and that of Henry Eddy, one mile and a half north from Masontown. The coal exhibits the following structure at the Posten mine:

	Ft. In.	Ft. In.
"Top" coal, impure, bony........................	2 9	
Coal, main bench	2 9	
"Little" slate...	0 2	
Coal, "mining ply"...................................	1 6	9 11
"Big" slate...	0 9	
Coal, "bottom" visible.............................	2 0	

The coal shows practically the same section at Henry Eddy's bank, nearby. The upper half of the "top" coal appears to be fairly pure, and it may furnish some good fuel, but the lower portion is interstratified with bony and slaty layers, so that probably all of the "top" coal will be lost in ordinary mine work. The "main bench" and the "mining ply" are both excellent looking here, as also the "bottom" division. The "big" slate is only six to twelve inches thick in this region, and hence, as the underlying coal is more than two feet thick, it may prove profitable to mine this bottom member.

The central line of the Ligonier basin crosses Cheat river near the mouth of Bull run, where the Upper Freeport coal is about 750-800 feet above the level of the water. It is mined by Forbes Blaney, Daniel Lyons, and several others in the hills which overlook Cheat river.

About four miles southeast from the central line of the Ligonier syncline, we come to the crest of the Laurel Hill anticlinal, and find the Upper Freeport capping a knob at Cameron Elliott's bank, on the very crest of the arch, exhibiting the following structure:

	Ft.	In.	Ft.	In.
Sandstone, massive, Lower Mahoning			20	0
"Top" coal	2	0		
Coal, main bench	2	6		
"Little" slate	0	2		
Coal, "mining ply"	1	3	9	4
"Big" slate	0	10		
Coal, two inches bone in center	2	7		

Here the "bottom" division of the coal is taken out, and is fairly good, except two inches of bony slate near the center.

On the Morgantown and Kingwood turnpike, this coal is mined by Davis Stutzel and William Miller, two and one-half to three miles east from Reedsville, where it exhibits practically the same section as those already given. West from the Miller and Stutzel mines, the coal dips rapidly to the northwest, and underlies Reedsville, in the center of the syncline, by a depth of 200 feet or more. The axis of the basis lies just west of Reedsville, and the coal soon begins to rise rapidly to the northwest. It underlies Deckers creek at the turnpike crossing, one mile west of Reedsville, by a depth of not less than 140 feet. One mile west from this, however, the coal gets up into the hills, and has been mined along the Morgantown road on the lands of the Keck heirs, John Sharp, and others, where it has the same structure as that already given.

Farther west the Chestnut Ridge anticlinal throws all of the Allegheny series into the air, and the Upper Freeport bed does not appear again till we come to Dalton's coal bank, in Monongalia county, six miles east from Morgantown, where it has long been mined for domestic supply, and has the same structure as in Preston county, except that the "top" and "bottom" coals are thinner. The "main bench" and "mining ply" still measure about four feet, however, and their coal is very bright and good.

Two large mining operations have recently been started on this bed along Deckers creek, on the Morgantown and Kingwood railroad, four miles southeast from Morgantown, by the West Virginia Coal Company and the Deckers Creek Coal & Coke Company, respectively. The former has its mines on the north bank of the stream and the latter occupies the south bank of the same.

The coal shows the following structure in the West Virginia Coal Company's mine:

	Ft.	In.	Ft.	In.
Gray shales				
Black slate	2	4		
Impure cannel....................	0	6		
Bony coal....	0	8		
Coal, "main bench"..................................	2	10		
"Little" slate, gray	0	2	13	0
Coal, "mining ply"	I	2		
"Big" slate (fireclay)	4	0		
Coal, "bottom"....................................	I	4		
Fireclay and sandy beds.............	10	0		
Limestone and iron ore, Upper Freeport	8	0		

It requires but a glance at this structure to perceive the same type as that shown in Preston county. The main mass of the "top" coal has changed to a black, cannelly slate, the bottom portion of which is genuine cannel with conchoidal fracture, while the "big" slate at the bottom has thickened up to four feet at the main opening, and within fifty yards is seen to thicken to ten feet of fireclay and sandy beds. The "main bench" and "mining ply" divisions remain constant, however, in both thickness and quality, separated by the "little" slate of the miners, a dark gray stratum one to two inches thick. The "main bench" varies from thirty-two to thirty-six inches, and the "mining ply" from twelve to sixteen inches, so that the average available coal is practically four feet. The bony coal at the top runs from six to nine inches in thickness, and is taken down only in the main entries.

The coal is soft, bright, and quite pure, a typical coking coal, and the West Virginia Coal Company is building 150 bee hive ovens (50 of which are now in operation) for the manufacture of coke.

Both the coal and coke have been analyzed by the Maryland Steel Company of Baltimore, with the following results:

COAL.

	Top.	Middle.	Mining Ply.	Gen. Sec.
Volatile matter	31.77	32.95	34.20	32.05
Fixed carbon	60.10	62.41	61.91	61.45
Ash	8.13	4.64	3.89	6.50
Totals	100.00	100.00	100.00	100.00
Sulphur	0.73	0.56	1.24	0.69
Phosphorus	0.316	0.014	0.003	0.165

The Maryland Steel Company also analyzed three samples of coke with the following results:

	I.	II.	III.	IV.
Volatile matter	0.96	1.02	0.70	1.24
Fixed carbon	85.45	86.49	87.85	88.48
Ash	13.59	12.49	11.45	10.28
Totals	100.00	100.00	100.00	100.00
Sulphur	0.67	0.76	0.75	0.57
Phosphorus	0.321	0.246	0.109	0.148

I., II., III., samples analyzed by Maryland Steel Company.

IV. sample analyzed by E. S. Stalnaker, Assistant Chemist, West Virginia Geological Survey.

Mr. Stalnaker also took a general sample of the coal across the "main bench" and "mining ply," which gave him the following results:

Moisture	1.55
Volatile matter	30.97
Fixed carbon	59.95
Ash	7.53
Total	100.00
Sulphur	0.895
Phosphorus	0.178
B. T. U.	14.008

These analyses all show a very superior coke in every respect, except as to phosphorus contents.   Mr. Davis Elkins, President of the West Virginia Company, to whose courtesy the Survey is indebted for the analyses made by the Maryland Steel Company, states that most of the phosphorus occurs in the upper portion of the "main bench,"and that by separating this portion of the coal, which is harder and bears shipment well, it will be possible to reduce the average phosphorus to less than one-tenth of one per cent.

The Upper Freeport limestone was uncovered in excavating for the coke ovens on the north side of the creek, and on top of it is one to two feet of lean carbonate of iron.   This ore was once stripped and used in the manufacture of iron, many years ago, at an old furnace a short distance above the coke plant.

On the south side of the creek the coal exhibits the following structure at the mines of the Decker's Creek Coal and Coke Company.

	Ft. In.	Ft. In.
Black slate		
Cannel	0 7	
Bone coal	0 8	
Coal, "main bench"	2 11	5 4
Slate, "little"	0 2	
Coal, "mining ply"	1 0	

The thickness of the black slate at the top, and of the "bottom" coal was not exposed at this mine.   The Deckers Creek Company is also building coke ovens and preparing to manufacture coke.

A sample of the coal taken from this mine by Mr. Stalnaker yielded him the following results:

Moisture	1. 32
Volatile matter	30. 02
Fixed carbon	60. 43
Ash	8. 23
Total	100. 00
Sulphur	1. 11
Phosphorus	0. 093
B. T. U.	14. 002

The strata dip rapidly northwest at these mines and soon carry the coal below water level, so that just below Rock Forge, less than one mile from the coke ovens, the coal is 163 feet below the surface, and exhibits the following section as determined by the test hole put down on the Gamble lot by Senator Elkins in 1901:

	Ft.	In.	Ft.	In.
Bone coal	0	2½		
Coal, "main bench"	3	4½		
Slate, "little"	0	2½	5	7
Coal, mining ply"	1	0		
Slate, "big"	0	3		
Coal, "bottom"	0	6½		

Here the "main bench" has thickened slightly, and the "big" slate of the miners has nearly disappeared.

The coal continues to dip to the northwest down into the center of the Connellsville basin, which crosses Decker's creek two miles below Rock Forge, half way between the latter point and Morgantown, where the coal would lie 250 feet below water level at the Harner bottoms. From this point it rises gently westward to the crest of the Indiana anticline, which passes across the measures just west from Morgantown; but the coal does not get up to water level until we come to the Eureka Pipe Line Pumping Station, two miles south from the mouth of Deckers creek. Here the coal was formerly (60-70 years ago) mined by stripping from the bed of the Monongahela at low water, and is reported to be three feet thick.

The coal keeps about level with the bed of the river up to the mouth of Booths creek, at Uffington, and there, on the east bank of the Monongahela, it rises above water level and has been mined by drifting, just under the B. & O. R. R. bridge, and only four or five feet above low water. The coal has also been stripped out of the bed of Booths creek, one-half mile above its mouth, where it is reported as three feet thick and quite pure.

About three-fourths of a mile above Uffington, the coal rises above the grade of the B. & O. R. R., near the "watch-box," and there exhibits the following structure on the land of Ed. S. Kinsley:

	Ft.	In.	Ft.	In.
Shales			5	0
Coal { coal	1	6		
slate	0	2	2	0
coal	0	4		

Here the "main bench" has thinned to only eighteen inches, and the "mining ply" to only four, while the "bottom" division has disappeared completely.

Just above the "watch-box" the river veers west and the coal dips down under it, and does not reappear until we come to two and one-quarter miles below Little Falls, where it emerges from the bed of the stream and has been mined on the land of Mr. Frum by stripping, just above low water, where it is about three feet thick, with a slate parting.

In the vicinity of Little Falls Station the coal has been mined by several parties for local use, and it exhibits a section like the following, seen one-fourth mile below the mouth of Joe's run, in the bluff above the B. & O. railroad track.

		Ft. In.	Ft. In.
Sandstone, massive, Lower Mahoning		20 0	
Shale, gray		0 6	
Coal .. { coal, "main bench"	2 2		
{ slate, "little"	0 2		3 2
{ coal, "mining ply"	0 10		
Fireclay, shales and limestone to railroad track		20 0	

Here both the "top" bony coal and the "bottom" divisions of the bed are entirely absent, but the "main bench," the "little" slate, and the "mining ply" remain. The Upper Freeport limestone is exposed in several layers, separated by shales, beginning about ten feet under the coal bed and extending down to track level.

A short distance above the mouth of Joe's run, the coal dips under the railroad tracks, and then under the Monongahela, and we see it no more in the direction of Fairmont.

In passing up Booths creek, the coal dips down into the Connellsville basin, and gets fifty to sixty feet below water level, until the center of that syncline is passed, three miles up the creek, when the southeastward rise soon brings the coal to the surface again on the land of Mr. Chisler, where it has been mined and is three feet thick. The coal continues to rise faster than the stream, and at Jackson's store, four miles above the mouth of Booths creek, gets thirty feet above water level and is mined on the land of Thomas Jackson, at whose bank the following succession is visible:

		Ft. In.	Ft. In.
Coal, "top"..	coal, bony	1 0	
	shale	0 8	
	coal, bony	0 7	4 1
	shale	0 5	
	coal, bony	0 5	
	shale	1 0	
Coal, "main bench"		1 11	
Slate, "little"		0 1	3 0
Coal, "mining ply"		1 0	

Here the "top" division of the coal makes its appearance, although it is only about one mile through the hills to Little Falls, where it is entirely absent, and the massive Lower Mahoning sandstone rests directly upon the "main bench" of the coal.

In passing up the right hand fork of Booths creek from Jackson's store, the rocks rise quite rapidly toward the Chestnut Ridge anticlinal, and carry the Upper Freeport coal high up in the hills, in the region of Clinton Furnace, one mile and a-half above Jackson's store. The O. C. Johnson bank, near Clinton Furnace, exhibits the following structure:

	Ft. In.	Ft. In.
Coal, "top," bony	2 0	
Coal, "main bench"	2 7	5 10
Slate, ' little"	0 2	
Coal, "mining ply"	1 1	

The "top" coal is mined for domestic use along with the other divisions below, but it is very poor coal and could not be used in a commercial way. The coal has now recovered the type seen everywhere in Preston county, and along Deckers creek in Monongalia, and it retains this type (which gives about four feet of good coal in the two divisions under the bony "top" coal) on eastward to and beyond the Preston county line, as well as northeastward to Deckers creek.

The coal has also been mined for local supply at the head of Booths creek, by Samuel Dalton, William Howell, Mr. Weaver, and others, in all of whose mines at least four feet of good coal occurs. The structure at Mr. Howell's mine, at the head of the left fork of Booths creek, is as follows:

	Ft. In.	Ft. In.
Bony coal, "top"	2 0.	
Coal, "main bench"	3 0	6 6
Slate, "little"	0 2	
Coal, "mining ply"	1 4	

The lower four inches of the "mining ply" division is slaty
and impure.

A sample of the coal at the Howell mine was analyzed by
Prof. Hite with the following results:

Moisture	1.39
Volatile matter	33.05
Fixed carbon	57.87
Ash	7.69
Total	100.00
Sulphur	2.40

A carload of this coal was coked in the ovens at Montana,
Marion county, and a sample of the coke, analyzed by Prof. Hite,
yielded the following results:

Moisture	0.06
Volatile matter	0.80
Fixed carbon	87.72
Ash	11.42
Total	100.00
Sulphur	1.50

The sulphur is rather high in this sample, but the farmers and
smiths of the region all agree that the Howell bank holds more
sulphur than any of the others.

Where this coal comes up to the surface, along the Valley river
in eastern Marion and western Taylor counties, on the crest of the
Chestnut Ridge anticlinal, it is not yet certainly identified, though
in the section at Valley Falls, Taylor county, given on page 355,
a bed of coal has been classed as the Upper Freeport, which occurs
nearly 200 feet above the Lower Kittanning.   This may be erroneous, however, and the thick coal bed seventy-nine feet lower,
only 120 feet above the Lower Kittanning, may possibly be the
Upper Freeport bed, instead of the Lower, as indicated in the
section.

This thick (6-7 feet) coal, only 120 to 130 feet above the Lower Kittanning bed, and containing much slate, bone, and impure
coal, is found over the entire area of the exposure, from where it
rises above the Valley river, one mile below Powell, until it dips
under the same again, just below Bush.   It will be described under the Lower Freeport coal, though it may turn out to be the Upper one.

At Bush, Taylor county, a coal bed occurs at forty-two feet above the coal just referred to, which exhibits the following structure at an old opening, where it was once mined for domestic supply:

	Ft. In.	Ft. In.
Coal	0 10	
Slate	0 1	
Coal	1 8	3 4
Slate	0 1	
Coal	0 8	

The coal is known locally as the "Four-foot" seam, and it reminds one of what has been termed the Mahoning coal, forty feet above the Upper Freeport bed, of the Philippi region, and if the coal now being opened up for shipment, forty-two feet lower, at Bush, should prove to be the Upper Freeport seam, then the "Four-foot" bed, at Bush, would be the Mahoning coal.

These questions of identity will be carefully worked out in the future county reports, since it has been impossible to make such detailed studies as would settle many of the doubtful cases of correlation like the present one.

This coal dips under the Valley river a short distance above Bush, and does not reappear until we pass up Three Fork creek, one mile beyond the Grafton station, where it comes above water level for a short distance and reveals two and one-half feet of coal under some coaly shales, twenty feet below a very massive sandstone.

On the Valley river, above Grafton, the Upper Freeport coal horizon does not rise over the tracks of the Grafton & Greenbrier branch of the B. & O. R. R. until we come to Sandy creek, eight miles from Grafton.

Near Cove run, eleven miles above Grafton, this coal changes to a bed of impure cannel, five to six feet thick, where it has been opened on the lands of Messrs. Whitescarver, Phelps, and others.

In the vicinity of Moatsville, at the mouth of Teter's creek, the Upper Freeport coal has been mined for local use on both sides of the Valley river. It lies on top of a very massive, pebbly sandstone, which makes great cliffs along Valley river, 125 feet above the water. On the west side of the river, the coal is mined along the public road, on the lands of John Wilson and others, where it exhibits the following structure:

	Ft. In.	Ft. In.
Coal, visible ....:...............	1 0	
Shale........	1 6	
Sandstone ....···············	3 0	10 8
Coal, good	3 0	
Fireclay shale...	1 2	
Coal, visible	1 0	

On the east side of the river, at Moatsville, the coal has been mined by Daniel Moore, Thomas Cline, Thomas Gener, and others, just above the great cliff of pebbly sandstone.

This coal is constantly above water level along Teter's creek, from its mouth, at Moatsville, up to the mouth of Brushy Fork, just below Nestorville, where it was once stripped out of the bed of the creek, forty feet under the Mahoning coal.

Above the mouth of Brushy Fork of Teter's creek, this coal dips under the stream into the southwestward extension of the Muddy creek basin of Preston county, and hence is below water level at Valley Furnace, until its horizon comes out again one mile above, and shows the following structure on the land of Mr. A. C. Keyser:

	Ft. In.	Ft. In.
Coal, bony	1 6	
Coal, good	1 6	
Shales	8 0	13 0
Coal, bony	0 6	
Coal	1 6	

This coal comes ten feet below a limestone which was once mined and used as a flux at the old Valley furnace. The limestone appears to be identical with the one seen in the roof shales of this coal, both at Moatsville and Meriden, below Philippi, and, according to preliminary identifications, would correlate with the Mahoning limestone of the Pennsylvania section.

At the headwaters of Sandy creek, in Preston county, south from the B. & O. R. R., the Upper Freeport coal swells up to a thickness of twelve feet, on the land of Jonas Wolf, where it has long been mined for local supply. The section measured there is as follows:

	Ft. In.	Ft. In.
Coal	2 0	
Gray shale..........	2 0	12 0
Coal, with some bone	8 0	

This is in the steep dip (15°) along the northwest slope of Big Laurel mountain.

The same coal is also mined on the Orr lands, farther to the northeast, but it is there only about six feet in thickness.

The steep dip along the foot of Big Laurel, extends from Sandy creek across Barbour and Randolph counties, through to the Valley river above the mouth of Roaring creek, and, although this region has been but little explored, it holds valuable areas of Upper Freeport coal along the entire distance. The bed is often split it into two distinct seams by three to ten feet of shales and sandy beds, and it frequently happens that the farmers open only one of them, and are not aware of the presence of the other.

This coal has been mined for several years in the vicinity of Arden, Barbour county, and used for coaling the B. & O. locomotives. It is also shipped east and west for general steam purposes.

The Laurel Coal Company's mine is one-half mile north from Arden, and there A. P. Brady reports the following structure:

	Ft. In.	Ft. In.
Sandstone		
Slate		
Draw slate		
Coal	2 8	
Bone coal	0 7	5 9
Coal	2 6	

Butts run S. 78° E.   Face S. 12° W.   Elevation 1326 feet A. T.

Analysis of sample reported by Prof. Hite as follows:

Moisture	0. 62
Volatile matter	31. 35
Fixed carbon	59. 58
Ash	8. 45
Total	100. 00
Sulphur	2. 60
Phosphorus	0. 006
B. T. U (Wil. Cal.)	13863

The Tygarts Valley Coal & Coke Company operates this coal at Arden, where A. P. Brady reports the following measurement:

	Ft. In.	Ft. In.
Sandstone		
Slate		
Draw slate	0 4	
Coal	2 2	
Bone coal	1 0	} 5 10
Coal ...., ...	2 4	

Butts and face same as preceding.   Elevation 1321 feet A. T.
Analysis of sample reported by Prof. Hite as follows :

Moisture	0. 66
Volatile matter..	30. 78
Fixed carbon	55. 39
Ash	13. 17
Total..100. 00	
Sulphur	2. 52
Phosphorus..................................	0. 010
B. T. U. (Wil. Cal.)	13474

The Philippi Coal & Mining Company operates this same coal
at Meriden, two miles below Philippi, and there A. P. Brady made
the following measurement in its No. 1 mine:

	Ft. In.	Ft. In.
Sandstone		
Slate		
Draw slate...	0 1	
Coal	2 3	
Bone coal..........	0 7	
Coal	2 4	} 5 7
"Mud seam"...	0 1	
Coal	0 4	

Butts and face same as preceding.   Elevation 1291 feet A. T.
Analysis of sample reported by Prof. Hite as follows :

Moisture	0. 53
Volatile matter..............................	29. 44
Fixed carbon	62. 92
Ash	7. 11
Total... 100. 00	
Sulphur	2. 51
Phosphorus...	0. 024
B. T. U. (Wil. Cal.)..	13896

The P. C. & M. Company, through one of its officers, (Hon.
A. G. Dayton), gives the following measurement of mine No. 1,
which appears to differ slightly from Mr. Brady's:

	Ft. In.	Ft. In.
Coal, upper bench	2 3	
Bone	0 3½	
Coal, mining bench	0 10	
Slate...	0 2	6 2
Coal, lower bench....	2 1½	
Fireclay, soft	0 2	
Bottom coal..	0 4	

The section at Mine No. 2 reads as follows, according to Mr. Dayton:

	Ft. In.	Ft. In.
Coal, upper bench...............	2 2½	
Bone.......	0 7	
Coal, mining bench	0 9½	
Parting slate...	0 1	5 8
Coal, lower bench....................................	1 7	
Fireclay, soft	0 2	
Coal, "bottom"	0 3	

There is another ply of coal, one and a-half to two feet thick, and ten to fifteen feet, below the coal as given above. It comes on top of the great sandstone deposit, which underlies the Upper Freeport coal, and forms the cliffs along the Valley river, between Arden and Moatsville.

As we pass up the Valley river from Meriden, the Upper Freeport coal dips under the level of the latter, and is ten to fifteen feet below it where the Clarksburg pike crosses the stream. The river soon veers to the south, however, and the coal rises above water level, and then above the B. & O. R. R. tracks, where it has been mined at Lilian, one mile above Philippi. The coal appears to hold more bony material at Lilian, however, since the mining plant established there has been idle for sometime.

The coal continues to rise up the Valley river southeastward to the crest of a broad anticlinal, which crosses the river at Clements, one mile above the mouth of Middle Fork of the Valley river, and elevates the coal to about 175 feet above water level, where it is over seven feet thick on the lands of Messrs. Brown, Enlow, and others, but contains much bony material, so far as one may judge from the outcrop, which is, of course, badly weathered.

From Clements southeastward, the coal dips down and passes under water level again, three miles below Belington. It is mined on the southside of the river, opposite Jones crossing, where it is over six feet thick, and interstratified with nearly a foot of bony material, in four different layers, as shown by the following section made by Mr. A. P. Brady at the mine of the Valley Coal & Coke Company:

	Ft. In.	Ft. In.
Sandstone		
Slate		
Draw slate		
Coal	0 10	
Bone coal	0 3	
Coal	0 9	
Bone coal	0 2	
Coal	1 6	6 3
Bone coal	0 2	
Coal	1 5	
Bone coal	0 2	
Coal	1 0	

Butts run S. 78° E.   Faces S. 12° W.   Greatest rise N. 45° W.

Analysis reported by Prof. Hite as follows:

Moisture	0. 60
Volatile matter	29. 38
Fixed carbon	54. 40
Ash	15. 62
Total	100. 00
Sulphur	3. 20
Phosphorus	0. 06

The coal makes a very poor showing, but of course may improve at other localities in the region.

From the mine just mentioned, on the Belington & Northern railroad, the coal dips rapidly under the Valley river, and at Belington, near the center of the deep syncline, which catches the Pittsburg coal in a few summits to the northeast, this Upper Freeport coal would probably be 100 feet or more below water level, and not very valuable, if one may judge from the character of the coal at Jones Crossing, and also by the thinned and slaty condition of the same where it emerges from the Valley river again, three miles above Belington.   It was formerly supposed that THICK coal would always be found in synclinal areas, but in West Virginia, with but few exceptions, the coal thins perceptibly in passing into the synclines, while its thickest measurements are found high up on the slopes, or on the crests of the anticlines.

The Junior Coal Company has mines on the Upper Freeport

coal, where it rises above the grade of the railroad at Junior station, four miles south from Belington, and there A. P. Brady made the following measurement:

	Ft. In.	Ft. In.
Sandstone...		
Coal and slate mixed...		
Coal...	1 9	
Slate...	0 2	
Coal...	0 8	
Slate...	1 0	8 6
Coal...	3 2	
Slate...	0 8	
Coal...	1 1	

Butts run S. 78° E.   Face S. 12° W.   Elevation 1735 feet A. T.

Analysis of sample reported by Prof. Hite as follows:

Moisture...	0. 81
Volatile matter...	28. 73
Fixed carbon...	61. 98
Ash...	8. 48
Total...	100. 00
Sulphur...	1. 07
Phosphorus...	0. 01
B. T. U. (Wil. Cal.)...	14080

Only the two lower divisions of the coal were in the sample analyzed. A sample of the coke manufactured at Junior gave the following results to Prof. Hite and his assistants:

Moisture...	0. 08
Volatile matter...	0. 90
Fixed carbon...	84. 97
Ash...	14. 05
Total...	100. 00
Sulphur...	0. 94
Phosphorus...	0. 018

This coke is first-class in every respect except a little too much ash. The Junior Coal Company also operates mines and makes coke from this same coal at Harding, Randolph county, four miles above Junior, where the coal lies about 200 feet above the Valley river. A. P. Brady made the following measurements there:

	Ft. In.	Ft. In.
Sandstone		
Slate		
Coal	0 6	
Slate	1 6	
Bone coal	0 3	
Coal	1 10	
Slate	0 2	
Coal	0 3	11 8
Slate	0 5	
Coal	3 2	
Slate	0 6	
Coal	1 9	
Fireclay	0 6	
Coal	0 10	

Butts run S. 82° E. Face S. 8° W.

Analysis of sample from only the two lower main benches reported by Prof. Hite as follows:

Moisture	0.74
Volatile matter	30.38
Fixed carbon	59.59
Ash	9.29
Total	100.00
Sulphur	1.65
Phosphorus	0.023
B. T. U. (Wil. Cal.)	13901

A sample of coke made in the Harding ovens, forty-eight hours burning, gave the following analysis according to Prof. Hite:

Moisture	0.12
Volatile matter	0.87
Fixed carbon	82.62
Ash	16.39
Total	100.00
Sulphur	1.24
Phosphorus	0.034

The Maryland Smokeless Coal Company operates the Weaver mine, on Beaver creek, Randolph county, where A. P. Brady made the following measurement of the Upper Freeport coal.

	Ft. In.	Ft. In.
Sandstone		
Slate		
Coal	3 6	
Draw slate	0 4	
Coal	3 4	9 6
Slate	0 4	
Coal	2 0	

Butts run S. 78° E.   Face S. 12° W.   Greatest rise, south.

A sample of the coal and coke from Weaver gave Prof. Hite the following:

	Coal.	Coke.
Moisture	0.62	0.23
Volatile matter	29.81	1.10
Fixed carbon	58.29	82.25
Ash	11.28	16.42
Totals	100.00	100.00
Sulphur	1.63	1.24
Phosphorus	0.031	0.021
B. T. U. (Wil. Cal.)	13785	

Only the coal from the two lower benches was in the sample taken for analysis, since the upper bench is apparently not mined.

A new mine opened near Monroe Junction is operated by F. P. Reese, where A. P. Brady reports the following structure.

	Ft.	In.	Ft.	In.
Coal	I	4		
Bone coal	0	0½		
Coal	I	1½		
Bone coal	0	0½		
Coal	0	3		
Bone coal	0	0½		
Coal	3	2	10	7
Slate	0	5		
Coal	I	8		
Fireclay	0	6		
Coal	2	0		

This structure appears to correspond exactly to that of the Upper Freeport coal in Preston county, and summarized would appear as follows:

	Ft.	In.	Ft.	In.
"Top" coal, bony	2	10		
"Main bench" coal	3	2		
"Little" slate	0	5	10	7
"Mining ply" coal	I	8		
"Big" slate	0	6		
"Bottom" coal	2	0		

Analysis of sample, which included all the layers of coal except the "bottom," reported by Prof. Hite as follows:

Moisture	0.63
Volatile matter	28.72
Fixed carbon	62.23
Ash	8.42
Total	100.00

Sulphur 1. 51
Phosphorus.. 0. 10

The Maryland Smokeless Coal Company has a mine in the Upper Freeport bed at Leiter, on the south side of Valley river, below the mouth of Roaring creek, where A. P. Brady reports the following structure:

	Ft.	In.	Ft.	In.
Coal	0	5		
Slate	0	5		
Coal	0	8		
Draw slate..	1	0		
Bone coal	1	2		
Draw slate..	0	2	10	0
Coal	3	2		
Slate	1	0		
Coal	1	6		
Fireclay...	0	1		
Coal	0	5		

Butts run S. 77° W. Face S. 13° E.

Analysis of sample reported as follows by Prof. Hite:

Moisture 0. 54
Volatile matter... 30. 82
Fixed carbon 60. 20
Ash 8. 44
————
Total... 100. 00

Sulphur 1. 86
Phosphorus.. 0. 025
B. T. U. (Wil. Cal.)... 13,749

A large fault, or "want," runs through this mine and cuts out the coal for an unknown width.

Mr. Reese operated the mines at Womelsdorf for Berwind, White & Company, when A. P. Brady visited the region, but all of these mining interests have since been purchased by Hon. Henry G. Davis, of Elkins, the principal owner of the Junior Coal Company.

Womelsdorf is on Roaring creek, seven miles south from its mouth, and at the foot of Rich mountain, near the Beverly and Buckhannon pike. The Upper Freeport coal at the Womelsdorf mine has the following structure, as measured by A. P. Brady:

	Ft.	In.	Ft.	In.
Coal	0	1		
Bone coal..	0	2		
Coal	2	2		
Slate	0	1½	7	7½

Coal	3	4
Slate	0	3
Coal	1	6

Butts run S. 80° E.   Face S. 10° W.   Elevation 2250 feet A. T.   Greatest rise S. 30° E.

Analysis of sample reported by Prof. Hite as follows:

Moisture	0.69
Volatile matter...	28.45
Fixed carbon	62.17
Ash..	8.69
Total..	100.00
Sulphur..	1.51
Phosphorus...	0.033
B. T. U. (Wil. Cal.)	13656

These sections and analyses of the Upper Freeport coal in what has been termed the "Roaring creek" field, reveal a coal bed which furnishes six to seven feet of good fuel after the removal of the slate and bony partings.   It also makes a good coke which is in great demand.

Eastward from the Roaring creek field, the Upper Freeport bed arches into the air over Rich and Big Laurel mountains, and does not descend into the West Virginia hills again, so far as known, except possibly in a small area of the Corinth basin, east from Terra Alta, Preston county, until it comes down along the eastern slope of Back Bone mountain, at the head of the North Potomac coal basin, in Tucker and Grant counties.

It has been mined for several years by the Davis Coal & Coke Company at Thomas, Tucker county, on the West Virginia Central and Pittsburg railroad, both by drifts and shafts.   S. D. Brady reports the following measurements of this coal in Nos. 1, 2 and 3 drifts at Thomas:

	No. 1 D. Ft. In.	No. 2 D. Ft. In.	No. 3 D. Ft. In.
Sandstone			
Black slate 1–15 0		3–8 0	1–10 0
Draw slate........................ 0 3		....	....
Coal 1 9		1 7½	1 11
Coal and bone 2 2½		2 8	2 5
Coal 3 4		3 6	3 6
Totals..................... 7 3½		7 9½	7 10
Elevation A. T. (feet)........2900		3065	2885
Greatest rise.......................S. 10° E.		S. 10° E.	S. 10° E.

The structure of the coal bed at Thomas resembles that in the Roaring creek field very much, except that the "mining ply" and "bottom" divisions appear to be absent. The "top" coal is fairly good, and the "main bench," at the bottom, is very fine, but the central two and one-half feet is made up of alternate layers of good coal and bony coal in such a mixture that the separation of the bone from the coal is hardly practicable by the methods of ordinary mining. The bed is locally known as the "Thomas" seam. Samples taken from each of the mines yielded the following results on analysis, as reported by Prof. Hite:

	No. 1 D.	No. 2 D.	No. 3 D.
Moisture	0.46	0.42	0.49
Volatile matter	21.11	22.81	22.71
Fixed carbon	71.23	70.30	70.62
Ash	7.20	6.47	6.18
Totals	100.00	100.00	100.00
Sulphur	0.43	0.51	0.52
Phosphorus	0.011	0.004	0.010
B. T. U. (Wil. Cal)	....	14,699	....

A sample of coke from No. 1 drift is reported by Prof. Hite as follows:

Moisture	0.18
Volatile matter	1.43
Fixed carbon	83.87
Ash	14.52
Total	100.00
Sulphur	0.70
Phosphorus	0.03

This basin is comprised within the great folds of the Allegheny mountain region, and hence its coal has suffered a partial metamorphism, so that the volatile matter is about one-third less than in the Preston, Barbour and Randolph areas, and the coal would be called semi-bituminous. It is low in ash and sulphur, and has a most excellent reputation for both steam and coke, its heat value being quite high, as shown by the calorimetric tests.

A very large area of this coal extends under the North Potomac basin, cropping against the Back Bone mountain on the west and the East Front Ridge of the Alleghenies on the east, through Tucker, Grant, and Mineral counties.

In the deep shaft of the Davis Coal & Coke Company at Henry, Grant county, this coal was struck at about 220 feet, and it exhibits the following structure, as measured by A. P. Brady:

	Ft. In.	Ft. In.
Sandstone		
Draw slate...		0 6
Coal	0 8	
Bone coal..	0 4	
Coal	0 4	5 4½
Bone coal..	0 4½	
Coal, good.................................	3 8	

Elevation A. T., 2428 feet.

The analysis of the sample collected here is reported as follows by Prof. Hite:

Moisture	0. 58
Volatile matter...	21. 89
Fixed carbon	69. 63
Ash	7. 90
Total...	100. 00
Sulphur	2. 60
Phosphorus...	0. 025

The large increase in the quantity of sulphur shown here, over that in the same coal at Thomas, is especially noteworthy. It is possible that the coal will make a better showing in this respect when the mine gets longer into operation, since it is new, and the sample may not fairly represent the sulphur contents of the coal.

This bed comes to the surface near Bayard, five miles below Henry, and gradually gets higher above the line of the West Virginia Central & Pittsburg railroad, until near Gorman, where it is about 100 feet above the same, and was once mined by drifting, just below the Northwestern turnpike, on the north bank of the Potomac, in the edge of Garrett county, Maryland. From this point through Mineral county to Piedmont, thirty odd miles below, the coal is constantly above water level, and often 300 to 400 feet above the same, though its thickness has diminished to such an extent that it is known as the "Four-foot" seam, instead of the "Big," "Eight," "Ten" or "Twelve-foot" seam of the other regions.

The Smith Coal Company has recently opened a mine on this bed, one-half mile south of Blaine, Mineral county, and there A. P. Brady made the following measurement:

	Ft. In.	Ft. In.
Bone coal	0 5	
Coal	0 5	
Slate	0 11	4 9
Coal	3 0	

Butts run E. Face S. Elevation 1950 feet A. T.
Analysis of sample reported by Prof. Hite as follows:

Moisture	0.67
Volatile matter	15.79
Fixed carbon	71.27
Ash	12.27
Total	100.00
Sulphur	3.20
Phosphorus	0.041

The same coal has also been opened by the Big Vein Coal Company, one mile and a-half north from Shaw, where A. P. Brady reports the following succession:

	Ft. In.	Ft. In.
Bone coal	0 8	
Coal	2 6	3 10
Bone coal	0 8	

Elevation 1600 feet A. T.

This is also called the "Four-foot" seam by Mr. Brady in his notes.

The analysis of sample gives the following results as reported by Prof. Hite:

Moisture	0.51
Volatile matter	16.68
Fixed carbon	71.37
Ash	11.44
Total	100.00
Sulphur	3.22
Phosphorus	0.036

The samples of these last two mines were taken from near the crop of the coal, and that possibly accounts for some, but not all, of the deficiency in volatile matter.

Dr. G. C. Martin, of the Maryland Survey, publishes a section of this coal, taken near Blaine, on page 196 of his Garrett County Report, which gives the bed the following structure :

	Ft.	In.
Coal	0	6
Shale	0	2
Coal	0	11
Shale	0	2
Bony coal	1	1
Coal	2	0
Total	4	10

Also a section on the same page from near Barnum, as follows:

	Ft.	In.	Ft.	In.
Bone	0	3		
Coal	1	7	2	1½
Shale	0	0½		
Coal	0	3		

Another section from four miles west of Bayard, given on page 197 l. c., shows the structure of the Upper Freeport coal there as follows:

	Ft.	In.	Ft.	In.
Coal	1	10		
Slate	0	4	6	0
Coal	3	10		

In the region of Piedmont and Westernport this coal is about six feet thick, but has nearly two feet of shale and sandy material near its center, and is generally known as the "split seam."

Returning now to the Roaring creek region of Randolph county, and passing westward to the waters of Middle Fork (of Valley) river, we find the Upper Freeport coal still an important bed, but not so thick as in the Roaring creek field. In the vicinity of Ford's Hotel, or the Half-way House, on the Beverly and Buckhannon pike, this coal exhibits the following structure on the land of G. F. Ford :

	Ft.	In.	Ft.	In.
Coal	0	6		
Shale, gray	1	1		
Coal	2	2	6	1
Slate, dark	0	9		
Coal	1	7		

One mile east from this the coal gets thicker, on the land of John Ford, at whose bank the following section was measured by the writer:

	Ft. In.	Ft. In.
Coal	o 6	
Slate, dark	o 2	
Coal	o 8	
Slate with coal streaks............................	o 10	
Coal	1 4	9 1
Dark slate and bone......	o 10	
Coal	1 11	
Slate	1 3	
Coal	1 7	

These parting slates, which make up more than three feet of the total thickness, may, of course, grow thinner when followed into the hills in mining operations, since it is a general law that the parting slates of coal beds show thickest at their outcrops. This area of thicker coal appears to trend southward to the Kettle creek region of the Middle Fork river, where the Upper Freeport bed has a fairly good development.

In the region of Kingsville, the coal has thinned to only four feet, or even less, and from there to Talbot's store, in the edge of Barbour county, it is occasionally mined by the farmers for domestic use, but is seldom more than three and one-half to four feet thick.

About one mile above Hall's Mill, on Middle Fork (of Valley) river, and three and one-half miles above its mouth, the Upper Freeport coal has been mined quite extensively for local supply on the land of O'Brien and others. It has the following structure at O'Brien's bank, 150 feet above Middle Fork river:

	Ft. In.	Ft. In.
Sandstone, massive, visible................................	20 0	
Cannel slate	o 10	
Coal	1 10	
Fireclay, sandy...........................	o 5	
Coal	o 6	6 2
Fireclay, sandy	o 9	
Coal	1 10	

A great sandstone makes cliffs directly below the coal, and at the mill the stream falls over it in cascades.

This coal is also stripped out of the flat, just opposite Hall's Mill, where only four feet of it is exposed.

On the north bank of Middle Fork, and about one mile above Hall's Mill, this coal is mined on the land of J. E. Strader, where the following structure is exhibited:

	Ft.	In.	Ft.	In.
Gray shale	1	0		
Cannel slate	0	4		
Gray shale	1	3		
Coal	1	10		
Fireclay	0	8		
Coal	0	8	6	6
Fireclay	0	10		
Coal	2	6		

About five miles southwest from Hall's Mill, this coal has been mined on the land of Samuel Price, where it exhibits the following section:

	Ft.	In.	Ft.	In.
Cannel slate	1	0		
Coal	1	6		
Shale	0	7		
Coal	0	4	7	10
Fireclay	1	0		
Coal	2	4		
Splinty cannel, impure	1	1		

The coal at the bottom of the bed is more of a "splint" than cannel, but it is called cannel by the farmers.

This coal has been mined at the head of Laurel fork of Sand creek, or Big Sand run, as it is often called, on the land of Richard Campbell, where the following section was measured:

	Ft.	In.	Ft.	In.
Black slate				
Coal	1	10		
Slate	0	5		
Coal	0	2		
Fireclay	0	10	5	11
Coal	2	0		
Slate	0	1		
Splinty coal	0	7		

The coal exhibits this split-up condition along Sand creek, where it is exposed in the bed of the same, between its mouth, at the Buckhannon river, and its head, several miles above.

The following section of this coal, taken on the right bank of Sand creek, one-half mile below the mouth of Laurel Fork, is a continuation downward of the section given on page 316 of this volume:

	Ft. In.	Ft. In.
Cannel slate	0 3	
Shale, gray...........................	2 0	
Slate, dark	0 6	
Coal	1 6	
Shale, gray...........................	0 10	7 7
Coal, slaty...........................	0 10	
Shale, gray...........................	0 8	
Coal	1 0	
Fireclay, impure...........................		6 0
Sandstone, very massive...........................		

Here the great sandstone which underlies this same coal in the Roaring creek region, is in the bed of Sand creek, while the exposures in the hills above, render it certain that this is the same bed as the "Roaring creek" coal, although it makes such a poor showing in the section just given.

One-half mile farther down Sand creek, the coal improves, however, and exhibits the following section at Creed Talbot's mine:

	Ft. In.	Ft. In.
Coal, bony at top	1 11	
Shale, gray...........................	1 0	
Coal	0 3	
Shale, gray...........................	0 7	7 4
Coal, bottom splinty	2 8	
Slate	0 1	
Coal, splinty...........................	0 10	

In passing down Sand creek, or Big Sand run, from the last opening in the coal, it is mined by two or three other parties near water level, and then dips under the same and continues below to the Buckhannon river, but as the latter turns eastward it soon comes up again, and has been mined at the mill, one mile below the mouth of Sand creek, where it exhibits the following structure:

	Ft. In.	Ft. In.
Sandstone, massive, Lower Mahoning...........................		
Coal	1 6	
Shale, gray...........................	0 8	
Coal	0 1	5 2
Shale, gray...........................	0 11	
Coal	2 0	

On down the Buckhannon, and just below where the Burnersville branch of the B. & O. R. R. crosses the river at Lemley Junction, this coal was once mined only a few feet above the level of the water, but the mine is now abandoned and the coal not fully exposed. About one-fourth mile east, however, the rapid rise of the strata in that direction brings the coal up to seventy-five feet above the Buckhannon, and it exhibits the following section on the land of B. E. McCray:

	Ft. In.	Ft. In.
Coal	3 0	
Slate	0 3	
Coal	0 6	
Shale, gray	0 8	
Coal and slate	0 10	9 9
Coal	0 8	
Shale, gray	0 3	
Coal	2 0	
Coal, hard, splinty	1 7	

This measurement approaches that of the Roaring creek region in point of thickness, and the quality of the coal is fairly good.

The coal keeps seventy-five to one hundred feet above the level of the Buckhannon from this point on down to its mouth, at the Valley river, five miles below, and has been mined occasionally by the farmers for domestic use.

In passing up the Buckhannon river from the mouth of Sand creek, or Big Sand run, the course bears westward and the northwest dip of the strata carries the Upper Freeport coal far below water level, between that point and the town of Buckhannon, where its horizon is probably not less than 300 feet below the bed of the river, since the Elk Lick coal is only 130 feet above the same, and the Pittsburg coal caps the hills one mile north of the town. At Buckhannon, however, the course of the river turns south as we ascend it, and the southeastward rise of the rocks brings the Upper Freeport coal to the surface, between Hampton and Sago, seven miles above. It rises above the level of the B. & O. R. R. at Sago, and was once mined near Sago station, where it exhibits the following structure on the land of G. W. Burner:

	Ft. In.	Ft. In.
Coal	1 6	
Bony coal	0 6	4 6
Coal	2 6	
Concealed		10 0
Sandstone, very massive, to bed of Buckhannon river		25 0

The sandstone under this coal is the one which makes the

great cliffs along Roaring creek, and along the Valley river, between Roaring creek and Moatsville. It is constantly in sight from Sago to the head of the Buckhannon river, getting higher and higher in the hills and protecting the same from erosion, until it escapes into the air from Turkey Bone mountain, Webster county, at an elevation of 3500 feet above the sea. Its bold, pebbly outcrop, often fifty to seventy-five feet in vertical height, enables the observer to keep hold of the overlying coal in passing up the Buckhannon river from Sago into the region of the thick Allegheny-Kanawha sediments appearing between Newlon and Pickens.

One mile and a-half above Sago, the Upper Freeport coal has been opened on the left bank of the Buckhannon by Peter Eagle, at whose mine the following structure is exposed:

	Ft.	In.	Ft.	In.
Black slate	2	0		
Bony coal	1	0	7	0
Coal	4	0		

The coal lies ten to twelve feet above a very massive, pebbly sandstone, which makes a bold cliff below the outcrop of the coal.

Two miles above this last locality, the coal has thickened greatly, and we see the following succession on the west bluff of the Buckhannon, at an opening on the land of Jesse H. Sharp, one mile and a-half below Ten Mile station.

	Ft.	In.	Ft.	In.
Coal blossom in clay				
Black slate, cannelly			3	0
Coal	3	7		
Shale, gray	2	0		
Coal, bony	0	6		
Shale, gray	1	2		
Coal, bony	1	0	11	11
Coal, good	2	0		
Shale	1	0		
Coal	0	8		
Concealed			10	0
Sandstone, massive, Roaring creek			50	0
Cannel slate			12	0
Coal, Lower Freeport { coal	2	0		
shale	2	0	5	0
coal	1	0		
Shale, gray			3	0
Concealed			10	0
Sandstone, massive, in bed of Buckhannon river			5	0

The portion of this section under the Roaring creek sandstone is exposed one-half mile further down the river than Mr. Sharp's coal opening, but as the great cliff sandstone and its underlying coal are constantly in sight along the cuts in the railroad between the two points, there can be no error in the relative position of the two coal beds.   It is interesting to compare the section of the Upper Freeport coal here with that at Sago, only three and one-half miles distant, since it has nearly tripled its thickness, and then there is more coal above the black slate that has not been included in the bed, which would probably increase the thickness to sixteen feet or more.

It is only a few miles northeast from this point, on Stone Coal branch of Big Sand run, or Sand creek, where this coal thickens up and forms the famous "Twenty-two foot" bed of coal, described in Bulletin 65, U. S. G. Survey, page 151, as follows:

	Ft.	In.	Ft.	In.
Black slate	2	6		
Coal	1	0		
Bony coal	0	8		
Coal	2	0		
Black slate	3	0		
Coal	1	0		
Gray slate	4	6		
Coal	1	5	22	0
Slate dark	1	4		
Coal	1	10		
Slate, dark	0	5		
Coal, slaty	0	5		
Slate, gray	0	6		
Coal	1	5		

This wonderful expansion of the Upper Freeport coal bed, takes place in the region where the great thickening of the Allegheny-Kanawha sediments begins, and, although the entire bed totals up twenty-two feet, yet only a little more than one-third of it is COAL, and practically none of that is in available form to mine under present conditions.

At Ten Mile station, thirteen miles above Buckhannon, this coal has been mined at one hundred feet above water level, and there the following measurement was made:

	Ft.	In.	Ft.	In.
Coal	1	3		
Shale, gray	4	0		
Coal	0	6		
Shale	1	4		

```
Coal ............................................................ 3   0  ⎫ 13  3
Black slate ................................................. 0   5  ⎪
Coal ............................................................ 1   0  ⎬
Slate ........................................................... 0   6  ⎪
Coal ............................................................ 1   3  ⎭
Concealed ....................................................... 10  0
Sandstone, massive, pebbly.................................. 40  0
Concealed to Buckhannon river..................... 50  0
```

Here there is an immense thickness of material, but only five feet of available coal in the entire bed.

From Ten Mile southward, this coal has been mined occasionally, especially in the vicinity of Alton, where it lies on top of the great Roaring creek sandstone, and just above it another (Lower Mahoning) massive, pebbly rock forms a bold escarpment along the hills.

From Alton southward, the rocks rise rapidly, and when we come to Alexander, at the mouth of the Left Fork of the Buckhannon, three miles above, the Upper Freeport coal is 275 feet above water level, and has been mined for use in the Alexander Lumber Company's mills. The section measured there is as follows:

```
                                                            Ft. In.  Ft. In.
Sandstone, Lower Mahoning, very massive, pebbly.. 60  0
Concealed ....................................................  5   0
                          ⎧ coal..................... 0   8 ⎫
                          ⎪ shales, gray............. 4   6 ⎪
                          ⎪ coal..................... 1   5 ⎪
                          ⎪ slate, hard, gray....... 0   3 ⎪
Coal, Upper Freeport ⎨ cannel, impure ....... 0   6 ⎬ 13  4
                          ⎪ slate ................... 2   0 ⎪
                          ⎪ coal..................... 0   4 ⎪
                          ⎪ fireclay ............... 1   2 ⎪
                          ⎩ coal ................... 2   6 ⎭
Concealed ....................................................  10  0
Sandstone, massive, pebbly, Roaring creek...............  60  0
Shale, dark...................................................  5   0
Coal, visible.................................................  2   0
Concealed and sandstone to level of the Buckhannon
    river .....................................................  200  0
```

The Upper Freeport coal has an elevation of about 2100 feet above tide at Alexander, and is rising quite rapidly to the southeast, so that it soon passes over the immediate hills along the Buckhannon river, but the coal is still caught in the higher summits, back from the stream, and on both sides of it, until we come to the summit of Turkey Bone mountain, on the divide between the Buckhannon and Elk river waters, where the bed has an elevation of 3550 feet above the sea, and has been dug into for local use.

About one mile and a-quarter west from Avondale, and five miles below Pickens, we find the crop of the Upper Freeport coal about 500 feet above Avondale, on the land of D. G. Thomas, and dipping rapidly to the northwest, so that when we come to Mayton, on the land of W. R. Thomas, the elevation of this coal is 300 feet lower.

It has the following structure where mined by W. R. Thomas:

	Ft.	In.	Ft.	In.
Coal, bony	1	8		
Coal, good	2	7		
Bone	0	9	7	6
Coal, good	2	6		

This is at the head of the Right branch of the Little Kanawha river, near the line between Upshur and Webster counties. There is a large area of this coal, where it has a thickness of six to seven feet, on the headwaters of the Little Kanawha river, in Webster and Upshur, though, of course, the bed always holds two or three partings of bony coal or slate.

The coal shows as follows at the McKissick bank, on Lynn Camp branch, near Kanawha Head:

	Ft.	In.	Ft.	In.
Coal, bony	2	0		
Coal, good	2	6		
Bony coal	0	9		
Coal, good	2	6	9	10
Slate	0	6		
Coal, visible	1	7		

The coal is overlain by a very massive sandstone, which makes bold cliffs along Cave run, and the valley of Lynn Camp.

Where this coal emerges from the bed of the Left Fork of the Little Kanawha, one-half mile below Georgetown or Stillman, it exhibits the following succession:

	Ft.	In.	Ft.	In.
Sandstone, massive				
Coal	1	0		
Shale	1	0		
Slaty coal	1	0		
Coal	0	6	7	0
Bone	0	6		
Coal, visible	3	0		

It is possible that there are other divisions of the coal on below the lowest portion exposed.

From this point, which is two miles from Rock Cave, the coal is above water level on down the Little Kanawha, and its tributaries of Cherry Fork, Glady, Trace, and others. In attains a great development in the region about the mouth of Cherry Fork, the measurement given on page 364 being from a locality a short distance below the mouth of Cherry, in the "Pan Handle" of Lewis county, between Upshur, Webster and Braxton.

The following measurement of this bed, from the land of James Rexroad, on Cherry, one mile above its mouth, will illustrate the great expansion of the bed in that region:

	Ft.	In.	Ft.	In.
Coal	1	2		
Shale, gray..	0	6		
Coal	2	0	4	7
Slate, dark	0	1		
Coal	0	10		
Sandy shale			0	11
Coal	0	12		
Slate and bone...	0	6		
Coal	1	0		
Bone	0	6	7	6
Coal, hard..	1	3		
Slate	0	5		
Coal	0	8		
Coal, splinty...	2	2		
Total...			13	0

The "sandy shale" division shown above is a constant feature of this region, and occasionally attains to eight feet in thickness, and then is often sandstone. In such cases, the farmers frequently mine one of the beds without knowing the presence of the other, either above or below, as the case may be. The rock parting is often only two feet in thickness, while the coal above it is about five feet thick and of a softer type than that below, which is frequently seven feet thick, and inclined to be "splinty" in its nature.

At Thomas Kincaid's, below the mouth of Glady, this rock parting thickens to eight feet, and at the head of Fallen Timber run, where the lower portion of the coal is mined on the land of Lorenz Farnash, it appears to be even thicker than eight feet.

On Little Wild Cat run, this coal is partially opened on the land of George Kincaid, and there the following interesting section was measured:

		Ft. In.	Ft. In.
Coal, Upper Freeport	coal	1 6	
	sandy shale	0 7	
	coal	0 3	
	coal, bony	0 4	6 3
	coal	1 1	
	splinty coal	2 6	
Concealed			5 0
Sandstone, massive, Roaring creek			85 0
Coal			0 8
Sandstone, flaggy			15 0
Shale			2 0
Coal, Lower Freeport	coal	0 7	
	shale, gray	1 2	
	slate, dark	1 4	
	coal	1 9	
	slate, dark	0 6	11 9
	coal	1 4	
	fireclay	3 0	
	coal	1 3	
	bone coal	0 7	
	coal	0 3	

This section was puzzling at first, since the coal at the bottom is so thick, but the finding of the Mahoning coal, on above the Upper Freeport, and the Mason bed still higher in the hills, made it certain that the coal at the top of the section is the Upper Freeport bed, and hence that the one under the great Roaring creek sandstone below, is the Lower Freeport coal, or the same one shown in the section below Ten Mile station, on the Buckhannon river.

The Upper Freeport coal has been partially opened by L. H. Malcomb, on the right bank of the Little Kanawha river, and 250-300 feet above water level, opposite the Devil's Backbone, where it exhibits the following:

	Ft. In.	Ft. In.
Coal	1 6	
Slate, gray	0 3	
Bony coal	0 4	6 2
Coal	0 9	
Shale, gray	1 4	
Coal, visible	2 0	

The underlying Roaring creek sandstone forms great cliffs here along the river.

This coal dips down to the northwest more rapidly than the river falls in descending the same, and when we come to the mouth of Short run, the coal is about 175 feet above water level, and gives the following succession on the land of Taylor Brohard:

		Ft. In.	Ft. In.
Sandstone, massive, pebbly		60 0	
Concealed and sandy shales		20 0	
Coal, Upper Freeport	coal 0 10		6 4
	coaly slate 0 6		
	coal 0 5		
	bone 0 6		
	coal 1 6		
	dark slate 0 3		
	coal 2 4		
Concealed			5 0
Sandstone, massive, Roaring creek			80 0
Slate, gray			0 7
Coal			1 8
Concealed to Little Kanawha river			50 0

The Upper Freeport coal thins down rapidly as we descend the river, and where it is last mined, one mile above the "Falls," has the following structure:

	Ft. In.	Ft. In.
Coal	2 10	4 9
Shale	0 8	
Coal	1 3	

The "Falls" of the Little Kanawha river is in Braxton county, and there the Upper Freeport coal has got down nearly to water level, as shown by the following section:

		Ft. In.	Ft. In.
Sandstone, massive, Lower Mahoning		20 0	
Slate, black, cannelly		1 0	
Shales and fireclay		20 0	
Coal, Upper Freeport	cannel slate 2 0		9 7
	shales 5 0		
	cannel slate 2 0		
	coal 0 7		
Fireclay			10 0
Shaly sandstone			10 0
Sandstone, massive, Roaring creek, in bed of Little Kanawha river			10 0

Here the great coal bed we have seen around the heads of the Little Kanawha, has practically disappeared in a mass of CANNELLY slates and shales, just before it dips down out of sight and passes under water level. The "Falls" is over the massive top of the great Roaring creek sandstone, which here rises from the water, and makes such a prominent feature in the topography southward along the waters of the Little Kanawha, and across to the Buckhannon and Valley rivers. Northward from this no coal is found except the thin (20″) Mason bed, which is mined about Bulltown, three miles below the "Falls," for local supply, until we come to the crop of the Pittsburg bed below Burnsville, twenty miles distant.

In passing southwestward from the Little Kanawha waters to Holly river, the Upper Freeport bed maintains its large size, as witness the following section of the coal at the bank of M. S. Chipps, on Williams Camp run, a tributary of the Right fork of the Little Kanawha river:

	Ft.	In.	Ft.	In.
Shale			5	0
Coal	1	4		
Bone coal	0	10		
Coal	0	3		
Slate	0	5		
Bony coal	0	7		
Dark, sandy shale	0	10		
Coal	1	2	9	11½
Slate	0	0½		
Splinty coal	2	4		
Slate	0	8		
Coal	1	2		
Bony coal	0	4		

The coal rises rapidly as we pass up the Right fork, and when we come to Cleveland, the top of the Pottsville is near water level, and the Upper Freeport bed is 500 to 600 feet higher in the hills, and has been mined on the land of Wilson Snyder, northwest of Cleveland one mile, at whose bank the following section is visible:

		Ft.	In.	Ft.	In.
Sandstone				5	0
	coal	0	4		
	slate	0	6		
	coal	0	3		
	slate	0	6		
	coal	0	2		
Coal, Upper Freeport...	slate	0	3	8	1
	coal, soft	1	0		
	slate	0	1		
	coal, splinty	2	6		
	slate, gray	0	9		
	coal	1	9		

At the working face of the coal, the following structure is visible:

	Ft. In.	Ft. In.
Slaty coal, top	....	
Coal	1 0	
Slate	0 1	
Coal, soft...	1 6	6 2
Coal, splinty.....................................	1 0	
Slate	0 10	
Coal	1 9	

The coal is here 400 feet above the Little Kanawha river, and rising toward it, so that at Cleveland its horizon would be at least 600 feet above water level, and possibly more, since the southeastward rise is quite rapid.

On Buffalo run and its tributaries, two miles southwest from Cleveland, the Upper Freeport coal has been opened on the land of Mr. Ferril and others, where it exhibits the following structure:

	Ft. In.	Ft. In.
Slaty coal..	1 0	
Coal	1 6	
Slate	0 1	4 8
Coal	1 0	
Slate	0 3	
Coal, visible	0 10	

The coal has an elevation of 700 feet above the river at Cleveland, and a very massive sandstone crops just below it in high cliffs. This is probably only the lower division of the coal, since the parting between the upper and lower half of the coal is often five to ten feet thick in the region between the Little Kanawha and Holly rivers. This is shown by the following section on the land of F. Wiedrig, near the Pickens and Hacker's valley road, in Webster county:

	Ft. In.	Ft. In.	Ft. In.
Coal	0 8		
Slate, dark	0 1	5 3	
Coal	4 6		
Sandy beds and concealed............		5 10	16 4
Coal	0 7		
Slate	0 7		
Coal	0 6		
Slate, gray	0 5		
Coal	1 0	5 3	
Slate, gray	0 2		
Coal	0 8		
Slate	0 0½		
Coal	1 3½		

On the land of Henry Spies, two miles east from Hacker's valley, the lower portion of this coal is exposed in the following section:

		Ft. In.	Ft. In.
Coal, blossom			
Shales, sandy			5 0
Coal, bony		1 3	
Coal		1 2	
Bone		0 1	
Coal		0 11	
Fireclay		0 7½	5 8
Coal		0 7½	
Slate, black		0 1½	
Coal		0 10½	

The blossom of coal in the clay above the five foot of sandy shales, shows there is more of this coal bed in the concealed interval above.

Farther down Holly river, this coal has been mined in the summits of the hills, near Allen Anderson's mill, and its structure there is shown in the section given on page 364 of this volume, though it probably is not fully exposed at that locality.

This coal is found in the hills along the Left fork of Holly river, below Anderson's mill, and has occasionally been mined by the farmers.

Mr. Heron has an opening in the coal along the road to Palmer, one mile northeast from Mollahan's mill, where the coal is only partly exposed. The rock parting is about three feet thick at Heron's opening, and there is thirty inches of coal above it, and four to five feet of coal below the same. The bed has an elevation of 640 feet above Holly river, which is flowing in the top of the Pottsville series at Mollahan's mill.

In passing down Holly river from Marpleton, at the forks of Holly, the rocks dip rapidly westward, and bring the Upper Freeport coal nearer water level, so that it is no longer in the summits of the hills, but only half-way to the summits, when we come to Palmer, at the mouth of Holly.

The coal has been mined by Mr. Salsbury, on Rock run, about one mile northeast from Palmer, where it exhibits the following structure:

	Ft. In.	Ft. In.	Ft. In.
Sandstone, massive			30 0
Dark shale			0 6

		Ft. In.	
Coal, "top"	coal	1 0	
	shale, dark	0 3	
	coal	1 0	4 5
	bone	0 4	
	coal	1 10	
Rock and slate parting		2 0	12 2
Coal, "bottom"	coal, slaty	1 6	
	fireclay & shale	2 3	5 9
	coal, good	2 0	

The coal has the same rock parting here that characterizes it farther up Holly, and on the head of the Little Kanawha in Braxton, Lewis and Upshur counties.

About one mile below Palmer this coal was once opened in the steep hill along Elk river, and an attempt made to mine it for use in the Holly River R. R. locomotives. Here we get the following section in descending from the summit to Elk river:

	Ft. In.	Ft. In.
Concealed and deep red marly shales		40 0
Sandstone, massive and concealed		140 0
Coal, Mason, bony at top		2 4
Concealed and massive, pebbly sandstone		130 0
Shales, dark		5 0
Coal, Upper Freeport { coal, with bone	4 0	
sandstone and shale	3 0	10 0
coal, slaty	3 0	
Concealed and massive sandstone		160 0
Concealed, with two coal beds		40 0
Sandstone, massive		40 0
Concealed to Elk river		50 0

The section extends up into the marly RED BEDS of the Conemaugh, and shows conclusively that the great double-bedded coal which has been followed from the Buckhannon river to the Little Kanawha, and across to Elk, can be nothing else than the Upper Freeport bed.

We are also here in the well developed Kanawha series of rocks, since along both Elk and Holly rivers, the interval between this double bed of coal at the summit of the section, and the top of the Pottsville, is more than 600 feet.

The Upper Freeport coal was transported down to the Holly River R. R. here through a chute constructed of boards, but the coal proved too slaty and poor to warrant its use in the locomotives, and the mine has been abandoned. The rock parting is about half sandstone at this locality.

There are two slaty and impure coal beds in the forty feet of concealed interval, 160 feet below the Upper Freeport coal, each two and one-half to three feet thick, and ten to fifteen feet apart. They have both been opened and show in the cuts of the railroad near Palmer Junction, one mile below this locality.

Where the B. & O. railroad leaves Elk river along Flatwoods run, three miles below Palmer Junction, a fine exposure of the Upper Freeport coal is made by the cutting along the steep hill side, and there the following section was measured between the top of the steep grade and Elk river at Gillespie, below:

		Ft. In.	Ft. In.
Sandstone, massive			20 0
Coal, Upper Freeport { coal	1 6		
shale	0 6		2 8
coal	0 8		
Dark shale			0 6
Fireclay and shales			10 0
Dark shales			10 0
Concealed			2 0
Sandstone, massive and concealed			80 0
Shales and concealed			50 0
Coal { coal	1 6		
shale	1 6		5 0
coal	2 0		
Sandy shales			15 0
Coal			1 3
Shales			6 0
Coal			0 3
Concealed to Elk river at Gillespie			10 0

The coal at the top of this section is all that is left of the Upper Freeport seam, which, with its rock parting, is ten feet thick only four miles distant, in the section below Palmer. The Lower Mahoning sandstone rests in immediate contact with the coal, and has evidently cut away the upper bench of the bed entirely.

As we pass down Elk river from Gillespie, the Upper Freeport bed dips rapidly, and goes under water level near the mouth of Bee run, two and one-half miles above Sutton, while the massive Mahoning sandstone makes a great cliff along Elk. The coal has been mined at the roadside, one mile above Bee run, where it is splinty and two and one-half to three feet thick, and all in one bed, unless, indeed, ten to twelve inches of coal thirty feet above, and directly under a great cliff of pebbly sandstone, could represent the upper division of the Freeport coal with the parting rocks greatly thickened.

Fletcher Morrison has a mine in this coal on Wolf creek, a short distance above its mouth, from which the town of Sutton, three miles below, is partly supplied. The coal is three feet thick and has about twelve inches of "splinty" coal near its center.

About four miles southward up Wolf creek from its mouth, this same coal thickens to five and one-half feet, and has been mined by Mr. Stalnaker just above a great cliff of massive sandstone, and 200 feet above water level. The coal is hard and splinty, with a slate parting two and one-half inches thick near the middle.

When the coal dips under the level of Elk river, above Sutton, it remains beneath the same until we pass the mouth of Strange creek, twenty-five miles below. There an anticlinal roll brings the coal once more above the level of Elk river, where it has been mined on the land of John Duffy, just below the mouth of Tate creek, and near the Clay-Braxton county line. It is about sixty feet above the water level of Elk river, and reported to be four feet thick.

It is this coal which thickens up to six feet at the mouth of O'Briens creek, two miles farther down Elk and has long been mined there for local supply. The thick coal is "pockety," however, since it thins away both up and down the river. Some of the coal at O'Briens creek is of the soft, coking type, which characterizes the bed in the northern end of the state. The opening had fallen shut when visited, so that no details of the structure could be obtained. That the deposit is local, however, is shown by the fact that, although the horizon of this coal is above water level along Elk, from O'Briens creek down to Clay Court House, eighteen miles below, no workings or openings exist on the bed, and at Clay it is a mere mass of black slate, in which we find only a few inches of coal, 90 to 100 feet above the river, and it continues unimportant on down Elk, so far as known.

Where the Charleston road leaves the immediate valley of Elk river, twelve miles below Clay, this coal is exposed on a little stream, and there the following section was measured:

	Ft. In.	Ft. In.
Sandstone, massive		15 0
Coal, slaty	0 6	
Fireclay shales	3 6	
Coal, bony	0 6	
Coal, splint, good	2 0	11 6
Bone	0 10	
Fireclay	1 6	
Bony coal	1 6	
Coal, good	1 2	
Dark shales and concealed to Elk river		35 0

This begins again to resemble the thick type of the coal seen on Holly and Elk rivers, except that the portion above the parting shales is thin and unimportant. In the hills at this locality, we come to the top of a great, massive sandstone, 430 feet above the Upper Freeport bed, and then come the RED BEDS of the Conemaugh series.

The Upper Freeport coal is seen for the last time as we descend Elk river, at the mouth of Porters creek, twenty-three miles below Clay Court House, and there the following interesting section was measured:

		Ft. In.	Ft. In.
Kanawha black flint			5 0
Dark, sandy shales			7 0
Coal, Upper Freeport	coal	0 3	
	slate	0 2	
	coal, good	1 0	
	shale, gray	1 0	
	coal, bony	2 0	
	shale, dark	3 0	12 5
	coal, splint	1 0	
	shale	0 3	
	coal	0 3	
	shale	2 0	
	coal, good	1 6	
Concealed to level of Elk river			20 0

On above this thick coal at about 200 feet, we find the outcrop of the Mason coal, and then at 420 feet we come to the lowest RED BEDS of the Conemaugh series, so that there can be no doubt that the thick bed of coal shown in this section is identical with the thick coal in Braxton, Webster, Upshur, Lewis, Randolph and Barbour, which we have now followed across the state until the Kanawha black flint appears in its roof, thus fixing the horizon of the flint at the base of the Conemaugh series.

On below Porters creek, the coal dips under the river silts, and soon gets below Elk river, since at Queen Shoals, three miles farther down, the BLACK FLINT itself goes under the Elk, and nothing more is seen either of it or the underlying coal until we come to Charleston, where both rise from the bed of the Great Kanawha, under the bridge across that stream, one-half mile or more above the mouth of Elk river.

The different phases of this coal bed in the Great Kanawha region, and beyond there to the southwest, we shall discuss when treating of the Allegheny-Kanawha series.

This coal has been opened on Buffalo creek, near the mouth of Sand Fork, in Clay county, by Mr. McMullens. The coal is only partially exposed at the digging by the roadside, and exhibits the following structure:

	Ft. In.	Ft. In.
Coal, blossom		
Shales, dark		5 0
Coal	0 3	
Shale	0 8	
Coal	0 5	4 7
Shale	0 9	
Coal, visible	2 6	

There is the appearance of coal in the clay above the five feet of dark shales, and this is most probably the upper bench of this coal.

The coal rises southward about as fast as the beds of the streams, and two miles up Dog run we see the following at an opening near the Clay-Nicholas road:

	Ft. In.	Ft. In.
Sandstone, massive		
Concealed		10 0
Blue shales		4 0
Coal .. coal	2 6	
shale, gray	3 4	7 2
coal, visible	1 4	

This is near the line between the Cameron-Brokerhoff land and that of W. T. Hamrick.

It has also been dug into one mile and a-half farther up Dog run, not far from the Clay-Nicholas county line, and 200 feet below the top of a very massive, pebbly sandstone deposit.

Where the Summersville road crosses the Lily fork of Buffalo creek, in the northern edge of Nicholas county, this coal and the overlying KANAWHA BLACK FLINT are both present, although the coal is quite thin, as shown by the following section:

		Ft. In.	Ft. In.
Kanawha black flint, visible		5 0	
Dark, sandy shale..		2 0	
Coal .. { coal	0 10		1 9
fireclay	0 3		
coal	0 8		
Fireclay...		2 0	
Sandstone to creek level................................		5 0	

About four miles southeast from this, and nearly 500 feet higher, this coal has been opened on the waters of Muddlety creek, by Joseph Robinson, just north from the Summersville road, and one-half mile from Muddlety creek. The coal is only partially exposed, but four feet of splinty coal is visible.

One mile below this, and opposite the old Valley Hotel, on the land of H. B. Herold, the Upper Freeport coal has been mined for local supply 400 feet above Muddlety creek, where the following measurement was made:

	Ft. In.	Ft. In.
Coal	1 6	
Shale	4 6	
Cannel, impure	0 8	13 4
Coal, soft.................................	2 6	
Slate, dark	1 8	
Coal, splint........	2 6	

Here the coal has recovered its great thickness shown in Lewis, Upshur, and Webster. It is possible that where it shows so thin under the BLACK FLINT, only five to six miles distant from this locality, more of the coal may be present under the sandstone, shown in the bed of the stream.

At the head of Glade creek, about three miles east from Herold's bank, a small area of this coal is caught in the summits of the hills, on the land of J. R. Tyree, where it has long been mined for local supply. The coal has the following structure at Tyree's bank :

		Ft. In.	Ft. In.
Sandstone and concealed from top of knob..............		75 0	
Coal, Upper Freeport { coal, soft	5 0		13 10
shale, gray, sandy...	2 0		
coal, splint.............	1 10		
bone	0 2		
coal, splinty........ ..	4 10		

The lower bench of the coal was mined for several years before it was known that there was any coal above, when finally a "fall-in" of the roof took place, and revealed the five feet of coal above. The upper bench is not mined, but it looks like good coal and is much softer than the lower bench, much of which is a genuine splint coal, and highly prized for domestic purposes.

This coal lies more than 500 feet almost vertically above McMillan creek, and along it K. B. McCue has opened a coal forty-two inches thick, with one inch of dark gray slate near its center. The coal is only fifteen feet above the level of the creek, and would be one of the Kanawha series, either the Cedar Grove, or uppermost division of the Campbell's creek bed.

At the head of Stroud creek, near the line between Webster and Nicholas counties, the Upper Freeport coal has been mined on the land of Dr. D. M. Lewis and others, and it exhibits the following succession at the Lewis mine:

		Ft. In.	Ft. In.	Ft. In.
Upper bench	cannel	0 5		
	coal, splinty	4 0		
	coal, soft	0 4	5 10	
	black slate	0 1		
	coal	0 6		
	black, coaly slate	0 6		
Parting slate, gray		3 0		12 10
Lower bench	coal, soft	1 10		
	fireclay	1 0		
	coal, soft	0 10	4 0	
	slate	0 1		
	coal	0 3		

In Powell mountain, Nicholas county, at the head of Muddlety (Mumble-the-Peg) creek, this coal has been mined for local use, and there the following section was observed in descending the Weston and Gauley Bridge Turnpike from the summit of Muddlety creek:

		Ft. In.	Ft. In.
Massive, pebbly sandstone from top of Powell Mt		180 0	
Coal, large blossom, *Mason*		5 0	
Concealed		5 0	
Sandstone, massive		85 0	
Coal, blossom, *Mahoning*			
Sandstone and shales		50 0	
Coal, U. Freeport..	coal, blossom	1 0	
	shales, gray	10 0	15 3
	Coal... { coal, splinty.. 2 0		
	black slate .. 0 3		
	coal, splinty.. 2 0		
Concealed, sandstone, and shales		50 0	

Coal { coal _____ 1 0 }	10	0
{ shales _____ 8 0 }		
{ coal _____ 1 0 }		
Sandstones, shales and sandstone _____	80	0
Coal _____	2	6
Sandstone and shales _____	50	0
Coal, blossom _____	1	6
Concealed and shales _____	30	0
Coaly slate _____	1	0
Sandstone and shales _____	30	0
Coal _____	2	0
Shales, sandy _____	15	0
Coaly streak and black slate _____	10	0
Concealed to bed of Muddlety creek _____	50	0
Total _____	672	3

Of this section, 325 feet at the top belong in the Conemaugh series, while the balance (347') is in the Allegheny-Kanawha series, and hence it is probably 200 feet or more down to the horizon of the Campbells creek coal, which comes out of the bed of Muddlety creek, four miles below the locality of the section, at 550 to 600 feet under the Upper Freeport coal.

From Powell mountain, this coal can be followed in the summits northeastward to Laurel creek, as shown in the section on page 366 of this volume, and thence to the Elk river and across to Holly, capping the Allegheny-Kanawha series at about 600-650 feet above the Pottsville, while above it, and crowning the highest peaks, we find 150 to 300 feet of the great cliffs of massive, pebbly sandstones, which everywhere form the base of the Conemaugh. From Holly to the Gauley river waters on Stroud creek, the Upper Freeport coal coming, as it does, high in the summits of the lofty hills, has been but slightly explored, though all of the farmers appear to be aware of its presence. When opened, only one bench of the coal is usually mined, so that its entire thickness is seldom seen within the region in question. About five to six feet of coal is generally reported at this horizon along Elk, Laurel, and Birch.

From Herold's, on Muddlety creek, southwestward, this thick coal can be followed in the summits of the hills across to Peters creek, and down the same until the KANAWHA BLACK FLINT again comes into its roof, and remains with it on southwestward to the Great Kanawha river, where this coal has been termed the STOCKTON CANNEL, and where we shall leave it now to be taken up again when we come to describe the Allegheny-Kanawha series.

MIDDLE FREEPORT COAL.

In the type section given from Freeport, Pennsylvania, page 342 of this volume, a small coal bed occurs at twenty-five feet below the Upper Freeport bed, and intermediate between the latter and the Lower Freeport coal. It is possible that this stratum is a local offshoot from the main Upper Freeport coal above, and represents the "bottom" member of the same below the "big" slate of Monongalia and Preston counties, since at one point on Deckers creek this parting slate is observed to thicken from four up to ten feet within a few yards.

Along the Valley river in the Philippi region, and also in the Roaring creek field farther south, there is often found a bed of coal, two to three feet thick, and only ten to twenty-five feet below the main Upper Freeport bed. It is possible, indeed quite probable, that this stratum represents the coal below the "big" slate of Preston county, and when separated so far from its parent bed, may be termed the Middle Freeport coal.

Although it has been noted at many points along the Valley river, it has been fully exposed and mined at only one, viz: at the plant of the Maryland Smokeless Coal Company, below Leiter, near the mouth of Roaring creek, Randolph county. Here it lies twenty-three feet below the Upper Freeport bed, and exhibits the following structure:

	Ft. In.	Ft. In.
Coal	0 10	
Bony coal	0 6	
Coal	1 8	4 11
Sandy shale and bone	0 8	
Coal	1 3	

The coal, as will be perceived from the section, contains much sandy and bony material, but the coal itself looks very rich and good.

There are doubtless other localities where this coal is thick enough to mine, but so far as known it has not been mined elsewhere separately from the Upper Freeport bed above.

THE BOLIVAR FIRECLAY.

The Bolivar fireclay, which is quite important at many localities in Pennsylvania, has not yet been developed to any extent in West Virginia.

On Deckers creek, near Dellslow, Monongalia county, this clay has been opened and tested at many localities on the Pixler farm, where it contains some very good hard, or flint clay, as well as several feet of soft, or plastic clay.

This horizon will doubtless furnish fireclay at many localities in the state when properly exploited and opened.

THE UPPER FREEPORT LIMESTONE.

Lying at an interval of five to twenty feet under the Upper Freeport coal, there occurs in Preston and eastern Monongalia a limestone of wide distribution in Pennsylvania, but so far as observed in West Virginia, with the exception of Hancock county at the north, is confined to the two counties mentioned. It has been quarried by the farmers at many localities in Preston, and burned into lime for agricultural purposes. It is usually found in several layers, separated by shales, the whole having a thickness of ten to fifteen feet. It is a fresh, or brackish water deposit, no marine fossils having been seen in it either in West Virginia or Pennsylvania.

The uppermost layers of the limestone are sometimes changed to carbonate of iron, as on Deckers creek, near Dellslow, where some iron ore was once mined and used in the old furnace there.

THE ROARING CREEK SANDSTONE.

(UPPER FREEPORT SANDSTONE.)

Cropping a short distance below the thick Upper Freeport coal, there occurs, over a wide area of the state, a very massive and often pebbly sandstone, which appears to come at the same horizon as the Upper Freeport sandstone of Pennsylvania. It is especially well developed and massive along Roaring creek, in Randolph county, forming the "falls" on that stream, fifty feet or more in heighth, which gave origin to the name of the creek. The stratum is frequently fifty to seventy-five feet in thickness, and occasionally, as near the mouth of Beaver creek on the Valley river, appears to unite with the next underlying sandstone, and form one solid mass of nearly 200 feet. It is this rock which comes out of the Valley river below Philippi, where the rapids in that stream begin, and forms a line of bold cliffs on either side of the valley for several miles down the river, being especially prominent at Moatsville and vicinity. The stratum is generally quite pebbly, and immense blocks of it, much resembling those from the Pottsville series, litter up the surface whenever its massive crop appears above water level. The upper portion of the stratum has been quarried to a small extent along the Valley river in the vicinity of Junior and above. It is quite hard and durable, though it does not split very regularly. It is this stratum which makes the "Falls" of the Little Kanawha in Braxton county, and it is especially massive on all of the headwaters of that stream, and across to the Buckhannon river, along which it makes a constant line of great cliffs, from where it rises above water level at Sago, until it passes into the air from the summits of the mountains above Pickens.

At many points along the Great Kanawha river, and across to the Tug fork of Big Sandy, a sandstone at this horizon assumes enormous proportions, often 200 to 300 feet in thickness, apparently, by coalescing with underlying sandy deposits. In such cases the coals which belong under the Roaring creek sandstone disappear entirely.

The rock is termed the Roaring creek sandstone in preference to Upper Freeport sandstone, since there is some doubt about the identity of the rocks in question, and then, too, the name "Upper Freeport" is already preoccupied by the coal and limestone beds above.

THE LOWER FREEPORT COAL.

At forty-five to seventy-five feet below the great coal deposit at the top of the Allegheny series, there generally occurs another coal horizon, which was also named from the town of Freeport, on the Allegheny river, by the First Geological Survey of Pennsylvania. The section from its type locality, given on pages 342-3 of this volume, shows that the LOWER FREEPORT COAL, like the Upper one, is also a multiple bed, and that possibly in other regions of Pennsylvania and West Virginia, it may have separated into two distinct seams, thus adding to the difficulty of the stratigrapher in the correlation of the coal beds.

In the northern Pan Handle of the state, the LOWER FREE-

PORT COAL overshadows the UPPER one in its development, since, according to the identifications of the Ohio geologists, the latter is thin or wanting entirely along the Ohio river, while the former is the "Roger" vein or main workable bed of the group. The writer accepts this identification tentatively, but is not entirely satisfied therewith, since it is possible that the rock intervals have thinned in the Allegheny series and that the "Roger" vein may be the UPPER FREEPORT BED. However, we shall call it the Lower Freeport for the present, and describe the "Roger" vein of the New Cumberland region, under the name of the Lower Freeport. It was formerly opened and mined at many places in the hills overlooking New Cumberland, but in recent years it has been neglected for the Mahoning coal, higher up in the hills. One small mine in operation on the land of William Chatman, along the old incline, up to the abandoned mine in the Mahoning coal, reveals the following structure:

		Ft. In.	Ft. In.
Mahoning coal		4 0	
Concealed		40 0	
Sandstone, massive		20 0	
Shales, sandy		30 0	
Coal, "Roger," *Lower Freeport*	coal 2 4		3 4
	slate 0 2		
	coal 0 10		

The upper bench is the better coal, there being more sulphur in the bottom. A section of the coal farther in the mine exhibits the following structure, which the miners say is more general than the one given above, from near the mine mouth:

	Ft. In.	Ft. In.
Coal	1 6	2 9
Slate	0 2	
Coal	1 1	

This coal lies only about 120 to 130 feet above the Lower Kittanning coal, with its great underlying fireclay, and it is this short interval, as well as the great interval, (330 feet) from it up to the Crinoidal limestone, in the summits of the hills, which induced the later Ohio geologists to correlate this bed with the Lower Freeport seam of Pennsylvania, although Dr. Newberry, in Vol. III, Ohio Geology, pages 756-762, holds to its equivalency with the Coal No. 6 of the Ohio series, which he elsewhere correlates with the Upper Freeport bed.

About one-half mile above the mouth of King's creek, which puts into the Ohio river three miles below New Cumberland, this coal is seen at the fine exposure made by Caspari's stone quarry. It is there only twenty to twenty-four inches thick, and 100 feet above the Middle Kittanning coal, which is exposed directly under the great quarry sandstone.

About two miles above the mouth of King's creek, this coal is at the roadside, where it has been mined and exhibits the following structure:

	Ft.	In.	Ft.	In.
Sandstone, massive, visible......................................	10	0		
Sandy shales, with iron ore nodules......................	15	0		
Coal ..{ coal	2	3		
{ slate, gray.......................	0	2	3	8
{ coal	1	3		

The coal is known as the "Four-foot" seam on King's creek, and has been mined near Osburn's mill for local supply, where it exhibits the following structure on the land of R. A. Osburn:

	Ft.	In.	Ft.	In.
Coal	2	9		
Slate, gray...............	0	2	4	3
Coal	1	4		

The coal varies from four to five feet in thickness, and has a very good reputation, both for steam and domestic purposes.

The coal is mined in this region by Frank Morrow, Hugh Forsha, David Henderson, and William Logan, and on the land of the latter it dips under King's creek, about three miles west from the Pennsylvania-West Virginia line.

About two miles south from the mouth of Kings creek, the southward dip of the rocks carries the horizon of this coal below water level of the Ohio river, and when we come to the Pan Handle Junction, opposite Steubenville, the coal is more than 100 feet below the bed of the Ohio, according to the late Dr. Newberry, who, in Geology of Ohio, Vol. III., page 759, states that this coal has been mined under the bed of the Ohio river to the West Virginia side of the same, by the Rolling Mill shaft of the Jefferson Iron Company, at Steubenville, and that the coal is 120 feet below low water on the Ohio side, and 140 feet below the same datum 2000 feet east, near the West Virginia side of the river.

The coal is stated to be three feet, eight inches thick, with a parting of slate nine inches above the bottom.   In the shaft of the Cincinnati Coal & Coke Company, near the Jefferson's, the coal is three feet, nine inches, to four feet in thickness, and has a parting of clay, one inch thick, twelve inches above the bottom. This structure, given by Dr. Newberry, agrees with that shown at New Cumberland, and on King's creek, and there is no doubt that the "Steubenville shaft" coal is the same as the "Roger" vein of the hill mines at New Cumberland, and opposite on the Ohio side.

This coal was once mined by a shaft at Wellsburg, Brooke county, which started on the river terrace about forty-five feet above low water.   No details of the structure of the coal are obtainable, but it is reported to be four feet thick at 235 feet below the mouth of the shaft, or about 190 feet below the bed of the Ohio river.

On the opposite side of the river, the LaGrange Coal Company (page 760, Vol. III, Ohio Geology) reports the coal as 183½ feet below low water, with the following structure:

	Ft. In.	Ft. In.
Coal	2 10	
Slate	0 1	
Coal	1 8	5 3
Slate	0 1	
Coal	0 7	

At this point the coal lies 540 feet below the Pittsburg bed, which crops in the hills above.

Farther south, at the Rush run shaft, this coal thickens locally to nine feet, according to Dr. Newberry, but it there has more slate partings, and is not so pure as when thinner.   The coal was formerly successfully coked, and used in the manufacture of iron at Steubenville, Mingo, and other points in the Ohio valley.

The following analyses by Prof. T. G. Wormley, of the Ohio Survey, quoted from page 779, Vol. III, l. c. will give an idea of the chemical composition of this coal along the Ohio Valley:

	I	II	III	IV	V	VI
Water	1. 40	1. 90	1. 77	1. 81.	2. 00	1. 40
V. M.	32. 30	31. 30	38. 73	39. 21	34. 60	30. 90
F. C	60. 60	62. 20	57. 21	53. 96	58. 60	65. 90
Ash	4. 80	4. 60	1. 65	3. 76	4. 80	1. 80

| Sulphur | 2.08 | 2.06 | 0.64 | 1.26 | 2.20 | 0.96 |
| Sulphur in coke | 1.12 | 0.96 | .... | .... | .... | 0.38 |

    I.   Upper bench at Rush run shaft.
   II. Lower   "   "   "
  III. Upper bench at LaGrange shaft,
  IV. Lower   "   "   "
   V. Mingo shaft.
  VI. Steubenville shaft.

These analyses reveal a coal very low in ash and of excellent quality generally, so that its importance to the future of the iron industry of the Ohio valley may be very great, especially in the vicinity of Wheeling, where this coal, as recorded by the boring at the Central Glass Company's works, occurs at a depth of about 450 feet below the level of the Ohio river, and 563 feet below the Pittsburg coal, with a reported thickness of seven feet. It is possible that in the near future the great iron industries of Wheeling may find it necessary to exploit this coal for coke as their cheapest source of supply, if proper exploration with the diamond drill should prove it to have commercial value.

It is probably from the base of this same coal bed at Linton, Columbiana county, Ohio, opposite the northern end of Hancock county, that Dr. Newberry discovered the rich Fish and Batrachian fauna described by Cope in Vol. II, Paleontology of Ohio, pages 351-411.

This coal is represented in eastern Monongalia county at the head of Booth's creek, where it is sixty feet below the Upper Freeport coal, and reported to be four feet thick, with a slaty parting below its middle, having formerly been mined on the land of Mr. Dalton and others.

This coal also shows in the cut at Deep Hollow, on the M. & K. R. R., near Dellslow, where it is only a foot thick and about fifty feet under the Upper Freeport bed. Its horizon is also indicated by a coaly streak on top of a fireclay deposit in the Gamble lot boring, (page 346) at fifty seven and one-half feet under the same coal.

In Preston county this coal is known as the "Three-foot" bed, and has been mined occasionally by the farmers. An old opening in this coal, on the land of D. K. Ryan, one mile east from Pisgah, shows it forty-five to fifty feet below the Upper Freeport bed, where the coal is reported to be three and one-half feet thick, and of good quality, though it has a slate parting one foot above the bottom.

On the south side of Cheat, in the river hills near the mouth of Bull run, this coal has been dug into on the land of Daniel Lyons, at sixty feet under his opening in the Upper Freeport coal. The bed is not fully exposed, but a slate parting is visible one foot above the bottom, and the coal is somewhat bony and slaty, on the crop at least.

In the Sanford Watson boring (page 346) this coal was struck at sixty-five feet below the Upper Freeport bed, but it was only thirteen inches thick, while in the sections at Cut 80 and Newburg (pages 348-9) its horizon is indicated only by fireclay and some coaly slate, at fifty-five and forty-five feet respectively below the Upper Freeport bed.

Where the Chestnut ridge arch crosses the Valley river, near the line between Marion and Taylor counties, we find a bed of coal, five to six feet thick, at 125 to 140 feet above the Lower Kittanning seam, which appears to correspond with the Lower Freeport coal, though, as stated on page 423, it may yet turn out to be the Upper one, with the interval between it and the Lower Kittanning bed greatly decreased. It is exposed for about six miles along the main line of the B. & O. R. R., from where it rises above water level, one mile below Powell siding, in Marion county, to where it again dips under the Valley river at Bush, in Taylor county.

This coal has recently been opened by the Valley Falls Coal & Coke Company, of Pittsburg, a short distance below Bush, Taylor county, where preparations are being made to coke the coal, as well as to ship it for fuel. The following sections, made in different portions of the mine, will exhibit the structure of the coal at Bush:

	I		II	
	Ft.	In.	Ft.	In.
Gray slate..............				
Cannel	0	3	0	4
Coal	1	3	1	4
Bony coal	0	7	0	8
Coal, good..	2	4	2	8
Totals.............	4	5	5	0

The upper bench of the coal is rather hard, and occasionally contains streaks of bone, but the lower bench is a beautiful, bright, pure-looking coal, and should make an excellent quality of coke, so far as one might judge from its physical appearance.

The dip is quite rapid to the southeast, and at the mouth of Wickwire run, one mile above the coke ovens, the coal is about 100 feet below the Valley river, thus indicating a dip of more than 150 feet to the mile.

At Valley Falls, two miles below Bush, this coal thickens up to nearly eight feet, but it contains much slate and bone, as shown in the section on page 355.

At Hammond, Marion county, two miles below Valley Falls, this coal has been opened up by the Hammond Brick Company, and it is there exposed in the following section:

		Ft. In.	Ft. In.
Sandstone, massive, Lower Mahoning......................			60 0
Shales and concealed, with a thin coal bed................			80 0
Coal, Lower Freeport { slaty cannel	1 0		6 0
{ coal	2 0		
{ shale, gray	1 0		
{ coal	2 0		
Concealed...			25 0
Coal .. { coal, good	2 0		3 6
{ coal and clay mixed....................	1 6		
Fireclay, plastic			8 0
Sandstone, massive, and concealed.............….......…..........100 0			100 0
Coal, Lower Kittanning ....…...........0–	3 0		
Fireclay ....…......................5–	10 0		
Concealed to level of B. & O. R. R. at Hammond, (formerly Nuzums) and to near the top of the Pottsville series.........…...............................…...........…			70 0

This section is quite puzzling, since it raises a doubt as to whether the coal called Lower Freeport, may not really be the UPPER one, the interval between it and the Lower Kittanning bed below, having thinned away. Of course, in that event, the coal twenty-five feet below it would be the Lower Freeport bed, and the blossom of the coal in the concealed interval above, would be the Mahoning instead of the Upper Freeport. This question is left open for future detailed studies to settle.

Near Powell siding, below Hammond, this coal shows the following structure in a section exposed in the steep hill along the B. & O. R. R., where once mined for domestic use:

		Ft. In.	Ft. In.
Sandstone, massive, pebbly (Upper Mahoning).........		50	0
Concealed, flaggy sandstone, and shales with lime- stone nodules........		95	0
Sandstone, massive, coarse.............................		10	0
Gray shales, sandy....................................		15	0

Coal, Lower Freeport
- cannel, impure 0 6
- coal 1 10
- bony coal................. 0 8
- coal 0 11
- slate 0 1
- coal 1 7

    5 7

	Ft. In.
Concealed and shales	40 0
Sandstone, massive..	22 0
Coal, visible	2 0
Concealed to level of Valley river......................	60 0

A mile below this point the coal dips under the bed of Valley river and we see it no more, in that direction, (west), until it re-appears on the other slope of the Appalachian basin, in Hancock county, as already described.

In the boring at Webster, Taylor county, the record of which is given on page 356, this coal was struck at a depth of 267 feet, and forty-four feet below the coal identified as the Upper Freeport bed. It has a thickness of nearly six feet there, and exhibits practically the same structure as in the last section, near Powell siding.

Just above Moatsville, Barbour county, two to three feet of coal occurs along the cuttings of the B. & O. R. R., and sixty-five to seventy feet under the Upper Freeport bed, which probably represents the Lower Freeport coal. It is squeezed out entirely at some places along the railroad, in the great mass of coarse sandstone, which appears there below the Upper Freeport coal.

In the Roaring creek basin, a thin coal is seen under the great sandstone, (Roaring creek) near the mouth of that stream, which may possibly represent the Lower Freeport bed.

On Buckhannon river, this coal first shows along the railroad, near the old mill, two miles above Sago, just beneath the great Roaring creek sandstone, and seventy-five to eighty feet below the Upper Freeport coal, both of which are shown in the section on page 443 of this volume. It crops near track level for about four miles, along the Buckhannon above this point, but nowhere has enough coal in one layer to be commercially valuable.

On Little Wild Cat run, in the Pan Handle of Lewis county, this coal swells up to a thickness of nearly twelve feet, where opened on the land of George Kincaid, as shown in the section on page 448, but more than half of this is slate and bony material, so that the bed is practically worthless. The coal is here about 108 feet below the Upper Freeport bed.

Near the mouth of Short run, on the Little Kanawha river, seven miles above the "Falls," a coal has been dug by stripping, on the land of Milton Rexroad, which probably represents this bed, since it comes about 100 feet below the Upper Freeport coal, and just under a massive sandstone. Only twenty inches of the coal is visible at the Rexroad stripping.

When traced across to the Great Kanawha river, this coal appears to correlate with the Coalburg bed, 80 to 100 feet below the KANAWHA BLACK FLINT, but it will be described in that portion of the state under the next chapter on the Allegheny-Kanawha series.

It is probably the Lower Freeport bed which is mined along the Elk river, in the vicinity of Clay Court House, Clay county.

In the North Potomac basin of Tucker, Grant, and Mineral counties, this coal is often represented by a thin bed at forty to sixty feet below the Upper Freeport seam, but it has never been mined on a commercial scale, so far as known, because it is seldom more than one to two feet in thickness. The place of this coal in the section together with its thickness in the Potomac basin is shown by the sections on pages 352 and 354 of this volume.

THE FLORA OF THE FREEPORT COALS.

Mr. David White, of the U. S. G. Survey, Washington, D. C. has studied the fossil plants found in the roof shales of both the Upper and Lower Freeport coal beds of Pennsylvania, and has published a list of the same in the Bulletin of the Geological Society of America, Vol. XI., pages 153-5, which is here quoted, as follows:

FREEPORT GROUP.

"*Plant beds and localities.*—The term "Freeport group" has been applied*to the remaining upper portion of the Allegheny series, including the two Freeport coals, and extending from the top of the Upper Kittanning coal to the top of the Upper Freeport coal. This division of the series is subject to considerable variation, chiefly by the expansion of the two Freeport sandstones; but in Clarion county it appears to average about 130 feet in thickness.

*Report of Progress, Second Geological Survey Pa., VV, pp. 33, 34.

"In considering the flora accompanying the Upper Freeport coal, I include the plants in the roof of that coal, though, strictly speaking, the shales belong to the base of the Mahoning sandstone, as that name is customarily, but often inappropriately, applied.　From the roof of the Lower Freeport coal, collections of plants have been made at Big Soldier run (R.) near Reynoldsville; Elk run (E. R.), and Horatio, (H.), near Punxsutawney, in Jefferson county, and at the Dubois shaft (Dub.) and the Shawmut mines (Shaw.), in Clearfield county.

"The roof of the Upper Freeport coal contains good plant fossils at the Brackenbush mines (Brack.) about two miles east of Freeport, at Shenley (Sh.), at the Gilpin (Gil.), and Haddon (Had.) mines near Bagdad, and at Pine run, near Vandergrift (Van.), all in the vicinity of Freeport, Armstrong county, and at Coal Glen, C. G.), in Jefferson county.

"*Species from the Freeport group.* —As in the preceding lists, the plants from each horizon may be separated by grouping the species according to the localities, as indicated in the abbreviated forms therein given.

Name.	Locality.
Mariopteris nervosa (Brongn.) Zeill	Shaw., Hor., Gil., E. R.
"　　　*sillimani* (Brongn) D. W.	R., Dub., Hor.
Pseudopecopteris squamosa (Lx.) (large)	Dub., Sh.
Sphenopteris pseudomurrayana Lx.?	Hor., E. R.
"　　　cf. *mixta* Schimp	Dub.
Pecopteris dentata Brongn	Hor.
"　　　*unita* Brongn	R., C. G.
"　　　*squamosa* Lx	
"　　　*villosa* Brongn.?	Hor., Dub., Gil., Sh., Had., E. R., Gil., R., Shaw.
"　　　*pennæformis* Brongn. [Lesq.]	Sh., C. G.
"　　　*oreopteridia* (Schloth.) Brongn	Hor., Dub., Gil., Sh., E. R., R., Shaw.
"　　　*polymorpha* Brongn	Hor., Dub., Had., E. R.
"　　　*pteroides* Brongn?	Dub.
Alethopteris serlii (Brongn.) Goepp	Hor., Gil.
"　　　*pennsylvanica* Lx	C. G.
Callipteridium neuropteroides Lx?	Dub.
Neuropteris ovata Hoffm	Brack., Gil., Sh., Hor., E. R. Dub., R., Shaw.
"　　　*clarksoni* Lx	Hor.
"　　　*scheuchzeri* Hoffm	Had., Brack., Gil., Sh., Hor. E. R., Shaw., P., Dub., C. G., R.
Linopteris obliqua (Bunby) Pot	Hor., E. R., R.
Calamites cistii Brongn	Sh., Hor.
"　　　sp	Dub.
Calamitina sp	R., Hor.
Asterophyllites equisetiformis (Schloth)Brongn.	Hor., E. R., Dub.

Annularia stellata (Schloth.) Wood ....Had , Hor.
     "   *sphenophylloides* (Zenk.) Gutb........Hor.
Sphenophyllum emarginatum Brongn..............Brack., Gil., R., Hor., E. R.,
                                                 Dub., C. G.
Lepidodendron lanceolatum Lx?.......................Dub.
     "   *dichotomum* Sternb?...................Van., Sh., R., Hor.
     "   *modulatum* Lx ....Hor., Dub.
Lepidostrobus cf. *variabilis* L. and H...............Had., Van.
     "   *geinitzii* Schimp? ....Hor.
Lepidophyllum cultriforme Lx............... ....R.   •
     "   *hastatum* Lx........... ....Sh.
     "   *lanceolatum* L. and H.............Hor.
Sigillaria comptotænia Wood......... ....R., Hor.
Cordaites sp ....
Rhabdocarpus (*Pachytesta*) cf. *mansfieldi* Lx ...Hor.

THE LOWER FREEPORT SANDSTONE.

Below the coal just described there occurs a great sandy horizon occupied in Pennsylvania by what was first called the Freeport sandstone, but which was later modified by Prof. Lesley into the term Lower Freeport sandstone after it was learned that a massive sandstone is often found ABOVE the Lower Freeport coal as well as BELOW that horizon. Both of these sandstones have a fine development in the Sanford Watson bore hole, near Masontown, Preston county, the record of which is given on page 344 of this volume, the Lower one having a thickness of 76 feet in one unbroken body of solid massive rock much of which is pebbly. This is one of the most persistent sandstone horizons in the Allegheny series. The Upper Freeport sandstone is often replaced by sandy shales, clays and limestones, but it is rare indeed that some hard, massive sandstone is not present at the horizon of this Lower Freeport stratum. The rock is usually quite hard, micaceous, and often pebbly, but does not split evenly and hence is seldom quarried for building purposes. It always makes a steep slope in the topography of the Allegheny series, and frequently crops in bold cliffs along the hills.

When it first enters West Virginia from Pennsylvania and Ohio in the northern Pan Handle of Hancock county, it is quite massive and often 75 to 100 feet in thickness. It crops in a bold bluff at New Cumberland, and is the great cliff rock at the "falls" on Harden run, one mile east from that town, where it is nearly 100 feet thick in one massive ledge.

It is also this same stratum that crops in high cliffs at the mouth of King's creek, three miles below New Cumberland, and which is quarried on a large scale by S. Caspari, one-half mile up that stream, where it shows an unbroken face of sandstone ninety-five feet in height. It yields stone of many grades, and much of it cannot be used, except for the coarser grades of rough foundation structures. This is the only locality in the state, known to the writer, where this rock has been successfully quarried.

Two miles below the mouth of Kings creek this stratum sinks below water level of the Ohio, and it is seen no more along that stream until we pass beyond the southwestern boundary of the state, where it finally comes up again and makes bold bluffs near Ironton, Ohio, as shown in the section given on page 379 from that locality.

To the east this stratum dips down into the Appalachian basin, and the oil well drillers call it by various names, such as "Gas sand," "Big Dunkard," "Second Cow Run Sand," etc. Occasionally, it has yielded some oil, as in the Youst well No. 1, at Amos, Marion county, and it is probably one of the oil sands in the "shallow" sand district of Washington county, Ohio, and Pleasants county, of West Virginia. Some gas is often found in this stratum, though not in commercial quantity, and hence its name of "gas" sand among the oil and gas well drillers.

When this horizon comes up to the surface on the western slope of the Chestnut Ridge anticlinal, in eastern Monongalia and Marion counties, it is not so thick and massive as in Hancock, and it frequently holds a coal bed (Upper Kittanning) near its center, but east from Chestnut Ridge, where it crops along Raccoon creek, above Austen, it thickens to seventy-five feet or more in one unbroken mass, and the same thickness was found in the Newburg shaft, a few miles west.

There is also much massive sandstone at this horizon along Valley river, between Powell and Bush, over the crown of the Chestnut Ridge arch, at the Marion-Taylor line.

This stratum is especially massive and pebbly between Grafton and Philippi, along the bed of the Valley river, on either side of Moatsville, where it occasionally appears to unite with the overlying Roaring creek sandstone, and form one solid mass more than 100 feet thick. The numerous rapids and cascades in the Valley river, in the vicinity of Moatsville, are made by this stratum.

Farther up the Valley river, between Junior and Harding, this sandstone again unites with the overlying one, and we get an unbroken mass of rock, in a nearly vertical cliff, 200 feet high, great boulders from which have broken away and encumber the bed of the stream below.

On the Buckhannon, the upper waters of Elk, between Gillespie and Webster Springs; across to Gauley and down its tributaries, from the north to the Great Kanawha, this is preeminently a sandstone horizon, and often weathers into "chimneys," "pinnacles," "turrets," and other fantastic shapes, so that the beds are frequently termed the "Chimney rocks." In Summersville mountain, Nicholas county, there appears to be nearly 300 feet of solid sandstone at this horizon, formed by the union of the Lower Freeport and Roaring creek beds. This enormous deposit of sandstone is especially massive in the lofty hills about the junction of the Gauley and New rivers, and along the Great Kanawha, where it forms long lines of vertical cliffs of the "Chimney rock" type for many miles down that stream, cutting out both the Coalburg and Winifrede coal seams when the thickness of the sandstone mass becomes so great.

This same sandstone extends to the Guyandot, and across to the Tug fork of the Big Sandy river, along both of which streams this horizon is one of the principal elements in making the steep slopes of the mountains, which enclose their narrow valleys, and those of their tributaries.

THE UPPER KITTANNING COAL.

When the Lower Freeport sandstone breaks up into two members by a parting of shales, a coal frequently makes its appearance therein at 90 to 120 feet below the top of the Allegheny series. This coal assumes much importance in Somerset and Cambria counties, of Pennsylvania, and has there been termed bed "D," as well as "C," and was finally called the Upper Kittanning by Mr. Platt and Prof. Lesley.

In northern West Virginia, there is frequently a coal bed at this horizon, but it is seldom of any economic importance, although in eastern Monongalia it attains a thickness of three feet on the waters of Booths creek, and has occasionally been mined by the farmers for domestic use. In the Gamble boring on Deckers creek, page 346, it was struck at 107 feet below the Upper Freeport coal, and is nearly three feet thick.

This coal does not appear in the bore hole on the Sanford Watson farm, near Masontown, page 344, its horizon being occupied entirely with the massive Lower Freeport sandstone.

On the crest of the Chestnut Ridge arch, near Hammond and Valley Falls, there is a coal at this horizon, shown in the section on page 355, which is of some economic importance in eastern Marion and western Taylor counties, though it has never been mined to any extent in a commercial way. It has a thickness of three to four feet along the Valley river, in the region referred to, and the coal looks well on its crop.

In the North Potomac basin this coal is occasionally present, and of commercial thickness. The section from near Harrison, Mineral county, given on page 351, shows the bed as three feet, seven inches thick, at forty-two feet above the Lower Kittanning coal, and 137 feet under the Upper Freeport coal:

In the hills at Piedmont and Westernport we find two feet of coal at this horizon, 100 feet under the Upper Freeport coal, and sixty-five feet above the Lower Kittanning bed.

On the head of the Buckhannon river, where the horizon of this coal comes up, we find a seam less than two feet in thickness, at 150 feet below the Upper Freeport coal, as shown in the section near Pickens, given on page 363.

On Elk river, at Gillespie, Palmer, and other localities in that region, a coal bed five to six feet thick, with much included bony and slaty material, occurs at 150 to 160 feet below the Upper Freeport coal, as exhibited in the section on page 454, and it probably belongs at the horizon of the Upper Kittanning seam.

The same coal has been opened on Wolf creek and Birch river where it also contains much slate and bone.

It is probably the same coal that is mined high up in Cottle Knob, Nicholas county, by John Woods, where it is three feet thick and contains two layers of bony coal, as shown on page 368.

Just what this Upper Kittanning coal may represent on the Great Kanawha, and in the region southwest from there, is as yet uncertain, but it appears to harmonize fairly well with the WINIFREDE SEAM, a detailed account of which will be given in connection with the discussion of the Kanawha coals.

MIDDLE KITTANNING COAL.

The interval between the coal last described and the next lower coal bed, is generally occupied by sandstone, which, in the southwestern portion of the state, especially along the Great Kanawha river, becomes very thick and massive. Just below it, we often find a coal bed, two to three feet thick, of great purity and general excellence. In western Pennsylvania and eastern Ohio, this coal occurs only twenty to thirty feet above the Lower, or main, Kittanning bed, and Prof. Lesley named it the Middle Kittanning coal.

Farther east, along the Allegheny river, the interval between it and the Lower Kittanning bed increases to sixty or seventy feet, as shown in the sections on pages 341-2.

The coal is of considerable economic importance in Hancock county, where it has been mined for use in the manufacture of brick and tile, by the Claymont Brick Company, and others. Where mined by the Claymont Company, just below the mouth of Holbert's run, it exhibits the following structure.

	Ft. In.	Ft. In.
Coal	1 0	
Slate, dark	0 1	2 11
Coal	1 10	

The coal is quite pure, making excellent fuel, and as it is underlaid by a bed of fireclay, which is mined for use in the brick plants, the coal, although thin, can be taken out to advantage.

Just north from the Claymont Company's mine on this coal, the great sandstone above comes down and cuts the coal out entirely, as we go up the river, but it soon comes in again, since on the Ohio side of the river at Freeman's station, opposite New Cumberland, it crops just above the grade of the C. & P. R. R., and is three and one-half feet thick.

At the mouth of King's creek, three miles below New Cumberland, this coal is well exposed in a cutting along the railroad grade, and exhibits the following structure:

	Ft. In.	Ft. In.
Sandstone, Lower Freeport	80 0	
Coal — coal	0 9	
shale	0 2	2 7
coal	1 8	
Fireclay to railroad level	10 0	
Concealed to Ohio river	40 0	

The coal passes under the bed of the Ohio river at Brown's Island, three-fourth's of a mile below the mouth of Kings creek, and we see it no more along that stream until it rises out of the water above Ironton, and becomes the important coal of that region.

The late Dr. Orton identified with this coal the main Hocking Valley seam, at Straitsville, New Lexington, and elsewhere, so that the Middle Kittanning bed is one of the most important coal beds in the Ohio column of Coal Measures.

The relation of this seam to the other members of the Allegheny series in the Ironton region, is shown by the section on pages 379-80. The numerous local names it has received in Ohio, according to Dr. Orton, of which the following is only a partial list, will serve to illustrate its wide distribution and importance in that state: "No. 4" in the Ohio and Yellow creek valleys; "No. 6" in Stark county and southwestward; "Hammondsville strip vein," "Onasburg," "Pike Run," "Dennison," "Coshocton," "Upper Zanesville," "Upper New Lexington," "Nelsonville," "Straitsville," "Great Vein" of the Hocking Valley, "Carbondale," "Mineral City," "Upper Zaleski," "Washington Furnace," "Sheridan, etc.

This coal does not appear to be represented in the Gamble boring (page 346) of eastern Monongalia county, and in the Watson boring (page 344), near Masontown, Preston county, it appears to be represented by a bed of bituminous slate, much resembling impure cannel.

This is a CANNEL COAL horizon in western Pennsylvania, since the great bed near Darlington, in Beaver county, as well as the thick deposits in Armstrong, Clarion, and Jefferson couties, belong at this geological level.

There is a bed of CANNEL COAL on the right fork of Holly river, seven miles above Palmer, Braxton county, which probably comes at this same horizon, but it is only one and a-half to two feet thick.

In the Newburg shaft, Preston county, this coal is only fifteen feet above the Lower Kittanning bed, and has the structure given on page 348.

In the region of Valley Falls and Hammond, a thin bed of coal, one to two feet thick, is found at fifteen to twenty feet above the Lower Kittanning seam, which most probably represents this Middle Kittanning bed.

In the North Potomac region of West Virginia and Maryland, this coal bed appears to coalesce with the Lower Kittanning coal below, by the thinning away of intervening shales, though at times the latter thicken to twenty feet or more.

This view is also maintained by Dr. G. C. Martin, of the Maryland Survey, as indicated in the section quoted from his Garrett County Report on page 351 of this volume. Hence at many localities in Mineral, Grant, and Tucker counties, this coal is believed to be represented by the uppermost ply of the "Davis," or Lower Kittanning seam, and it is included in the measurements given for the latter bed through the region in question.

In the Great Kanawha valley this coal would correlate with the "Cedar Grove" seam, at an interval above the Lower Kittanning or Campbells creek coal varying from sixty to one hundred and fifty feet.

On McMillen's creek, Nicholas county, a bed of coal two and one-half feet thick has long been mined by the Baker heirs and others, for local domestic supply, which would appear to come at this same horizon. It is a beautiful, bright, and soft coal, of the coking type, and contains only a thin streak of bone, six inches below the top.

In Hancock county, as well as in Beaver and Columbiana counties, adjoining, the rock interval separating the Middle Kittanning coal from the one next below, is only twenty to thirty feet thick, as already stated, and consists largely of dark shales, filled with plant remains. Nodules of iron ore are also present in considerable quantity, and occasionally a bed of fireclay underlies the coal.

Mr. David White, of the United States Geological Survey, has made a study of the fossil plants found in connection with the several Kittanning coals of Pennsylvania; and in his paper on the "Relative Ages of the Kanawha and Allegheny Series," published in the Bulletin of the Geological Society of America, Volume XI., pages 150-153, he gives a list of these, with some general remarks on the same, which may be appropriately quoted here, as follows:

KITTANNING GROUP.

"*Plant beds of the group.*—That portion of the series extending from the top of the Ferriferous limestone to the top of the Upper Kittanning coal has been termed the Kittanning group.   In the typical region this group embraces about 120 feet, including the three Kittanning coals, the middle one of which is very rarely of workable thickness.   That portion in the vicinity of the Lower and Middle Kittanning coals is usually largely occupied by dark shales, often black and fissile, whose more common fossils are marine or brackish water mollusks.   Plant remains, except fragments of the more indestructible tissue, are generally very rare and very poorly preserved.   The upppermost portion of the series is more arenaceous and phytiferous.

"Since the plants of the shales forming the immediate roof of the Upper Kittanning coal mark the date of the latter, I include that flora in the same group.   From the shales accompanying the Lower Kittanning coal, or the "Dagus" coal, which is generally regarded as equivalent thereto, fossil plants have been collected near Snowshoe, (Sn.), Center-county, the Dagus mines, Elk county, and Hommers (Hom.) in Clearfield county.   The Miller coal from the roof of which plants were collected at Trout run (T.R) Cambria county, is supposed to represent the same horizon.   Plants have been found at the horizon of the Middle Kittanning near Logansport Log.), Armstrong county, and along the railway between Powelton and Electric (El. ', in Clearfield county.   The environing shales of this coal generally contain little but stem and Lycopodineous leaf fragments.   The roof shales of the Upper Kittanning are, however, frequently the matrix of well preserved plant remains   Fossils have been collected at this level at Kittanning (Kit.) and Kelleys station (K. S.), Armstrong county; Euclid (Eu.), Butler county; Fairmount (Fair.), Clarion county; and along Toby creek (T. C.), in Clearfield county.   The very rich flora from Cannelton (Can.), Beaver county, described in "The Coal Flora" by Lesquereux, is said by Dr. I. C. White † to have come from the floor of the Darlington coal, which is correlated by Dr. White with the Upper Kittanning coal.

"*Species from the Kittanning group.*—In the following list of species from the Kittanning group those marked with the asterisk (*) are, so far as is known, characteristic of the post-Pottsville terranes in the Pennsylvanian sections.   A large portion of the species from Cannelton are cited on the authority of Prof. Lesquereux.

Name.	Locality.
Rhacopteris elegans (Ett.) Shimp. [Lesq.]†......Can.	
Pseudopecopteris macilenta (L. and H.) Lx. typ..Can.	
" *squamosa* (Lx.)*.......................T. C., Can.	
" *hispida* (Lx, '..........................Can.	
" *nummularia* (Gutb.) Lx. *.........Can.	
" *plukenetii* (Schloth) Lx.*[Lesq].Can.	

†Report of Progress, Second Geol. Survey Pa., Q, pp. 51, 54.

Mariopteris sillimanni (Brongn.)*......................T. C., Can.
    "   *nervosa* (Brongn.) Zeill................Sn., Can.
    "   *newberryi* (Lx.)*.......................Can.
Sphenopteris stipulata Gutb. [Lesq.] ....Can.
    "   *canneltoni* D. W.*.........................Can.
    "   *subalata* Weiss* [Lesq.].................Can.
    "   *chærophylloides* (Brongn.) Presl*.....Can.
    "·   *goniopteroides* Lx?* ....El.
Aloiopteris winslovii D. W. * ....Sn., T. R., Can.
    "   *erosa* (Gutb.)?................................Can.
Pecopteris dentata Brongn.* ....Sn., T. R., Can.
Neuropteris rarinervis Bunby. * ....Can.
    "   *ovata* Hoffm. *.............................Kit., Log., En., Fair., Sn.,
                                    Hom., T. R., El., T. C.,
                                    Can.
    "   *fimbriata* Lx. *...............................Sn., Can.
    "   *vermicularis* Lx. *..........................K. S.. El., T. C., Can.
    "   *aspera* Lx. ....Can.
    "   *scheuchzeri* Hoffm.*.......... ....Kit., T.C., En.. K.S., Fair.,
                                      Sn., T. R., Can.
    "   *clarksoni* Lx. *.............. ....K. S., Can.
    "   *oblongifolia* Lx. * ....Can.
    "   *rogersi* Lx.*...................................Can.
    "   *agassizi* Lx.* [Lesq.] ....Can.
    "   *crenulata* Brongn?* [Lesq.]............Can.
Linopteris obliqua (Bunby.) Pot.* ....Fair., El., T. C., En., Can.
Odontopteris cornuta Lx.*.................................Can.
Caulopteris mansfieldi Lx.*..............................Can.
    "   *oblecta* Lx.*.......................................Can.
    "   *cistii* (Brongn.) Presl*.......................Can.
Rhachiopteris squamosa Lx.................................Can.
Aphlebia adnascens (L. and H.) Presl...............Can.
    "   *cornuta* (Lx.) [Lesq.] ....Can.
    "   *filiciformis* (Gutb.) [Lesq.] ....Can.
    "   *trichomanoides* (Goepp.) [Lesq.]......Can.
    "   *tricoidea* (Lx.) [Lesq.]...................Can.
    "   *thalliformis* (Lx.)............................Can.
Calamites ramosus Artis.................................Can.
    "   *suckowii* Brongn ....Sn., Can.
    "   *approximatus* Brongn...... ....Can.
Asterophyllites equisetiformis (Schloth.) Brongn*.Can.
Annularia ramosa Weiss ....Can.
    "   *stellata* (Schloth.) Wood* ....T. C., Can.

---

†"Lesq." in brackets indicates identification or interpretation of the species by Prof. Lesquereux.

*Series characteristic of the post-Pottsville beds.

Annularia sphenophylloides (Zenk.) Gutb.* ....T. C., Sn., T. R.,
Can.

Calamostachys brevifolius Lx. ....Can.
Sphenophyllum majus Brongn.......................Sn., Hom., Can.
   "   *emarginatum* Brongn* ...............K.S., Sn., T.R., T.C., El.,
Can.
   "   *schlotheimii* Brongn.* [Lesq.] ...Can.
Lepidodendron cf. *brittsii* Lx*.....................Kit.
   "   *dichotomum* Sternb...............Log., Fair., Eu., Can.
   "   *aculeatum* Sternb.........................Can.
   "   *modulatum* Lx.*.................Sn., Dag., Can.
   "   *rigens* Lx.................................Can.
Lepidophloios auriculatus Lx*.......................Can.
   "   *dilatatus* Lx*..............................Can.
Halonia mansfieldi Lx*......... ....Can.
Lepidostrobus cf. *variabilis* L. and H. ....Sn., Hom., Can.
   "   *butleri* Lx.*............................Can.
   "   *goldenbergii* Schimp.* [Lesq.] ...Sn., Can.
   "   *spectabilis* Lx*.........................Can.
Lepidophyllum cultriforme Lx,* ....Can.
   "   *foliaceum* Lx ....El.?, Eu.?, Kit., Can.
   "   *lanceolatum* L. and H.* ....Can.
   "   *mansfieldi* Lx*.........................Can.
Lepidocystis truncatus Lx............. .... Can.
   "   *vesicularis* Lx.............................Can.
Sigillaria camptotænia Wood*.....................T. C., Can.
   "   *tesselata* (Steinh.) Brongn. [Lesq.] ..Sn.
Tæniophyllum brevifolium Lx* ....Can.
   "   *deflexum* Lx*.........................Can.
   "   *decurrens* Lx*.........................Can.
Desmiophyllum gracile Lx ....Can.
Dolerophyllocarpum pennsylvanicum Dn* ....Can.
Cordaites borassifolius (Sternb.) Ung. [Lesq.]...Can.
   "   *mansfieldi* Lx*.........................Can.
   "   *serpens* Lx. *....   Can.
   "   *costatus* Lx. * ....Can.
   "   *radiatus* Lx. *.........................Can.
Cordaistrobus grand'euryi Lx. *................ ....Can.
Cordianthus ovatus Lx. *.........................Can.
   "   *mansfieldi* Lx.*............................Can.
   "   *costatus* Lx.*.........................Can.
Cordaicarpon gutbieri Gein.* ....Sn., Can.
   "   *ovatum* Gr'Ey.* [Lesq.] ....Can.
   "   *cinctum* Lx.*...........................Can.
   "   *costatum* Lx.*.........................Can.
Cardiocarpon marginatum (Art.) Gein. *..........Can:
   "   *ellipticum* (Sternb.) Lx.*..............Can.
   "   *pusillum* Lx.* ....Can.

Trigonocarpon adamsii Lx.*........................... Can.
   "   *menzelianum* Geopp. and Berg.
            [Lesq.] ....Can.
   "   *grande* Lx. ....Sn., El., Can.
   "   *schultzianum* Goepp. and Berg.
            [Lesq.] ....Can.
Rhabdocarpus arcuatus Lx. ....Can.
   "   *subglobosus* Lx.................... ......Can.
   "   *tenax* Lx.* ....Can.
   "   *inflatus* Lx .... Can.
   "   *beinertianus* Goepp and Berg.........Can.
   "   *jacksoniensis* Lx.*[Lesq.] ....Can.
   "   (*Pacuytesta*) *mansfieldi* Lx. *.........Can.
   "   *abnormalis* Lx.......................Can.
   "   *mammillatus* Lx.*.....................Can.
Dicranophyllum dichotomum Lx. *......... ....Can.
   "   *dimorphum* Lx.* ....Can.
Carpolithes cerasiformis Presl. [Lesq.]............Can.
   "   *minimus* Sternb....... ....Can.
   "   *perpusillus* Lx ....Can.

The locality near Cannelton, Beaver county, Pennsylvania, which has furnished so many fossil plants in this list, was discovered by Hon. I. F. Mansfield, of Beaver county, and the rich flora given above, from the pavement of the Middle Kittanning coal, was collected entirely through his efforts, and identified by the eminent paleobotanist, Prof. Leo Lesquereux.

THE LOWER KITTANNING COAL.

One of the most persistent coal beds of the Allegheny series in Pennsylvania, was long ago named the Kittanning coal, by the First Geological Survey of Pennsylvania, from the town of that name on the Allegheny river, in Armstrong county. The structure of this coal at its type locality is given on page 342. When Prof. Lesley remodeled the Pennsylvania coal nomenclature, by adding the names Upper and Middle Kittanning to the same, he gave the name, Lower Kittanning, to the coal bed which had previously been the only member to bear the name, Kittanning.

This coal, while so regular and widely extended in Western Pennsylvania, and persistent entirely across the Ohio coal field, is not so regular and persistent in West Virginia, being frequently interrupted and absent entirely as a workable bed in many regions of the state.

In the Gamble and Watson borings of eastern Monongalia and western Preston counties, respectively, pages 344 and 346, only traces of this coal were found, although the coal appears to be present in the section at the head of Booths creek, given on page 347.

The Newburg shaft, in Preston county, found a good thickness of this coal, as shown on page 348, at a depth of 360 feet below the surface. The coal proved an excellent fuel for steam and domestic use, and was successfully coked, but a disastrous explosion and poor mine engineering led to the abandonment of the workings.

There is doubtless a large area of this valuable coal under the Newburg region, and to a considerable distance to the southwest, since Mr. Sliney found six feet of good coal at this horizon in a boring made several miles southwest from Newburg, on the land of Jonas Wolf.

Where brought to the surface by the Chestnut Ridge arch, at Hammond and Valley Falls, on the Tygarts Valley river, this coal has a thickness of five feet, as shown in the section on page 354, but it is subject to great and rapid changes, being cut out entirely at many localities by the underlying fireclay.

In the New Cumberland region of Hancock county, this coal is present over the great bed of fireclay mined there, but it is thin and impure, being only two to three feet thick, and sometimes it is cut out completely by the overlying sandstone. It is not mined there on a commercial scale, except that in some of the fireclay entries it is taken down and used in burning the brick and tile.

A small area of this coal is caught in the eastern edge of Preston county, at Corinth, where the deep first bituminous basin of Pennsylvania enters the state from Garrett county, Maryland. The coal is mined at Corinth by the Oakland Coal and Coke Company, at whose mine A. P. Brady made the following measurement:

	Ft.	In.	Ft.	In.
Sandstone, ...				
Sandy slate			0	4
Coal	2	7		
Slate	0	1		
Coal	0	9	10	1
Fireclay	3	0		
Coal, reported	3	8		

Butts run S. 70° E. Face S. 20° W. Elevation 2430′ A.T.

The bottom coal was not seen by Mr. Brady, but its thickness was given him by the mine boss. It is not taken out, the overlying fireclay shales being too expensive to remove. The sample for analysis was taken from the two plys of coal above this bottom member, and the composition is reported as follows by Prof. Hite:

```
Moisture ................................................. 0.64
Volatile matter ......................................... 22.43
Fixed carbon ............................................ 65.37
Ash ..................................................... 11.56
                                                         _____
     Total .............................................100.00

Sulphur ................................................. 1.39
Phosphorus .............................................. 0.055
B. T. U. (Wil. Cal.) .................................... 13876
```

This coal has also been successfully coked, but the ovens (56) were not in operation when the plant was visited by Mr. Brady. As this Corinth region is just east from the first great ridge of the Alleghany mountains, it is, of course, within the area of the semibituminous coals, as shown by the low percentage of volatile matter.

Passing eastward over the great Backbone mountain of the Alleghany range, we come to the North Potomac coal basin at its southern end, where the measures come to the surface on Glady fork of Blackwater (Cheat), in Tucker county, along the line of the West Virginia Central & Pittsburg railroad. This coal has been mined very successfully for both fuel and coke, by the Davis Coal & Coke Company, for twenty years, in the vicinity of Coketon and Thomas, Tucker county, and in this region S. D. Brady made the following measurements:

	Ft. In.	Ft. In.	Ft. In.	Ft. In.
	I	II	III	IV
Sandstone.............				
Fireclay				
Coal	1 3	1 6	0 9	1 9
Slate	0 3	0 4	0 3	0 3
Coal	0 11	0 3	1 7	1 2
Slate	0 2	0 3	0 2	0 2
Coal	3 6	3 6	3 5	3 7
Slate	3 6	3 6	1 6	2 0
Coal	......	......	2 10	3 0
Totals...............	9 7	9 4	10 6	11 11
Greatest rise........	S. 10° E.	S. 10° E.	S. 10° E.	S. 10° E.
Elevation A. T.......	2850	2870	2850	2713

ANALYSES.

Moisture	0. 22	0. 29	0. 50	0. 48
Volatile matter	21. 70	23. 15	21. 42	20. 72
Fixed carbon	71. 99	70. 53	70. 76	72. 29
Ash	6. 09	6. 03	7. 32	6. 51
Totals	100. 00	100. 00	100. 00	100. 00
Sulphur	0. 65	0. 62	0. 59	0. 82
Phosphorus	0. 019	0. 021	0. 21	0. 02
B. T. U. (Wil. Cal.)	14520	14728	14506	....

I.   No. 1 mine, Coketon.
II.   No. 2 mine, Coketon.
III.   No. 3 mine, Coketon.
IV.   Thomas shaft, 187 feet deep.

These analyses reveal a coal of exceptional purity, especially in its low percentage of sulphur, and this has given it a splendid reputation as a smithing-coal, for which purpose it is shipped to every portion of the United States, and even to Mexico and Canada. The bottom member of the coal is separated from the rest of the bed by an impure fireclay shale, varying in thickness from two to five feet, and as this lower coal is not so pure as the other plys, it is not mined. In the Thomas shaft, this bottom coal has the following structure:

	Ft. In.	Ft. In.
Coal	1 8	
Sulphur band	0 2	} 3 0
Coal	1 2	

The sample of this coal from above and below the "sulphur band," collected by Mr. Brady, yielded the following results on analysis by Prof. Hite:

Moisture	0. 57
Volatile matter	22. 15
Fixed carbon	67. 01
Ash	10. 27
Total	100. 00
Sulphur	2. 13
Phosphorus	0. 005
B. T. U. (Wil. Cal.)	14024

While this coal is much higher in both ash and sulphur than the rest of the bed, it would make a fairly good steam and general fuel.

The Lower Kittanning bed is also mined by the Cumberland Coal Company, at Douglas station, one mile below Coketon, where A. P. Brady made the following measurement:

	Ft. In.	Ft. In.
Sandstone		
Blue slate..........	3· 10 0	
Draw slate...	0 6	
Coal .... I 7		
Slate 0 2½		
Coal 0 10		
Slate.. 0 2		9 9½
Coal 3 6		
Slate (fireclay)................................... I 10		
Coal .... I 8		

Butts run S. 75° W.   Face S. 15°E.   Elevation 3000 feet A. T.   Greatest rise, west.

The bottom ply is not mined, as the slate above varies from eight to thirty-six inches in thickness.

Analysis of sample reported by Prof. Hite as follows:

Moisture	0. 63
Volatile matter	23. 18
Fixed carbon	68. 94
Ash	7. 25
Total	100. 00
Sulphur	0. 58
Phosphorus	0. 019

This coal has been very successfully coked at Thomas, Coketon and Douglas, Tucker county, in connection with the mines from which the samples of coal were taken for analysis. Mr. Brady also sampled the coke made at these mines, and the analyses of the same, reported by Prof. Hite, read as follows:

COKE (LOWER KITTANNING COAL.)

Analyses No.	Mois.	V. M.	F. C.	Ash.	Total.	Sul.	Phos.	Coking Time.
I	0. 15	0. 74	90. 02	9. 09	100.	0. 63	0. 0310	... hrs.
2	0. 11	0. 44	91. 27	8. 18	100.	0. 62	0. 0460	72 hrs.
3	0. 12	I. 17	88. 68	10. 03	100.	0. 74	0. 0270	.. hrs.
4	0. 11	0. 57	87. 22	12. 10	100.	0. 89	0. 0180	72 hrs.
Average	0. 13	0. 83	89. 29	9. 85	100.	0. 72	0. 0280	

LOCATION OF SAMPLES.

1. From No. 2 ovens, Thomas shaft, Thomas, Tucker county.

2. From No. 2 ovens, No. 2 mine, Coketon, Tucker county, two miles south of Thomas.

3. From Coketon No. 3 ovens, Coketon, Tucker county, two miles south of Thomas.

4. From Douglas ovens, Douglas, Tucker county, three miles south of Thomas.

These results reveal a coke of most excellent quality in every respect, except that it contains a little more phosphorus than is desirable for the manufacture of iron and steel. It is possible that this could be reduced by eliminating some particular layer of the coal, which may hold the principal portion of the phosphorus.

The main upper bench of this coal is supposed to represent the Middle Kittanning coal, since just above it comes seventy-five to eighty feet of massive, pebbly, Lower Freeport sandstone, and then, near Davis, this upper ply of coal separates from the main bench by twenty feet or more.

The Lower Kittanning coal underlies a wide area in the North Potomac basin, and, being so near tide water, must prove of great value in the future history of the coal and coke industry. This bed is locally known as the "Davis" seam, while the Upper Freeport seam, 190 feet higher, is termed the "Thomas" seam.

At Henry, Grant county, near the North Potomac river, and one-half mile east from the center of the basin, this coal is mined by a shaft, sunk by the Davis Coal & Coke Company to a depth of over 400 feet, at the bottom of which A. P. Brady reports the coal exhibiting the following structure:

	Ft. In.	Ft. In.
Sandstone		
Fireclay		
Coal	2 1	
Slate	0 10	
Coal	4 2	7 2
Bone coal	0 1	

Butts run S. 54¼° W. Face S. 35¼° E. Greatest rise S. 54° E. Elevation, 2231 feet A. T.

Analysis of sample reported by Prof. Hite as follows:

Moisture	0.65
Volatile matter	18.46
Fixed carbon	68.64
Ash	12.25
Total	100.00
Sulphur	2.21
Phosphorus	0.014

In a bore hole near this shaft the coal has the following structure:

	Ft.	Ft.	In.	In.
Coal	0	2		
Shale.....	0	1		
Coal	2	9½		
Shale, gray.............	0	4½		
Bone	0	7½	8	5½
Coal	2	0		
Shale	0	1½		
Coal	2	0		
Shale........	0	1		
Bone.......	0	2½		
Shale			19	2½
Rough coal and shale.........			2	1½

The "rough coal" at the bottom of this section is most probably the same as the "bottom" division of the bed at Thomas and Coketon, but here separated farther from the main bed. This is the view held by Dr. G. C. Martin, of the Maryland Survey, who identified this division with a similar coal in Garrett county, known as the "Split-six," the main Lower Kittanning bed being generally termed the "Six-foot" seam in that county.

Where this coal comes out to the surface, near Stoyer, Garrett county, twenty miles below Henry, the following structure is exhibited, as measured by Dr. G. C. Martin, page 119, Geology of Garrett county, Md:

		Ft.	In.	Ft.	In.
	coal	0	4		
	bone	0	1		
Coal, M. Kittanning..	coal	0	9	3	8
	bone	1	0		
	coal	1	6		
Shale				8	4
	coal	0	5		
	bone	0	1		
	coal	0	5		
Coal, L. Kittanning..	bone	0	1½	4	4
	coal	0	4		
	bone	1	0		
	coal	1	11		
Shale				1	0
Limestone, Ferriferous				1	0

Here the two coal beds, which are practically one in the Henry shaft, and in the mines at Thomas and Coketon, are separated by eight feet of dark shales.

William Taylor has a mine in what A. P. Brady identifies as the Lower Kittanning coal, one mile and a-half northwest of Emory, Mineral county, where the following structure is found:

		Ft. In.	Ft. In.
Sandstone			
Slate			
Coal	bone coal	0 7½	
	coal	1 4	4 8½
	slate	0 0½	
	coal	2 8½	

Elevation A. T., 1900 feet.

Mr. Brady refers this to the Lower Kittanning bed doubtfully, and hence it may be some other coal, since the structure is more like that of the Upper Freeport bed along the Potomac.

The analysis of this coal is reported as follows by Prof. Hite:

Moisture	0.56
Volatile matter	15.35
Fixed carbon	75.78
Ash	8.31
Total	100.00
Sulphur	2.54
Phosphorus	0.022

The Smith Coal Company has a mine in the Lower Kittanning bed, one-half mile south from Blaine, Mineral county, and there A. P. Brady made the following measurements:

		Ft. In.	Ft. In.
Sandstone, massive			
Slate			1 0
Coal	coal	2 0	
	slate	1 2	
	coal	0 7	5 0½
	slate	0 0½	
	coal	1 3	

Butts run E.   Face S,   Elevation, 1710 feet A. T.
Analysis of sample reported as follows by Prof. Hite:

Moisture	0.85
Volatile matter	15.40
Fixed carbon	72.55
Ash	11.20
Total	100.00

Sulphur .... 2.

Phosphorus .... 0.03.

This coal has long been mined in the vicinity of Piedmon. Westernport, and Bloomington, where it is known as the "Six-foot" seam.

Near Piedmont, the Piedmont & Potomac Coal Company operate a mine called the "Virginia," and there A. P. Brady made the following measurements:

		Ft. In.	Ft. In.
Sandstone			
Fireclay 5-		6 . 0	
Draw slate..........		0 3	
Coal ..	coal...	0 10	
	bone coal............... -	0 4	
	coal...........................	1 9	
	slate	0 0¾	5 7
	coal...............................	1 10	
	sulphur	0 0½	
	coal.........................	0 9	

Elevation A. T., 1215 feet.

Analysis of sample reported by Prof. Hite as follows:

Moisture 0.52

Volatile matter.. 15.29

Fixed carbon 74.13

Ash 10.06

Total.... ....100.00

Sulphur 1.76

Phosphorus:.. 0.031

The Davis Coal and Coke Company mines this Lower Kittanning bed at its "Hampshire" mine, where A. P. Brady reports the following structure:

		Ft. In.	Ft. In.
Draw slate...........		0 2	
"Soapstone".............		0 1	
Coal ..	bone coal.....................................	0 2	
	coal.	0 5	
	bone coal......	0 5	
	coal	1 8	5 1½
	slate ... .:................................	0 1	
	coal	2 4½	

Greatest rise S. 65° E.   Elevation A. T., 1248 feet.

Analysis of sample reported by Prof. Hite as follows:

Moisture	0. 64
Volatile matter.............................	15. 98
Fixed carbon	71. 41
Ash	11. 97
Total..100. 00	
Sulphur	1. 39
Phosphorus...............................	0. 055

These last three analyses, from the lower end of the Potomac basin, exhibit a marked decrease in the quantity of volatile matter over that shown for the same coal bed in the vicinity of Thomas and Coketon.

In the bore hole at Webster, Taylor county, the record of which is given on page 356, this coal appears to be cut out entirely by the development of massive, pebbly sandstones, and when this horizon comes to the surface along the Valley river, above the mouth of Roaring creek, in Randolph county, the coal cannot be certainly recognized, since it is thin and of no commercial value, so far as can be determined by the borings put down, near the mouth of Beaver creek, the records of which are given on pages 360-1-2.

The same state of affairs is found at the head of the Buckhannon river, in the vicinity of Pickens and below, where the Allegheny-Kanawha series has thickened up to nearly 600 feet. A coal bed occurs there at about 450 feet below the top of the series, which may represent the Lower Kittanning bed, but it has been impossible to demonstrate the supposed identity. It has been mined for local supply on the lands of James Pickens, and others, and is two and one-half to three feet thick, while above it, twenty to twenty-five feet, is another coal two feet thick. The Pickens coal is most probably identical with the Campbells creek coal, of the Great Kanawha, since it can be followed from Pickens to Holly river, and across from Elk to Gauley waters, and down the latter stream to its mouth, in the Great Kanawha, but whether or not the Campbells creek bed represents the Lower Kittanning coal is only conjectural. This matter will be discussed later in connection with the chapter on the Kanawha coals.

In the deep oil and gas well borings of Marion county, around Mannington, a thick coal is frequently noted at the horizon of the Lower Kittanning bed, about 800 feet below the Pittsburg seam, and some coal is reported at this horizon in the adjoining counties of Harrison and Monongalia, but it does not appear to be thick enough for commercial purposes, so that the Marion area of thick coal may be of limited extent, like that in the Newburg region of Preston county.

THE KITTANNING FIRECLAY.

Directly below the coal just described, there is nearly everywhere, in western Pennsylvania and eastern Ohio, a very valuable bed of fireclay, which in Hancock county has given rise to an extensive brick, sewer pipe, and pottery industry. The clay is mostly of the plastic variety, though some flint clay is nearly always found, and the whole bed varies in thickness from five to fifteen feet.

In only one other region of the state, outside of the New Cumberland region of Hancock county, has the Kittanning fireclay been mined and utilized, and that is at Hammond, in eastern Marion county, where the great Chestnut Ridge anticlinal brings this horizon 100 feet or more above the level of the Valley river. The clay has a thickness of five to eight feet, and one to three feet of it, is hard, or flint clay, while the rest is plastic.

When the clay is in good development, the overlying coal is absent, and vice versa. The presence of this clay deposit at Hammond makes the identification of the horizon certain when taken in connection with the associated beds.

THE FERRIFEROUS (VANPORT) LIMESTONE.

The marine type of the Ferriferous limestone of Pennsylvania, now known as the Vanport limestone, does not appear anywhere within the boundary of West Virginia, so far as known, except in Hancock county, where it is thin and impure, and underlies the Lower Kittanning coal by an interval of sixty feet, the most of which is sandy shales and shaly sandstone. This stratum and its overlying iron ore have been traced entirely across the Ohio coal field, however, from Mahoning and Columbiana counties on the east, to where it emerges from the Ohio river silts, three or four miles above Ironton in Lawrence county, and about the same distance from the southwest corner of West Virginia at Kenova, so that the marine type of the limestone very probably underlies the adjoining portion of Wayne county at the southwestern extremity of the State, although the stratum is below water level.

Where this horizon is exposed at Valley Falls and Hammond in Taylor and Marion counties, some iron ore is present, but no limestone, and the same is true of the exposures in Preston and elsewhere in the northern portion of the State.

. In the Potomac basin, however, a limestone of fresh water origin, makes its appearance at a few feet below the Lower Kittanning coal, carrying on its top a layer of carbonate ore just like the "Buhrstone" iron ore of Pennsylania and Ohio, and hence this limestone and iron ore have been referred to the Ferriferous and Buhrstone horizons of Pennsylvania. The relation of the limestone and its ore to the other members of the series may be seen in the section on page 354 from Coketon, where both are well exposed in the cuttings along the W. Va. C. & Pgh. R. R.

The same limestone is also visible in a small stream near Stoyer in Garrett county, where it lies much closer to the Lower Kittanning coal, as shown by the section quoted from Dr. Martin on page 489. In the Great Kanawha valley there are two limestones in the lower half of the series, either one of which may be the representative of the Ferriferous, viz., the Campbells creek limestone, 20-30 feet above the coal of the same name, or the Cannelton Cement limestone below the coal in question, seventy-five to one hundred feet. If the Campbells creek coal be the representative of the Clarion of Pennsylvania, then the limestone ABOVE it would represent the Ferriferous horizon, but if it be the Lower Kittanning coal, then the Cannelton Cement limestone would come at the horizon referred to.

THE CLARION SANDSTONE.

In Pennsylvania and in the northern Pan Handle of West Virginia, a massive sandstone, much resembling the top of the Pottsville, occasionally makes its appearance in the interval between the Lower Kittanning coal and the next underlying coal, to which the name Clarion sandstone has been given by the Pennsylvania geologists. It is seldom present except when the Ferriferous limestone is absent, or but poorly developed.

Other localities in West Virginia, outside of Hancock county, at which this sandstone can be identified with a fair degree of certainty, are at Valley Falls, near the Marion-Taylor line, where it forms a massive ledge over the Clarion coal, just above the "Falls" in the Valley river; also along Cheat river in Preston and Monongalia, and in the North Potomac basin of Tucker, Grant and Mineral counties, where a massive sandstone is frequently present at this horizon.

THE CLARION COAL.

On the Allegheny river, the lowest bed of coal above the top of the Pottsville was named the CLARION by the First Geological Survey of Pennsylvania. True, there is occasionally a thin coal (Scrub Grass) above it, and sometimes there was supposed to be another one, the Brookville, below it, but H. M. Chance has shown that the former is only a "split" from the Clarion, and has called the Scrub Grass bed the Upper Clarion, and the main division of the coal, the Lower Clarion, and it is very probable that the Brookville coal bed is simply a local phase of the Clarion, since along the Allegheny river, the type locality for the series, there are certainly no other coals than the Upper and Lower Clarion beds between the Ferriferous or Vanport limestone, and the top of the Pottsville series.

On Bee Run, near the line between Preston and Monongalia counties, a coal bed has been mined on the land of Z. C. Gibson, about one mile south from Cheat river, which appears to represent the Clarion coal. The section there is as follows:

		Ft. In.	Ft. In.
Sandstone, massive, Clarion	....	20 0	
Coal .. { coal	3 0	}	6 0
{ fireclay............	1 0		
{ coal	2 0		

The upper bench of the coal varies from three to three and one-half feet, while the parting fireclay shale varies from six to eighteen inches within a short distance, and the lower bench of the coal is equally variable. The coal has been opened at several localities farther up the Run from the Gibson bank, and appears to be of fair quality. The dip is to the southeast, and the position of the coal is 190 feet below the Upper Freeport bed, which is opened in the hill on the land of Forbes Blaney, one mile east, so that it interval vertically below the latter coal cannot be less than 250 to 300 feet.

In the Sanford Watson boring (page 344), near Masontown, Preston county, the top of this coal was struck at 245 feet under the Upper Freeport bed, and it is split into two divisions by six and one-half feet of fireclay shales, while in the Gamble lot boring (page 346) it is single bedded and 221 feet below the Upper Freeport coal. Where the B. & O. R. R. turns west from Cheat river in Preston county, this coal lies almost in direct contact with the uppermost member of the Pottsville series, and has the structure shown in the section on pages 349-50 of this volume, in which, as will be observed, it is still split into two benches by five feet of fireclay.

About one mile farther down Cheat river from the outcrop on the B. & O. R. R. in Preston county, just referred to, this coal has been opened and exhibits the following structure:

	Ft.	In.	Ft.	In.
Coal, slaty	2	10		
Fireclay shales	7	0	12	8
Coal	2	10		

Here the parting has thickened to seven feet of fireclay and sandy shales. The upper bench of the coal is rather slaty and bony on its crop, but the lower one appears to be of fair quality. A great cliff of sandstone (Pottsville series) crops immediately under the coal bed.

At Valley Falls, near the Marion-Taylor line, this coal has been mined for local use on the south side of the valley river, only a few feet above water level near the "Falls" in the stream, where it has the structure shown on page 355. The coal is also double bedded at this locality, though the parting is only one half foot thick, and the coal appears to be of fair quality.

On the North Potomac river, the position of this coal is revealed in the section near Harrison, Mineral county, measured by Dr. G. C. Martin, of the Maryland Geological Survey, and quoted on page 351 of this volume. The coal is generally present in the North Potomac basin at seventy-five to eighty feet below the Lower Kittanning bed, but is usually coarse in texture and inclined to be impure and bony.

At the head of the Buckhannon river a bed of coal occurs about 100 feet under the Pickens seam, and is known as the "Gimmel" vein, which would represent this coal if the "Pickens" bed should prove to be the Lower Kittanning, as seems probable, or possible at least.

This same coal crops along the left fork of Holly and has been mined near its head by Henry Spies for use in the locomotives on the narrow guage R. Rs. which lead from Pickens across the divide to the head waters of Holly and Elk rivers. The coal lies a few feet below a very massive sandstone, and is about three feet thick with a slate or bony parting below the center. The same coal is also mined below Hacker's Valley by Charles Curry, Dr. Elliott and others, and also at Allen Anderson's mill, where it lies 522 feet below the Upper Freeport bed, and has the structure given in the section on page 365. This coal on Holly river can be traced through to the Great Kanawha, where it appears to correlate with the Eagle seam of that region; so that if the bed which crops along the left fork of Holly between Mollahan's Mill and its head, is the Clarion, then the Eagle bed of the Kanawha series is also the same. We shall refer to this Holly river coal again under the chapter on the Kanawha coals.

A thick bed of fireclay often underlies the Clarion coal in Pennsylvania, and the same is true in the Watson and Gamble borings near Masontown, Preston county, and Rock Forge, Monongalia county, but so far as known it has not been utilized anywhere in West Virginia.

The horizon of the Clarion coal and its underlying clay is covered by the Ohio river silts in the northern end of Hancock county, so that although the coal is above water level, nothing is known of its thickness or quality in that region.

Mr. David White gives the following RESUME of the flora of the Clarion group in the Bulletin of the Geological Society of America, Vol. XI, pages 148-150:

CLARION GROUP.

"*Plant beds of the group*--The interval embracing the lower portion of the Allegheny series, from the top of the Homewood sandstone (Pottsville formation) up to the top of the "Ferriferous limestone," is known as the Clarion group. The ordinary thickness of this group is about seventy or seventy-five feet in the Allegheny valley. Two coals—sometimes three or more, two of which are locally workable—are usually present in this section.

"In the Clarion group of western Pennsylvania determinable fossil plants are generally very rare, most of the scarce material from this region being badly macerated and abraded. Nevertheless, specimens have been collected from the roof of the Brookville coal, which usually occurs within a few feet of, or almost on the top of, the Pottsville formation at Point Barnett, near Brookville (Br.), and from the roof shales of the Clarion coal at Somerville (Som.) near the Clarion county line. Fossil plants occur in this group in Butler and Mercer counties, where they have been collected at Grove City (G. C.), Pardoe (Par.), and Filer (Fil.), from above the "Pardoe" coal. This coal is regarded by Dr. I. C. White as equivalent to the Brookville coal, though it is thought that it possibly represents the Clarion coal. Its reference to the Clarion group is, however, certain.

"*Plants of the Clarion group.*—For the sake of economy of space, the species collected from the relatively small stratigraphic interval included in the Clarion group, may be combined in one list, from which the plants of each horizon may be separated by referring to the abbreviations given above. The identifications are the result of a preliminary study, and are, as such, subject to revision."

Name.	Locality.
Mariopteris cf. *aspera* Brongn	Fil.
Pecopteris villosa Brongn*	Fil., Som.
" cf. *vestita* Lx.*	Br.
Alethopteris serlii (Brongn.) Goepp	G. C.
Neuropteris desorii Lx.*	Fil.
" *rarinervis* Bunby*	G. C., Par.
" *ovata* Hoffm.*	Br., Fil., G. C., Som.
" *vermicularis* Lx.*	Som.
" *scheuchzeri* Hoffm.*	Br., Fil., G. C., Som.
Caulopteris sp	Fil.
Annularia stellata (Schloth.) Wood*	Fil.
" *sphenophylloides* (Zenk.) Gutb.*	Par.
Sphenophyllum emarginatum Brongn.*	Br.
Lycopodites meekii Lx	Par.
Lepidodendron dichotomum Sternb	Fil.
" cf. *andrewsi* Lx.*	Par.
" *clypeatum* Lx	Fil.
Lepidostrobus geinitzii Schimp*	Fil.
Lepidophyllum lanceolatum L. and H.*	Par., Som.
Polysporia sp	Fil.

*Forms characteristic of post-Pottsville beds.

Sigillaria cf. *brardii* Brongn............................Fil.
    "   (*Rhytidolepis*) sp ....Fil.
Cordaites lacoei Lx.?*......... ....Fil.
Cardiocarpon sp...... ....Fil., G. C.
Rhabdocarpos multistriatus (Sternb.) Lx.*.........Fil.

"The species in the above list comprise a flora representative of the lower portion of the Allegheny series."

—————————————————————————————————

*Forms characteristic of post–Pottsville beds.

CHAPTER VI.

THE KANAWHA SERIES.

As already stated many times in this report, the Allegheny series of Pennsylvania and Ohio, and its principal members are easily recognized and readily identifiable in the northern region of West Virginia, and even at the southwestern end of the state, just across the line in Lawrence county, Ohio. Yet when we attempt to follow the Allegheny series along its eastern crop across the state, from Monongalia and Preston counties through Barbour, Randolph, Upshur, Webster, Nicholas, and Fayette, to the Great Kanawha, we find the interval between the Upper Freeport bed, at the top, and the undoubted Pottsville below, expanding to twice, thrice, and finally four times its average thickness at the Pennsylvania border, so that while there appears to be a general agreement and harmony as to the number of coal beds on the Great Kanawha, with those in the typical Allegheny series of Pennsylvania, yet the correlations below the highest member of the series, are not yet altogether conclusive, and hence it has been considered best to describe the coals of these thickened deposits under a separate chapter, and term them for the present the KANAWHA SERIES with the understanding that the deposits in question include not only the ALLEGHENY SERIES, but also any beds intermediate between the latter and the Pottsville, which may have made their appearance as we pass from the Pennsylvania border southwestward to the Great Kanawha river. This treatment of the matter is also desirable since Mr. David White, the eminent authority on fossil plants of Coal Measure age, has recently claimed (Bulletin of the Geological Society of America, Vol. XI, pages 145 to 178) that the Kanawha coals are distinctly older than the Allegheny series, and represent a group of strata heretofore unrecognized in America, viz., the Lower Coal Measures of Europe, thus coming in between the Allegheny series proper and the top of the Pottsville. From this standpoint Mr. White would place practically all of the Kanawha series, as here defined, below the Allegheny, since he states in the paper to which reference has been made, that the STOCKTON COAL at the very top of the Kanawha series would appear to be no higher in the geologic time scale than the CLARION COAL of the Allegheny series (see page 170 l. c.).

The writer has given reasons (Bulletin of the Geological Society of America, Vol. XIII, pages 119-126) for dissent from this conclusion of David White, as to the horizon of the Stockton coal of the Kanawha valley, which, as shown in this report, is believed by the writer to represent the Upper Freeport coal at the TOP of the Allegheny series instead of the Clarion coal, as claimed by David White, at the BASE of the Allegheny beds. But as to the other members of the Kanawha series below the Stockton coal, the writer has not been able to trace them with such certainty as the one referred to (Upper Freeport), and hence the question as to their equivalency is left open for future and more detailed study than it has been possible to devote to the solution of the problems involved.

Regarding the Kanawha series as a whole, we find along the Great Kanawha river, between the KANAWHA BLACK FLINT bed and the top of the Pottsville series, six coal beds which appear to be persistent over considerable areas. These six beds have received local names along the Kanawha valley and are as follows, with their supposed equivalents in the Allegheny series:

Stockton (Cannelton) = Upper Freeport.

Coalburg = Lower Freeport.
Winifrede = Upper Kittanning.
Cedar Grove = Middle Kittanning.
Campbells Creek = Lower Kittanning.
Eagle = Clarion.

Other local names like "Lewiston," "Peerless," "Coal Valley," "No. 2 Gas," "Blacksburg," "Tunnel Seam," etc., are also in use, but these are for the most part synonyms of those already given, or of different phases of the same bed named where identity has not been recognized.

The foregoing is the correlation suggested by the writer in Bulletin No. 65 of the U. S. G. Survey, 1891, and previously, in a paper published in "The Virginias" for January, 1885. This last was the first serious attempt to correlate the coals of the Kanawha valley with those in the Allegheny series, and the studies upon which the results were founded were made during the summer of 1884.

The writer does not insist that this order suggested above has been demonstrated with a reasonable degree of certainty, except for the coal at the summit of the series, in fact future detailed stratigraphic work may overturn or greatly modify the suggested correlations, but they are presented as a working hypothesis to remain as probable until they are shown or demonstrated to be erroneous.

As already stated in a former chapter, Prof. Wm. B. Rogers long ago (1838) described the KANAWHA BLACK FLINT, and discerned its value as a key rock in the study of the Kanawha coals, as well as its place in the stratigraphic order, separating two important coal series from each other.

The coals above the BLACK FLINT in the Kanawha valley have already been described under the Conemaugh series, as the MASON and MAHONING, or "No. 5 Block" coal, and we shall now give a series of sections along the Great Kanawha river from Charleston, where the BLACK FLINT bed first appears above water level, on southward to where it passes into the air from the summit of Ganley mountain at Ansted.

As stated under the Conemaugh series, the PITTSBURG COAL comes into the summits of the hills a short distance northwest from Charleston, and a connected nearly vertical measurement of the

rocks puts its horizon about 800 feet above the level of the KA-
NAWHA BLACK FLINT, as shown by the section on pages 239-40.
There can be no doubt that the Two Mile limestones shown in that
section represent the horizon of the AMES, or GREEN CRINOIDAL bed
of the Huntington region, only fifty miles distant, though these
limestones contain only fresh water types of fossils like SPIRORBIS
CARBONARIUS at Charleston.

The hills surrounding the city of Charleston extend far up
into the RED BEDS of the Conemaugh series, while the lower bluffs
of the valley are made by the Mahoning and other massive sandstones, which form the basal members of the Conemaugh. The
following section measured from the summits at the head of Coal
branch run, a small tributary of Elk river, a short distance above
Charleston, will serve to show the character of the rocks above the
KANAWHA BLACK FLINT:

Ft.

Sandstone, massive, pebbly	30
Concealed and *limestone*, Two Mile	30
Deep red shales, with iron ore	20
Shales and concealed, with iron ore nuggets	160
Sandstone, massive	40
Concealed, shales and fireclay	20
Sandstone, very massive	70
Concealed, with thin *coal* (Mason)	5
Sandstone, massive	40
Coal and shale	1
Sandstone, massive	35
Concealed to the horizon of the *Kanawha black flint*, below the bed of Elk river	60

The Two Mile limestone horizon is also caught in the summits
of the hills at the head of Porter's run on the south side of the
Kanawha, above Charleston, where the BLACK FLINT is above water
level, and the limestone has been quarried and burned on the lands
of Capt. Swan. In descending Porter's run from the limestone
quarry the following succession was measured:

		Ft. In.		Ft. In.		Ft. In.	
Sandstone, massive						20	0
Shales						10	0
Limestone, Two Mile { limestone		1	8				
shales, gray		6	0	}		9	0
limestone		1	4				
Red shale, with iron ore nuggets						35	0
Concealed						65	0
Sandstone, pebbly						25	0
Concealed and massive sandstone						150	0

Coal, Mason						2	0
Concealed						50	0
Sandstone, massive						50.	0
Sandy shales						30	0
Kanawha black flint						5	0

Stockton coal horizon	coal ... {	coal 0 6		} 3 6		} 25 0
		slate 0 6				
		coal 2 6				
	shale, gray 5 0					
	black slate 0 8					
	shales, blue 14 0					
	coal, splint...................... 1 6					
	black slate 0 4					

Sandstone, massive		35	0
Coal, slaty, impure...		1	3
Shales and flaggy sandstone		20	0
Coal, Coalburg { coal, slaty at top.............. 2 0	} 2 11		
fireclay.... .... 0 6			
coal and slate........ .... 0 5.			
Shales..		3	0
Sandstone, massive			

This section in itself shows the improbability of the hypothesis that the KANAWHA BLACK FLINT represents the horizon of the FERRIFEROUS LIMESTONE of Pennsylvania and Ohio, and that consequently, the ALLEGHENY SERIES of coals, except the lowest or CLARION, must be looked for above the BLACK FLINT. The Charleston people have looked very diligently for coal above this horizon, and with the exception of the small bed (Mason) noted in the section, they have found no coal of value between the Black Flint and the Two Mile limestones at the top of the section, and indeed none of any importance until they pass 375 feet or more above the latter and reach the PITTSBURG BED northwest from the city; so that if the ALLEGHENY SERIES is to be found above the BLACK FLINT, two very strange things have occurred in the Charleston region, viz., 1st, practically all of its five coal beds (Upper and Lower Freeport, Upper, Middle and Lower Kittanning) have disappeared, while at the same time, in a region where all the other underlying formations have expanded many fold, the ALLEGHENY SERIES has SHRUNK to half its normal thickness, since even in northern West Virginia and western Pennsylvania, the ordinary interval between the AMES LIMESTONE and the FERRIFEROUS LIMESTONE is 550 feet, while here at Charleston this same interval would be only a little over 400 feet if the BLACK FLINT represents the FERRIFEROUS LIMESTONE, as claimed by Mr. David White in the publication to which reference has been made. The ordinary interval from the Ames limestone to the top of the Allegheny series, or Upper Freeport coal, is about 300 feet in the northern portion of West Virginia and the adjoining region of Pennsylvania, and as it is only slightly over 400 feet from the horizon of the AMES LIMESTONE here to the STOCKTON COAL, it is not a violent assumption, to say the least, to consider that this interval has increased by only 100 feet, while, as is well known, the underlying Kanawha and Pottsville series have each quadrupled in thickness in passing from the northern end of the state to the Great Kanawha valley.

Aside from any evidence derived from the direct tracing of the beds, the measurements themselves, and the character of the intervening strata at Charleston, where we can pass directly from the undisputed Pittsburg coal, in the summits of the hills along Two Mile creek, within sight of Charleston, to the BLACK FLINT ledge, where it emerges from the bed of the Kanawha, near the C. & O. railroad station, would seem to be conclusive in placing the latter stratum at the base of the CONEMAUGH SERIES, as the writer has done on stratigraphical evidence, instead of at the base of the ALLEGHENY SERIES, as Mr. David White has done on paleobotanical evidence.

Of course, it is POSSIBLE for most of the five coal beds, above the Ferriferous limestone, to disappear, and the measures themselves to shrink to only half their normal thickness, in a region where all other rock series are expanding many fold, but it hardly seems PROBABLE, and hence, until more evidence can be adduced in favor of Mr. David White's hypothesis, we must continue to regard the BLACK FLINT of this section as the basal member of the Conemaugh series, and the underlying Stockton coal as equivalent to the Upper Freeport bed of the Allegheny series.

In this section along Porters run, the lower portion of it was measured between the mouth of the stream and the mouth of Lick run, next above. The Stockton coal is here split by slate and shales, and spread through an interval of twenty-five feet. This is made plain by a section on the north side of the river, only a mile and a half distant, where the following succession is found in descending from the summits of hills, on the land of Mr. Ruffner, one-half mile below the mouth of Wilsons run:

	Ft. In.	Ft. In.
Sandstone, massive, coarse	30 0	
Concealed	20 0	

		Ft.	In.
Sandstone, massive, gray..		40	0
Concealed......		40	0
Sandstone, very hard, white......................................		5	0
Concealed (contains *Mason coal*)		25	0
Sandstone. massive		100	0
Concealed		20	0
Kanawha black flint..		4	0
Shales, sandy, dark gray............................		7	0

		Ft.	In.		Ft.	In.
Coal, Stockton	coal, slaty.........................	0	10			
	shale, dark	0	5			
	coal, bony in center..........	3	0			
	shale...................................	0	1		5	10
	black slate	0	5			
	shale, dark gray................	0	8			
	coal, bony.......................	0	5			

		Ft.	In.
Sandy shale		0	2
Sandstone, massive		40	0
Concealed to level of Great Kanawha river................		125	0

The Stockton coal was once mined at this locality by Mr. Ruffner, but it contained much slaty and bony material along with some impure cannel in the center of the main bench.

The COALBURG COAL, locally known as the "Brooks" vein, belongs in the concealed interval about sixty feet below the Stockton seam.

The rocks rise rapidly southward, and at the mouth of Wilsons run, the following measurement was made, which reveals another coal bed under the Coalburg seam:

	Ft.	In.	Ft.	In.
Kanawha black flint			5	0
Concealed, with coal blossom....................................			12	0
Sandstone, gray, micaceous..			45	0
Concealed...			75	0
Sandstone			15	0
Coal			1	6
Fireclay			1	0
Sandstone			20	0
Coal, "Point" seam, blossom				
Concealed to Kanawha river...................................			35	0

Here a thin coal, the representative of the WINIFREDE BED, makes its appearance at 147 feet below the BLACK FLINT. It has been mined for local use on Wilsons run, but as it does not exceed twenty inches in thickness it is of little economic importance. The coal twenty feet below the Winifrede bed has been mined on the south side of the river near the mouth of Chapel run, where it is locally known as the "Point" seam, and has the relation to the BLACK FLINT shown in the following section:

			Ft. In.	Ft. In.

Kanawha black flint 5 0
Coal, Stockton 5 0
Concealed 140 0
Coal, Winifrede 2 0
Sandstone 25 0

Coal, "Point" seam .. { coal 0 7
"niggerhead" .... 0 9 } 3 3
coal 1 11

Concealed to Kanawha river..................................145 0

The Kanawha miners give the name "Niggerhead" to any hard black slate or bone in the coal seams of the region. The "Point" seam was once mined on Chapel run by the late Dr. Hale of Charleston, who gave me the structure for it shown above. The STOCKTON coal was also mined near the mouth of Chapel run but it proved slaty and impure.

Black Hawk run puts into the north bank of the Kanawha river nearly opposite the mouth of Chapel run, and descending the steep hill one-fourth mile up the former stream, the following section was measured:

			Ft. In.	Ft. In.

Massive sandstone and concealed 285 0
Shales and concealed................................. .... 20 0
Kanawha black flint 5 0
Sandy shales.. .... 5 0
Coal, Stockton, and concealed........... .... 5 0
Fireclay and sandy shales 5 0
Sandstone, massive 60 0

Coal, Coalburg, "*Brooks vein*" { coal, slaty 0 1
shale, blue 0 4
coal 0 10
fireclay...................... .... 2 0
shale, sandy 1 3
coal 1 0
shale and fireclay 1 6
coal .... 1 4 } 8 4

This coal is locally known as the "Brooks" seam, and it has been mined quite extensively for use in the old Daniel Boone salt furnace. Its horizon is midway between the Stockton coal and the Winifrede bed.

The STOCKTON COAL was also once mined here in Black Hawk hollow for use in the salt furnaces by Dr. Hale, who reported it as three and one-half to four feet thick but very slaty and sulphurous.

Campbells creek puts into the north bank of the Great Kanawha four miles above Charleston, and at its mouth a very important and widely persistent coal bed rises from the bed of the river, and has been extensively mined along Campbells creek. The following section was measured in descending from the summit of a steep hill, one mile and a-half above the mouth of Campbells creek:

	Ft.	In.	Ft.	In.
Concealed from summit			45	0
Sandstone, very hard, white			10	0
Coaly slate			2	0
Sandstone, coarse, soft			50	0
Sandstone, bluish gray, hard			40	0
Concealed			40	0
Kanawha Black flint			5	0
Concealed, with blossom of *coal* near top			90	0

		Ft.	In.	Ft.	In.
Coalburg, or "Brook's" coal	coal, splinty	1	6		
	"niggerhead"	0	6		
	coal, good	1	6	5	0
	shale	0	6		
	coal, slaty	1	0		

	Ft.	In.	Ft.	In.
Concealed			135	0
Sandstone, massive			125	0
Coal, "Arno" (Cedar Grove)			1	3
Shales, sandy			15	0
Limestone silicious, Campbells creek			1	0
Shales and sandstone			34	0

		Ft.	In.	Ft.	In.
Coal, Campbell's creek	coal, splint	1	10		
	slate	0	1		
	coal	1	1		
	slate	0	1	5	8
	coal	0	10		
	shale	0	6		
	coal	1	3		

The interval between the CAMPBELLS CREEK COAL and the BLACK FLINT, foot up 406 feet as measured with the aneroid barometer, and Mr. Lovell of the Pioneer Coal Co., reports an accurate instrumental determination of 410 feet for the same, made by the mine engineer.

Here we get three new elements appearing in the Kanawha series, viz., the Cedar Grove coal, locally known as the "Arno" or "Trimble" seam, a silicious limestone, exhibiting cone-in-cone structure, and the most important coal of the Kanawha series, the Campbells creek bed.

This coal as mined along Campbells creek often presents the following structure:

	Ft.	In.	Ft.	In.
Coal	4	0		
Shale	1	0	6	6
Coal	1	6		

In which there are only two benches, the upper one solid coal with no partings, and separated from the lower bench by a parting of gray shale which varies in thickness from six inches to three feet, even in the same mine, and as we pass up the Great Kanawha, thickens to twenty and even thirty feet, thus separating the Campbells creek coal into two distinct beds of coal, both of which have been mined, as we shall see later.

Georges creek puts into the north bank of the Kanawha at Malden, one mile above the mouth of Campbells creek, and in descending a steep hill, one-half mile above the mouth of the former the following section was obtained:

		Ft. In.	Ft. In.
Sandstone, massive, coarse			50 0
Concealed			20 0
Kanawha black flint			5 0
Concealed			25 0
Sandstone, massive, micaceous			50 0
Concealed			25 0
Sandstone, massive			85 0
Concealed			60 6
Sandstone, massive			110 0
Concealed			80 0
Coal, Campbells creek	coal	2 6	
	shale	0 8	
	coal	0 6	5 3
	shale	0 4	
	coal, visible	1 3	
Concealed			3 0
Shales, blue, sandy			15 0
Sandstone, massive, visible			25 0
Concealed to Kanawha river			45 0

On the south side of the Kanawha at Malden, and a short distance above the C. & O. R. R. station, the following section was obtained in descending from the summit of the hill:

	Ft. In.	Ft. In.
Sandstone, massive		90 0
Concealed		20 0
Kanawha black flint		5 0
Concealed, with *coal* blossom (Stockton)		15 0
Sandstone, massive		50 0
Concealed		30 0
Sandstone, massive, micaceous		65 0
Shale, sandy, gray		3 0
Concealed		20 0
Sandstone, massive, micaceous		50 0
Shales, sandy		2 0

			ft.	in.
Coal, "Point" seam	coal	0	8	
	"niggerhead"	0	11	} 3 8
	coal	2	1	
Fireclay, sandy			2	0
Concealed			55	0
Sandstone, massive			130	0
Coal, Cedar Grove, "Arno," etc.			0	8
Concealed and shales			15	0
Sandstone			2	0
Shales, sandy			10	6
Limestone, Campbells creek			1	0
Shales and sandstone			35	0
Coal, Campbells creek	coal	2	0	
	fireclay shale	1	2	
	coal	0	4	
	fireclay shale	1	10	} 8 8
	slaty coal	0	8	
	coal	0	10	
	slate	0	2	
	coal	1	8	
Fireclay and sandy shale			7	0
Coal	coal, slaty	0	6	
	fireclay	1	2	} 1 11
	coal	0	3	
Shale			2	0
Sandstone, massive, visible			25	0
Concealed to Kanawha river			50	0

Here we get an immense development of massive sandstone which increases the interval between the Campbells creek coal and the BLACK FLINT to 489 feet, and throws the "Point" seam seventy feet farther below the BLACK FLINT than it was at Chapel and Wilson runs, two and one half miles north.

In this general thickening of the measures the parting slates of the Campbells creek coal bed also appear to participate, and the little coal seven feet under the main bed is most probably only a "split" from the former.

The "Point" seam was once extensively mined here for use in the old salt furnaces. The coal is rather hard and some of it bony. It is possible that this bed may sometimes have been mistaken for the Winifrede seam which belongs above it.

The rocks continue rising southeastward up the Kanawha river until we come to the vicinity of Brownstown and Burning Springs run, nine miles above Charleston, where the BLACK FLINT attains an elevation of 700 feet above water level, and in descending from a high point on Burning Springs run to the Kanawha river, the following succession was measured:

	Ft. In.	Ft. In.
Sandstone, massive...	45 o	
Kanawha black flint...	5 o	
Concealed.........	5 o	
Sandstone, massive...	45 o	
Concealed and sandstone...430 o		
Coal, Campbells creek { coal .... 2 6 / shales and concea'd.20 o / coal .... 2 4 }		24 10
Sandstone, massive.........	35 o	
Shales and concealed...	35 o	
Coal, Brownstown	2 o	
Fireclay and shales...	5 o	
Sandstone, massive..	15 o	
Sandy shales...	10 o	
Coaly slate...	o 5	
Sandy shales	15 o	
Coaly shale..	o 6	
Concealed to level of Kanawha river.......................	50 o	

Here the Campbells creek coal has separated into two well defined beds exactly twenty feet apart, and both have been opened and mined at several localities along Burning Springs run. The upper portion of the bed, which farther up the river becomes the "Peerless" coal, is 480 feet below the BLACK FLINT, while the lower member is 502½ feet below the same datum, thus showing a thickening of nearly 100 feet between these two horizons in the four miles from Campbells creek.

At the mouth of Rush creek, below Brownstown, on the south side of the Kanawha, the following section is exposed:

	Ft. In.	Ft. In.
Coal, probably Campbells creek.................................		
Concealed	80 o	
Sandstone, massive, visible	20 o	
Shales, sandy...	25 o	
Coal, slaty......	o 6	
Sandstone and sandy shales...................................	15 o	
Limestone, silicious, Cannelton (Stockton)	1 o	
Sandy shales and sandstone...................................	40 o	
Concealed	5 o	
Coal, (Eagle), reported in bed of Rush creek	3 o	

Two other members of the Kanawha series make their appearance here near the bottom of the section, viz., a limestone which appears to be identical with the one at Cannelton, which Mr. Stockton once burned for cement, and hence is often termed the STOCKTON CEMENT BED. Then below this, in the bed of Rush creek, a coal, with a thickness of three feet, is reported to have been found when the C. & O. R. R. piers for the bridge across that stream were built. This would come at the horizon of the EAGLE SEAM found at Cannelton and southward.

On the north side of the Kanawha just opposite the Brownstown ferry, the following section was measured from the top of the steep adjoining hill:

	Ft. In.	Ft. In.
Concealed from summit		30 0
Kanawha black flint		5 0
Coal and shale, *Stockton*		5 0
Concealed		10 0
Sandstone, massive		95 0
Shales and concealed		30 0
Sandstone, massive		40 0
Sandy shales and concealed		25 0
Sandstone, massive, micaceous		160 0
Shales, sandstone, and concealed, with *Campbells creek coal* near base		130 0
Sandstone, massive		40 0
Concealed		35 0
Coal, Brownstown		
Concealed to river level		150 0

This is the crest of the anticlinal wave which crosses the Great Kanawha at Brownstown, and carries the BLACK FLINT to an elevation of 720 feet above water level. From this point southeastward up the river, the rocks decline and the FLINT comes down to within 600 feet or less above the Kanawha river a few miles above.

On Simmons creek, which puts into the north bank of the Great Kanawha just above Brownstown, the Cedar Grove coal has been mined, and there the following succession was observed:

	Ft. In.	Ft. In.
Sandstone, massive		
Coal, Cedar Grove		3 4
Concealed		75 0
Fireclay		2 0
Concealed		23 0
Coal, Campbells creek		
Sandy shales and concealed		40 0
Sandstone, massive		40 0
Sandy shales and concealed		25 0
Coal, blossom		
Shales		5 0
Sandstone, massive		30 0
Sandy shales and flaggy sandstone		35 0
Limestone, silicious		1 0
Shales, sandy		15 0

Slate, black ....   o   6
Shales.. 7   o
Sandstone, flaggy, to creek level.............................. 20   o

At the mouth of Simmons creek both the Cedar Grove bed and one of the benches of the Campbells creek bed have been mined and exhibit the following relations to each other:

	Ft. In.	Ft. In.
Sandstone, massive..		25 o
Coal, Cedar Grove		3 4
Concealed		10 o
Sandstone, massive..		15 o
Concealed		75 o
Coal, Campbells creek		..
Concealed		20 o
Sandstone, massive		30 o
Concealed		25 o
Coal, Brownstown		
Shales and concealed..................................		5 o
Sandstone, massive		35 o
Concealed		45 o
Sandstone, massive..		25 o
Concealed to level of Kanawha river.....................		45 o

About one mile and a-quarter above the mouth of Simmons creek the following section was measured near the mouth of a small stream:

	Ft. In.	Ft. In.
Sandstone, massive..		100 o
Concealed		20 o
Kanawha black flint		5 o
Concealed		20 o
Sandstone, very massive..		75 o
Shales and concealed..............		65 o
Gray shales..		5 o
Coal, Winifrede, visible		2 o
Concealed and massive sandstone........		100 o
Coal, blossom..		
Concealed and sandstone		190 o
Sandstone, massive		50 o

Coal, Campbells creek
   coal .... o   5
   shale............ .... o   6 }   3   1
   coal 2   2
   shale.. 10   o
   coal ....

	Ft. In.	Ft. In.
Concealed		7 o
Sandstone, massive		35 o
Concealed and sandy shales............................... ...		35 o
Coal, Brownstown		
Shales..		5 o
Sandstone, massive..		25 o
Concealed to level of Kanawha river.....................		65 o

In this section the Campbells creek coal is found at 507 feet below the BLACK FLINT, and the latter at 692 feet above the Kanawha river, instead of 720 as at Brownstown, thus showing that the dip has changed to the southeast. Both benches of the Campbells creek coal have been opened here, but the lower opening had fallen shut and the thickness of that member could not be measured.

Witchers creek puts into the north bank of the Great Kanawha two miles and a-half above Simmons creek, and along this stream between its mouth and Laurel branch two miles above, Mr. C. C. Lewis of Charleston, once constructed a very accurately leveled section of the strata which reads as follows, beginning at the highest summit.

	Ft. In.	Ft. In.
Sandstone, hard, white, pebbly		35 0
Coal, Mason, blossom		
Concealed		175 0
Kanawha black flint		5 0
Concealed		18 0
Coal, Stockton		2 6
Concealed and sandstone		23 0
Coal, hard, Lewiston		4 0
Sandstone and concealed		54 0
Coal, Coalburg { coal	2 0	
slate	1 0	4 0
coal	1 0	
Concealed		50 0
Coal Winifrede { coal	2 4	
slate, gray	0 1	
coal	2 0	6 6
slate, black	0 1	
coal	2 0	
Sandstone, massive and concealed		78 1
Cannel coal and bituminous slate		2 6
Concealed and shaly sandstone		21 6
Coal, streak		
Concealed		18 1
Coal		1 2
Concealed (steep bluff)		86 8
Coal, Cedar Grove		3 7
Concealed to level of Laurel run		77 0
Interval to Kanawha river		120 0

This measurement puts the Cedar Grove coal 370 feet below the BLACK FLINT.

The coal called Lewiston is probably only a "split" from the Stockton seam above. The original "Lewiston" bed was the one now called Winifrede, but by a singular popular error the name has been transferred to the horizon in question.

Macfarlane's old coal works are about one-half mile above the mouth of Witchers creek, and in descending the steep hill at that locality the following section was measured:

			Ft.	In.	Ft.	In.
Concealed to top of knob					200	0
Kanawha black flint						
Concealed					15	0
Sandstone, visible					30	0
Concealed					180	0
Coal Winifrede	coal, soft	0	8			
	splint coal	1	8			
	coal, soft	1	4		4	2
	shale	0	2			
	"gray" splint	0	4			
Concealed					175	0
Sandstone, massive					20	0
Coal, Cedar Grove					2	0
Concealed					100	0
Coal, Campbells creek						
Concealed to river level					85	0

About one mile southeast from this last locality, and at the mouth of Fields creek or Winifrede junction, the Winifrede coal was once extensively mined, and in descending from the summit there the following section was constructed:

			Ft.	In.	Ft.	In.
Sandstone, massive					25	0
Concealed					20	0
Kanawha black flint					5	0
Concealed					170	0
Coal, Winifrede					3	6
Concealed, (mostly sandstone)					45	0
Coal, "Point" seam	coal	0	8			
	cannel slate	1	0			
	shale, gray	2	6		6	4
	coal	0	10			
	shale, gray	0	2			
	coal	1	2			
Concealed					45	0
Sandstone, massive					5	0
Concealed and shaly sandstone					50	0
Coal, blossom						
Shaly sandstone and concealed					90	0
Limestone, silicious					1	0
Sandstone, massive					20	0
Concealed					20	0
Coal, blossom						
Shales, sandy and concealed					35	0
Limestone, silicious					1	0
Sandstone, massive					25	0
Coal, Peerless, upper bench of Campbells creek					2	4
Fireclay					1	3
Concealed and sandstone					25	0

Coal, Blacksburg. Cleaver bench of Campbells creek
bed 4   0
Concealed to Kanawha river 50   0

The interval here between the BLACK FLINT and the upper or "Peerless" member of the Campbells creek coal foots up 517 feet, and the elevation of the FLINT above the Kanawha river is about 600 feet, or 120 feet less than at Brownstown, on the crest of the anticlinal.

Two well defined members of the Campbells creek coal have been opened and mined here, though the upper one, called the Peerless seam, is the better of the two, being very free from slate and a rich gas coal.

About half-way between Brawleys run and Coalmont a small stream descending the steep hillside has uncovered a fine section in the lower portion of the Kanawha series as follows:

	Ft. In.	Ft. In.
Sandstone		10 0
Limestone, silicious		1 0
Shales and shaly sandstone		20 0
Coal		0 6
Shales		20 0
Coal, Cedar Grove?		1 2
Concealed		40 0
Sandstone and sandy shale		7 0
Coaly slate and fireclay		1 0
Shales, gray, fossil plants		8 0
Coal, Peerless		2 6
Fireclay, sandy		2 0
Sandstone, shaly		8 0
Coal and coaly shale		1 4
Sandy shales		10 0
Coal, Blacksburg { coal	1 6	
shale	0 8	
coal	0 2	4 4
shale	1 2	
coal	0 10	
Sandstone, massive, to C. & O. R. R. level		10 0

All of the coal from the Peerless bed down, belongs at the horizon of the Campbells creek coal bed.

Near Brawley's run the following section was measured:

	Ft. In.	Ft. In.
Kanawha black flint		5 0
Concealed		5 0
Coal, blossom, Stockton		
Sandstone and concealed		85 0

```
Coal, blossom, Coalburg..................  .................
Concealed and  sandstone.........................................  65   o
Coal ......................................................... ....  o   8
Shales..............  ..............................................  6   4
              ⎧ coal .................... o   1  ⎫
              ⎪ draw slate ...............  o   8  ⎪
Winifrede coal ⎨ "niggerhead" ................ o   1¼ ⎬  3   9
              ⎪ coal ...................... 2   9  ⎪
              ⎩ slaty coal................. o   1¼ ⎭
Concealed .........................................:............. 365   o
Coal, Peerless (Campbells Creek) .................... ....  2   6
Concealed to C. & O. R. R .................................... 30   o
Concealed to Kanawha river  ....... ......... .. ........... 47   o
```

The interval from the BLACK FLINT to the upper member ("Peerless") of the Campbells creek coal is 530 feet, and the BLACK FLINT is 610 feet above the Kanawha river in this section.

On the north bank of the Kanawha river, at Lock No. 4, a fine exposure of the strata has been made by the Government quarry, and in descending the hill at this point the following interesting section is exposed:

```
                                            Ft. In.  Ft. In.
Sandstone, massive....................................  30   o
Concealed ......................... ..................  20   o
Sandstone ................ ...........................  5   o
Shales, gray..........................................  5   o
              ⎧ coal, impure .. ............. o   6 ⎫
Cedar Grove coal ⎨ shale........................... o   4 ⎬  3   o
              ⎩ coal .......... ........ ... ... 2   2 ⎭
Shales and concealed..................................  40   o
Limestone, Campbells creek...........  ...............  1   o
Shales, sandy.........................................  20   o
              ⎧ coal ...... ............... 1   3 ⎫
              ⎪ sandy shales........... 7   0 ⎬  9   9 ⎫
              ⎪ coal ................... 1   6 ⎭      ⎪
Coal,         ⎪ fireclay, sandy........ 2   0 ⎫      ⎪
Campbells     ⎨ sandstone.............14   0 ⎬ 22  6 ⎬ 44  1
creek.        ⎪ sandy shales........... 6   6 ⎭      ⎪
              ⎪ coal ...................... o  10 ⎫   ⎪
              ⎪ shales, sandy..........10   8 ⎬ 11 10⎪
              ⎩ coal ...... ............ o   4 ⎭      ⎭
Concealed to Kanawha river............................- 75  o
```

By the thickening up of parting slates the Campbells creek coal occupies 44 feet of rock interval at this locality, while possibly some other layers below are not included. The top portion of the bed represents the "PEERLESS COAL," extensively mined on the opposite side of the Kanawha river as a gas coal. The CAMPBELLS CREEK LIMESTONE exhibits the cone-in-cone structure and is impure and sandy.

One mile above this last locality, Mr. C. C. Lewis of Charleston, many years ago leveled a section from the summits of the lofty hills opposite Coalburg, to the Kanawha river, securing a nearly complete exposure of the different strata. This section was published in "The Virginias," page 137, Sept. 1882, and is as follows:

	Ft. In.	Ft. In.
Sand rock, top of river bluff	33 6	
Slate	12 0	
Conglomerate rock	11 0	
Coal, "Big" bed, (Mason) — coal 0 8; slate 2 0; coal 2 0; "niggerhead" 0 4; coal 4 6; soapstone 3 0; coal 4 6		17 0
Limestone nodules	1 6	
Hard sand rock	39 0	
Rotten sandstone	17 6	99 6
Coarse, white sand rock	37 6	
Red sandstone	3 0	
Fireclay	1 0	
Coal (Mahoning, No. 5 Block, etc.)		2 0
Coarse sandstone		64 8
Iron nodules		1 6
(Kanawha) black flint ledge		7 0
Hard sandstone	13 6	
Coal 2 6; White sandstone 4 5; Coal, "Lewiston" 4 6 (Stockton)	11 5	
Slate	2 6	
Sandstone	32 4	150 3
Coal, Coalburg	4 0	
Slate	8 0	
Coal, outcrop showing	2 0	
Sandstone	76 6	
Coal, slate and iron ore mixed (Winifrede)		5 0
Slate	2 0	
Sandstone	44 5	
Slate, with iron ore nodules	23 9	
Coal, outcrop	2 0	
Sandstone	59 9	
Slate	3 6	220 1
Iron ore	1 0	
Coal, outcrop	1 0	
Sandstone	71 4	
Dark slate	11 4	
Coal, Cedar Grove		2 8
Fireclay	5 0	
Friable sandstone	42 9	74 3
Coal	1 0	
Sandstone	25 6	
Coal, Campbells creek, upper (Peerless)		3 0
Sandstone		15 6

Coal, Campbells creek, lower ('middle) bed 3 0
Sandstone 15 0
Coal, Blacksburg, (Campbells creek, lower)............. 4 6
Concealed to low water of Kanawha river.............. 26 6
_____
       Total............... ....830 0

From *black flint* to top of *Campbells creek coal* 452 3
   "   "   bottom   "   "   " 493 3
Kanawha black flint above Kanawha river..............519 6

The names in parentheses were added by the writer, otherwise the identifications are those made by Mr. Lewis.

This section shows beyond any question that the Campbells creek coal is represented by the "Peerless" and "Blacksburg" seams of this region, with frequently an intermediate bed. Also that the "Lewiston" bed is simply a "split" from the Stockton seam.

The interval given by Mr. Lewis between the BLACK FLINT and the COALBURG SEAM is less than the writer found in this region, and it probably resulted from his not finding the Coalburg bed opened immediately below the crop of the FLINT, since near this same locality, the writer's measurement foots up ninety feet between the Coalburg bed and the base of the BLACK FLINT. With this correction, which would add about thirty-five feet to the interval in question, and put the top of the Campbells creek coal (Peerless member) 487 feet below the FLINT, the section will agree fairly well with that published on page 300, and made in this same region, or rather one mile above. This addition would make the interval between the black flint and the base of the Blacksburg bed 515½ feet, or only twenty-two and a-half feet more than that given (493).

Between Coalburg and East Bank, on the south side of the Kanawha river, the following section was measured:

	Ft. In.	Ft. In.
Sandstone, massive..	25 0	
Coal -- { coal	0 3	
shale	0 8	
coal...	0 6	I 11
black slate..	0 6	
Kanawha black flint.............	5 0	
Concealed with coal blossom (*Stockton*)	40 0	
Coal, Lewiston -- { "niggerhead"	0 3	
coal, splint	2 7	2 10
Concealed, sandstone and shales	45 0	
Coal, Coalburg { coal, splint	0 8	
"niggerhead"...................	0 8	
coal, splint	2 4	6 2
slate, gray........................	I 4	
coal, soft	I 2	

Concealed 50   0
Coal, splint, Winifrede...   1   8
Concealed..200   0 ⎫
Sandstone, massive 24   0   ⎥
Shales and concealed.................. 23   0   ⎥
Limestone, silicious.......................................   1   6   ⎬260   0
Sandstone, massive ....·····   8   6   ⎥
Shales, gray, full of fossil plants ···········   3   0   ⎭
Coal, Cedar Grove   2   11
Fireclay   2   0   ⎫
Concealed and shales.................... 35   0   ⎥
Coal   0   6   ⎥
Shales, sandstone, and concealed 35   0   ⎥
Coal, streak..   ⎬ 93   6
Shales ....,... 10   0   ⎥
Limestone, Campbells creek.................... ..   1   0   ⎥
Shales and concealed.................... 10   0   ⎭

	coal, Peerless..................			1	8	⎫
	shales........................			10	0	⎥
Coal,	*coal* ...	{	coal .0	3 }		⎥
Campbells creek		{	shale..4	0 }	4 7	30 1
		{	coal .0	4 }		⎥
	shales, bluish.............			10	0	⎥
	coal	{	coal .1	10 }		⎥
	Blacks-	{	slate.0	4 }	3 10	⎥
	burg	{	coal .1	8 }		⎭

Concealed and sandstone 30   0
Sandy shales and shaly sandstone to Kanawha river.. 20   0

This section gives a complete exposure of the three members
of the Campells creek coal and also shows an interval of 502 feet
between the BLACK FLINT ledge and the top (Peerless) member of
that multiple bed.

About half way between Crown Hill and Paint creek stations,
the following section was measured in descending the steep point
above the old Doddridge coal openings:

			Ft. In.	Ft. In.
oal, blossom..........................				
Kanawha black flint..................................			5 0	
Concealed and massive sandstone........			25 0	
Coal, Lewiston..	{	coal, splint 0 8	⎫	
	{	"niggerhead" 0 2	⎬ 4 3	
	{	coal, splint 3 5	⎭	
Concealed and sandstone....................................			100 0	
Coal, Coalburg	{	coal, splint 1 0	⎫	
	{	"niggerhead"................. 0 4	⎥	
	{	coal, splint 3 0	⎬ 6 2	
	{	shale................. 0 10	⎥	
	{	coal, soft 1 0	⎭	
Concealed and sandstone			50 0	

		Ft. In.	Ft. In.
	coal, slaty .... o 4		
	shale.......................... 2 o		
	coal, slaty .... o 6		
Coal, Winifrede	shale........................... o 6	8 7	
	coal, slaty .... o 3		
	fireclay, impure............ 1 8		
	coal, splint 3 4		
Concealed to Kanawha river level............................465 o			

The elevation of the BLACK FLINT is here 659 feet above the level of the Kanawha river. The center of a syncline crosses the river near Cedar Grove and East Bank, since the rocks rise to the southeast quite rapidly above those points, the FLINT being seventy-seven feet higher from water level in the last section than in the one near East Bank.

On the north side of the Kanawha, and just below Cedar Grove, the following section was measured:

		Ft. In.	Ft. In.
Sandstone, massive, gray...			30 o
Sandy shales			25 o
Coal			1 o
Fireclay and sandy shales.................................			5 o
Sandstone			10 o
Shales.......................			5 o
Coal			o 4
Shales			5 o
Coal, Cedar Grove..	coal, soft.................. o 6		
	coal, splint.............. 2 5	3 1	
	coal, softer .... o 2		
Concealed			100 o
Coal, Blacksburg................			4 o
Concealed to Kanawha river................			25 o

This is the type locality of the CEDAR GROVE COAL which, although thin, has been extensively mined in this region on both sides of the river.

The BLACKSBURG division of the Campbells creek bed was once mined here by a tunnel under the public road, and hence has been frequently called the "Tunnel" seam.

Three miles above Cedar Grove the following section was measured near Lock No. 3 at the Government quarry:

	Ft. In.	Ft. In.
Sandstone, flaggy..		10 o
Shales, sandy..		4 o
Coal		o 4
Shales...........		4 o
Coal, Cedar Grove		2 10

	Ft.	In.
Concealed	75	0
Coal, blossom, *Peerless*		
Sandy shales	12	0
Coal	2	0
Fireclay and shales	17	0
Coal, Blacksburg	2	4
Fireclay and shales	10	0
Sandstone, massive, gray	20	0
Concealed to Kanawha river	80	0

About one-half mile above Lock No. 3, a very high point rises abruptly from the river, and in descending the same the following section was measured:

		Ft.	In.	Ft.	In.
Concealed from top of knob				75	0
Sandstone, massive, pebbly				25	0
Concealed and sandstone				75	0
Sandstone hard, gray				55	0
Coal, Mason, visible				2	0
Concealed				20	0
Sandstone, gray, massive				130	0
Shale, sandy and concealed				15	0
Coal, blossom					
Shales, sandy				5	0
Sandstone, massive				25	0
Shale, sandy				10	0
Coal				1	0
Kanawha black flint				7	0
Sandy shales				35	0
Coal, Lewiston	coal, bony	0	4		
	coal, splint	2	5½		
	slate	0	0½		
	coal	0	4	5	2
	"niggerhead"	0	2		
	coal, splint	1	10		
Shales				10	0
Sandstone				2	0
Fireclay				1	0
Coaly slate				1	0
Shale				5	0
Coal, Coalburg	splint	4	9		
	slate	0	1	5	4
	splint	0	6		
Concealed				15	0
Sandstone, massive				45	0
Concealed				15	0
Coal, blossom, *Winifrede*					
Concealed and massive sandstone		30	0		
Concealed		20	0		
Sandstone, massive		20	0		
Coal, blossom					
Concealed		20	0		
Sandstone, massive		10	0		
Shales and concealed		5	0	250	0
Coal, blossom					
Shales		15	0		
Sandstone, massive		10	0		

Shale 20	0	
Sandstone........................ 25	0	
Concealed 70	0	
Shale, fossil plants................................. 5	0	
Coal, Cedar Grove	3	0
Concealed	30	0
Limestone, Campbells creek, impure.......................	1	0
Concealed	25	0
Coal, Peerless...	2	6
Concealed	35	0

	coal 2 10	
Coal, Blacksburg { shale............... 0 8 }	4	6
coal 1 0		

Concealed to river level..............................,............145   0

    This section exhibits one of those sudden changes in the intervals, separating important strata, for which the Kanawha region is noted. The upper member of the Stockton coal is gone entirely, while the interval separating the Lewiston division of the Stockton coal from the Coalburg bed,. is reduced to only nineteen feet, thus putting the latter bed only fifty-nine feet below the BLACK FLINT, instead of 90 to 100 feet, its customary distance, unless indeed the coals could both be members of the Stockton bed, which hardly appears possible in view of the short interval between the BLACK FLINT and BLACKSBURG COAL, viz., 486 feet, instead of 515½ as given by the section on page 300, thus indicating a thinning of the intervals in the Kanawha measures, possibly as a correlative of the thickened intervals shown by the great sandstone deposits above the BLACK FLINT, since the immense sandstone below the MASON COAL stands out in a giant wall, 130 feet high without a break. The coal blossom, fifteen feet below that great sandstone, probably represents the "No. 5 Block" seam of the region, although it is only forty-one feet above the FLINT, instead of sixty to seventy feet, the usual interval.

    Another low anticlinal wave crosses the Kanawha river at the mouth of Paint creek, and the rocks dip to the southeast slowly for about three miles as we pass up the river.

    Just above Dego we see a concretionary limestone deposit at about sixty feet under the BLACKSBURG COAL, and ten feet above the C. & O. R. R. grade. This would represent the CANNELTON limestone, or cement bed.

    About two and a-half miles above Dego, we get the following section of the measures in descending from the summit of the hill on the south bank of the river:

		Ft. In.	Ft. In.
Kanawha black flint			5 0
Concealed and shales			60 0
Coal, Coalburg	coal, splint	1 9	
	"niggerhead"	0 2	
	coal, splint	0 10	3 10
	dark slate	0 3	
	coal, soft	0 10	
Concealed			70 0
Sandstone			5 0
Coal, Winifrede	coal, splint	3 0	
	slate, hard, sandy	0 4	4 2
	coal	0 10	
Concealed			375 0
Coal, Blacksburg	coal, gas	2 4	
	slate and impure coal	0 4	
	coal	1 4	8 4
	fireclay	3 6	
	coal	0 10	
Concealed to river level			75 0
Flint first above Kanawha river			601 4
" " Blacksburg coal			518 0

About three-fourths of a mile above this last locality, we come to the property of the Kanawha Mining Co., and there get the section already given on page 373. This is a very important section, since it reveals the Stockton seam separated from the BLACK FLINT by an interval of twenty-five feet, and also shows that the "Lewiston" bed is simply a "SPLIT" from the main Stockton coal, here fully developed. Then, too, in their proper order below, come the Coalburg, Winifrede and the multiple bedded Campbells creek coal, the basal member of which, the Blacksburg division, is here beginning to assume much importance.

About one-fourth of a mile above the last locality, the following section was measured at the Union Coal Co.'s works;

		Ft. In.	Ft. In.
Sandstone, massive			25 0
Concealed			35 0
Kanawha black flint			5 0
Concealed			175 0
Coal, Winifrede	coal, soft	0 6	
	splint	0 3	
	coal, soft	0 10	
	splint	0 3	
	coal, soft	0 8	
	splint	0 4	
	coal, soft	0 10	5 5
	slate, gray	0 4	
	coal, soft	0 3	
	black rock	0 4	
	splint	0 2	
	coal, soft	0 8	

Fireclay 2 0
Concealed 20 0

		Ft. In.	Ft. In.
Coal ..	coal	0 6	
	shale...	0 2	
	coal	1 2	2 10
	shale....................	0 2	
	coal	0 10	

Concealed..330 0

		Ft. In.	Ft. In.
Coal, Blacksburg	coal	0 10	
	coal, hard, splinty.........	0 6	
	coal	0 8	
	shale.............................	0 4	
	coal	0 1	6 7
	shale.........	0 2	
	coal	2 8	
	shale.............................	0 6	
	coal	0 10	

Concealed to level of Kanawha river 125 0

The Winifrede bed exhibits layers of soft bituminous coal alternating with the hard splint coal, the whole making an admirable steam fuel.

The Blacksburg bed is shipped as a gas coal, except the splinty layer near the top, which is separated for fuel. The whole bed is termed the "No. 2 Gas" seam in this region. The Peerless member of the Campbells creek coal occurs fifteen to twenty feet above the BLACKSBURG member, but was not visible in the immediate line of the section.

On the north side of the Kanawha river, just opposite the mouth of Paint creek, the following section was measured in descending the steep hillside:

	Ft. In.	Ft. In.
Kanawha black flint		5 0
Concealed..		.400 0
Sandy shales...		20 0
Coal, Cedar Grove.................		3 0
Concealed..		30 0
Limestone, Campbells creek (cone-in-cone)............		2 0
Shales and sandstone...		18 0
Coal, Peerless...		2 0
Sandy shales.......		25 0
Coal, blossom...		--
Shales...		10 0
Coal, Blacksburg .... ,.........		3 0
Shales, sandstone, and concealed to Kanawha river...135 0		

The CAMPBELLS CREEK LIMESTONE in the section, exhibiting the "cone-in-cone" structure, which characterized it all along the valley, is an important witness to the correctness of the stratigraphic correlations shown in these sections.

At the quarry where the stone for Lock No. 2 was obtained, one mile below Cannelton, on the north side of the Kanawha river, the following section was measured:

	Ft. In.	Ft. In.
Coal, blossom, *Peerless*..		
Shales..	40 0	
Coal	0 4	
Shales..	15 0	
Coal, Blacksburg { coal .... 4 6 slate .... 0 4 coal .... 0 8 }		5 6
Fireclay and sandy beds..	5 0	
Sandstone, massive	35 0	
Coal..	1 8	
Concealed and shales...	35 0	
Limestone, Cannelton (Stockton cement)...................	2 4	
Shales and concealed to Kanawha river	55 0	

About one-fourth of a mile above the locality of this last section, and at the mouth of Staten run, the following section was measured:

	Ft. In.	Ft. In.
Coal, blossom, *Cedar Grove*.......................................		
Concealed	5 0	
Sandstone, massive	40 0	
Shales, sandy...	25 0	
Coal	0 10	
Shales..	5 0	
Coal and shale..	0 10	
Sandy shales, with nuggets of cone-in-cone limestone near center	10 0	
Coal, slaty..	0 8	
Shales, sandy.	15 0	
Coal, Peerless..	1 9	
Shales..	10 0	
Coal	0 4	
Shales, sandy...	15 0	
Coal, Blacksburg..	5 0	
Concealed and sandstone..	35 0	
Coal .. { coal .... 1 6 fireclay and shale .... 2 0 coal .... 0 6 }		4 0
Shales and sandstone...	35 0	
Limestone, Cannelton	2 3	
Shales and sandstone...	35 0	
Coal, top only visible in bed of run	1 0	
Concealed to Kanawha river.....................................	20 0	

Here a bed of coal appears in the bottom of Staten run, which comes at the horizon of the "Eagle" seam, mined farther up the river.

The limestone above it is the one formerly burned into cement by Mr. Stockton, and hence often called the Stockton Cement bed, but which was named by the writer the Cannelton limestone, from the town of Cannelton just above where this section was made.

A short distance above Staten run we come to the town of Cannelton, and the plant of the Cannelton Coal Co., which mines, or at least formerly mined, the Stockton cannel coal in the summit of the mountain, as well as the "No. 5 Block" coal on above it, and where the writer once measured the section given on page 372. This is the locality where the coal at the summit of the Kanawha series received the name "Stockton," and which was later termed the Lower Cannelton coal by the writer in his "Virginias" paper, heretofore mentioned. The name Stockton, however, has been retained by the U. S. G. Survey, and is still used by many of the operators, so that the name, Cannelton, has been discarded in this report, and the old one (Stockton) used instead.

The BLACKSBURG division of the Campbells creek coal has been extensively mined at Montgomery and on Morris creek, which puts into the south bank of the Kanawha just below that town. On this stream the interval of twenty feet or more, which often separates the Peerless division of the Campbells creek bed from the lower or Blacksburg member, is seen to thin away almost completely about one mile from the Kanawha river, as shown in the following sections, the first of which, at the Excelsior Company's mine, shows the usual section thus:

		Ft. In.	Ft. In.
Coal, Peerless		2 6	
Shales		20 0	
Coal, Blacksburg	coal 0 5		
	shale 0 1		
	coal 0 10		
	splint 0 2		
	coal 0 8		
	"black band" 0 0¼		9 9¼
	coal 0 3		
	shale 0 2		
	coal 3 2		
	shale 2 6		
	coal 1 6		
Concealed		75 0	
Limestone, Cannelton		2 0	
Concealed to creek level		5 0	

At the Eureka mine, three-eighths of a mile farther up Morris creek, the following section is exposed:

			Ft. In.	Ft. In.
Sandy shales				30 0
Coal, Peerless				2 8
Shale and black slate				1 6
Coal, Blacksburg	coal	2 0		
	shale	0 3		
	coal	0 3		5 10
	shale	0 4		
	coal	3 0		
Fireclay shales				2 0
Concealed				10 0
Coal	coal	0 8		
	shale	0 6		2 0
	coal	0 10		
Shales and sandy beds				10 0
Coal				1 8
Fireclay and shales				15 0

Here the twenty feet of shales separating the Peerless bed from the Blacksburg coal of the previous section, has thinned down to only one foot and a-half, while just across the creek, at an abandoned mine, the interval thins to only six inches, and the Peerless bed was once mined along with the main Blacksburg division below, but farther back in the mine, the intervening shale thickened up rapidly, and the Peerless division could no longer be mined with the Blacksburg bed. We know that this upper coal is the PEERLESS, because this division of the Campbells creek coal has a peculiar physical structure unlike any other members of this multiple seam, and hence there can be no doubt that the coal bed which is twenty feet above the Blacksburg seam, at the Excelsior opening, is only one foot and a-half above the latter at the Eureka mine.

As a correlative for this thinning ABOVE the Blacksburg bed, it is quite probable that the two and a-half feet of shales separating the bottom member from the main seam at the Excelsior mine, has thickened to twelve feet at the Eureka. These facts are given as an illustration of what is a common feature of the Kanawha series, viz., sudden changes in the intervals which sepapate not only the different coal beds of the series, but also the several members of the same coal bed.

In the region of Montgomery (formerly called Coal Valley) this Blacksburg coal is often termed the Coal Valley seam, as well as "No. 2 Gas" coal, since the Eagle bed below is frequently called "No. 1 Gas," because it is the lowest workable coal of the Kanawha series, and in order to distinguish it from the "splint," or "block" coals found at the horizon of the Winifrede, Coalburg, Stockton, etc.

A short distance above Montgomery the Blacksburg coal has long been mined by the Coal Valley Coal Company, and the following section was measured in descending from the summits of the hills at that point:

		Ft. In.	Ft. In.
Coal (No. 5 Block) blossom			
Sandstone, massive.................................		50	0
Concealed		15	0
Kanawha black flint		5	0
Concealed		18	0
Coal, Stockton.	cannel, visible.................. 0 10		
	shales 6 0		
	coal and slate................. 2 0	16	10
	shale with streaks of coal...... 4 0		
	coal, slaty. *Lewiston*............ 4 0		
Sandstone, massive and concealed.................		90	0
Coal, blossom, *Coalburg*.............................			
Concealed		10	0
Sandstone, massive and concealed.................		90	0
Coal, Winifrede......	coal 0 2		
	shale 2 10		
	coal 0 2	5	4
	shale 0 2		
	coal 2 0		
Concealed and sandstone		40	0
Coal, blossom.............................			
Concealed and sandstone		55	0
Coal, slaty, blossom.............................			
Concealed.............................		120	0
Coal, Cedar Grove	coal 1 4		
	slate 0 2	2	6
	coal 1 0		
Concealed.............................		145	0
Coal, Blacksburg	coal, bony..................... 0 4		
	slate 0 0½		
	coal, soft..................... 0 6		
	coal, splint..................... 1 0		
	slate 0 0½		
	coal, soft..................... 0 6	7	0½
	shale..................... 0 2		
	coal, soft..................... 3 0		
	shale..................... 0 8		
	coal 0 10		
Concealed		115	0
Coal, Eagle	coal..................... 1 2		
	shale 0 4	3	6
	coal..................... 2 0		
Concealed to Kanawha river.................		50	0

Interval of *black flint* above Kanawha river..............768 feet.
"   "   "   Blacksburg coal............592 "

Here the development of massive sandstones has thickened up the interval between the BLACK FLINT and the BLACKSBURG coal by nearly 100 feet over what it is within a few miles north, as may be observed from the sections given.

The Eagle coal was opened by Mr. Thoma, the superintendent of the Coal Valley Company, who reported its thickness and structure. It comes near the C. & O. R. R. track level, and 115 feet of debris was passed through before the crop of the coal was found.

As we go south from Montgomery, the strata continue to rise rapidly, and we soon get exposures below the Eagle coal, the following section being visible a short distance below Edgewater (formerly Frederick):

		Ft.	In.	Ft.	In.
Shaly sandstone				5	0
Coal, Peerless				2	0
Shales, dark blue				15	0
Coal, Blacksburg	coal, sulphurous	0	5		
	slate	0	0½		
	coal, gas	0	6		
	splint	0	11	5	4
	parting	0	0¼		
	coal, gas	0	7		
	slate	0	0¼		
	coal, gas	2	10		
Fireclay				5	0
Concealed				100	0
Sandstone				5	0
Shales, sandy				5	0
Coal, Eagle	coal	0	3		
	"niggerhead"	0	2		
	coal	0	9		
	slate	0	1	4	7
	coal	0	3		
	slate	0	3		
	coal	2	10		
Fireclay and sandy beds				6	0
Sandstone				6	0
Sandy shales				8	0
Coal, Little Eagle				1	8
Fireclay, impure				5	0
Sandstone and sandy shale				50	0
Limestone, Eagle (black marble)				1	0
Shales, dark, fossiliferous, to C. & O. R. R. level				10	0

The Eagle coal is soft and a typical coking coal. The BLACKS-BURG BED was formerly mined principally for gas making purposes, the layer of "splint" coal shown in its section being separated for fuel.

The "Little Eagle" bed exposed twenty feet below the main Eagle seam, is a beautiful coal of the coking type, and is the lowest coal bed seen by the writer in the Kanawha series, there being nothing but sandstone and shales, with some black slates on below the section just given, until we come to the top of the Pottsville.

The EAGLE LIMESTONE is known locally as the "BLACK MARBLE," but it is simply an impure limestone darkened with carbon, and exhibiting the "cone-in-cone" structure.

The bituminous shales under it are filled with marine fossils, PRODUCTUS NEBRASCENSIS P. LONGISPINUS, SPIRIFER CAMERATUS, EUOMPHALUS RUGOSUS, and many other forms being present.

Near Eagle station, two miles above Montgomery, Fayette county, the Eagle coal has the following structure at its type locality, where first mined and named by Mr. Weyant:

	Ft.	In.	Ft.	In.
Coal	0	2		
"Niggerhead"	0	2		
Coal	0	10		
Shale	0	1		
Coal	0	2½	4	6½
Shale	0	3		
Coal	2	4		
Cannel	0	2		
Coal	0	4		

The streak of cannel near the bottom of the seam is not always present.

One mile farther south we come to the mouth of Armstrong creek, and in that vicinity find the section already given on pages 371-2, where the Pottsville makes its appearance in the bed of the Kanawha, and the entire Kanawha series, over 1,000 feet thick, is exposed between the BLACK FLINT in the top of the mountain, and low water, below.

In the Mt. Carbon region, one mile above the mouth of Armstrong creek, several openings in the Blacksburg coal reveal the same condition of affairs with reference to the PEERLESS COAL, as on Morris creek, near Montgomery, viz., a great variation in the thickness of the shale separating it from the Blacksburg member. This interval is fourteen feet at the main entry, but within 100 feet thins to eight, and in one-half mile farther to the southwest is only six inches, as shown in the following section:

	Ft. In.	Ft. In.

Shales... 10 0
Coal, Peerless.. 2 11
Shales... o 6

Coal, Blacksburg
- coal .... o 3
- shale........................... o 5
- coal 1 2
- shale........................... o 4
- coal .... 3 o

} 5 2

Shales and sandstone 40 0

Coal, Brownstown
- coal 1 4
- shale .... o 3
- coal .... o 4
- shale .... 1 o
- coal .... o 8

} 3 7

Concealed, sandstone, and shales........................... 80 0

Coal, Eagle
- coal .... o 2
- shales .... o 8
- coal 2 10

} 3 8

Shales and sandy beds 20 0
Coal, Little Eagle 2 0
Concealed to top of Pottsville 300 0
Concealed to level of Kanawha river....................... 50 0

The coal termed BROWNSTOWN here, is possibly the same bed which thickens up and is mined on Armstrong creek under the name of the "Powellton" seam.

At the mouth of Armstrong creek the BLACK FLINT has an elevation of about 1,625 feet above tide, but as the rocks rise rapidly to the southeast, it gets higher and higher above water level, and when we come to the junction of the Gauley with New river, six miles east, its position is nearly 1,500 feet above water level, or 2,200 feet above tide.

Messrs. Clark and Krebs, civil and mining engineers of Kanawha Falls, W. Va., have measured a section exposed along Sand branch, which puts into the Gauley, one mile above its junction with New river, and have kindly given the Survey a copy of the same. The section, while accurately leveled, is made from west to east, without taking into account the rapid dip, and hence some of the intervals are much too large. The coals were numbered, from the lowest one found in the Kanawha series up to its top at the BLACK FLINT, and the section as compiled by them reads as follows:

Ft.

Kanawha black flint..
Interval 77. 9

Coal, No. 14 (thickness not given)............................
Interval 19. 7
Coal, No. 13, splint coal 12. 5
Interval 182. 7
Coal No. 12, Coalburg seam..................................... 4. 2
Interval 55. 5
Coal No. 11 .... 0. 5
Interval 58. 2
Coal No. 10, Winifrede seam.................... .... 4. 0
Interval 72. 2
Coal No. 9... 0. 5
Interval 16. 5
Coal No. 8 .... 1. 0
Interval 26. 0
Coal No. 7 .... 2. 0
Interval 64. 3
Coal No. 6, soft (Cedar Grove) 3. 7
Interval 75. 4
Coal No. 5, soft, (Peerless) 4. 5
Interval 37. 9

Coal No. 4, Ansted $\begin{Bmatrix} \text{coal.. .. 3 0} \\ \text{slate .. ..0 11} \\ \text{coal.........0 6} \\ \text{slate ....0 7} \\ \text{coal ....4 0} \end{Bmatrix}$ (Blacksburg) 9. 0

Interval, fireclay and sandstone............................ 61. 1
Coal No. 3, soft (Brownstown, Powellton)............ 4. 0
Interval 54. 6

Coal, No. 2, Eagle $\begin{Bmatrix} \text{coal.........2 6} \\ \text{slate ....0 4} \\ \text{coal.........3 0} \end{Bmatrix}$ 5. 10

Interval 49. 0
Coal No. 1 (Little Eagle).. .... 1. 0
Interval, sandstone, etc., to C. & O. R. R., Twenty
Mile branch, at mouth of Sand branch.............. 589. 0

Total... 1494. 7

Interval from *black flint* to Anstead (Blacksburg,
Campbells creek) coal.. 750. 6
Interval from *black flint* to top of Pottsville series
(by adding 300 feet for Kanawha series below Coal
No. 1...................... .... 1245. 9

The words in parentheses have been added by the writer. The measurements, as stated, make the intervals too large, and hence probably 100 feet or more, should be deducted from the interval (750.6) between the BLACK FLINT and the Ansted or Blacksburg coal. Owing to this uncertainty, the writer can give no opinion as to the correctness of the identification of the Coalburg and Winifrede seams by Messrs. Clark and Krebs.

Nos. 13 and 14 most probably represent the Stockton coal, including its lower division, the "Lewiston," or "Crown Hill" splint coal.

Maj. Wm. N. Page, C. E., President of the Gauley Mountain Coal Company, has also measured a section from the top of Gauley Mountain at Ansted to the bed of the New River at Hawks Nest on the C. & O. R. R.   Through the courtesy of Maj. Page, a copy of this interesting section is published herewith, along with the following explanatory letter:

ANSTED, FAYETTE COUNTY, W. VA., April 1, 1903.

DR. I. C. WHITE, State Geologist,
                              Morgantown, W. Va.

MY DEAR DOCTOR:—

I am just in receipt of your favor of the 30th ult., and enclose herewith a section from the New River level at Hawks's Nest station to the top of Gauley Mountain, above the Ansted mines, which is capped with the Mahoning sandstone.   The elevations on this section are all taken by actual level, referred to the Chesapeake & Ohio tide water datum line, as taken from the Hawk's Nest bridge seat, and is correct with the exception of a correction on account of dip of strata.   From the starting point at New River to the Ansted seam, an interval of 980 feet, the distance is a little more than two miles in a straight line, the direction being very nearly due north, in which line of direction the dip here would be about seventy feet to the mile. From the Ansted seam to the top of Gauley mountain, or to the Mahoning sandstone, is very steep, and the dip may be practically ignored.

Trusting that the section may be of some service to you, I remain
                              Very truly and sincerely yours,
                                        WM. N. PAGE.

	Ft.	In.	Ft.	In.
Sandstone and concealed			321	0
Coal ("No. 5 Block," Mahoning, etc.)......................			9	0
Concealed			90	0
Kanawha black flint			4	0
Slate..	10	0		
Coal (Stockton)	9	0		
Concealed	50	0		
Coal (Lewiston?)........	3	6		
Soft sandstone and shale............. 137	137	0		
Coal (Coalburg)	10	0		
Shale	27	6		
Coal	2	6		
Sandstone	49	4		
Coal (Winifrede).....................................	4	8		
Concealed	54	0	641	1
Sandstone, massive..................................	80	0		
Concealed	20	0		
Shales, dark...	15	0		
Sandstone	60	0		
Coal (Cedar Grove?)	0	7		
Shale, black	3	0		

Sandstone.. 15   0 ⎫
Shale 17   0 ⎪
Sandstone 50   0 ⎪
Limestone, hydraulic (Campbells creek)... 2   0 ⎬
Slate, argillaceous 21   0 ⎭
Coal (Ansted, Campbells creek)............................. 11 0
Slate... 3   0 ⎫
Shaly sandstone 27   0 ⎪
Coal (Brownstown, Powellton)................. 3   0 ⎪
Sandstone, gray, massive........ 58   0 ⎪
Shale 2   0 ⎪
Coal (Eagle).................................... 2   0 ⎪
Shale 28   4 ⎪
Coal (Little Eagle)............................ 1   8 ⎪
Shale 35   0 ⎪
Slate, black 3   0 ⎪
"*Black Marble*" (Eagle limestone) 2   0 ⎬ 400 0
Shale, dark.................................... 10   0 ⎪
Shale 52   0 ⎪
Coal 3   0 ⎪
Shale 30   0 ⎪
Slate, black.................................... 18   0 ⎪
Sandstone, gray, shaly.......................... 20   0 ⎪
Shale, hard....................................... 10   0 ⎪
Coal... 2   0 ⎪
Shale 4   0 ⎪
Sandstone, argillaceous............. 32   0 ⎪
Shale 5   0 ⎪
Coal... 4   0 ⎭
Shale, ferriferous...... 45   0 ⎫
Sandstone, massive, top of Pottsville 167   0 ⎪
Shale 10   0 ⎪
Coal 3   0 ⎪
Shale, soft....................................... 45   0 ⎬ 403 0
Sandstone, massive............................108   6 ⎪
Shale soft 15   0 ⎪
Sandstone, massive.......................... 50   0 ⎪
Slate, black 5   0 ⎭
Coal (Sewell, Nuttall, etc.)............................ 3 4
Slate, laminated 30 0
Coal......... .... 0 6
Shale 54 6
Sandstone, hard (Raleigh) to level of New river at
   780 feet A. T.... ... . 60 0

Kanawha black flint to Ansted coal 641 1
   "   "   to top of Pottsville series........1051 1

The words in parentheses in this section have been introduced by the writer. Maj. Page has not shown the parting slates in any of the coal beds, but has simply given the gross measurements, including partings, etc., thus giving the several coal beds of workable size much more thickness than they actually have of minable coal.

Comparing this section with the one on pages 371-2, from the mouth of Armstrong creek, we see that the interval between the

BLACK FLINT and the CAMPBELLS CREEK COAL has increased by practically 100 feet in the Gauley section, or 250 feet over that at the mouth of Campbells creek, where the coal of that name first appears above the Kanawha river, thirty miles in an air line to the northwest.

The PEERLESS division of the Campbells creek bed is separated from the others at Ansted by an interval of only two feet or less, and was formerly taken out with the lower members, but the parting shale thickens up to several feet, and this portion of the coal is not now mined, though it is included in the eleven feet given by the section for the thickness of the Ansted seam.

It is important to note in this connection, that Mr. David White admits this 250 feet of thickening, on page 160 of his Kanawha Coal paper, heretofore referred to, and is even inclined to add over 100 feet more to it, when he states that the fossils of the Ansted seam ally it with the Cedar Grove coal, the horizon of which is more than 100 feet above the Campbells creek bed. Since Mr. White admits that the Kanawha series has thickened up 250 to 350 feet within thirty miles, is it unreasonable to suppose that the Allegheny series could thicken twice this amount in more than 100 miles? There is nothing in stratigraphic geology more certain than that the Ansted seam and the Campbells creek, Coal Valley, No. 2 Gas, etc., are all one and the same bed, instead of the Cedar Grove, so that the testimony of the fossil plants, as interpreted by Mr. White, cannot be right in this case, as any one may see who will follow the sections given along the Kanawha Valley. Of course the bearing of such points as these upon the larger question, which Mr. White attacked, viz., the relation of the Allegheny series to the Kanawha series, is so obvious that it needs no further discussion.

Mr. E. E. Fillmore of Cedar Grove, W. Va., assistant mining engineer for the Kanawha and Hocking Coal and Coke Company, has made a general section of the Kanawha series, which he has kindly placed at my disposal, and it reads as follows:

	Ft. In.	Ft. In.
Kanawha black flint		
Interval		41 0
Lewiston coal	1½–	3½0
Interval		73 0
Coalburg coal	3–	5½0
Interval		28 0

"Split" from Coalburg seam..........................1½– 3 0
Interval 24 0
Kanawha (Winifrede) coal.......................1½– 3 0
Interval 293 0
Cedar Grove coal 2½– 3 0
Interval 130 0
"No. 2 Gas" (Campbells creek) coal 3– 6 0
Interval 120 0
"No. 1 Gas" (Eagle) coal........................3– 5½0
Interval from *black flint* to "No. 2 Gas" (Campbells
    creek) coal..603 0
Interval from *black flint* to bottom of "No. 1 Gas"
    (Eagle) coal...731 0

If we add to Mr. Fillmore's figures 300 feet for the interval from his "No. 1 Gas" (Eagle) coal to the top of the Pottsville, it gives 1,031 feet for the thickness of the Kanawha series, a result in complete harmony with the measurements of the writer, as well as those of Maj. Page, and Clark and Krebs, with proper allowances for uncorrected dip. The names in parentheses are given by the writer.

Mr. Fillmore adds the following interesting notes with reference to the Kanawha coals on the north side of the river:

"THE KANAWHA (WINIFREDE) AND LEWISTON COALS do not show up in workable shape on this side of the river, so they have been omitted."

NO. 5 OR TOP SEAM (MAHONING).

"Good domestic and fair steam coal. Top of very hard sandstone, sometimes accompanied by a crust of iron pyrites, making it impossible to pick jack holes for machines. Seam is very variable, in some places the sandstone entirely disappears and the top is of bastard slate."

COALBURG SEAM.

"From three and a-half to five and a-half of splint coal, fair steam and good domestic coal. Top sandstone with an overlying stratum of slate (white streak). In some places (particularly Mine No. 108 on Kelly's creek) the sandstone is eroded, leaving slate top, the erosive action generally producing a want in the coal."

CEDAR GROVE SEAM.

"From 2' 10" to 3' of clean coal. Bottom of slate (indurated fireclay) which is "shot" to make mule height. Top of argillaceous shale (excellent top, requiring but little propping in entries, which are driven 18' wide to make room for the gob). Rooms worked double, with two rows of posts 60' wide.

"Tough fibrous coal, excellent for steaming purposes, coking, making good foundry coke but not supporting enough for furnace purposes."

NO. 2 GAS SEAM (CAMPBELLS CREEK).

"Upper layer of splint (fine domestic coal) and lower layer of gas coal.
Splint mines in large blocks with little slack. Gas coal very soft in some
places; it jams on machines, making machine cutting difficult. Coal increases toward southeast. Top, slate, gray streak."

NO. I GAS SEAM (EAGLE).

"Entire seam of gas coal. Top 2½' to 3' slate, white streak, tender, falls
in thin slabs. Excellent steam coal and fine coking coal. "

This Kanawha series of coals, as illustrated in the sections already given between Charleston and Gauley mountain, can be
followed southwestward from the New and Kanawha rivers to Big
and Little Coal, and thence to the Guyandot and Tug Fork of Big
Sandy at the Kentucky line in Mingo county, with practically the
same great thickness (1,000 feet or more) as shown by these last
sections. True, the BLACK FLINT, so unfailingly present along the
Kanawha from Charleston to where it escapes into the air at Ansted,
soon fades out of the section when one goes southwest from the
Kanawha valley, but the main coals of the series, the Stockton,
Coalburg, Winifrede, Campbells creek and Eagle, remain, capped
at the top with the great sandstone group (Mahoning, Buffalo,
etc.) which everywhere overlies the BLACK FLINT horizon, so that
the stratigrapher has plenty of guides left after the FLINT has disappeared from the section.

Having now traced the Kanawha series as a whole along the
river of that name, throughout the entire outcrop of the beds in
question, which is typical of the series from Nicholas and Webster
counties southwestward to the Kentucky line, especially along the
eastern crop of the series, we shall consider some of the principal
coals of these measures more in detail, beginning with the highest.

THE STOCKTON COAL.

As already illustrated by the Kanawha river sections, the Stockton coal, the first bed below the KANAWHA BLACK FLINT, splits up
in coming southwestward from Webster and Nicholas counties in
Fayette and Kanawha, often forming two entirely distinct seams,
the Stockton proper and the Lewiston, separated by several feet of
shale or sandstone, as the case may be.

As revealed by these sections just given, this Stockton coal is
not of much value along the Kanawha river, since it is often thin
and unimportant, and even when thick, like that shown in the

Handley section, page 373, it is a mere mass of dirty coal so mixed up with slate, bone and rock material as to be almost valueless under present mining conditions. Of course the time will come in the far-off future, when the large quantity of good coal mixed up with so much impurities, even in a bed like that of the Stockton at Handley, will be crushed, washed and winnowed from its rocky partings, and form a business quite as profitable as that now pursued with the purer beds of coal. When this time comes, as come it surely will, then the Kanawha series will yield nearly as much coal from the beds that are now neglected, on account of their interstratified impurities, as is now obtained from the better class of coals.

The Stockton coal was formerly mined in a small way for fuel at the salt factories between Charleston and Brownstown, but the coal is poor and sulphurous, and its use has practically ceased with the closing of the salt factories many years ago, so that unless the cannel deposit opposite Montgomery is yet in operation, there is at the present time, only one mine shipping coal from the main portion of the Stockton bed in the Kanawha valley.

There are a few mines on the lower division of the Stockton or Lewiston coal, which is generally of the "splint" variety.

One of these mines is that of the Belmont Coal Company, one-half mile west from Crown Hill, Kanawha county, where R. W. Edmonds collected a sample for analysis, and reports the following structure for the Lewiston coal:

	Ft.	In.	Ft.	In.
Shale				
Coal	0	6		
"Niggerhead"	0	2		
Coal	0	7		
Gray splint	0	4		
Coal	1	7	4	9
Coal, softer	0	4		
Gray splint	0	3		
Coal	1	0		

Butts S. 60° W., Face S. 30° E. Elevation 1,163 feet A. T.

"Gray splint" is a term used by the Kanawha miners to designate a splint coal having a slight tinge of gray, and often containing more impurities than the regular black splint, of which the most of this bed is composed.

Analysis of sample reported by Prof. Hite as follows:

Moisture	1.33
Volatile matter	35.26
Fixed carbon	59.09
Ash	4.32
	——
Total	100.00
Sulphur	0.71
Phosphorus	0.004
B. T. U. (Wil. Cal.)	14441

A coal is mined one mile north from Mammoth, Kanawha county, which S. D. Brady reports as the Lewiston, with the following structure:

	Ft.	In.	Ft.	In.
Sandstone				
Slate			5	0
Coal	1	0		
"Niggerhead"	0	2		
Coal	1	9		
"Niggerhead"	0	1	7	4
Coal	0	6		
Slate and coal	2	8		
Coal	1	2		

Butts run S 80° E.   Face S. 10° W.   Elevation 1,135 A. T. Greatest rise S. 15° W.

Analysis reported as follows by Prof. Hite:

Moisture	0.49
Volatile matter	34.84
Fixed carbon	54.97
Ash	9.70
	——
Total	100.00
Sulphur	0.42
Phosphorus	0.042
B. T. U. (Wil. Cal.)	13614

The structure of this coal is quite different from the customary type of the "Lewiston" seam, and it may possibly represent the main Stockton coal.

On Falling Rock creek, a tributary of Elk river, in Kanawha county, the Falling Rock Cannel Coal Company mines a bed of coal which is most probably identical with the Stockton seam. The mine is six miles up from the mouth of the stream, and R. W. Edmonds reports the structure as follows:

	Ft. In.	Ft. In.
Sandstone		
Slate ....o–	1 0
Cannel	0 8	
Shale, bituminous...............................	0 5	
Cannel	1 8	4 10
Slate	0 10	
Coal, soft..	1 3	

Elevation A. T. 840 feet.

Analysis reported by Prof. Hite as follows:

Moisture	0. 83
Volatile matter..	46. 22
Fixed carbon	41.14
Ash	11. 81
Total...	100. 00
Sulphur...	2. 59
Phosphorus..	0. 005

The coal is shipped north for steam purposes.

On the waters of Coal river, in Boone county, there is some very thick coal high up in the hills that Prof. Lyman of Philadelphia, has identified with the Pittsburg bed, which is very probably the Stockton seam, for certainly it is not the Pittsburg, since the soft rocks which underlie it could not exist on the lofty summits where the coal in question occurs, and besides, it is well known that these high ridges (mountains) along the head waters of Coal river are all made by the great sandstone (Mahoning, etc.) mass, which overlies the KANAWHA BLACK FLINT horizon.

On the Guyandot river, the Stockton coal rises above water level about two miles above the "Falls" dam, and is first opened and mined at the mouth of Stone Coal run, where it exhibits the following structure:

	Ft. In.	Ft. In.
Coal	0 4	
Slate	0 2	
Coal	0 7	3 6
Slate and bone...................................	0 9	
Coal, visible	1 8	

Another opening a short distance farther up Stone Coal run, which possibly belongs just above the last coal, exhibits the following:

	Ft. In.	Ft. In.
Sandstone, massive	25 0	
Cannel slate	1 0	
Slate	0 3	5 3
Coal	4 0	

Throughout this region, in Lincoln and Wayne, this coal is
known as the "Big bed." It contains some good coal, but also a
large number of partings, as exhibited by the following section on
the Caldwell tract opposite the mouth of Camp Branch:

	Ft. In.	Ft. In.
Sandstone	10 0	
Coal, slaty..	1 0	
Coal	1 6	
Slate..	0 1	
Coal	2 0	
Slate..........	0 2	10 5
Coal	0 9	
Shale.............	0 9	
Coal	0 8	
Slate	0 6	
Coal	3 0	

In passing westward from the Guyandot to the waters of
Twelve Pole, this coal appears to split into two distinct beds, just
as it does on the upper Kanawha river, only on Twelve Pole the
lower division is CANNEL instead of SPLINT coal, like the Lewiston
bed. The rock parting attains a thickness of thirty feet.

On Cave creek, Wayne county, the following succession occurs
near Cave P. O., where the coal has been mined for local supply:

	Ft. In.	Ft. In.
Coal, visible	2 0	
Shales and sandstone 30 0		
Shales	0 6	36 10
Coal .. { coal, splint 1 8		
{ cannel 1 4	4 4	
{ coal, bony...................... 1 4		

The basal portion of the bed is a bony cannel, and on the opposite side of the stream turns to good cannel and we get the following structure at another mine:

	Ft. In.	Ft. In.
Coal	0 6	
Slate	0 4	5 4
Coal	1 6	
Cannel	3 0	

From this point a narrow belt of cannel coal extends in a western direction nearly across Wayne county, being found on all of the main branches of Twelve Pole. It is possibly identical with the Moses Fork cannel of Kentucky. The belt varies much in width, but it is frequently two to three miles wide, and while the cannel is sometimes absent, yet it is fairly persistent, and seldom less than twenty inches in thickness, being generally of good quality, comparing favorably with the cannel from the Stockton coal horizon opposite Montgomery on the Great Kanawha.

The structure of this coal in the top of the hills near Dingess, at the southern line of Wayne county, has already been given on pages 378-9, where the coal has a thickness of eight feet with several partings.

Another opening in that region exhibits the following succession:

	Ft.	In.	Ft.	In.
Coal	2	0		
Slate, dark	o	6½		
Coal	o	9		
Coal, slaty	1	2		
Coal	o	2		
Slate	o	1½	9	6
Coal	o	1		
Bone	o	4		
Coal	1	10		
Fireclay	o	3½		
Coal, bony	o	5½		
Coal	1	9		

An opening on Bear Trace, a branch of Twelve Pole, gives the following succession:

	Ft.	In.	Ft.	In.
Coal, bony	1	o		
Slate	o	8		
Coal, good	2	4		
Bone	o	9		
Coal, slaty	2	o	11	3
Fireclay	o	4		
Bone	o	8		
Coal, good	3	6		

Where this coal first rises out of Twelve Pole creek, above Wayne, it is thin and impure, and efforts to mine it on the N. & W. R. R., near Radnor, have proven unsuccessful. It appears to thicken up eastward, however, just like the New river and Pocahontas coals of the Pottsville series below, and furnishes a belt of thick coal in the summits of the hills overlooking the region where the Pottsville coals pass below water level and thin away.

In recent years, a very important coal bed has been opened high up in the lofty hills along the Tug Fork of Big Sandy river in southern Mingo county, adjoining the Kentucky border. The coal is shipped to market over the Norfolk & Western R. R., and as it was first opened for commercial shipments near Thacker, it has taken the name of that village. It has not been possible to determine certainly whether the Thacker coal is the Stockton bed, or the Coalburg, eighty to ninety feet lower, but it is certainly one or the other of these important Kanawha seams, as may be seen from the general sections given on pages 376-8 of this volume. The preponderance of evidence is in favor of its correlation with the Stockton bed, and we shall describe it in this connection, even if it should finally turn out to represent the Coalburg seam.

About three-fourths of a mile south from Thacker station, Mingo county. on a small stream, the Thacker Coal and Coke Company has a mine in the Thacker seam at an elevation of 650 feet above the level of Tug River, and there A. P. Brady made the following measurements:

	Ft. In.	Ft. In.
Sandstone		
Slate	0 8	
Sandstone	1 6	
Draw slate	1 8	
Coal	4 8	
Slate	0 0½	
Coal	0 11	
Slate	0 1½	8 0
Coal	0 8	
Slate	0 1	
Coal	1 6	

Elevation, 1,300 feet A. T. Greatest rise, S. E.
Analysis reported by Prof. Hite as follows:

Moisture	0. 41
Volatile matter	36. 33
Fixed carbon	58. 09
Ash	5. 17
Total...	100. 00
Sulphur	0. 86
Phosphorus...	0. 0025
B. T. U (Wil. Cal.)	14738

The Logan Consolidated Coal Company's Maritime mine is one-fourth mile west from Thacker, and there S. D. Brady reports the following:

	Ft. In.	Ft. In.
Sandstone		
Coal, "rider"		1 2
Slate		8 0
Draw slate		
Coal, soft	1 10	
Coal, splint	1 8	
Coal, soft	1 0	4 6
Slate	?	
Coal	?	

Elevation, A. T. 1,250 feet.   Greatest rise, S. E.
Analysis reported by Prof. Hite as follows:

Moisture	0. 47
Volatile matter	35. 38
Fixed carbon	59. 48
Ash	4. 67
Total	100. 00
Sulphur	1. 06
Phosphorus	0. 002

The lower half of the coal is not taken out at this opening, the parting slates being too thick.

The "Lick Fork" mine of the Logan Company, one mile and a-half southeast from Thacker station, exhibits the following structure, according to S. D. Brady:

	Ft. In.	Ft. In.
Sandstone		
Slate		
Coal, soft	1 1	
Splint	2 0	
Coal, soft	1 2	
Splint	1 7	
Coal, soft	0 3	
Bone	0 0½	8 10
Spint	0 3	
Coal, soft	1 3	
Splint	0 2½	
Coal, soft	1 0	
Slate	? ?	
Coal reported		4 0

Elevation A. T. 1,559.   Greatest rise S. E.
Analysis reported as follows by Prof. Hite:

Moisture	0. 37
Volatile matter..	34. 37
Fixed carbon	60.63
Ash	4. 63
Total..	100. 00
Sulphur	1. 13
Phosphorus	0. 013
B. T. U. (Wil. Cal.)	14981

Mr. Brady reports four feet more coal beneath fireclay and
shales, but it is not taken out in this mine. The section illustrates
the alternation of splint layers with ordinary bituminous coal, the
mixture of which makes this such an admirable steam fuel.

The Grape Vine Coal Company's mine, just east from Thacker,
gave the following results on measurement by S. D. Brady:

	Ft.	In.	Ft.	In.
Splint and soft coal, mixed..........	4	9		
Bone	0	0½		
Coal	2	2		
Slate..	0	7		
Coal, soft...................................	0	6		
Slate, black................................	0	1		
Coal	0	1		
Slate, black................................	0	1	12	7¼
Coal	0	3		
Slate..	0	0½		
Coal	1	10		
Slate..	0	2		
Coal	1	6		
Slate..	0	0¼		
Coal	0	6		

Elevation 1,389 A. T., or 700 feet above Tug river. Greatest
rise, S. E.

Analysis reported as follows by Prof. Hite:

Moisture	0. 84
Volatile matter...	34. 92
Fixed carbon	58. 79
Ash	5. 45
Total..	100. 00
Sulphur	0. 93
Phosphorus	0. 06
B. T. U. (Wil. Cal.)	14657

The measurement of the coal given above was taken at a different locality in the Grape Vine mine from that of the writer's,

given on page 376, but they each reveal a total thickness of more than twelve feet for this great bed, when both the upper and lower members are fully exposed.

The Lynn Coal and Coke Company has a mine in the Thacker bed, on a stream which puts into Tug river near Matewan, and there A. P. Brady measured the following section:

	Ft. In.	Ft. In.
Sandstone		
Coal, "rider"	1 6	
Slate	10 0	
Coal	4 5	
Fireclay		

Elevation A. T. 1,240 feet.   Greatest rise S. E.

Sample for analysis reported as follows by Prof. Hite:

Moisture	0.42
Volatile matter	34.61
Fixed carbon	59.32
Ash	5.65
Total	100.00
Sulphur	0.93
Phosphorus	0.0035
B. T. U. (Wil. Cal.)	14864

The Logan Consolidated Coal Company has two mines in the Matewan region, viz., the "Logan" mine, where the upper member is four feet seven inches thick, and the "Red Jacket" mine, where it is four feet eight inches, the upper bench only being mined.   The analyses of samples taken from each are reported as follows by Prof. Hite:

	Logan.	Red Jacket.
Moisture	0.99	1.00
Volatile matter	34.78	34.69
Fixed carbon	59.23	58.32
Ash	5.00	5.99
Totals	100.00	100.00
Sulphur	0.90	0.88
Phosphorus	0.004	0.004
B. T. U. (Wil. Cal.)		14525

The Glen Alum Coal Company has a mine in the Thacker coal, according to S. D. Brady, four miles up Alum creek from Glen Alum station, where the upper bench is the only one mined, and it has a thickness of six feet, at 1,545 feet above tide.

The analysis of sample from Glen Alum mine is reported as follows by Prof. Hite:

```
Moisture ................................................... 0. 45
Volatile matter ........................................... 32. 36
Fixed carbon .............................................. 61. 25
Ash ....................................................... 3. 94
                                                          _____
      Total ..............................................100. 00

Sulphur ................................................... 0. 67
Phosphorus ................................................ 0. 0115
B. T. U. (Wil. Cal.) . ................................... 14709
```

These analyses reveal a coal of most excellent quality, being low in both ash and sulphur, while the fixed carbon and volatile matter are in such proportions as to form an ideal fuel for steam purposes.

There is evidently a large area of this coal between the Tug, Guyandot, and Coal rivers, covering a belt not more than ten to fifteen miles wide along the eastern crop of the coal, but becoming patchy and interrupted west of this belt, since nothing is known of the coal at Williamson, though it comes in again near Naugatuck, at the mouth of Pigeon creek, as shown in the section on page 377.

THE COALBURG COAL.

The interval separating the Stockton coal, or its lower division, the Lewiston seam, from the Coalburg bed, varies greatly both in thickness and character, occasionally nothing but shales intervene, and then the interval is small, only twenty to forty feet, and again, when massive sandstones appear in this interval, it thickens to 100 feet or more, but the average distance of this coal below the KANAWHA BLACK FLINT is eighty to ninety feet.

This bed is mined at Coalburg, Kanawha county, by the Robinson Coal Company, where R. W. Edmonds reports the following structure for this coal at its type locality:

	Ft. In.	Ft. In.
Coal	0 9	
"Niggerhead"	0 7	
Coal	1 4½	
Bone	0 1	
Coal	0 11	5 8½
Slate	0 3	
"Niggerhead"	0 2	
Coal	1 7	

Butts run N. 45° E: Face N. 45° W.

Elevation 1,125 feet A. T. Greatest rise S. 32° E.

Analysis reported by Prof. Hite as follows:

Moisture	0. 77
Volatile matter	36. 79
Fixed carbon	56. 22
Ash	6. 22
Total...	100. 00
Sulphur...	0. 85
Phosphorus	0. 0045
B. T. U. (Wil. Cal.)	14051

The most of the coal is of the splinty type, and is highly valued as a steam and domestic fuel. In the Coalburg region there is generally a seam of soft coal one to two feet thick, at a few inches to eight feet below the main bed.

The following sections of this coal, measured by the writer in the Robinson mine, will show this feature:

	Ft. In.	Ft. In.	Ft. In.
	I	II	III
Coal, splint.........................	0 4	0 6	0 6
"Niggerhead"	0 6	0 6	0 7
Splint	2 10	2 8	2 11
Gray shale	0 9	8 0	0 2
Soft coal	1 8	1 8	1 8
Totals.........	6 1	13 4	5 10

I. Measurement at Drum House.

II. Measurement one mile and a-half in mine S. W.

III. Measurement at Blackberry entry, three miles from Drum House.

This coal is mined by the Black Hawk Coal Company, three miles above Charleston on the K. & M. R. R., where S. D. Brady reports the following structure:

	Ft. In.	Ft. In.
"Niggerhead"	0 2	
Coal	1 8	
Slate	0 2½	
Coal	0 8	4 2
Slate	0 4½	
Coal	1 3	

Butts run S. 85° E.   Face S. 5° W.

Analysis of sample reported by Prof. Hite as follows:

Moisture	1. 67
Volatile matter	38. 10
Fixed carbon	54. 48
Ash	5. 75
Total	100. 00
Sulphur	0. 50
Phosphorus	0. 005
B. T. U. (Wil. Cal.)	13877

The Kanawha and Hocking Coal and Coke Company mines the Coalburg seam near Mammoth, Kanawha county, and there S. D. Brady made the following measurements:

	Ft. In.	Ft. In.
Sandstone		
Coal	1 4	
"Niggerhead"	0 3	
Coal	1 2	4 10
"Niggerhead"	0 6	
Coal	1 7	

Elevation 1,075 feet A. T.   Greatest rise S. E.

Analysis of sample reported as follows by Prof Hite:

Moisture	0. 56
Volatile matter	36. 63
Fixed carbon	56. 38
Ash	6. 43
Total	100. 00
Sulphur	0. 51
Phosphorus	0. 004
B. T. U. (Wil. Cal.)	13855

This bed has been extensively mined on Cabin creek, near Ronda, Kanawha county, by the Coalburg Colliery Company, and there R. W. Edmonds made the following measurement:

	Ft. In.	Ft. In.
Sandstone		
Slate, black		1 0
Slate, gray		2 0
Splint	1 0	
"Niggerhead"	0 10	
Splint	3 0	7 7
Coal, soft	2 0	

Butts run S. 30° W.   Face S. 60° E.   Greatest rise N. 40° W. Elevation 1,325 A. T.

Separate samples were collected from the splint coal and the soft coal below, the analyses of which are reported as follows by Prof. Hite:

	Splint Coal.	Soft Coal.
Moisture	0. 52	0. 69
Volatile matter	35. 78	35. 56
Fixed carbon	56. 84	58. 43
Ash	6. 86	5. 22
Totals	100. 00	100. 00
Sulphur	0. 86	0. 93
Phosphorus	0. 005	0. 004
B. T. U. (Wil. Cal.)	14298	14738

Several miles farther up Cabin creek, the Stevens Coal Company has a mine one-half mile above Acme, in what is believed to be the Coalburg bed, and R. W. Edmonds reports its structure as follows:

	Ft. In.	Ft. In.
Draw slate		0 6
Coal, soft	1 7	
Gray splint	0 3	
Coal, soft	2 4	5 6
Slate	0 2	
Coal	1 2	

Butts run S. 30° W.   Face S. 60° E.   Greatest rise S. 30° E. Elevation 1,785 feet A. T.

Analysis of sample reported as follows by Prof. Hite:

Moisture	0. 72
Volatile matter	33. 88
Fixed carbon	60. 81
Ash	4. 58
Total	100. 00
Sulphur	0. 61
Phosphorus	0. 0085
B. T. U. (Wil. Cal.)	14645

The bottom division of the coal was not in the sample analyzed.

The Crown Hill Coal Company has a mine in the Coalburg seam at Crown Hill, Kanawha county, according to R. W. Edmonds, in which he made the following measurements:

	Ft.	In.	Ft.	In.
Sandstone				
Slate			0	3
Coal	2	0		
Slate	0	4		
Coal	1	0	4	9
Sulphur band	0	4		
Coal	1	1		

Butts run N. 60° E.   Face N. 30° W.   Greatest rise S. 37° E. Elevation 1,093 feet A. T.

Analysis of sample reported as follows by Prof. Hite:

Moisture	0. 86
Volatile matter	36. 88
Fixed carbon	56. 72
Ash	5. 54
Total	100. 00
Sulphur	0. 67
Phosphorus	0. 003
B. T. U. (Wil. Cal.)	14525

The Belmont Coal Co. has a mine in this bed, one-half mile west from Crown Hill, and there R. W. Edmonds reports the following measurement:

	Ft.	In.	Ft.	In.
Sandstone				
Slate, hard			2	6
Draw slate			0	8
Coal	0	8		
"Niggerhead"	1	1		
Splint	3	0		
Slate	0	2	7	0
Splint	0	6		
Slate	0	2		
Coal, soft	1	5		

Butts run N 60° E. Face N. 30° W.
Elevation 1,103 feet A. T.

Analysis of sample reported as follows by Prof. Hite:

```
Moisture ..................................................................   1. 21
Volatile matter........................ ...................... ...   37. 67
Fixed carbon ...................................... .............   57. 93
Ash .......................................................................   3. 19
                                                                        _____
     Total .................................................... ....100. 00
Sulphur ...................................................... .............   0. 64
Phosphorus............................................   .  .........   0. 003
B. T. U. ( Wil. Cal.) ..........................................   14856
```

The Scranton Splint Coal Company operates the Coalburg seam near Pratt, four miles up Paint creek from the Kanawha river, and there R. W. Edmonds made the following measurement.

```
                                               Ft. In   Ft. In.
Sandstone .........................................·.... .........
Shale................................................... .. 2   0
Splint ...............................................  1   8  ⎤
"Niggerhead" ........................... ..........   0   2  ⎟
Coal ................................................   0   4  ⎟
"Niggerhead" . ..... .........................   0   2  ⎬ 8  6
Coal .................................................   4  10  ⎟
Slate ................................................   0   7  ⎟
Coal .................................................   0   9  ⎦
```

Butts run N. 30° E.   Face N. 60° W.
Analysis of sample reported as follows by Prof. Hite:

```
Moisture.........................................................   0. 46
Volatile matter.... ...............................................   36. 09
Fixed carbon ........... ...... ...............................   54. 79
Ash ................................................. ...............   8. 66
                                                                        _____
     Total................. ..........  .........................100. 00
Sulphur ......................................................   0. 74
Phosphorus............................................   0. 0037
B. T. U.  Wil. Cal.)............................................   14166
```

The Bell Creek Coal Company has a mine near Belva, at the Fayette- Nicholas county line, which is very probably in the Coalburg seam, although it may possibly be the Winifrede bed.   A. P. Brady reports the coal as having the following structure:

```
                                               Ft. In.   Ft. In.
Sandstone .....................................................
Slate ...........................................................
Coal .........................................  ..............   0   6  ⎤
Slate ......................................... ..............   0  10  ⎟
Splint ............................................. ..........   2   3  ⎟
Bone coal .........................................   0   0¼ ⎬ 4  7¾
Coal ........ .....................  .............. .....   1   8  ⎟
Slate  .....................................   0   2  ⎟
Coal ........................................ .............   0   2  ⎦
```

Runs on S. 58° W.   Face S. 22° E.

Elevation 740 feet above the R. R.

Analyses of sample reported as follows by Prof. Hite:

Moisture	0.65
Volatile matter	33.73
Fixed carbon	55.87
Ash	9.75
Total	100.00
Sulphur	0.70
Phosphorus	0.008

Mr. Filmore, the mining engineer of Cedar Grove, gives the following as the average section of the Coalburg seam, on the north side of Kanawha river:

	Ft.	Ft.
Shaly coal	0.7	
Coal	1.6	
Niggerhead	0.2	
Coal	1.1	5.2
Niggerhead	0.6	
Coal	1.0	

Some of the mines about to be described under the Winifrede coal may in reality belong at the horizon of the Coalburg seam, since the beds are seldom both workable in the same hill, and the intervals separating each from the BLACK FLINT "key" rock are quite variable.

As heretofore stated, it is possible that the Thacker coal, described under the Stockton bed, may prove to be the Coalburg, when the detailed geology of the region can be carefully studied with the aid of the new and better topographic maps with which it is designed to cover the entire State, and hence the final solution of these questions of identity must be deferred for the present.

From these quite variable rock intervals, it results that the Coalburg bed has not been traced and certainly identified very far beyond the immediate region of the Great Kanawha valley.

On the Elk river, a coal comes up ninety to one hundred feet under the BLACK FLINT horizon, between Queen Shoals and Clay, that appears to represent the Coalburg bed. It has been mined for local use in the vicinity of Yankee Dam, and hence is locally known by that name.

Near the mouth of Little Beechy, this coal has been opened by Mr. Thompson, where it has the following structure:

	Ft. In.	Ft. In.
Sandstone, massive		
Coal	0 4	
Shale..	0 3	
Coal	0 9	
Bone	0 3	5 5
Coal	1 0	
Coal and slate.................................	0 9	
Coal	2 1	

The coal is about 150 feet above the level of Elk river, and over 300 feet below the Mason, or Queen Shoals coal, which has been opened high in the hills above the great cliffs, which rise in an almost solid wall to 450 feet above the Elk.

This coal has been mined for many years on the south side of Elk river at Clay, the principal supply for the town having been secured here, where it exhibits the following structure:

	Ft. In.	Ft. In.
Sandstone		
Draw slate..	0 3	
Splint	2 6	
Coal, bony	0 6	
Coal, soft......................................	0 6	
Splint	0 2	6 3
"Niggerhead"	0 1	
Coal, soft......................................	2 6	
Concealed to Elk river	15 0	

The coal has the following structure at the Scott & Price mine, one mile below Clay, on the north side of Elk river:

	Ft. In.	Ft. In.
Sandstone, massive, micaceous		
Coal	0 6	
Dark shales.................................	1 0	
Splint	2 4	
Shale	0 8	
Coal	0 4	9 2
Shales and bone	1 0	
Coal, soft...................................	1 6	
Shale, gray....................	0 4	
Splint, impure	1 6	

The thickness of impurities nearly or quite exceeds that of the good coal at this mine, but this may possibly change for the better when farther under the hill. The coal, when freed from its stony partings, is quite good, and makes an excellent steam and domestic fuel.

The Coalburg bed will doubtless furnish much valuable fuel on the waters of Big and Little Coal rivers, the Guyandot, and Tug, when those regions are fully opened up for railway traffic.

THE WINIFREDE COAL.

At 150 to 225 feet below the KANAWHA BLACK FLINT, another bed of excellent coal is frequently present in the Kanawha series. It has long been successfully mined on Fields creek, near the town of Winifrede, Kanawha county, and has taken its name from that locality. It comes in the middle of the great sandstone mass, which underlies the Coalburg bed along the Kanawha river, and would therefore appear to represent the Upper Kittanning bed of the Allegheny series. One of the curious things in connection with this Winifrede bed, is that it is rarely of workable dimensions and quality when the Coalburg bed above is in good condition, and VICE VERSA, especially along the Great Kanawha, indeed so frequently is this true that the writer has sometimes suspected it possible that the Coalburg and Winifrede beds might be one and the same, but with greatly changing intervals below the BLACK FLINT. However, there are so many stratigraphic arguments against such a supposition that it has never been seriously entertained.

This coal was first mined on a commercial scale near Lewiston, Kanawha county, and for several years was known as the "Lewiston" seam, but by some popular misconception the name "Lewiston" was transferred to a coal above the Coalburg bed, more than 100 feet higher in the geologic column than the one which first bore this name.

The Winifrede Coal Company has long mined this coal at the head of Fields creek, Kanawha county, and has now extended its mining operations through the divide to the waters of Coal river. The coal is not thick but it is very pure, and seldom surpassed both for steam and domestic purposes. There are three principal mines operated by the Winifrede Company at the head of Fields creek, and R. W. Edmonds made the following measurements at each. The "South" mine shows this structure:

	Ft. In.	Ft. In.
Sandstone		
Draw slate		o 1

		Ft.	In.	Ft.	In.
Coal		o	10	}	
"Gray splint"		o	4	}	
Coal		I	6	}	5 I
Slaty coal		o	6	}	
Slate		o	6	}	
Coal		I	11	}	

The "North" mine shows the following:

	Ft.	In.	Ft.	In.
Sandstone				
Slate			2	o
Coal	I	2	}	
"Gray splint"	o	4½	}	
Coal	I	4	}	
Slaty coal...., ...	o	I	}	4 8½
Slate	o	3	}	
Coal	I	6	}	

The "Machine" mine is just northwest from the last, and the coal has the following structure there:

	Ft.	In.	Ft.	In.
Sandstone				
Shales....			o–11	
Coal	o	10	}	
Sulphurous coal	o	2	}	
Coal...	I	I	}	4 3
Slate	o	4	}	
Coal...	I	10	}	

The samples analyzed from each mine are reported as follows by Prof. Hite:

	South Mine.	North Mine.	Machine Mine.
Moisture	1. 07	1. 09	1. 02
Volatile matter ...	35. 79	36. 59	36 ·05
Fixed carbon	55. 69	58. 42	58. 34
Ash	6. 45	3. 90	4. 59
Totals............	100. 00	100. 00	100. 00
Sulphur..............	0. 77	0. 65	0. 69
Phosphorous........	0. 006	0. 003	0. 003
B.T.U. (Wil.Cal)..	14304	14347	14435

Butts run N. 26¼° E.   Face N. 63¼° W. in all of the mines, and the elevation is 1,000 to 1,020 feet A. T., while the greatest rise is S. 35° E.

At Quincy, Kanawha county, the Quincy Coal Company mines a seam, the elevation of which would make it the Winifrede bed, although it is popularly supposed to be the "Lewiston." The coal was measured by S. D. Brady, who reports the following structure:

	Ft. In.	Ft. In.
Sandstone		
Slate	1	6
"Niggerhead"	0	5
Coal	3	0

Elevation 980 feet A. T.   Greatest rise N. W.
Analysis of sample reported by Prof. Hite as follows:

Moisture	0.70
Volatile matter	36.73
Fixed carbon	58.26
Ash	4.31
Total	100.00
Sulphur	0.80
Phosphorus	0.004
B. T. U. (Wil. Cal.)	14692

The New Diamond Mining Company operates on this same coal, three-fourths of a mile below Quincy, and there S. D. Brady made the following measurement:

	Ft. In.	Ft. In.
Sandstone		
Slate		
"Niggerhead"	0	4
Coal	3	1

Elevation 950 feet A. T.   Greatest rise N. W.
Analysis of sample reported by Prof. Hite as follows:

Moisture	0.56
Volatile matter	38.64
Fixed carbon	57.67
Ash	3.13
Total	100.00
Sulphur	0.77
Phosphorus	0.003
B. T. U. (Wil. Cal.)	14844

The Marinet Company has mines on Lens creek, Kanawha county, and one of these is identified by R. W. Edmonds as the Winifrede bed with the following structure:

```
Slate ...................................... .... ..................................
Coal ............................................................... 3   0 ⎫
Slate..........,.............. ..................... .....  0   1 ⎬  4  7
Coal .................. ...... .................................. 1   6 ⎭
```

Butts run N. 60° E.   Face N. 30° W.

Elevation 230 feet above level of branch of R. R. (C. & O.) at Marinet.

Analysis of sample reported as follows by Prof. Hite:

```
Moisture ................................................. ..........  ......   0. 65
Volatile matter ..................................... ......................... 37. 06
Fixed carbon .................................................. ... ..........  56. 70
Ash ......................................................................... 5. 59

    Total ......................................................100. 00

Sulphur.......... ...........................................   0. 65
Phosphorus........ ...................................................  0. 015
B. T. U. (Wil. Cal.)............................................. 14543
```

The Crown Hill Coal Company mines the Winifrede bed at Crown Hill, Kanawha county, under the name of the "Kanawha" seam, a term used to designate this coal in the region around Handley, and there R. W. Edmonds measured the following structure:

	Ft.	In.	Ft.	In.
Slate				
Gas coal.. ..	1	0		
Splint ..... :.......	0	5		
Gas coal..	1	1	3	8
Splint	0	8		
Gas coal.............	0	6		

Butts run N. 45° E.   Face N. 45° W.

Elevation 1,053 feet A. T.   Greatest rise S. 38° E.

Analysis of sample reported by Prof. Hite as follows:

```
Moisture ......... ............................................. ......   0. 98
Volatile matter............ ................................. 35. 49
Fixed carbon ...................................... ...... ......... 60. 76
Ash ..... ..................................................... ........  2. 77

    Total ...................................................100. 00
Sulphur ...................... .................................   0. 65
Phosphorus................................................  0. 003
B. T. U. (Wil. Cal. ) ........ ............................... 14767
```

The term "gas coal" is used in the Kanawha valley to designate any ordinary bituminous coal not of the splint type.

.The Chesapeake Mining Company has a mine in a coal bed, one-half-mile south from Handley, Kanawha county, where R. W. Edmonds reports the following structure:

	Ft. In.	Ft. In.
Sandstone		
Splint	4 4	
Sandstone, dark gray.............................	0 3½	5 6½
Splint	0 11	

Butts run N. 50° E.   Face N. 40° W.
Elevation 1,131 feet A. T.   Greatest rise S. 30° E.
Analysis of sample reported as follows by Prof. Hite:

Moisture	0. 77
Volatile matter	35. 23
Fixed carbon...	59. 79
Ash	4. 21
Total...	100. 00
Sulphur..	0. 62
Phosphorus..	0. 003
B. T. U. (Wil Cal.)..................................	14912

The elevation given for the coal by Mr. Edmonds would make it the Winifrede, or "Kanawha" seam, but the structure of the coal bed, and the character of the coal, is more like that of either the Lewiston seam or the Coalburg bed.   It is possible that it is one of these instead of the Winifrede.

The Davis Creek Coal Company mines a bed of coal on Davis creek, Kanawha county, a few miles south from Charleston, that possibly belongs at the horizon of the Winifrede seam, since Hon. Neil Robinson, the well known mining expert of Charleston, W. Va., informs me that it lies at least 200 feet below the horizon of the KANAWHA BLACK FLINT.

R. W. Edmonds gives it the following structure at the Davis creek mine:

	Ft. In.	Ft. In.
Rock		
Coal	2 8	

Analysis of sample reported as follows by Prof. Hite:

Moisture	1. 08
Volatile matter	37. 69
Fixed carbon	55. 48

Ash 5. 75
_____
Total...100. 00
Sulphur........................ .... 0. 66
Phosphorus... 0. 004
B. T. U. (Wil.Cal.)..

This coal is called the "Black Band" seam, since it was opened
for mining operations many years ago in connection with a bed of
impure BLACK BAND IRON ORE, but the ore proved too lean and
variable for successful use, and the company, organized to manufacture iron, went into the coal business.   The coal is of the splinty
type, and has an excellent reputation both for steam and domestic
purposes.

This coal bed doubtless exists on Coal and Guyandot rivers
and their tributaries in Boone and Logan counties, but as the coals
of that region have not been opened up for mining, except in a
very limited way as domestic fuels, it has not been possible to identify this coal with certainty in the district referred to.

On the Tug river, at Williamson, Mingo county, a coal is
mined in the hills 250 feet above water level, which appears to
come at the horizon of this coal.   It exhibits the following section
at the mine of Wallace Williamson, one-half mile northwest from
the N. & W. R. R. station:

	Ft. In.	Ft. In.
Coal	0 9	
Shale, gray......................	0 1	
Coal	1 8	3 8
Bone	0 4	
Coal	0 10	

The coal is of the splinty type and makes an excellent domestic fuel.

The Hatfield Colliery Company has recently opened a bed of
coal one mile above Nolan, Mingo county, which comes at the
horizon of the Winifrede bed, and much resembles its Kanawha
type in the alternations of splint, and softer coal, as shown by its
section already given on page 378.

The Jackson Coal Company has also recently opened this coal a
short distance north from the Hatfield Company's mine, where
the bed exhibits the following structure:

	Ft. In.	Ft. In.
Shales, gray..		5 0
Coal	0 7	
Slate	0 2	
Splint	2 0	
Coal, soft..	0 5	3 10
Bone	0 1	
Splint .... ·	0 7	

These mines were opened too late to furnish samples for analysis, but the coal is of excellent quality for either steam or domestic purposes.

In the Kanawha valley another coal, much split up with
shales, fireclay, and other impurities, is frequently found at twenty-five to fifty feet below the Winifrede bed. It was once mined
for use in the old salt furnaces a few miles above Charleston, and is
locally called the "Point" seam, but so far as known the coal has not
been mined on a commercial scale in recent years, and appears to
be very sporadic and irregular in thickness, so that it does not appear to be of much economic importance. It is possible that the
"Point" seam may occasionally have been confused with the
Winifrede bed, especially when the latter is not of workable dimensions.

THE CEDAR GROVE COAL.

Between the Winifrede coal and the next lower regular and
valuable seam of the Kanawha series, (the Cedar Grove coal), there
intervenes 250 to 300 feet of sandy measures. .These rocks, when
broken by interbedded shales often contain thin and irregular seams
of coal of little economic importance, and the sandstones frequently
become massive, forming immense cliffs of gray, micaceous sandstone that occasionally, uniting with those above the Winifrede coal,
form long lines of bold cliffs, which weather into many fantastic
shapes of the "chimney rock" type. These sandstones have a
gnarly, irregular stratification, and are seldom quarried for building purposes, resembling in this respect the Upper and Lower Freeport sandstones of the Allegheny series, with which they would
seem to correlate in a general way. They always make conspicuous bluffs above the horizon of the Cedar Grove coal, and have been
a prominent factor in shaping the steep slopes and lofty hills of
this southwestern region of the State. These sandstones have not
been given any special name in this report, because it was con-

sidered desirable to await their further detailed study in the region between the Kanawha and Tug Fork of Big Sandy, where they are so well developed, before attempting to give them geographical designations.

As stated above, the Cedar Grove coal is the first workable seam below this great sandstone mass, in the Kanawha valley at least, having received its name from the village of Cedar Grove at the mouth of Kelly's creek, Kanawha county, where the bed was first mined on a commercial scale.

The Kanawha and Hocking Coal and Coke Company mines this coal on Kellys creek, near the village of Cedar Grove, and there S. D. Brady made the following measurement: .

	Ft. In.	Ft. In.
Sandstone		
Shales, gray	18 0	
Coal	2 10	
Fireclay	5 0	
Sandstone		

Greatest rise S. 45° E.   Elevation 775 feet A. T.
Analysis af sample reported by Prof. Hite as follows:

Moisture	0. 79
Volatile matter	36. 04
Fixed carbon	58. 92
Ash	4. 25
Total...	100. 00
Sulphur	0. 46
Phosphorus......................................	0. 003
B. T. U. (Wil. Cal.).........	14767

The coal is quite hard but not of the splinty type, being rather intermediate between that and the "gas" coals below.   There is a thin streak of bony coal one foot below the top at this mine, but it burns up completely, and is not separated from the rest of the bed, all of which makes a steam coal of great excellence.

The Cedar Grove Colliery Company also mines this bed near Cedar Grove, and there the section is as follows, according to S. D. Brady:

	Ft. In.	Ft. In.
Sandstone		
Coal..	0 3	
Slate	0 3	
Coal .... I 4		
Coal, very hard................. .... 0 2	}	3 2
Coal .... I 8		

Greatest rise S. E.   Elevation 725 A. T.
Analysis of sample reported as follows by Prof. Hite:

```
Moisture ....................................................  0.82
Volatile matter ...........................................  36.44
Fixed carbon ..............................................  58.40
Ash .........................................................  4.34
                                                          _____
       Total ..............................................  100.00
Sulphur ....................................................  0.52
Phosphorus...............................................  0.004
B. T. U. (Wil. Cal. ).................................  14554
```

The Kanawha and Hocking Coal and Coke Company's mine
No. 110 is also in this same coal, and there S. D. Brady reports
the following structure:

	Ft. In.	Ft. In.
Sandstone		
Slate	5	0
Coal, "rider"...	0	4
Slate	1	3
Coal	2	8

Greatest rise S. E.   Elevation 765 feet A. T.
Analysis of sample reported as follows by Prof. Hite:

```
Moisture .................................................  .064
Volatile matter ...........................................  36.76
Fixed carbon ..............................................  57.97
Ash .........................................................  4.63
                                                          _____
       Total ..............................................  100.00
Sulphur ....................................................  0.48
Phosphorus...............................................  0.003
B. T. U. (Wil.Cal.)......................................  14656
```

This section exhibits a feature often present with this coal,
viz., a thin "rider" coal in the roof of the main bed, from which
it is separated by shales, a few inches to several feet in thickness.
These shales, both above and below the "rider" coal, are usually
very rich in fossil plant remains.

The Mile Branch Coal Company has a mine in the Cedar
Grove coal near Monarch, Kanawha county, and there S. D. Brady
made the following measurement:

	Ft. In.	Ft. In.
Slate	10	0
Coal, "rider"...	0	2½
Slate	0	10
Coal	3	1

Greatest rise S. E.　Elevation 705 feet A. T.

Analysis of sample reported by Prof. Hite as follows:

```
Moisture ........................................................ 0. 69
Volatile matter ........ ..................................... 35. 92
Fixed carbon ................................ .... ........ 59. 24
Ash ........................................................... 4. 15
                                                             _____
Total........................ .............. .... .........100. 00
Sulphur....................................................... 0. 58
Phosphorus.................................................. 0. 003
B.T.U. (Wil.Cal.).. ....................................... 14693
```

On the south bank of the Kanawha river this coal is mined by the Robinson, East Bank, and Crown Hill Coal Companies at Coalburg, East Bank, and Crown Hill respectively. R. W. Edmonds reports the coal as two feet eight inches thick at Coalburg and Crown Hill, and two feet nine inches at East Bank.

The analyses of samples from each of these mines are reported as follows by Prof. Hite:

	Coalburg.	East Bank.	Crown Hill.
Moisture	1. 27	0. 76	1. 07
Volatile matter	35. 66	37. 37	35. 96
Fixed carbon	55. 95	57. 41	57. 07
Ash................................	7. 12	4. 46	5. 90
Totals.........	100. 00	100. 00	100. 00
Sulphur	0. 81	0. 66	0. 74
Phosphorus......................	0. 007	0. 006	0. 004
B.T. U. (Wil. Cal.)	14071	14649	14535

These several analyses reveal a coal of most excellent quality, very low in sulphur, phosphorus and ash. Although averaging only two feet eight inches to two feet ten inches in thickness, yet it has been very successfully mined, thus furnishing a good object lesson as to what thickness of pure fuel will warrant mining operations when not complicated by the removal of included bone, "niggerhead," or other slaty partings.

There is doubtless a large area of this coal in the region southwest from the Kanwaha valley, as well as northeast from it, since the same coal exists in Nicholas county, having been dug into at 100 feet above the main coal (Campbells creek) around Summersville, and it has also been mined by the Baker heirs, on McMillans creek, a branch of Muddlety.

On Tug river, the Mingo Mining Company works a coal bed at

Alma, two miles west of Matewan, which belongs 300 to 400 feet below the Thacker bed, and it is possible that this coal is a representative of the Cedar Grove seam. It is reported as follows by A. P. Brady:

	Ft. In.	Ft. In.
Sandstone		
Slate		
Coal		3 5

Elevation 890 feet A. T.

Analysis of sample reported as follows by Prof. Hite:

Moisture	0. 62
Volatile matter	35. 24
Fixed carbon	57·43
Ash	6. 71
Total	100. 00
Sulphur	0. 55
Phosphorus	0. 003

The similarity in chemical composition with the Cedar Grove seam, revealed by the above analysis, while not of much weight in a question of identity, is still of some little significance.

If the Kanawha series is simply the expanded Allegheny, then, as already stated, the Cedar Grove coal would correlate with the Middle Kittanning coal of the latter series.

CAMPBELLS CREEK LIMESTONE.

The interval between the Cedar Grove coal and the next underlying coal bed (Campbells creek) consists largely of alternating shales and sandstones, sometimes containing thin seams of coal, and often a peculiar earthy limestone, the whole varying in thickness from fifty to over one hundred feet. The limestone in question was first observed by the writer near the mouth of Campbells creek, and was named from that locality, where it occurs at an interval of thirty-four feet above the coal of the same name. It frequently takes the form of lens-shaped concretions, and often exhibits the "cone-in-cone" structure, which is itself of concretionary origin. This limestone horizon is rather persistent in the Kanawha valley, though the stratum is seldom more than a foot in thickness.

THE CAMPBELLS CREEK COAL.

At an interval below the BLACK FLINT, varying from 410 feet at Campbells creek on the north, to 640 feet at Ansted, thirty odd miles to the southeast, we find the most important coal of the Kanawha series. It received its name from the stream along which it first appears above water level in passing southeastward from Charleston, and which puts into the north bank of the Kanawha river, four miles above that city. The general section at the mouth of Campbells creek, given on page 508, shows the relation of this important coal to the other members of the Kanawha series above it, and the remaining sections which follow that one to page 536, will reveal its relation to the beds below, as well as to those above it along the Kanawha valley. They show it to be a multiple seam at its type locality, and that it also splits up and becomes even more complex to the southeast along the Kanawha river, the upper portion separating from the lower, and locally becoming an entirely distinct coal bed, which has been separately mined under the name of the "Peerless" seam, which, after getting twenty to thirty feet away from the lower member, the Blacksburg seam, or "No. 2 Gas," again approaches the latter within a few inches on Morris creek, near Montgomery. These different phases of the original Campbells creek coal are fairly illustrated in the sections given above, but the complete evidence for the splitting of the Campbells creek bed into the Peerless and Blacksburg members, and their coming practically together again near Montgomery, can only be realized by actual examinations in the field.

The Campbells creek coal is different in type from the hard, splint coals like the Winifrede and Coalburg above, and hence is generally known as a "gas" coal, or "No. 2 Gas" to be specific; the coal from this bed having long been used for gas making purposes. Being soft in texture this coal also cokes well, so that the type is entirely different from all of the coals above the Cedar Grove bed in the Kanawha valley, although there is frequently a few inches of splint coal in the upper portion of the "No. 2 Gas," or Blacksburg member of the Campbells creek bed.

The following section of the Campbells creek coal at the Calderwood mine of the Campbells Creek Coal and Coke Company, near the mouth of Campbells creek, made by S. D. Brady, will illustrate the complex character of the bed at its type locality:

	Ft. In.	Ft. In.
Sandstone		
Slate	o 2	
Coal	2 3	
Black slate	o 4	
Coal ....,..	o 11	
Slate	o 1	7 o½
Coal	o 11½	
Slate	1 1	
Coal	1 5	

Butts run S. 85° W.   Face S. 5° E.

Elevation 610 feet A. T.   Greatest rise, S. E.

Analysis of sample reported by Prof. Hite as follows:

Moisture	1. 12
Volatile matter...	36. 63
Fixed carbon	55. 05
Ash..	7. 20
Total... ....100. 00	
Sulphur	1. 16
Phosphorus...	0. 005
B. T. U. (Wil. Cal.)	13755

"Bottom coal taken out only in portions of the mine where intervening slate is not too thick to remove."

The Spring Fork mine of the same company is located on the south side of Campbells creek, one mile above its mouth, and there S. D. Brady made the following measurement:

	Ft. In.
Sandstone	
Slate...	o 3
Coal	2 2
Slate	o 1
Coal	2 7
Slate	1 o
Coal, not exposed.......	

Analysis of sample reported as follows by Prof. Hite:

Moisture	0. 96
Volatile matter	37. 42
Fixed carbon	57. 66
Ash..	3. 96
Total 100. 00	
Sulphur	0. 54
Phosphorus	0. 002
B. T. U. (Wil. Cal.)	14278

The "bottom" member of the coal was not in this sample.

From this point southeastward the parting slates of the Campbells creek coal begin to thicken, and just above Malden station on the C. &. O. R. R., only one mile and a-half from the mouth of Campbells creek, we find the bed extending through an interval of seventeen and a-half feet, ten feet of which is fireclay and sandy shales, as shown in the section on page 510. These intervening shales increase still more as we go up the Kanawha, apparently by the thickening of the "one foot ten inch fireclay and shale" of the Malden section referred to, and separate the Campbells creek coal into two well defined beds, which are twenty feet apart at Brownstown, and mined separately, as shown in the section on page 511, the upper member of which becomes the "Peerless" coal, and the lower one the Blacksburg bed.

One of these beds, probably the lower, is mined by the Kanawha and Coal River Coal Company at Carkin, one mile above Malden station, where R. W. Edmonds made the following measments:

	Ft.	In.
Sandstone		
Draw slate	0	4
Coal	0	6
Bone	0	1
Coal	2	6

Butts run N. 60° E.   Face S. 30° W.
Elevation 641 feet A. T.
Analysis of sample reported as follows by Prof. Hite:

Moisture	0. 94
Volatile matter	34. 19
Fixed carbon	57. 53
Ash	7. 34
Total	100. 00
Sulphur	0. 12
Phosphorus	0. 008

The upper or "Peerless" member of the Campbells creek bed is mined at the mouth of Fields creek by the Lewiston Coal Company at its Peerless mine, near the village of Peerless, the type locality for this coal, and there R. W. Edmonds reports a thickness of two feet three inches at 640 feet A. T.   This is at the locality of the general section given on the lower half of page 515, where the lower division of the Campbells creek bed appears at twenty-six feet below the Peerless seam.   The same coal is mined by the Winifrede Coal Company at its "Arbuckle" mine, three miles up Fields creek, according to Mr. Edmonds, who found it there two feet eight inches thick, at 710 feet A. T.   The samples from each of these mines yielded the following results as reported by Prof. Hite:

	Lewiston.	Arbuckle.
Moisture	0. 62	1. 07
Volatile matter	37. 33	38. 69
Fixed carbon	58. 41	57. 25
Ash	3. 64	2. 99
Totals	100. 00	100. 00
Sulphur	0. 83	1. 25
Phosphorus.........................	0. 003	0. 0025
B.T.U.(Wil. Cal.).....................	14768	14641

This is a beautiful coal, single bedded, and having the columnar structure of typical coking coal.   It is very rich in volatile matter, and highly prized as a gas coal, and also for steam.

The Pine Grove Coal Company has a mine one-half mile up Cabin creek, which Mr. Edmonds thinks is in the Peerless seam, and he reports its structure as follows:

	Ft.	In.
Sandstone		
Slate	3	0
Coal...........................	2	10
Slate . ...…	0	2½
Coal ....…...	0	6½

Butts run S. 15° E.   Face N. 75° E.   Greatest rise S. 75° E. Elevation 695 A. T.
Analysis reported by Prof. Hite as follows:

Moisture	0. 59
Volatile matter................................	35. 76
Fixed carbon	58. 87
Ash	4. 78
Total...	100. 00
Sulphur	1. 05
Phosphorus......................	0. 002

It is possible that this is the Blacksburg member instead of the Peerless, since, as a rule, the latter has no slate or bony partings whatever.

At Acme, near the head of Paint creek, Kanawha county, the Stevens Coal Company has two mines in the Blacksburg member of this coal, one the "Empire," three-fourths of a mile below Acme, and the other, the "Keystone," one-fourth of a mile above Acme. R. W. Edmonds reports the structure at each as follows:

	Empire.		Keystone.	
	Ft.	In.	Ft.	In.
Soft coal	2	7	3	0
Gray splint	0	8	0	4
Soft coal	0	5	0	3
Slate	0	0½	0	0½
Soft coal	1	8	0	10
Totals	5	4½	4	5½

Elevations: (Empire) 1,235 feet A. T. (Keystone) 1,275 feet A. T.

ANALYSES.

	Empire.	Keystone.
Moisture	0. 76	0. 53
Volatile matter	34. 70	33. 08
Fixed carbon	59. 82	59. 32
Ash	4. 72	7. 07
Totals	100. 00	100. 00
Sulphur	1. 18	2. 52
Phosphorus	0. 003	0. 007
B. T. U. (Wil. Cal.)	14715	

The lower division (Blacksburg) of the Campbells creek bed thickens up in the region of Handley, and becomes a very important coal bed. There is always some "splint" coal near the top and two to four layers of "gas" coal in the seam, separated by thin slates or bones, the main bench of the bed being from three to three and a-half feet thick. The section of this coal given on page 529, near Montgomery, will serve as a type of the bed over a wide region, although frequently there are fewer divisions.

Mr. Fillmore, the mining engineer of Cedar Grove, gives the following as the most common section of this coal:

	Ft.	Ft.
Cannel, thin...		
"Gas" coal...	0. 2	
Bone..	0. 2	4. 8
Splint	1. 2	
"Gas" coal	3. 2	

The following table of analyses reported by Prof. Hite from samples collected by R. W. Edmonds and A. P. Brady, will show the chemical character of this coal in the upper Kanawha region:

BLACKSBURG, NO. 2 GAS COAL, CAMPBELLS CREEK LOWER BED.

Analyses No.	Mois.	V. M.	F. C.	Ash.	Sul.	Phos.	B.T.U.
1................	0. 41	34. 13	57. 36	8. 10	1. 07	0. 055	14323
2................	0. 59	33. 63	62. 59	3. 19	0. 95	0. 054	14985
3................	0. 53	35. 73	55. 17	8. 57	1. 06	0. 005	
4................	0. 61	37. 66	57. 97	3. 76	1. 28	0. 0085	
5................	0. 69	35. 90	61. 13	2. 28	0. 66	0. 014	
6................	0. 53	35. 87	57. 45	6. 15	0. 54	0. 006	
7................	0. 63	37. 74	56. 20	5. 43	0. 60	0. 005	14700
8................	0. 72	36. 65	60. 95	1. 68	0. 76	0. 0035	15183
9................	0. 47	35. 77	60. 22	3. 54	1. 25	0. 0135	14915
10...............	0. 47	35. 41	58. 47	5. 65	1. 06	0. 004	14637
11...............	0. 74	34. 66	58. 57	6. 03	1. 30	0. 032	14554
12...............	0. 70	35. 33	58. 59	7. 38	0. 69	0. 010	
13...............	0. 51	31. 93	57. 07	10. 49	0. 71	0. 012	
14...............	0. 62	35. 34	58. 18	5. 86	2. 48	0. 008	14674
15...............	0. 71	34. 04	61. 79	3. 46	0. 98	0. 017	
16...............	0. 63	34. 39	60. 44	4. 54	1. 34	0. 033	
17...............	0. 63	35. 47	57. 14	6. 76	1. 64	0. 012	14462
18...............	0. 63	35. 63	55. 50	8. 24	1. 23	0. 005	
19...............	0. 59	33. 39	52. 57	13. 45	1. 04	0. 007	
20...............	0. 43	33. 58	60. 80	5. 19	1. 84	0. 004	14694
21...............	0. 37	34. 81	60. 39	4. 43	1. 77	0. 0055	14669

LOCATION OF SAMPLES.

Analyses No.

1. Splint coal, from Harewood mine, Harewood, Fayette county, W. Va., K. &. H. C. & C. Co.

2. Gas coal, from Harewood mine, Harewood, Fayette county, K. &. H. C. & C. Co.

3. Splint coal, from Long Acre mine, Long Acre, Fayette county, W. Va., K. & H. C. &. C. Co.

4. Gas coal, from Long Acre mine, Long Acre, Fayette county, W. Va., K. & H. C. & C. Co.

5. Gas coal, from Carbondale mine, one mile northeast of

Cannelton, Fayette county, K. & H. C. & C. Co.

6. Splint coal, from Carbondale mine, K. & H. C. &. C. Co.

7. Splint coal, from National mine, one and one-half miles northeast of Cannelton, K. & H. C. &. C. Co.

8. Gas coal, from Carbondale mine, 1½ miles northeast of Cannelton, K. &. H. C. & C.. Co.

9. Gas coal, from No. 2 mine, one and one-half miles northeast of Cannelton, Cannelton C. Co.

10. Splint coal, from No. 2 mine, one and one-half miles northeast of Cannelton, Cannelton C. Co.

11. From No. 2 mine, Crescent, Fayette county, W. R. Johnson.

12. From No. 117 mine, Glen Ferris, Fayette county, K. & H. C. & C. Co.

13. Eureka mine, two miles southeast of Montgomery, Fayette county, Davis-Gordon Co.

14. Digby mine, three-fourths of a mile east of Mt. Carbon, Fayette county, G. K. C. Co.

15. From No. 2 mine, Mt. Carbon, Fayette county, G. K. C. Co.

16. From No. 1 mine, one-half mile up Boomer Br. R. R., Fayette county, Boomer C. & C. Co.

17. Splint coal from Kanawha Gas Coal Co.'s mine, three-fourths of a mile above Cannelton.

18. From Raven mine, at mouth of four-mile of Smithers creek, Fayette county.

19. From No. 2 Edgewater mine, Edgewater, Fayette county, Carver Bros.

20. From No. 2 mine, Eagle, Fayette county, St. Clair C. & C. Co.

21. From Diamond mine, one mile west of Mt. Carbon, Fayette county, Diamond and Forest Hill Colliery Co.

The "gas" divisions of this coal make a very good coke, and some of the Kanawha plants engage in its manufacture as well as the shipment of steam coal from the splinty layers of the bed. The coke at the several plants was sampled by Messrs, Edmonds and Brady (A. P.), and Prof. Hite reports the following results of the analyses:

COKE FROM NO. 2 GAS COAL.

Analyses No.	Mois.	V. M.	F. C.	Ash.	Sul.	Phos.	Coking time.
1................	0.40	1.66	87.26	10.68	0.69	0.0075	72 hours.
2................	0.13	1.95	89.26	8.66	1.05	0.0215	72 "
3................	0.12	1.02	91.53	7.33	0.91	0.0135	72 "
4................	0.15	0.69	86.43	12.73	1.15	0.0750	48 "
5................	0.17	0.87	82.56	16.40	1.04	0.0250	72 "
6................	0.22	1.64	88.59	9.55	1.14	0.0105	72 "
7................	0.14	1.61	84.85	13.40	0.75	0.009	72 "

LOCATION OF SAMPLES.

Analyses
No.

1. From East Bank ovens one-fourth of a mile south of East Bank, Fayette ceunty, 12 ovens.
2. From one and a-half miles northeast of Cannelton, Fayette county, Cannelton Coal Co., 90 ovens.
3. From Carbondale mine, one mile northeast of Cannelton, Fayette county, 50 ovens.
4. From Harewood mine, Harewood, Fayette county, K. & H. C. & C. Co., 80 ovens.
5. Kanawha ovens, Mt. Carbon, Fayette county, G. K. C. Co., 69 ovens.
6. Long Acre ovens, Long Acre, Fayette counto, K. & H. C. & C. Co., 100 ovens.
7. Ansted ovens, Gauley Mt. C. & C. Co., Fayette county, 150 ovens.

The Nos. 4, 5 and 7 samples were evidently not representative, since the corresponding coal analyses do not agree with the high percentages of ash. Also the coal analyses Nos. 13 and 19 are too high in ash to be representative of the coal, as one may see by comparing them with the other analyses.

The "splint" layers appear to be uniformly higher in ash than the "gas" coal divisions of the bed.

The Gauley Mountain Coal Company has a mine in the Campbells creek seam, near Ansted, Fayette county, 1000 feet above the bed of New river, at Hawks Nest, and there R W. Edmonds measured the following section at the "Nova Scotia" mine of the Company:

	Ft. In.	Ft. In.
Coal		1 8
Slate		2 0
Draw slate		0 6
Coal		1 6

```
Slate and coal.................................................................  0   6
Coal ..............................................................................  3   5
                                                                         ____
   Total.......................................................................  9   7
```

Butts run N. 45° W.   Face N. 45° E.
Elevation A. T. 1730 feet.
Greatest rise S. 25° E.
Analysis of sample reported by Prof. Hite as follows:

```
Moisture ....................................................................  0. 89
Volatile matter..........................................................  32. 29
Fixed carbon ............................................................  65. 41
Ash .............................................................................  1. 41
                                                                         _____
Total..........................................................................100. 00

Sulphur ......................................................................  0. 91
Phosphorus...............................................................  0. 003
B. T. U. (Wil. Cal.)..................................................  14951
```

The uppermost bench of this coal appears to represent the "Peerless" member of the Campbells creek bed, with the slate interval thinned down to only two feet. When this interval is thin the coal is taken out, but when it thickens, (as it does to several feet in many portions of the Gauley Mt. Company's mine), this portion of the bed is then abandoned.

A coal bed which appears to be identical with the Campbells creek seam, has been mined to a considerable extent around the town of Summersville, Nicholas county. It occurs at an interval of 140 to 160 feet above the top of a very massive sandstone which looks like the Pottsville, and about 600 feet under the Kanawha black flint.

The bed has the following structure at Alex. McMillan's bank, one mile southwest from the town:

```
                                                   Ft. In.   Ft. In.

Coal, soft...................................................  1   2  ⎤
Slaty coal..................................................  0   5  ⎥
Coal, soft...................................................  2   8  ⎬   4   6
Coal, splinty, hard...................................  0   9  ⎦
```

This is the type of the coal at all of the mines (Jos. A. Alderson's, Mrs. Alderson's, Duffy's, Brown's, Grove's, Remley's, etc.) in the vicinity. There is frequently an inch or two of bony cannel at the top, and the slaty coal, one foot below the top, varies from three to ten inches in thickness. It appears to correspond to the "splint" coal in the upper half of the Blacksburg, or "No.

2 Gas'' coal of the Kanawha valley. The coal in the bottom is usually hard and splinty, or even bony in type.

This coal is also well developed on Bryants branch of Muddlety, northeast from Summersville, where it is stripped out of the run on the land of J. C. P. Duffy, and, with its parting slates, has a thickness of six feet, while fifty to sixty feet higher. is another coal nearly four feet thick, which is mined both by Mr. Duffy and also by Richard Bryant, just above. The higher one may be the Cedar Grove coal. It has two thin parting slates and is a very fair coal.

At Hon. Theo. Horan's bank, near the Thornton school house, on Peters creek, the Summersville coal has the following structure:

	Ft. In.	Ft. In.
Shale, gray		2 0
Cannel, bony	0 3	
Coal, soft	0 10	
Slaty coal	0 5	4 6
Coal, soft	2 6	
Coal, hard	0 6	

The same coal is opened by many farmers along Peters creek, including Curtis Stevenson, Charles Drennen, Jane Johnson and many others, where it has substantially the structure given above. It is a bright, rich fuel, and will prove quite valuable when Nicholas county secures shipping facilities.

The Campbells creek coal has a fine development on the upper waters of Coal and Guyandot rivers, including their tributaries in Boone, Lincoln, Logan, and southern Wyoming counties. The bed is multiple in that region, as everywhere else, and exhibits a fairly good thickness along the Spruce Fork of Little Coal river, where the writer has traced it from the mouth of Laurel to where it goes under, on the Garland branch of Spruce. The coal exhibits the following structure at the mouth of Ben's branch, a short distance above the mouth of the Laurel Fork of Spruce:

	Ft. In.	Ft. In.
Coal, blossom		
Shales		5 0
Coal		4 0
Fireclay		1 0
Coal, visible		1 0
Concealed to Spruce		55 0

Near the mouth of Rockhouse branch, this coal exhibits the following structure on the land of Sydney Chambers:

	Ft. In.	Ft. In.
Coal		0 5
Shales		5 0
Coal		0 2
Fireclay		1 8
Coal		5 8

The main bench has only one bony layer, two inches thick, near the middle, and is very good coal.

Near the mouth of Old House run the following exposure shows the relations of this coal to the thin coals above:

		Ft. In.
Sandstone, massive		20 0
Coal		1 0
Shale and concealed		35 0
Coal		0 2
Shales and fireclay		5 6
Coal	5 0	}
Fireclay	1 3	} 7 11
Coal	1 8	}
Concealed and sandstone to Spruce		75 0

Near the mouth of Whites Trace branch this coal has the following structure:

	Ft. In.	Ft. In.
Coal	3 4	}
Fireclay	0 4	} 6 10
Coal	3 2	}

When this bed emerges on Buffalo creek, a tributary of the Guyandot, which heads up against the Garland branch of Spruce, it attains a good development, as exhibited by the following section, measured two miles below the mouth of Mud Lick run:

		Ft. In.	Ft. In.
Soft shales			2 0
Coal	coal	4 0	}
	fireclay	0 3	}
	coal	0 1	} 8 0
	fireclay	0 2	}
	coal	3 6	}
Concealed sandstone and shales to Buffalo creek			110 0

At the mouth of Buffalo creek, which puts into the Guyandot

about ten miles above Logan Court House, the following section was measured on the land of Dr. Doss:

	Ft. In.	Ft. In.
Massive sandstone, and concealed from summit 275	o	
Coal, large blossom, *Stockton?*		
Concealed and massive sandstone.........................210	o	
Sandy shales 55	o	
Coal, Winifrede? 4	10	
Concealed 2	o	
Sandstone, massive 35	o	
Concealed 20	o	
Sandstone, massive....................................... 40	o	
Shales and concealed...................................... 10	o	
Sandstone, massive....................................... 80	o	
Concealed 20	o	
Sandstone, massive....................................... 65	o	
Sandy shales.. 5	o	

Coal, Campbells creek { coal .... 3 0 ; fireclay .... 0 8 ; coal, visible .... 1 0 } 4 8

Concealed and massive sandstone 190	o	
Coal, Eagle?.. 1	8	
Sandy shales and sandstone............................... 25	o	
Coal .... o	6	
Dark, sandy shales to level of Buffalo creek............ 15	o	

In the region of Oceana, Wyoming county, the Campbells creek coal is known as the "Cook," or "Big bed," and it crops high up in the mountains, 700 to 800 feet above the level of the Clear Fork of the Guyandot.

Near the mouth of Cow creek, above Oceana, this coal has an elevation of 2110 feet above tide, on the land of George Cook, according to the levels of the Guyandot Coal Land Association, and there it exhibits the following structure:

	Ft. In.	Ft. In.
Sandstone 5	o	

Coal, Cedar Grove { coal .... 2 0 ; slate .... 0 1 ; coal .... 0 6 } 2 7

Concealed 80	o	
Shale, gray.. 6	o	

Coal, Campbells creek { coal .... 2 2 ; shale .... 1 2 ; coal .... 1 6 ; shale .... 1 2 ; coal .... 4 0 } 10 0

Concealed, with massive sandstone, to level of Guyandot river, in the Pottsville series 825	o	

The Guyandot Coal Land Association, under the supervision of Capt. M. A. Miller, its chief engineer of Richmond, Va., and the late Major Jed. Hotchkiss, its general manager, made a large number of openings on the Campbells creek bed, in Wyoming county, in 1884-5, all of which were placed at the writer's disposal through the courtesy of Major Hotchkiss. One of these, on Toney's Fork, above Oceana, will illustrate the type of the Campbells creek bed on that stream, as follows:

	Ft. In.	Ft. In.
Slate		
Coal		0 7
Slate		6 6
Coal	1 7	
Slate	0 2	
Coal	1 4	
Slate	2 11	12 10
Coal	4 0	
Slate	0 8	
Coal	1 2	

Elevation above tide at base 2266 feet.

Capt Miller adds this note to his Toney Fork work:

"On the line of the St. Albans and Boone County R. R. Survey, which crosses the Guyandot mountains at Walnut Gap, the "Big" (Campbells creek) coal occurs on the north side (Little Coal river) of the mountains, at 1718 feet A. T., and what I believe to be the same coal occurs on the south side along the waters of Toneys Fork, at an elevation of 2210 feet A. T., a rise of 492 feet in a distance of a mile and two thirds, or approximately 300 feet to the mile in a direction S. 36° E."

Crane Fork of Guyandot (Clear Fork) puts into the latter seven miles above the mouth of Toneys Fork, heading up against the corners of Raleigh, Boone, and Wyoming counties, and on the Rock Lick branch of Crane, Mr. Miller measured the following interesting section:

		Ft. In.	Ft. In.
Slate			
Coal			1 0
Slate			10 0
Coal, Campbells creek	coal	1 8	
	slate	0 6	
	coal	1 2	
	slate	0 4	13 9
	coal	4 0	
	slate	5 3	
	coal	0 10	
Interval			157 0

		Ft. In.	Ft. In.
Coal	coal	1 7	
	slate	1 4	
	coal	0 2	
	slate	0 8	
	coal	0 4	7 7
	slate	0 4	
	coal	0 6	
	slate	1 8	
	coal	1 0	
Interval			65 0
Coal, Eagle	coal	3 4	
	slate	0 4	5 4
	coal	2 0	

Base of Eagle coal 2380 feet A. T.   Capt Miller adds:

"This middle coal occupies the position which elsewhere in Wyoming county, a coal occurs only twelve to fourteen inches thick. "

In Ramp hollow of Crane Fork the Campbells creek coal has the following section:

	Ft. In.	Ft. In.
Coal	1 8	
Slate	0 2	
Coal	1 5	
Slate	1 1	11 1
Coal	4 6	
Slate	1 0	
Coal	1 3	

Base of coal above tide, 2640 feet.

Another opening in Pole hollow of Crane Fork district, exhibits the following structure for the Campbells creek coal, as measured by Capt. Miller:

	Ft. In.	Ft. In.
Coal	2 8	
Slate	2 0	
Coal	3 7	
Slate	1 4	13 0
Coal	0 9	
Slate	2 0	
Coal	0 8	

The uppermost division of the coal in this section appears to represent the Peerless member of the Kanawha valley.

On the right hand fork of Upper Gap branch, near Oceana, the Campbells creek coal has been opened on the land of Thomas Cook, at an elevation of 700 feet above the Guyandot, and there it exhibits practically the same section as those already given for this region, the main bench of the coal being about four feet thick, and very rich and pure looking.

On the waters of Big Huff creek, north from Oceana, the Campbells creek coal appears to be split into a large number of divisions, none of which are very thick, as shown by the following section, measured near the mouth of Laurel branch:

	Ft. In.	Ft. In.
Shales, dark		10 0
Coal	1 3	
Shale and coal	0 3	
Coal	0 11	
Sandy beds	9 0	
Coal	1 10	18 7
Shale, gray	3 0	
Coal	0 6	
Shale, gray	0 4	
Shale and coal	0 6	
Coal	1 10	

Island creek puts into the Guyandotte river at Logan Court House, and a bed which appears to be identical with the Campbells creek coal has a good development along this stream. An opening in this seam at the mouth of Copperas Fork of Trace Fork of Island creek, shows the following structure according to A. S. Brady:

	Ft. In.	Ft. In.
Black slate		
Coal	0 3	
Slate	0 1	5 10½
Coal	3 6½	

Elevation above tide, 785 feet.

Analysis of sample reported by Prof. Hite as follows:

Moisture	0. 17
Volatile matter	37. 14
Fixed carbon	59.37
Ash	3. 32
Total	100. 00
Sulphur	0. 82

The same coal at the mouth of Mill branch of Island creek exhibits the following structure as measured by A. S. Brady:

                                           Ft. In.   Ft. In.

Slate ....
Coal .... 2 11 ⎫
Slate .... o o¾ ⎬ 6 10¾
Coal .... 3 11 ⎭

Analysis of sample reported by Prof. Hite as follows:

Moisture .... o. 23
Volatile matter 37. 93
Fixed carbon.. .... 58. 62
Ash 3. 22
                                                          ─────────
    Total 100. 00
Sulphur .... o. 76

Mr. Frank Haas, chief chemist for the Fairmont Coal Company, has recently visited the Island creek district and made a few interesting observations on the coals of the region, which he has embodied in the following notes:

"I spent only one day in the Island creek region, and most of my time was taken up in going to and from. Detailed measurements I could not make, because the coal was not opened up sufficiently. At only a few points could I get sectional measurements of the seam, and I did not attempt to construct a column of intervening stratification.

"The principal seam, from an operating standpoint, locally known as the "seven foot" seam, showed the following section about three-fourths of a mile up Stone House branch from its junction with Island creek. My barometer showed the seam to be 100 feet above Island creek at this point:

                                           Ft. In.   Ft. In.

Coal 3   6 ⎫
Clay parting............................... .... o   2 ⎪
Coal .... o   6 ⎪
Clay parting... o   2 ⎬ 7 10½
Coal .... o   7 ⎪
Bone coal.. o   2½⎪
Coal 2   9 ⎭

"This section is the main part of the seam; it was covered with a slate, followed by more coal, the thickness of which I could not determine. This is the one I understood you to say corresponded with the Campbells creek.

"Below this, some fifty feet, a seam, locally known as the "five foot," was seen. At no point was it fully faced up. I saw four feet of it without a parting, and am inclined to believe that it is fully, if not more, than the reported (five feet) thickness.

"Fifty feet, more or less, below this, a seam was exposed at the lower end of the creek, at several places, with the following section:

	Ft. In.	Ft. In.
Coal	I 5	
Clay parting..	o 7	
Coal	o 4	
Clay parting...	o 7	6 5
Coal	o 10	
Cannel	o 6	
Coal	2 2	

"While these partings and cannel coal were present in all openings, they were not uniform in thickness.

"Above the "seven foot" seam, but within 100 feet, two more seams were found—the top seam, about four feet thick, was rather a soft coal without a parting; the lower, a three foot seam, was not examined.

"Finally, near the top of the mountain, 740 feet above the "five foot" seam, a ten-foot, four-inch seam was found; it had not been opened up and was badly weathered. I could see that there were no thick partings; but but cannot say whether any small partings were present or not.

"This coal lies between two heavy ledges of sandstone, both of which form the peculiar weathered effects seen on top of all the mountains in this neighborhood."

The middle, or "five foot" seam, is probably the Brownstown or Powellton coal, while the one near the mouth of Island creek, with the cannel in its basal division, is most probably the Eagle seam of the Kanawha valley, since, according to A. S. Brady, it lies 105 feet below the "five foot" seam.

A few miles west from Island creek, we come to the Dingess mining region, at the head of Twelve Pole river, in Mingo county. Here a coal bed, which appears to be identical with the Campbells creek coal, has been mined quite extensively and shipped over the N. & W. R. R., both east and west, as a steam coal.

The Pearl Coal and Coke Company, and the Camp Branch Coal ond Coke Company, both mine this Dingess seam near the station of that name, and there Mr. A. P. Brady made the following measurements at the respective mines:

	Pearl.	Camp Branch.
	Ft. In.	Ft. In.
Coal	I 2	I 3
Bone	o 2	o 2
Coal	2 4	I 10
Bone	o I	o 3
Coal	o 10	o 8
Totals...........	4 7	4 2

Elevation above tide: Pearl, 1000 feet; Camp Branch, 1030 feet.

ANALYSES.

	Pearl.	Camp Branch.
Moisture	1.17	0.65
Volatile matter	35.67	38.60
Fixed carbon	53.96	51.22
Ash	9.20	9.53
Totals	100.00	100.00
Sulphur	0.67	3.61
Phosphorus	0.006	0.005
B. T. U. (Wil. Cal.)	13594	13497

Two miles north from Dingess, the Freeport Coal Mining Company operates a coal which Mr. Brady (A. P.) thinks is the same as the one at Dingess, but it has a very different structure, as witness the following section measured there by Mr. Brady:

	Ft.	In.	Ft.	In.
Sandstone				
Coal	3	0		
Shale	1	2		
Coal	1	8	9	5
Bone	1	3		
Coal	2	4		

Analysis of sample reported by Prof. Hite as follows:

Moisture	1.30
Volatile matter	34.49
Fixed carbon	54.04
Ash	10.17
Total	100.00
Sulphur	0.56
Phosphorus	0.0055
B. T. U. (Wil. Cal.)	13486

The position of this coal is not certain since the Warfield anticlinal crosses Twelve Pole at Dingess, and the dips on either side of it are quite rapid.

The Campbells creek coal is most probably the same as the Warfield coal of Kentucky, which has also been mined on the West Virginia side of Tug river opposite Warfield, where it shows the following structure:

		Ft. In.	Ft. In.
Coal		o 4	
Slate..............................		o 10	5 2
Coal		4 0	

It is probably this same coal that has been mined at Dunlow, in Wayne county, where it is only three feet thick, with a bony layer near the center.

The Campbells creek coal has not been certainly identified along the upper portion of Tug river, after it goes under water level on its southeast dip above Warfield, Ky., but there is a coal fifty feet above the N. & W. track, one mile below Devon, which appears to come at the horizon of this bed. It has the following structure:

		Ft. In.	Ft. In.
Coal, soft...		I o	
Coal, splinty ....•...........		o 10	
Coal, soft...		o 6	3 6
Bone..		o 2	
Coal .... ·		I o	

This coal (if the Campbells creek) soon passes under the railroad track to the north, and is not visible again so far as known, until brought up by the Warfield anticlinal

As already stated, the Campbells creek coal, on the basis of the Kanawha series being simply the expanded Allegheny, would correlate with the lower Kittanning bed of the latter series.

THE BROWNSTOWN COAL.

In the sections given along the Kanawha river, a coal bed is frequently present nearly midway between the Campbells creek coal and the Eagle coal below, and for lack of any other suitable term it has generally been named the Brownstown coal, from its occurrance near the village of that name in Kanawha county. It does not appear to attain any economic importance along the Kanawha, however, unless a bed known as the Powellton seam, mined by the Mt. Carbon Co., Lt., should turn out to be this bed.

It is also possible that the "Five-foot" vein mentioned by Mr. Haas, page 582, as occurring next below the Campbells creek bed on Island creek, Logan county, may be this same coal.

Two samples of this Island creek coal were collected by A. S.

Brady, one at the mouth of Trace Fork, where the bed is four feet, and another near the mouth of Ellis Fork, where the coal is four and a-half feet thick with no slate nor bone. Prof. Hite reports the analysis of the samples as follows:

	Trace.	Ellis.
Moisture	0.26	0.27
Volatile matter	36.27	37.51
Fixed carbon	56.82	51.65
Ash	6.65	10.57
Totals	100.00	100.00
Sulphur	1.72	1.26

These analyses reveal a coal of good quality, except that they carry slightly more sulphur than the average coal of the Kanawha series.

THE CANNELTON (STOCKTON) LIMESTONE.

The interval between the Campbells creek coal and the Eagle coal is occupied by sandstones and shales, with the exception of the coal bed noted above, and a thin bed of impure limestone which appears to be quite persistent in the Kanawha valley. It was once manufactured into cement at Cannelton, Fayette county, by Mr. Stockton, and hence it is often termed locally the "Stockton" cement bed. It is usually quite silicious, frequently exhibits the "cone-in-cone" structure, and is non-fossiliferous, so far as the writer knows. Its usual place is seventy-five to one hundred feet below the Campbells creek coal, and forty-five to fifty feet above the Eagle seam. If the Eagle coal represents the Clarion bed of the Allegheny series, then the Cannelton limestone would correspond to the Ferriferous limestone of western Pennsylvania.

In this interval between the Campbells creek and Eagle coals there is also an important sandstone deposit which comes only a short distance under the Campbells creek coal, having frequently been quarried for use in building the Government locks and dams on the Kanawha river between Brownstown and Montgomery, and is generally known as the Brownstown sandstone. It is usually twenty-five to thirty-five feet in thickness, and makes an excellent building stone.

THE EAGLE COAL, NO. 1 GAS.

At several points along the Kanawha river, where the Campbells creek coal is 150 or more feet above water level, there are "reports" of the finding of a coal of good quality in foundation piers of bridges, low down in the silt covered valleys. Whether there is any valuable coal at this "horizon" reported in the beds of Rush, Lens, and other streams, where crossed by the C. & O. R. R. bridges, and their foundation piers, is not certainly known, but above Montgomery, the southward rise of the strata soon carries the Campbells creek, or "No. 2 Gas" coal, high above water level, and at 120 to 150 feet under it, we find another very important coal, which was first mined on a commercial scale in the Kanawha valley at Eagle station, two miles above Montgomery, by Mr. Weyant, who named it the Eagle coal early in the '80s, a term it has ever since borne, except that occasionally it is locally called "No. 1 Gas" coal, since it is the lowest bed of the Kanawha series that has been mined along the Kanawha river.

The Eagle seam is a soft coal of the "gas" type, as compared with the "splint" coals in the upper half of the Kanawha series, having the columnar structure of typical coking coal without any splinty layers whatever. Its physical character very much resembles the Pottsville coals of New river, and hence we find it making excellent coke, as well as a good steam coal. It contains less volatile matter, but more fixed carbon than the Campbells creek, or "No. 2 Gas" coal above it, with practically the same percentages of ash, sulphur and phosphorus.

This coal first comes up to the level of the C. & O. R. R. a short distance above Montgomery, where it is mined by the Coal Valley Mining Company, in whose "Straughan" mine A. P. Brady made the following measurements:

	Ft.	In.	Ft.	In.
Sandstone				
Slate	5	9	9	0
Coal	0	2½		
Bone coal	0	1½		
Coal	0	8		
Slate	0	2	3	3½
Coal, soft	0	9		
Coal, hard	0	8½		
Coal	0	8		

Butts run N. 77° E.   Face N. 13° W.   Elevation above tide, 635 feet.

One-half mile south from this, the same (Eagle) coal is mined at Crescent station by W. R. Johnston, and at his No. 1 mine, A. P. Brady made the following measurements:

	Ft.	In.	Ft.	In.
Slate				
Coal	1	1½		
Slate	0	3	3	7
Coal	2	2½		

Butts run N. 77° E.   Face N. 17° W.   Elevation above tide, 683 feet.

The coal is coked as well as shipped for steam coal.

The Carver Bros. operate this coal at Edgewater, two-thirds of a mile above Crescent, and there A. P. Brady made the following measurements at their No. 1 mine:

	Ft.	In.	Ft.	In.
Sandstone				
Slate	1	6		
Coal	0	4		
Slate	0	0½		
Coal	1	1	4	8½
Slate	0	3		
Coal	3	0		

Butts run N. 77° E.   Face N. 18° W.   Elevation above tide, 709 feet.

The St. Clair Coal and Coke Company has mines at Eagle, one-half mile above Crescent, and there, at Mine No. 1, the type locality for the Eagle coal, A. P. Brady made this measurement:

	Ft.	In.	Ft.	In.
Sandstone				
Draw slate...				
Coal	1	4		
Fireclay	0	3		
Coal	0	2	4	9
Slate	0	4		
Coal	2	8		

Butts run N. 77° E.   Face N. 13° W.   Elevation above tide, 836 feet.

The greatest rise is S. 50° E., in each of these four mines from Montgomery to Crescent.

Boomer branch puts into the north bank of the Kanawha one mile above Eagle, and about one mile and a-half up the branch, the Boomer Coal and Coke Company has mines, where R. W. Edmonds made the following measurements:

	Ft. In.	Ft. In.
Sandstone		
Draw slate.............................	0 3	
Coal	3 11	
Slate	0 3	6 2
Coal	2 0	

Butts run N. and S.   Face E. and W.   Elevation 1050 feet above tide.

This coal rises quite rapidly to the southeast, and when we come to the Vulcan mine of the Mt. Carbon Company, Limited, on Armstrong creek, three miles south of Powellton, the elevation is 1600 feet above tide, and the coal has the following structure, according to A. P. Brady:

	Ft. In.	Ft. In.
Sandstone		
Draw slate............................:......................	1- 20 0
Bone	0 5	
Coal	2 4	
Slate	0 3	6 6
Coal	3 6	

Butts run N. 77° E.   Face N. 13° W.

The analyses of the samples collected from each of these six mines on the Eagle coal, are reported by Prof. Hite as follows:

	Mois.	V. M.	F. C.	Ash.	Sul.	Phos.	B. T. U.
Coal Valley..........	0. 86	32. 27	56. 82	10. 05	0. 85	.017	14172
W. R. Johnson..........	0. 97	33. 36	60. 90	4. 77	0. 85	.009	14671
Carver Bros	0. 71	32. 00	60. 12	7. 17	1. 00	.009	14422
St. Clair C. & C. Co..	0. 81	31. 66	61. 36	6. 17	1. 06	.017	14422
Boomer C. & C. Co....	0. 79	32. 90	61. 05	5. 26	0. 76	.009	14933
Mt. Carbon C. Co.,Lt	0. 71	31. 38	64. 37	3. 54	0. 75	.004	14997

This Eagle coal has been coked very successfully at several points in the Kanawha valley, and samples of coke taken by A. P. Brady are reported by Prof. Hite to have the following composition:

COKE (EAGLE SEAM.)

Analyses No.	Mois.	V. M.	F. C.	Ash.	Sul.	Phos.	Coking time.
1	0.21	1.76	81.37	16.66	0.76	.020	72 hours.
2	0.17	0.87	84.71	14.25	0.83	.020	"
3	0.20	1.39	84.64	13.77	1.24	.0125	"
4	0.05	0.64	91.49	7.82	0.72	.0013	"

LOCATION OF SAMPLES.

Analysis No.

1. From W. R. Johnson's ovens, Crescent, Fayette county, W. Va.
2. From Carver Bros.' ovens, Edgewater, Fayette county, W. Va.
3. From St. Clair Co.'s ovens, Fayette county, W. Va.
4. From Mt. Carbon Co.'s ovens, Powellton, Fayette county, W. Va.

The first three samples appear to be higher in ash than the corresponding coal analyses would warrant, but it is probably due to the fact that some fine slate particles get into the screenings which are used in the ovens.

Mr. E. E. Fillmore, of the K. & H. C. & C. Co., Cedar Grove, gives the following as the average structure of the Eagle, or "No. 1 Gas" coal, on the north side of the Kanawha river:

	Ft.	Ft.
Gas coal	0.3	
"Niggerhead"	0.1	
Gas coal	1.4	
Slate	0.1	5.0
Gas coal	0.3	
Slate	0.3	
Gas coal	2.5	

There is probably a large area of this coal around the southeastern crop of the Kanawha series, that will prove sufficiently pure and thick to warrant mining operations.

It is probably this coal that is mined along the left branch of Holly river, from Mollahan's mill to near Hacker's Valley P. O., where it varies in thickness from two and a-half to four feet, and always has a slate or bone near the middle. It is this coal at Anderson's mill on Houdon, at Dr. Elliott's and Henry Spies', near the head of Fall run, where it is mined for use in the engines of the narrow guage railroads which cross from Pickens to the heads of Elk and Holly rivers.

This coal would also correspond to the "Gimmel" bed on the Buckhannon river, three miles below Pickens.

In Wyoming county and adjacent regions, there is a coal bed known as the "coking" seam that, with its parting slates, has a thickness of five to six feet, which corresponds to the Eagle bed. It has been opened on Crane Fork of the Clear Fork of the Guyandot, by Captain M. A. Miller of the Guyandot Land Association, and its structure is given on page 579 of this volume. The interval between the Campbells creek seam and what appears to be the Eagle bed in Wyoming county, has increased by nearly 100 feet over that found on the Kanawha river, since the section in question shows 235 feet from the base of one to the base of the other, but as this is in the direction in which all other intervals thicken, the result is what would be expected, and is no argument against identity.

On Upper Mill Hollow of Crane Fork, this same coal has the following structure, according to Captain Miller:

	Ft. In.	Ft. In.
Olive slate		5 0
Coal	3 2	
Slate	0 3	5 6
Coal	3 0	

Elevation 2,340 feet A. T.

About four miles north from Oceana, at the mouth of Dingess branch of Big Huff creek, this same coal has been exploited by Captain Miller, where it exhibits the following structure:

	Ft. In.	Ft. In.
Coal	2 5	
Shale	0 3	3 11
Coal	1 3	

About 200 yards farther up Big Huff creek this coal exhibits the following structure:

		Ft. In.	Ft. In.
Shales			15 0
Coal	coal	2 1	
	shales	0 9	4 0
	coal	1 2	

The coal has a columnar structure very much resembling that of the Eagle coal on the Kanawha, and at this point lies about 200 feet under the Campbells creek bed, which has been opened in the hills above. The coal comes twenty to thirty feet above water level at the mouth of Dingess branch.

The coal, with the cannel in its lower bench, noted by Mr. Haas (see page 583 above) near the mouth of Island creek, Logan county, would most probably be identical with the Eagle seam of the Kanawha valley.

On the Tug river, one-half mile below Devon, Mingo county, a coal bed, which may possibly represent the Eagle seam, is exposed in the cuts of the N. & W. R. R. as follows:

		Ft. In.	Ft. In.
Sandstone, massive...			
Shales, gray, sandy			10 0
Coal	coal	2 0	
	slate	0 3	
	coal	0 4	5 4
	fireclay...	2 0	
	coal	0 10	
Fireclay and shales...			3 0
Sandstone, massive to railroad..................................			15 0

A short distance below this the same coal has the following structure:

		Ft. In.	Ft. In.
Shales			10 0
Coal	coal	1 8	
	shale	0 4	
	coal	0 6	3 8
	fireclay...	0 8	
	coal	0 6	
Fireclay			1 6
Sandstone, massive, to water level			40 0

This coal passes under the N. & W. R. R. track at the 448th mile post from Norfolk.

Southward from this point the rocks rise rapidly, and near the mouth of Knox creek, the blossom of this coal is high in the hills, 500 feet or more above the level of Tug river.

THE LITTLE EAGLE COAL.

At about twenty feet below the Eagle coal on the Kanawha, there is generally present a very pure seam of soft coking coal, but only eighteen to twenty inches thick, and hence has never been mined in a commercial way. In Wyoming and adjoining regions across to Tug river in Mingo county, there is also a soft, very pure, single-bedded coal, twenty-four to twenty-seven inches thick at fifty-five to sixty-five feet below the "coking" seam, the interval having increased, like that between the Campbells creek and Eagle coals above, by the development of massive sandstones, and hence if the "coking" seam is the Eagle, then this next lower one would represent the Little Eagle coal.

THE EAGLE LIMESTONE, "BLACK MARBLE."

Below the Little Eagle coal in the Kanawha valley, no other coal beds are visible in the 250 to 300 feet of shales and sandstones which intervene down to the top of the Pottsville series, although as we pass eastward some lower, thin coals appear to come in, as shown in the section of Major Page between Ansted and Hawks Nest, and the same is true of the section in Wyoming county. A very interesting bed of fossiliferous, impure, "cone-in-cone" limestone occurs, however, at an interval of seventy-five feet below the Eagle coal at Eagle, Fayette county, and the bed in question has been designated from that locality. The local name for the rock is "Black Marble," since it has a very dark color, and as it often occurs in the midst of bituminous slates, its mottled "cone-in-cone" structure in contrast with the latter, has suggested the name in question. The limestone itself contains marine fossils, and the enclosing shales are crowded with them, all of the common, Coal Measures type, so far as a cursory examination could determine. This limestone and its enclosing shales occur on Twenty-mile creek, and along Gauley river at some localities, but outside of these points the writer has not recognized this horizon, so that the deposit is probably confined to the Kanawha region.

AGE OF THE KANAWHA SERIES.

Mr. David White has investigated the fossil flora of the Kanawha series, and the results of his careful studies have already been given, pages 326-7, with reference to the highest member (Stockton coal) of the series, but his results in the study of the lower group from the Cedar Grove bed to the Eagle inclusive, remain to be considered. On pages 157-168, Bulletin of the Geological Society of America, Vol. XI, March, 1900, Mr. White has given a very interesting account of the flora in this lower portion of the Kanawha series, which is here quoted as follows:

DIVISION OF THE KANAWHA COALS INTO TWO GROUPS.

COMPOSITION OF THE GROUPS.

"In their discussion of the type section of the Kanawha formation, Messrs. Campbell and Mendenhall * have found it most convenient to divide the coals of the formation into two groups

" 'The lower group includes the Ansted, Eagle, Gas, Cedar Grove, Tunnel, Peerless, Brownstown, Campbells creek, and the associated thin seams. The principal coal seams of the upper group are the Stockton or Crown Hill, the Coalburg, and the Kanawha Mining or Winifrede seams. Between these two groups are about 300 feet of practically barren strata.' "

"The correlations of the developments in the upper group have led to little or no differences of opinion, the Winifrede coal being generally regarded as identical with the Kanawha Mining seam. With reference to the identities of the coals in the lower division, there is, however, some difference of opinion, as may be seen by a consultation of the two memoirs just cited. With these differences we have, at present, little to do, since in these papers the floras are treated only in a most general way, and from a broad point of view. I shall, therefore, not here consider the correlation of the individual coals, though I may add that the final systematic treatment of the fossil plants, of the several horizons, promises to throw light on a number of points now in dispute.

"So far as concerns the stratigraphic positions of the coals in the lower group, it is sufficient for present purposes to state that the Eagle, the lowest workable coal, is about 330 feet above the base of the formation as that boundary has, largely on lithologic evidence, been traced. The Gas coal is about 155 feet above the Eagle coal. There is doubt as to the equivalence of the Gas coal, as well as to the relations of the other coals of the lower group to it. For paleontologic reasons, I am slightly disposed to regard the Tunnel coal, mined at Cedar Grove, as identical with the Gas coal. It certainly cannot be far from the same stratigraphic level. The Cedar Grove coal is but 125 feet above the Tunnel bed. Twenty-five feet above the Cedar Grove bed, another one-foot coal is found. It is important to note that a slope from the latter to the Tunnel coal cuts no less than five coals, each of which is from one to four feet in thickness. The painstaking stratigraphic studies, carried on by Messrs. Campbell and Mendenhall, show † that within the interval of 140 feet, traversed by this slope, there must fall the horizons of the Gas, Peerless, Brownstown, and Campbells creek coals, as well as the Cedar Grove and Tunnel beds.

"Within the relatively short period represented by the deposition of the 140 feet of the formation, no marked floral changes are to be expected, and for the purpose of broad correlation the local floras may be combined. I

---

*Geologic section along the New and Kanawha rivers in West Virginia. Seventh Ann. Rept. U. S Geol. Survey, part 2, 1896, pp. 473-511, pls xxxix-xlix.

†Op. cit., p. 502.

may add, however, that on account of certain peculiarities and minor phases of the local floras, I am inclined to place the roof shales of the Peerless coal not far from the level of the Gas coal, or the Tunnel bed.   To the interval between the latter and the Cedar Grove, I would refer the coals mined at Ansted and Cotton hill.   They are, perhaps, most closely related, paleontologically, to the Cedar Grove coal. ''

FLORAS OF THE LOWER GROUP OF COALS.

Localities.—''The roof shales of the principal coals in the lower group along the Kanawha river, usually contain abundant carbonized plant remains, which are beautifully impressed.   As representative of the floras of the principal coal horizons of the lower group of coals, collections will be cited from the following localities * along the Kanawha river:

1.   ''Six feet below the Eagle coal at Crescent (Cresc. E.) and from the roof of the Eagle coal at the Eagle mine (Eag. E.), and at St. Clair (St. C. E.)

2.   ''Five feet below the Gas coal at Forest hill (F. H. G.) mine near Edgewater; also from the roof of the same coal at the Diamond mine (Diam. G.) one mile below Mount Carbon; at Crescent ¡Cr. G.), and two mines near the mouth of Morris creek (M. C. G.)

3.   ''Tunnel coal in slope at Cedar Grove ¡C. G. T.) and at the mouth of Kelleys creek (K. C. T.)

4.   ''Roof shales of the Peerless coal at Peerless (P.P.); from a drift one-half mile below Cedar Grove (C. G. P.) Little fork of Slaughter creek (Sl. P.); the Black Diamond mine near Lewiston (B. D.P.); shaft at the Monarch mine (Mon. P) near Peabody; as probably coming not far from the same horizon we may include the fossils from the roof shales at Handley (Hand.) and the roadside near the incline at the Black Cat mine (B. C.)

5.   ''Roof of the Cedar Grove coal at Cedar Grove ¡C. G. C.), Kelleys creek, below the mouth of Hurricane branch (H.C. G.); the Big Mountain mine, near the mouth of Kelleys creek (K. C. G.) East Bank (E.C.G.), Black Cat (Bl.C.G.)and from the roof of a coal supposed to be the Cedar Grove seam at the Riverside mine opposite Crown Hill (R.C. G.)

6.   ''The coal mined at Ansted (Anst.) and Cotton hill (C. H.) also belongs to the lower group.

''The greater portion of the ferns accompanying the lower group of the Kanawha coals, consists either of species not yet described from our American Coal Measures, or of phases and varieties clearly different from the familiar or typical forms.   A part of the flora is composed of the survivors of the floras in the upper portion of the Pottsville; that is Sewell and Fayette formations. †   As neither the latter, nor the floras of the Kanawha forma-

---

*In this paper only the localities typical of the coal bearing horizons will be reviewed.

†Campbell and Mendenhall, op. cit., pp. 494, 497.

tion are yet completely elaborated systematically, the identifications recorded below must be considered as tentative, or often comparative, and subject
to revision in the full systematic report on the floras of the two formations,
which is now in preparation.

Plants at the horizon of the Eagle coal. —"As indicating the frequent
occurrence of the Pottsville survivors, or of modified forms of Pottsville
species, as high as the Eagle coal in the Kanawha formation, I have designated such species with an asterisk in the following list † of plants from the
horizon of that coal. "

Name.	Locality.
Eremopteris n. sp*.	Eag. E.
" cf. *lincolniana* D. W.*	St. C. E.
Pseudopecopteris trifoliolata (Artis)	Cresc. E. , Eag. E., St. C. E.
Mariopteris muricata (Schloth.) Zeill*	Eag. E., St. C. E.
" *nervosa* (Brongn.)Zeill	Eag. E.
" *acuta* (Brongn.) Zeill	Cresc. E., Eag. E., St. C. E.
" *inflata* (Newb.)*	Eag. E.
Sphenopteris spinosa Goepp. *	Eag. E., St. C. E.
" *furcata* Brongn. * (small)	Cresc. E.
" *linkii* Goepp. *	Cresc. E.
" cf. *dubuissonis* Brongn. [Lesq.]	St. C. E.
" *tracyana* Lx. *?	Eag. E.
" *schatzlarensis* Stur.?	Cresc. E., St. C. E.
" cf. *microcarpa* Lx. *	Eag. E., St. C. E.
Pecopteris sp. cf. *integra* Andra.	Cresc. E.
Alethopteris decurrens Artis.	Cresc. E.
" *serlii* (Brongn.) Goepp.	Eag. E., St. C. E.
Neuropteris cf. *zeilleri* Pot.*	Cresc. E.
" cf. *flexuosa* Sternb. ‡	Eag. E., St. C. E.
Calamites ramosus Artis.	St. C. E
Asterophyllites minutus Andr. *	Cresc. E.
" *rigidus* Sternb.	Eag. E.
Annularia ramosa Weiss	Cresc. E., St. C. E.
" *acicularis* (Dn.) Ren. *	Cresc. E., Eag. E.
Calamostachys ramosus Weiss.	St. C. E.
Sphenophyllum furcatum Lx.* (slender)	Cresc. E., Eag. E.
" *cuneifolium* (Sternb.) Zeill. (lax form.)*	Eag. E., St. C. E.

---

†Although the list is hardly complete, it shows approximately the proportions of the zonal elements.

‡The plant in hand approaches very closely to the Old World type,
though it is specifically different from the forms from the Anthracite and
Northern bituminous basins identified under the same name.

Lepidodendron sp. cf. *dichotomum* Sternb?...... Cresc. E., Eag. E.

"   *obovatum* Sternb. .... Eag. E.

Bothrodendron n. sp* ....……......... St. C. E.

Lepidostrobus variabilis L. & H............……...... Eag E., St. C. E.

Lepidophyllum campbellianum Lx*............... Eag. E., St. C. E.

Rhabdocarpos sulcatus Goepp. and Bein.. ...... Eag E.

"A comparison of the Eagle flora with the flora of the Clarion group (p. 149) shows but a very small percentage of identical elements in common. Most important is the total absence, at or below the Eagle horizon in the Kanawha formation, of the everywhere common and characteristic species which, in the Allegheny series, range from the Brookville coal upward. This disparity is the more striking since the Eagle coal, which has been correlated with the Clarion coal of Northwestern Pennsylvania, is over 300 feet above the top of the Pottsville, as the upper boundary of the latter formation has, by all geologists, been located along the Kanawha river. It may here be remarked, that between the Pottsville series (Fayette, Sewell, Raleigh, etcetera, formations,) of southern West Virginia and the Allegheny series in the typical region, there is hardly a distinct fern species in common,* although, as will later be seen, identical or modified forms of species in the Fayette and Sewell formations, penetrate the entire lower group of the Kanawha. The plants from horizons below the Eagle coal, as, for example, the so-called "black marble at Ansted,† which is correlated by local experts with the Eagle limestone, or in the beds at the mouth of Paint creek, show a much stronger impregnation of Upper Pottsville types. On the other hand, by the time we rise to the Cedar Grove horizon, the Virginian Pottsville fern types have either disappeared almost completely, or they are represented only by well marked modifications.

Plants accompanying the higher coals of the lower group.—"To avoid a large number of lists, the plants from the horizons of the other coals all of which fall in an interval of not over 150 feet in the lower group, will be combined in one list. These horizons are the Gas, Tunnel, and Peerless, which have been regarded by the state geologists‡ as splits of the Lower

---

*The differentation of the Lycopodiales and Equisetales is easily recognizable, though in these groops of plants, which possess less stratigraphic value, it is less marked than in the ferns.

†*Archæopteris* cf. *stricta* Andr.,* *Eremopteris* sp.,* *Mariopteris pygmæa* D. W.,* *Mariopteris muricata* (Schloth.) Zeill.,* *Sphenopteris* cf. *linearis* Brongn. *Pecopteris plumosa* (*serrulata* Hartt),* *Neuropteris*, n. sp.,* *Megalopteris* sp.,* *Calamites approximatus* Brongn., *Asterophyllites minutus* Andr.,* *Annularia cuspidata* Lx.,* *Calamostachys* sp., *Sphenophyllum saxifragæfolium* Sternb. [Lesq.],* *Lepidodendron* cf. *rushvillense* Andr.,* *Lepidostrobus variabilis* L. and H., *Lepidophyllum* sp., *Cardiocarpon cornutum* Dn. ?*

The species marked by the asterisk are closely allied to or identical with species of the Pottsville formation in the type region.

‡L. C. White: Bulletin U. S. Geological Survey, No. 65, page 140.

Kittanning coal of the Allegheny valley; the Cedar Grove, similarly corre-
lated§ with the Middle Kittanning of Pennsylvania; and the Ansted-Cotton
Hill coals."

Name.	Locality.
Eremopteris sp.†	P. P., C.G.P., Hand, Eb. C.G., R. C. G., Anst., C. H.
" cf. *sanveuri* Stur. †	Eb. C. G.
Pseudopecopteris trifoliolata (Artis) Lx......	F. H. G., Tunn. T., P. P. Sl. P., B. D. P., Mon. P., Hand., B. C.
" *obtusiloba* Sternb. var. *dilatata* Lx	Eb. C. G., Bl. C. G., C. H.
Mariopteris muricata (Schloth.) Zeill†	F. H. G., P. P., C. G. P., Sl. P., B. D. P., Mon. P., Hand, C. G. C., H. C. G., Eb. C.G., Bl. C. G., R. C. G., C. H.
" cf. *jacquoti* (Zeill.)†	C. G. C.
" *inflata* Newb. †	Diam. G., P. P. ?, Anst.
" *nervosu* (Brongn.) Zeill.*†........	Diam. G., Eb. C. G., Anst.
" *sphenopteroides* (Lx.) Zeill. n. var.	Eb. C. G.
" *acuta* (Brongn.) Zeill	C. G. P., Sl. P., B. D. P.
" *adræana* (Roehl.) [Lesq.]	P. P., Eb. C. G., Bl. C. G., Anst.
Sphenopteris sp. cf. *hildreti* Lx. †	Eb. C. G., C. H.
" *spinosa* Goepp.?	C. G. P., Sl. P., B. C.
" cf. *geniculata* Germ. and Kaulf.†..	Eb. C. G., Bl. C. G.
" cf. *schatzlarensis* Stur.	P. P., Mon. P.
" cf. *canneltonensis* D. W	Mon. P.
" *delicatnla* Sternb. [Lesq.]	Anst.
" cf. *dubuissonis* Brongn. *[Lesq.].	F. H. G., P.P, Hand., B. C.
" cf. *microcarpa* Lx. †	Tunn.T., P.P., Mon.P., Hand., B. C., C. G. C., Eb. C.G., Bl. C. G.
" n. sp. cf. *crepini* Boul	P. P., Anst.
Oliogocarpia sp. †	Hand.
" *alabamensis* Lx. ?†	C. G. C.
Pecopteris plumosa Artis*†	Diam. G., Cr. G., M. C. G., Tunn. T., Anst.
" n. sp. cf. *crenulata* Brongn	Diam. G., Cr. G., M. C. G., Tunn. T., K. C. T., Anst., C. H.
" cf. *aspera* Brongn. †	C. H.

§ Op. Cit., p. 167.

‖The species in the list may be separated by referring to the abbreviations, each of which ends with the initials of the nearest coal. See p. 160.

*Identical with species in the Allegheny series.

†Idenfical with or modification of Upper Pottsville forms.

Alethopteris serlii (Brongn.) Goepp.† ....Diam. G., F. H. G., M. C. G.,
Tunn. T. ,, P. P. , Sl. P. ,Mon.
P., Hand., B. C. H. C. G.,
K. C. G., Eb. C. G., Bl. C. G.,
R. C. G. , Anst.

"   *lonchitica* (Schloth.) Goepp. ....C. G. P. ,   C. G. C. ,   Eb. C. G. ,
Bl. C. G. , Anst.

Neuropteris sp. cf. *gigantea* Sternb.† ....Eb. C. G. , Anst.

"   *flexuosa* Sternb.‡.......... _.........F. H. G. , Diam. G. , Cr. G. ,
M. C. G. , Tunn. T. , P. P. ,
C. G. P. , Sl. P. , B. D. P. ,
Mon. P. , Hand., B.C., C. G.
C., Eb.C.G., Bl. C. G,, Anst.,
C. H.

"   n. sp. , No. I................................P. P.

"   n. sp. , No. 2†...... ....Sl. P. , Hand. , Bl. C. G. , Anst.

"   *cistii* Brongn. ? ....Eb. C. G. , R. C. G.

Calamites ramosus Artis* ....F. H. G., Eb. C. G., P. P., C.H.

"   *suckowii* Brongn. *.....................F. H. G. , Eb. C. G. , Bl. C. G. ,
Anst.

"   *cistii* Brongn. *.....................Eb. C. G. , Anst.

"   *approximatus* Brongn* ....C. H.

Calamitina sp................................M. C. G.

Calamodendron sp......... ....P. P.

Annularia ramosa Weiss. *........................P. P., C. G. P., Sl. P., Hand. ,
Eb. C. G. , Anst., C. H.

"   *radiata* Brongn. * ....P. P. , C. G. P., Sl. P. , Eb. C.
G. , Anst., C. H.

"   *acicularis* Dn. † ....F. H. G. , P. P. , Eb. C. G

Asterophyllites rigidns Sternb. *.................M. C. G. , H. C. G.., K. C. G.,
Eb. C. G.

"   cf. *minutus* Andr.†.....................C. G. P. , Hand.

"   *lycopodioides* Zeill.....................Eb. C. G

Calamostachys ramosa Weiss. * ....P. P.

Sphenophyllum cuneifolium (Sternb.) Zeill.₰† F. H. G. , M.C.G. , Tunn. T. ,
P. P. , C. G. P., Hand. , C. G.
C., H.C.G., Bl. C.G., R.
C. G., Anst.

"   *furcatum* Lx. (form)†..........Hand.

Lycopodites simplex Lx.?†............... ....P. P. , Eb. C. G. , C. H.

---

*Identical with species in Allegheny series.

†Identical with or modification of Upper Pottsville form.

‡The form from this group is specifically different from that reported from the Allegheny series under the same name.

₰Very narrow lax form figured by Lesqereux (Coal Flora, iii, pl. xciii, fig. 9) as *S. saxifragæfolium.*

Lepidodendron cf. *acuminatum* (Geop.)
Ung.†..Cr. G.
Lepidodendron sp. cf. *brittsii* Lx...../............F. H. G., Mon. P.
"   *veltheimii* Sternb. *†..........M. C. G., Hand.
"   cf. *magnum* Wood..............Diam. G.
"   *clypeatum* Lx. *†..............H. C. G.
"   *obovatum* Sternb. ?..............Diam. G., Tunn. T.
Lepidophloios sp. cf. *laricinus* Sternb.........M. C. G., Hand., Anst.
Bothrodendron n. sp., *minutifolium* Boul. ..F. H. G., M. C. G., P. P., C. G.,
                           P., Sl. P., Mon. P., Hand.,
                           B. C., C. G. C.,K. C. G., Eb.
                           C. G., Anst.
Lepidostrobus variabilis L. and H..............F. H. G., Diam. G., C. G. P.
                           Mon. P., Hand., H. C. G.,
                           Anst., C. H.
"   *ornatus* L. and H. ?†.........Tunn. T., K. C. T.
"   sp. nov. ?.............................K. C. G.
Lepidophyllum acuminatum Lx. *†............P. P.
"   cf. *campbellianum* Lx†........F. H. G., Diam. G., M. C. G. P.
                           P., C. G. P., H. C. G., Anst.
"   cf. *cultriforme* Lx..............Diam. G., M. C. G., K. C. T.
Lepidocystis obtusis Lx.†*..........................M. C. G., K. C. T.
Ulodendron majus L. and H. *................Eb. C. G., Anst.
Sigillaria cf. *reticulata* Lx.†......................M. C. G.
"   sp. cf. *ichtyolepis* Sternb..............Tunn. T.
Cordaites borassifolius (Sternb.) Ung. *......
Cardiocarpon minor (Newb)†....................Tunn. T.
Rhabdocarpos amygdalæformis Geop. and
Berg. *..Mon. P.
"   *sulcatus* (L. and H.) Schimp*F. H. G., M. C. G., C. H.
"   *multistriatus* (Presl) Lx. *..Anst., C. H.
Carpolithes fragarioides Newb. †................P. P., Anst.

RELATIVE AGES OF THE LOWER KANAWHA GROUP AND THE ALLEGHENY SERIES.

"In the preceding list the asterisk (*) marks species which appear to be identical in form with material examined from the Allegheny series. It should, however, be noted that while these species, which constitute but a small percentage in the ferns, occur also in the Allegheny series, they do not include forms that are characteristic of that series. On the contrary, they comprise species which are either of wide range or which in most cases originate in the upper zone of the Pottsville formation. Referring again to the list, the species distinguished by the dagger (†) are either identical with or

---

*Identical with the species in the Allegheny series.
†Identical with or modification of Upper Pottsville forms.

they are modifications of Upper Pottsville forms. The much greater percentage of species in the latter category falls far short of indicating the really very intimate connection of the floras of the lower group of the Kanawha series with those of the Pottsville formation, both in West Virginia and in the type district.

"An examination of the combined floras from the lower half of the Kanawha series reveals at once the absence of both the characteristic and the omnipresent ferns of the Clarion and succeeding groups in northern Pennsylvania. The unfailing forms of the Neuropterids, the common and characteristic Annulariæ and Sphenophylla* which predominate at the base of the Allegheny series, as well as the entire group of higher Pecopterids, appear, so far as my inspection of more than 100 collections has extended, to be entirely absent from the lower half of the Kanawha series in southern West Virginia.

"The plant life of the lower half of the Kanawha formation in southern West Virginia differs from that of even the lower portion of the Allegheny series of northern Pennsylvania, not only by the almost entirely different forms in the fern flora, but by the still more important relations of the flora as a whole. The fern (Annularian and Sphenophyllean) elements in the flora of the Allegheny series are essentially totally different from those in the Virginian Pottsville and offer a well marked contrast to the types found below the Homewood sandstone in the Allegheny valley, or below the Fuck Mountain conglomerate in the Pottsville district of the southern Anthracite field of Pennsylvania. The floras of the Allegheny series are by their composition bound to the higher coal measures. The plant associations in the Freeport group are, as may be noted in a scrutiny of the list (page 154 , characterized by the development of the higher Pecopterid flora. The ferns of the Kittanning (page 151), like those of Mazon creek, Illinois, and Henry county, Missouri,† show the almost entire absence of Pottsville types, and while not so highly developed, especially in Pecopterids, they still compose a flora that is in close agreement with those at the base of the Upper Coal Measures, or the Middle Coal Measures of the Old World. The flora of the Clarion group (see list page 148) is characterized by a smaller proportion of the higher Pecopterid elements, and a consequent reduction in richness, rather than by any considerable representation of Pottsville ferns, Annulariæ or Sphenophylla. The flora of this, the lowest group of the Allegheny series, with its abundant *Neuropteris ovata, Neuropteris scheuchzeri*, and *Pcopteris villosa (?)*,' as well as *Annularia stellata, Annularia sphenophylloides*, and *Sphenophyllum emarginatum*, is still bound to the higher floras, and is comparable to the Middle Coal Measures of Great Britian, or the upper zone of the Valenciennes, or the upper portion of the Westphalian series of the Old World.

---

*The form of *Sphenophyllum cuneifolium* in the Allegheny series is broad leaved, often irregularly dissected in narrow tapering teeth, while that from the Lower Kanawha group, and the Sewell formation, has narrow, long, lax leaves, rarely cut in more than four relatively broad, obtusely pointed teeth.

†Age of the coals of Henry county, Missouri. Bull. Geol. Soc. Am. vol. 8, 1897, pp. 287-304. Flora of the Lower Coal Measures of Missouri. Mon. U. S. Geol. Surv. vol. xxxvii, 1899.

"In contrast to the composition and affinities of the floras of the Allegheny series, we find the floral associations in the lower half of the Kanawha series, including the lower group of coals, to be almost totally lacking in the characteristic elements of the Allegheny flora. The Lower Kanawha flora is distinctly largely of Pottsville derivation or affinity. Many of its elements are but slight modifications of types characteristic of the Pottsville of Virginia or of the southern Anthracite field, while the greater part of the remaining stratigraphic species either are closely allied to Pottsville plants or they are unfamiliar in our American Paleozoic floras. The comparative reference of a considerable number of the species in the latter category, to the types described from the Valenciennes series, or the Schatzlar series of the Old World, is in itself a suggestion of the most intimate relations of the floras. It needs but a cursory examination of the magnificent and voluminous illustrations published by Zeiller* and Sturt to at once reveal the homotaxial significance of the floral composition of the Lower Kanawha flora, and its exact reference to the Westphalian or Lower Coal Measures of the European basins. Thus not only does the Lower Kanawha flora appear by its composition and relations, when compared with the floral succession in the Pennsylvania section, to distinctly antedate the flora of the Clarion group in the lower portion of the Allegheny series, but the same relative positions for the two series are indicated also by a paleontological comparison of both with the Old World paleobotanical sections. In short, the plant life of the lower half of the Kanawha formation, with its new or unfamiliar types, forms an elaborate connecting link between the typical Pottsville or Millstone Grit floras and the Clarion flora in the Allegheny series.

"That the flora under discussion preceded the typical Allegheny floras, at least in the Virginia region, is further shown by the occurrence of the normal and characteristic plant associations of the Clarion and Kittanning groups at a higher stage in the Kanawha section."

FLORAS OF THE UPPER GROUP OF COALS IN THE KANAWHA FORMATION.

Plant horizons—"As described by Campbell and Mendenhall, an interval of usually barren and arenaceous strata, which attains to a thickness of about 300 feet, lies between the lower and upper groups of coals in the Kanawha formation. Reference to their published sections shows these sandstones themselves to occur within the upper half of the entire thickness of the formation. The three exploited coals of the upper group are locally known as (1) the Kanawha Mining seam; (2) the Coalburg seam, and (3) the Stockton seam. They have been respectively correlated and named by the geologists of West Virginia as identical with the Upper Kittanning, the Lower Freeport, and the Upper Freeport of the Allegheny valley.

Plants from the Kanawha Mining and Coalburg coals.—"The roof shales of the Kanawha Mining and Coalburg coals do not appear generally to con-

---

Flore foscile de la bassin houiller de Valenciennes, 1886 and 1888.
†*Die Carbon-Flora der Schatzlarer Schichten*, 1885 and 1887.

tain well preserved plants. From the rock dump at the Chesapeake mine,
Lower creek, near Handley, specimens of *Lepidodendron modulatum* Lx.
and a Sigillaria belonging to the *mamillaris* group have been obtained. *Lepidodendron modulatum* affords a slight indication of Allegheny age, although the Lycopodiales of the Carboniferous flora are of inferior stratigraphic value. The plant fragments from the horizon of the Coalburg seam
at the Belmont mine, near Crown hill, and at Ronda, on Cabin creek, represents a very delicate, deeply dissected Sphenopteris, more lax than *Sphenopteris hildreti* Lx.; a Sphenopteris of the form identified in the unpublished
work of Prof. Lesquereux as *Sphenopteris delicatula* Broun; two species of
Neuropteris, one of which is probably identical with *Neuropteris flexuosa*
Sternb., while the other belongs to the group represented by *Neuropteris
gigantea* Sternb., *Calamites suckowii* Brongn., and *Lepidodendron* cf. *obovatum* Sternb. The plant representations from the levels of these two coals are
too scanty to permit an attempt at correlation. They contain little that
points distinctly to a position in the Allegheny series, while, on the other
hand, the fern species differ in their facies from the forms in the Clarion or
the higher groups in northwestern Pennsylvania."

In a recent letter (May 7, 1903) to the writer, Mr. White gives
a brief account of new and additional evidence bearing upon the
age of the Kanawha series, saying that a collection of ferns from
140 feet (Winifrede coal horizon) below the KANAWHA BLACK FLINT,
at Kendalls Mills on Blue creek, Kanawha county, will not go into
the Allegheny series, and suggests that the Kanawha series may
represent the Mercer group of Pennsylvania enormously expanded,
since he finds many plant forms common to both. If this view of
the case should prove to be the true one, it would follow that the
great sandstone mass which comes in below the BLACK FLINT horizon, and weathers into the "chimney rock" type along the Kanawha, is the real top of the Pottsville series, as heretofore limited,
and that the Allegheny ends, say, with the Lewiston coal horizon,
and hence the correlations instead of being as the writer has suggested on pages 501-502, would read as follows:

Mason coal = Upper Freeport.
"No. 5 Block" coal = Upper Kittanning.
Stockton coal = Lower Kittanning or Clarion.

This view also leads to the inevitable conclusion, that while
the Pottsville and all other series of rocks below it, have expanded
enormously in the Kanawha region, the Allegheny has actually
dwindled in size, and its coals become of minor importance, since
at Charleston, just before the BLACK FLINT passes below drainage,
there is actually no merchantable coal from thirty feet below the

latter stratum up to the Pittsburg bed, while the interval from the
Mason coal to the base of the Stockton is only 140 to 160 feet, and
it is never more than 200 feet anywhere along the Kanawha.

This state of affairs, while improbable from general considerations, is not impossible, as already stated on pages 502 and 505,
and if Mr. White's paleobotanical studies in the region farther to
the northeast on Holly, and the Buckhannon shall confirm his Kanawha results, the stratigraphic column must be rearranged to bring
the two into harmony, since there can be no serious disagreement
when all of the facts are known.

It is possible that the suggestion made by the writer on page
357, in connection with the record of the Diamond drill hole at
Webster, Taylor county, as an alternative explanation of the curious results obtained therein, has actually taken place in the
northern region of the State south from the B. &. O. Railroad,
viz., that the Allegheny series thins away to only half its normal
size, against the swelling deposits of the Pottsville, and thus crowds
the coals much closer together, thus rendering it probable that the
big, multiple coal of the Philippi region is not the Upper Freeport
bed, but may be the Lower Kittanning instead, or even the Middle
and Lower Kittanning beds combined, while the Upper Freeport
would be the insignificant Mason bed, only 120 feet higher.   This
rearrangement of correlations would make the Roaring creek coal,
the Lower Kittanning bed, and the equivalent of the "Davis"
seam of the Allegheny mountain region of Tucker and Grant counties, with which it exhibits some striking similarities.   The thick
coal on the head of the Buckhannon, Little Kanawha, and Holly
would also fall into this category, as well as the southwestward extension of the same bed through Webster and Nicholas counties.

If we accept this view of the identity of the thick coal now
mined in the Philippi and Roaring creek regions of Barbour and
Randolph counties, viz., that it represents the Middle and Lower
Kittanning rather than the Upper Freeport bed, then the section
at Philippi, published on page 312, must have the following interpretation (instead of the one given), the former identifications being placed in parentheses:

	Ft. In.	Ft. In.
Sandstone, massive (Buffalo), Mahoning................	40	0
Shales and concealed................................	30	0

```
Coal (Mason), slaty, Upper Freeport................... 3  o  ⎫
Concealed .......................................................25  o  ⎪
Sandstone (Upper Mahoning), massive, flaggy at           ⎪
  base, probably Freeport.................................50  o  ⎪
(Mahoning) coal  ⎧Coal ................... 3  o ⎫               ⎪
Upper Kittanning..⎨Bone .................. o  2 ⎬ 4  3          ⎪
                 ⎩Coal ........... ... 1  1 ⎭               ⎬ 155  3
Concealed (shales, sandstone and limestone)......40  o  ⎪
(Upper Freeport) Middle and Lower Kittanning            ⎪
  coal ............................................................. 6  o  ⎪
Shales.................................................................15  o  ⎪
Coal (Middle Freeport), Clarion................. ........ 2  o  ⎪
Shales to top of Pottsville (Roaring creek sand-        ⎪
  stone) .............................................................10  o  ⎭
```

The section is continued on down to the top of the great Roaring creek sandstone, which comes out of the Valley river below Philippi, and which, on the basis of the Philippi coal's being the Lower Kittanning, instead of the Upper Freeport, would be the top member of the Pottsville, instead of the Upper Freeport sandstone, an interpretation which accords more closely with its physical aspect, although it cuts off 100 feet from the usual thickness of the Allegheny series in Preston county, a few miles northeast from Barbour.

This interpretation will also explain the curious results found in the Webster, Taylor county, bore hole (page 356), where the rocks immediately below what was supposed to be the Lower Freeport coal, assume the aspect of the Pottsville series. If we take the full record of this bore hole, given partly on page 232-3, and page 356, and interpret the same on the basis of that just given for the Philippi region, we should have the following for the total thickness of the Allegheny series in the Webster boring:

```
                                              Ft. In.  Ft. In.
Coal, Upper Freeport............................... 2  o
Fireclay and sandy shales......................... 19 11
Limestone. dark greenish gray (Freeport)........ 7  o
Shale and fireclay, with lime nodules............ 14  o
Sandy shale and micaceous sandstone.. ......... 12  1
                   ⎧coal.................... o  1 ⎫
                   ⎪black slate ........... o  2 ⎪
Coal, Lower Freeport⎨coal......... ......... o  4 ⎬ 4  9
or Upper Kittanning..⎪gray shale ........... 1  2 ⎪
                   ⎪black slate ........... 1  6 ⎪
                   ⎩coal ........... ....... 1  6 ⎭
Dark slate and sandy shales......... ........... 13  4
Limestone...........................................  9  6
Shale ................................................ 10  o
Black slate, thin seams of coal.................. .. 2  o
Fireclay ......... .................................... 2  4
```

Shales, sandy.. 6 10

Coal Lower Kittanning
{
coal 0   2
black slate........... 1   2
bony coal 0   2
coal................... 2   4
bony coal 0   4
coal 1   8
}
5 10

Fireclay, hard 6   0
Shale, sandy, some limestone to top of Pottsville series   4   0
_____

Total thickness of the Allegheny series....... ....119 7

Below this the drill brought up only very hard sandstone, much of which was pebbly, with some streaks of coal, and a little sandy shale, ending in very hard conglomerate at a depth of 217 feet below the base of this section, so that if the lowest coal given above, be the Lower Kittanning, there is no escape from the conclusion that the entire Allegheny series is there (at Webster, Taylor county,) compressed into an interval of only 120 feet, since in the hills above the Webster well, the Crinoidal limestone and its underlying red shales crop to the surface, while the great Pittsburg coal caps the highest knobs, leaving but 624 feet for the Conemaugh series, and hence nothing more can be taken from it to add to the Allegheny beds.

Now, if this suggested interpretation of the Webster and Philippi sections be correct, and the Allegheny series should continue in this thinned condition across to the Great Kanawha valley, instead of expanding PARI PASSU with the other measures below, as has heretofore seemed most probable, then the apparent differences between the results of stratigraphy and those derived from paleobotanic evidence would be reduced to very narrow limits.

The future detailed work of the Survey in the several counties of the State along the crop of the Allegheny series, viz., Preston, Taylor, Barbour, Randolph, Upshur, Braxton, Webster, Nicholas, Clay, Kanawha, and Fayette, between the northern line of the State and the Great Kanawha river, may be expected to solve these mooted questions of identity, and correlation, which are of more theroetic than economic interest, since all the valuable coal beds are known and have been described, whether they belong in the Kanawha, Allegheny, or Conemaugh series.

In the event that the correlations here considered possible should prove correct, then the name, MASON COAL, from Barbour county southwestward to the Kanawha river and beyond, would be replaced by UPPER FREEPORT COAL, while for the latter name, over the same region covered by this report, the name, LOWER KITTANNING, should be substituted.

CHAPTER VII

THE POTTSVILLE SERIES, No. XII.

Beneath the Allegheny series, along the river of the same name, and most everywhere else in western Pennsylvania, there comes a group of very hard, gray or white, massive, pebbly sandstones, so different in lithological appearance from the rocks above that they were classified in a separate series by the geologists of the First Geological Survey of Pennsylvania, and given the names "Seral" Conglomerate, "Great" Conglomerate, No. XII, etc.

The conclusions of the early geologists appear to have been that this division of the Coal Measures was one great mass of pebbly sandstone or conglomerate, with few, if any, divisions of interstratified shales or coal beds. To them it was simply a great sheet of lithified sand and gravel forming the basal member of the Coal Measures upon which rested the column of rocks holding coal of commercial value. It remained for the Second Geological Survey of Pennsylvania to show that beneath the Allegheny series, as defined by H. D. Rogers and his assistants of the First Survey, there came not ONE stratum of conglomerate, or massive sandstone, but SEVERAL, separated by shales, and holding important coal beds.

These facts were first set forth, and the series definitely classified in Vols. Q, QQ and QQQ of the Second Geological Survey of Pennsylvania, published in 1878, '79, and '80 respectively. In these publications, the field notes for which were taken during 1876 and '77, it is shown that in Beaver, Lawrence, and Mercer counties of Pennsylvania, and the adjoining regions of Columbiana, Mahoning, and Trumbull counties of Ohio, the "Seral" or No. XII conglomerate of the First Survey, is very complex, and its several sandstones, coals and limestones were duly named and described. To this series of deposits Prof. Lesley gave the name, Pottsville, from the great development (1000 feet) at Pottsville in the southern anthracite field of Pennsylvania. This name has now been adopted by the U. S. G. Survey, and the Maryland Survey, so that it has supplanted all of the other and older terms, including the name, "New River," given to the series by Prof. Wm. M. Fontaine, from its great development along the stream of that name in West Virginia, where it contains important coal beds.

The series exhibited in western Pennsylvania, as given by the writer in Vol. QQQ (page 33), of the Second Geological Survey of that State, is as follows:

	Ft.	In.
Sandstone, Tionesta (Homewood)	50	0
Shales	5	0
Iron ore	2	0
Limestone, Upper Mercer	2	6
Coal Upper Mercer	2	6
Shales	25	0
Iron ore	2	0
Limestone, Lower Mercer	2	6
Shales	10	0
Coal, Lower Mercer	2	6
Shales	10	0
Iron ore	1	0
Shales	5	0
Sandstone, Upper Connoquenessing	40	0
Shales, with iron ore	10	0
Coal, Quakertown	2	0
Shales	40	0
Sandstone, Lower Connoquenessing	30	0
Shales Sharon, iron bearing	30	0
Coal, Sharon	4	0
Fireclay and shales	5	0
Sharon, conglomerate, base of No. XII (Pottsville)	20	0
Total	301	0

From this section it will be observed that between the sand-

stone at the top, and the next underlying massive rocks, there is a
shale, coal and limestone group of seventy feet in thickness. While
this shale interval extends eastward to the Allegheny river, it appears not to increase in that direction; on the contrary, it loses
both of its limestones, one of its coals, and decreases somewhat in
thickness, and the overlying sandstone remains massive.   But
when traced westward into Ohio, the shales, coals and limestones,
iron ores, etc., hold their places and thickness in the series
from Mahoning county entirely across the State, to where their
outcrops pass into Kentucky from the Hanging Rock District in
Lawrence county, beyond the southwest boundary of West Virginia, while at the same time, the Tionesta or Homewood sandstone grows thin and inconspicuous to such an extent that the Ohio
geologists have never recognized it as a member of the underlying
conglomerate series, but have included it along with even the
Connoquenessing sandstones below, in one series, the Lower Coal
Measures, extending from the Upper Freeport coal to the Sharon
conglomerate, the latter stratum being the only member recognized
as included in the "Great" or "Seral" conglomerate of Rogers.
In view of what Mr. David White claims with reference to the
Kanawha series, viz., that its great thickness is largely composed
of sediments which belong in the top of the Pottsville at the north,
it would probably be more philosophical to extend the Allegheny
series down to the top of the Upper Connoquenessing (U. Massil-
lon) sandstone, since, if the Kanawha series is really the expanded
Mercer coal group of western Pennsylvania, the sediments reveal
such an intimate resemblance to the Allegheny beds that they
should all be classed in one series.   As thus limited, the Pottsville
series is everywhere in West Virginia very distinct in its physical
aspect, and in the character of its sandstones and coals, from the
overlying Allegheny and Kanawha, its sandstones being harder,
whiter and more conglomeratic than those in the Allegheny above.

The change in lithology at the base of the series is most pronounced, the hard white sandstones of the Pottsville being in
striking contrast to the RED SHALES, and green micaceous sandstones
of the underlying Mauch Chunk series.   There is no perceptible unconformity in the dip of the two series, yet there is much
evidence of erosion at their contact line, while the great change in
the character of both animal and plant life in passing from one to
the other is evidence of actual unconformity.

The Pottsville series being composed mainly of very hard and often pebbly sandstones, the grains of which are cemented by silica and peroxide of iron, becomes almost indestructible by ordinary atmospheric agencies, and it has thus proved a most important factor in shaping the topography around the margins of the Carboniferous system. Wherever these beds come to the surface in West Virginia, wild scenery and rugged topography are sure to be found. Rapid streams, high water falls, "rock cities," great cliffs, precipitous slopes, and barren regions generally mark the lines where these rocks emerge to daylight. The lofty peaks of the Alleghany mountains owe their origin to this friendly mantle, while its upturned edges have preserved many coal basins from complete erosion. The deep gorges, narrow canyons, and wild scenery of the Cheat, North Potomac, Tygarts Valley, Little and Big Kannawhas, Guyandot, and Tug rivers are all carved from these rocks. The "Falls" of both Kanawhas, the Black Water and Stony rivers are over these rocks, as well as the "Roughs" of Tug and Guyandot. A belt of evergreen vegetation, laurel, hemlock, pines, etc., marks the soil (usually too poor, stony and infertile for agriculture) derived from this series.

It was formerly supposed that this hard white sandstone series at the base of the Coal Measures held no coal beds of commercial value, but the investigations of recent years have revealed the fact that some of the purest and most valuable coals of the entire Appalachian field are bound up between the great cliffs of the Pottsville series, along its southeastern crop across the State, so that on the New and Tug rivers this series now furnishes some of the purest coal and cokes of the State. One of the peculiarities of the Pottsvile coals, in which they resemble the Allegheny-Kanawha series above, is their distribution in a comparatively narrow belt, only twenty-five to thirty miles wide around the southeastern border of the Appalachian field, since in passing northwestward these early coals thin away and disappear in a mass of pebbly sandstones and sandy beds in which no coal of commercial value is found. This same state of affairs is true along the northwestern crop of the Pottsville series across western Pennsylvania and southeastern Ohio, and hence there is no reason for believing that West Virginia has any Pottsville coals of much commercial value outside the counties of McDowell, Wyoming, Mercer, Raleigh, Summers, Fayette, Nicholas, Greenbrier, Webster, Randolph, Tucker, Grant, and eastern Preston.   True, the Pottsville rock series underlies all the region of the State west from the counties named, but it consists largely of coarse sandstone and conglomerates in which the drill of the oil and gas seeker reports no coals of commercial value, except an occasional sporadic seam which may hold more slate than coal.

Another peculiarity of the coals in the Pottsville series of West Virginia is their soft, columnar, and typical coking structure, as opposed to the dry or "block" coal type found in the coals of the same series like the Sharon, Wellston, Jackson Hill, etc, occurring along the northwestern margin of the Appalachian field, across western Pennsylvania and southeastern Ohio.

The purity of these early coals is also another characteristic, the percentages of both ash and sulphur being very low, and probably due to the fact that just previous to the spread of the early coal marshes, the floor of the Appalachian region had been sheeted with a thick deposit of clean gravel and sand, thus effectually covering up the muddy deposits of a previous epoch, so that the streams of that time which drained into the Carboniferous bogs were pure and clear like our mountain brooks of the present.

The thickness of the Pottsville series varies greatly in the different portions of the State along its eastern crop.   At the Pennsylvania line, both in Preston and Monongalia, the thickness of this series seldom exceeds 250 to 300 feet, but as we pass southwestward the beds begin to swell, and when we reach New river a thickness of 1400 feet has been attained, and this is increased to nearly 2000 feet at the Kentucky line in McDowell, according to the measurements of the U. S. Government Survey, while, if we accept the view of David White that the Kanawha series is simply the Mercer group enormously expanded, 1000 feet more must be added to the thickness in the Tug and New river regions.

Under all of the great Appalachian basin of the State these sandstones form a continuous floor for the Coal Measures, and the oil and gas drillers nearly always find it in two or three divisions separated by intervening shales.   They generally term it the "salt sand" since it often holds salt water as well as oil and gas.

A few sections will now be given to illustrate the character and thickness of the Pottsville series, where it is exposed to view between ;the Pennsylvania and Maryland line at the north, and the Kentucky line at the southwest.   The typical section of the Pottsville series in western Pennsylvania and eastern Ohio has already been given on page 609 above.

Dr. G. C. Martin of the Maryland Survey, reports the following complete section of the Pottsville series, as measured by him at Swallow Falls, Garrett county, a few miles northeast from the Preston county line, page 103, Geology of Garrett County:

	Ft.	In.	Ft.	In.
Massive sandstone, Homewood			50	0
Shale			0	0
Fireclay, Mount Savage			4	0
Coal, Mount Savage.. { coal	0	4		
bone	0	8		
coal	1	4	3	●
shale	0	2		
coal	0	6		
Shale			5	0
Sandstone			5	0
Coal, Lower Mercer			0	10
Conglomeratic sandstone, Upper Connoquenessing			75	0
Black shale			2	0
Coal, Quakertown			1	6
Shale			0	6
Concealed			0	8
Massive, conglomeratic sandstone, Lower Connoquenessing			75	0
Concealed			60	0
Shale			5	0
Coal, Sharon.. { coal	0	5		
shale	0	6	1	4
coal	0	5		
Shale			0	6
Sandstone			25	0
Total			327	8

Dr. Martin has also measured a complete section of the Pottsville series just below Westernport, opposite Piedmont, Mineral county, which is given on page 104, Geology of Garrett County, Maryland, as follows:

	Ft.	In.
Massive sandstone, Homewood	26	0
Concealed, but with abundant fragments of flint fireclay in the talus	64	0
Massive sandstone	6	0
Concealed	29	0
Massive quartzose sandstone	20	0
Sandstone	4	0
Concealed	28	0
Black shale	5	0
Sandstone	1	0
Dark shales	12	0
Coal	1	0
Dark gray shale	4	0
Coal	1	6
Dark gray shale	4	0
Sandstone	4	0

	Ft.	In.
Concealed	16	o
Dark gray shales...	10	o
Sandstone	1	o
Concealed	40	o
Massive sandstone	20	o
Shale..	2	o
Sandstone	10	o
Black shales	25	o
Coal		8
Black shale	4	o
Sandstone	25	o
Shale and sandstone..	6	o
Coal	1	3
Sandstone	4	o
Mauch Chunk shales		
Total 374		5

This section foots up about seventy feet less thickness than the one the writer measured near Piedmont, and published in Bulletin 65, U. S. Government Survey, page 186, but as Dr. Martin's section was measured with much care, it is very probably the more accurate one.

An almost complete exposure of the Pottsville series is revealed along the cuts of the B. & O. Railroad, in descending its Cheat river grade near Anderson, Preston county, from the top of the gorge to Buckhorn wall, and there the writer once measured the following section:

		Ft.	In.		Ft.	In.
Sandstone, massive (Homewood), Tionesta...............					60	o
Coal ..	coal	o	5			
	shales, sandy	6	o		6	10
	coal	o	5			
Shales, brown, sandy.................................					45	o
Coal, slaty..					2	o
Shales..					3	o
Sandstone, massive.................................					25	o
Sandstone, flaggy..................................					15	o
Sandstone, massive, grayish white					20	o
Sandstone, filaggy.................................					8	o
Shales, brown......................................					4	o
Sandstone, grayish white...........................					20	o
Shale, brown					3	6
New River coal beds..	coal ....-...	o	5			
	shale, gray.............	4	o			
	coal	o	4			
	shales, sandy	8	o			
	iron ore	o	6			
	shales	5	o		55	1
	coal	1	o			
	shales	10	o			
	coal	o	4			
	shales, sandy	25	o			
	coal	o	6			

```
Shales, brown ......................................................... 20  0
Sandstone ............................................................. 15  0
Shales, buff, sandy................................................. 20  0
Sandstone, massive, pebbly.................................... 20  0
Concealed and shales to the top of Mauch Chunk red
    beds ............................................................... 20  0
                                                              ───────
    Total ...............................................362  5
```

Along the gorge of Deckers creek in western Preston and eastern Monongalia counties, where the entire Pottsville series is exposed, it appears to be almost solid, white sandstone 200 to 250 feet thick, some of the layers of which produce excellent glass sand.

On the Black Water branch of Cheat river below Coketon in Tucker county, the late James Parsons, chief engineer of the West Virginia Central and Pittsburg Railroad, measured a section of the Pottsville, which gives these measures a thickness of 734 feet, as published in Bulletin 65, U. S. G. Survey, page 187. This measurement seems excessive for the region, however, and Mr. Parsons may have duplicated some of the beds, since the exposures are not continuous.

The records of the two oil well borings near Philippi, published on pages 358 and 359 of this volume, give the thickness and constitution of the series under the Philippi region, although 100 to 150 feet should be added to the Pottsville beds from what has been classed as Allegheny sediments, if the main Philippi coal proves to be the Lower Kittanning bed instead of the Upper Freeport, as suggested on a previous page.

In passing southwest from the Philippi region, the Pottsville thickens rapidly, and when we come to Elk river below Webster Springs, a thickness of over 800 feet of shales and massive sandstones interstratified with thin coal beds, is found between the base of the Kanawha series above, and the top of the red Mauch Chunk shales below.

Still farther southwest from Elk river, and at Camden-on-Gauley, in Webster county, we know the constitution of the Pottsville series from the well drilled for gas by Hon. J. N. Camden, the record of which was very carefully kept by J. W. Bonner, chief clerk for the Gauley Lumber Company. The boring begins on the bank of Gauley river, about 250 feet below the base of the Kanawha series, and shows the following succession through the rest of the Pottsville:

	Ft.
Sand and gravel (surface)	25
Black slate	6
Gray sandstone	4
Coal .:...	3
Sandstone, white..	5
Black slate	8
Sandstone, dark..	9
Coal	1
Slate, brown..	5
Sandstone, gray, hard..	16
Slate, light colored...	6
Sandstone, dark, shaly.......................................	32
Black slate	40
Coal	2
Sand, gray, pebbly, very hard (Raleigh)..............	92
Shales, light and dark colored...........................	72
Sandstone, white, fine-grained...........................	39
Black slate	18
Sandstone, white...	17
Coal	5
Sandstone, white, hard...	20
Black slate	33
Coal	1
Sandstone, gray, hard..	10
Black slate	51
Coal	5
Black slate	5
Sandstone..	66
Shales, sandy, light colored	25
Coal	3
Sandstone, white, hard	47
Slate, gray	18
Sandstone, white, hard, base of Pottsville............	11
Shale, red, *Mauch Chunk*	

Total...700

To which, if we add 250 feet for the portion of the Pottsville up to the base of the Kanawha series, we get 950 feet for the thickness of undoubted Pottsville beds.

Southwestward from Camden-on-Gauley, the Pottsville series continues to thicken, and when we come to the Nuttall region on New river, Fayette county, the following succession is revealed in that great canyon:

	Ft.	In.	Ft.	In.
Sandstone, massive, pebbly (Nuttall)			110	0
Shales..			60	0
Coal			1	0
Sandy shales and sandstone			75	0
Sandstone			25	0
Black slate			2	0
Coal			1	0
Shales and sandstone			75	0

Coal	0	10
Shales, sandstone and shales	50	0
Coal, Sewell (Nuttall)	3	6
Shales and slates...................	75	0
Sandstone, massive, Raleigh....................................	155	0
Slates, dark ....….....	10	0
Concealed and shales...............	120	0
Coal	3	6
.Shales and sandstone	130	0

Coal, Quinnimont Fire Creek.	coal........................ 1 0 slate .... 0 3 coal .... 2 0 slate .... 0 2 coal 1 0		4	5

Shales and sandstone........	35	0
Coal, slaty..............….......................	2	4
Shales	40	0
Coal ....….........	1	5
Shales ....,........	10	0
Concealed	30	0
Sandstone, massive ....…................................	125	0
Concealed and sandstone ....,.........	60	0
Sandstone, massive	140	0
Concealed and sandstone to base of Pottsville and top of Mauch Chunk red shale ....….......	55	0
Total.. ,.....................1400		0

The portion of this section below the Raleigh sandstone, was obtained at Sewell, three miles above Nuttall.

The BECKLEY COAL, according to M. R. Campbell of the U. S. G. Survey, comes immediately below the great Raleigh sandstone, and a bed only ten inches thick was observed in that position near the line of section. The coal, at 130 feet above the one identified as the Fire Creek or Quinnimont, was opened and prospected by Mr. McGoffin of the Longdale Coal and Coke Company, but, although showing nearly four feet thick at the outcrop, it thinned away completely when mined into the mountain a few hundred feet. It may possibly represent the Beckley coal, but its interval below the Sewell bed would appear to be too great for that seam.

In the Raleigh folio recently (1902) issued by the U. S. G. Survey, Mr. M. R. Campbell gives two generalized sections of the Pottsville series, one from the northern half of the Raleigh quadrangle, representing the conditions in southern Fayette and northern Raleigh counties, and the other from the southern half of the quadrangle, representing the measures in southern Raleigh, northern Wyoming, and Mercer counties.

The northern section reads as follows:

	Ft.
Nuttall sandstone lentil	0– 200
Sandy and argillaceous shale and sandstone, containing Harvey conglomerate lentil and Sewell coal near base	600– 625
Raleigh sandstone..............	75– 150
Beckley coal	
Quinnimont shale, sandy.....	180– 200.
Quinnimont coal........	
Sandstone and shale, Thurmond, to top of red beds (Mauch Chunk).....................................	450– 550
Total (not including Nuttall lentil)............1305–1525	

The average of which, 1405 feet, agrees almost exactly with the writer's measurement in the vicinity of Nuttall, made in 1884.

For the southern half of the Raleigh quadrangle Mr. Campbell gives the following generalized section:

	Ft.
Sandy and argillaceous shale and sandstone, containing Harvey conglomerate lentil and Guyandot sandstone lentil......................................	650– 700
Raleigh sandstone, coarse	75– 150
Beckley coal	
Quinnimont shale..........	200– 225
Quinnimont coal................................	
Sandstone and shale (Thurmond) with *Pocahontas* (*No. 3*) *coal* near middle.............	600– 725
Totals 1525–1800	

This last section gives an average thickness of 1663 feet, which shows a considerable thickening southward from the New river region.

The Pocahontas quadrangle of the U. S. G. Survey lies directly south from the Raleigh quadrangle, and includes the extreme southern portion of Wyoming and Mercer counties, as well as the southeastern part of McDowell. The top of the Pottsville series has there been lost by erosion so that Mr. M. R. Campbell reports only 100 feet of measures remaining above the Raleigh sandstone. But if we give his Sewell beds the same thickness as he reports for the southern half of the Raleigh quadrangle in the section above, and add the rest of the Pottsville series, as published by him in the Pocahontas folio, 1897, the following measurements result for the region in question:

Ft.

Sandy and argillaceous shale and sandstone (from
   base of Kanawha series) 650- 700
Raleigh sandstone, coarse 80
Quinnimont shale, containing thin sandstone and
   a few coal seams... 300
Quinnimont coal...:....
Sandstone, heavy beds at top and bottom, with
   some shale and coal seams 380
Pocohontas (No. 3) coal................... .. ..
Gray and green argillaceous sandstone and sandy
   shale (to base of Pottsville and top of *red shale*,
   Mauch Chunk)... 360

    Total... 1795

This section shows a slight (132 feet) increase in thickness toward the south, over the measurement given for the southern half of the Raleigh quadrangle.

The Tazewell quadrangle lies immediately west from the Pocahontas, and includes the main portion of McDowell county, as well as the adjoining regions of Virginia and Kentucky. The general section of the Pottsville series as described in the Tazewell folio, by M. R. Campbell, in 1897, gives the following succession:

Ft.

Dotson sandstone, coarse, with sandy shale at base...... 180
Bearwallow conglomerate, coarse sandstone................. 60
Sandstone and shale, with several important coal seams
   and Dismal conglomerate lentil near center of forma-
   tion in western area... 490
Raleigh sandstone, sometimes conglomeratic.............. 100
Sandstone and shale, with many seams of workable
   coal 700
Coal, Pocahontas, No. 3.................. ....
Sandstone and shale, with thin seams of coal (to base
   of Pottsville series and top of Mauch Chunk *red beds*) 360

    Total 1890

This measurement reveals an increase in these measures of 100 feet over that given by Mr. Campbell for the Pocahontas quadrangle, so that on the Virginia and Kentucky line, at the southwestern corner of the State, the Pottsville series has a thickness approximately six times as great as where it enters West Virginia from Maryland and Pennsylvania, 200 miles to the northeast.

The writer measured a section at Welch, McDowell county, which, supplemented by the record of a boring near the mouth of Browns creek, at the miners' Hospital, just below Welch, gives the following results in that region:

	Ft. In.	Ft. In.
Concealed, sandstone and shales..........................		150 0
Coal, Sewell? { coal		2 6
{ shales, sandstone and concealed........		40 0
{ coal		2 0
Shales and concealed		60 0
Coal, "Welch"... { coal	1 4	
{ bone	0 2	3 1
{ coal	1 7	
Shales and concealed		10 0
Sandstone, Raleigh		190 0
Shales, sandstone and concealed		160 0
Coal, Quinnimont 1½–		2½0
Concealed and sandstone, with one or two thin coals to level of boring near mouth of Browns creek...		180 0
Sandstone and slate in bore hole............ ..:.........		38 1
Coal and bone		0 11½
Slate, sandstone, etc.................................		117 7½
Coal		0 9
Sandstone and slate........		142 6½
Coal, No. 4....................................		3 5
Sandstone and slate.................................		61 4
Coal, Pocahontas, No. 3 { coal.................	1 9	
{ bone	0 6	5 2
{ coal.................	2 11	
Sandstone and slate.................................		27 5½
Coal, slate and bone ("split" from No. 3)................		1 9
Slate and sandstone.................................		10 10½
Coal, No. 2		0 7
Slate and sandstone..............................		47 0
Coal, No. 1....		0 9
Sandstone and slate to top of red beds (Mauch Chunk)		202 2
Total...................................		1287 6½
Add interval up to Kanawha series.....................		473 0
Gives		1770 6½ as

the total thickness of the Pottsville in the region of Welch, by
adopting Mr. M. R. Campbell's measurement (730 feet) for the
thickness of Pottsville beds above the horizon of the Raleigh sandstone, given in the Tazewell folio.

This great thickness of Pottsville sediments around the southeastern margin of the Appalachian field, thins away quite rapidly
to the northwestward, as we learn from the records of wells drilled
for oil and gas. For instance, at the Dingess well in Mingo county,
about forty-five miles northwest from Welch, the Pottsville series
is thus recorded by Messrs. Gibson and Giles, the contractors for
the Dingess gas well:

	Ft.
Sandstone, white	130
Slate, black	48
Slate, white	41
Sandstone, white	473
Slate, black	11
Coal, Quinnimont?	6
Slate, black	4
Sand, white (water), to base of Pottsville	308
Total	1021

The coal reported from this boring may possibly represent the Quinnimont horizon, since that is one of the very persistent beds in the Pottsville series, and the coal in question comes at the proper level for that bed.

A few miles northeast from Dingess, a well drilled at the mouth of Harts creek on the Guyandot river, reveals a still further reduction in the thickness of the Pottsville series as follows:

	Ft.
Sandstone, white	20
Sandstone, gray	80
Sandstone, black	13
Sandstone, white	290
Slate, blue	20
Sandstone, black	4
Sandstone, gray	18
Slate, blue	6
Sandstone, yellow, hard	18
Slate, black	6
Slate, blue	39
"Salt sand" (water) to bottom of Pottsville series	182
Total	716

The mouth of Harts creek is only about fifty miles in a northwestern direction from Welch, and yet it reveals a thinning of 1000 feet in the Pottsville series, or say, at the rate of twenty feet to the mile.

Charleston is nearly due north from Welch, and only sixty-three miles distant in an air line, and there the Pottsville series has thinned to only 580 feet, as we learn by the record of Edwards well No. 3, while at the Ohio river, forty miles farther to the northwest, the same series has returned to its normal thickness in western Pennsylvania of 200 to 300 feet, and this it maintains over all the region west from the Monongahela, and the tier of counties southwest from that area.

The detailed measurement of the Pottsville in a well bored at Powellton, Fayette county, twenty-five miles southeast from Charleston, of which a careful record was kept, beginning 1053 feet below the KANAWHA BLACK FLINT, reads as follows:

	Ft.
White sandstone.........	195
Coal...........	2
Sandstone	9
Shale........	5
Sandstone, white, hard........	11
Shales........	265
Shale, black, limy........	18
Lime, gray	4
Lime, sandy, buff colored........	3
Sandstone	3
Lime, sandy, white	43
Slate, black........	3
Limestone.........	23
Sandstone, white, pebbly........	93
Slate, black, and shale........	50
Shale and sandy lime........	12
Lime and slate........	23
Sandstone, pebbly (gas slight), to base of Pottsville series	10
Total	813

From Powellton to Nuttall, where these sediments are 1400 feet thick, or 600 more than at the former locality, is only fifteen miles in a southeast course, which gives a rate of thickening equal to forty feet per mile in that region.

Borings on the head of the Little Kanawha, near the mouth of Trace fork in Lewis county, make the interval from the base of the Kanawha series to the base of the Pottsville about 450 feet, with a coal bed reported midway in the series.

Some coal is also found in the Pottsville series along Middle Fork river, a branch of the Tygarts, Valley river in Randolph county, as shown by the following sections put down with a core drill along Middle Fork, under the supervision of S. D. Brady, for Hon. S. B. Elkins, to whom the Survey is indebted for copies of the records. The wells begin 150 to 200 feet below the top of the Pottsville series, and all but one go down to the RED SHALES of the Mauch Chunk series. The one (No. XI) farthest down the Middle Fork, near the mouth of Three Fork creek, begins at an elevation of 2137 feet above tide, and reads as follows.

	Ft.	In.
Surface boulders and sand	6	3
Fireclay, broken up, soft	2	9
Coal	2	2
Coal and slate mixed	1	0
Fireclay, broken up	18	0
Fireclay, little streaks of gray sandstone	11	0
Slate and fireclay	3	2
Fireclay and gray sandstone mixed	23	9
Sandy slate	11	11
Gray sandstone, streaks of slate	10	8
Sandy slate	2	8
Gray sandstone	6	11
Sandy slate	2	8
Gray sandstone	11	0
Fireclay and slate mixed, and trace of coal	23	8
Bone coal	0	2½
Fireclay	8	0
Bone and coal mixed, streaks of slate	1	9
Slate	2	5
Gray sandstone	15	7
Conglomerate, very coarse	0	6
Sandy slate	1	2
Gray sandstone	0	5
Coarse conglomerate	1	0
Gray sandstone	5	8
Coarse conglomerate	2	7
Sandy slate	2	9
Green sandstone and shale	58	9
Gray sandstone	43	1
Fireclay, greenish cast	9	0
Gray sandstone to red beds, base of Pottsville	5	4
Total	295	10

Bore Hole No. XII, at the mouth of Stone Coal run, elevation 2257 feet above tide, gave the following record:

	Ft.	In.
Surface boulders and sand	11	0
Gray sandstone, streaks of slate	1	7
Gray sandstone, streaks of slate	8	6
Cray sandstone	6	3
Slate, spotted with gray sandstone	5	3
Fireclay	4	0
Slate and fireclay	13	3
Bone coal	0	2
Fireclay, very soft	6	3
Slate and sandstone mixed	9	5
Coal	0	3
Sandstone, and streaks of fireclay	9	0
Slaty fireclay, little streaks of gray sandstone	38	6
Slate	37	2
Coal, slate mixed	2	4
Fireclay and slate, mixed, very soft	6	1
Sandstone and fireclay mixed	25	2
Gray sandstone	5	0

	Ft.	In.
Fireclay, very soft.............................. ....:....................	2	0
Coal, very good..	4	1½
Fireclay and slate................................	20	1½
Sandstone and fireclay	4	2
Gray sandstone...	18	2
Fireclay, spongy, very hard to drill..................... ..	3	8
Gray sandstone, very hard..	2	7
Gray sandstone and lime mixed................................	1	8½
Gray sandstone	9	3
Fireclay and sandstone mixed..................................	1	11
Gray sandstone, trace of coal at bottom.....................	5	0
Sandy slate, full of seams, broken up.....................	0	8½
Sandy slate, full of seams, broken up	5	6
Gray sandstone	22	7
Gray sandstone and pea conglomerate.......................	42	0
Fireclay, sandy and spongy, very hard to drill.........	7	0
Fireclay, broken up and would not make score........	3	1
Gray sandstone, with pea conglomerate, very hard...	18	10
Sandstone, conglomerate mixed, very hard................	15	11
Sandstone, very hard..................................	9	8
Sandstone and fireclay mixed to red beds.................	5	6
Total 395	395	8

Still farther up the Middle Fork, at the mouth of Laurel branch, and approximately 2300 feet above tide, Bore Hole No. XIV gave the following record:

	Ft.	In.
Surface clay, sand and boulders...........	4	2
Gray sandstone, streaks of slate..........................	7	6
Slate, little streaks of gray sandstone.......................	12	0
Fireclay........	2	11
Slate and fireclay ....……	0	10
Coal	1	0
Fireclay, broken up, very soft................................	12	10
Gray sandstone and fireclay mixed..........................	10	7
Slate and fireclay mixed	4	7
Fireclay	1	10
Gray sandstone..................	3	7
Gray sandstone..	19	11
Slate ....:	26	7
Coal and slate mixed............	1	8
Fireclay	6	6
Gray sandstone	34	3
Gray sandstone and pea conglomerate mixed, very hard	12	9
Pea conglomerate, very hard................................	4	0
Coal	0	2
Pea conglomerate, very hard	1	9
Coal	0	2
Pea conglomerate, very hard	0	4
Fine grained gray sandstone, very hard.....................	7	9
Gray sandstone	4	3
Slate, fireclay, sandstone, broken up	9	6
Gray sandstone, broken up, very hard.....................	11	0

	Ft.	In.
Gray sandstone, full spots of fireclay, sulphur.......	3	10
Gray sandstone	19	0
Conglomerate	4	3
Gray sandstone, and streaks of slate..................	4	10
Gray sandstone	30	9
Gray sandstone	7	4
Sandy slate and fireclay..............................	13	3
Fireclay	3	6
Fireclay and green shale mixed........................	5	11
Fireclay, very soft	7	0
Fireclay and green shale mixed...................	5	0
Fireclay and streaks of green sandstone......	13	6
Gray sandstone......	9	1
Gray sandstone, mixed.................................	14	2
Conglomerate and sandstone mixed........	3	5
Gray sandstone, spots of conglomerate	28	6
Fireclay and sandstone mixed to red beds	3	11
Total	379	8

The fourth and last (No. XIII) of these bore hole records was located at West Huttonsville, elevation 2377 feet above tide, and its record reads as follows:

	Ft.	In.
Surface, boulders and sand	7	7
Slate and little seams of gray sandstone........ ...	7	1
Coal	1	7
Slate..	13	11
Gray sandstone, broken up.....	14	8
Gray sandstone.....	17	10
Slate, fireclay, spots of gray sandstone....................	5	6
Slate......	17	1
Gray sandstone, streaks of slate.............	14	9
Fireclay and slate..	3	4
Coal ....,.......................	1	0
Slate...	0	7½
Coal, bony	0	4½
Fireclay, very soft, broken up	10	3
Dark sandstone and fireclay	5	8
Gray sandstone, dark	25	10
Slate and fireclay.......................................	12	8
Gray sandstone and streaks of slate	10	9
Slate and bony coal	0	4½
Fireclay, very sandy	5	8½
Fireclay and slate.............	15	2
Gray sandstone	16	6
Gray sandstone and little trace of coal	6	8
Fireclay	5	8
Coal, slaty...........................	2	7
Fireclay	8	5
Gray sandstone	29	6
Slate and streaks of gray sandstone........................	2	7
Gray sandstone and streaks of slate........................	21	8
Slate	4	2
Slate and sandstone, mixed......................	4	2
Gray sandstone and streaks of slate mixed..............	3	5
Gray sandstone, very hard to bottom........................	23	10
Total...............................	318	11

This boring did not reach the base of the Pottsville by probably sixty to seventy feet.

These records illustrate in an admirable manner the ever changing structure and character of the beds which make up the Pottsville series, and they also reveal the fact that this series has a thickness of 500 to 600 feet along the Middle Fork of Tygarts Valley river. They show, too, that the inclosed coal beds in the Middle Fork region have not the horizontal extent that would render them of much value commercially, although they may thicken up occasionally to three or more feet, like the coal bed on Beech creek, near Star, at the head of Middle Fork, or the one near the mouth of Cassiday, both of which are fair coals of the coking type.

COALS OF THE POTTSVILLE SERIES.

In the northern end of the State, the coal beds of the Pottsville are not of much importance, being thin and much split up with slate, as shown in the sections on Cheat river, page 614, and near Piedmont, page 613. Occasionally, however, the coal under the Homewood or Tionesta sandstone will thicken up to three or four feet of good fuel, as it does on the arch of Chestnut Ridge along the line between Preston and Monongalia county.

This coal has been mined on the land of the late Judge R. L. Berkshire, near the line between Preston and Monongalia counties, where it is three and a-half to four feet thick, and a very good steam and domestic fuel, according to Prof. S. B. Brown of the State University, who has examined the bed.

Along the North Potomac river for several miles southward above Piedmont, a coarse, bony and irregular coal bed is frequently visible in the cuts of the West Virginia Central & Pittsburg Railroad, and hence is known locally as the "Railroad" seam. It belongs in the Mercer group, but whether it represents the Upper or Lower one of thes coals, one can only conjecture, since neither of the corresponding limestones is present. The coals in the Mercer group of the northern end of the State are of only local value, and have never been mined on a commercial scale. Should the contention of David White ever be established, however, viz., that the Kanawha series is largely made up of the expanded Mercer group, then the latter would take its place as one of the most important members of the Carboniferous system.

It was formerly supposed that the great sandstone which caps the New river canyon at Hawks Nest and Nuttall, was a representative of the Homewood or Tionesta sandstone, but if the Kanawha series is older than the Allegheny, then no one yet knows what would represent the Tionesta sandstone on the Great Kanawha, or where the coal beds would belong that underlie the massive sandstones between Summersville and the Gauley river in Nicholas county.

A bright, soft, pure looking coal has been mined under a massive, white sandstone at Beaver Mills, Nicholas county, and on the head of Birch river, near Cowen, Webster county, as well as under the quarry rock below the Court House at Summerville, Nicholas county, which the writer would correlate with the Mercer horizon, since it underlies the Campbells creek bed of the Kanawha series by an interval of approximately 200 feet, and comes immediately below a massive, grayish, or reddish white sandstone, which much resembles the top of the Pottsville series in western Pennsylvania and the northern portion of West Virginia.

It may be this same Beaver Mills coal horizon that furnishes the coal at the mouth of Cassiday on the Middle Fork river, where it has been mined on Kerns, Rutherford and others, and is three to three and a-half feet thick, rich and lustrous.

Just beyond the eastern border of Preston county, a coal bed of excellent quality occurs near the base of the Pottsville, and only twenty to thirty feet above the red shales of the Mauch Chunk. It is soft, and of the regular New river or coking type, but is only two and a-half to three feet thick, and may not have much horizontal extent.

A coal of the same character and thickness crops along the steep grade of the West Virginia Central & Pittsburg Railroad, where it passes through the Pottsville series below Point Look Out, Tucker county.

In the summit of Rich mountain, five miles west from Beverly, one of these Pottsville beds has long been mined for local supply. The coal is three and a-half to four feet thick, with slaty layers in the lower half, very pure and much prized for domestic purposes. It comes about 100 feet above the base of the Pottsville series, and is one of the New river beds, possibly the Sewell, which David White correlates with the Sharon coal, on the basis of fossil plants. It is probably identical with the bed referred to in Preston county,

The ____ ____ the base of the Pottsville by proba-____

____ in an admirable manner the ever ____ and character of the beds which make up the ____ and ____ the fact that this series has a ____ ($54) ____ feet along the Middle Fork of Tygarts Valley. They show ____ that the inclosed coal beds in the Middle Fork ____ the ____ extent that would render ____ commercially, although they may thicken up ____ a ____ or more feet. Like the coal bed on Beech ____ near the ____ of Middle Fork, or the one near the ____ ____ most of which are fair coals of the coking type.

COALS OF THE POTTSVILLE SERIES

In the northern end of the State the coal beds of the Pottsville ____ minor importance, being thin and much split up ____ as shown in the sections on Cheat river, page 614, and ____ page ____ Occasionally, however, the coal under ____ sandstone will thicken up to three or ____ feet ____ in the arch of Chestnut Ridge ____ between Preston and Monongalia county.

____ mined in the land of the late Judge R. L. ____ the line between Preston and Monongalia counties, ____ and ____ is four feet thick, and a very good ____ according to Prof. S. B. Brown of the ____ who has examined the bed.

____ the North Potomac river for several miles southward ____ a ____ heavy and irregular coal bed is frequently ____ the West Virginia Central & Pittsburg Railway ____ is known locally as the "Railroad" seam. It belongs in the lower group, but whether it represents the Upper or lower coal, one can only conjecture, since neither of ____ limestones is present. The coals in the Mercer ____ State are of only local ____ ____ cial scale. ____ ablished, how____ ____ of the ____

t
'
on
of
rty-
ayne
mined
ve Elk
k Fork

re coals of
coke. The
the former is
ive sandstones.
feet, and only
omes another coal
mething like that
mrick, and Charles
times thinning away

, the Pottsville coals
of Cranberry and Cherry
to five feet along these

and it very probably extends along the steep dips of Rich mountain for a long distance, although nothing but a "blossom" of it appears to exist in Big Laurel, north from the Valley river.

On the Shavers Fork of Cheat, near the Club House, some openings have been made in these Pottsville coals, but while the coal is good the beds are thin, and much split with slate partings. They also occur several miles below the Club House, as well as above it, and may eventually furnish coal of commercial value, though no bed more than two feet thick in one bench has yet been exploited.

Near the head of Mill creek, Randolph county, a coal bed with the following structure is referable to the Pottsville series:

	Ft.	In.	Ft.	In.
Coal	1	8		
Shale, dark	0	8		
Coal	2	3		
Slate	0	1	7	4
Coal	0	6		
Black slate	1	6		
Coal	0	8		

The coals at Shifflet's, Anderson's, and Currence's banks, two and a-half to three and a-half feet thick, are also most probably in the Pottsville series.

As we pass southwestward from the head of Mill creek to the Point mountain region, the Pottsville coals begin to increase in number, size and purity, as the series itself swells up to 800 to 900 feet in thickness. These coals have been opened and mined for domestic purposes by William Vandevener, H. B. Marshall, G. W. Saulsbury and others. The main coal is five to six feet in thickness and comes about 150 feet above the base of the Pottsville. It has the following structure in Vandevener's mine:

	Ft.	In.	Ft.	In.
Coal	2	3		
Bone	0	2½		
Coal	1	3½	5	9
Slate and coal	2	0		

This is most probably the same coal as the one mined just west from the top of Rich mountain, on the Beverly and Buckhannon turnpike.

One mile west from Vandevener's, H. B. Marshall's opening

on a tributary of Elk river, exhibits four and a-half feet of beautiful coal, presumably the same bed as the one on Vandevener.

These same coals have been exploited in the summits of the mountains along Elk river below the mouth of old Field Fork, and on Bergoo and other streams which head up toward the Gauley river mountains, and at least one good coal, which Mr. Edwards of Charleston, believes is the same as the Fire Creek of New river, exists wherever the proper horizon is exposed. Its thickness varies from three and a-half to five and a-half feet, and it generally has some slaty layers near its base.

On the Back Fork of Elk river, Pottsville coals have been opened of a thickness varying from three to four feet. One of these has been mined for local supply by Robert Cougar near the mouth of Little Sugar creek, where it is three and a-half to four and a-half feet thick, with only a few bony streaks.

In the vicinity of Webster Springs, Webster county, the Pottsville beds cap the summits of the mountains 1200 to 1500 feet above Elk river, and hold three beds of coal. The upper one, known as the "Dorr vein," has been mined for village supply on the land of Hon. C. P. Dorr, where it lies 150 above the base of the Pottsville, and varies in thickness from twenty inches to forty-five inches. Below it, ninety to one hundred feet, is the "Payne vein," four and a-half to five feet thick, which has also been mined for local supply on the land of the Payne heirs, 900 feet above Elk river, and at many other localities along Elk and the Back Fork of the same.

The "Dorr" and "Payne" veins are both soft, pure coals of the typical New river facies, and would make excellent coke. The "Payne" bed is more regular and persistent, since the former is frequently pinched to a few inches between two massive sandstones.

Below the "Payne" bed, twenty-five to thirty feet, and only twenty feet above the MAUCH CHUNK RED BEDS, comes another coal known as the "Three-foot" bed, since it has something like that thickness. It has been mined by Willis Hamrick, and Charles Boran, but is not regular in thickness, sometimes thinning away to less than two feet.

Southwestward from Webster Springs, the Pottsville coals come out of Gauley river at the mouths of Cranberry and Cherry rivers, and exhibit a thickness of three to five feet along these streams.

Below Cherry and New rivers, the Gauley Coal Land Association of Boston, Mass., owns a very large area of these Pottsville
coals, upon which Mr. E. V. d'Invilliers, the eminent coal expert
of Philadelphia, has recently completed an elaborate report, having made a large number of openings, analyses, etc., on all the
coals in the Pottsville series.   From this report the Survey is permitted to quote much that is of permanent and general interest,
through the courtesy of the president of the Gauley Company,
Mr. H. L. Higginson, of Boston, as follows:

TOPOGRAPHY.—"Reference to the printed sheets and folios of the
United States Geological Survey will best show the extremely mountainous
character of the entire district.

"The Gauley river, joining New river at Gauley bridge, roughly marks
the northern boundary of the property between Cherry and Meadow rivers.
Though its course through Nicholas county is not marked by the canyon-
like topography of New river, along the Chesapeake and Ohio railroad, nevertheless it flows through a tortuous channel of sandstone bluffs, generally
above the *Gauley* (*Sewell*) *coal seam*, making somewhat precipitous cliffs of
from 500 to 700 feet high, and rendering railroad development along this
stream exceedingly difficult.

"Its drainage area is enormous, for the waters of every stream on the
property eventually find their way into the Gauley river, through some one
of its principal tributaries, Cranberry, Cherry, Hominy, or Meadow rivers.

"The main dividing mountain of the district makes an irregular topographic break extending rudely east and west in a sinuous line through
the southern side of the property, mainly in Greenbrier county, from Cold
Knob, on the east, to the Sugar Grove Knob, on the west, in Nicholas county, beyond which point the ridge breaks away westward to the gap of Meadow river, at Bays Ferry, near the Nicholas-Greenbrier line.

"The elevation of this great regional divide is approximately 4400 feet
A. T. on the east at Cold Knob, and holds an elevation of 4000 feet to Beach
Knob.   From here west it declines to 3864 feet at the Bush Place; 3588 feet
at the low gap at Grassy Knob; 3392 feet at Buck Knob, where the Nicholas
road crosses the mountain, and from there westward holds an elevation of
about 3000 feet to Sugar Grove Knob.   Meadow river cuts down to the base
of this ridge at 1905 feet above tide, and in its flow northward erodes an ever
deepening channel to its mouth at the Carnefix ferry, on Gauley river, at
1184 feet above tide.

"Therefore the elevations at this point (1184 feet) and that of Cold
Knob (4384 feet), a difference of just 3200 feet, represent all the changes of
topography within the limits of the property, the whole country gradually
rising southeastward from the Gauley river canyon on a long slope for 24
miles, to the dividing ridge, a total rise of 2400 feet, or 100 feet per mile.
But from this summit, down the southeast slope to the same elevation of
2000 feet on the Greenbrier river, the descent is made in eight miles, or just
three times as rapidly, 300 feet per mile. ....

"Meadow creek occupies the same strategic importance for access to the proper development of the western portion of the property and district as Big Laurel occupies with reference to the eastern side, and fortunately each presents no engineering difficulties whatever to provide for the entire development of these lands. Both of these valleys present many excellent sites for mining operations, especially along Meadow creek, where the principal mining seam of the district outcrops at a convenient elevation above the stream nearly to its head; and it is through this valley that connection should eventually be made with the extensive outcrop along the waters of Hominy.

STRUCTURE.—"The structure of this coal field, viewed from every possible standpoint, could scarcely be more favorable for economic development and mining; it is everywhere simple and regular. Indeed, if this had not been the case, it would have been well nigh impossible to have so generally succeeded, during the past season, in opening the several coal seams in so many places; for, with very few exceptions, the coal beds are so firm and weather-resisting that the whole country, prior to development, was a coal field *without outcrop*. There were no 'benches' marking the topography, save those made by massive beds of sandstone, and scarcely any 'blossoms' of coal beds to indicate the possible presence of the concealed coal.

"Therefore, what was at first an almost hopeless task, to accomplish in one brief season's field work, proved to be altogether feasible through the perfect regularity of the geological structure of the coal measures. After a few starting points were secured, it was found entirely feasible to locate the approximate position of the outcrops by barometric leveling from ravine to ravine, from hillside to hillside, and ultimate development at such locations rarely failed to show the coal seam, save where surface wash or boulders were encountered.

"While throughout the area there appears to be no exception to the prevalently accepted theory of a *northwest* dip, or inclination of the measures from the dividing ridge on the south, toward the Gauley river, the rate of dip, or percentage of fall, is neither constant nor uniform; but even in this respect the resulting structural effects are always favorable to the preservation of the mineral wealth of this property, and rather aid, than retard, the cheap mining of its included coal beds...

"Without repeating in detail the several minor flexures, developed along Big Laurel, it was clearly shown, by the carefully taken levels at the various coal openings there, that a coal-level line, or line of no dip, had a bearing of about N. 40° E. and S. 50° W., or practically parallel to the Nicholas-Greenbrier county line; on a course of S. 40° W., there is a slight rise to the southwest, varying from 1.5 per cent. to 2.5 per cent.

"The practical effect of this structure on mining in this special region, is that all the coal contained between the several western branches of Big Laurel—and along both sides of the main stream itself—can be opened and mined from the Big Laurel front, thereby entailing a minimum amount of lateral railroad construction, instead of having to go to the heads of these streams for economical locations of plants.

"At right angles to the coal level line, on a course of N. 40° W., the coal shows its *greatest average dip*, though this dip naturally varies in strength in a field of such extent.

"The average dip along Big Laurel was found not to exceed 4.5 per cent., which is an exceedingly favorable one for mining operations. Towards the head of the stream, near the Job's Knob dividing ridge, the initial dip is only 2.5 per cent., succeeded northward down the next three miles by a dip of less than half of one per cent. to near the county line. Thence to Pack Fork it increases to 2.7 to 3 per cent., beyond which the coal remains nearly level for some distance, the coal falling only 100 feet in the mile between openings 26 and 22. From this point the coal bed contours indicate a very regular, gentle slope to the northwest, gradually declining in strength towards the Gauley river, so that in all the wide, unbroken coal area, watered by Taylor and Panther creeks, the measures evidently lie in a most favorable condition for economical mining.

"The total fall from opening No. 1, on the Gauley seam, above the mouth of Big Laurel, to opening No. 451, where that coal passes below water level, on Gauley river, is 617 feet, and the distance seven miles; if there be no irregularity of structure between these two points, the average dip of 88' per mile, or roughly 1.5 per cent., would enable the rapid development of this district on very cheap mining plans, and, indeed, a very large portion of the entire district, over to Hominy creek, could be made tributary to drift mines from Panther creek.

"A moment's inspection of the Structural Map Plate No. 5, will show the extreme regularity of the coal field to the south, over a belt three miles wide in Nicholas county, from Big Laurel creek across to Leivasy and Hominy Falls, the dip averaging about 5 per cent. The same structure prevails southward, for a mile and a-half into Greenbrier county, until the great anticlinal flat is reached, marked by Beech Knob and Pollock Mountain, where the contours show a wide area of coal at 3500 feet A. T.

"The interpolation of the 3550 foot contour line on this part of the map, has more sharply defined the structure, and lends character to the dominating feature of the coal topography. At opening No. 35, on Big Laurel creek, the Gauley seam has an elevation of 3577 feet A. T., and virtually marks the crown of this anticlinal arch, from which the coal dips northwest on a gradually declining slope to Gauley river.

"On the south side of this arch, however, the anticlinal is succeeded by a narrow synclinal basin, marked generally by the trough of Big Clear creek, from a mile north of Duo down to the mouth of Brown's creek, the coal falling 100 feet in 1½ miles southeast from Beech Knob, and then rising in gentle waves out of the basin to the final outcrop in the county........

"The *Beech Knob anticlinal axis* expires at the southwest end of Pollock mountain, in which knob the coal also reaches a maximum elevation of about 3575 feet A. T., so that in descending the valley of Big Clear creek, below Brown's creek and toward Rupert, there is no cessation in the pronounced southeast rise of the measures, as the contours plainly show. Between Mill creek and Big Clear creek, along Meadow river, this dip amounts to 700 feet in an air line distance of 2½ miles, a rate of 300 feet per mile, or 6 per cent., and this accounts for the lifting of the red shales high in the ridges here, and the absence of all but the lowest coal measure rocks on Big mountain and Little ridge.

"The structure in the Burdets and Toms creek district, west of Meadow creek, shows a distinct flattening in the dip, the measures falling northwest 150 feet per mile, or 3 per cent. as far as Burdets creek, and then 75 feet per mile, or 1.5 per cent., to the disappearance of the Gauley seam below water level on Meadow river.

"What modifications of structure future developments will eventually show to prevail along the Nicholas–Greenbrier county line, to the west of the Nicholas road and Hominy creek, cannot now be determined, but the cross-section derived along the west side of Hominy, taken in connection with the structure prevailing along Burdets creek, would seem to suggest perfect regularity of structure in this area between these limits.

"The Price fork of Hominy creek, and the main stream itself, shows most interesting structural conditions, which continue well into the head of the fork into the Peaser's ridge territory; but despite the development of sharper curves here from the determined levels at many coal openings, the crop is so open, and the average rate of dip so uniform, that this whole area of thick coal should be won with great economy and ease in mining, especially as it is all self-draining..

GEOLOGY.—"As the object of the recent development of this property was solely to ascertain its commercial values, the number and extent of its coal beds, and the chemical quality of the several seams, a brief reference to the geological features is all that seems pertinent.

"In Pennsylvania, where perhaps more attention has been paid to the correlation and sub-division of the Carboniferous Formation than in other states, the coal measure series has been divided into the following groups:

1. Upper Productive Coal Measures.   (Monongahela River Series.)
2. Barren Measures.   (Elk River Series of West Va.)
3. Lower Productive Coal Measures.   (Allegheny River Series.)
4. Pottsville Conglomerate Measures.   (New River - Pocohontas Series of West Va.)

"In this Gauley-New River Field, all the commercial values attach to the fourth, or *Conglomerate* (New River) *Series*, the other groups not being present on your property.

"The series in Pennsylvania rarely exceeds 250 feet in thickness, and, except in the extreme western portion of the state, is devoid of commercial coal. The same formation entering West Virginia, rapidly increases in thickness, until along the Gauley and its tributaries, on New and Guyandot rivers, and along the Elkhorn in the Pocahontas district, it presents a massive formation of sandstone and included shales 1200 to 1400 feet thick.

"All the well known steam and coking coals of the Gauley, New River, and Pocahontas-Flat Top coal districts are germane to this group. No complete correlation of the coal seams in these three districts has as yet been perfected, mainly because of the varying thickness and commercial value of the different individual coal seams, even within some one field, but

much excellent work has been done in recent years to eliminate the erroneous idea that there were a great number of seams of equal value in these
several fields and measures. And it is the rule, rather than the exception,
to find some one coal seam of such preeminent stability and value, as to
overshadow all others, at least in an economic sense.

"Thus in the Elkhorn-Sandy River district, to the south, the *No. 3 or
Pocahontas coal seam*, near the base of the group, supplies fully 95 per cent.
of all the tonnage won from the Conglomerate Series—a truly magnificent
seam of coal, and one whose reputation is so firmly established as to form a
standard for comparison in other portions of the country.

"The New River district, commercially speaking, yields the tonnage
from two coal seams—the *Sewell* or *Nuttall* above, and the *Fire creek* or
Quinnimont below— separated by about 350 to 375 feet of measures, and in
places by only 260 feet.

"As the Gauley district, covered by the lands of your Association, is
a direct northeastern prolongation of the New River field, the geological
features are, in the main, very similar, though there was no opportunity for
connecting the outcrops of the coal seams across the belt of 25 miles, separating Meadow and New rivers.

"Both the *Fire creek* and *Sewell coals* have been extensively mined
through the canon of New river, and the general excellence of their fuel is
now very widely recognized; but as these coals must naturally form the basis
for both a geologic and commercial comparison with the coals of the Gauley
field, it may be well to review the data secured as the result of mining developments there.

"The *Fire creek* seam is mined at numerous points on New river,
among which may be mentioned Quinnimont, Prince, Slater, Alaska, Claire-
mont, Beechwood, Dimmock, Rush Run, Red Ash, Central, Firecreek, and
at the lower mines at Stonecliff and Beury. These mines are mostly shown
on the Key Map, page 2, and at all of them the identity of the seam mined
is emphasized by its occurrence at from 250 to 300 feet below the *top* of the
Raleigh Conglomerate sandstone, a persistent and valuable bench mark
from which to measure *down* to the Firecreek and *up* to the Sewell coal.
This rock caps the edge of the gorge for 20 miles up New river from Firecreek station.

"The coal is described as :

'usually firm, bright, of excellent coking
quality, and well adapted for steam purposes; but its great irregularity in
thickness is frequently a serious drawback in the commercial development
of the seam. It appears to lie in swamps or basins, in which the coal ranges
from 3 to 5 feet in thickness; but the swamps are usually surrounded by areas
in which it is very much thinner, and in places is wanting altogether.'*

"Some idea of its variation in thickness may be judged from the following.

	Ft. In.	Ft. In.
Quinnimont	2 0	to 4 6

*17th Annual Report, U. S. C. G., p. 492, Mendenhall and Campbell.

Prince..................................	3	6	" 4	0
McKendree : abandoned : coal found only......	1	6		
Slater : old mines very thin : new mines up creek ....……….....	2	0	" 4	0
Alaska : carries a heavy band of top pyrites : average .... ……......	4	0	" 6	0
Thurmond........	3	6		
Rush Creek	5	8		
Red Ash...				
Rush Run: varies greatly from a very thin section up to			5	0
Fire creek (too thin to mine below this point)	2	0	" 5	0

"The *Sewell formation*, above the Raleigh sandstone, is a mass of shales and sandstones of variable thickness. At Cotton Hill, where its base passes below water level in New river, it is but 280 feet; at Gaymont 320 feet; at Fayette 370 feet; and at Caperton 500 feet. The top member of this massive sandstone makes the Kanawha Falls as it disappears in the bed of New River at Gauley bridge.

"The *Sewell coal* in this formation occurs about 70 feet above the base of the group, or, roughly, 320 to 370 feet above the lower *Fire creek coal*. It is the most important and valuable seam of the *Conglomerate series* on New river, and the fairly constant thickness and wide persistency it maintains, renders it of greater economic value than the *Fire creek seam* in this region.

"It is mined at Stonecliff, Thurmond, Beury, East Sewell, Sewell, Caperton, Nuttall, Fayette, Elmo, Sunnyside, and Gaymont, besides on Keeney creek, at Clifftop, and on Dunloop creek.

"Through all this large area it holds a fairly regular thickness, but thins gradually towards the northwest, and disappears altogether before its horizon passes below water level at Cotton Hill.

"In the high land, in the bend between Sewell and Meadow creek, it has been frequently opened, but it is thin and poor. Farther west, opposite McKendree, it shows 4 feet, and on the head waters of Loop creek 5 feet to 6 feet. In passing eastward from Thurmond, it averages about as follows: Beury, 3 feet and 6 inches to 4 feet and 6 inches; Keeny creek, 3 feet and 5 inches; Nuttall, 3 feet and 6 inches; Elmo, 3 feet; Sunnyside 3 feet; Gaymont, 2 feet and 10 inches, and Hawk's Nest, 2 feet and 6 inches................

"While, as previously stated, no attempt has been made to correlate the coals of the two sections, their parallelism is sufficiently palpable to permit a tentative identity between the *Sewell seam* of New river and the *Gauley seam* of Greenbrier and Nicholas counties. This suggested correlation cannot be carried further, for, as there is no great river cutting a passage through and down to the base of the coal measures in this northern field, as is the case along the Chesapeake and Ohio railroad, the exposure of the coals *below* the "Gauley seam" is confined largely to the south end of the district, along the tributaries of Big Clear creek, Mill, Laurel, and Meadow creeks.

"It is, perhaps, too soon to express a final opinion with regard to the special characteristics of the coal seams themselves; but the field examination, just completed, leaves no doubt of the general harmony of the two districts, or of the prevailing excellence and general superiority of the upper coal bed in each.

"Both, in fact, are integral parts of one great coal field, stretching from *Pocahontas*, on the south, through McDowell, Wyoming, Raleigh, Fayette, Greenbrier, and Nicholas counties, but limited north, *commercially*, by Big Laurel creek.

"Throughout this area, each commercial district presents the same characteristic features of marginal development, and none is exempt from the general rule of presenting coals that are thicker and of more uniform bed section, along the southeastern margin of the field, than they are to the northwest, where the coal beds, germane to these measures, sink beneath the water level... ....

"Hence it is that the coal, exposed in the dividing ridge at the head of Meadow river, Clear creek, Hominy, and Big Laurel, appears to be much thicker, and more regular in section, than it is in the central portion of the district, around Leivasy and Hominy Falls, and these latter probably thin away as they pass under cover northwestward toward the Gauley.

"Nevertheless, the coal itself always presents a fuel of remarkable purity and excellence, so that it is possible to say that no better or cleaner steam and coking coal is mined today anywhere in the United States than is found so widely distributed on this property..................... . ...

"It is, perhaps, only too manifest that all of it will not be equally productive; that portions of it will yield more coal per acre than others. But the important fact stands out clearly, that whatever of coal value there is germane to the Carboniferous system of rocks, between the Gauley river and the eastern edge of the field, is all contained within the boundaries of the Association property.. ....

"Meadow river, Big Clear creek, Hominy and its tributaries, Grassy and Brushy Meadow creeks, and the large area drained by Big Laurel, offer innumerable and excellent sites for mining operations. Coal of workable thickness, great purity and of high grade steam and coking quality, outcrops for miles above water level on these various streams, everywhere accessible under the most favorable conditions for economical mining.........................

"Finally, reference has been made to the existence of special areas of 'thin coal' in this district, which, with relation to the *Gauley coal seam*, is more conspicuously the case on Big Laurel approaching Cherry river, around and below Hominy Falls and Leivasy; at the head of the Elijah branch of the north fork of Big Clear creek, and especially, in the Burdets creek area approaching the loop in Meadow river, where the seam has evidently split.

"This is inevitable in any large coal field, and of course, the importance of these changes is magnified where the average coal section does not exceed 4 feet in thickness, but the same conditions prevail along the New river, as already shown, and even as far south as Pocahontas, and in this Gauley district (as elsewhere) there is always a compensation. Where the mining seam is cut down below 3 feet, the thinner coat almost invariably yields the best quality, and moreover, the good coal, in thinned sections, frequently carries above or below a certain thickness of laminated coal and slate, not fit for shipment, but of distinct economic value in providing cheap headroom in mining.

"This coal always carries a slate roof (except in isolated cases along the limited outcrop on Gauley river), and over the entire district has an abundant cover above its outcrop...

"*DEVELOPMENTS.* The work of development on the lands of your Association was carried through a period of about six months, and without reference to your property lines, or the lines of intervening reservations. In other words, the several coal outcrops were followed irrespective of property lines, with the end in view of presenting a complete exposition of the size, section and value of the several coal seams in the entire district...................

"This statement applys more specifically to the outcrop of the *Gauley* (*Sewell*) *seam*, because more attention was given it in development, from the fact that it was more persistent and widespread. The *lower coals* vary so greatly both in section and interval, as to render it very difficult to follow them successfully from one part of the region to another. Their correlation, as shown on the map, is therefore only tentative and approximate; they create values where the *Gauley seam* is absent. ....

"The *Record Map* contains two different tints of Payne's gray:

"*1st.* The darkest of the two to show the outcrop and area of the principal and uppermost mining seam of the district, the so called *Gauley coal bed*, which may be tentatively correlated with the *Sewell seam* of the New river district.

"*2nd.* The lighter tint indicates approximately the position, area and relation of the lowest workable coal of this region, provisionally called the *Echols coal bed*, which is the fourth seam below the Gauley, and 200 feet above the red shale.

"It is needless to say that this seam has a much larger area geologically, than the Gauley, and in addition to occupying a very large territory to the south of the *Gauley area*, where that overlying seam is absent, it also necessarily underlies all the region to the northwest, tinted to represent the area of the upper coal. Its economic condition there, however, is of course unknown and problematical, for as it occurs on an average of about 600 feet *beneath* the Gauley coal, it is largely concealed wherever the upper seam occupies the country.

"Between, above, and below these two controlling seams of the section, there are additional coal beds, whose value and interval vary constantly through this large coal field..

"It might be said that throughout the district, there is no *commercial coal* anywhere *above* the Gauley seam, or *below* the Echols. But the intermediate coals, between these two well defined horizons, frequently become of commercial size and importance, especially in the southern portion of the field, on the waters of Big Clear creek, Laurel, and Mill creek, and while they nowhere possess the persistency, integrity of section, or the high fuel value of the *Gauley seam*, they will undoubtedly furnish a large future auxiliary tonnage. Reference to the chapter on the 'Chemistry of the Coals,' will show their general inferiority as compared with the *Gauley seam*, especially in contents of sulphur and ash; still, they suffer chiefly through comparison with this coal of unusual purity and constancy, rather than from any inherent lack of merit as fairly good steam coals.

"What they lack principally, is constancy of section and character, and this, together with their varying interval in their relation to each other, and to the upper and lower standard coal horizons, has made their identification in many places difficult and imperfect, especially as time did not permit the thorough development of their outcrops.

"Two of these intermediate seams, noted in the section plate as *Coal No. 2*, or *first* below the Gauley, and *Coal No. 3*, or *second* below the Gauley, are really the only intermediate coals of any value, and where they show commercial size at all, they often yield good coal. With but few notable exceptions, both rarely show seams of mining value in the same locality, and in general it may be said that the upper of the two, or the *No. 2 seam*, is of the least importance, showing best in isolated patches on Joe's Knob and Briery Knob, south of the South fork of Big Clear creek. Its interval beneath the Gauley ranges from 160 feet to 190 feet, except on Big Laurel, where it is 130 feet±.

"The *No. 3*, or *Second Lower seam*, shows workable character and dimensions on *Laurel*, *Mill* and *Browns creeks*, where it is locally known as the "*Laurel vein*," and is roughly 300 feet beneath the *Gauley seam*. In the Big and Little Clear creek territory its mining value is quite variable, sometimes good but more often inferior. And while it holds its general average interval of 300 feet beneath the *Gauley bed*, the interval of 150 feet ± between it and the next higher, *No. 2 seam*, is extremely variable, averaging about 100 feet, but only 10 feet to 30 feet on Joe,s Knob in Little Clear creek mountain. It is practically worthless on Big Laurel, where its section is spoiled by frequent partings. On stratigraphic grounds it may be assumed to represent the impoverished horizon of the *Fire creek seam* of New river, and like that seam, is uncertain and sporadic in occurence. It shows, however, some excellent sections at widely separated points.

"The *Echols bed* is in some respects one of the most remarkable seams of the series, but it can in no sense be considered to have regional commercial value, though showing excellent sections and good quality at many places.

"At the five widely separated points, where it was sampled, to-wit: opening No. 588, on Smokehouse branch of Big Clear creek, above the Manspile place; No. 594, the *Echols bank* above the Rupert-Duo road; No. 596, towards the head outcrop on Browns creek, and Nos. 609 and 610, on opposite sides of Hickory mountain, in the Buffalo mountain area, it shows a favorable section from 3 feet to 4 feet 4 inches thick, and yielding from 3 feet to 4 feet of good coal. These points are all well separated, showing a wide range of commercial possibility; but at a large number of other points, its section is by no means so favorable, its special drawback being its characteristic sandstone roof instead of slate, which almost invariably results in irregularity and imperfection.

"Occupying an average interval of 175 to 200 feet above the red shale measures of the *Greenbrier formation*, its stratigraphic position in the series can be fairly well defined by reason of the great change in color and lithology of the rocks, but it is often a thin seam of impure coal, too sporadic and too impoverished to warrant serious attention, save in connection with the development of superior overlying coals. As a geologic horizon to define and limit the base of the coal measures, it is of great usefulness.

"*CHEMISTRY OF THE COAL.*   Prior to the beginning of the preliminary investigation of this property, in the late autumn of 1900, there was absolutely no knowledge whatever of the chemical quality of the several coal beds, and indeed no record of any samples having been taken.

"There were perhaps a dozen openings from which coal had been dug for the local wants of the small population spread over this property, but otherwise, the entire area of this great 175,000 acre tract was totally undeveloped, its coal beds unopened and their presence only inferred. Every latitude was therefore asked and readily accorded, not only to open the several coal seams, but to carefully sample and have analyzed the developed sections, and this has been done without stint, without selection, and with only one object in view, viz., to arrive at a just and definite conclusion as to the *commercial character* of the fuel this coal field could furnish, in competition with the other well known steam and coking coals, annually going to market from the more highly developed *New river* and *Pocahontas fields* on the south.

"Fully ninety-five per cent of the samples secured were cut from coal beds merely faced on the outcrop, and the results recorded under the column of moisture or 'water,' in the succeeding tables of analyses, will clearly indicate the effect this necessity has involved. Nevertheless, in a majority of cases these beds show good, firm, commercial coal at their very outcrop. so that there will be little or no waste, or allowance to be made for rusty crop.

TABLE No. 1.

Coals sampled 1900.   Gauley Coal Land Association.

GAULEY (SEWELL) COAL SEAM.

Samples taken by E. V. d'Invilliers; duplicate check analyses by Mr. A. S. McCreath, Harrisburg, and N. M. Randall, Chemist Maryland Stee Company, Baltimore, 1900.

Map No.	Water.	V. M.	F. C.	Sul.	Ash.	Phos.	Total Sec. In.	Coal Sam. In.
2.	.926	27.014	67.372	.658	4.030	.010	38.5	38.5
		26.80	69.20	.630	4.00	.008		
18.	3.162	28.298	64.279	.571	3.690	.005	38.5	38.5
		23.90	72.60	.575	3.50	.004		
3.	2.344	27.556	65.584	.536	3.980	.023	45.0	45.0
		28.80	67.37	.616	3.90	.017		
19.	.802	26.928	68.871	.719	2.680	.017	48.0	46.0
		27.60	69.60	.616	2.80	.018		
4.	.846	27.314	66.960	.670	4.210	.016	47.5	47.5
		26.30	69.60	.617	4.10	.015		
5.	3.114	25.986	67.101	.779	3.020	.007	52.0	48.0
		27.40	69.40	.616	3.80	.003		
7.	1.466	26.404	64.135	.595	7.400	.008	39.0	39.0
		23.20	68.90	.496	7.90	.008		

8.	1.012	27.078	65.195	.695	6.020	.020	55.5	55.5
		26.30	66.90	.630	6.80	.013		
26.	1.260	28.660	66.513	.847	2.720	.009	47.0	45.0
		23.20	74.10	.524	2.70	.008		
27.	2.702	28.498	66.065	.575	2.160	.015	33.0	33.0
		28.40	69.45	.479	2.15	.012		
30.	1.206	29.144	67.196	.674	1.780	.003	32.0	32.0
		28.40	70.00	2.640	1.60	.002		
447.	1.082	27.738	68.684	.536	1.960	.003	32.0	32.0
		38.00	60.00	.507	2.00	.004		
424.	1.682	27.818	67.036	.584	2.880	.006	51.0	48.0
		28.50	68.80	.466	.270	.061		
422.	.916	27.814	68.482	.588	2.200	.007	47.0	47.0
		28.20	69.90	.575	1.90	.008		
31.	9.690	27.600	58.203	.477	4.030	.003	37.0	37.0
		34.20	62.30	.520	3.50	.003		
38.	2.482	28.558	64.313	.787	3.860	.008	46.0	44.0
		25.90	69.70	.670	4.40	.010		
39.	1.356	26.934	64.884	.856	5.970	.096	65.0	56.0
		26.20	68.50	.604	5.30	.044		
40.	.854	27.696	65.291	1.789	4.370	.017	50.0	50.0
		26.00	69.60	1.580	4.40	.010		
Average	1.601	27.614	66.351	.718	3.720	.010	45.2	44.0
"		27.620	68.660	.742	3.710	.0104		

"The exceedingly close agreement in these results leaves little doubt as to the accuracy of the chemical determinations, and this suite of analyses, representing a breadth of outcrop of nearly 15 miles, should clearly show the commercial character of the *Gauley seam* in this district.

"However, in order to pursue additional investigations on the ultimate ingredients of this coal, eight more samples of 40 pounds each, were secured by Mr. F. H. Anschutz, selected from the same openings.

"These samples, taken independently in December, 1900, were sent directly to the Maryland Steel Company, who reported the following interesting results:

Map No.	V. M.	F. C.	Sul.	Ash.	Phos.	Nitro.
2.	28.57	68.14	.620	3.29	.012	1.10
19.	26.90	69.90	.580	3.20	.018	1.18
4.	26.50	71.10	.375	2.40	.012	1.16
8.	27.10	67.20	1.040	5.70	.024	1.18
26.	28.00	69.45	.590	2.55	.009	1.20
30.	28.25	70.05	.540	1.70	.002	1.22
422.	26.80	71.40	.561	1.80	.002	1.18
31.	28.00	70.50	.480	1.50	.004	1.16
Average	27.51	69.72	.598	2.77	.0104	1.17

"On a ten hours' burning test these coals yielded an average of 16.44 lbs. Ammonium Sulphate per ton of coal, 127.20 lbs of tar, 9469 cubic feet of gas and 74.25 per cent. coke by weight.

"The next step was to make a reconnoissance of the whole field in February, 1901, when openings throughout the whole field (exclusive of the Big Laurel district) were sampled by S. E. Fairchild, Jr., assistant, and analyzed by Mr. McCreath.

TABLE No. 2

Coal samples 1901.   Gauley Coal Land Association.

GAULEY COAL SEAM.

Map No.	Water.	V. M.	F. C.	Sul.	Ash.	Total Sec. In.	Coal Sam. In.
57.	.612	26.428	69.082	1.098	2.780	49	49
158.	.670	26.030	71.678	.532	1.090	48	48
189.	.476	24.812	67.490	.960	6.260	67	51
180.	.504	24.656	70.141	.959	3.740	84	54
416.	.648	28.432	68.551	.559	1.810	64	40
308.	.576	28.024	68.976	.594	1.830	49	49
370.	.554	26.686	67.459	11.91	4.110	74	60
Average	.577	26.439	69.054	.842	3.090	62	50

TABLE No. 3.

Coals sampled 1901.   Gauley Coal Land Association.

GAULEY COAL SEAM.

Map No.	Water.	V. M.	F. C.	Sul.	Ash.	Phos.	Total Sec. Ft. In.		Coal Sam. Ft. In.	
187.	3.866	27.334	64.169	.791	3.840	.006	6	4	6	4
195.	3.320	27.340	63.683	.657	5.000	.006	6	2	6	0
183.	2.308	25.472	68.675	.615	2.930	.020	5	11	4	9
210.	2.960	28.160	66.432	.588	1.860	.003	5	5	5	5
202.	5.060	28.180	62.290	.540	3.930	.008	6	5	6	0
177.	.940	25.230	71.372	.698	1.760	.009	7	0	4	8
446.	.950	28.150	68.326	.514	2.060	.003	4	2	4	2
443.	.932	28.038	67.625	.585	2.820	.005	3	3	3	3
280.	1.000	28.060	67.387	.523	3.030	.002	3	7	3	7
306.	.900	29.210	67.306	.544	2.040	.006	5	0	4	9
297.	.876	29.314	67.835	.595	1.380	.003	6	7	4	2
50.	2.000	25.790	62.213	.697	9.300	....	3	6	3	6
54.	1.360	26.130	68.857	.813	2.840	.004	4	1	4	1
71.	1.030	26.490	67.670	1.080	3.730	.014	4	6	3	10
72.	1.204	26.226	64.700	.730	7.140	.011	4	10	4	2
76.	1.010	29.310	66.293	1.637	4.750	.031	5	10	4	10
82.	1.426	26.944	66.651	.809	4.170	.012	4	6	3	6
88A.	1.160	26.170	68.124	.646	3.900	....	5	11	3	4
362.	1.020	26.650	67.955	.865	3.510	.002	5	0	5	0
353.	2.440	26.680	65.436	1.344	4.100	.011	6	1	4	10
375.	1.174	27.176	69.162	.578	1.910	.004	5	9	3	0
379.	.956	26.104	69.962	.748	2.230	.002	4	9	4	0
396.	1.060	26.010	69.731	.679	2.520	.005	3	11	3	11
403.	1.060	27.000	69.420	.660	1.860	.002	4	8	4	1
157.	1.580	25.880	70.781	.589	1.170	.002	3	4	3	4
154.	1.980	25.680	67.114	.796	4.430	.024	5	2	5	1
125.	3.200	25.650	63.703	1.147	6.300	.002	5	0	5	0
120.	1.546	25.154	68.029	1.121	4.150	.003	4	5	4	5
131.	.820	27.590	66.502	.988	4.100	.008	3	10	3	10
145.	3.860	27.460	64.012	.708	3.960	.006	4	8	4	8
394.	.874	27.726	68.762	.738	1.900	.003	4	2	4	1
204.	4.360	26.880	64.591	.629	3.540	.002	6	8	6	3
385.	.930	26.510	68.119	.711	3.730	.008	6	7	6	7

No.	Water	V. M.	F. C.	Sul.	Ash	Phos.	Total Sec.	Coal Sam.
168.	1.810	24.920	68.278	.692	4.300	0.07	10 2	4 7
452.	1.122	30.408	65.800	.600	2.070	......	8 0	4 4
460.	.870	29.930	63.939	1.641	3.600	......	3 10	3 10
10.	1.080	28.180	66.800	.690	3.250	.014	4 0	4 0
309.	5.790	26.170	64.449	.511	3.080	.003	5 6	5 0
315.	.690	27.810	69.172	.698	1.630	.003	7 11	4 6
322.	2.050	27.360	66.540	.820	3.230	.004	5 6	4 10
348.	4.310	28.390	61.979	1.031	4.290	.008	5 9	4 1
345.	3.456	28.714	64.647	.563	2.620	.004	6 1	4 8
271.	1.584	26.196	62.491	1.189	8.540	....	2 10	2 10
47.	1.120	26.520	64.892	.928	6.540	......	4 2	4 2
55.	1.832	26.178	66.136	1.474	4.380	......	3 8	3 8
457.	.710	29.985	66.044	.791	2.470	.003	3 8½	3 8½
254.	2.420	26.915	66.947	.693	3.025	.008	4 7	3 9
Average	1.830	27.114	66.617	.801	3.615	.007	5 2	4 5

"The above determinations dried at 212 Fahr., were made by Mr. A. S. McCreath, Chemist, of Harrisburg, which is a sufficient guarantee of the chemical part of the work. The sampling I stand personally responsible for, and the workable portion of each bed sampled is shown in the last column of figures.

CHEMISTRY OF THE LOWER COAL SEAMS.—"In addi" tion to the samples secured from the *upper*, or *Gauley* seam, reported in the previous tables, samples were taken at various places where good exposures of the underlying coal seams were made, in order to arrive at some valuation of the chemical character of this auxiliary tonnage.

"These underlying seams outcrop above water level only at the southern end of the field, on the waters of Clear creek and tributaries of Meadow river, and, to a large extent, on the head waters of Big Laurel; there is also a closed outcrop of the first commercial seam below the Gauley on the waters of Hominy creek.

"The results of analyses are recorded in the following table, in the order in which these coals occur beneath the Gauley seam:

TABLE NO. 4.

Analyses of No. 2 Seam, or First Lower Coal.

Coals sampled 1901.   Gauley Coal Land Association.

Map No.	Water.	V. M.	F. C.	Sul.	Ash.	Total Sec. In.	Coal Sam. In.
472.	2.100	26.550	64.904	1.396	5.050	39	39
477.	4.800	26.500	63.763	.887	4.050	51	51
480.	1.040	23.470	63.807	1.473	10.210	60	60
495.	.900	26.400	67.234	1.066	4.500	34	32
501.	1.600	25.440	56.899	1.511	14.550	33	33
503.	.860	25.580	58.469	2.781	12.310	36	36
Average	1.883	25.657	62.513	1.519	8.428	42	42

Analyses of No. 3 Seam, or Second Lower Coal.

517.	3.450	28.650	59.251	.949	7.700	51½	46
520.	3.300	28.100	60.680	.770	7.150	46	45½

526.	2. 850	25. 900	63. 475	. 625	7. 150	54	53
534.	1. 600	26. 900	63. 655	1. 245	6. 600	54	53
536.	1. 350	27. 200	63. 631	. 869	6. 850	59½	54½
552.	2. 900	25. 400	58. 158	1. 492	12. 050	43½	42
568.	1. 100	23. 850	70. 788	. 612	3. 650	41	41
Average...2. 364		26. 572	62. 805	. 952	7. 307	50	48

Analyses of No. 4 (Echols) or Third Lower Coal.

588.	. 700	25. 370	68. 216	. 814	4. 900	36	36
593.	1. 540	23. 720	64. 520	. 890	10. 330	52	46
596.	. 700	25. 950	64. 750	1. 300	7. 300	43	37
609.	3. 950	25. 600	67. 656	. 694	2. 100	33	33
610.	1. 950	25. 500	65. 294	1. 506	5. 750	48	45
Average...1. 768		25. 028	66. 087	1. 041	6. 076	42½	39½

TABLE NO. 5.

Comparative Analyses of Pocahontas, New River and Gauley Coals, all from the same Conglomerate Coal Measure Seams.

COAL DISTRICT.	Water.	V. M.	F. C.	Sul.	Ash.	Phos.
1. *Pocahontas—Flat Top* [1]...... . 987 Elkhorn Dist. :22 samp.		18. 455	74. 429	. 701	5. 428	
2. *Pocahontas—Flat Top* [2]...... ..968 Dry Fork Dist. :9 samp.		19. 581	73. 354	. 856	5. 240	
3. *New River* [3] 4 samp........... . 683		19. 242	74. 390	. 664	4. 935	

Samples taken from the "Gauley" Coal Seam.

4. *Gauley (Big Laurel)* [4].......1. 601 average 18 samp.		27. 614	66. 351	. 718	3. 720	. 010
4a. ditto: ditto: [5]		27. 620	68. 660	. 742	3. 710	. 0104
5. ditto: ditto: [6]		27. 510	69. 720	. 598	2. 770	. 0104
6. *Gauley: Meadow River* [7] ... . 577 average 7 samp.		26. 439	69. 054	. 842	3. 090	
7. *GAULEY DISTRICT* [8]..1. 830 average 47 samp.		27. 114	66. 617	. 801	3. 615	. 0070

Composition of Seams below the Gauley Coal: Gauley Coal Land Ass'n.

8. *First Lower Seam* [9]............1. 883 average 6 samp.		25. 657	62. 513	1. 519	8. 428	
9. *Second Lower Seam* [9].........2. 364 average 7 samp.		26. 572	62. 805	. 952	7. 307	
10. *Third Lower (Echols)* [9]......1. 768 average 5 samp.		25. 028	66. 087	1. 041	6. 076	

Notes: [1] Sampled by A. S. McCreath—E. V. d'Invilliers: analyzed by A. S. McCreath.
[2] Sampled by E. V. d'Invilliers; analyzed by A. S. McCreath.
[3] Includes two samples by S. E. Fairchild 1901: analyzed by A. S. McCreath.
[4] Sampled by E. V. d'Invilliers 1900 analyzed by A. S. McCreath.
[5] " " " " 1900 " Md. Steel Co.
[6] " F. H. Anschutz 1900 " "
[7] " S. E. Fairchild, Jr. 1901 " A. S. McCreath.
[8] " E. V. d'Invilliers 1901 " "
[9] " " " " 1901 " E. K. Landis.

"Its unitormity of composition can probably be better shown graphically in tabular form:

Volatile Matter,.........	72 samples:	extremes	24. 656 pr. ct.	and	30. 408 pr. ct.
Fixed Carbon.............	71* "	"	61. 979	"	71. 678
Sulphur	72 "	"	. 477	"	1. 789
Ash..........................	72 "	"	1. 090	"	9. 300
Phosphorus	40 "	"	. 002	"	. 096

"On still further analyzing these results we find that:—

Volatile Matter:	1 sample	yields	more than			30 pr. ct.
	37 samples	yield	between	27	and	30
	31 "	"	"	25	"	27
	3 "	"	less than			25
Fixed Carbon:	4 "	"	more than			70 pr. ct.
	49 "	"	between	65	"	70
	19 "	"	"	60	"	65
Sulphur:	12 "	"	more than			1 pr. ct.
	59 "	"	between	.5	"	1
Ash:	4 "	"	"	7	"	9
	6 "	"	"	5	"	7
	62 "	"	less than			5
Phosphorus:	16 "	"	more than			.010
	20 "	"	between	.005	"	.010
	22 "	"	less than			.005

"The several tables of analyses, presenting without exclusion, determinations of every sample secured from all parts of the Gauley Coal Land Association, call for no very extended comment.

"Naturally, importance attaches principally to the *Gauley seam*, for it is at once the thickest, most persistent and most generally accessible bed of the New river (Conglomerate) series in this district; moreover, it is everywhere a bed of commercial size, as well of general excellence and purity.

"During the progress of the field examinations, from the Autumn of 1900 to the close of the season in 1901, seventy-two samples for analysis were taken from this one seam, thoroughly representing all portions of the field where this coal outcrops above water level. These samples were cut with the sole object of representing the commercial character of the coal, and represent the workable portions of the same as it would be mined on a commercial scale.

"A general average of the seventy-two samples shows a coal of the following excellent composition:

Water...	1. 660 per ct.	
Volatile matter...27. 162		"
Fixed carbon........ ....66. 786		"
Sulphur 784		"
Ash 3. 590		"
Phosphorus ....:............................. . 008		"

"A coal of such a chemical composition needs no commendation, for

---

*Excluding one sample from opening No. 31, at Lile P. O., McMillian creek, where 9. 690 per cent moisture indicates an abnormal weathering at this point.

there is nothing better in the market today. This is a strong assertion, but the results demand such an expression as a frank tribute to the great purity of this fuel.

"The special points of merit about this coal, for steam purposes, are its favorable percentage of fixed carbon in connection with its extremely low ash; and for coking, the additional feature of possessing such a sufficiency of volatile hydrocarbons as to render the coking effects complete, without necessarily consuming some of the fixed carbon in the process. In practice, a coal of this composition should produce not less than 70 per cent. yield.

"The element of low phosphorus is also most important as indicating a wide range of consumption for the coke for all classes of metallurgical use. In every respect, therefore, this coal yields a first-class steam and coking fuel, which will merit for it a ready market, both east and west.................

DETAILED DESCRIPTION OF THE DIFFERENT AREAS.

BIG LAUREL DISTRICT.—"The Gauley seam outcrops continuously along the west bank of Big Laurel, and everywhere within the property shows a high grade coal and of commercial thickness. Its section varies from about 3 feet, 3 inches up to 5 feet, 8 inches, gradually increasing in thickness going south up stream towards the margin of the field.

"Between these extreme points, however, there is a local thinning over a narrow belt, extending east and west from below Pack branch, in which the coal is under 3 feet thick, but its quality is excellent.

"On the east bank of the creek, the coal is generally thick as far south as the Nixon place, and under Kerless Knob, where it shows a beautiful section of four feet thick, and of very superior quality. As the crop swings around Little Kerless Knob, to extend down Little Laurel, every attempt to develop good commercial coal failed.

"There is a limit to everything, of course, but the conditions of topography in the Big Mountain all so strongly favor the presence of a splendid coal area (especially in connection with the results obtained on its west side along Big Laurel) that the inference is rather towards a belief in the presence of coal here than its absence, and the wide, saucer-like erosion of the hill, at the head of Little Laurel, makes the uncovering of coal extremely difficult and expensive.

"To the south of Kerless Knob the *Gauley seam* is present only in remnants, six such patches showing on the Record Map along the Jettsville road, west of View school house, represented by sections 14, 15 and 16. The Chew opening, No. 14, represents an area of 60 to 75 acres, with less than 100 feet of covering, at 3620 feet A. T.; but the coal is still good, showing in all a thickness of 3 feet and 8 inches, with 4 inches of slate parting 4 inches below the roof.

"In openings 15 (3660 feet A. T.) and 16 (3708 feet A. T.) the coal has dwindled to 2 feet and 7 inches and 2 feet and 2 inches, respectively, while its last remnant catches in a small knob on the road near Boone's place, at

No. 17, (3872 feet A. T.), where the coal is but two feet. Hence this point marks both the geological and commercial limit of the *Gauley seam* in this whole region, none of the hills to the northeast or southeast rising high enough to hold it.

"*Seam No. 2* or *First Lower coal* in the Big Laurel area has been sparingly developed, its interval below the *Gauley seam* averaging 140 feet.

"Geologically, it extends from below the mouth of Pack branch, south to the head of Big Laurel, but while a number of test openings were made on it during 1900, they were not considered of sufficient importance to locate instrumentally then, and do not, therefore, appear on the Record Map. The sections on McMillian creek, at the Gwinn banks Nos. 463 and 464, show from 3 feet to 3 feet and 6 inches of coal, the top 2 feet good and the bottom bony and impure. At opening No. 465, above the Hunt cabin, it shows 3 feet of very pretty soft coal, 200 feet above the creek.

"On Hog Camp ridge, to the south, there are additional openings where the coal swells to nearly 6 feet, but the integrity of its section is spoiled by carrying a 2 foot fireclay slate parting below the roof. A second opening, farther south, shows 8 inches bony top coal; 20 inches slate; 6 inches coal; 1 inch bone, and 3 inches coal: in all 3 feet and 2 inches. On Lynn branch the section is 4 feet, but streaked with thin seams of slate and bands of sulphur.

"On the east side of Big Laurel creek, this coal is first recognized at opening No. 516, south of Kerless Knob, where it yields only a thin section of 8 inches of coal, and from there east its crop should extend across the Richwood road into the highest land in the Lost Flat area under Manning Knob. It is extremely doubtful whether this coal bed is caught in any of the property to the south, a district of great ruggedness and devoid of culture, except possibly in a patch in Cold Knob opening No. 515, where the bed is 3 feet and 2 inches thick.

"*Seam No. 3*, or *Second Lower coal*, has a somewhat larger area, due to its position, 150 to 200 feet, below the *First Lower bed*. Very little of it shows commercial proportions, though diligent search was made for it along many of the tributaries of Big Laurel.

"Rising from water level on the main stream near the Nicholas-Greenbrier county line, it is first opened at the Robinson place opening No. 517, a coal which has been variously claimed to represent the *Gauley seam*. This has not been definitely disproved by the location and opening of the higher seam above it. The Robinson coal shows a mixed section of coal and slate for something over three feet below the roof, and 41 inches of fair coal in the lower bench, its analysis yielding 1.55 per cent. sulphur, and but 4.75 per cent. ash.

"East to the Richwood road, its horizon was repeatedly tested without success, and at opening No. 518, on the road between Manning and Blue Knob, it shows 30 inches top coal, six inches slate, and 1½ inches coal, of fair quality.

"At the two openings, Nos. 519 and 520, on the south flank of the Lost Flat ridge, it suddenly thickens to good proportions and yields first-rate coal, the bed yielding about 4 feet; but it apparently loses this value on the north side of the ridge, where only 16 to 20 inches were found. Its condition in all the country south, around Blue and Cold Knobs, is unknown; but in Nunly mountain it is worthless.

"On the west side of Big Laurel, this seam was opened in several places during the season of 1900, but it was located at only one place—opening No. 522 on the south side of Beech run and east of Hunt's cabin, and at the head of a small branch called Rocky fork. Its imperfect section showed 16 inches top coal, 4 inches slate, and 40 inches bottom coal: in all 5 feet of section.

"In the Hog Camp ridge section it is split up with 6 inches top coal, 20 inches slate, 6 inches coal, 1 inch bone, 3 inches coal: in all 3 feet thick, and, as nowhere else on the east side of Big Laurel was it found, even if this was good it may be assumed worthless for mining in this valley.

"*The Echols*, or *Third Lower seam*, was rarely found. In all the hollows of the Middle and Coldspring branches were mere thin seams of coal at its horizon, though this country was difficult to prospect in. On Hog Camp it occurs 130 feet below No. 3 coal with 39 inches of top coal, 9 inches slate, and 19 inches of bone and slate at the bottom.

BIG CLEAR CREEK DISTRICT.—"This area embraces all the territory from the drainage of the North fork of Big Clear creek south to the Buffalo mountain, at the southern end of the property, and from the main Trout Run-Richwood road, passing Cold Knob on the east, to the road running between Rupert and Duo on the west. It is entirely a mountainous district, the many long ridges and spurs reaching elevations of 4000 feet A. T., while the separating valleys, watered by fine perennial branches of Big Clear creek, have been cut down to elevations of from 3500 to 3000 feet above tide.

"The geological section developed here extends from the coal about 150 feet above the *Gauley seam*, to the *Greenbrier red shale* formation, below the Coal Measures. The red shales reach high up both flanks of the Buffalo mountain, up Little Clear and Big Clear creeks nearly to their head springs, but for only a short distance up the North fork of the latter stream. This is the direct result of the structure of the district, and explains why the *Gauley coal*, and everything above it, has no representation in the high ridges south of the South fork of Big Clear creek.

"The seam of coal overlying the *Gauley bed* is persistent in Job Knob and Shell Camp ridge, with a thickness of 4 feet at opening No. 48; 3 feet at No. 82, and 2 feet at No. 37; it is everywhere variable as to section, and is not of commercial value.

"*The Gauley seam*, in the northern portion of the district, has been cut at many places along it entire outcrop, and exists in commercial condition at nearly all points. At the several typical openings, where the seam has been exposed with care, and with a view to permanency, it shows an average of about 50 inches, with partings of from 3 to 15 inches always occurring under the main bench of the seam, which runs from 38 inches to 43 inches...

"The opening on Elijah branch of Big Clear creek, northwards from

99, would indicate a decided local deterioration of the seam.   From opening No. 88A to the head of Big Clear creek, notwithstanding variation in the whole section, the seam maintains a fairly uniform main bench section, and closely represents conditions found along the entire crop line. At openings 61 and 58, together with those already mentioned as typical of the region, this main bench yields 46 inches and 50 inches of very clean, bright coal of most excellent chemical character.

"*The First Lower seam* (*No. 2*) occurs at from 110 to 188 feet below the *Gauley bed*, and is persistent through all the northern section except near the point of Shell Camp ridge, at the low place known as the Vaughn farm.   Its average thickness is about 40 inches.   Its character is well shown at opening No. 507, near the forks of Big Clear creek and Elijah branch, with 3 feet and 4 inches of coal, and farther up Big Clear creek to its head.

"On Shell Camp ridge, at opening No. 498. it shows in the field, north of the old Deitz place, 3 feet and 7 inches, and again near the Sublet house.   On Smokehouse it was cut at No. 494, showing top coal 7 inches, slate 2 inches, coal 22 inches.

"Its outcrop extends into Rock Camp ridge, at the head of the South fork, and back on the south side along Little Clear creek mountain to openings Nos. 474 and 475, at Knight meadow.   Here the crop turns south to No. 471, near Humes' camp, and thence through Big and Little Coon ridges, Point, Lick and Nunly mountains, where the seam has dwindled to only 12 inches.   It has a considerable area and good cover in the Buffalo mountain district, though its condition there is not known.

"In the two isolated areas on Joe and Briery Knobs it shows, perhaps, its best sections, and is, moreover, only separated from the next lower seam here by 10 to 30 feet of measures.   The seam in these knobs has swelled to a great extent, showing from 3 feet, 3 inches to 5 feet of good coal; but, unfortunately, its area is small, perhaps 40 acres in Briery Knob, and 150 acres in Joe Knob.   On Little Clear Creek mountain, opening No. 482 shows 5 feet and 6 inches, but whether such a section is maintained through the 600 to 700 acres on this ridge, is questionable.

The Second Lower, or *No. 3 seam*, occurs on an average of only 60 feet below the last described coal in this area, though in the Pollock mountain-McClung field, this interval is 150 feet.

"At the Ford crossing of Clear creek, below Duo, it shows a hard, thin coal under a sandstone cliff, but as it takes water near this point its crop line on the east bank of Big Clear creek is not very well defined.   However, it is opened on the Vaughn farm, on Shellcamp ridge, 2 feet and 10 inches thick, and again on Smokehouse branch, at Nos. 543 and 544, showing 2 feet and 10 inches to 4 feet and 2 inches.

"On Rock Camp ridge, openings 538 and 539 furnish very fine representative sections, showing 38 and 34 inches of clean, bright coal.   On Briery Knob of Little Clear creek mountain, this seam thickens with the one above it, as shown in openings Nos. 535, 536 and 535a, which yield respectively 5 feet and 2 inches, 4 feet and 6 inches, and 6 feet and 2 inches, excluding partings.   On the south side of Joe's Knob, a nearby opening, No. 527, shows a thickness of 5 feet and 3 inches of very good coal, and it seems to hold a good thickness through Point and Lick mountains, with the thinning in Nunly mountain as in the upper seam. In Buffalo mountain its area is about the same as the No. 2 seam, with its character represented in openings 577 and 578, the first with 35 inches and the second split by 20 inches of slate and yielding only two bands of coal 4 inches each.

"*The Echols*, or *No. 4 seam*, averages in this field about 270 feet below the last coal, and perhaps 200 feet above the red shale. It appears above water level about two miles above the forks of Big Clear creek, and continues above water level in the southern part of the district to near the base of Rock Camp ridge. Its thickness here is variable.

"On Briery Knob, openings 583 and 584 show about 30 inches of fair coal, with an inch slate parting. On Little Clear creek, between Point and Lick mountains, opening 580 shows only 20 inches of clean coal. Through Nunly mountain it loses all character and thickness, and its position there can only be placed with reference to the red shales.

"In the Buffalo mountain district, openings 610, 611, 612, and 615 show an irregular seam with a band of slate running through the center, which varies from 1½ inches to 15 inches, with from 15 inches to 30 inches of coal on top, and about 15 inches below; but in the eastern Buffalo mountain, at the Burr opening 614, it shows a 4-inch slate parting dividing an upper bench of 15 inches from a lower 16 inches thick. At opening 609, the coal is clean 33 inches thick, and was sampled here, as well as on the south side of Hickory mountain, at 610.

McCLUNG DISTRICT.—"This general area embraces the territory south from the main ridge, dividing the waters of Hominy from the drainage of Meadow river, and from Big Clear creek along the Rupert-Duo road, on the east, over to the main Meadow river, at the loop at Bays Ferry.

"In the high ridges of Pollock mountain and Rich Knob, a thin and valueless coal, of little area, has been found 400 feet above the Gauley seam, yielding good clean coal 20 inches thick. In all, three openings were made on this seam, for purposes of identification and possible correlation with other isolated openings in the Wilderness district, north.

"The coal bed occurring about 150 feet above the Gauley seam, in the Big Clear creek district, is likewise present here, yielding 12 to 25 inches of good clean coal, and in two places 30 inches. The *Upper Rider coal* to the Gauley seam (see plate of vertical sections) was opened in six places; it is very constant through this district, and the field generally, but always thin, 15 to 18 inches.

"The Joe Amick coal opening, No. 616, on Angling's creek, is also an unidentified higher coal seam, which may have representation in the Wilderness district to some extent. It was found to be so inferior (chemically) at this point of best development, that very little further attention was given to its area, save to ascertain that it nowhere yielded over 3 feet of coal.

"An analysis of a sample taken from this opening gave:

Water... .800 per ct.
Volatile matter...28.950 "
Fixed carbon........ ....53.503 "
Sulphur .... 3.597 "
Ash ....13.150 "

"*The Gauley seam*, in this area, shows its very best development, and in scores of openings presents an extremely favorable section, and is uniformly of good quality. It is everywhere commercial, and in some places yields fully 7 feet of clean coal of the highest grade. Its average thickness will be, perhaps, 4 feet; only four openings show sections that are not commercial. From opening No. 99, on Big Clear creek, following the crop around Sam ridge, Pollock mountain, Huggins ridge, down Browns creek around Big mountain and its many spur ridges, through and down the upper Hominy water; on both sides of Meadow creek and Little fork it is always a beautiful seam of coal, and will yield at least 4 feet of clean coal.

But in the Burdets creek district these conditions begin to change. Three miles west of the McClung postoffice, around Adam Pitzenberger's, a slate parting suddenly thickens to 7 or 8 feet, splitting a seam of 40 inches into two sections, 28 inches above and 13 inches below, as shown at openings 226 and 227. The lower split was not found at Nos. 227 and 228. The seam at opening 254, and possibly 253 and 252, shows commercial sections; but nowhere else on the crop around Burdets and Toms creeks are the sections as favorable, the coal thinning down to 12 inches, with 5 to 6 feet of black, laminated coal and slate under it, not fit to mine.

"The *No. 2 seam*, 125 to 150 feet below the *Gauley* (*Sewell*), shows only two commercial sections, Nos. 549 and 548, on Mill creek mountain, in isolated knobs, where the coal is but 30 inches thick. The best sections on this seam in Pollock mountain average only 20 inches of coal; elsewhere the bed is also thin and interleaved with slate bands. It corresponds, geologically, with the "*First Lower coal*, already described on the Big Clear creek waters.

"The *No. 3*, or *Laurel seam*, 300 feet below the *Gauley bed*, is of more consistent thickness, and frequently shows fairly good sections in widely separated parts of this district. Quite a number of openings were made in it on Pollocks mountain, which show the coal at its best, especially at the south end of the ridge.

"Going up Brown and Sam creeks, the seam thins to 18 or 20 inches. On Laurel creek, openings No. 567, 568, 569, 566 and 565, all show good height and quality, and the seam hereabouts should yield a very acceptable fuel, with good acreage.

"On Pollock mountain an additional seam—not uniformly present—was opened at three places, Nos. 618, 619 and 617, one of which, No. 618, shows a beautiful section of coal over 4 feet thick; but the other two are thinner and dirty.

"The *No. 4*, or *Echols seam*, about 600 feet below the Gauley, shows commercial thickness on Browns creek at opening 596, and on Big Clear creek at opening 593. Very few of the other openings, made on the spurs of Big mountain, show commercial value. The T. A. Hall opening, No. 600, on the Big mountain road, shows a characteristic section of 30 inches, with two thin bands of bone, and is only 160 feet above the red shales at this point.

HOMINY FALLS–LEIVASY DISTRICT. *The Gauly seam* shows on the Laurel branch of Grassy creek, beginning at the Pack Laurel gap opening 447, with a thin section of beautiful coal for some distance down this stream, with an increasing section up to an average of about 4 feet of clean coal, with extremes of 36 inches at opening 449, and 50 inches at 446. On the west branch of this creek the seam carries about the same thickness, but the section shows a soft fireclay parting 12 inches to 16 inches from the top, running from 5 inches in thickness at 441, to 9 inches at 440.

"The seam goes below water level about one-quarter mile below the forks, and is highest above the stream (80 to 90 feet) at 446. Its condition in all the country north on Grassy and Panther creeks, must be determined by drilling, as its outcrop there is everywhere concealed.

"Its probable section cannot be judged from the conditions exhibited along the Cherry river outcrop, where the sides of the whole valley of that stream are disturbed by slips and slides, which make it extremely doubtful whether the coal found there yields its full thickness. But the excellent sections yielded at openings 451 and 459, along the limited outcrop exposed on Gauley river, and on lower Panther and Taylor creeks, with 4 feet of handsome, clean coal, gives reason to the belief that a considerable portion of the large area to the south, until the coal rises to daylight on Laurel and Brushy Meadow creeks, will contain this *Gauley seam* in good commercial condition. If so, this region would be one of special value, as the coal would be present in an unbroken body, and could be reached at numerous places by shallow shafts, as well as worked largely by drifts from the outcrops on Taylor and Panther creeks.

"On Brushy Meadow creek this coal shows from 3 to 4 feet thick, though still carrying the same irregular fireclay parting, as on the west branch of Laurel, a parting somewhat unusual, and largely confined to this district. At a number of openings this parting totally disappears, leaving the section clean, and presenting a coal of high grade quality. In the extreme head of the stream, at No. 425, the upper bench of the section is wanting, and the good coal 31 inches thick.

"Following the outcrop westward from 425, the seam shows its normal section of 4 feet of coal with a 4 inch parting, at the Sang Point opening 424, which parting at opening 423 entirely disappears, leaving the section clean and 4 feet thick. At the next two openings, the section shows the unique feature of a thin 2 inch sandstone parting, and without associated fireclay at No. 420, and with 3 inches of sandstone below 14 inches of fireclay at 418.

"At the Perry Amick opening 416, the parting is all fireclay slate 14 inches, leaving 1 foot 1 inch of good coal above the parting, and 3 feet 4 inches below. From this point the bed passes over to Hominy creek waters, being cut out of the Brushy Meadow-Hominy divide between the Sam Joby Odell house, and a point a half mile south of the J. O. McClung opening 308, except for a few acres in a knob at Perry Amick's, as shown on the map.

"Northward on the left bank of Brushy Meadow creek, there is no parting whatever, openings 308, 307 and 306 showing respectively 4 feet 1 inch,

3 feet 10 inches, and 4 feet 8 inches; but below this region the parting reappears as a thin 2 inch band in openings 428, 303 and 301, increasing to 4 inches at 431, and 12 inches at 300.

"Along the east branch of the creek the parting is present 3 to 4 inches thick on the south bank, and 8 inches thick at 437, except at openings 433 and 435, where there is no parting, and coal 43 inches.

"On the west branch of Brushy Meadow there are two closed outcrops, where the coal occurs under about the same conditions; for, while in places the parting is thicker (10 inches at 293, and 23 inches at 294) elsewhere at the head of the stream, this band is only 5 inches, and the coal thickens at openings 295, 296 and 297 to 4 feet 3 inches, 3 feet 10 inches, and 5 feet 9 inches respectively, opening No. 97 showing an especially fine section of clean coal 4 feet 2 inches thick below this parting.

"In this district a large proportion of the total number of openings made are readily found and reached, being located near public roads and well defined paths ....

"On Hominy creek the general character of the *Gauley seam* is continued, always, however, with improving bed sections going south towards the dividing ridge between Hominy and Meadow creeks, where this seam reaches splendid proportions and is universally of good quality. The parting fireclay slate still shows occasionally, and the clean coal, due to the variation of this parting, has extremes of 25 inches at 413, to 5 feet 2 inches at 407.

"At opening 403 the parting reappears, three sections at this point all figured under the same number, and but 30 feet apart, showing it to vary from 2 inches to 18 inches, continuing with great fluctuations to opening 398, where the seam has lost its upper bench entirely; all of the white fireclay by enlargement; a considerable increase in the thickness of the coal, and the appearance for the first time of a black laminated coal and slate.

"This parting (with some variations from pure slate to pure coal) remains a characteristic feature of the coal bed section, to the extreme northern point to which this seam was traced, and it thickens below Hominy Falls as the whole coal bed thins and effects the destruction of the otherwise commercial value of the seam. At No. 398 this parting is but 4 inches thick, and the coal 5 feet 7½ inches thick, and with such characterizing features it shows all through the area south on Big Clear creek, and along Meadow river and its numerous tributaries. While this laminated coal and slate parting can rarely be considered as adding anything of commercial value to the seam, it will prove of great usefulness in assisting the mining where the coal bench has become thin, and thus enable all of the coal itself to be won.

"The six openings from 383 to 376, show an average of 4 feet 8 inches of coal and 4 inches of slate. At Nos. 373 and 374 the upper parting increases to 4 feet, and the lower to 22 inches, leaving just about 3 feet of beautiful clean coal between, to represent the commercial portion of the seam. At the L. M. Helem opening 370, there is 4 feet of clean coal above, and 1 foot of coal below a 10 inch parting, and from this point around the crop to No. 351 inclusive, the sections show an average of 5 feet of coal and 7 inches of parting; or omitting parts of seam cut off by partings, an average of 3 feet 4 inches of clean coal between openings 370 and 364, and an average of 5 feet four inches clean coal between openings 363 and 352.

"Towards the mouth of Price fork the parting increases again to an average of 3 feet in thickness, leaving about 34 inches of clean coal. The seam appears to be split for part of the distance between 309 and 312, otherwise the openings from 309 to 324, near the Wade McClung place, and including 345 on the west side of Hominy, show an average of four feet of coal and 10½ inches partings; or omitting one parting and the coal cut off by it, an average of 46 inches coal and 8½ inches of parting, in which section there is 36 inches of clean coal in one bench.

"In this district the only opening on coal lower than the *Gauley seam*, is that noted on the map as 346a, which probably represents *Seam No. 2* on the *First Lower Coal*, as its interval here is just about 140 feet below the *Gauley bed*. It shows 3 feet 4 inches of rusty coal, but partially opened, and its outcrop in the open area on upper Hominy has been interpolated on this basis. ....

"*THE WILDERNESS DISTRICT* is a name given to all that portion of the property lying south of the Gauley river, and between Hominy and Meadow rivers, extending back, southward, to a line connecting Bays Ferry, on the latter stream, and the point of Hominy creek, where developments ceased on the *Gauley seam* opening 260, by the reason of the thinning of that coal bed, and the general limit of the property having been reached.

"The development of the outcrop of the *Gauley seam* to its points of commercial disappearance, to the south of this line, surely indicated the futility of anticipating any areas of that coal bed being found above water level in this district; but it was thought that with its disappearance some higher coal bed might enter the region and assume commercial proportions and quality. This may still be found true at local places, but hardly probable, so that all values in this district, as along the waters of upper Panther and Taylor creeks, must be sought for by drilling the horizon of the *Gauley coal*.

"In traversing this district, by way of the Nicholas road to Summersville, which practically follows the general dip of the coal, it was not found possible to develop the complete structure of the field from the rock exposures, owing to their characteristic variation along such a line; but at a number of points there was found an outcrop of a persistent small coal.

"This bed shows first at opening No. 626,* just north of Fowler Knob postoffice, on the Nicholas road, at 2287_ feet A. T., by barometer; again at No. 625, about two miles farther northwest, at an elevation of 260 feet lower, or 2127 feet A. T., indicating a dip between these two points of about 80 feet per mile. Finally, at No. 623, in the road as it descends to Hughes Ferry, on the Gauley, at approximately 1737 feet A. T., or a dip of about 100 feet per mile for the entire distance of five miles, between the first and last places.

*None of the openings described in this Wilderness district were located instrumentally, and levels are barometric.

"This would seem to correlate this small seam with the coal found on Pollock mountain and Rich Knob, about 400 feet above the *Gauley coal bed*. The last opening at the Hughes Ferry is still 200 feet above the river, so that assuming the above structure and correlation to be correct, the Gauley seam should be found at a maximum depth of 200 feet below the river at this ferry.

"The most conspicuous feature of the Gauley river topography is the heavy ledge of sandstone that forms the river cliffs, which seems to make continuous bluffs, as along the New river canyon, and such outcrops were noted at Brocks, Hughes, and Carnefix ferries and still show prominently on Hominy creek, at Haynes mill, at the lowest crossing of that stream.

"The small coal mentioned occurs just above this rock stratum, which may, therefore, represent the heavy sandstone boulder remnants of this formation which were so frequently noted in the hills above the *Gauley seam* to the south.

"At opening 622 on the Long Point, below this rock formation, and 40 feet above the river, a lower coal outcrops with a top bench of 18 inches, slate parting 4 inches, and a bottom coal bench of 6 inches, which again agrees, stratigraphically, with a persistent coal bed found 150 feet above the *Gauley seam* in the Big Clear creek-McClung districts to the south; and the same seam is reported to show at two places, under similar conditions, on the river to the south of Rucker's bend.

"Opening No. 624, on the east bank of Hominy, about two miles from the river, is also thought to represent this coal from its relative location under the cliff, and the character of the coal scattered on the waste pile; the opening was closed.

"Opening No. 627, on Jim branch of Deer creek, has been provisionally identified with the higher seam outcropping at Nos. 623, 625 and 626, before mentioned, a section of which shows 2 feet of clean coal at an elevation of about 2125 feet A. T.

"Between the Hughes and Carnefix ferries, Gauley river falls about 300 feet, through an ever-deepening canyon, in an air line distance of about six miles, on a course generally parallel to the strike of the measures, but about eleven miles by the bends of the river. With this rate of fall on this line it would seem as if the *Gauley seam* should outcrop, if it be only 200 feet below the river at Hughes ferry, providing it remained at a constant level between these two extreme points, but this coal is not clearly in evidence, unless it should be represented by the impoverished section of the lower of the next two beds described.

"Between the river and the top of the cliffs (500 feet high at Carnefix ferry) two seams of coal were found, openings 620 and 621 yielding respectively coal 10 inches, fireclay 3 feet, coal 13 inches; and the second one but 14 inches of coal. No. 620 is by barometer 130 feet above the river, and No. 621 about 200 feet higher, with a prominent ledge of sandstone separating the two seams. It is just possible, therefore, that the lower coal may be the *Gauley bed*, especially as its character and structure somewhat resemble that seam in the Lower Hominy district. Its bed section, however, did not seem to warrant extensive developments to prove it.

"Around Summersville, across the river from Brocks ferry, there are openings in a seam of coal of some character, which, however, must certainly overlie and be absent from the district covered by land of the Association south of Gauley river. To the north and south of the village, at an elevation approximately 2000 feet A. T., three openings in evidently the same seam showed 36 to 41 inches of good coal, underlaid by 6 to 10 inches of bone coal.

"Around Gad postoffice, four miles to the southwest, and about one mile north of the river at the point of Ruckers bend, a seam of quite similar section and character (36 inches of coal with a 3 inch parting near the top) outcrops at an elevation of just 100 feet lower than the Summersville bed. A line connecting the coal at these two places is just about parallel with the line connecting Hughes and Carnefix ferries; by inference, therefore, the coal measures show a gentle southwest slope of about 40 to 50 feet per mile, which inclination would be quite sufficient to place a coal out-cropping at Hughes ferry nearly 300 feet lower at Carnefix ferry, and, therefore, correlate the coals showing at these two places, and still leave the Gauley seam well below water level at the mouth of Meadow river. If the Gauley seam does outcrop on Gauley river, after disappearing below Panther creek with a handsome section of four feet of good coal, its exposure is without commercial value, so far as the developments of last season permit this general statement to be made. "

The SEWELL or GAULEY COAL, as it is termed by d'Invilliers, is above water level at the mouth of Meadow river, and is one of the thin coals under the huge sandstone mass which forms the great cliff, whose base is about 130 feet above the river at the point in question.

For many years it has been questioned by some geologists as to whether there are TWO or THREE workable coals in the Pottsville series of the New river district, but in the recently published Raleigh folio, Mr. M. R. Campbell admits that there are THREE, viz., the SEWELL, BECKLEY and QUINNIMONT (FIRECREEK) BEDS, the intermediate or BECKLEY SEAM, coming nearly midway between the other two, but generally nearer the Sewell bed than the Quinnimont.

Mr. Campbell has given the name NUTTALL SANDSTONE to the great cliff of massive, pebbly sandstone which caps the walls of the New river canyon at Nuttall and below, but which fades out of the section, as a massive rock, to the southward. It is especially massive northward from Caperton and along the Gauley river, where it is the principal cliff rock in the narrow canyon of that rapid stream, and is so conspicuous at Hughes', Brock's and other ferries, the writer formerly correlated this sandstone with the

Homewood, or Tionesta bed of the northern region of the State, and if it does not come at that horizon, it could not belong farther down in the Pottsville series than the Connoquenessing sandstone group.

The RALEIGH SANDSTONE is a name given by Mr. Campbell to the great ledge of massive sandstone, which underlies the Sewell coal by an interval of fifty to seventy-five feet, and which was termed the upper Piney Creek conglomerate in a paper by David White, on "The Pottsville Series Along New River," published in the Bulletin of the Geological Society of America, Vol. VI, pages 303-320, Dec. 28, 1894.

This great pebbly sandstone, often 150 feet thick, forms the summit or uppermost wall of the New river canyon south from Sewell, for many miles, as well as the floor of the country generally across Raleigh, northern Mercer and southern Wyoming counties, through McDowell to the Kentucky line. It is the one sandstone horizon of the Pottsville series, which Mr. Campbell has identified from New river to the Elkhorn at Welch, in McDowell county, and thus made it possible to correlate some of the members of the New river section with the McDowell county phase of the Pottsville. The other sandstones of the series are too variable to trace for any considerable distance, and hence cannot be used as key rocks like the Raleigh, though some of them have been given distinctive names by Campbell, like the Dotson sandstone, Harvey, Bearwallow, and Dismal conglomerates, etc.

The statement of Mr. d'Invilliers in the paragraph at the head of page 636, viz., that the Pottsville coals are limited northward COMMERCIALLY by Big Laurel creek, it should be explained, applies only to those coals as exploited on the lands of the Gauley Coal Land Association, all of which lie southwest from Cherry river, since it is well known that between Cherry river and Elk river, there is a large area of the Pottsville measures, in which there is much valuable coal belonging at the horizon which Hon. William H. Edwards of Charleston (who has done much prospecting in this wilderness region), believes to be mostly identical with the Quinnimont seam of New river. The coal varies from four to five feet in thickness, and is very probably the same bed as that at Vandevener's, in Point mountain, Randolph county, and which extends along the northwest slope of Rich mountain, to and beyond the Beverly-Buckhannon turnpike.

THE SEWELL (NUTTALL) COAL.

The first coal of the Pottsville series on New river to receive commercial development, was the uppermost one of the New river group of coals in Sewell mountain, 400 feet below the top of the Nuttall sandstone.   This first commercial development was made by John Nuttall, who came from Pennsylvania into the New river gorge, and established the mining town of Nuttallburg, soon after the C. & O. Railroad was constructed.   This coal, which Mr. Nuttall first began mining, is locally known as the Nuttall seam, and the writer so designated it in his first paper on the New river coals, published in "The Virginias," pages 7-16, January, 1885.   The coal had previously been mined for local use, however, near the top of Sewell mountain, and hence the name "Sewell" became attached to the coal and refuses to be separated therefrom, thus illustrating the tendency of the first names given to any coal bed or other stratum, to adhere to the same.

The structure and character of this important coal bed in southern Nicholas, northern Greenbrier and eastern Fayette counties has been fully and adequately described by d'Invilliers, in his report to the Gauley Coal Land Association, from which the Survey has quoted so freely in the preceding pages, so that it only remains to describe briefly the development and character of this coal in the region along either side of New river.

The commercial development of the Sewell bed is confined almost entirely to the New river district of the State, since east from it no railroad facilities were at hand, until the B. & O. extended its Gauley branch into the Cherry river region of Nicholas county, from which shipments from the Sewell seam will soon begin, while southwest from it, no shipping facilities are at hand along the crop of the Sewell coal, until we come to the Norfolk & Western Railroad at the Kentucky border.

This SEWELL BED is a type of the best Pottsville coals in all of the southwestern region of the State, and, being low in moisture, volatile matter, ash, sulphur and phosphorus, they are necessarily high in fixed carbon, constituting ideal steam and domestic fuels, since they are practically smokeless, with proper devices for securing good combustion.   They are the only coals in the United States which equal or surpass in effective heating results for steam, domestic and general fuel purposes, the best grades of Cardiff coal from southern Wales.

With the exception of one or two mines in northern McDowell county, on the N. & W. Railroad, all the commercial mines of the Sewell coal are located in Fayette county. Samples across the entire section of the coal bed in thirty-four different mines, operating on the Sewell coal in this county, were taken by A. P. Brady and R. W. Edmonds, which samples were analyzed by Prof. Hite and his assistants, with the following results:

ANALYSES OF THE SEWELL COAL SEAM.

Anal. No.	Mois.	V. M.	F. C.	Ash.	Sul.	Phos.	Th'nss of Seam. Ft. In.	B. T. U.
1.	0. 82	26. 83	70. 87	1. 68	0. 54	0. 023	2 10	15258
2.	0. 75	26. 54	70. 37	2. 34	0. 55	0. 055	3 0	15348
3.	0. 63	25. 74	71. 21	2. 42	0. 62	0. 005	3 6	15274
4.	0. 61	25. 51	69. 46	4. 42	0. 75	0. 005	3 2	15156
5.	0. 49	25. 99	71. 49	2. 03	0. 57	0. 005	3 9	15571
6.	0. 56	25. 52	70. 80	3. 12	0. 63	0. 006	3 10	15109
7.	0. 70	26. 17	70. 49	2. 64	0. 68	0. 017	3 7	15443
8.	1. 01	25. 53	71. 37	2. 09	0. 73	0. 006	3 2	15600
9.	0. 67	25. 31	70. 95	3. 07	0. 65	0. 005	2 8½	15130
10.	0. 61	25. 45	72. 17	1. 77	0. 73	0. 005	3 11	15439
11.	0. 73	23. 98	73. 11	2. 18	0. 54	0. 003	3 9	15573
12.	0. 71	24. 12	73. 21	1. 96	0. 51	0. 004	4 2	15504
13.	1. 04	24. 85	72. 63	1. 48	0. 62	0. 005	4 1	15620
14.	0. 75	24. 39	70. 88	3. 98	0. 73	0. 005	3 7	15048
15.	0. 74	28. 58	66. 36	4. 32	0. 98	0. 018	3 9	14893
16.	0. 50	24. 61	67. 49	7. 40	0. 79	0. 015	3 9	14281
17.	0. 74	27. 09	70. 58	1. 59	0. 53	0. 005	3 9	15359
18.	0. 67	23. 40	71. 04	4. 89	9. 68	0. 010	2 10	15021
19.	0. 96	25. 14	71. 15	2. 75	0. 56	0. 005	3 9	14965
20.	0. 87	26. 91	69. 78	2. 44	0. 85	0. 004	3 7	15203
21.	0. 89	22. 54	74. 58	1. 99	0. 61	0. 005	5 0	15517
22.	0. 53	19. 41	74. 08	5. 98	0. 98	0. 005	5 0	14992
23.	0. 48	22. 09	74. 28	3. 15	0. 68	0. 002	4 10	15426
24.	0. 73	20. 67	76. 46	2. 14	0. 59	0. 003	5 2	15446
25.	0. 71	24. 23	73. 34	1. 72	0. 55	0. 006	5 1	15576
26.	0. 61	21. 31	69. 78	8. 30	2. 54	0. 008	5 10½	14389
27.	0. 77	21. 29	74. 58	3. 36	0. 77	0. 006	5 11	15225
28.	0. 67	21. 37	74. 33	3. 63	0. 71	0. 011	5 2	15095
29.	0. 67	22. 91	74. 10	2. 32	0. 61	0. 006	5 5	15463
30.	0. 76	21. 18	74. 92	3. 14	0. 69	0. 006	5 1	15321
31.	0. 76	21. 55	71. 63	6. 06	0. 86	0. 003	5 6	14891
32.	0. 54	21. 50	74. 51	3. 45	0. 91	0. 005	5 1	15419
33.	0. 64	21. 33	72. 21	5. 82	0. 79	0. 005	5 1	14804
34.	0. 46	21. 46	75. 12	2. 96	0. 69	0. 005	5 1	15219
A'v'g	0. 69	23. 95	72. 04	3. 22	0. 74	0. 008		

LOCATION OF SAMPLES IN FAYETTE COUNTY, W. VA.

Analyses
No.

1. From Cook mine, Cook & Sons, Gaymont.
2. From Elmo mine, New River Mining Co., Elmo.
3. From Michigan mine, Michigan C. Co., one-half mile below Fayette station.
4. From Newlyn mine, Newlyn C. Co., three-fourths mile below Fayette station.
5. From Nuttallburg mine, Nuttallburg C. & C. Co., Nuttallburg.
6. From South Nuttall mine, Brown C. Co., South Nuttall.
7. From Boone mine, Boone C. &. C. Co., Boone.
8. From Keeneys Creek mine, Nuttallburg C. &. C. Co., Keeneys Creek.
9. From Chapman mine, Chapman C. & C. Co., three-fourths of a mile west South Caperton.
10. From New Sugar Camp mine, Victoria C. & C. Co., South Caperton.
11. From South Caperton mine, Victoria C. & C. Co., South Caperton.
12. From Cunard mine, Cunard C. Co., Sewell.
13. From Brooklin mine, Brooklin C. & C. Co., East Sewell.
14. From Quarrier mine, Bothwell C. Co., one-fourth mile northwest of Dubree.
15. From Dubree mine, Bothwell C. Co., Dubree.
16. From No. 1 mine, Ballinger C. Co., Ballinger.
17. From Smokeless mine, Smokeless C. Co., Winonia.
18. From Longdale mine, Longdale Iron Co., Clifftop.
19. From Kay-Moor mine, Low Moor Iron Co., Kay Moor.
20. From Blume mine, Blume C. & C. Co., Lookout.
21. From No. 2 mine, W. P. Rend, two miles up Rush creek.
22. From Sugar Creek mine, Sugar Creek C. & C. Co., one-half mile northwest of Mt. Hope.
23. From Killside mine, McKell C. & C. Co., Killside.
24. From Sun mine, Sun C. & C. Co., one-fourth mile south of Sun.
25. From No. 3 mine, Thurmond C. Co., one mile west of Thurmond.

26. From Derryhale mine, McKell C. & C. Co., two miles south of Thurmond.

27. From Turkey Knob mine, Turkey Knob C. & C. Co., ten miles south of Thurmond.

28. From No. 1 mine, Prudence C. & C. Co,, one-half mile south of Harvey.

29. From No. 1 mine, Harvey C. & C. Co., one-half mile south of Harvey.

30. From Star mine, Star C. & C. Co., Red Star.

31. From No. 2 mine, Collins Colliery Co., Glen-Jean.

32. From No. 1 mine, Dunloop C. & C. Co., Dunloop.

33. From White Oak mine, White Oak Fuel Co., one-half mile southeast of Oak Hill.

34. From McDonald mine, McDonald Colliery Co., McDonald.

The averages of these analyses compare as follows with those obtained by McCreath and the Maryland Steel Company, for the same coal bed on the Gauley waters farther east:

	Hite, 34 samps.	McCreath, 47 samps.	McCreath, 18 samps.	Md. Steel C. 18 samps.
Moisture	0.69	1.830	1.601	....
Volatile Matter	23.95	27.114	27.614	27.620
Fixed Carbon	72.040	66.617	66.351	68.660
Ash	3.320	3.615	3.720	3.710
Sulphur	0.740	0.801	0.718	0.742
Phosphorus	0.008	0.007	0.010	0.0104

These results agree very closely, except as to moisture and volatile matter, and of course the increase in these for the Gauley coal, is accompanied by a proportional decrease in the amount of FIXED CARBON.

The excess of moisture shown for the Gauley coals, is due to the fact that the samples were in all cases taken from the crop of the beds, where they had absorbed much more than the normal amount of water consequent upon their weathered condition, and the only wonder is that the amount was not larger. The increase in volatile matter is due to a regional increase to the northeast, the same regional decrease being continued southwestward to Mc-Dowell county, where the same bed (Sewell), as well as all the other Pottsville coals, has about five to six per cent less volatile matter than it has in the central or New river district, as may be observed by the analyses given on subsequent pages, for the Mc-Dowell county coals.

The Sewell coal in the New river mining district varies in thickness from two to six feet, and rarely has any parting slates, except where it attains a thickness of five to six feet, when a thin (two to three inches) slate often makes its appearance eight to ten inches above the bottom of the bed, while frequently there is a thin bony layer at the extreme top of the seam.

The pavement of this bed, unlike any of the other Pottsville seams below it, is extremely smooth and regular, quite as much so as that of any beds in the Kanawha or Allegheny series above, and this feature adds greatly to the coal as a mining proposition, and thus permits of successful mining ventures on this coal when not more than two feet thick.

This bed is mined by some deep shafts in the region of Glen-Jean, Fayette county, along the waters of Dunloup creek and its tributaries.

The following record of a diamond drill hole bored for E. B. Hawkins near Oak Hill, Fayette county, and kindly given the Survey by Messrs. Clark and Krebs, civil and mining engineers of Kanawha Falls, will serve to show the rock succession in these deep shafts:

	Ft.	In.
Surface	13	7
Sandstone, very hard and broken up	98	5
Conglomerate, spots of fireclay	5	2
Coal	0	6
Conglomerate, spots of fireclay	6	2
Gray sandstone	18	11
Fireclay	3	11
Fine gray sandstone, seams of slate	62	11
Slate, seams of gray sandstone	5	6
Slate	11	11
Sandstone and slate mixed	6	0
Slate and fireclay	10	0
Sandstone, streaks of slate	95	2
Coal	0	2
Gray sandstone	8	2
Sand, slate, and slate mixed	2	10
Coal, Sewell	4	4
Slate	0	10
Fine gray sandstone, broken up	44	8
Fine gray sandstone, slate mixed	5	4
Slate, spongy	17	4
Sandstone and slate, mixed	2	8
Slate, little streaks of sandstone	8	7
Fireclay and slate, mixed	11	8
Gray sandstone and pea conglomerate (*Raleigh*)	72	2

Gray sandstone, seams of coal, spots of fireclay 5 10
Slate   8   0
Coal (Beckley)   4   2
Slate and fireclay.............................   6   3
——————
Total......... 541   2

The coal near the base of this section is supposed to be the BECKLEY BED, otherwise known as the WHITESTICK SEAM, from its occurrence along the creek of that name, in Raleigh county.

· The Sewell seam is caught in the high knobs around Beckley, but has not been mined to any extent, since it does not appear to be more than two feet thick, judged by the "blossom" it makes along the public road between Beckley and McDonald.

Just what area and thickness of coal may occur at the horizon of the Sewell seam, between the New and Tug rivers through Raleigh, Wyoming and McDowell counties, no one can yet say, but there is no reason why a large area of it may not exist, since this seam is reported by M. R. Campbell as present on the Winding Gulf branch of Rock Castle creek, a tributary of the Guyandot river in Wyoming county, where it exhibits the following structure:

                                                   Ft. In.   Ft. In.

Sandstone ....
Coal .... 0 10 ⎫
Shale 0   9 ⎬ 3 11
Coal 2   4 ⎭

The inference that it is persistent southwestward to a greater or less extent, is also strongly supported by its northeastern extension from New river through Nicholas, Greenbrier and Webster counties, and possibly as far north as the Rich mountain region just west from Beverly, in Randolph county.

The mining operations on New river have illustrated the fact that this coal may be counted as commercially valuable, on account of its great purity, when not more than two feet thick, and since this coal is found in McDowell county, on the Tug river, with a thickness of two feet and more, there must be much of the intermediate region where its thickness will exceed this minimum figure.

In the section at Welch, McDowell county, given on page 620, it appears to be split by forty feet of shales and sandstones into two beds, both of which have been opened and found to be good coal, but neither of which has yet been mined.

About four and a-half miles below Welch, both the Davy Crockett and the Antler Coal Companies have mines on the SEWELL SEAM, sixty feet above the Welch bed. It is there four to four and a-half feet thick, but split with several inches of shale near the middle. It is possible that the two distinct seams shown in the Welch section, page 620, have here come together.

The Sewell coal is most probably the one mined by Dr. Iaeger, near the mouth of Nigger branch, two and a-half miles below Jaeger station, McDowell county, where it is only thirty feet above track level, and soon disappears under Tug river to the west.

The coal has the following structure at Dr. Iaeger's bank:

```
                                                  Ft. In.   Ft. In.
Sandy shales, fossil plants.......................... 10   0
Coal ...................................................  1   9  ⎫
Slate ..................................................  0   3  ⎬  2  10
Coal ...................................................  0  10  ⎭
```

Above the coal, at eighty feet, a succession of great massive sandstones begin and extend to 500 feet above the Jaeger coal bed, where we come to the base of a great coarse, brown, iron stained cliff, 100 feet high, which appears to be the top of the Pottsville series, and probably the Dotson sandstone of Campbell.

The Sewell seam, having the composition shown by the analyses given above, is naturally an excellent coking coal, since it everywhere possesses the soft, columnar structure, typical of good coking coals. The following analyses are reported by Prof. Hite, from samples of Sewell coke collected by Messrs. A. P. Brady and R. W. Edmonds, in the New river district:

COKE FROM SEWELL SEAM.

Analyses No.	Mois.	V. M.	F. C.	Ash.	Sul.	Phos.	Coking time.
1	0.05	0.84	93.94	5.17	0.68	0.010	72 hrs.
2	0.11	1.17	89.87	8.85	0.63	0.013	"
3	0.12	0.59	91.82	7.47	0.76	0.011	48 hrs.
4	0.07	0.78	90.37	8.78	1.02	0.005	"
5	0.06	0.81	91.33	7.80	0.81	0.009	72 hrs.
6	0.11	0.68	92.71	6.50	0.80	0.006	"
7	0.16	0.93	92.03	6.88	1.06	0.006	"
8	0.08	0.73	92.89	6.30	0.66	0.014	"
9	0.10	t.27	91.89	6.74	0.60	0.008	"
10	0.07	1.18	88.60	10.15	0.54	0.012	"
11	0.13	0.92	92.09	6.86	0.56	0.007	48 hrs.
12	0.52	2.83	87.73	8.92	0.83	0.013	72 hrs.

LOCATION OF SAMPLES, ALL FROM FAYETTE COUNTY.

Analyses
No.
1. From Victoria C. & C. Co. ovens, one-half mile east of Caperton.
2. From Longdale Iron Co. ovens, Sewell.
3. From Harvey C. &. C. Co. ovens, Harvey.
4. From Collins Colliery Co. ovens, Glen-Jean.
5. From Turkey Knob C. & C. Co. ovens, Turkey Knob. .
6. From McDonald Colliery Co. ovens, McDonald.
7. From Sun C. & C. Co. ovens, Sun.
8. From W. P. Rend ovens, two miles up Rush creek.
9. From Brooklyn C. & C. ovens, Brooklyn.
10. From Low Moor Iron Co. ovens, Kay-Moor.
11. From Chapman C. & C. Co. ovens, Chapman.
12. From Low Moor Iron Co. ovens, Fayette.

The average of these twelve samples gives the following:

Moisture 0. 14
Volatile matter 1. 06
Fixed carbon 91. 26
Ash... 7. 54
Sulphur 0. 75
Phosphorus.. 0. 0095

A result which speaks for itself in revealing a coke of the highest purity, which could be mixed to great advantage with those having more ash, and consequently greater sustaining power in the blast furnace. For all purposes for which coke is desired, except where great weight is to be sustained, in the very high iron furnaces, no better or purer coke can be found, though of course, the Quinnimont (Firecreek), Pocahontas and other Pottsville coals of West Virginia, furnish coke of practically the same quality.

As already stated, Mr. David White, the eminent paleobotanist, correlates the Sewell coal bed with the famous Sharon coal horizon of western Pennsylvania and eastern Ohio, from a wide study of the fossil plants, and also with the horizon of the main Sewanee coal of Tennessee, and the "coal bearing shale" of Washington county, Arkansas.* Mr. White gives the following list of fossil plants found by him in the shales accompanying the Sewell coal at the several mines in the New river district:

---

*See Mr. White's interesting paper on "The Pottsville Series Along New River," published in the Bulletin of the Geological Society of America, Vol. VI., pp. 305-320.

Species.	*Localities.
Eremopteris cf. *elegans* (Ett.) Schimp. , form	H.
" *cheathami*, Lx	N, C.
Sphenopteris hoeninghausii, Brongn	Th.
" cf. *larischii* (Stur.)Lx	H.
" *microcarpa*, Lx	H.
" *flexicaulis*, Lx	H.
" cf. *royi*, Lx	N.
" *communis*, Lx	N.
Pseudopecopteris muricata (Brongn.) Lx. , form	Th, H, C.
" " " " "	C.
" *macilenta* of Lesquereux, form	Th, N.
" *dimorpha*, Lx	Th, TK.
Neuropteris elrodi, Lx., form	Mc, Th, C.
" n. sp. , Lx	Mc
" *biformis*, Lx., form	Mc, C.
" *smithsii*, Lx., form	Mc, TK, SC, H, N.
" n. sp	Th.
Odontopteris newberryi, Lx. (?)	Mc.
Callipteridium n. sp. , Lx..	C, N.
" n. sp	C.
Alethopteris cf. *lonchitica*, (Schl.) Goepp	Th, Mc, N.
" *evansii*, Lx.	C, N.
Pecopteris (?) *serrulata* Hartt, non Herr, nec (Lx.) Schimp	Th.
Calamites. sp	Th, N.
Asterophyllites erectifolius, Andr	Mc, TK, H, Th.
" *gracilis*, Lx. , nec (Stb.) Brongn	Mc.
Annularia cf. *ramosa*, Weiss	Mc, Th.
" *radiata* (Brongn.) Stb	Th.
Calamostachys lanceolata, Lx	Th, H.
Macrostachya, n. sp	C.
Shenophyllum, n. sp	H.
Lepidodendron veltheimianum, Stb. , form	C, N.
" *sternbergii*, Brongn	SC.
Lepidophyllum, n.sp	Th.
" *campbellianum*, Lx	SC.
Sigillaria, cf. *reticulata*, Lx., nec (Stb.)Mill	C.
" *dentata*, Newb. (?)	Mc.
Whittleseya elegans, Newb	Mc.
Rhabdocarpus n. sp	TK, Mc, H, SC, Th.
" n. sp. , Lx	Mc, SC.
Trigonocarpus oliviæformis, L. and H. (?)	TK, Mc (?), H. Th.
Cardiocarpus elongatus, Newb	Mc, TK.
" *minor*, Newb. (?)	TK.
" cf. *bicuspidatus*, (Stb.) Newb	SC.

* C—Cunard ; H—Harveys; Mc—McDonald; N Nuttall; SC—Stone Cliff; Th—Thurmond; TK—Turkey Knob.

THE WELCH COAL.

In the New river region no coal beds are known between the Sewell seam and the top of the Raleigh sandstone fifty to seventy-five feet below, but in McDowell county, and the adjoining region in Tazewell county, Virginia, M. R. Campbell describes an important coal horizon which comes just above the great Raleigh sandstone, and attains its thickest development on Dismal creek, Tazewell county, where it is much split with shale and bony partings. The same coal, according to Mr. Campbell, occurs in the hills at Welch, where it lies nearly 600 feet above Tug river, and is mined for local supply by J. H. Mitchell & Co. It has been designated from this locality as the WELCH COAL, since this is a better term than "Dismal creek," which Mr. Campbell indirectly suggests as its name. The coal shows the following structure at the Mitchell mine:

	Ft. In.	Ft. In.
Coal	1 3	
Bone	0 4	3 1
Coal	1 6	

The upper bench of the coal is the better fuel, having less ash and bony material than the lower.

The Tazewell folio, by Mr. Campbell, gives the following analysis of the coal at Welch:

Moisture	0. 21
Volatile matter	19. 32
Fixed carbon	70. 42
Ash	10. 05
Total	100. 00
Sulphur	0. 73
Phosphorus	trace

This coal is mined on a commercial scale by several companies below Welch, at Short creek, Davy, Roderfield, Twin Branch, Big Sandy, Tug river and other localities, where it has descended to within 200 to 250 feet above the level of Tug river. The coal varies in thickness from three to three and a-half feet, and usually has one or two slate partings in its lower half. Although thin, it furnishes a coal of great excellence, as may be seen from the analyses of samples collected by S. D. and A. P. Brady, and reported by Prof. Hite as follows:

Name of Mine.	Mois.	V. M.	F. C.	Ash.	Sul.	Phos.	B. T. U.
Cambridge	.16	18.75	75.22	5.87	1.34	.0058	15230
Big Sandy	.12	18.90	77.50	3.48	0.58	.0027	15487
Tug River	.25	18.72	77.52	3.51	0.65	.005	15584
Short Creek..................	.21	17.70	78.17	3.92	1.63	.0025	15308
Davy Crockett	.29	17.42	78.00	4.29	0.54	.004	15340
Twin Branch	.16	17.49	78.63	3.72	0.59	.005	15272

This coal, which is locally termed the "Tug River Smokeless" seam, is not mined at present west from the plant of the Cambridge Coal Co., below Roderfield, and it doubtless decreases in thickness, and becomes too thin for commercial mining before its horizon passes under the Tug river, not far below Iaeger.

It is possibly this bed which occurs in a cut, one mile and a-half above Wilmore, where two layers of good coal are visible, the upper twelve inches thick, and the lower one fifteen inches,. but separated by twelve feet of shales and sandy beds.

About one mile and a-half below Iaeger, a coal bed split with three to four feet of shales, and lying five feet above a very massive sandstone, dips under the track and is seen to the west no more. It is probably this same Welch coal, since one-half mile farther below, and sixty feet higher, we find a coal bed mined by Dr. Iaeger which would correspond to the Sewell seam.

THE BECKLEY COAL.

In the region around Beckley, Raleigh county, and especially along the Whitestick branch of Piney creek, a coal occurs a short distance below the Raleigh sandstone, which appears to have considerable importance. It is extensively mined by the Raleigh Coal and Coke Company, M. T. Davis & Company, and others, and varies in thickness from three to six feet, being generally single bedded. Mr. A. P. Brady gives it the following section at the No. 2 mine of the Raleigh Coal and Coke Company, near Beckley:

	Ft.	In.
Sandstone		
Slate		
Coal	0	0¼
Slate	0	0½
Coal	6	0

Analysis of sample reported by Prof. Hite as follows:

```
Moisture ...................    .....................................   0. 58
Volatile matter ....................... ...........................  18. 04
Fixed carbon ............................................····.......... 78. 95
Ash .........................................................  ............  2.43
                                                                      ─────
   Total........................................................100. 00

Sulphur .............................................. ...............    .77
Phosphorus.......... · ............... ...................................   .005
B. T. U ........ .......... ............. ....... ...... ................  15534
```

Some operators claim that the Beckley coal is none other than the Quinnimont, or Fire creek seam, with the interval between it and the Sewell bed greatly diminished, but Mr. Campbell gives a series of sections in the Raleigh folio, which would appear to demonstrate the correctness of his views, viz., that the BECKLEY COAL belongs directly under the Raleigh sandstone, and approximately 200 feet above the Quinnimont bed.

The coal is locally known as the "Whitestick" seam, from its development along the waters of that creek.

Messrs. Clark and Krebs of Kanawha Falls, who have prospected much in Raleigh and adjoining counties, report this coal as having a very large development southward from Beckley.

Mr. M. R. Campbell states (in the Raleigh folio, page 8) that this bed occurs on Rock Castle creek, near Pineville, Wyoming county, where it exhibits the following structure:

```
                                                              Ft. In.
Sandstone ...............    .......................................
Shale and bone................................ ....................  0  9
Coal .................................. .............................  2  2
```

Throughout the Gauley coal field described by d'Invilliers, the coal which he names No. 2 or FIRST BELOW the Gauley (Sewell) seam, at an interval of 130 to 190 feet, would correspond to this Beckley coal bed, and hence it does not appear to have much importance east from New river.

THE QUINNIMONT (FIRE CREEK) COAL.

At an interval of about 200 feet below the Beckley seam, and 375 feet below the Sewell bed, there occurs along New river an im-

portant and widely persistent coal bed, which was first mined on a
commercial scale high up in the New river hills, at Quinnimont,
Fayette county, 1000 feet above the level of New river, and 620
feet above the top of the Mauch Chunk red shales.   Hence the coal
in question has generally been called the QUINNIMONT SEAM, although the mine in the summit of the mountain near Quinnimont,
its type locality, has long since been exhausted and abandoned.

Later in the mining history of New River, a coal bed was
opened in the hills along Fire creek, which puts into New river
sixteen miles below Quinnimont, and as the coal operators were
not sure of its identity with the Quinnimont bed, they called it
the FIRE CREEK SEAM.   Subsequent mining developments in the
New river district appear to leave no doubt about the identity of
the two beds, since both lie at the same (600 feet) interval above
the Mauch Chunk red shales, and this stratigraphic determination
is confirmed by the fossil plants, according to the results obtained
in their study by Mr. David White, so that the term FIRE CREEK
should give way to QUINNIMONT on the basis of priority, the name
first given the coal by Prof. William M. Fontaine, although the
term FIRE CREEK is so much used by the operators that it will probably remain in common use.

The coal bed, as mined in the old workings at Quinnimont, is
split with two or three layers of shale and fireclay slates, and the
available coal varies in thickness from two and a-half to four and
a-half feet.   The mining operations now in progress upon this bed
along the main valley of New river, and up its tributary streams,
reveal this coal generally as a single bedded seam of most excellent quality, and varying in thickness from two and a-half feet to
five feet.   It, like the Beckley and Sewell seams above, thins away
and fades out of the section in passing down New river northwestward, long before its horizon dips down to water level.

The upper portion of the seam is generally a little softer than
the rest of the bed, so that it has usually been termed "top" coal,
for twelve to fourteen inches, by Messrs. A. P. Brady and R. W.
Edmonds, who collected the samples for analysis, and measured
the thickness of this coal at the several mines (all of which are in
Fayette county, except the two last, which are in Raleigh), given
in the following table, showing the composition of the coal, as
reported by Prof. Hite:

QUINNIMONT (FIRE CREEK) COAL.

Analyses No.	Mois.	V. M.	F. C.	Ash.	Sul.	Phos.	Th'nss of seam. Ft. In.		B. T. U.
1	0.82	20.55	74.11	4.52	0.55	0.024	3	6	15098
2	0.51	20.27	76.67	2.55	0.58	0.007	3	6	15500
3	0.57	20.95	72.36	6.12	0.95	0.130	4	2	14758
4	0.70	21.64	76.46	1.20	0.64	0.002	3	3	15504
5	0.57	21.35	74.31	3.77	0.91	0.007	4	4	15327
6	0.44	20.73	77.20	1.63	0.77	0.003	3	1½	15476
7	0.82	20.08	74.65	4.45	0.63	0.056	4	11	15125
8	0.38	20.71	72.21	6.70	0.48	0.020	4	1	14964
9	0.75	19.16	75.63	4.46	0.63	0.008	3	9	15101
10	0.62	18.03	76.59	4.76	0.71	0.019	3	11½	15080
11	0.83	19.26	70.95	8.96	0.96	0.152	4	4	14833
12	0.44	21.43	74.21	3.92	0.55	0.033	3	11	15147
13	0.59	17.88	78.57	2.96	0.52	0.010	3	5	15334
14	0.69	19.29	75.42	4.60	0.77	0.046	4	0	15455
15	0.61	19.72	75.37	4.30	0.60	0.006	5	6	15208
16	0.62	18.57	78.36	2.45	0.62	0.014	3	4½	15438
17	0.56	18.36	75.73	5.35	0.59	0.063	4	0	15182
Average	0.60	19.93	75.20	4.27	0.67	0.035			

LOCATION OF SAMPLES.

Analyses No.

1. From Fire Creek mine, Fire Creek C. & C. Co., one-half mile east of Fire Creek.

2. From Central mine, Central Coal Co., three-fourths of a mile below Beury.

3. From Echo mine, Echo C. & C. Co., Beury.

4. From Big Bend mine, Big Bend C. Co., at Dimmick, two miles west of Thurmond.

5. From No. 2 mine, Thurmond C. Co., one mile west of Thurmond.

6. From No. 1 mine, Beury C. & C. Co., Stone Cliff.

7. From Beechwood mine, Beechwood C. & C. Co., Claremont.

8. From Alaska mine, Alaska C. & C. Co., Alaska.

9. From Robins mine, Robins C. Co., three miles east of Quinnimont.

10. From Laurel Creek mine, Laurel Creek C. Co., four miles east of Quinnimont.

11. From Big "Q" mine, Quinnimont C. Co., five miles east of Quinnimont.

12. From No. 1 Buffalo mine, Ephraims Creek C. & C. Co., one-half mile west of Thayer.
13. From Slater mine, New River Colliery Co., Thayer.
14. From Greenwood mine, Greenwood C. Co., Lawton.
15. From No. 5 mine, W. P. Rend, one-half mile up Rush creek.
16. From Royal mine, Royal C. & C. Co., south side of river at Prince.
17. From No. 8 mine, Wright C. & C. Co., three miles south of Prince.

These analyses reveal a coal of very high character, the impurities of all kinds being quite low, and thus comparing favorably with the Sewell coal. The volatile matter in the Quinnimont bed is about four per cent. lower than in the Sewell seam of the same region, and hence the former exceeds the latter in the quantity of fixed carbon.

The Quinnimont coal also makes an excellent coke, as may be seen by the following analyses reported by Prof. Hite, from samples collected by A. P. Brady and R. W. Edmonds, the ovens all being located in Fayette county:

COKE FROM QUINNIMONT (FIRE CREEK) SEAM.

Analyses No.	Mois.	V. M.	F. C.	Ash.	Sul.	Phos.	Coking time.
1	0.07	0.92	90.17	8.84	0.54	0.063	72 hrs.
2	0.04	1.34	92.30	6.32	0.45	0.0675	"
3	0.29	1.02	92.19	6.50	0.76	0.009	"
4	0.15	0.96	93.21	5.68	0.60	0.075	"
5	0.11	0.67	90.68	8.54	0.86	0.099	"
Average	0.13	0.98	91.71	7.18	0.64	0.0627	

LOCATION OF SAMPLES.

Analyses No.

1. From Fire Creek C. & C. Co. ovens, Fire Creek.
2. From Beechwood C. & C. Co. ovens, Claremont.
3. From Beury C. & C. Co. ovens, Stone Cliff.
4. From Greenwood C. Co. ovens, Lawton.
5. From Quinnimont C. Co. ovens, Quinnimont.

This coke compares favorably with that from the Sewell bed, the fixed carbon, ash, and sulphur being practically the same, while the phosphorus is considerably higher in the Quinnimont coke.

East from New river, on the tributaries of Meadow river and the Gauley waters generally, this coal would represent the "Laurel vein" of d'Invilliers' report, or the SECOND BELOW the Sewell seam. It appears to be of considerable importance in the high plateau east from Cherry river, and between that stream and the waters of Elk, where it frequently has a thickness of four to five feet, though generally containing some slaty layers in its lower half. It is most probably this coal that has been mined in Point mountain, Randolph county, by Vandevener, Marshall and others, to which reference has already been made, and if the coal in the summit of Rich mountain west from Beverly, is lower than the Sewell bed, it would represent the Quinnimont seam.

Traced southward, Mr. Campbell identifies this bed with a large seam that has been opened on the Guyandot river near the western edge of the Raleigh quadrangle, having the following section:

	Ft. In.	Ft. In.
Coal	4 11	
Bone	0 1½	
Coal	0 10½	7 7
Bone and sulphur	0 3	
Coal	1 5	

The same coal, according to Mr. Campbell, is frequently exposed on the head waters of Piney creek, Raleigh county, showing three to three and a-half feet where opened on Boyer Fork, the bottom portion being occasionally bony, while on main Piney, above the mouth of Laurel, it is forty-two inches thick with no bone. Just west from this last locality, the Quinnimont coal has the following structure on the Laurel fork of Stone Coal creek, according to Mr. Campbell:

	Ft. In.	Ft. In.
Coal	2 11	
Shale and bone	0 8	5 7
Coal	2 0	

Near the Wyoming-Raleigh county line at Basin Spring, on the Devil Fork of the Guyandot river, the same authority reports the coal as five feet thick, and generally present with a good devel-

opment on the head of Barker creek and along the southern portion of the Raleigh quadrangle.

In the Tazewell folio, Mr. Campbell, while identifying the
overlying Raleigh sandstone at Welch and other localities in Mc-
Dowell county, hesitates to identify the QUINNIMONT COAL, and adds
a new name, "Upper Horsepen," for the coal at Welch, which
occupies the horizon of the Quinnimont bed at an interval of 350
feet below the top of the Raleigh sandstone, 420 feet below the
Sewell coal, and 500 odd feet above the POCAHONTAS No. 3 coal.

This coal at Welch, which appears to represent the Quinnimont bed, is only eighteen to thirty inches thick, and not very
good, but was formerly mined to supply the town, at an opening
200 feet above the level of Elkhorn.

Mr. Campbell gives the following analysis of the coal in question at Welch:

Moisture	2.46
Volatile matter	18.45
Fixed carbon	62.93
Ash	16.16
Sulphur	0.54
Phosphorus	trace.

If the Upper Horsepen coal be the same as the bed at Welch
(which is very doubtful), it appears to grow quite important in the
region along the McDowell-Tazewell county line, in the vicinity of
Horsepen, and eastward, where it is eight to nine feet thick, and
has been confused with the Pocahontas seam several hundred feet
below. The coal grows thinner toward the north, however, being
only two feet thick at Peeryville, according to Campbell.

In his paper on the Pottsville series of the New river region,
heretofore cited, Mr. David White gives the following list of fossil
plants which he has found at the horizon of the Quinnimont coal:

PLANTS OF QUINNIMONT-FIRE CREEK COAL.

Species.	*Localities.
Adiantites cf. *tenuifolius*, (Goepp.) Schimp	P, RR, D, N, FR, H.
Eremopteris cf. *elegans*, (Ett.) Schimp	RR, FR, H.
" *microphylla*, Lx. (?)	N.
Sphenopteris hoeninghausii, Brongn	Q, P, RR, Bw, H.
" *dicksonioides*, (Goepp.) Schutze, form.	FC.
" *microcarpa*, Lx.	Q(?), FR, RR, By(?).
" *divaricata* of Lesquereux	P, 8C.

Sphenopteris patentissima, (Ett.) Schimp., nec Goepp P, RA, FR.
" cf. *goepperti*, (Ett.) Schimp. non Dunk.,
nec (Munst.) Gein.................. .....SC, N.
Pseudopecopteris muricata, (Brongn.) Lx., form.....Bw, RA, P, RR, D, N.
" " " " D, RR, RA.
" cf. *dimorpha*, Lx................ ....FR, P, N.
" *latifolia*, (Brongn.) Lx., form.......D, RR, H.
Megalopteris sewellensis, Font., (?)...................FR, N.
" cf. *dawsoni*, Hartt ....Q.
Neuropteris smithsii, Lx., original......... ....N, D, P, SC, RR.
" " " form ....H, SC, N, P.
Alethopteris, sp........ ....Q, SC, N, P.
Bornia radiata, (Brongn.) Schimp.....................P, RR.
Calamites, sp ....A, D, Q.
Asterophyllites minutus, Andr. (?)...................RR, D, H.
Equisetites cf. *occidentalis*. Lx.....................D, H.
Calamostachys lanceolata, Lx., form ....RR.
Annularia cf. *ramosa*, Weiss ....D, H, RR.
" n. sp ....RR.
Sphenophyllum, n. sp.............................D.
Lycopodites, n. sp., Lx................. ....P, SC, D, RR
Lepidodendron sternbergii, Brongn., form.............D, A, P.
" cf. *acuminatum*, (Goepp.) Newb. nec
Rost...........................RR.
" *veltheimianum*, Stb.......................Q, RR, H, RA, SC.
Lepidostrobus variabilis, L. and H. (?), form...........SC.
Lepidophyllum, n. sp.............................D, RR.
" *campbellianum*, Lx...................D, RR.
Ulodendron, sp.....................................D, Q. Bw.
Halonia, sp........................ ....RR.
Sigillaria, sp ....By.
" cf. *dentata*, Newb....... ....By, Bw.
Trigonocarpus clavatus, Stb........... ....:Q, D.
Rhabdocarpus, n. sp ....FR, RR, D.
Carpolithes, n. sp., Lx ....SC.

HORSEPEN COAL GROUP.

Mr. Campbell describes a group of coals which attain commercial development or thickness, in the southern portion of McDowell county and the adjoining region of Virginia, under the term, Horsepen Group, of which there are four beds, viz.:
Lower Horsepen seam, 150 feet above Pocahontas No. 3.

---

*A—Alaska; Bw—Beechwood; By—Beurys; D—Dimmock; FC—Fire Creek; FR—Fayette; H—Harveys(R. R.); N—Nuttall; P—Princess station; Q—Quinnimont; RA—Red Ash; RR—Rush Run.

War Creek seam, 270 feet above Pocahontas No. 3.

Middle Horsepen seam, 389 feet above Pocahontas No. 3.

Upper Horsepen seam, 449 feet above Pocahontas No. 3.

The Lower Horsepen seam varies from three and a-half to five feet in thickness, and is much split up with slate. Its distribution is confined to the region around Horsepen at the McDowell-Tazewell county line, and the valley of Big creek just north. It is evidently local in distribution, and of no great economic importance, unless it be the same as the No. 5 coal, along the eastern slope of Flat Top mountain, which on Simmons, Crane, Flipping and other streams in Mercer county, has a thickness of four to five feet at 180 feet above the Pocahontas seam.

The WAR CREEK SEAM is a much better coal than the Lower Horsepen, and has a thickness of four and a-half to five feet without shale partings, as exposed along War creek, and on Dry Fork near Peeryville, where it has been dug from the bed of the stream for domestic use.

The MIDDLE HORSEPEN bed, like the lower one, is frequently much split with shale partings, although at Horsepen it has four feet of clean coal, and gives the following analysis, according to Campbell:

Moisture	0.15
Volatile matter	25.61
Fixed carbon	68.54
Ash	5.70
Sulphur	0.94
Phosphorus	trace.

The distribution of this coal is confined to the southern portion of McDowell county.

The UPPER HORSEPEN coal, as already stated, cannot be the same as the Quinnimont seam, unless Mr. Campbell is correct in identifying it with the thin seam in the hills at Welch. Of this, there is much doubt, however, since Mr. Campbell gives the horizon of the Upper Horsepen coal as only 449 feet above the Pocahontas No. 3 bed, while the section at Welch, published on page 620 of this volume, shows that the coal which Mr. Campbell identifies with the Upper Horsepen there, comes 545 feet above the Pocahontas bed. Of course, a northward INCREASE in these separating intervals is possible, but the rule is a DECREASE in that direction.

In the diamond drill boring near Welch, which forms the low-

er half of the section on page 620, three coal beds are found
within an interval of 326 feet above the Pocahontas seam, and they
most probably represent some of the Horsepen beds.

Just what the ECHOLS COAL of d'Invilliers' Gauley report, represents, in the New river and Welch sections, is not certain, possibly either the Lower Horsepen or the War creek horizon, since it
comes 160 to 200 feet above the RED BEDS, and 300 feet below the
Quinnimont coal.   It would appear to be too high in the Measures
for the Pocahontas No. 3 bed, since David White and Mr. Campbell identify this horizon quite confidently on Piney creek, Raleigh
county, as coming a little more than 100 feet above the RED BEDS,
and 400 feet below the Quinnimont coal, and since all of these intervals DECREASE northeastward, the Pocahontas coal could hardly
get 200 feet above the RED BEDS on the Meadow river (Gauley)
waters.

COAL No. 4, OR POCAHONTAS No. 4.

In the section at Pocahontas, Virginia, a coal bed of some importance occurs at eighty to ninety feet above the great No. 3 SEAM,
and it has always been designated as coal No. 4, or Pocahontas No.
4.   It is mined on a commercial scale by the Tidewater and Big
Four C. & C. Companies in the region west from Vivian, McDowell
county, where it lies sixty to sixty-five feet above the No. 3, or main
POCAHONTAS SEAM, having the following structure, as measured by
A. P. Brady:

	Tidewater Mine.		Big Four Mine.	
	Ft.	In.	Ft.	In.
Coal	1	7	1	9
Slate	0	0¾	0	1
Coal	0	8	0	9½
Slate	0	1	0	2
Coal	1	5	1	3
Totals	3	9¾	4	0½

Analyses of samples reported by Prof. Hite as follows:

	Tide Water.	Big Four.
Moisture	0. 17	0. 22
Volatile matter	17. 07	17. 12
Fixed carbon	73. 99	78. 36

Ash... .	8.77	4.30
Totals....................................	100.00	100.00
Sulphur..	0.74	0.55
Phosphorus....................................	0.058	0.002
B.T.U...	14612	15336

This coal was struck at a depth of 182 feet in the bore hole put down for the Watson Coal Company at Helena, or Huger, on Elkhorn creek, two miles above Welch, and was there four feet one inch in thickness, and sixty-four feet four inches above the Pocahontas seam, while in the boring at the mouth of Browns creek, just below Welch, the same coal is three feet five inches thick and was struck at a depth of 299 feet eleven and a-half inches, sixty-four feet nine inches above the top of the Pocahontas No. 3. In the boring one-half mile east from the mouth of Browns creek, the No. 4 COAL was struck at a depth of 248 feet two and a-half inches, sixty-two feet seven inches above the top of the Pocahontas No. 3, and had the following structure:

	Ft. In.	Ft. In.
Coal	1 0	
Bone	0 1½	4 8½
Coal	3 7	

This coal appears to be quite persistent along the southeastern margin of the Pottsville series, over a belt several miles in width. In Flat Top mountain and along Crane creek, it lies eighty to ninety feet above the No. 3 or Pocahontas bed, and is four to five feet in thickness. If Mr. Campbell is correct about the position (150 feet above) of the Lower Horsepen coal, with reference to the main Pocahontas seam, the No. 4 bed could hardly be identical with it.

This bed will doubtless furnish a large area of good fuel in southern McDowell and Mercer counties, provided it is mined in conjunction with the No. 3 bed below, or at least before the surface is permitted to fall in and dislocate the overlying strata.

THE POCAHONTAS COAL, No. 3.

Below the last described coal, at an interval of sixty to ninety eet, there comes the most important coal of the Pottsville series,

and next to the great Pittsburg seam, the most valuable mineral
deposit in the entire Appalachian field.   True, its area is limited,
compared to the spread of the Sewell seam, 700 to 800 higher, but
it surpasses the latter so greatly in thickness that the smaller area
overbalances the larger one in value.   Then, too, there is a considerable body of the Pocahontas coal in the adjoining counties of
Virginia and Kentucky, where it has a fine development, so that
considering its purity, thickness and area, it is the only rival to the
celebrated Pittsburg seam.

As a workable coal, so far as known, the Pocahontas bed in
West Virginia is confined to the counties of Mercer, Raleigh, Wyoming and McDowell.

Probably only the extreme southern corner of Raleigh holds
any of this Pocahontas seam, say twenty to thirty square miles,
while the northern border of Mercer possibly fifty to seventy-five
square miles, and about an equal area in southern Wyoming may
be productive.

It is in McDowell county where the great body of this coal occurs, since its productive area covers more than half of the county
north from the Virginia line, or something like 500 square miles,
thus making in all an area somewhere between 600 and 700 square
miles of this coal bed in the southwestern portion of the State,
where the seam has a valuable thickness before it fades away northward, like all the other Pottsville beds above, and becomes too thin
for present commercial purposes.   It is possible that future explorations with the diamond drill may extend this belt of commercial
coal a few miles northward from its supposed limit, but so far as
known at present, the width of the productive zone is not over
twenty miles.

To the late Major Jed. Hotchkiss of Staunton, Va., is due
more than to any other one man, the credit of discovering and
making known to the world this immense area of valuable coal.

As a soldier on General Lee's staff in the Confederate army,
he first observed the rich treasures of coal that lay hidden along
the eastern base of Flat Top mountain, and although it was in a
series which is practically devoid of merchantable coal in the Pennsylvania regions, yet his quick perception and keen geologic faculty
convinced him that here, in what was then a wilderness region, lay
a great wealth of the best fuel in America.   He was the leading
spirit in organizing the Flat Top Coal Land Association, that led to

the building of the Norfolk & Western Railroad into the field, and first opened it up to market, making the value of this remarkable fuel known to the world. In the columns of his geological journal, "The Virginias,'" he persistently advocated its merits as a steam and coking coal of the highest grade, until the latter were fully recognized, and the shipments from the Flat Top district, beginning with a few tons in 1883, have now grown into millions, and the country along the Norfolk & Western Railroad become one of the most important coal and coke producing regions of America.

The POCAHONTAS COAL, as well as all the other coals of the Pottsville series, whether in the Gauley, New river, or Flat Top district, is an ideal steam fuel. Low in volatile matter and high in fixed carbon, while very low in ash, sulphur and moisture, these coals give off an intense heat with a nearly smokeless combustion. The small proportion of sulphur they contain insures safety from spontaneous combustion on shipboard, so that they have become the ideal fuel for steamship and general naval purposes, and their use in these lines is constantly increasing.

Mr. Charles Catlett, the geologist and mining expert of Staunton, Va., who has studied the Pottsville coals in all the West Virginia districts, has kindly consented to prepare a special paper upon their coking and steaming qualities for the benefit of the Survey, and it is given herewith as follows:

THE COKING AND STEAMING QUALITIES OF THE POCAHONTAS-NEW RIVER-GAULEY COALS.

By Charles Catlett, M. E.

"An examination of the State Survey map will disclose that the coals developed on the line of the Norfolk and Western Railway, and which are in the market under the trade name of "Pocahontas," and the coals which go into the market over the Chesapeake & Ohio Railway, and are known under the trade name of "New River," come from the same geological measures, and that these measures extend so as to cover the headwaters of the Gauley river. The coal from the latter portion of the field has not yet reached the markets. Of course, these measures occur elsewhere; but, so far as is known, there is no point outside of this comparatively restricted area (closely located on the Geological map of the state) where they carry coal in any quantity; so that the limits of their existence and ultimate developments are well defined. The field is practically confined to West Virginia, a small portion of it being found across the line in Virginia at and near the town of Pocahontas. Within this territory, wherever these measures are found, are one or more coal seams differing somewhat among themselves, and in the same seam from point to point; but the similarity at all points is greater towards each other than to the coals of the higher and succeeding measures, which are found so extensively developed in the state, and differentiates them into a class of their own. Their special qualities, and their geographical position towards the eastern outcrop of the coal measures of the state, give them a relative advantage with reference to export shipments, which are destined to be the great balance wheel of the coal trade; and it is evident that the ultimate development of West Virginia's resources in the way of export must mainly come from these coals. The shipments have already been large, and, while temporarily suspended, must necessarily become great in the future. One feature of the export trade, which has so far not been considered, is of special applicability to these coals. The fact that they are coking coals will enable their shipment abroad for the manufacture of coke; and the extensive use there of retort ovens eliminates all objections which might otherwise be raised to such a course.

"These various facts warrant a brief consideration of the qualities which these coals, wherever found, possess in common.

"The most marked changes in the bed from point to point, though subject to numerous local exceptions, are an irregular but progressive thinning of the beds from any point on the southeastern outcrop to the corresponding point on the northwest, where they go below the water level, and a gradual thinning of the beds from the southwestern end of the field towards the northeastern end of the field. In illustration of the latter, reference is made to the reports of the Flat Top Coal Land Association (recently purchased by the Norfolk & Western Railway), whose lands are located near the southwestern extremity of the field, and the thickest portion of whose coal is now being operated. They give, as the average thickness of the coal mined by its lessees, from the opening of the mines in 1883 up to January 1, 1899, as 7.11 feet. The average for the year 1898 is given as 6.55 feet.

"Passing to the northeastern end of the field, in the Gauley basin, recent explorations by the geologist, d'Invilliers, give, as an average thickness of several hundred openings, a little less than 4 feet.

"There seems to be no marked change in chemical or physical properties, from the eastern edge to the corresponding western water-line of the field; but there seems to be a progressive change from the southwestern end to the northeastern end. As a whole the coals carry less ash, less carbon, and more volatile matter towards the northeastern limits of the field. McCreath reports, as an average of eight samples taken by himself from the No. 3 seam of the Pocahontas district, from the southwestern edge of the field: water, .699 per cent.; volatile matter, 18.756 per cent.; fixed carbon, 73.406 per cent.; sulphur, .752 per cent.; ash, 6.388 per cent.

"The same party reports, as a result of a series of seven samples, selected in person by d'Invilliers, from the outcrops in the Gauley basin: moisture, 1.25 per cent.; volatile matter, 27.47 per cent.; fixed carbon, 67.05 per cent.; sulphur, .61 per cent.; ash, 3.61 per cent.

"The general purity of the coals from these measures, wherever found, is remarkable; and the writer has examined numerous picked samples which ran less than one per cent. in ash.

"These coals have the unusual distinction in possessing, in an eminent degree, three qualities, any one of which should command marked recognition:

"Superior steaming qualities.

"Relatively smokeless qualities.

"Superior coking qualities.

"The value of a coal as a steam producer is determined, primarily, by the total amount of heat it will produce on combustion; but in view of the very crude way in which we burn our fuel, even more depends on the manner in which it responds to ordinary conditions of handling and firing.

"The total heating value can be determined with a fair degree of accuracy by a calorimeter; but the form of the sample, the particular instrument used, and the individuality of the operator, all affect the result; and no single determination, no matter how carefully conducted, can, therefore, be accepted as a basis of comparison.   Taking the published reports of a large number of determinations, and making comparisons with the same operator, instrument, and the relative amount of waste material in the coal as marketed, enough work has been done to demonstrate that the coals from this field may be counted on to average, in this respect, equal to, if not above, any of the other coals which can be bought in quantity on the markets of the world today. They will probably average in shipments over 15000 B. T. U. per pound of coal.

"In actual use, these coals seem to possess all of the qualities which go to make up good steaming coal.   The ash is small in amount, heavy and compact, dropping from the coal as the latter burns, thus leaving a fresh surface for combustion. The ash makes a comparatively small amount of unobjectionable clinker.   The coal burns with a short, white flame, which deposits a minimum amount of soot in the flues.   By judicious handling, it exhibits, without excessive draft, great liveliness, so that a plant may be pushed if desired; while its combination of free burning and coking qualities makes it possible to retain small fires for a long time without becoming "dead. " The fine coal, properly dampened and handled, gives results equal to the lump, and is especially adapted for use where fine sizes are desirable. The equal purity of the fine coal with the lump, coupled with plasticity at a comparatively low temperature, gives good promise that in time it will be largely used for the manufacture of briquettes (*without needing binding material*) for those markets which prefer it in that shape.   In the form of small briquettes, it will furnish a most effective grate fuel.

"In considering the evaporating qualities of any coal under actual conditions of work, it is exceedingly hard to make comparisons, owing to the great difference of the conditions under which the tests may be made, and uncertainty as to whether the conditions were normal or abnormal. A series of working tests, made for the city of Cincinnati in 1897 and 1898, at their pumping station, with a view to determining the city's contracts, are probably of especial service, in view of the uniform character of the experiments, though higher results are recorded elsewhere from these coals. Thirty-five samples of coal were bought in the open market, and the tests of each coal extended over a period of 16 hours firing. The New River and Pocahontas coals showed an actual evaporation of 10. 60 to 10.77, from and at 212 degrees Fahrenheit. The next nearest coal showed 10. 18 and 10.13; and all others less than 10.

"There seems no question, from the published reports available, that these coals in actual use bear out the calorimetric tests, and may be depended on to give, under ordinary conditions of service, higher results than any of the other steam coals which are available on the market in quantity.

"Messrs. Castner, Curran and Bullit, who have been the selling agents for the "Pocahontas" coal, which reaches the market from the southwestern portion of the field over the Norfolk and Western road, ever since the first shipment in 1883, have shown remarkable skill and energy in making known to the world at large the valuable properties of their specialty. Today the Pocahontas coal is known all over the world. I submit their rules for firing their coal, as equally applicable to the coals from the other sections of the field, as follows:

FIRING STATIONARY BOILERS.

'1. Whenever possible, the fire should be banked at night, or whenever the plant is shut down. The best way to do this is to clean the fire thoroughly, push the remaining fire against the bridge wall, put a few lumps on this, and then cover it all over with fine coal. The ash pit doors and dampers should be closed, and fire door left open.

When getting ready to start up, if the fire has been banked, it should be spread carefully and so as to cover, as nearly as possible, every part of the grates. Before spreading, see that all ashes and clinkers are cleaned off grates and that the air spaces are open. If rocking grates are used, shake them well before spreading. After spreading, use lumps to put on the fire, as fine coal would be liable to fall through grates; and be careful not to allow green coal to get on the bare places on grates.

'2. There are three methods most commonly used in firing—the "Coking System," the "Spreading System," and the system of "Alternate Firing."

'The "Coking Method" is as follows: Having moistened the coal, fire the fresh coal near the door, to let it give off the volatile matter and what little smoke is in it; then push the coal with the hook or the scraper to the back end of the grates, where it makes a white, bright fire. This part of the grates should be kept covered with this kind of a fire. Then, when needed, fire again at the door, in this way making the gases, etc., pass over the white heat at back, and preventing the formation of smoke, as well as assisting in burning the gases from the freshly fired coal. With this method some air must be admitted above the fire, or else carbonic oxide will be formed instead of carbonic acid, which means a loss of heat.

'3. The "Spreading System' is the one commonly used and generally considered the best. It is as follows: Fire a little at a time and throw the coal where it will be quickly coked, being careful not to put too much coal at one place. The brigh-st spots are, as a rule, the places where fresh coal coal is most needed. Fire regularly, and close the doors every time coal is put on fires. Keep the fire level—that is, do not allow holes to burn in fire, and do not allow the fire to get heaped up in the middle. Pay particular attention to keeping a good fire next the sides of the fire box, especially if the boiler is of the locomotive type.   If holes are allowed to burn in the fire, not only may too much air be admitted, thus keeping down the heat of the fire, but when fresh coal is put on, some of it will fall through on grates, and is liable to form clinkers which would not be formed otherwise.   If in this way green coal does get on grates, it should be carefully worked off.   It is sometimes a good plan to wet the coal before using, especially where there is much fine coal, the idea of this plan being that not only is dust kept down, but the coal gives a longer flame when burning, by the heat decomposing the water into oxygen and hydrogen, which are afterwards burned in the flues.   This plan is, therefore, used when the flues are long.   In Hawley down-draft furnaces it is claimed by the makers that coal should be dripping wet in order to get the best results.

'4.   "Alternate Firing."   This system consists of putting on fresh coal, first on one-half of the grates, then on the other half, alternately, at equal intervals of time. After each addition of fresh coal, the volatile gases arising from it meet the current of hot gas coming from the partly burned fire on the other side of the grates.   The combustion chamber should be large enough to allow two currents of gas to be thoroughly mixed.

'5.   Keep the flame of a white, bright color all over the fire if a very hot fire is desired, especially next the bridge wall or flue sheet.   Always carry as light a fire as possible; never more than ten inches thick.   From four to six inches will be sufficient ordinarily, but be sure that, when carrying a very thin fire, it does not get too light at the sides.   As a general rule, it may be stated that the fire that will make the most steam is the most economical.

'6.   Do not throw large lumps of coal in the fire box, but break them up to about the size of half a brick, the reason of this being that so much more surface of the coal is exposed to the fire, and that the combustion is more rapid.   Besides, throwing a large lump in the firebox will make a bad spot in the fire.   The broken up lumps and fine coal should be mixed together as much as possible before firing.   All coal should be carefully watched, and any foreign substances that might cause the fire to get dirty thrown aside.

'7   Do not be in too much of a hurry to close the fire box doors after firing, especially with a boiler that is steaming freely.   Smoke can often be kept down by leaving the door slightly open a few seconds after firing.

'8.   Do not stir the fire except when absolutely necessary, as stirring the fire unnecessarily may help to form clinkers by mixing small pieces of fusible ash together; and it also wastes coal by causing the smaller particles to fall through grates.   If you see that the fire needs hooking, do it at once, and do not wait until steam pressure falls from fire not being in the proper condition.   Usually, when the fire needs stirring, the result to be accomplished is to have the fire level, not black in one place and bright in another, but showing the same white heat all over.   This can be done best by using a two pronged hook and running it over top of fire.

'9.   Watch the fire closely, see when the brightest flames appear with the least amount of smoke, and try to keep the fire in that condition.

'Do not put any coal on the fire until it is actually needed, and always see where the coal is needed before it leaves the shovel.

'Do not fire aimlessly.

'More coal is wasted and more smoke made by unnecessary firing than in any other way.   There is a great deal of heat lost by firing too much at a time and at too long intervals.   As little coal as possible at a time, firing often and putting coal just where it is needed, and no where else, is a good rule.

'By actual experiment under a boiler, it has been shown that by firing

13 pounds of coal at a time, instead of 55 pounds, an increased efficiency was obtained of 8. 19 per cent., and this notwithstanding the fact that it was, of course, necessary to open the doors more frequently with the smaller amount of coal.

'10.   Try to keep the fire so that the steam pressure will vary as little as possible, and do not allow steam to blow off at the safety valves, this being a waste of coal, water and labor.   This latter point must be closely watched, especially when the boiler makes steam freely.   With such a boiler, the tendency with many firemen is either to keep too hot a fire and waste steam at safety valves, or else let the fire go too long without attention.

'11.   In order to get the best results from this coal it is necessary to pay close attention at all times to the condition of the fire.   Every time the fire door is opened look at every part of the fire, and note any change in its condition.   If the steam pressure varies, try to find out what made it vary.   When the demand on the boiler for steam is steady, such variation in pressure is always due to the fire.   At some plants the demand on the boiler for steam varies so much that it is not always possible to keep an even, steady pressure, and it is therefore all the more necessary at such places to watch the fire closely.

'12.   There are several ways of cleaning the fire, any one of which may be used; the most common way being to clean first one side of the fire box and then the other.   But whatever way is used, be sure to clean it thoroughly, especially next the bridge wall or flue sheet; leave as much fire as possible and try not to pull out any partly burned coal.   Whenever the fire is drawn, examine the grates carefully; see that they are in proper position and that the air spaces are open.   .

'13.   See that the appliances for regulating the draft and admission of air to the fire are in good working order.

'The supply of air to be admitted to the fire depends on the condition of the fire and amount of coal burned.   A bright, clean fire will not require as much air as a dirty fire, nor will a thin fire need as much as a thick fire.   The firemen should always try to find out the peculiarities of each boiler—what kind of fire will make most steam, and the supply of air that will give the best results.   A semi-bituminous coal will not require as much air as one that is higher in volatile matter or gases, because it contains a larger amount of carbon, which does not need as much oxygen for perfect combustion as do the hydro-carbons or gases.

'The amount of air needed for perfect combustion is 11. 3 pounds per pound of carbon, or for coals like Pocahontas about 10. 58 per pound of coal. But in practice from 18 to 24 pounds will be necessary with ordinary hand-firing.   Where ash pits are below the level of the floor, it is thought to be a good plan to keep them partly filled with water, the object in so doing being to keep the grates cool, putting out fire that may fall through grates, and allowing vapor to rise against grates.   It is also easier for the firemen.   It is of no assistance to combustion, however, as is sometimes claimed, as the vapor takes as much heat to decompose it as it afterwards makes by mixing with the gases of the coals.

'14.   It will be found highly advantageous to the user of coal to keep it under cover, protected from the action of the weather.   Coal may lose in actual weight, as well as in heating power, if exposed for any length of time to the action of the sun and rain.   This is due to the fact that by chemical action the quantity of carbon and hydrogen in coal is reduced, and the amount of oxygen is increased by being absorbed in the pores of the coal.

FIRING LOCOMOTIVES.

'1.   Before going into yard to couple to train, see that all the firing tools are on the engine and in good order; examine the grates, see that they are in good condition, and that both grates and ash-pan are clean.

'2. While waiting in yard, keep ash-pan dampers closed. Do not allow engine to blow off, and try to make as little smoke as possible. It is not necessary to get a hot fire in your engine until a short time before your train is to leave. But always try to get engine hot gradually, as this will not be so hard on flues and fire-box as getting up steam quickly.

'3. Before starting, the blower should be put on, and a good, solid fire of well-burned coal be made ready for the start. When building up the fire the door should be left partly open—as far as the first notch on the catch— until smoke disappears.

'4. After leaving a station or stop of any kind, do not open fire-box door to throw coal on or hook the fire until reverse lever is hooked back. If firing is begun as soon as the throttle is opened, and when the engine is working hard, a great deal of cold air will be drawn into the fire-box and against the flues. This is not only hard on the flues and sheets, but it is apt to cause steam pressure to fall. There should be enough coal on fire before starting to avoid this.

'5. Do not throw on the fire at one time more coal than is absolutely needed. Two or three shovelfulls at one time should always be enough; and generally one will be enough with careful firing.

'Always see where coal is needed before it leaves the shovel.

'Do not fire aimlessly.

'More coal is wasted by unnecessary firing than in any other way. There is a great deal of heat lost by firing too much at a time, and at too long intervals. As little coal as possible at a time, firing often, and putting coal just where needed, will give more steam and use less coal. By putting a large amount of coal in the fire-box at a time heat is wasted, as the supply of air needed cannot mix with the coal fast enough to burn it properly.

'6. Always try to keep down smoke as much as possible. This is an easy matter with Pocahontas coal. When steam is about to be shut off, open door just a little before throttle is closed, and if necessary, put on blower a little.

'When using steam, smoke can be prevented by keeping a white heat, firing a little at a time, and holding door open about an inch for a few seconds after firing. But the fire-box door should never be left wide open, especially when using steam or when blower is on.

'7. Do not allow steam to blow off if it can possibly be avoided. Steam blowing off means a waste of coal, water and labor. It can always be prevented while using steam by watching the gauge closely, and closing a damper, and opening door on the latch before pop valve raises. Try to keep the fire so that the steam pressure will vary as little as possible. By doing so the engine will use less coal, and there will be less strain on the fire-box and boiler, owing to the temperature being more even. While on side tracks, or at a long stop, both dampers should be kept closed.

'8. Always carry as light a fire as possible, as by doing so more heat can be obtained from the coal than with a heavy fire. It takes a certain amount of air to mix with a quantity of coal so as to get out of the coal all the heat there is in it. If a very heavy fire is carried it will be difficult to get sufficient air to enable it to mix thoroughly with the gases.

'Keep the fire free from holes, especially next the fire-box sheets. That part of the fire nearest flue-sheets should always be carefully watched, as cold air coming up through grates at that point will do more to cause steam to fall than any other one thing, besides being hard on the flues. This is especially the case where brick arches are used.

'The unpleasant noise sometimes made when standing still or running with a light, clean fire, known as "drumming," should always be prevented. This is caused by a series of minute explosions of oxyhydrogen gas, due to having a hole or holes in the fire, and can be stopped by closing dampers or filling up holes.

'9. Keep the flame of a bright, white color all over fire-box if a hot fire is desired, especially in front of the fire-box. Watch the fire closely, see when the flame is brightest, with least amount of smoke, and try to keep it that way.

'10. Have the ash-pan dampers kept in order, and pay strict attention to their proper use. Always bear in mind that these dampers regulate the supply of air for the fire and that a proper amount of air is required, just as much as a proper amount of coal, as coal will not burn without air. The dampers should be kept closed when engine is not using steam, whether standing still or running, and whenever you shake the grates. Regulate the supply of air according to the condition of the fire; a clean, light fire will not require as much air as a thick or dirty one.

'11. Grates should be shaken only when absolutely necessary, and the best time to do this is when steam is shut off, or when the draft through fire is lightest. They should not be shaken too hard, as the object to be accomplished is merely to shake ashes into ash-pan and away from grates, so as to give more air to fire. Unnecessary shaking of grates will cause a loss of fuel, and partly burned coal falling into ash-pan is liable to warp it. Ash-pans should be examined frequently and should not be allowed to fill up.

'12. Keep the coal moist all the time. This keeps the dust from flying and the coal will coke better.

'13. The engineman should handle the water supply so that the fire man can fire the engine regularly and with economy. The best me hod of doing this is to supply water continuously and as regularly as possible; but the injector should never be left on when starting. The fireman should watch closely the way in which the engine is handled, especially the injectors, so as to regulate his firing accordingly.

'Before coming to a heavy pull, get the fire in shape in plenty of time; do not keep a light fire until you start for the hill and then try to get a heavier fire while engine is being worked hard.

'14. The fireman should always arrange to do his firing either on a straight piece of track or on a curve towards the engineman's side, so that when going around a curve on which the engine man cannot see ahead, the fireman can do the looking out. Always keep a sharp lookout ahead when not firing.

'15. Always try to save as much coal as possible. A few shovelfulls saved each trip means a large amount saved in a year.

FIRING MARINE BOILERS.

'If the draught is light, grate moderately large, and lots of steam needed, carry a thin fire, say 6 or 8 inches in depth, and loosen your fire often by rocking the bars if they are so arranged, if not, then by running the slice bar under the fire over the bars, and raising up first one end and then the other of the fire.

'If the fire door is so arranged that you cannot use a slice bar in this way, take a two-pronged rake and break up the fire with it from the top.

'Always clean the ashes out from under the fire by either rocking or shaking the bars, or by using the single thin-bladed hook up through the bars from the under side. Never try to push or work the ashes down through the bars from above, but get them out from underneath. This will prevent choking up the grate bars and prevent the possible formation of any clinkers.

'When there are a number of fires to the same boiler, or battery of boilers, fire them in regular turn, and keep the doors open as short a time as possible.

'The admission of air over the fire should be just enough to stop the appearance of black smoke and no more, unless the boilers are making too much steam, then of course more air can be let in over the fire by the dampers, or by opening the doors a little, so as to check the draught and prevent waste.

'If the boilers are not steaming well with a thin fire, and the dampers over the fire are open, shut all top draughts and make all the air go through the grates.

'On vessels working under forced draught, experience can be the only guide to obtain the best results. But begin by spreading a thin fire of 8 or 10 inches thickness and use a light air pressure, increasing the depth of fire and strength of the blast gradually until a point is reached when the boilers are easily able to supply the steam needed.

'Watch to see that the dampers are always shut before the corresponding fire doors are open, to prevent the rush of air to the flues; keep the fires loose, and clean out any dull spots by working the ashes out from underneath.'

"The existence of a reasonable amount of volatile matter, which is so desirable in steaming coals, necessarily implies that these bituminous coals burn with more or less smoke, as their gases cannot be perfectly consumed without unusual care, But the amount and character of the smoke is a direct function of the character of the coals and of the combustible gases, even if the conditions of firing also greatly affect the result. With some coals, complicated smoke-consumers and the most careful attention, are necessary to produce good results; while with others the simplest appliances produce perfect combustion, and reasonable care under ordinary methods of firing, produces results which are comparatively unobjectionable. The small amount of smoke produced by these coals under ordinary conditions of firing, is a guarantee that no costly or complicated appliances will ever be made necessary by their use, even where the strictest smoke regulations are in force.

"The writer, some years ago, made a number of rough but fairly accurate tests, in the firing of the boilers of the 500-barrel flouring mill at Staunton, Va. The tests were taken for a period of from one to two hours each day, and extended over a number of days. The slightest changes which could be noted from the bottom of the shaft were recorded. These tests indicated that with anything like reasonable care, no smoke could be seen from the bottom of the shaft for 90 per cent. of the time, and that probably four per cent. of the time was the extreme limit that smoke of an objectionable nature could be detected. The worst of this objectionable smoke, while called black for want of a better name, had somewhat of a brownish cast, and was not the jet black color of the smoke derived from the more highly bituminous coals. It did not seem to be in large volume, did not hang together, and soon became dissipated in the atmosphere.

"These coals have established a reputation as superior coking coals. In chemical composition they leave nothing to desire, being low in ash, very high in fixed carbon, very low in sulphur, and low in phosphorus, while there is not a washer in the entire field. As a whole, the coal is so pure that no special care is exercised in discarding adventitious mixtures of inferior material, and the coke is not as pure as it could be made. It will usually average from 90 per cent. to 92 per cent. in fixed carbon, from 6 per cent. to 8 per cent. in ash, and between 0.50 per cent. and 0.75 per cent. in sulphur. While extensively used for furnace purposes, it is preeminently valuable as a foundry coke, its low ash, low sulphur, and high melting power making it especially appreciated.

"Unfortunately, coke making in this section has been subordinated to shipments of coal for other purposes, and has been usually introduced as a means of utilizing the finer sizes of coal. The physical character of the coke, and the best methods of handling, have, with a few shining exceptions, been almost totally neglected. Taking the New river and Pocahontas districts as a whole, much improvement may be produced in these respects; and it is greatly to be hoped that the entrance, into the latter district, of the United States Steel Corporation, whose operations will be entirely for the purpose of making coke, will result in marked improvement in these respects.

"The writer's own observations are, that while additional care is needed in all particulars, it is more especially true in regard to the questions of yield of coke from the coal, and in defective physical properties due to insufficient control of heat in the ovens. With proper care, it is possible to make a coke from these coals which, in the aggregate of its good features, cannot be surpassed.

"There is submitted a test of coal from this field in the Semet-Solvay ovens, as of interest:

SIX OVENS CHARGED.

Total weight coal charged. 52,220 pounds.	Per cent. moisture. 5. 5	Weight dry coal. 49,348 pounds.

Total weight coke (large.) 37,200 pounds.	Per cent. moisture. 3. 01.	Weight dry coke. 36,081 pounds.	Yield. 73. 11 per cent.

Weight of breeze. 1,645 pounds.	Per cent. moisture. 22. 4	Weight dry breeze 1,277 pounds.	Yield. 2. 56 per cent.

                                                              Per cent.

Yield of large coke... 73. 11
Yield of breeze.. 2. 58
                                                                    ———
    Total yield of coal 75. 69

"The coke produced was of very good quality, sound and hard.
"The time of coking was twenty-four hours.
"The following are the yields of by-products per 2,000 pounds coal:

Sulphate of ammonia, pounds......... 19. 58   . 979 per ct.
Tar, pounds .... 90. 70   4. 53 per ct.
Gas, cubic feet.............................. 8,500

"The following are the analyses of coal and coke:

	Coal. Per cent.	Coke. Per cent.
Volatile matter	26. 16	. 89
Fixed carbon	69. 64	93. 79

Ash 4. 20   5. 52

.   ──────   ──────
                                                      100. 00   100. 00

Sulphur 63   .46

(Signed) J. D. PENNOCK.
March 21, 1899.

R. M. ATWATER,
SECRETARY SEMET-SOLVAY CO.

"The best Connellsville coke in the same make of ovens is reported by
Fulton to give 71. 03 per cent. of large coke. Unfortunately the by-products
are not reported; but the Connellsville coke is reported (Fulton) as giving,
in the Otto–Hoffman ovens, 71. 1 per cent. of large coke, and the following
by-products per ton of 2,000 pounds: Sulphate of ammonia, 1.07 per cent.;
tar, 4. 00 per cent.; gas, 9,321 cubic feet. These figures will serve in some
sense as a comparison with those obtained from the Pocahontas-New river-
Gauley coals, as noted above.

The section of the Pottsville series exposed in the high spur
of Flat Tot mountain, at the town of Pocahontas, Tazewell county,
Virginia (where the Pocahontas coal bed received its name), is
given by Mr. W. A. Lathrop in "The Virginias," for June, 1884,
page 97, as follows:

	Ft. In.	Ft. In.
Top of State-line ridge (Flat Top)		2747 0 A. T.
Concealed		40 0
Coal No. 7..		2 0
Concealed		20 0
Coal No. 6.....		1 6
Concealed		80 0
Coal No. 5 { coal.............. 2 6 / bone and dirt.......... 2 0 }		4 6
Concealed		91 0
Coal No. 4..		2 0
Concealed		90 0
Sandy fireclay		6 0
Coal No. 3, Pocahontas { coal.............. 10 0 / slate .... 0 3 / coal..... .. .. 1 0 }		11 3
Fireclay		6 0
Shales and sandstone		61 0
Coal No. 2 { coal............. . ... 1 0 / shale................................. 2 0 / coal................................. 1 0 }		4 0
		────────
		419 3
Concealed to level of Pocahontas station (2315 feet A. T.)		12 6

Record continued from here in diamond drill hole.

Gray sandstone	15	4
Coal No. 1	1	0
Slate	2	0
Sandstone	27	6
Slate	3	0
Gray sandstone	35	4
Sandstone, with streaks of coal	8	8
Sandstone and shale	27	2
Gray sandstone	4	0
Gray sandstone and shale	8	5
Fireclay and shale	8	10
Blue slate	7	10
Sandstone and shale	15	1
Gray sandstone	17	0
Dark slate	27	1
Blue sandstone	26	3
Blue sandstone, very hard	26	4
Slate	1	0
Gray sandstone	23	10
Dark shale, lighter at bottom	102	7
Gray sandstone	3	0
Gray shale	2	4
Gray sandstone	1	6
Gray shale	2	0
Red shale to bottom	7	6
Total section	836	4

The POTTSVILLE SERIES is supposed to end at the top of the 102 feet seven inches of dark shale, thus giving a thickness of 717 feet five inches of Pottsville sediments, and making the horizon of the Pocahontas seam 369 feet above the base of the same, or 488 feet above the RED BEDS. The measurements were barometric down to Coal No. 5, but from there down to top of the bore hole they were made with the transit level.

Coal bed No. 5 of this section would probably represent the Lower Horsepen seam of Campbell.

The No. 4 COAL, which has an interval of sixty odd feet above the POCAHONTAS SEAM No. 3, where it is mined near Vivian, and also in the diamond drill holes at Welch and Huger, is here ninety-six feet above the same datum, while the great Pocahontas bed, which is only 290 feet seven inches above the top of the RED MAUCH CHUNK SHALES at Welch, is here at Pocahontas eighteen miles southeast from Welch, 488 feet above the top of the red beds, or 369 feet above the base of the Pottsville series, thus illustrating the eastward thickening of these Pottsville measures. This section is an important one, since it is the type one at Pocahontas, from which the series of coals in the Flat Top district were originally numbered.

The writer's measurement of the great Pocahontas seam is as follows:

	Ft.	In.	Ft.	In.
Coal	9	6		
Shale	0	4	10	8
Coal	0	10		

Mr. S. D. Brady's measurement of the coal in the "West" mine at Pocahontas, shows the following structure:

	Ft.	In.	Ft.	In.
Sulphurous coal	0	3		
Coal, not mined	1	3		
Coal	7	2	9	8
Slate, black	0	2		
Coal	0	10		

The following section of this coal at the "Reliance" mine of the Booth-Bowen Coal and Coke Company, as measured by S. D. Brady on Simmons creek, Mercer county, is a type of the Pocahontas bed when thick:

	Ft.	In.	Ft.	In.
Coal	2	0		
Bone	0	4		
Coal	2	3		
Sulphur band	0	1	10	0
Coal	4	4		
Slate and bone	0	2		
Coal	0	10		

On Flipping creek, Mercer county, east from Simmons creek, the upper half of the Pocahontas bed either disappears entirely, or else the bed "splits," as is popularly supposed, and the upper half is separated from the lower by a rock interval several feet in thickness. The remaining portion of the coal has the following structure, as reported by S. D. Brady at the "Goodwill" mine on that stream:

	Ft.	In.	Ft.	In.
Coal	1	3		
Sulphur band	0	1	4	9
Coal	3	5		

This same condition of affairs is shown on Crane creek and northward into Wyoming county, where this seam comes out of the Guyandot river at the mouth of Long branch, with the following section, according to M. R. Campbell, in the Raleigh folio.

	Ft. In.	Ft. In.
Coal	0 10	
Bone	0 2½	
Coal	0 9	3 9½
Bone	0 3	
Coal	1 9	

Farther up the river, at an opening below the mouth of Joe branch, Mr. Campbell measured the following section of this bed:

	Ft. In.	Ft. In.
Coal	0 10	
Shale	0 3	4 1
Coal	3 0	

Five miles northeast from this last locality, Mr Campbell measured a section of the Pocahontas coal on Slab fork, near the mouth of Cedar creek, which is exactly like the one at Joe branch.

On the Jim branch, of Barker creek this coal has the following section, according to Campbell:

	Ft. In.	Ft. In.
Coal	1 0	
Bone	0 5½	4 3½
Coal	2 10	

In the southern portion of Raleigh county this seam occurs on Devil fork, Tommy creek, Stone Coal, Bragg branch, and many other streams, with a thickness of three to three and a-half feet.

Where the Pocahontas coal dips under Pinnacle branch of the Guyandot, about one mile above the mouth of Beartown branch in southern Wyoming, it exhibits the following structure:

	Ft. In.	Ft. In.
Sandstone, massive		25 0
Coal		1 4
Fireclay		3 0
Sandy shale		5 0
Coal		5 4

The coal eight feet above the main seam of this section is a "split" from the top of the bed.

In the borings around Welch, McDowell county, a "split" is found at twenty-seven to forty-one feet below the Pocahontas seam in the borings made there, which is considered a "split" from the bottom of the No. 3 bed by the local mining engineers.

The Pocahontas seam, as mined along Elkhorn and its tributaries in McDowell county, generally has a "sulphur band" of one to three inches near the top of the seam, and a bony layer two to four inches thick at three and a-half to four and a-half feet above the bottom of the coal.

This bed passes under Elkhorn creek at Kimball, McDowell county, and when we come fo Helena, or Huger, three miles below (west) or five miles by the N. & W. Railroad, the coal is far beneath water level, as shown by the following record of a bore hole put down for the Watson Coal Company, which begins, say twenty feet above Elkhorn creek:

Surface			20	0	
Soft slate	1	2			
Slate	8	0			
Coal	0	9			
Slate	0	4			
Sandstone	10	8			
Slate	0	3			
Sandstone	3	8			
Coal	1	6			
Fireclay	0	6			
Sandstone	10	0			
Slate	0	6			
Sandstone	6	7			
Slate	0	8			
Sandstone	23	1	182	1	
Broken sandstone and coal seams	2	9			
Sandstone	7	9			
Hard, broken sandstone	11	6			
Sandstone	4	0			
Sandstone and mixed slate	0	10			
Sandstone	32	6			
Sandstone and mixed slate	77	2			
Sandstone	1	5			
Sandstone and mixed slate	3	3			
Broken sandstone	1	6			
Sandstone streaked with slate	6	2			
Sandstone	11	8			
Sandstone streaked with coal	3	5			
Sandstone	0	6			
Coal, No.4			4	1	
Black slate	0	1			
Fireclay and shale	3	2			
Sandy slate	4	0			
Sandstone and slate	6	9			
Sandy slate	2	0			
Sandstone	13	6			
Slate	3	1			
Sandstone	2	6	64	4	
Sandy slate	4	6			
Slate	0	9			

Sandstone and slate............................... 7   4 ⎫
Sandstone 2   0 ⎪
Slate.......... 4   6 ⎬
Slate... 5   0 ⎪
Slate and sulphur.................................. 5   2 ⎭
Coal (No. 3) Pocahontas   5   0
Black slate   0   2
Slate   5   0
Sandstone   4   4
                                                         ──────
Total..265   0

The record of another boring kindly furnished by M. J. Caples, Superintendent of the Pocahontas Coal and Coke Company, shows the thickness and depth of this seam on Browns creek, •near Welch, as follows:

		Ft. In.	Ft. In.
Sandstone.......................................		90 4 ⎫	
Coal, slaty.................		0 9 ⎬	258 3½
Sandstone and slate............................		157 2½ ⎭	
Coal, No. 4	coal	1 0 ⎫	
	bone	0 1½ ⎬	4 8½
	coal	3 7 ⎭	
Slate and sandstone............................			57 10½
Coal No. 3, Pocahontas	coal	1 6½ ⎫	
	bone	0 2½ ⎬	4 4
	coal	2 7 ⎭	
Sandstone and slate............................		27 5½ ⎫	
Coal, "split No. 3"...........................		1 9 ⎪	
Slate and sandstone............................		10 10½ ⎬	87 8
Coal, No. 2		0 7 ⎪	
Slate and sandstone............................		47 0 ⎭	
Coal, No. 1			0 9
Sandstone and slate to top of *red beds*....................			202 2

Total... 605   9½

This record shows that at Welch we are approaching the north-western limit of the workable area of the POCAHONTAS No. 3 COAL, which is here surpassed in size by the overlying No. 4 bed. It is possible that the latter may continue a few (five to ten) miles farther to the northwest before it, too, thins below commercial size, but of course only the diamond drill can determine this matter.

On Tug river, the Pocahontas seam rises above water level, just above the mouth of Mill creek, five miles south from Welch, and has there the following structure, according to M. R. Camp-bell:

		Ft. In.	Ft. In.
Bony coal		1 8	
Coal		0 3	
Bone		0 1	
Coal		2 2	
Bone		0 1	8 9
Coal		3 5	
Bone		0 1	
Coal		1 0	

Where this coal first comes above the level of Dry fork of Tug river, one mile and a-half below the mouth of Kewee creek, it is only three feet three inches thick and quite slaty, according to Campbell, but farther south, at the mouth of Vall creek, it has increased to four feet seven inches, with a shale parting seven inches thick below the center. South from this it gets thicker, and to the northeast a few (six) miles on Long branch, the Pocahontas Company reports it as ten feet eleven inches, while at the mouth of Cucumber creek Mr. Campbell measured six feet two inches of clean coal, as the bed section of the Pocahontas seam at 180 feet above water level.

Messrs. S. D. and A. P. Brady took accurate samples of this Pocahontas seam entirely across the bed, at thirty-eight different mines in every portion of the Flat Top district, thus securing representative specimens of the coal shipped from the several mines, and including any bony layers not separated from the same in mining. The thickness of the seam and its partings was also measured, and the result of these measurements, minus the bone and slate partings, is given in the subjoined table of analyses, reported by Prof. Hite as the composition of the samples as follows:

POCAHONTAS (No. 3) COAL.

Anal. No.	Mois.	V. M.	F. C.	Ash.	Sul.	Phos.	Th'nss of Seam. Ft. In.	B. T. U.
1.	0.41	18.21	76.38	5.00	0.50	0.005	4 10	15249
2.	0.36	17.02	78.22	4.40	0.54	0.004	5 1	15261
3.	0.15	17.37	76.86	5.62	0.47	0.003	4 6	14934
4.	0.26	17.45	76.93	5.36	0.55	0.005	5 2	15386
5.	0.30	17.25	78.85	3.60	0.67	0.019	5 2	15344
6.	0.19	17.03	78.40	4.38	0.54	0.0025	5 5	15337
7.	0.24	16.06	77.87	5.83	0.53	0.0045	5 7	15025
8.	0.13	15.82	79.34	4.71	0.72	0.005	6 6	15251
9.	0.27	15.73	79.80	4.20	0.61	0.0045	6 5	15413
10.	0.39	15.92	78.16	5.53	0.56	0.0065	6 3	15038
11.	0.31	16.82	76.41	6.46	0.70	0.006	5 6	14978
12.	0.23	16.81	78.61	4.35	0.70	0.009	5 10	15235

No.									
13.	0.27	16.54	76.49	6.70	0.65	0.007	6	0	14738
14.	0.23	16.03	74.16	9.58	0.65	0.012	6	4	14272
15.	0.14	16.73	76.58	6.55	0.67	0.0147	7	3	14851
16.	0.22	16.47	78.00	5.31	0.59	0.005	6	9	14997
17.	0.20	16.42	76.49	6.89	0.59	0.0038	6	2	14883
18.	0.12	15.70	79.40	4.78	9.64	0.0045	6	6	15141
19.	0.21	16.25	79.12	4.42	0.78	0.005	6	3	15121
20.	0.21	15.67	78.99	5.13	0.57	0.005	6	9	15140
21.	0.34	17.97	76.74	4.95	0.61	0.004	7	3	15059
22.	0.30	18.03	77.77	3.90	0.53	0.003	8	7	15307
23.	0.26	16.55	80.01	3.18	0.54	0.0025	8	7	15375
24.	0.42	18.29	77.02	4.27	0.64	0.030	7	5	15240
25.	0.19	17.15	77.00	5.66	0.53	0.0035	7	6	14984
26.	0.31	19.13	77.21	3.35	2.48	0.002	7	1	14935
27.	0.32	16.42	79.88	3.38	0.56	0.0022	7	8	15376
28.	0.32	18.27	77.78	3.63	0.55	0.002	8	0	15229
29.	0.18	17.36	80.12	2.34	0.53	0.002	8	1	15543
30.	0.23	19.03	77.71	3.03	0.54	0.0025	8	1	15486
31.	0.36	19.04	77.24	3.36	0.56	0.0025	4	5	15403
32.	0.13	17.22	79.30	3.35	0.68	0.0025	4	8	15518
33.	0.14	18.82	77.11	3.93	0.87	0.008	10	7	15239
34.	0.65	17.78	74.58	6.99	0.67	0.004	8	5	14874
35.	0.16	18.85	77.52	3.47	0.54	0.001	9	5	15384
36.	0.16	17.33	77.75	4.76	0.87	0.006	7	9	15296
37.	0.17	18.05	79.01	2.77	0.88	0.002	9	5	15550
38.	0.21	19.62	76.61	3.56	0.69	0.006	9	3	15398

LOCATION OF SAMPLES, MCDOWELL COUNTY.

Analyses
No.

1. From Ashland mine, Ashland C. &. C. Co., Ashland.
2. From McDowell mine, McDowell C. & C. C., McDowell.
3. From Roanoke mine, Roanoke C. & O. Co., one-half mile below McDowell.
4. From Indian Ridge mine, Indian Ridge C. & C. Co., one mile and a-half below McDowell.
5. From Arlington mine, Arlington C. & C. Co., Arlington.
6. From Greenbrier mine, Greenbrier C. & C. Co., one mile south of Greenbrier.
7. From Rolft mine, Rolft C. & C. Co., Rolft.
8. From Algoma mine, Algoma C. & C. Co., Algoma.
9. From Elk Ridge mine, Elk Ridge C. & C. Co., North Fork.
10. From Tidewater No. 3 mine, Tidewater C. & C. C., one-half mile west of Vivian.
11. From Bottom Creek mine, Bottom Creek C. & C. Co., one-fourth mile west of Vivian.
12. From Peerless mine, Peerless C. & C. Co., Vivian.
13. From Empire mine, Empire C. & C. Co., one mile west of

Landgraf.

14. From Shawnee mine, Shawnee C. & C. Co., one-half mile west of Eckman.
15. From Eureka mine, Eureka C. & C Co., Eckman.
16. From Pulaski mine, Pulaski Iron Co., one-fourth mile south of Eckman.
17. From Keystone mine, Keystone C. & C. Oo. Keystone.
18. From Gilliam mine, Gilliam C. & C. Co., one mile and three-fourths east of North Fork.
19. From Lynchburg mine, Lynchburg C. & C. Co., Kyle.
20. From Powhatan mine, Powhatan C. & C. Co., one-half mile west of Powhatan.
21. From Upland mine, Upland C. & C. Co., one-half mile west of Elkhorn.
22. From Housted No. 1 mine, Housted C. & C. Co., Elkhorn.
23. From Turkey Gap mine, Turkey Gap C. & C. Co., one-third mile west of Ennis.
24. From Crozer mine, Crozer C. & C. Co., one-third mile west of Ennis.
25. From Lick Branch Colliery mine, Norfolk C. & C. Co., Ennis.
26. From Angle mine, Norfolk C. & C. Co., one mile north of Maybeury.
27. From Delta Colliery mine, Norfolk C. & C. Co., Switch Back.
28. From Norfolk Colliery mine, Norfolk C. & C. Co., Switch Back.
29. From Shamokin mine, one-fourth mile west of Maybeury.
30. From Elkhorn mine, Elkhorn C. & C. Co., Maybeury.
31. From Louisville mine, Louisville C. & C. Co., Goodwill.
32. From Goodwill mine, Goodwill C. & C. Co., one mile from Goodwill.
33. From Mill Creek mine, Mill Creek C. & C. Co., one-fourth mile west of Ruth.
34. From Coaldale mine, Coaldale C. & C. Co., one-fourth mile west of Coaldale.
35. From Reliance mine, Booth-Bowen C. & C. Co., one mile and one-half from Simmons.

36. 　From Buckeye mine, Buckeye C. & C. Co., one mile and one-half from Simmons.
37. 　From Caswell mine, Caswell Creek Co., Caswell Creek.
38. 　From Pocahontas "West Mine," Pocahontas Collieries Co., Pocahontas, Va.

This coal is also coked on an extensive scale in every portion of the Flat Top and Elkhorn districts. The coke was sampled by the Messrs. Brady at thirty-two different points in the several regions, and the composition of these samples is reported by Prof. Hite as follows:

COKE—POCAHONTAS (No. 3) VEIN.

Analyses No.	Mois.	V. M.	F. C.	Ash.	Sul.	Phos.	Coking time.
1	0.14	0.91	90.18	8.77	0.78	0.009	48 hrs.
2	0.10	0.98	92.70	6.22	0.68	0.0125	"
3	0.06	0.71	92.68	6.55	0.67	0.0045	"
4	0.05	0.98	91.47	7.50	0.72	0.005	"
5	0.14	1.12	89.14	9.60	0.56	0.0055	72 hrs.
6	0.08	1.17	88.30	10.45	0.65	0.006	48 hrs.
7	0.05	0.82	94.46	4.67	0.51	0.0035	"
8	0.09	0.93	91.95	7.03	0.58	0.006	"
9	0.05	0.84	93.49	5.62	0.50	0.0035	"
10	0.14	0.90	92.73	6.23	0.63	0.0045	"
11	0.09	1.21	83.57	15.13	0.44	0.0105	72 hrs.
12	0.06	1.07	90.67	8.20	0.44	0.0065	"
13	0.14	0.88	86.69	12.29	0.48	0.0065	"
14	0.04	1.01	88.63	10.32	0.39	0.007	"
15	0.14	0.98	88.82	10.06	0.43	0.006	"
16	0.11	1.30	85.81	12.78	0.49	0.0085	48 hrs.
17	0.08	0.64	90.30	8.98	0.49	0.0055	72 hrs.
18	0.08	1.05	88.00	10.87	0.54	0.097	48 hrs.
19	0.14	1.16	92.58	6.12	0.64	0.0067	72 hrs.
20	0.06	0.79	93.77	5.38	0.61	0.0045	"
21	0.21	0.92	92.80	6.07	0.65	0.0075	"
22	0.08	0.82	93.13	5.97	0.55	0.0096	"
23	0.07	0.89	92.38	6.66	0.67	0.0025	48 hrs.
24	0.04	0.83	93.09	6.04	0.54	0.004	"
25	0.05	1.10	91.15	7.70	0.55	0.005	"
26	0.08	0.97	91.92	7.03	0.62	0.0065	72 hrs.
27	0.10	0.93	92.59	6.38	0.66	0.005	"
28	0.12	1.29	92.38	6.21	0.60	0.0065	48 hrs.
29	0.15	1.13	88.00	10.72	0.60	0.0055	"
30	0.10	1.21	91.92	6.77	0.58	0.005	"
31	0.05	0.69	92.66	6.60	0.68	0.004	"
32	0.09	1.10	93.67	5.14	0.62	0.0035	"

LOCATION OF SAMPLES, McDOWELL COUNTY.

Analyses
　No.

1. 　From Tidewater C. & C. Co. ovens, one-half mile west of

Vivian.

2. From Peerless C. & C. Co. ovens, Vivian.
3. From Houston C. & C. Co. ovens, Elkham.
4. From Keystone C. & C. Co. ovens, Keystone.
5. From Gilliam C. & C. Co. ovens, one mile and three-fourths east of North Fork.
6. From Powhatan C. & C. Co. ovens, Powhatan mine.
7. From Elkhorn C. & C. Co. ovens, Elkhorn mine.
8. From Lynchburg C. Co. ovens, Lynchburg mine.
9. From Shamokin C. C. ovens, Shamokin mine.
10. From Turkey Gap C. & C. Co. ovens, Turkey Gap mine.
11. From Ashland C. & C. Co. ovens, Ashland.
12. From McDowell C. & C. Co. ovens, McDowell.
13. From Roanoke C. & C. Co. ovens, one-half mile below McDowell.
14. From Indian Ridge C. & C. Co. ovens, one mile and one-half below McDowell.
15. From Arlington C. & C. Co. ovens, Arlington.
16. From Rolft C. & C. Co. ovens, Rolft.
17. From Greenbrier C. & C. Co. ovens, one mile south of Greenbrier.
18. From Louisville C. & C. Co. ovens, Goodwill.
19. From Algoma C. & C. Co. ovens, Algoma mine.
20. From Elk Ridge C. & C. Co. ovens, Elk Ridge mine.
21. From Eureka C. & C. Co. ovens, Eureka mine.
22. From Shawnee C. & C. Co. ovens, Shawnee mine.
23. From Buckeye C. & C. Co. ovens, Buckeye mine.
24. From Norfolk C. & C. Co. ovens, Switch Back.
25. From Norfolk C. & C. Co. ovens, Lick Branch mine.
26. From Upland C. & C. Co. ovens, Upland mine.
27. From Crozer C & C. Co. ovens, Crozer mine.

MERCER COUNTY.

28. From Coaldale C. & C. Co. ovens, Coaldale.
29. From Goodwill C. & C. Co. ovens, Goodwill mine.
30. From Booth-Bowen C. & C. Co. ovens, Simmons creek.
31. From Mill Creek C. & C. Co. ovens, Ruth.
32. From Pocahontas Collieries Co. ovens, "Baby mine," Pocahontas.

Taking the average of these analyses of the Pocahontas coal, and its resulting coke, and comparing them with the average of Prof. Hite's analyses of the coal and coke from the Sewell bed, we get the following table:

	Pocahontas. Coal.	Sewell. Coal.	Pocahontas. Coke.	Sewell. Coke.
Moisture	0. 23	0. 69	0. 09	0. 14
Volatile Matter..	17. 43	23. 95	0. 98	1. 06
Fixed Carbon.....	77. 71	72. 04	90. 99	91. 26
Ash..	4. 63	3. 32	7. 94	7. 54
Sulphur...........	0. 62	0. 74	0. 58	0. 75
Phosphorus........	0. 0057	0. 008	0. 0061	0. 0095

These averages speak for themselves in revealing coals and cokes of the highest types, and where each has so many excellent qualities, it is a difficult matter to decide between them purely on chemical grounds, and the final judgment as to which is superior, must be delegated to the arbitration of actual results achieved in the practical use of each.

In some parts of the THICK COAL region, one to two feet of coal is left in the roof of the Pocahontas seam as a support for the overlying shales. A sample of this coal was collected from the two feet left in the roof of the Buckeye mine on Simmons creek, the composition of which is reported by Prof. Hite as follows.

Moisture	0. 45
Volatile matter	18. 47
Fixed carbon	77. 39
Ash..............	3. 69
Total...	100. 00
Sulphur..	0. 63
Phosphorus	0. 006
B. T. U...	15226

A result which reveals a very pure coal, really better than that from the main portion of the seam (see sample No. 36 of the table, page 696).

As already stated, both David White and M. R. Campbell concur in the opinion that the Pocahontas coal horizon is represented on Piney creek, in the New river region, by a thin, insignificant coal more than 400 feet below the Quinnimont seam, and a little more than 100 feet above the top of the RED BEDS, so that no valuable extension of the No. 3 VEIN need be expected very far northeast from the southern portion of Raleigh county. Mr.

White reaches this conclusion from the finding on New river of some forms of NEUROPTERIS, SPHENOPTERIS, and RHABDOCARPUS peculiar to the Pocahontas flora.

The No. 2 and No. 1 COALS below the Pocahontas bed are both too thin to be of much economic importance, since neither one seldom exceeds two feet, though in southern McDowell, Campbell reports a coal as showing a thickness of two feet eight inches, and not entirely exposed, 150 feet above the red beds, near the mouth of Vall creek, while one (No. 2), sixty feet below No. 3, has the same thickness at Tug river P. O., and on Adkins branch near by, shows a section of three feet eight inches, so that it is possible some commercial coal may exist at the horizons of COALS Nos. 1 and 2 below the Pocahontas seam in southern McDowell county.

Just what relation the "Payne" and "Three-foot" beds, which lie so close to the RED BEDS near Webster Springs, Webster county, sustain to the Pocahontas or higher beds of the Flat Top and New river districts, is not yet known, but David White's researches into their fossil flora now being made, may be expected to throw some light upon the question. From the fact that in passing southwestward, successively lower, and lower coals appear in the Pottsville series, one would infer that the Webster coals must belong in the New river group, and that none of them are lower than the Quinnimont bed, though it is possible the "Echols" bed of d'Invilliers may be represented.

CHAPTER VIII.

THE POCONO COALS, OR "FALSE" COAL MEASURES. STATISTICS OF COAL AND COKE PRODUCTION, ETC.

THE POTTSVILLE SERIES, just described, is the oldest and the lowest of the true Coal Measures. The beds of the latter lie unconformably upon the eroded surface of the next underlying series of red and green shales, green sandstone, etc., which make up the Mauch Chunk series, containing a very different fauna and flora. True, there is practically no discordance in the dip of the Pottsville, and that of the Mauch Chunk beds, but evidence of erosion at the line of contact is clear, and the break in life forms is very marked, so that none of the conglomerates on New River, or elsewhere, which come below the top of the RED REDS, should be included in the Pottsville series. No coal beds, of workable thickness, are known in this Mauch Chunk series under the Pottsville, so that when the basal beds of the latter are reached, all hope of finding coal in commercial quantity, should be abandoned.

Below the MAUCH CHUNK RED BEDS and the underlying Green-brier limestone, ("Big Lime" of the oil well drillers), there comes the Pocono sandstone series of rocks which occasionally hold some irregular, impure, sporadic coal seams, of a nature approaching anthracite. These coals have excited much interest in western Berkeley, eastern Morgan, Greenbrier and other counties, along the line between Virginia and West Virginia. This is the same geological formation as the "Big Injun" oil sand of the western portion of the state, and when coal bearing, is usually referred to as the "False" Coal Measures, since the appearance of coal in them raises hopes, in those who do not know their unreliable nature, that can never be realized.

The Dora coal field, of Augusta county, Virginia, is of the same age, and it is well known that several fortunes, amounting to several hundreds of thousands of dollars, have been hopelessly spent in attempting to develop commercial mines in the delusive coal beds of that field. One of the peculiar features of these Pocono coals is their extreme variability in thickness. They may show eight to ten feet at one point, and within as many yards thin away to only a few inches. Then, too, they are always interstratified with much slate and bony material, and as they occur in the regions where the strata are highly folded, and often overturned, the coal is always much crushed, and the basins of very limited extent, so that even if any good coal could be found, there would not be enough of it to warrant the large expenditure necessary to market it on a commercial scale from the usual high and inaccessible mountain regions of its occurrence.

Quite recently there has been much newspaper discussion of the coal which occurs in these Pocono beds along the line between Berkeley and Morgan counties, and farther west and southwest. The writer paid a brief visit to the region, but could see no coal of commercial value, except for local uses, and even for that purpose it will cost much more to procure, than to purchase the best grades of Pennsylvania anthracite.

Mr. William Griffith, an eminent mining engineer, who has had much experience in the anthracite fields of Pennsylvania, has studied the Morgan and Berkeley deposits, and in a paper published in "Mines and Minerals." pages 293-4, February, 1893, has given an interesting description of these coals, which is herewith quoted in full, as follows:

THE ANTHRACITE

Of the Third Hill Mountain, West Virginia. —The effect of Crushing

Movements on the Quality of the Coal.

By William Griffith, Mining Engineer.[*]

Situation. —"The Third Hill and Sleepy Creek mountains are located in Berkeley and Morgan counties, West Virginia. They extend nearly north and south (N 25° E), the northerly end being about 13 miles west of Martinsburg, 7 miles east of Berkeley Springs. Sleepy Creek Station, on the Baltimore and Ohio railroad, is the nearest point by rail, being 3 or 4 miles north of the northerly end of the mountains, while Cherry Run Station (the junction point of the Baltimore and Ohio railroad and Western Maryland railroad) is 6 miles distant. This station is 124 miles by rail from Baltimore. 84 miles from Washington, 68 miles from Cumberland, 18 miles from Hagerstown, and 200 miles from Pittsburg.

Topography. —" As before stated, these mountains extend southward from near the Potomac river, having general directions of about S 25° W and are nearly parallel, being separated by the valley of Meadow Branch, which rises near the southerly end of the valley on the slope of Middle Ridge (a hill which gradually rises from the center of the valley, and increasing in height southward, unites the two mountains). From Middle Ridge, the Meadow Branch flows northward and empties into Sleepy Creek, a stream of considerable size, which drains the valley lying west of Sleepy Creek mountain. The Back Valley, to the east of Third Hill, is drained by Back Creek and its tributaries, and flows also into the Potomac west of Martinsburg. A good idea of the relative positions of these mountains can be obtained from the sketch map by noting that their general outline somewhat resembles a fish, Sleepy Creek mountain forming the back, Third Hill the belly, and Middle Ridge uniting the two at the base of the tail. Their southern extension, including Brush Creek Valley, forms the tail, while the nose and mouth are formed by the north end of Sleepy Creek mountain and Short mountain, the latter being a detached portion of Third Hill. The crests of Third Hill and Sleepy mountain are about 1000 feet above the general level of Sleepy Creek and Back Creek valleys, and about 500 feet above Meadow Branch valley, which latter, at Tom Meyer's, 11 or 12 miles south of the Baltimore and Ohio railroad, is 600 feet higher than Sleepy Creek Station.

"The coal beds, which are the especial object of this paper, are found in the rocks which flank the east side of Third Hill. At the southern end, i. e., near the fish's tail, the outcrops are near the crest of the mountain; but to the north, the rocks containing them gradually separate from the main hill, forming Short mountain, above mentioned. The space between Short mountain and the main ridge is occupied by soft red shales, forming a sort

---

*Paper read before the Franklin Institute, Philadelphia, Jan. 8, 1902.

of valley, in which several mountain streams have their source, which have cut channels or passes through Short mountain, thus dividing it into a chain of ridges lying end to end, parallel to Third Hill proper; and as the crests of these ridges are formed by the hard and almost vertical strata in which the coal is found, it will be seen that the coal outcrop runs lengthwise of the highest crest of Short mountain and across the passes, through which the Cherry run and other brooks flow, as above mentioned, and that the coal beds are very accessible by water-level drifts, lengthwise of the seam, from the creek beds.

Geology. —"A knowledge of the geology of this region is of the utmost importance in determining the value of the anthracite coal in the Third Hill; for if we know positively their geological position, we have gone a long way toward determining their economical value. The following ideal cross-section will illustrate :

"In the first place, we find that both Sleepy Creek and the Back Creek valleys are occupied by the soft red and yellow shales and black slates of the middle and upper Devonian measures, the lowest rocks of the series being in each valley farthest from the mountain in question, while the highest rocks of the Devonian Age (the red shales of the Catskill group, or No. IX of Pennsylvania Geological Survey), are found flanking the west slope of Sleepy Creek mountain and the east slope of Third Hill. The crest of both these mountains is formed by a ridge or spine of hard white and gray sandstone, being the lowest rocks of the subcarboniferous or Pocono measures, and these same rocks form the mountain sides sloping down to Meadow Branch.

"The rocks in the crest and in the east flank of Third Hill and in the Back Creek valley are overturned or inverted, as shown by their decided dip to the east, while in Sleepy Creek mountain and valley the rocks are regular and dip also to the east. Thus we see that the two mountains are formed by a long, narrow, canoe-shaped trough or basin of hard Pocono sandstone, resting upon the soft red rocks of the valley. Through this basin Meadow Branch flows, breaking through a precipitous gorge at the northerly end. Now, while there are coal openings on the west side of Meadow Branch in a number of places, those in Third Hill are particularly interesting in this paper, and we will confine ourselves to the developments along its crest.

"Anthracite coal has long been known to exist in Third Hill, and in fact has been found far to the southward and also to the northward in the same general range of Pocono rocks at various places. At Third Hill, however, more than any other one locality, the coal has been proved by many test pits dug into the outcrop along the crest of the mountain for 12 or 15 miles, and while these provings have been very alluring to prospectors, and considerable time and money have been spent, both in shafting and boring with diamond drills, as yet no coal beds have been found of sufficient value to warrant the expense necessary for their development. The true Carboniferous formation, which includes the productive coal measures of Pennsylvania and West Virginia, is much higher in the geological series of rocks than the Pocono (in which the coal in question is found). And in Pennsylvania no anthracite coal of workable thickness has ever been found in the Pocono rocks. It is true that in a few localities, notably in Kentucky and Tennessee, and in one or two special points in Pennsylvania, bituminous coal is mined in the lower Carboniferous measures. At the same time, these beds are not so regular as to thickness and are more subject to faults and disturbances, and, consequently, are more costly to mine than beds of the true Carboniferous age. As a rule, when bituminous coal exists, the measures are not much disturbed or distorted, and the coal lies flat or on moderate dips, very much as originally deposited; while in the case of anthracite coal, the conditions are quite different, as it only occurs in highly disturbed measures, where the coal (originally supposed to have been bituminous) has been coked or distilled under the heat and great pressure, due to the distortion of the rock formation in which it exists. The anthracite beds of Pennsylvania are, therefore, found to contain more slaty refuse and are more subject to faulty squeezes, crushed coal, etc., than the bituminous beds of the same age. Again, the Pocono rocks are known to be false-bedded and much more irregular in their stratification, and more liable to faults, crushes and other irregularities, than the rocks of the true coal measures.

"As a result of the above facts, and the known geological position of the beds of Third Hill, in connection with their steep dips; usually inverted) and the evident distortion and folding of the measures, we must expect to find the coal beds more or less crushed throughout the region, and in much the same state as the crushed and faulty coal of the Pennsylvania anthracite beds. In addition to this, the beds would probably be found more irregular and erratic as to thickness and continuity, existing more or less as "pockets,' and very uncertain as a basis upon which to make a large investment of capital necessary to development for railroad shipment.

"The provings noted on Third Hill were made many years ago, the most recent provings west of Shanghai and near the source of Cherry Run, and it was impossible to get fresh samples of coal from the seam for analysis or tests. It is reported that a number of wagon loads of coal were hauled away from the various shafts and sold, and found to give very good satisfaction as fuel, and apparently equal to Pennsylvania anthracite. Analyses of fresh coal have been shown me, which average about as follows:

Volatile matter............................... .... about 10 per cent.
Fixed carbon............ ....about 84 per cent.
Ash......... .... about 6 per cent.

"From this we should take the coal to be a semi-anthracite, free-burning, white ash, approaching in quality the coals of Shamokin and Bernice, Pa., which are classed as anthracites. It is probable that the above analysis is from picked samples of pure coal, and that the average of the seam would show much higher percentage of ash, owing to the bony coal and slate which would remain intermingled with it, even after careful preparation. The coal does not yield readily to the influence of the atmosphere, as is shown by the good condition of coal exposed 10 or 15 years at the proving shafts.

"The rocks of the mountain in the south end, where the recent Shanghai provings were made, are much disturbed, and the coal bed in the proving shaft is inverted and the coal badly crushed.

"At this point a distinct basin is found in the hard Pocono rocks near the crest of the mountain. This basin is about 500 feet wide, and shallow. The proving shaft was about 8 feet square, 50 or 60 feet deep, and sunk in the coal outcrop on the east margin of the basin. The writer was lowered into the shaft by means of a bucket and rope attached to the hoisting engine, and found the coal bed—which was supposed to be about 10 feet thick—much crushed and faulty, as has before been mentioned, and practically worthless. Near the bottom of the shaft the bed seemed to be parted by layers of fire-clay and slate, and in worse condition than at the top. This shaft was shortly afterwards abandoned.

"On the western outcrop of this narrow basin the rocks were regular, dipping to the east about 40 degrees. A short tunnel had been driven west-ward into the hill, cutting a bed of coal about 2½ feet thick. The writer examined this seam, after having the tunnel cleaned out, and found that though the dip was regular and the bed right side up, the coal was in much the same condition as in the shaft; and that while a small quantity had evi-dently been mined out and used locally by the farmers in the valley, the bed was virtually valueless for general development.

"Previous to sinking the shaft above mentioned, much money had been spent in driving a tunnel horizontally into the east flank of the mountain, about half way down, all the way through the red rocks of No. IX, in hopes of cutting the vertical coal bed 200 or 300 feet below the surface. The tun-nel (about 7 feet x 8 feet) was driven several hundred feet into the moun-tain, and at its end diamond drill holes were bored horizontally 100 feet or more, until the water pressure forced the drills out and stopped the further progress of the work. This tunnel would not cut the coal if it had been ex-tended clear through the mountain, as it was probably far below the bottom of the shallow basin containing the bed. A diamond drill hole had also been bored in the top of the mountain, but outside of the coal basin.

"As noticed above, as we go north from the Shanghai provings, the ridge containing the eastern coal outcrop gradually separates from the main ridge, and if the same basin structure is maintained it becomes wider and deeper, allowing an area of red shale between Short mountain and the main range, as priorly noted, and permitting the coal to cut down as low as the bottom of the lowest creek beds in the foot hills near the valley. At the provings north of Shanghai, the rocks seemed to be more regular, in some places vertical or with slight westerly dip, and not being inverted, owing perhaps to their being higher and nearer to the summit of overturn. The coal, except on the dumps, which had been taken from the shaftings, showed slightly better fracture, though much crushed and faulted. Farther to the northward, in the vicinity of the lands near the head of Cherry Run, about the same conditions are found, the strata dipping about 80 degrees to the eastward and inverted. The outcrop has recently been cut by a drift on the north side of Cherry Run gap of Short mountain, and more recently at a shaft in the gap southwest of Norrington's peach orchard. This shaft is about 5 feet x 8 feet, and it is said to be over 50 feet deep. Coal was struck about half-way down, and it is said to be about 4 or 5 feet thick. A number of tons was sold to the farmers nearby for upwards of $4 per ton, and was pronounced of satisfactory quality. Although this shaft was filled with water—and we were not permitted to examine the coal in place—we were able to judge of its structure and condition by the heap of coal, dirt, etc., still piled near the top of the shaft. It is unquestionably in the same crushed and faulted condition as found at every other point of the region, where openings have been made.

"As to the thickness and general condition of the coal in the beds north of Shanghai, I cannot say, except from inference, as all the openings were long since filled. We noticed, however, that the pieces of slate exposed on the dumps had not the flat laminated structure of the interstratified slate of the Pennsylvania anthracite beds, but had the same shape and crushed appearance that characterized the coal, and was hard to distinguish from the coal, except by its greater weight or by breaking. This fact is an indication of the crushed, faulty condition of the beds, and of the great pressure to which they must have been subjected, and it is evident that the pressure was sufficient to crush not only the coal but the slate also, and force it out of its true stratified condition. The slate carries considerable iron and is much heavier than coal. Owing to this fact it could be readily separated from the coal by the process of jigging, common in Pennsylvania anthracite regions. The writer had a proving hole dug into the outcrop of a bed of coal in the Meadow Branch valley, west of Tom Meyer's house, and found it 3½ to 4 feet in thickness, lying in good position between regular dipping rocks, but the coal was of the same crushed and slippery character referred to above; and while the coal would probably burn good, the crushed condition would cause an excessively large percentage of fine coal, such as pea, buckwheat and dust, which would reduce the market value of the product, as would also its soft and friable nature; on account of which it could not stand much handling, but would readily crumble, causing much culm and waste.

"Our investigations of this curious coal field have led us to regard the coal beds of Third Hill as a sort of natural curiosity or geological freak, and, owing to uncertainty as to thickness and continuity, and probable unreliable or "pockety" and faulty nature of the beds, their ecomical value is small. There can be no doubt that the above-described crushed condition of the coal beds extends throughout the region, including the deeper parts of the seam, far below the surface, as well as near the outcrop. Of course, if the coal beds in Third Hill were proved to be 3 or 4 feet thick or more, continuous and reliable, the large investment required to develop for railroad shipment would be justifiable, notwithstanding the crushed condition of the coal, for the location, excellent railroad facilities, and good market, at high prices, would go a long way toward counterbalancing the loss due to poor fracture or faulty coal. But to attempt to prove the reliability of these seams as to thickness, continuity, etc., would require a considerable expenditure, which would, in the writer's opinion, be very likely to result unfavorably."

This unbiased report of an expert on anthracite coal should convince most people that the fuel locked up in the summits of

the mountains of Berkeley, Morgan, and other counties southwestward to Greenbrier, is not now commercially available. Of course,
in the remote future, when the Pennsylvania anthracite is largely
exhausted and the cheaply mined bituminous coals have all been
used up, it may be possible to mine these crushed and irregular
beds of anthracite in Berkeley and Morgan, and separate the coal
from its interstratified slate, bone, and other impurities, in such a
way as to yield a profitable return on the large investment that
will be necessary, but so far as one can now judge that time is
many years in the future.

Mr. David White has examined the fossil plants occurring
with these coals, and unhesitatingly pronounces them of Pocono
age, in entire agreement with the conclusions of Prof. William B.
Rodgers, who first examined and described the coal beds in his annual reports on the Geological Survey of Virginia, sixty odd years
ago.

The writer had hoped that some of these basins might contain
coal of Pottsville age instead of Pocono, but David White's conclusions from the flora effectually disposes of any such possibility.

STATISTICS OF COAL AND COKE PRODUCTION.

The growth of coal production in West Virginia has been constantly increasing during the past thirty years, with the exception
of two years due to prolonged strikes. Beginning with only 672,-
000 short tons in 1873, the first year for which we have definite
statistics, production has grown until the present year bids fair to surpass 25,700,000 short tons, barring any serious strikes or labor difficulties. The time must soon come when West Virginia will pass
Illinois and become the second State in coal production instead of
third, a place she has held since 1895, when Ohio was left behind.
Just when West Virginia will pass Pennsylvania and become first
in bituminous coal production, depends largely upon the rate of
exhaustion of the latter's coal fields. That she will surpass Pennsylvania sometime during the present century is practically sure,
since the vast production of the latter State must lead to rapid exhaustion of her limited area, and the fuel for her great industries
must necessarily come from the adjoining State, where so much
coal can be floated down the Monongahela directly to the greatest
manufacturing district in the world.

The following account of West Virginia's coal production, quoted from the annual volume of the U. S. G. Survey on the Mineral Resources of the country for 1901, will prove of interest:

WEST VIRGINIA.

"Total production in 1901, 24,068,402 short tons; spot value, $20,848,184.

"The coal production of West Virginia in 1901 shows an increase of 1,421,-195 short tons, or 6.3 per cent. in amount, and of $2,431,313, or 13 per cent. in value. The record of West Virginia as a coal-producing State is one without parallel in the history of our development. During the last twenty-one years there has been only one instance in which the production of West Virginia was less than that of the preceding year. This was in 1895, and was due to two causes. One was the general strike which prevailed in the Pocahontas region, and which resulted in a decrease of 1,150,000 in the counties of McDowell and Mercer, and the other was the general business depression which affected the coal-mining industry, and all industries in every State during that year. Notwithstanding the loss of 1,150,000 tons in McDowell and Mercer counties, and the general depression, the total production of the State decreased in that year only 240,000 tons. During the twenty-one years that the history of coal production has been recorded in the volumes of Mineral Resources of the United States, the coal production of West Virginia has increased an average of over 1,000,000 tons each year. Notwithstanding its decreased production in 1895, West Virginia in that year exceeded the output of Ohio, which, up to that time, held third place as a coal producer. Since that time West Virginia has been gradually approaching Illinois, which ranks second to Pennsylvania, but has not fulfilled a prediction made some years ago, that by the beginning of the present century West Virginia would rank next to Pennsylvania as a coal-producing State.

"There is another respect in which the coal-mining industry of West Virginia stands distinctly alone. This is in the fact that although its production now approaches 25,000,000 tons per year, the amount of this fuel consumed within the State's borders is almost insignificant, if the amount consumed by the transportation companies is excluded. There are some iron and steel manufacturing industries in Wheeling and vicinity, which utilize West Virginia coal, but except for these, the manufacturing industries in the State are almost entirely undeveloped, and by far the greater proportion of the fuel taken from West Virginia mines goes to feed and support the manufacturing enterprises of neighboring States. This has probably been the result of the fact that the railroad companies penetrating the coal fields have been identified with the coal mining interests, and have been glad to get the advantage of long hauls in the way of transportation.* Some of the West Virginia coals are highly prized, both for steam raising and coke making. They are used to a large extent by the United States Government for naval

---

*The principal factor is the abundance of natural gas which annually displaces a large tonnage of coal in all of the principal cities of the State, and in the manufacturing industries. —(I. C. W.)

vessels, and are shipped either in the form of coal or coke to blast furnaces and steel works as far from the coal regions as Chicago and Milwaukee, in competition with fuels mined almost in the immediate vicinity of these cities·

"The statistics of the use of mining machines in West Virginia show that there were 403 machines in use in 1901, and that they produced a total of 4,817,943 tons, as compared with 327 machines which produced 3,418,377 tons in 1900, and 154 machines which produced 1,181,125 tons in 1899.

"The details of production in 1900 and 1901, by counties, with the distribution of the product for consumption, are shown in the following tables:

Coal production of West Virginia in 1900, by counties.

County.	Loaded at mines for shipment.	Sold to local trade and used by employes.	Used at mines for steam and heat.	Made into coke.	Total production.	Av'r-age price per ton.
	short tons	sh'rt t'ns	sh'rt t'ns	sh'rt t'ns	short tons	
Barbour..	189,031	1,796	3,050	22,254	216,231	$0. 68
Brooke	46,905	13,965	100	....	60,970	. 89
Fayette	4,896,223	47,903	39,560	758,452	5,742,138	. 88
Harrison	912,837	11,227	9,092	12,799	945,955	. 74
Kanawha	1,930,930	38,704	11,991	81,116	2,062,741	. 91
McDowell	3,203,626	26,510	22,181	1,668,918	4,921,235	. 80
Marion	2,806,370	17,173	24,652	393,480	3,241,675	. 79
Marshall	209,296	17,417	4,858	....	231,571	. 95
Mason	112,953	28,710	546	....	142,209	. 91
Mercer......... .	744,604	5,977	3,941	255,014	1,009,536	. 76
Mineral	609,412	31,522	222	....	641,156	. 70
Mingo .....·...........	567,338	4,914	1,904	....	574,156	. 74
Monongalia	71,766	616	1,386	13,632	87,400	I. II
Ohio	84,577	51,964	1,255	....	137,796	. 92
Preston	369,960	1,148	3,203	7,636	381,947	. 78
Putnam	137,285	185	400	....	137,870	I. 12
Randolph	159,108	443	765	19,272	179,588	. 65
Taylor	514,330	7,696	1,232	....	523,258	. 75
Tucker	711,898	42,866	11,313	413,976	1,180,053	. 66
Hancock & Raleigh	69,713	18,315	420	16,274	104,722	. 90
Small mines............	....	125,000	....	....	125,000	....
Total...............	18,348,162	494,051	142,071	3,662,923	22,647,207	. 81

Coal Production of West Virginia in 1901, by Counties.

County.	Loaded at mines for shipment.	Sold to local trade and used by employes.	Used at mines for steam and heat.	Made into coke.	Total production.	Average price per ton.
	short tons	sh'rt t'ns	sh'rt t'ns	short tons	short tons	
Barbour	266,048	11,287	18,111	17,930	313,376	$0.73
Brooke	68,279	4,838	81	....	73,198	.96
Fayette.................	5,090,139	80,602	66 202	815,446	6,052,389	.90
Harrison	1,728,008	7,996	18,880	7,679	1,762,563	.79
Kanawha	1,878,056	35,747	17,981	52,119	1,983,903	.90
McDowell	3,386,075	40,063	34,187	1,535.186	4,995,511	.90
Marion	3,089,516	17,054	45,053	259,974	3,411,597	.80
Marshall	181,638	31,147	4,452	....	217,237	.88
Mason	74,322	42,109	13,533	....	129,964	.90
Mercer	676,112	7,736	4,944	275,186	964,028	.86
Mineral..............	593,529	3,706	541	....	597,776	.74
Mingo	567,626	4,851	4,409	....	576,886	.79
Monongalia	89,019	699	184	20,899	110,801	.85
Ohio	87,011	103,404	1,346	....	191,761	.94
Preston	470,877	1,408	4,076	12,878	489,239	1.39
Putnam	237.163	4,270	1,356	....	242,789	.98
Randolph	139.339	1,187	679	20,356	161,561	.77
Taylor	371,595	7,127	1,868	....	380,590	.73
Tucker	713,645	6,273	16,846	360,576	1,097,340	.71
Hancook & Raleigh	151,812	38,242	839	....	190,893	.93
Small mines...........	....	125,000	....	....	125,000	.. ..
Total	18,859.809	574.746	255,618	3,378,229	24,068,402	$0.87

"The distribution of the total product since 1889 has been as follows:

Distribution of the coal product of West Virginia from 1889 to 1901 inclusive.

Year.	Loaded at mines for shipment.	Sold to local trade and used by employees.	Used at mines for steam and heat.	Made into coke.	Total product.	Average price per ton.
	short tons	sh'rt t'ns	sh'rt t'ns	shr't tons	short tons	.
1889......................	4,764,900	493,287	37,368	936,325	6,231,880	$0. 82
1890......................	5,614,752	438,527	30,594	1,310,781	7,394,654	. 84
1891......................	6,887,151	429,878	47,163	1,856,473	9,220,665	. 80
1892......................	7,560,790	441,159	49,563	1,687,243	9,738,755	. 80
1893......................	8,591,962	390,689	46,898	1,679,029	10,708,578	. 77
1894......................	9,116,314	428,202	64,126	2,019,115	11.627,757	. 75
1895......................	8,858,256	445,023	50,595	2,034,087	11,387,961	. 68
1896......................	9,838,053	426,441	56,395	2,555,407	12,876,296	. 65
1897......................	11,312,408	446,795	58,694	2,430,262	14,248,159	. 63
1898......................	12,965,903	471,796	61,176	3,202,124	16,700,999	. 61
1899......................	15,044,272	476,996	87,022	3,644,705	19,252,995	. 63
1900......................	18,348,162	494,051	142,071	3,662,923	22,647,207	. 81
1901......................	19,859,809	574,746	255,618	3,378,229	24,068,402	. 87

"The principal coal-producing regions of West Virginia may be divided into four distinct districts. These may be distinguished by certain geo‐graphic or physiographic features. They do not include all of the coal-producing counties of the State, but do include the more important ones, and they contribute nearly 90 per cent. to the total output of the State. Two of these districts are in the northern part of the State, and two in the south‐ern portion. The two in the northern portion of the State are designated, respectively, the Fairmont or Upper Monongahela district, and the Elk Gar‐den or Upper Potomac. Those in the southern portion of the State are the • Pocahontas or Flat Top district, and the New and Kanawha River district. The Upper Monongahela district is penetrated by the Baltimore and Ohio Railroad, and sends its coal to market over that highway. The Upper Poto‐mac region is also reached by the Baltimore and Ohio Railroad, and is pen‐etrated by the West Virginia Central and Pittsburg Railroad. The Poca‐hontas or Flat Top region is tributary to the main branch of the Norfolk and Western Railroad. All of the product of this district goes either west or to tidewater over that line. The New and Kanawha River district is named from the two rivers which drain it, the coal being shipped partly by the Chesapeake and Ohio Railroad which passes through it, and partly by barges on the Kanawha river. The most important district from the productive point of view, is the New and Kanawha River, which embraces the counties of Fayette and Kanawha. The coal from these two counties is drawn from two different areas, most of the coal from Kanawha county being from a higher geologic horizon than that of Fayette county, but the district is prac‐tically compact and continuous, is drained by the same waters and reached by the same railroad, so the two areas are considered as one district in this report. The production of the two counties in 1901.amounted to 8,036,292 short tons, as compared with 7,804,879 short tons in 1900.

"The Pocahontas or Flat Top district embraces the counties of McDow‐ell and Mercer in West Virginia, and Tazewell county in Virginia. The openings to the mines in Tazewell county are in Virginia, and it has been customary to credit that county and State with the total production, although it is known that most of the coal is taken from the West Virginia side of the line. Because of this the production of Tazewell county has been included in the following table with the Pocahontas or Flat Top district. The de‐creased production in Tazewell county in 1901, which was mentioned in con‐nection with the discussion of Virginia's production, caused a falling off in the total output of the district for last year to 6,736,107 short tons, from 6,901,637 short tons in 1900.

"The Fairmont region, which embraces Harrison and Marion counties, and includes the mines around Clarksburg and Fairmont, has shown the largest ratio of increase of all the coal-producing districts of West Virginia. The production of this district in 1901 was nearly thirteen times that of 1886, fifteen years before; four and one-half times that of 1891, and about three times that of 1896. As compared with 1900 it shows an increase of nearly 1,000,000 tons, not quite 25 per cent. The total product in 1901 amounted t o 5,174,160 short tons, as compared with 4,187,630 tons in 1900.

"The Upper Potomac or Elk Garden district, is a part of an isolated basin which lies to the east of the main Appalachian field, and which includes the Cumberland region of Maryland, the Somerset district of Pennsylvania, and the Piedmont region of West Virginia. The counties in West Virginia included in this district are Mineral, Grant, Tucker, and Randolph· Most of the coal mined is drawn from what is known as 'Big Vein,' which has furnished the greater portion of Maryland's product. The production in 1901 was slightly less than that of the preceding year, being 1,856,677 short tons, as compared with 1,999,797 short tons in 1900. The production of the four principal districts of West Virginia since 1886 is shown in the following table:

Coal production of the principal districts of West Virginia since 1886.

[Short tons.]

Year.	New and Kanawha River district.	Pocahontas or Flat Top district.	Fairmont or Upper M'nong'la district.	Upper Potomac or Elk G'rd'n district.
1886	2,290,563	968,484	406,976	383,712
1887	2,379,296	1,357,040	520,064	503,343
1888	2,840,630	1,912,695	473,489	518,878
1889	2,669,016	2,290,270	456,582	666,956
1890	3,012,414	2,702,092	600,131	819,062
1891	3,632,209	3,137,012	1,150,569	1,052,308
1892	3,773,021	3,503,260	1,141,430	942,154
1893	4,099,112	3,815,280	1,255,956	1,129,397
1894	3,650,971	5,059,025	1,655,532	927,220
1895	4,399,623	4,044,998	1,550,256	1,125,601
1896	4,650,455	4,608,113	1,743,590	1,245,012
1897	4,921,701	4,859,373	2,074,663	1,425,026
1898	5,947,272	5,521,160	2,525,294	1,531,562
1899	6,544,956	6,033,344	3,374,183	1,786,009
1900	7,804,879	6,901,637	4,187,630	1,999,797
1901	8,036,292	6,736,107	5,174,160	1,856,677

"In order to show how steady the coal-mining industry of West Virginia has been during the past twenty-one years, the following table has been prepared, which shows the increase each year since 1880. There has been only one break in the series, and the average annual increase for twenty-one years has exceeded 1,000,000 tons.

Annual increase in the coal production of West Virginia since 1880.

[Short tons.]

Year.	Quantity.	Year.	Quantity.
1881 over 1880	112,000	1894 over 1893	919,179
1882 over 1881	560,000	Total increase in 14 y'rs	10,059,757
1883 over 1882	95,833	Decrease in 1895.........	239,796
1884 over 1883	1,024,167		
1885 over 1884	9,062	Total increase in 15 y'rs	9,819,961
1886 over 1885	636,734		
1887 over 1886	875,824	1896 over 1895	1,488,335
1888 over 1887	617,180	1897 over 1896	1,371,863
1889 over 1888	733,080	1898 over 1897	2,452,840
1890 over 1889	1,162,774	1899 over 1898	2,551,996
1891 over 1890	1,826,011	1900 over 1899	3,394,212
1892 over 1891	518,090	1901 over 1900	1,421,195
1893 over 1892	969,823	Total increase in 21 y'rs	22,500,402
		Average annual increase	1,071 448

"The annual production of coal in West Virginia is shown in the following table:

Coal production of West Virginia since 1873.

[Short tons.]

Year.	Quantity.	Year.	Quantity.
1873........	672,000	1889........	6,231,880
1874...................................	1,120,000	1890...............................	7,394,654
1875..............................	1,120,000	1891...............................	9,220,665
1876................................	896,000	1892	9,738,755
1877................................	1,120,000	1893...............................	10,708,578
1878................................	1,120,000	1894...............................	11,627,757
1879........	1,400,000	1895...............................	11,387,961
1880..........	1,568,000	1896...............................	12,876,296
1881...........................	1,680,000	1897........	14,248,159
1882..........	2,240,000	1898...............................	16,700,999
1883..........	2,335,833	1899...............................	19,252,995
1884................................	3,360,000	1900........................	22,647,207
1885................................	3,369,062	1901...............................	24,068,402
1886................................	4,005,796	1902*.............................	24,307,387
1887................................	4,881,620	1903* (Estimated).........	25,760,000
1888................................	5,498,800		

*Given by Hon. J. W. Paul, State Mine Inspector for West Virginia.

INDEX.

———

A

CPSIA information can be obtained at www.ICGtesting.com
Printed in the USA
BVOW06s0951250314

348701BV00008B/186/P

9 781271 625307